Fodors98
New York City

The complete guide, thoroughly up-to-date

Packed with details that will make your trip

The must-see sights, off and on the beaten path

What to see, what to skip

Vacation itineraries, walking tours, day trips

Smart lodging and dining options

Essential local do's and taboos

Transportation tips

Key contacts, savvy travel advice

When to go, what to pack

Clear, accurate, easy-to-use maps

Books to read, videos to watch, background essay

Fodor's Travel Publications, Inc.
New York • Toronto • London • Sydney • Auckland
www.fodors.com/

Fodor's New York City

EDITOR: David Low

Editorial Contributors: Robert Andrews, Hannah Borgeson, David Brown, Audra Epstein, Matthew Lore, Amy McConnell, Anastasia Mills, Margaret Mittelbach, Jennifer Paull, Heidi Sarna, Helayne Schiff, M. T. Schwartzman (Gold Guide editor), Dinah Spritzer, J. Walman, Stephen Wolf

Editorial Production: Janet Foley

Maps: David Lindroth, *cartographer*; Steven K. Amsterdam, *map editor*

Design: Fabrizio La Rocca, *creative director*; Guido Caroti, *associate art director*; Jolie Novak, *photo editor*

Production/Manufacturing: Robert B. Shields

Cover Photograph: Poul Lange

Copyright

Special Sales

CONTENTS

Contents

Maps

ON THE ROAD WITH FODOR'S

WE'RE ALWAYS THRILLED to get letters from readers, especially one like this:

It took us an hour to decide what book to buy and we now know we picked the best one. Your book was wonderful, easy to follow, very accurate, and good on pointing out eating places, informal as well as formal. When we saw other people using your book, we would look at each other and smile.

Our editors and writers are deeply committed to making every Fodor's guide "the best one"—not only accurate but always charming, brimming with sound recommendations and solid ideas, right on the mark in describing restaurants and hotels, and full of fascinating facts that make you view what you've traveled to see in a rich new light.

About Our Writers

Our success in achieving our goals—and in helping to make your trip the best of all possible vacations—is a credit to the hard work of our extraordinary writers.

The editor of *Fodor's New York City,* **David Low,** is a native New Yorker (born in Queens) who makes his living as a fiction writer and book editor. He also revised the Arts chapter and the Chelsea, Greenwich Village, East Village, SoHo and Tribeca, Little Italy, and Chinatown exploring tours. Mr. Low has had an obsessive interest in theater, movies, and other performing arts in the city since he saw his first Broadway play, *Baker Street,* a musical about Sherlock Holmes. He lives around the corner from the Strand Book Store, where he has spent many hours searching for bargains.

Editor and freelance writer **Hannah Borgeson** will do just about anything to see New York City streets auto-free, from the Five Borough Bike Tour to the New York City Marathon. Is kayaking next? She also enjoys walking tours of Manhattan neighborhoods and reading about and visiting interesting architectural sites throughout the city, all of which helps her in updating portions of the Exploring Manhattan chapter. On the last Friday of every month, she bikes the less-traveled paths of Central Park on the Moonlight Ride.

Brooklyn updater **Matthew Lore** has lived in Park Slope for three years. Most mornings before turning up as an editor at Fodor's, he runs in Prospect Park, the neighborhood's treasured green oasis. He can frequently be found on Saturday mornings browsing among the veggies and plants at the Grand Army Plaza Greenmarket. "It's great once you get there," he loves to tell Manhattanites who think Brooklyn is just too far away.

Fodor's editor **Amy McConnell,** who worked on the chapters on Lodging and Exploring the Other Boroughs, has spent many a night evaluating the softness of mattresses and the deepness of bathtubs in New York City's swankiest hotels. In her waking hours, she likes to ride the subway to the farthest corner of the city to see what lies beyond Manhattan.

Anastasia Mills, Fodor's editor and the Nightlife updater, has taken full advantage of New York City's clubs and bars since the early '80s. She mourns the passing of Limelight and the Ritz but celebrates the continued existence of such intimate venues as the Bottom Line and Irving Plaza.

Freelance writer **Margaret Mittelbach** is a Los Angeles native who has lived in New York for the past nine years. She updated the chapters on Exploring New York City with Children and Outdoor Activities and Sports. Because she recently co-authored a book about New York's wildlife and wild places, she has been spending a lot of time in the city's marshes, woods, and underground passageways. Her favorite spots in New York are Brooklyn's Park Slope, where she lives and works in a brownstone, and the Jamaica Bay Wildlife Refuge, where she has been seen stalking butterflies without a net.

Shopping updater (and Fodor's editorial staff member) **Jennifer Paull** would like to thank her family for her exasperating consumer profile—half Yankee frugality ("I could get that for $10 in a thrift store in

Vermont"), half devil-may-care extravagance ("But it's Italian"). Both tendencies wreak havoc on her wallet.

Syndicated travel, food, and wine journalist **J. Walman,** who wrote the Dining chapter, dispenses culinary advice to the 2 million listeners of WEVD-AM, writes regularly for *Chocolatier* and *Troika Magazines,* and is president of Punch In–International Syndicate, an interactive electronic publishing company specializing in travel, restaurants, entertainment, and wine. He prefers to skip breakfast (rather than exercise), take vitamins (instead of giving up martinis), and is married to a beautiful, intelligent woman who shares his enthusiasm for travel, food, and wine—not necessarily in that order.

Whether it's scrutinizing a photograph of old New York to travel back in time or stopping to take in the rush-hour crush at Grand Central Station or walking the streets in the brilliant late-afternoon light, Fodor's editor **Stephen Wolf,** who updated a few lower- and upper-Manhattan sections of this guide, always has an eye out for that perfect New York moment.

New This Year

This year we've added terrific Great Itineraries that will lead you through the best of the city, taking into consideration how long you have to spend.

And this year, Fodor's joins Rand McNally, the world's largest commercial mapmaker to bring you a detailed color map of New York City. Just detach it along the perforation and drop it in your tote bag.

On the Web, check out Fodor's site (http://www.fodors.com/) for information on major destinations around the world and travel-savvy interactive features. The Web site also lists the 80-plus radio stations nationwide that carry the Fodor's Travel Show, a live call-in program that airs every weekend. Tune in to hear guests discuss their wonderful adventures—or call in to get answers for your most pressing travel questions.

How to Use This Book

Organization

Up front is the **Gold Guide,** an easy-to-use section divided alphabetically by topic. Under each listing you'll find tips and information that will help you accomplish what you need to in New York City. You'll also find addresses and telephone numbers of organizations and companies that offer destination-related services and detailed information and publications.

The first chapter in the guide, Destination: New York City, helps get you in the mood for your trip. What's Where gets you oriented, Pleasures and Pastimes describes the activities and sights that really make New York City unique, Great Itineraries helps you plan your days, Fodor's Choice showcases our top picks, and Festivals and Seasonal Events alerts you to special events you'll want to seek out.

The Exploring chapters are subdivided by neighborhood; each subsection recommends a walking tour and lists neighborhood sights alphabetically. The remaining chapters are arranged in alphabetical order by subject (arts, dining, lodging, nightlife, outdoor activities and sports, and shopping).

At the end of the book you'll find Portraits, with a memorable essay about New York City by V. S. Pritchett, followed by suggestions for pretrip reading, both fiction and nonfiction, and movies on tape with New York City as a backdrop.

Icons and Symbols

★	Our special recommendations
✕	Restaurant
▧	Lodging establishment
♻	Good for kids (rubber duckie)
☞	Sends you to another section of the guide for more information
✉	Address
☎	Telephone number
♾	Opening and closing times
💵	Admission prices (those we give apply to adults; substantially reduced fees are almost always available for children, students, and senior citizens)

Numbers in white and black circles that appear on the maps, in the margins, and within the tours correspond to one another.

Credit Cards

The following abbreviations are used: **AE,** American Express; **D,** Discover; **DC,** Diners Club; **MC,** MasterCard; and **V,** Visa.

Please Write to Us

You can use this book in the confidence that all prices and opening times are based on information supplied to us at press time; Fodor's cannot accept responsibility for any errors. Time inevitably brings changes, so always confirm information when it matters—especially if you're making a detour to visit a specific place. In addition, when making reservations be sure to mention if you have a disability or are traveling with children, if you prefer a private bath or a certain type of bed, or if you have specific dietary needs or other concerns.

Were the restaurants we recommended as described? Did our hotel picks exceed your expectations? Did you find a museum we recommended a waste of time? If you have complaints, we'll look into them and revise our entries when the facts warrant it. If you've discovered a special place that we haven't included, we'll pass the information along to our correspondents and have them check it out. So send us your feedback, positive *and* negative: email us at editors@fodors.com (specifying the name of the book on the subject line) or write the New York City editor at Fodor's, 201 East 50th Street, New York, New York 10022. Have a wonderful trip!

Karen Cure
Editorial Director

New York City Area

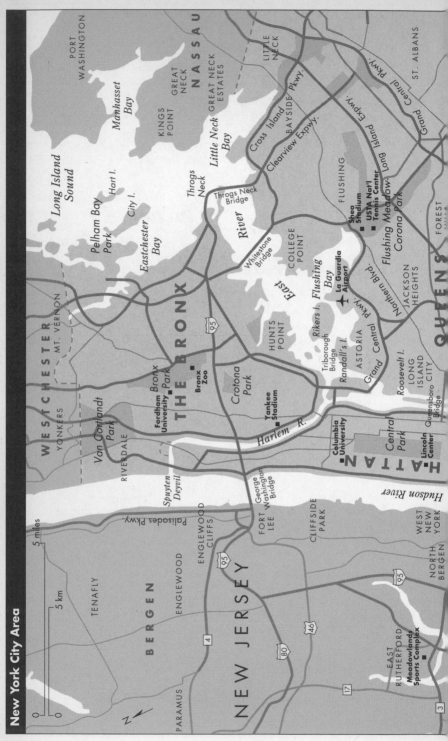

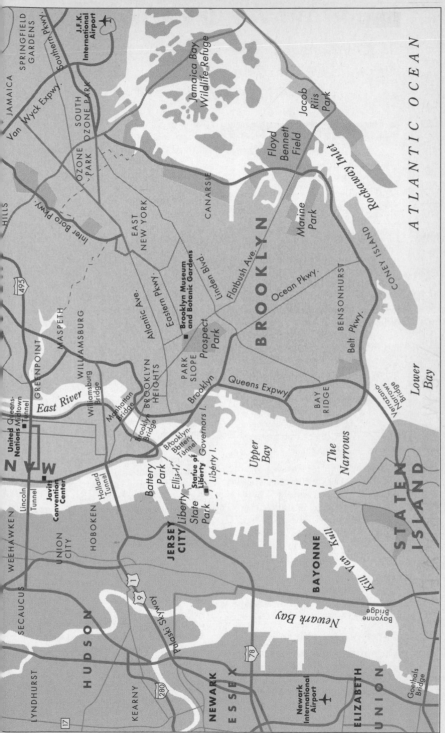

SMART TRAVEL TIPS A TO Z

Basic Information on Traveling in New York, Savvy Tips to Make Your Trip a Breeze, and Companies and Organizations to Contact

A

AIR TRAVEL

MAJOR AIRLINE OR LOW-COST CARRIER?

Most people choose a flight based on price. Yet there are other issues to consider. Major airlines offer the greatest number of departures; smaller airlines—including regional, low-cost, and no-frill airlines—usually have a more limited number of flights daily. Major airlines have frequent-flyer partners, which allow you to credit mileage earned on one airline to your account with another. Low-cost airlines offer a definite price advantage and fewer restrictions, such as advance-purchase requirements. Safety-wise, low-cost carriers as a group have a good history, but **check the safety record before booking** any low-cost carrier; call the Federal Aviation Administration's Consumer Hotline (☞ Airline Complaints, *below*).

➤ MAJOR AIRLINES: **America West** (☎ 800/235–9292). **American** (☎ 800/433–7300). **Continental** (☎ 800/525–0280). **Delta** (☎ 800/221–1212). **Northwest** (☎ 800/225–2525). **TWA** (☎ 800/221–2000). **United** (☎ 800/241–6522). **US Airways** (☎ 800/428–4322).

➤ SMALLER AIRLINES: **Carnival Air Lines** (☎ 800/824–7386). **Midway** (☎ 800/446–4392). **Midwest Express** (☎ 800/452–2022).

GET THE LOWEST FARE

The least-expensive airfares to New York are priced for round-trip travel. Major airlines usually require that you **book in advance and buy the ticket within 24 hours,** and you may have to **stay over a Saturday night.** It's smart to **call a number of airlines, and when you are quoted a good price, book it on the spot**—the same fare may not be available on the same flight the next day. Airlines generally allow you to change your return date for a fee $25–$50. If you don't use your ticket you can apply the cost toward the purchase of a new ticket, again for a small charge. However, most low-fare tickets are nonrefundable. To get the lowest airfare, **check different routings.** If your destination or home city has more than one gateway, compare prices to and from different airports. Also price off-peak flights, which may be significantly less expensive.

To save money on flights from the United Kingdom and back, **look into an APEX or Super-PEX ticket.** Both sorts should be booked in advance and have certain restrictions, though they can sometimes be purchased right at the airport.

DON'T STOP UNLESS YOU MUST

When you book, **look for nonstop flights** and **remember that "direct" flights stop at least once.** Try to **avoid connecting flights,** which require a change of plane. Two airlines may jointly operate a connecting flight, so ask if your airline operates every segment—you may find that your preferred carrier flies you only part of the way.

USE AN AGENT

Travel agents, especially those who specialize in finding the lowest fares (☞ Discounts & Deals, *below*), can be especially helpful when booking a plane ticket. When you're quoted a price, **ask your agent if the price is likely to get any lower.** Good agents know the seasonal fluctuations of airfares and can usually anticipate a sale or fare war. However, waiting can be risky: The fare could go *up* as seats become scarce, and you may wait so long that your preferred flight sells out. A wait-and-see strategy works best if your plans are flexible, but if you must arrive and depart on certain dates, don't delay.

AVOID GETTING BUMPED

Airlines routinely overbook planes, knowing that not everyone with a ticket will show up, but sometimes everyone does. When that happens, airlines ask for volunteers to give up their seats. In return these volunteers usually get a certificate for a free flight and are rebooked on the next flight out. If there are not enough volunteers the airline must choose who will be denied boarding. The first to get bumped are passengers who checked in late and those flying on discounted tickets, **so get to the gate and check in as early as possible,** especially during peak periods.

Always **bring a photo ID to the airport.** You may be asked to show it before you are allowed to check in.

ENJOY THE FLIGHT

For better service, **fly smaller or regional carriers,** which often have higher passenger-satisfaction ratings. Sometimes you'll find leather seats, more legroom, and better food.

For more legroom, **request an emergency-aisle seat**; don't however, sit in the row in front of the emergency aisle or in front of a bulkhead, where seats may not recline.

If you don't like airline food, **ask for special meals when booking.** These can be vegetarian, low-cholesterol, or kosher, for example.

To avoid jet lag try to maintain a normal routine while traveling. At night **get some sleep.** By day **eat light meals, drink water (not alcohol), and move about the cabin** to stretch your legs.

COMPLAIN IF NECESSARY

If your baggage goes astray or your flight goes awry, **complain right away.** Most carriers require that you file a claim immediately.

➤ AIRLINE COMPLAINTS: **U.S. Department of Transportation Aviation Consumer Protection Division** (✉ C-75, Washington, DC 20590, ☎ 202/366–2220). **Federal Aviation Administration (FAA) Consumer Hotline** (☎ 800/322–7873).

AIRPORTS & TRANSFERS

The major gateways to New York City are La Guardia Airport (☎ 718/533–3400) and JFK International Airport (☎ 718/244–4444), both in the borough of Queens, and Newark International Airport (☎ 201/961–6000) in New Jersey.

TRANSFERS FROM LA GUARDIA AIRPORT

Taxis cost $17–$29 plus tolls (which may be as high as $4) and take 20–40 minutes. Group taxi rides to Manhattan are available at taxi dispatch lines just outside the baggage-claim areas during most travel hours (except on Saturday and holidays). Group fares run $9–$10 per person (plus a share of tolls).

Carey Airport Express buses depart for Manhattan every 20–30 minutes from 6:45 AM to midnight, from all terminals. It's a 40-minute ride to 42nd Street and Park Avenue, directly opposite Grand Central Terminal. The bus continues from there to the Port Authority Bus Terminal, the New York Hilton, Sheraton Manhattan, Holiday Inn Crowne Plaza, and Marriott Marquis hotels, among others. A short cab ride will get you anywhere else in midtown. The bus fare is $10; pay the driver.

The Gray Line Airport Shuttle Minibus serves major Manhattan hotels and Port Authority directly to and from the airport. The fare is $13.50 per person; make arrangements at the airport's ground transportation center or use the courtesy phone.

The Delta Water Shuttle runs between La Guardia Airport's Marine Air Terminal and the East Side, including a stop at Wall Street (Pier 11). The trip lasts just under half an hour. The fare is $15.

The most economical way to reach Manhattan is to ride the M-60 public bus (there are no luggage facilities on this bus) to 116th Street and Broadway, across from Columbia University. From there, you can catch Subway 1 or 9 to midtown. Alternatively, you can take Bus Q-33 to either the Roosevelt Avenue–Jackson Heights station, where you can catch Subway E or F, or the 74th Street–Broadway station, where you can catch Subway 7. Allow 90 minutes for the entire trip to midtown; the total cost is two tokens ($3). You can use exact change for your bus fare, but you will have to purchase a token to enter the subway.

➤ BUS AND SUBWAY INFORMATION: **Carey Airport Express** (☎ 718/632–0500). **Gray Line Airport Shuttle Minibus** (☎ 212/315–3006 or 800/451–0455). **New York City Transit** (MTA, ☎ 718/330–1234).

➤ FERRY INFORMATION: **Delta Water Shuttle** (☎ 800/543–3779).

TRANSFERS FROM JFK INTERNATIONAL AIRPORT

Taxis cost $30–$38 plus tolls (which may be as much as $4) and take 35–60 minutes.

Carey Airport Express buses depart for Manhattan every 20–30 minutes from 6 AM to midnight, from all JFK terminals. The ride to 42nd Street and Park Avenue (Grand Central Terminal) takes about one hour. The bus continues from there to the Port Authority Bus Terminal, the New York Hilton, Sheraton Manhattan, Holiday Inn Crowne Plaza, and Marriott Marquis hotels, among others; it's a short cab ride to other midtown hotels. The bus fare is $13; pay the driver.

The Gray Line Airport Shuttle Minibus serves major Manhattan hotels and Port Authority directly from the airport; the cost is $16.50 per person. Make arrangements at the airport's ground transportation counter or use the courtesy phone.

New York Helicopter offers private charter flights between the airport and one of four heliports in Manhattan. Helicopters leave from the General Aviation Terminal and set you down in the city 10 minutes later. The one-way fare is $299 for up to five people.

The cheapest but slowest means of getting to Manhattan is to take the Port Authority's free shuttle bus, which stops at all terminals, to the Howard Beach subway station, where you can catch the A train into Manhattan. Alternatively, you can take Bus Q-10 (there are no luggage facilities on this bus) to the Union Turnpike–Kew Gardens station, where you can catch Subway E or F. Or you can take Bus B-15 to New Lots station and catch Subway 3. Allow at least

two hours for the trip; the total cost is one token ($1.50) if you use the shuttle or two tokens ($3) if you use the Q-10 or B-15. You can use exact change for your fare on the Q-10 and B-15, but you will need to purchase a token to enter the subway.

➤ BUS AND SUBWAY INFORMATION: ☞ Transfers from La Guardia Airport, *above.*

➤ HELICOPTER RESERVATIONS: **New York Helicopter** (☎ 800/645–3494, FAX 516/756–2694).

TRANSFERS FROM NEWARK AIRPORT

Taxis cost $34–$38 plus tolls ($10) and take 20–45 minutes. "Share and Save" group rates are available for up to four passengers between 8 AM and midnight; make arrangements with the airport's taxi dispatcher.

New Jersey Transit Airport Express buses depart for the Port Authority Bus Terminal, at 8th Avenue and 42nd Street every 15 minutes on weekdays from 4:45 AM to 3:45 AM; on weekends, service runs nearly as frequently from 4:45 AM until 3 AM. From Port Authority, it's a short cab ride to midtown hotels. The ride takes 30–45 minutes. The fare is $7; buy your ticket inside the airport terminal.

Olympia Airport Express buses leave for Grand Central Terminal and Penn Station about every 20 minutes, and 1 World Trade Center (WTC) about every 30 minutes, from around 6 AM to midnight. The trip takes roughly 45 minutes to Grand Central and Penn Station, 20 minutes to WTC. The fare is $7. At press time, a new route was planned between Port Authority and Newark. Buses will run every 20 minutes 5 AM–midnight. The fare is $10.

The Gray Line Airport Shuttle Minibus serves major Manhattan hotels and Port Authority directly to and from the airport. You pay $14 per passenger; make arrangements at the airport's ground transportation center or use the courtesy phone.

You can also take New Jersey Transit's Airlink buses, which leave every 20 minutes from 6:15 AM to 2 AM, to Penn Station in Newark. The ride takes about 20 minutes; the fare is $4. (Be sure to have exact change.) From there, your can catch PATH Trains, which run to Manhattan 24 hours a day. The trains run every 10 minutes on weekdays, every 15–30 minutes on weeknights, every 20–30 minutes on weekends; trains stop at the WTC and at five stops along 6th Avenue—Christopher Street, 9th Street, 14th Street, 23rd Street, and 33rd Street. The fare is $1.

➤ BUS AND TRAIN INFORMATION: **Gray Line Airport Shuttle Minibus** (☎ 212/315–3006 or 800/451–0455). **New Jersey Transit** (☎ 201/762–5100). **Olympia Airport Express** (☎ 212/964–6233 or 718/622–7700).

TRANSFERS FROM ALL AIRPORTS

Car services are a great deal because the driver will often meet you on the concourse or in the baggage-claim area and help you with your luggage. You ride in late-model American-made cars that are comfortable, if usually a bit worn. New York City Taxi and Limousine Commission rules require that all be licensed and pick up riders only by prior arrangement. **Call 24 hours in advance for reservations,** or at least a half day before your flight's departure.

➤ CAR RESERVATIONS: **All State Car and Limousine Service** (☎ 212/741–7440, FAX 212/727–2391). **Carey Limousines** (☎ 212/599–1122 or 800/336–4646). **Carmel Car and Limousine Service** (☎ 212/666–6666). **Dav-El Services** (☎ 212/645–4242 or 800/922–0343). **Eastside Limo Service** (☎ 212/744–9700, FAX 718/937–9400). **Greenwich Limousine** (☎ 800/385–1033 or 212/868–4733). **London Towncars** (☎ 212/988–9700 or 800/221–4009, FAX 718/786–7625). **Manhattan International Limo** (☎ 718/729–4200 or 800/221–7500, FAX 718/937–6157). **Sherwood Silver Bay Limousine Service** (☎ 718/472–0183 or 800/752–4540, FAX 718/361–5693). **Skyline** (☎ 212/741–3711 or 800/533–6325). **American Media Tours** (☎ 212/255–5908) for business accounts car services.

B
BUS TRAVEL

Long-haul and commuter bus lines feed into the Port Authority Terminal on Broadway between 40th and 42nd streets.

The George Washington Bridge Bus Station is at Fort Washington Avenue and Broadway between 178th and 179th streets in the Washington Heights section of Manhattan. Six bus lines, serving northern New Jersey and Rockland County, New York, make daily stops there from 5 AM to 1 AM. The terminal connects with the 175th Street Station on Subway A, making it slightly more convenient for travelers going to and from the West Side.

➤ BUS TERMINAL INFORMATION: **George Washington Bridge Bus Station** (☎ 212/564–1114). **Port Authority Terminal** (☎ 212/564–8484).

➤ INTERSTATE BUSES: **Greyhound Lines Inc.** (☎ 212/971–6404 or 800/231–2222). **Adirondack, Pine Hill,** and **New York Trailways** (☎ 800/225–6815) from upstate New York. **Bonanza Bus Lines** (☎ 800/556–3815) from New England. **Martz Trailways** (☎ 800/233–8604) from Philadelphia and northeastern Pennsylvania. **New Jersey Transit** (☎ 800/556–3815) from around New Jersey (☎ 800/556–3815). **Peter Pan Trailways** (☎ 800/343–9999 or 413/781–2900) from New England. **Vermont Transit** (☎ 802/864–6811 or 800/451–3292) from New England.

WITHIN NEW YORK

Most buses follow easy-to-understand routes along the Manhattan grid. Routes go up or down the north–south avenues, or east and west on the major two-way crosstown streets. Most bus routes operate 24 hours, but service is infrequent late at night. Buses are great for sightseeing, but traffic jams—a potential threat at any time or place in Manhattan—can make rides maddeningly slow. Certain bus routes now offer "Limited-Stop Service"; buses on these routes stop only at major cross streets and transfer points and can save traveling time. The "Limited-Stop" buses usually run on weekdays and during rush hours.

THE GOLD GUIDE / SMART TRAVEL TIPS

Actually finding the bus stop will be much easier than in the past. New bus stop signs were introduced in the fall of 1996 and should be in place throughout the city by 1998. **Look for a light-blue sign (or green for an express bus)** on a green pole; bus numbers and routes are listed, with the current stop's name underneath. Bus fare is the same as subway fare: $1.50 at press time, in coins (no change is given) or a subway token or MetroCard. When using a token or cash, you can **ask the driver for a free transfer coupon,** good for one change to an intersecting route. Legal transfer points are listed on the back of the slip. Transfers have time limits of at least two hours, often longer. You cannot use the transfer to enter the subway system. However, you can **transfer free from bus to subway or subway to bus with the MetroCard.** You must start with the MetroCard and use it again within two hours to complete your trip.

Route maps and schedules are posted at many bus stops in Manhattan and at major stops throughout the other boroughs. Each of the five boroughs of New York has a separate bus map, and they are scarcer than hens' teeth. They are available from some subway token booths, but never on buses. The best places to obtain them are the Convention and Visitors Bureau at Columbus Circle or the information kiosks in Grand Central Terminal and Penn Station.

➤ SCHEDULE AND ROUTE INFORMA-TION: **New York City Transit** (MTA, ☎ 718/330–1234), available daily 6–9. **Status information hot line** (☎ 718/243–7777), updated hourly 6–9.

BUSINESS HOURS

New York is very much a 24-hour city. Its subways and buses run around the clock, and plenty of services are available at all hours and on all days of the week. It's always a.

Banks are open weekdays 9–3 or 9–3:30; a few branches in certain neighborhoods may stay open late on Friday or open on Saturday morning.

Post offices are open weekdays 10–5 or 10–6. The main post office on 8th Avenue between 31st and 33rd streets is open daily 24 hours.

Museum hours vary greatly, but most of the major ones are open Tuesday–Sunday and keep later hours on Tuesday or Thursday evenings.

Stores are generally open Monday–Saturday from 10 to 5 or 6, but neighborhood peculiarities do exist. Most stores on the Lower East Side and in the diamond district on 47th Street close on Friday afternoon and all day Saturday for the Jewish Sabbath while keeping normal hours on Sunday. Sunday hours, also common on the West Side and in Greenwich Village and SoHo, are the exception on the Upper East Side.

C

CAMERAS, CAMCORDERS, & COMPUTERS

Always **keep your film, tape, or computer disks out of the sun.** Carry an extra supply of batteries, and **be prepared to turn on your camera, camcorder, or laptop** to prove to security personnel that the device is real. Always **ask for hand inspection of film,** which becomes clouded after successive exposure to airport X-ray machines, and **keep videotapes and computer disks away from metal detectors.**

➤ PHOTO HELP: **Kodak Information Center** (☎ 800/242–2424). *Kodak Guide to Shooting Great Travel Pictures,* available in bookstores or from Fodor's (☎ 800/533–6478; $16.50 plus $4 shipping).

CAR RENTAL

Rates in New York City begin at $46 a day and $205 a week for an economy car with air-conditioning, automatic transmission, and unlimited mileage. This does not include tax on car rentals, which is 13¼%.

➤ MAJOR AGENCIES: **Avis** (☎ 800/331–1212; 800/879–2847 in Canada). **Budget** (☎ 800/527–0700; 0800/181181 in the U.K.). **Dollar** (☎ 800/800–4000; 0990/565656 in the U.K., where it is known as Eurodollar). **Hertz** (☎ 800/654–3131; 800/263–0600 in Canada; 0345/555888 in the U.K.). **National InterRent** (☎ 800/227–7368; 0345/222525 in the U.K., where it is known as Europcar InterRent).

CUT COSTS

To get the best deal, **book through a travel agent who is willing to shop around.** When pricing cars, **ask about the location of the rental lot.** Some off-airport locations offer lower rates, and their lots are only minutes from the terminal via complimentary shuttle. It is usually cheaper to rent a car at Newark Airport than at the New York City airports. You also may want to **price local car-rental companies,** whose rates may be lower still, although their service and maintenance may not be as good as those of a name-brand agency. Remember to ask about required deposits, cancellation penalties, and drop-off charges if you're planning to pick up the car in one city and leave it in another.

Also **ask your travel agent about a company's customer-service record.** How has it responded to late plane arrivals and vehicle mishaps? Are there often lines at the rental counter, and, if you're traveling during a holiday period, does a confirmed reservation guarantee you a car?

Be sure to **look into wholesalers,** companies that do not own fleets but rent in bulk from those that do and often offer better rates than traditional car-rental operations. Prices are best during off-peak periods.

➤ Rental Wholesalers: **Auto Europe** (☎ 207/828–2525 or 800/223–5555).

NEED INSURANCE?

When driving a rented car you are generally responsible for any damage to or loss of the vehicle. You also are liable for any property damage or personal injury that you may cause while driving. Before you rent, **see what coverage you already have** under the terms of your personal auto-insurance policy and credit cards.

New York has outlawed the sale of collision- or loss-damage waiver (CDW or LDW), which limits your liability for damage to the rented car. You pay only for the first $100 of damage. However, if you do not have auto insurance or an umbrella policy that covers damage to third parties, purchasing liability insurance is highly recommended.

BEWARE SURCHARGES

Before you pick up a car in one city and leave it in another, **ask about drop-off charges or one-way service fees,** which can be substantial. Note, too, that some rental agencies charge extra if you return the car before the time specified on your contract. To avoid a hefty refueling fee, **fill the tank just before you turn in the car,** but be aware that gas stations near the rental outlet may overcharge.

MEET THE REQUIREMENTS

In New York you must be 18 to rent a car, and rates may be higher if you're under 25. You'll pay extra for child seats (about $3 per day), which are compulsory for children under five, and for additional drivers (about $2 per day). Residents of the United Kingdom will need a reservation voucher, a passport, a U.K. driver's license, and a travel policy that covers each driver in order to pick up a car.

CHILDREN & TRAVEL

CHILDREN IN NEW YORK

Children under six travel free on subways and buses; children over six must pay full fare.

Be sure to plan ahead and **involve your youngsters** as you outline your trip. When packing, include things to keep them busy en route. On sightseeing days try to schedule activities of special interest to your children. If you are renting a car, don't forget to **arrange for a car seat** when you reserve.

➤ Baby-Sitting: The **Baby Sitters' Guild** (✉ 60 E. 42nd St., Suite 912, ☎ 212/682–0227) can take your children on sightseeing tours. Rates start at $12 an hour for one or two children over age one, plus a $4.50 transportation charge ($7 after midnight); there are special rates for infants under one year and for foreign language (over a dozen languages are spoken among the staff). Minimum booking is for four hours.

The **Avalon Registry** (✉ Box 1362, Radio City Station, New York, NY 10101, ☎ 212/245–0250) is prepared to take very young children off your hands—at least for the day. Rates are $10 an hour for one child of any age; rates increase $2 per hour for each additional child. There is also a $3 transportation charge ($8 after 8 PM).

➤ LOCAL INFO: *Where Should We Take the Kids? Northeast* ($18), available from Fodor's Travel Publications (☎ 800/533–6478) and in bookstores.

For calendars of children's events, consult *New York* magazine, *Time Out New York,* and the weekly *Village Voice* newspaper, available free at Manhattan newsstands and bookstores. The Friday *New York Times* "Weekend" section also provides a good listing of children's activities. Other good sources of information on happenings for kids are the monthly magazines *New York Family* (✉ 141 Halstead Ave., Suite 3D, Mamaroneck, NY 10543, ☎ 914/381–7474) and the *Big Apple Parents' Paper* (✉ 36 E. 12th St., New York, NY 10003, ☎ 212/533–2277), which are available free at toy stores, children's museums and clothing stores, and other places around town where parents and children are found.

➤ STROLLER RENTAL: **AAA-U-Rent** (✉ 861 Eagle Ave., Bronx, NY 10456, ☎ 718/665–6633).

HOTELS

Most hotels in New York allow children under a certain age to stay in their parents' room at no extra charge, but others charge them as extra adults; be sure to **ask about the cutoff age for children's discounts.**

FLYING

As a general rule, infants under two not occupying a seat fly free. If your children are two or older **ask about children's airfares.**

In general the adult baggage allowance applies to children paying half or more of the adult fare.

According to the Federal Aviation Administration (FAA), it's a good idea to use safety seats aloft for children weighing less than 40 pounds. Airlines, however, can set their own policies: U.S. carriers allow FAA-approved models but usually require that you buy a ticket, even if your child would otherwise ride free, since the seats must be strapped into regular seats. Airline rules vary regarding their use, so it's important to **check your airline's policy about using safety seats during takeoff and landing.** Safety seats cannot obstruct any of the other passengers in the row, so get an appropriate seat assignment as early as possible.

When making your reservation, **request children's meals or a freestanding bassinet** if you need them; the latter is available only to those seated at the bulkhead, where there's enough legroom. Remember, however, that bulkhead seats may not have their own overhead bins, and there's no storage space in front of you—a major inconvenience.

CONSUMER PROTECTION

Whenever possible, **pay with a major credit card** so you can cancel payment if there's a problem, provided that you can provide documentation. This is a good practice whether you're buying travel arrangements before your trip or shopping at your destination.

If you're doing business with a particular company for the first time, **contact your local Better Business Bureau and the attorney general's offices** in your state and the company's home state, as well. Have any complaints been filed?

Finally, if you're buying a package or tour, always **consider travel insurance** that includes default coverage (☞ Insurance, *below*).

➤ LOCAL BBBs: **Council of Better Business Bureaus** (✉ 4200 Wilson Blvd., Suite 800, Arlington, VA 22203, ☎ 703/276–0100, FAX 703/525–8277).

CUSTOMS & DUTIES

ENTERING THE U.S.

Visitors age 21 and over may import the following into the United States: 200 cigarettes or 50 cigars or 2 kilograms of tobacco, 1 liter of alcohol, and gifts worth $100. Prohibited items include meat products, seeds, plants, and fruits.

ENTERING CANADA

If you've been out of Canada for at least seven days you may bring in C$500 worth of goods duty-free. If you've been away for fewer than seven days but more than 48 hours, the duty-free allowance drops to C$200; if your trip lasts 24–48 hours, the allowance is C$50. You may not pool allowances with family members. Goods claimed under the C$500 exemption may follow you by mail; those claimed under the lesser exemptions must accompany you.

Alcohol and tobacco products may be included in the seven-day and 48-hour exemptions but not in the 24-hour exemption. If you meet the age requirements of the province or territory through which you reenter Canada you may bring in, duty-free, 1.14 liters (40 imperial ounces) of wine or liquor *or* 24 12-ounce cans or bottles of beer or ale. If you are 16 or older you may bring in, duty-free, 200 cigarettes and 50 cigars; these items must accompany you.

You may send an unlimited number of gifts worth up to C$60 each duty-free to Canada. Label the package UNSOLICITED GIFT—VALUE UNDER $60. Alcohol and tobacco are excluded.

➤ INFORMATION: **Revenue Canada** (✉ 2265 St. Laurent Blvd. S, Ottawa, Ontario K1G 4K3, ☎ 613/993–0534; 800/461–9999 in Canada).

ENTERING THE U.K.

From countries outside the European Union, including the United States, you may import, duty-free, 200 cigarettes or 50 cigars; 1 liter of spirits or 2 liters of fortified or sparkling wine or liqueurs; 2 liters of still table wine; 60 milliliters of perfume; 250 milliliters of toilet water; plus £136 worth of other goods, including gifts and souvenirs.

➤ INFORMATION: **HM Customs and Excise** (✉ Dorset House, Stamford St., London SE1 9NG, ☎ 0171/202–4227).

D

DISABILITIES & ACCESSIBILITY

ACCESS IN NEW YORK

Many buildings in New York City are now wheelchair-accessible. The subway is still hard to navigate, however; people in wheelchairs do better on public buses, most of which have wheelchair lifts at the rear door and "kneel" at the front to facilitate getting on and off.

➤ LOCAL RESOURCES: The **Mayor's Office for People with Disabilities** (✉ 52 Chambers St., Office 206, New York, NY 10007, ☎ 212/788–2830, TTY 212/788–2842) has brochures and helpful information. The **Andrew Heiskell Library for the Blind and Physically Handicapped** (✉ 40 W. 20th St., New York, NY 10001, ☎ 212/206–5400) has a large collection of Braille, large-print, and recorded books, housed in a layout specially designed for easy access for people with vision impairments.

TIPS AND HINTS

When discussing accessibility with an operator or reservationist, **ask hard questions.** Are there any stairs, inside *or* out? Are there grab bars next to the toilet *and* in the shower/tub? How wide is the doorway to the room? To the bathroom? For the most extensive facilities meeting the latest legal specifications, **opt for newer accommodations,** which are more likely to have been designed with access in mind. Older buildings or ships may offer more limited facilities. Be sure to **discuss your needs before booking.**

➤ COMPLAINTS: **Disability Rights Section** (✉ U.S. Dept. of Justice, Box 66738, Washington, DC 20035-6738, ☎ 202/514–0301 or 800/514–0301, FAX 202/307–1198, TTY 202/514–0383 or 800/514–0383) for general complaints. **Aviation Consumer Protection Division** (☞ Air Travel, *above*) for airline-related problems. **Civil Rights Office** (✉ U.S. Dept. of Transportation, Departmental Office of Civil Rights, S-30, 400 7th St. SW, Room 10215, Washington, DC 20590, ☎ 202/366–4648) for problems with surface transportation.

TRAVEL AGENCIES & TOUR OPERATORS

The Americans with Disabilities Act requires that travel firms serve the needs of all travelers. That said, you should note that some agencies and operators specialize in making travel arrangements for individuals and groups with disabilities.

➤ TRAVELERS WITH MOBILITY PROBLEMS: **Access Adventures** (✉ 206 Chestnut Ridge Rd., Rochester, NY 14624, ☎ 716/889–9096), run by a former physical-rehabilitation counselor. **CareVacations** (✉ 5019 49th

Ave., Suite 102, Leduc, Alberta T9E 6T5, ☎ 403/986–6404; 800/648–1116 in Canada), organizing group tours and cruise vacations. **Hinsdale Travel Service** (✉ 201 E. Ogden Ave., Suite 100, Hinsdale, IL 60521, ☎ 630/325–1335), a travel agency that benefits from the advice of wheelchair traveler Janice Perkins. **Wheelchair Journeys** (✉ 16979 Redmond Way, Redmond, WA 98052, ☎ 206/885–2210 or 800/313–4751), for general travel arrangements.

➤ TRAVELERS WITH DEVELOPMENTAL DISABILITIES: **Sprout** (✉ 893 Amsterdam Ave., New York, NY 10025, ☎ 212/222–9575 or 888/222–9575, FAX 212/222–9768).

DISCOUNTS & DEALS

Be a smart shopper and **compare all your options before making a choice.** A plane ticket bought with a promotional coupon may not be cheaper than the least expensive fare from a discount ticket agency. For high-price travel purchases, such as packages or tours, keep in mind that what you get is just as important as what you save. Just because something is cheap doesn't mean it's a bargain.

LOOK IN YOUR WALLET

When you use your credit card to make travel purchases you may get free travel-accident insurance, collision-damage insurance, and medical or legal assistance, depending on the card and the bank that issued it. American Express, MasterCard, and Visa provide one or more of these services, so **get a copy of your credit card's travel-benefits policy.** If you are a member of the American Automobile Association (AAA) or an oil-company-sponsored road-assistance plan, always **ask hotel or car-rental reservationists about auto-club discounts.** Some clubs offer additional discounts on tours, cruises, or admission to attractions. And don't forget that auto-club membership entitles you to free maps and trip-planning services.

DIAL FOR DOLLARS

To save money, **look into "1-800" discount reservations services,** which use their buying power to get a better price on hotels, airline tickets, even car rentals. When booking a room, always **call the hotel's local toll-free**

number (if one is available) rather than the central reservations number—you'll often get a better price. Always ask about special packages or corporate rates.

➤ AIRLINE TICKETS: ☎ 800/FLY-4–LESS. ☎ 800/FLY-ASAP.

➤ HOTEL ROOMS: **Accommodations Express** (☎ 800/444–7666). **Central Reservation Service (CRS)** (☎ 800/548–3311). **Hotel Reservations Network (HRN)** (☎ 800/964–6835). **Quickbook** (☎ 800/789–9887). **Room Finders USA** (☎ 800/473–7829). **RMC Travel** (☎ 800/245–5738). **Steigenberger Reservation Service** (☎ 800/223–5652).

SAVE ON COMBOS

Packages and guided tours can both save you money, but don't confuse the two. When you buy a package your travel remains independent, just as though you had planned and booked the trip yourself. Fly-drive packages, which combine airfare and car rental, are often a good deal. In cities, ask the local visitors bureau about hotel packages. These often include tickets to major museum exhibits and other special events.

JOIN A CLUB?

Many companies sell discounts in the form of travel clubs and coupon books, but these cost money. You must use participating advertisers to get a deal, and only after you recoup the initial membership cost or book price do you begin to save. If you plan to use the club or coupons frequently you may save considerably. Before signing up, find out what discounts you get for free.

➤ DISCOUNT CLUBS: **Entertainment Travel Editions** (✉ Box 1068, Trumbull, CT 06611, ☎ 800/445–4137; $28–$53, depending on destination). **Great American Traveler** (✉ Box 27965, Salt Lake City, UT 84127, ☎ 800/548–2812; $49.95 per yr). **Moment's Notice Discount Travel Club** (✉ 7301 New Utrecht Ave., Brooklyn, NY 11204, ☎ 718/234–6295; $25 per yr, single or family). **Privilege Card International** (✉ 201 E. Commerce St., Suite 198, Youngstown, OH 44503, ☎ 330/746–5211 or 800/236–9732; $74.95 per yr). **Sears's Mature Outlook** (✉

Box 9390, Des Moines, IA 50306, ☎ 800/336–6330; $14.95 per yr). **Travelers Advantage** (⊠ CUC Travel Service, 3033 S. Parker Rd., Suite 1000, Aurora, CO 80014, ☎ 800/548–1116 or 800/648–4037; $49 per yr, single or family). **Worldwide Discount Travel Club** (⊠ 1674 Meridian Ave., Miami Beach, FL 33139, ☎ 305/534–2082; $50 per yr family, $40 single).

DRIVING

If you plan to drive into Manhattan, try to time your arrival for late morning or early afternoon. That way you'll avoid the morning and evening rush hours (a problem at the crossings into Manhattan) and lunch hour.

The deterioration of the bridges linking Manhattan, especially those spanning the East River, is a serious problem, and repairs will be ongoing for the next few years. Don't be surprised if a bridge is entirely or partially closed.

Driving within Manhattan can be a nightmare of gridlocked streets and predatory motorists. Free parking is difficult to find in midtown, and violators may be towed away literally within minutes. All over town, parking lots charge exorbitant rates—as much as $15 for two hours in some neighborhoods. If you do drive, **don't plan to use your car much for traveling within Manhattan.** Instead, try to park it in a guarded parking garage for at least several hours; the sting of hourly rates lessens if a car is left for a significant amount of time.

➤ AUTO CLUBS: In the United States, **American Automobile Association** (☎ 800/564–6222). In the United Kingdom, **Automobile Association** (AA, ☎ 0990/500600), **Royal Automobile Club** (RAC, ☎ 0990/722722 for membership inquiries, 0345/121345 for insurance).

E

EMERGENCIES

Dial **911** for police, fire, or ambulance in an emergency (TTY is available for the hearing impaired).

➤ DOCTOR: **Doctors On Call** (☎ 212/737–2333), 24-hour house-call service. **St. Luke's-Roosevelt Hospital** (59th St. between 9th and 10th Aves.,

212/523–6800) and **St. Vincent's Hospital** (7th Ave. and 12th St., ☎ 212/604–7997), both near midtown, have 24-hour emergency rooms.

➤ DENTIST: **Emergency Dental Service** (☎ 212/679–3966; 212/679–4172 after 8 PM) will make a referral.

➤ HOT LINES: **Victims' Services** (☎ 212/577–7777). **Mental Health** (☎ 212/219–5599 or 800/527–7474 for information after 5 PM). **Sex Crimes Report Line** (☎ 212/267–7273).

➤ 24-HOUR PHARMACY: **Kaufman's Pharmacy** (Lexington Ave. and 50th St., ☎ 212/755–2266) is open around the clock, but prices are exorbitant. **Genovese** (2nd Ave. at 68th St., ☎ 212/772–0104) has reasonable prices. Before 10 or 11 PM look for a pharmacy in a neighborhood that keeps late hours, such as Greenwich Village or the Upper West Side, for better deals.

F

FERRIES

Ferries run from Battery Park's Castle Clinton to the Statue of Liberty and Ellis Island. The fare is $7. The Staten Island Ferry departs from the tip of Manhattan and crosses New York Harbor to Staten Island. The ride is free. NY Waterway has Yankee Clipper ferries taking passengers from Manhattan ($10) and New Jersey ($15) to Yankee Stadium.

➤ FERRY INFORMATION: **Castle Clinton** (☎ 212/269–5755). **Staten Island Ferry** (☎ 718/390–5253). **NY Waterway** (☎ 201/902–8700 or 800/533–3779).

G

GAY & LESBIAN TRAVEL

➤ LOCAL INFO: The **Lesbian and Gay Community Services Center** (⊠ 208 W. 13th St., New York, NY 10011, ☎ 212/620–7310) offers the free "Lesbian & Gay Center Welcome Packet," which contains everything from HIV services to cultural listings, plus the Center's monthly event calendar.

➤ PUBLICATIONS: *Fodor's Gay Guide to New York City* ($11; Fodor's Travel Publications, ☎ 800/533–6478 and in bookstores) is a comprehensive resource for gay and lesbian visitors to the Big Apple. *Fodor's Gay Guide to the USA* ($19.50; Fodor's Travel Publications) covers New York in a detailed chapter. *Metro Source* (✉ 180 Varick St., 5th floor, New York, NY 10014, ☎ 212/691–5127; $15 for 4 issues) has up-to-date news on gay- and lesbian-oriented hotels, restaurants, shops, and nightspots in New York City. The premier international travel magazine for gays and lesbians is *Our World* (✉ 1104 N. Nova Rd., Suite 251, Daytona Beach, FL 32117, ☎ 904/441–5367, FAX 904/441–5604; $35 for 10 issues). The 16-page monthly newsletter "Out & About" (✉ 8 W. 19th St., Suite 401, New York, NY 10011, ☎ 212/645–6922 or 800/929–2268, FAX 800/929–2215; $49 for 10 issues and quarterly calendar) covers gay-friendly resorts, hotels, cruise lines, and airlines.

▶ TOUR OPERATORS: **Toto Tours** (✉ 1326 W. Albion Ave., Suite 3W, Chicago, IL 60626, ☎ 312/274–8686 or 800/565–1241, FAX 312/274–8695) for groups.

▶ GAY- AND LESBIAN-FRIENDLY TRAVEL AGENCIES: **Advance Damron** (✉ 1 Greenway Plaza, Suite 800, Houston, TX 77046, ☎ 713/682–2002 or 800/695–0880, FAX 713/888–1010). **Club Travel** (✉ 8739 Santa Monica Blvd., West Hollywood, CA 90069, ☎ 310/358–2200 or 800/429–8747, FAX 310/358–2222). **Islanders/Kennedy Travel** (✉ 183 W. 10th St., New York, NY 10014, ☎ 212/242–3222 or 800/988–1181, FAX 212/929–8530). **Now Voyager** (✉ 4406 18th St., San Francisco, CA 94114, ☎ 415/626–1169 or 800/255–6951, FAX 415/626–8626). **Yellowbrick Road** (✉ 1500 W. Balmoral Ave., Chicago, IL 60640, ☎ 773/561–1800 or 800/642–2488, FAX 773/561–4497). **Skylink Women's Travel** (✉ 3577 Moorland Ave., Santa Rosa, CA 95407, ☎ 707/585–8355 or 800/225–5759, FAX 707/584–5637), serving lesbian travelers.

I

INSURANCE

Travel insurance is the best way to **protect yourself against financial loss.** The most useful policies are trip-cancellation-and-interruption, default,

medical, and comprehensive insurance.

Without insurance you will lose all or most of your money if you cancel your trip, regardless of the reason. It's essential that you **buy trip-cancellation-and-interruption insurance,** particularly if your airline ticket, cruise, or package tour is nonrefundable and cannot be changed. When considering how much coverage you need, look for a policy that will cover the cost of your trip plus the nondiscounted price of a one-way airline ticket, should you need to return home early. Also **consider default or bankruptcy insurance,** which protects you against a supplier's failure to deliver.

Medicare generally does not cover health-care costs outside the United States, nor do many privately issued policies. If your own policy does not cover you outside the United States, **consider buying supplemental medical coverage.** Remember that travel health insurance is different from a medical-assistance plan.

Citizens of the United Kingdom can buy an annual travel-insurance policy valid for most vacations during the year in which it's purchased. If you are pregnant or have a preexisting medical condition, make sure you're covered. According to the Association of British Insurers, a trade association representing 450 insurance companies, it's wise to buy extra medical coverage when you visit the United States.

If you have purchased an expensive vacation, comprehensive insurance is a must. **Look for comprehensive policies that include trip-delay insurance,** which will protect you in the event that weather problems cause you to miss your flight, tour, or cruise. A few insurers sell waivers for preexisting medical conditions. Companies that offer both features include Access America, Carefree Travel, Travel Insured International, and Travel Guard (☞ *below*).

Always **buy travel insurance directly from the insurance company;** if you buy it from a travel agency or tour operator that goes out of business you probably will not be covered for the agency or operator's default, a

THE GOLD GUIDE / SMART TRAVEL TIPS

major risk. Before you make any purchase, **review your existing health and home owner's policies** to find out whether they cover expenses incurred while traveling.

➤ TRAVEL INSURERS: In the United States, **Access America** (✉ 6600 W. Broad St., Richmond, VA 23230, ☎ 804/285–3300 or 800/284–8300), **Carefree Travel Insurance** (✉ Box 9366, 100 Garden City Plaza, Garden City, NY 11530, ☎ 516/294–0220 or 800/323–3149), **Near Travel Services** (✉ Box 1339, Calumet City, IL 60409, ☎ 708/868–6700 or 800/654–6700), **Travel Guard** whether they cover expenses incurred while traveling.

➤ TRAVEL INSURERS: In the United States, **Access America** (✉ 6600 W. Broad St., Richmond, VA 23230, ☎ 804/285–3300 or 800/284–8300), **Carefree Travel Insurance** (✉ Box 9366, 100 Garden City Plaza, Garden City, NY 11530, ☎ 516/294–0220 or 800/323–3149), **Near Travel Services** (✉ Box 1339, Calumet City, IL 60409, ☎ 708/868–6700 or 800/654–6700), **Travel Guard International** (✉ 1145 Clark St., Stevens Point, WI 54481, ☎ 715/345–0505 or 800/826–1300), **Travel Insured International** (✉ Box 280568, East Hartford, CT 06128-0568, ☎ 860/528–7663 or 800/243–3174), **Travelex Insurance Services** (✉ 11717 Burt St., Suite 202, Omaha, NE 68154-1500, ☎ 402/445–8637 or 800/228–9792, ℻ 800/867–9531), **Wallach & Company** (✉ 107 W. Federal St., Box 480, Middleburg, VA 20118, ☎ 540/687–3166 or 800/237–6615). In Canada, **Mutual of Omaha** (✉ Travel Division, 500 University Ave., Toronto, Ontario M5G 1V8, ☎ 416/598–4083; 800/268–8825 in Canada). In the United Kingdom, **Association of British Insurers** (✉ 51 Gresham St., London EC2V 7HQ, ☎ 0171/600–3333).

L

LIMOUSINES

If you want to ride around Manhattan in style, **rent a chauffeur-driven car** from one of many limousine services. Companies usually charge by the hour or offer a flat fee for sightseeing excursions.

➤ LIMOUSINE SERVICES: **All State Car and Limousine Service** (☎ 212/741–7440). **Bermuda Limousine International** (☎ 212/249–8400). **Carey Limousines** (☎ 212/599–1122). **Carmel Car and Limousine Service** (☎ 212/666–6666). **Chris Limousines** (☎ 718/356–3232 or 800/542–1584). **Concord Limousine Inc.** (☎ 212/230–1600 or 800/255–7255). **Eastside Limo Service** (☎ 212/744–9700). **Greenwich Limousine** (☎ 212/868–4733 or 800/385–1033). **London Towncars** (☎ 212/988–9700 or 800/221–4009).

LODGING

APARTMENT RENTALS

If you want a home base that's roomy enough for a family and comes with cooking facilities, **consider a furnished rental.** These can save you money, however some rentals are luxury properties, economical only when your party is large. Home-exchange directories list rentals (often second homes owned by prospective house swappers), and some services search for a house or apartment for you and handle the paperwork. Some send an illustrated catalog; others send photographs only of specific properties, sometimes at a charge. Up-front registration fees may apply.

➤ RENTAL AGENTS: **Europa-Let/Tropical Inn-Let** (✉ 92 N. Main St., Ashland, OR 97520, ☎ 541/482–5806 or 800/462–4486, ℻ 541/482–0660). **Hometours International** (✉ Box 11503, Knoxville, TN 37939, ☎ 423/690–8484 or 800/367–4668). **Property Rentals International** (✉ 1008 Mansfield Crossing Rd., Richmond, VA 23236, ☎ 804/378–6054 or 800/220–3332, ℻ 804/379–2073). **Vacation Home Rentals Worldwide** (✉ 235 Kensington Ave., Norwood, NJ 07648, ☎ 201/767–9393 or 800/633–3284, ℻ 201/767–5510). **Hideaways International** (✉ 767 Islington St., Portsmouth, NH 03801, ☎ 603/430–4433 or 800/843–4433, ℻ 603/430–4444).

HOME EXCHANGES

If you would like to exchange your home for someone else's, **join a home-exchange organization,** which will send you its updated listings of available exchanges for a year and will include your own listing in at least one of them. Making the arrangements is up to you.

➤ EXCHANGE CLUBS: **HomeLink International** (✉ Box 650, Key West, FL 33041, ☎ 305/294–7766 or 800/638–3841, FAX 305/294–1148) charges $83 per year.

M

MONEY

ATMS

Before leaving home, **make sure that your credit cards have been programmed for ATM use.**

➤ ATM LOCATIONS: **Cirrus** (☎ 800/424–7787). **Plus** (☎ 800/843–7587).

P

PACKING FOR NEW YORK

Jackets and ties are required for men in a number of restaurants—and in general, New Yorkers tend to dress a bit more formally than their west coast counterparts for special events like the theater. Jeans and sneakers are acceptable for casual dining and sightseeing just about anywhere in the city. Always **come with sneakers or other flat-heeled walking shoes** for pounding the New York pavement.

Do **pack light,** because porters and luggage trolleys can be hard to find at New York airports. And **bring a fistful of quarters to rent a trolley.**

Bring an extra pair of eyeglasses or contact lenses in your carry-on luggage, and if you have a health problem, **pack enough medication** to last the trip. It's important that you **don't put prescription drugs or valuables in luggage to be checked,** for it could go astray. To avoid problems with customs officials, carry medications in the original packaging. Also, don't forget the addresses of offices that handle refunds of lost traveler's checks.

LUGGAGE

In general you are entitled to check two bags on flights within the United States. A third piece may be brought on board, but it must fit easily under the seat in front of you or in the overhead compartment.

Airline liability for baggage is limited to $1,250 per person on flights within the United States. On international flights it amounts to $9.07 per pound or $20 per kilogram for checked baggage (roughly $640 per 70-pound bag) and $400 per passenger for unchecked baggage. Insurance for losses exceeding these amounts can be bought from the airline at check-in for about $10 per $1,000 of coverage; note that this coverage excludes a rather extensive list of items, which is shown on your airline ticket.

Before departure, **itemize your bags' contents** and their worth, and label the bags with your name, address, and phone number. (If you use your home address, cover it so that potential thieves can't see it readily.) Inside each bag, **pack a copy of your itinerary.** At check-in, **make sure that each bag is correctly tagged** with the destination airport's three-letter code. If your bags arrive damaged or fail to arrive at all, file a written report with the airline before leaving the airport.

PASSPORTS & VISAS

CANADIANS

A passport is not required to enter the United States.

U.K. CITIZENS

British citizens need a valid passport to enter the United States. If you are staying for fewer than 90 days on vacation, with a return or onward ticket, you probably will not need a visa. However, you will need to fill out the Visa Waiver Form, 1-94W, supplied by the airline.

➤ INFORMATION: **London Passport Office** (☎ 0990/21010) for fees and documentation requirements and to request an emergency passport. **U.S. Embassy Visa Information Line** (☎ 01891/200–290) for U.S. visa information; calls cost 49p per minute or 39p per minute cheap rate. **U.S. Embassy Visa Branch** (✉ 5 Upper Grosvenor St., London W1A 2JB) for U.S. visa information; send a self-addressed, stamped envelope. Write the **U.S. Consulate General** (✉ Queen's House, Queen St., Belfast BTI 6EO) if you live in Northern Ireland.

R

REST ROOMS

Public rest rooms in New York run the gamut when it comes to cleanliness. Facilities in Penn Station, Grand Central Terminal, and the Port Authority bus terminal are often quite dirty and are inhabited by homeless people. Rest rooms in subway stations have largely been sealed off because of vandalism and safety concerns.

As a rule, **head for midtown department stores, museums, or the lobbies of large hotels** to find the cleanest bathrooms. Public atriums, such as the Citicorp Center and Trump Tower, also provide good public facilities, as does the newly renovated Bryant Park and the many Barnes & Noble bookstores. Restaurants, too, have rest rooms, but usually just for patrons. If you're dressed well and look as if you belong, you can often just sail right in. Be aware that cinemas, Broadway theaters, and concert halls have limited amenities, and there are often long lines before performances, as well as during intermissions.

S

SAFETY

Despite New York's bad reputation in the area of crime, most people live here for years without being robbed or assaulted. Nevertheless, as in any large city, travelers make particularly easy marks for pickpockets and hustlers, so **be cautious.**

Do **ignore the panhandlers** on the streets (some aggressive, many homeless), people who offer to hail you a cab (they often appear at Penn Station, Port Authority, and Grand Central Terminal), and limousine and gypsy cab drivers who offer you a ride. Someone who appears to have had an accident at the exit door of a bus may flee with your wallet or purse if you attempt to give aid; the individual who approaches you with a complicated story is probably playing a confidence game and hopes to get something from you. Also **beware of strangers jostling you in crowds,** or someone tapping your shoulder from behind. Never play or place a bet on a sidewalk card game, shell game, or guessing game—they are all rigged to get your cash.

Keep jewelry out of sight on the street; better yet, **leave valuables at home.** Don't wear gold chains or gaudy jewelry, even if it's fake. Women should **never hang a purse on a chair in a restaurant** or on a hook in a rest-room stall. Men are advised to **carry wallets in front pants pockets** rather than in their hip pockets. Many New Yorkers carry a "mugging wallet"—a cheap wallet with a small amount of money inside, which you won't mind relinquishing—just in case.

Be sure to **avoid deserted blocks in out-of-the-way neighborhoods.** If you end up in an empty area or a side street that feels unsafe, it probably is. A brisk, purposeful pace helps deter trouble wherever you go.

Although the subway runs round the clock, it is usually safest during the day and evening. Most residents of the city have a rough cut-off time—10 or 11 PM—past which they avoid riding the subway trains. The subway system is much safer than it once was, but to **err on the side of caution,** you may want to travel by bus or taxi after the theater or a concert. If you do take the subway at night, ride in the center car, with the conductor, and wait among the crowds on the center of the platform or right in front of the token clerk. Watch out for unsavory characters lurking around the inside or outside of stations, particularly at night. When you're waiting for a train, **stand away from the edge of the subway platform,** especially when trains are entering or leaving the station. Once the train pulls into the station, **avoid empty cars.** When disembarking from a train, **stick with the crowd** until you reach the comparative safety of the street.

Though they're slower, buses are often more pleasant than subways, particularly when you sit next to a window and can view the passing street life. Buses are usually safer than the subways.

SENIOR-CITIZEN TRAVEL

To qualify for age-related discounts, **mention your senior-citizen status up front** when booking hotel reservations (not when checking out) and before you're seated in restaurants (not when paying the bill). Note that discounts may be limited to certain menus, days, or hours. When renting a car, **ask about promotional car-rental discounts,** which can be cheaper than senior-citizen rates.

➤ EDUCATIONAL TRAVEL PROGRAMS: Elderhostel (⊠ 75 Federal St., 3rd floor, Boston, MA 02110, ☎ 617/426–7788).

SIGHTSEEING

➤ BOAT TOURS: A **Circle Line Cruise** (⊠ Pier 83, west end of 42nd St., ☎ 212/563–3200) is one of the best ways to get a crash orientation to Manhattan. Once you've finished the three-hour, 35-mi circumnavigation of Manhattan, you'll have a good idea of where things are and what you want to see next. Narrations are as interesting and individualized as the guides who deliver them. The fare is $18. The Circle Line operates daily March–mid-December.

Express Navigation (⊠ Pier 11, 2 blocks south of South Street Seaport, ☎ 800/262–8743) has a hydroliner to show you the island of Manhattan in 75 minutes. The fare is $15. Boats depart May–September weekdays and Saturday at noon and 2 PM.

NY Waterway (⊠ Pier 78, W. 38th St. and 12th Ave., ☎ 800/533–3779) also offers a harbor cruise; the 90-minute ride costs $16. The StarLight Cruise follows the same route (for the same price) at night, providing excellent views of the lit-up skyline. The harbor cruise runs daily April–early December, while the StarLight Cruise operates nightly from late May–late August, and on Friday and Saturday nights from early September–late October.

The Spirit of New York (⊠ Pier 62, at W. 23rd St. and 12th Ave. on the Hudson River, ☎ 212/742–7278) sails on lunch ($29–$34) and dinner ($53–$65) cruises; the meal is accompanied by live music and dancing. There are also occasional moonlight cocktail ($20) cruises. All can be scheduled year-round.

World Yacht Cruises (⊠ Pier 81, W. 41st St. at Hudson River, ☎ 212/630–8100) serves Sunday brunch

($39) on two-hour cruises, and dinner (Sun.–Fri. $62; Sat. $75; drinks extra) on three-hour cruises. The Continental cuisine is restaurant quality, and there's music and dancing on board. The cruises run daily year-round, weather permitting.

At South Street Seaport's Pier 16 you can take hour-and-a-half- or three-hour voyages to New York's past aboard the cargo schooner *Pioneer* (☎ 212/748–8786); cruises depart daily May–September. **Seaport Liberty Cruises** (☎ 212/630–8888) also offers daily, hour-long sightseeing tours of New York Harbor and Lower Manhattan, as well as two-hour cruises with live jazz and blues on Wednesday and Thursday nights. Boats run between March and December.

➤ BUS TOURS: **Gray Line New York** (⊠ 900 8th Ave., ☎ 212/397–2620) offers a taste of yesteryear with its "NY Trolley Tour" on coaches replicating New York trolleys of the '30s, in addition to a number of standard city bus tours in various languages, plus cruises and day trips to Atlantic City. On weekdays between May and October, Gray Line's Central Park Trolley Tour tempts visitors to explore parts of the park that even native New Yorkers may never have seen.

New York Doubledecker Tours (⊠ Empire State Bldg. at 34th St. and 5th Ave., Room 4503, ☎ 212/967–6008) runs authentic London double-deck buses year-round, 9–6 in summer, 10–3 in winter, making stops every 15–30 minutes at the Empire State Building, Greenwich Village, SoHo, Chinatown, the World Trade Center, Battery Park, the South Street Seaport, the United Nations, and Central Park. Tickets, which are valid for boarding and reboarding all day for two days, cost $15 and can be purchased at the Empire State Building. An uptown loop, which costs $25, makes stops at Lincoln Center, the Museum of Natural History, Harlem, Museum Mile, and Central Park. Hop on and off to visit attractions as often as you like.

New York Visions (⊠ 1697 Broadway, at W. 53rd St., ☎ 212/956–0517) has tours lasting roughly four to five hours, including "New York

Lights at Night," featuring dinner in Little Italy, a tour of downtown New York, and a glittering skyline from the Empire State Building.

➤ HELICOPTER TOURS: **Island Helicopter** (✉ Heliport at E. 34th St. and East River, ☎ 212/683–4575) offers four fly-over options, from $44 per person (for 7 mi) to $129 per person (for the "Ultimate Delight, 34 mi).

From the West Side, **Liberty Helicopter Tours** (✉ Heliport at W. 30th St. and Hudson River, ☎ 212/465–8905) has four pilot-narrated tours ranging from $49 to $155 per person.

➤ SPECIAL-INTEREST TOURS: **Art Tours of Manhattan** (☎ 609/921–2647) custom-designs walking tours of museum and gallery exhibits as well as artists' studios and lofts; most center on the SoHo area.

Backstage on Broadway (☎ 212/575–8065) is a talk about the Broadway theater held in an actual theater, given by a theater professional. Reservations are mandatory; tour groups of 25 or more only.

Bite of the Apple Central Park Bicycle Tour (☎ 212/541–8759 or 212/603–9750) organizes two-hour bicycle trips through Central Park with several stops along the way, including Strawberry Fields and the Belvedere Castle.

Gracie Mansion Conservancy Tour (☎ 212/570–4751) will show you the 1799 house, official residence of New York City mayors since 1942. The mansion is open to the public on Wednesday; the tours run between late March and mid-November, and reservations are mandatory.

Grand Central Station (☎ 212/818–1777) provides the setting for architectural tours that take you high above the crowds and into the Beaux Arts building's rafters.

Harlem Spirituals, Inc. (☎ 212/757–0425) and **Penny Sightseeing Harlem Tours** (☎ 212/410–0080) offer bus and walking tours and Sunday gospel trips to Harlem. Also in Harlem, you can trace the history of jazz backstage at the **Apollo Theater** (☎ 212/222–0992).

The **Lower East Side Tenement Museum** (☎ 212/431–0233) offers tours through former immigrant communities.

Madison Square Garden (☎ 212/465–6080) has tours of the sports mecca's inner workings.

Manhattan Tours (☎ 212/563–2570) leads customized, behind-the-scenes tours inside fashion and interior-design showrooms, theaters, restaurants, and artists' lofts.

The Metropolitan Opera House Backstage (☎ 212/769–7020) offers a tour of the scenery and costume shops, stage area, and rehearsal facilities.

Quintessential New York (☎ 212/501–0827) has over a dozen specialty tours; the trump card is the behind-the-scenes take. For example, during "The Artist Colony: SoHo" tour, guests visit an artist's studio and an antique dealer's workshop. Another plus is the chauffered car.

Radio City Music Hall Productions (☎ 212/632–4041) schedules behind-the-scenes tours of the theater.

Rock and Roll Tours of New York (☎ 212/941–9464) visits the places where rock stars hung out, recorded, lived, and died. Tours are conducted by bus and are restricted to groups of 30 or more.

Sax & Company (☎ 212/832–0350) tours include visits to museums, theaters, and artists' studios and private collections.

The **South Street Seaport Museum** (☎ 212/748–8590) has tours of historic ships and the waterfront, as well as predawn forays through the bustling Fulton Fish Market.

➤ WALKING TOURS: **Adventure on a Shoestring** (☎ 212/265–2663) is an organization dating from 1963 that explores New York neighborhoods. Weekend tours are scheduled periodically and cost $5 per person; reservations are a must.

Big Onion Walking Tours (☎ 212/439–1090) has theme tours on weekends throughout the year, and on selected weekdays from April to late November: try "From Naples to Bialystock to Beijing: A Multi-Ethnic Eating Tour."

Citywalks (☎ 212/989–2456) offers two-hour walking tours exploring various neighborhoods in depth; weekends at 1 PM for $12.

The **Municipal Art Society** (☎ 212/935–3960) operates a series of walking tours on weekdays and both bus and walking tours on weekends. Tours highlight the city's architecture and history.

The **Museum of the City of New York** (☎ 212/534–1672) sponsors primarily historical and architectural walking tours on Sunday afternoons from April–early October.

New York City Cultural Walking Tours (☎ 212/979–2388) focuses on the city's architecture, landmarks, memorials, outdoor art, and historic sites, including 5th Avenue's "Millionaires' Mile." Public tours are offered every Sunday, while private tours can be scheduled throughout the week.

The **92nd Street Y** (☎ 212/996–1100) often has something special to offer on weekends and some weekdays.

River to River Downtown Walking Tours (☎ 212/321–2823) specializes in lower Manhattan for 2½-hour walking tours.

Urban Explorations (☎ 718/721–5254) runs tours with an emphasis on architecture and landscape design; Chinatown is a specialty.

The **Urban Park Rangers** (☎ 212/427–4040) offer free weekend walks and workshops in city parks.

Walks of the Town (☎ 212/222–5343) will tailor a tour to your interests; special themes include "Cops, Crooks, and the Courts." Tours are available by appointment only.

Among other knowledgeable walking-tour guides are **Joyce Gold** (☎ 212/242–5762), whose history tours include "The Vital Heart of Harlem," "The Women of Washington Square," and "When China and Italy Moved to New York," and **Arthur Marks** (☎ 212/673–0477), who creates customized tours on which he sings about the city.

➤ SELF-GUIDED WALKING TOURS: A free "Walking Tour of Rockefeller Center" pamphlet is available from the information desk in the lobby of the **GE Building** (30 Rockefeller Plaza).

Heritage Trails New York (☎ 212/269–1500) is a wanderer's version of connect-the-dots. Four color-coded sidewalk trails wind through the downtown area, guiding visitors to the New York Stock Exchange, Trinity Church, and other points of interest.

Pop one of the **Talk-a-Walk** cassettes (✉ Sound Publishers, 30 Waterside Plaza, Suite 10D, New York, NY 10010, ☎ 212/686–0356; $9.95 per tape, plus $2.90 packing and shipping for up to 4 tapes) into your Walkman and start strolling to an in-your-ear history of lower Manhattan or the Brooklyn Bridge.

STUDENTS

To save money, **look into deals available through student-oriented travel agencies.** To qualify you'll need a bona fide student ID card. Members of international student groups are also eligible.

➤ STUDENT IDs AND SERVICES: Council on International Educational Exchange (✉ CIEE, 205 E. 42nd St., 14th floor, New York, NY 10017, ☎ 212/822–2600 or 888/268–6245, FAX 212/822–2699), for mail orders only, in the United States. **Travel Cuts** (✉ 187 College St., Toronto, Ontario M5T 1P7, ☎ 416/979–2406 or 800/667–2887) in Canada.

➤ HOSTELING: **Hostelling International—American Youth Hostels** (✉ 733 15th St. NW, Suite 840, Washington, DC 20005, ☎ 202/783–6161, FAX 202/783–6171). **Hostelling International—Canada** (✉ 400-205 Catherine St., Ottawa, Ontario K2P 1C3, ☎ 613/237–7884, FAX 613/237–7868). **Youth Hostel Association of England and Wales** (✉ Trevelyan House, 8 St. Stephen's Hill, St. Albans, Hertfordshire AL1 2DY, ☎ 01727/855215 or 01727/845047, FAX 01727/844126). Membership in the United States, $25; in Canada, C$26.75; in the United Kingdom, £9.30).

➤ STUDENT TOURS: **Contiki Holidays** (✉ 300 Plaza Alicante, Suite 900, Garden Grove, CA 92840, ☎ 714/740–0808 or 800/266–8454, FAX 714/740–0818).

SUBWAYS

The 714-mi subway system operates 24 hours a day and, especially within Manhattan, serves most of the places you'll want to visit. It's cheaper than a cab and, during the workweek, often faster than either cabs or buses. The trains have been rid of their graffiti (some New Yorkers, of course, miss the colorful old trains), and air-conditioned cars predominate on every line. Still, the New York subway is not problem-free. Many trains are crowded and noisy. Although trains usually run frequently, especially during rush hours, you never know when some incident somewhere on the line may stall traffic. Don't write off the subway—some 3.5 million passengers ride it every day without incident—but stay alert (☞ Safety, *above*).

Subway fares are $1.50, although reduced fares are available for senior citizens and people with disabilities during nonrush hours. If you're just taking a few trips, you should pay with tokens; they are sold at token booths that are *usually* open at each station, as well as at token vending machines. It is advisable to **buy several tokens at one time** to avoid having to wait in line later. For four or more subway trips, you might find it easier to use the New York City Transit (MTA)'s new MetroCard Gold, a thin, plastic card with a magnetic strip; swipe it through the reader at the turnstile, and the cost of the fare is automatically deducted. Most major subway stations accept the cards, and all 469 stations are scheduled to accept MetroCard by the end of 1997. They are sold at all subway stations where they are accepted and at some stores—look for an "Authorized Sales Agent" sign. You can buy a card for a minimum of $3 (two trips) and a maximum of $80, in $6 increments. You can add more money to a card, and more than one person can use the same card: Swipe it through the turnstile once for each rider. Both tokens and Metro-Cards permit unlimited transfers within the system. When you use the MetroCard, you can transfer free from bus to subway or subway to bus within two hours. There are no discounts offered for either tokens or MetroCards.

Most subway entrances are located at street corners and are marked by lampposts with globe-shaped green lights. Subway lines are named for numbers and letters, such as the 3 line or the A line. Some lines run "express" and skip lots of stops; others are "locals" and make all stops. Each station entrance has a sign indicating the lines that run through the station; some stations are also marked "uptown only" or "downtown only." Before entering subway stations, **read the signs carefully**—one of the most frequent mistakes visitors make is taking the train in the wrong direction—although this can be an adventure, it can also be frustrating if you're in a hurry. Maps of the full subway system are posted on trains near the doors and at stations. You can usually pick up free maps at token booths, too.

For route information, **ask the token clerk, a transit policeman, or a fellow rider.** Once New Yorkers realize you're harmless, most bend over backward to be helpful.

➤ SCHEDULE AND ROUTE INFORMATION: **New York City Transit** (MTA, ☎ 718/330–1234), available daily 6–9.

T
TAXIS

Taxis are usually easy to hail on the street or from a taxi rank in front of major hotels, though finding one at rush hour or in the rain can take some time. You can tell if a cab is available by checking its rooftop light; if the center panel is lit and the side panels dark, the driver is ready to take passengers. Taxi fares cost $2 for the first ⅓ mi, 30¢ for each ⅕ mi thereafter, and 20¢ for each minute not in motion. A 50¢ surcharge is added to rides begun between 8 PM and 6 AM. There is no charge for extra passengers, but you must pay any bridge or tunnel tolls incurred during your trip (sometimes a driver will personally pay a toll to keep moving quickly, but that amount will be added to the fare when the ride is over). Taxi drivers expect a 15% tip.

To avoid unhappy taxi experiences, **try to have a general idea of where you want to go.** A few cab drivers are dishonest; some are ignorant; some can barely understand English. If you have no idea of the proper route, you may be taken for a long and costly ride.

TELEPHONES

Make sure that the pay phone is labeled as a NYNEX telephone; the unmarked variety are notorious change-eaters. There are also public credit-card phones scattered around the city. If you want to consult a directory or make a more leisurely call, pay phones in the lobbies of office buildings or hotels (some of which take credit cards) are a better choice.

The area code for Manhattan is 212; for Brooklyn, Queens, the Bronx, and Staten Island, it's 718. Pay telephones cost 25¢ for the first three minutes of a local call (this includes calls between 212 and 718 area codes); an extra deposit is required for each additional minute.

LONG-DISTANCE

AT&T, MCI, and Sprint long-distance services make calling home relatively convenient and let you avoid hotel surcharges; typically, you dial an 800 number in the United States.

➤ To Obtain Access Codes: **AT&T** USADirect (☎ 800/874–4000). **MCI** Call USA (☎ 800/444–4444). **Sprint** Express (☎ 800/793–1153).

TIPPING

The customary tipping rate is 15%–20% for taxi drivers and waiters (*see* Chapter 6 for further tipping advice); bellhops are usually given $2 in luxury hotels, $1 elsewhere. Hotel maids should be tipped around $1 per day of your stay.

TOUR OPERATORS

Buying a prepackaged tour or independent vacation can make your trip to New York less expensive and more hassle-free. Because everything is prearranged you'll spend less time planning.

Operators that handle several hundred thousand travelers per year can use their purchasing power to give you a good price. Their high volume may also indicate financial stability. But some small companies provide more personalized service; because they tend to specialize, they may also be more knowledgeable about a given area.

A GOOD DEAL?

The more your package or tour includes, the better you can predict the ultimate cost of your vacation. Make sure you know exactly what is covered, and **beware of hidden costs.** Are taxes, tips, and service charges included? Transfers and baggage handling? Entertainment and excursions? These can add up.

If the package or tour you are considering is priced lower than in your wildest dreams, **be skeptical.** Also, **make sure your travel agent knows the accommodations** and other services. Ask about the hotel's location, room size, beds, and whether it has a pool, room service, or programs for children, if you care about these. Has your agent been there in person or sent others you can contact?

BUYER BEWARE

Each year consumers are stranded or lose their money when tour operators—even very large ones with excellent reputations—go out of business. So **check out the operator.** Find out how long the company has been in business, and ask several agents about its reputation. **Don't book unless the firm has a consumer-protection program.**

Members of the National Tour Association and United States Tour Operators Association are required to set aside funds to cover your payments and travel arrangements in case the company defaults. Nonmembers may carry insurance instead. Look for the details, and for the name of an underwriter with a solid reputation, in the operator's brochure. Note: When it comes to tour operators, **don't trust escrow accounts.** Although there are laws governing charter-flight operators, no governmental body prevents tour operators from raiding the till. For more information, *see* Consumer Protection, *above.*

➤ Tour-Operator Recommendations: **National Tour Association** (✉ NTA, 546 E. Main St., Lexington, KY 40508, ☎ 606/226–4444 or 800/755–8687). **United States Tour Operators Association** (✉ USTOA,

342 Madison Ave., Suite 1522, New York, NY 10173, ☎ 212/599–6599, FAX 212/599–6744).

USING AN AGENT

Travel agents are excellent resources. When shopping for an agent, however, you should **collect brochures from several sources**; some agents' suggestions may be skewed by promotional relationships with tour and package firms that reward them for volume sales. If you have a special interest, **find an agent with expertise in that area** (☞ Travel Agencies, *below*). Don't rely solely on your agent, who may be unaware of small-niche operators. Note that some special-interest travel companies only sell directly to the public and that some large operators only accept bookings made through travel agents.

SINGLE TRAVELERS

Prices for packages and tours are usually quoted per person, based on two sharing a room. If traveling solo, you may be required to pay the full double-occupancy rate. Some operators eliminate this surcharge if you agree to be matched with a roommate of the same sex, even if one is not found by departure time.

GROUP TOURS

Among companies that sell tours to New York, the following are nationally known, have a proven reputation, and offer plenty of options. The classifications used below represent different price categories, and you'll probably encounter these terms when talking to a travel agent or tour operator. The key difference is usually in accommodations, which run from budget to better, and better-yet to best.

➤ DELUXE: **Globus** (✉ 5301 S. Federal Circle, Littleton, CO 80123-2980, ☎ 303/797–2800 or 800/221–0090, FAX 303/347–2080).

➤ FIRST CLASS: **Gadabout Tours** (✉ 700 E. Tahquitz Canyon Way, Palm Springs, CA 92262-6767, ☎ 619/325–5556 or 800/952–5068).

➤ BUDGET: **Cosmos** (☞ Globus, *above*).

PACKAGES

Like group tours, independent vacation packages are available from major tour operators and airlines. The companies listed below offer vacation packages in a broad price range.

➤ AIR/HOTEL: **Continental Vacations** (☎ 800/634–5555). **Delta Dream Vacations** (☎ 800/872–7786, FAX 954/357–4687). **United Vacations** (☎ 800/328–6877). **US Airways Vacations** (☎ 800/455–0123). **Amtrak's Great American Vacations** (☎ 800/321–8684).

➤ CUSTOM PACKAGES: **Amtrak's Great American Vacations** (☎ 800/321–8684).

➤ HOTEL ONLY: **SuperCities** (✉ 139 Main St., Cambridge, MA 02142, ☎ 800/333–1234).

Also contact **Amtrak's Great American Vacations** (☎ 800/321–8684).

FROM THE U.K.

➤ TOUR OPERATORS: **Americana Vacations Ltd.** (✉ 11 Little Portland St., London W1 5ND, ☎ 0171/637–7853). **Jetsave** (✉ Sussex House, London Rd., East Grinstead, West Sussex RH19 1LD, ☎ 01342/312033). **Key to America** (✉ 1–3 Station Rd., Ashford, Middlesex, TW15 2UW, ☎ 01784/248–777). **Premier Holidays** (✉ Westbrook, Milton Rd., Cambridge CB4 1YQ, ☎ 01223/516–688). **Trailfinders** (✉ 42–50 Earls Court Rd., London W8 6FT, ☎ 0171/937–5400; ✉ 58 Deansgate, Manchester M3 2FF, ☎ 0161/839–6969). **Travelpack** (✉ Clarendon House, Clarendon Rd., Eccles, Manchester M30 9AL, ☎ 0990/747–101).

➤ TRAVEL AGENCIES: **Trailfinders** (✉ 42–50 Earls Court Rd., London W8 6FT, ☎ 0171/937–5400). **Travel Cuts** (✉ 295a Regent St., London W1R 7YA, ☎ 0171/637–3161; ☞ Students, *above*). **Flight Express Travel** (✉ 77 New Bond St., London W1Y 9DB, ☎ 0171/409–3311).

THEME TRIPS

➤ CULTURAL TOURS: **IST Cultural Tours** (✉ 225 W. 34th St., New York, NY 10122-0913, ☎ 212/563–1202 or 800/833–2111, FAX 212/594–6953).

➤ PERFORMING ARTS: **Dailey-Thorp Travel** (✉ 330 W. 58th St., #610, New York, NY 10019-1817, ☎ 212/307–1555 or 800/998–4677, FAX 212/974–1420). **Keith Prowse Tours** (✉ 234 W. 44th St., #1000, New York, NY 10036, ☎ 212/398–1430 or 800/669–8687, FAX 212/302–4251). **Sutherland Hit Show Tours** (✉ 370 Lexington Ave., #411, New York, NY 10017, ☎ 212/532–7732 or 800/221–2442, FAX 212/532–7741).

➤ SPAS: **Spa-Finders** (✉ 91 5th Ave., #301, New York, NY 10003-3039, ☎ 212/924–6800 or 800/255–7727).

➤ TENNIS: **Championship Tennis Tours** (✉ 7350 E. Stetson Dr., #106, Scottsdale, AZ 85251, ☎ 602/990–8760 or 800/468–3664, FAX 602/990–8744). **Dan Chavez's Sports Empire** (✉ Box 6169, Lakewood, CA 90714-6169, ☎ 310/920–2350 or 800/255–5258). **Esoteric Sports Tours** (✉ 2005 Woods River La., Duluth, GA 30155, ☎ 770/622–8872 or 800/321–8008, FAX 770/622–8866). **Spectacular Sport Specials** (✉ 5813 Citrus Blvd., New Orleans, LA 70123-5810, ☎ 504/734–9511 or 800/451–5772, FAX 504/734–7075). **Steve Furgal's International Tennis Tours** (✉ 11828 Rancho Bernardo Rd., #123-305, San Diego, CA 92128, ☎ 619/675–3555 or 800/258–3664).

TRAIN TRAVEL

Amtrak trains from points across the United States arrive at Penn Station (✉ W. 31st to 33rd Sts., between 7th and 8th Aves.). For trains from New York City to Long Island and New Jersey, take the Long Island Railroad and New Jersey Transit respectively; both operate from Penn Station. Metro-North Commuter Railroad trains take passengers from Grand Central Terminal (✉ E. 42nd St. at Park Ave.) to points north of New York City, both in New York State and Connecticut.

➤ TRAIN SCHEDULES: **Amtrak** (☎ 800/872–7245). **Long Island Railroad** (☎ 718/217–5477). **Metro-North Commuter Railroad** (☎ 212/340–3000). **New Jersey Transit** (☎ 201/762–5100). **PATH** (☎ 800/234–7284).

TRANSPORTATION

When it comes to getting around New York, you'll have your pick of transportation in every neighborhood. The subway and bus networks are thorough, although getting across town can take some extra maneuvering. If you're not pressed for time, **take a public bus**; they make more stops than subways, but you can also see part of the city as you travel. True to the city's reputation, you'll see as many yellow cabs as personal cars, and while just getting into a taxi costs more than a subway or bus ride, the convenience can be worth it. Depending on the time of day and your destination, walking might be the easiest and most enjoyable option. During weekday rush hours (from 7:30 to 9:30 AM and 5 to 7 PM, **avoid the jammed midtown area, both in the subways and on the streets**; travel time can easily double.

TRAVEL AGENCIES

A good travel agent puts your needs first. **Look for an agency that specializes in your destination, has been in business at least five years, and emphasizes customer service.** If you're looking for an agency-organized package or tour, your best bet is to choose an agency that's a member of the National Tour Association or the United States Tour Operators Association (☞ Tour Operators, *above*).

➤ LOCAL AGENT REFERRALS: **American Society of Travel Agents** (✉ ASTA, 1101 King St., Suite 200, Alexandria, VA 22314, ☎ 703/739–2782, FAX 703/684–8319). **Alliance of Canadian Travel Associations** (✉ 1729 Bank St., Suite 201, Ottawa, Ontario K1V 7Z5, ☎ 613/521–0474, FAX 613/521–0805). **Association of British Travel Agents** (✉ 55–57 Newman St., London W1P 4AH, ☎ 0171/637–2444, FAX 0171/637–0713).

TRAVEL GEAR

Travel catalogs specialize in useful items, such as compact alarm clocks and travel irons, that can **save space when packing.**

➤ MAIL-ORDER CATALOGS: **Magellan's** (☎ 800/962–4943, FAX 805/568–5406). **Orvis Travel** (☎ 800/

541–3541, FAX 540/343–7053).
TravelSmith (☎ 800/950–1600, FAX 800/950–1656).

U
U.S. GOVERNMENT

The U.S. government can be an excellent source of inexpensive travel information. When planning your trip, **find out what government materials are available.**

➤ ADVISORIES: **U.S. Department of State American Citizens Services Office** (✉ Room 4811, Washington, DC 20520); enclose a self-addressed, stamped envelope. Interactive hot line (☎ 202/647–5225, FAX 202/647–3000). Computer bulletin board (☎ 202/647–9225).

➤ PAMPHLETS: **Consumer Information Center** (✉ Consumer Information Catalogue, Pueblo, CO 81009, ☎ 719/948–3334) for a free catalog that includes travel titles.

V
VISITOR INFORMATION

Contact the New York City visitors information offices below for brochures, subway and bus maps, a calendar of events, listings of hotels and weekend hotel packages, and discount coupons for Broadway shows. For a free "I Love New York" booklet listing New York City attractions and tour packages, contact the New York State Division of Tourism.

➤ CITY INFORMATION: **New York Convention and Visitors Bureau** (✉ 2 Columbus Circle, New York, NY 10019, ☎ 212/484–1200, FAX 212/484–1280), weekdays 9–5. **New York City Visitors Information Center** (☎ 212/397–8222).

➤ STATEWIDE INFORMATION: **New York State Division of Tourism** (✉ 1 Commerce Ave., Albany, NY 12245, ☎ 518/474–4116 or 800/225–5697).

W
WALKING

The cheapest, sometimes the fastest, and usually the most interesting way to explore this city is by walking. Because New Yorkers by and large live in apartments rather than in houses, and travel by cab, bus, or subway rather than by private car, they end up walking quite a lot. As a result, street life is a vital part of the local culture. On crowded sidewalks, people gossip, snack, browse, cement business deals, make romantic rendezvous, encounter long-lost friends, and fly into irrational quarrels with strangers. It's a wonderfully democratic hubbub. Also sharing some streets, however, are panhandlers, some aggressive, some friendly, and others more or less insane.

A typical New Yorker, if there is such an animal, walks quickly and focuses intently on dodging around cars, buses, bicycle messengers, construction sites, and other pedestrians. Although this might make natives seem hurried and rude, they will often cheerfully come to the aid of a lost pedestrian, so **don't hesitate to ask a passerby for directions.**

WHEN TO GO

At one time, it seemed New York's cultural life was limited to the months between October and May, when new Broadway shows opened, museums mounted major exhibitions, and formal seasons for opera, ballet, and concerts held sway. Today, however, there are Broadway openings even in mid-July, and a number of touring orchestras and opera and ballet companies visit the city in summer. In late spring and summer, the streets and parks are filled with ethnic parades, impromptu sidewalk concerts, and free performances under the stars. Except for regular closing days and a few holidays (such as Christmas, New Year's Day, and Thanksgiving), the city's museums are open year-round.

CLIMATE

➤ FORECASTS: **Weather Channel Connection** (☎ 900/932–8437), 95¢ per minute from a Touch-Tone phone.

Although there's an occasional bone-chilling winter day, with winds blasting in off the Hudson, snow only occasionally accumulates in the city. Summer is the only unpleasant time of year, especially the humid, hot days of August, when many Manhattanites vacate the island for summer homes. Most hotels are air-conditioned, but if you're traveling in the summer and choosing budget accommodations, it's a good idea to **ask whether your room has an air conditioner.** Air-conditioned stores, restaurants, theaters, and museums provide respite from the heat; so do the many green expanses of parks. Subways and buses are usually air-conditioned, but subway stations can be as hot as saunas.

When September arrives—with its dry "champagne-like" weather—the city shakes off its summer sluggishness. Mild and comfortable, autumn shows the city off at its best, with yellow and bronze foliage displays in the parks.

The following table shows each month's average daily highs and lows:

Jan.	38F	3C	May	72F	22C	Sept.	76F	24C
	25	–4		54	12		60	16
Feb.	40F	4C	June	80F	27C	Oct.	65F	18C
	27	–3		63	17		50	10
Mar.	50F	10C	July	85F	29C	Nov.	54F	12C
	35	2		68	20		41	5
Apr.	61F	16C	Aug.	84F	29C	Dec.	43F	6C
	44	7		67	19		31	–1

1 Destination: New York City

DISCOVERING NEW YORK

I N 1925, the youthful songwriting team of Richard Rodgers and Larry Hart wrote "Manhattan," arguably the loveliest city anthem ever. "We'll have Manhattan, the Bronx, and Staten Island, too," it promises, drawing its images from the merry scramble that was the city more than 60 years ago: "sweet pushcarts," "baloney on a roll," a subway that "charms," Brighton Beach, Coney Island, and the popular comedy *Abie's Irish Rose.* "We'll turn Manhattan into an isle of joy," coos the refrain.

Several decades later, in 1989, an album called simply *New York,* by aging enfant terrible rocker Lou Reed, viewed the same city with glasses fogged by despair and cynicism: Drugs, crime, racism, and promiscuity reigned in what Reed considered to be a sinkhole of "crudity, cruelty of thought and sound." His voice brittle with weary irony, he sang, "This is no time for celebration." Manhattan's "sweet pushcarts" now apparently overflow with deadly vials of crack.

So, whom to believe—Larry or Lou?

The truth of the matter is slippery, for New York has long been a mosaic of grand contradictions, a city for which there has never been—nor ever will be—a clear consensus. Hart himself took the city to task in another song, "Give It Back to the Indians," whose lyrics count off a litany of problems that still exist: crime, dirt, high prices, traffic jams, and all-around urban chaos. Yet for all that, millions live here, grumbling but happy, and millions more visit, curious as cats to find out what the magnificent fuss is all about.

I was in eighth grade in suburban Detroit when I first really became aware of New York. A friend's Manhattan-born mother subscribed to the Sunday *New York Times,* and at their house I'd pore over the "Arts and Leisure" section, as rapt as an archaeologist with a cave painting. The details of what I read there have blurred, but I remember vividly the sensation I felt while reading: a combined anticipation and nostalgia so keen it bordered on pain. Although I had never been there, I was homesick for New York.

It's my home now, yet I can still appreciate the impulse that draws visitors here. In a city so ripe with possibilities, we are all more or less visitors.

I think of this on an uncharacteristically warm day in late March, as fellow New Yorkers and I escape from the hives of offices and homes to celebrate spring's first preview. We unbutton our jackets, leave buses a stop or two before our usual destinations, quicken our resolve to visit that new exhibit at the Met or jog around the Central Park Reservoir. A jubilant sense of renewal infects us all, and I overhear one happy fellow saying to a friend, "I felt just like a tourist yesterday."

Whenever I get the New York blues, the best tonic for me is to glimpse the city through the eyes of a visitor. One day, after subway construction had rerouted me well out of my usual path, I found myself in the grimy Times Square station—hardly the place for a spiritual conversion. As usual I had that armor of body language that we New Yorkers reflexively assume to protect ourselves from strangers bent on (1) ripping us off, (2) doing us bodily harm, (3) converting us, (4) making sexual advances, or (5) being general pains-in-the-butt just for the hell of it. But that day, tucked away in a corner, was a group of musicians—not an uncommon sight in New York—playing the guitar, organ, and accordion with gusto and good spirits behind a homemade sign that dubbed them the Argentinean Tango Company. Like many other street musicians in Manhattan, they were *good,* but I was only half listening, too intent on cursing the city. Just as I passed the band, however, I noticed four teenagers drawn to the music—visitors, surely, they were far too open and trusting to be anything else. Grinning as widely as the Argentineans, they began to perform a spontaneous imitation of flamenco dancing—clapping hands above their heads, raising their heels, laughing at themselves, and only slightly self-conscious. Passersby, myself included, broke into smiles. As I made my way to the subway platform, buoyed by the impromptu show, I once again forgave New York. This minor piece of magic was apology enough.

I wonder whether that was the moment one of those teenagers happened to fall in love with the city. It *can* happen in a single moment, to a visitor or to a longtime resident. Perhaps it hits during a stroll through Riverside Park after a blanketing snowfall, when trees have turned to crystal and the city feels a hush it knows at no other time; or when you turn a corner and spy, beyond a phalanx of RVs and a tangle of cables and high-beam lights, the filming of a new movie.

That moment could also come when the house lights dim at the Metropolitan Opera, and the chandeliers make their magisterial ascent to the ceiling; or when you first glimpse the Prometheus statue in Rockefeller Center, gleaming like a giant present under the annual Christmas tree as dozens of skaters cut swirls of seasonal colors on the ice below. You may even be smitten in that instant when, walking along the streets in the haze of a summer afternoon, you look up above the sea of anonymous faces to see—and be astonished by—the lofty rows of skyscrapers, splendid in their arrogance and power. At times like these it is perfectly permissible to stop for a moment, take a breath, and think, "Wow! *This is New York!*" We who live here do it every so often ourselves.

For some, of course, that special moment comes when they spot a street or building made familiar by movies or television, from *I Love Lucy* to *On the Waterfront*. At the Empire State Building, who can help but remember King Kong's pathetically courageous swing from its pinnacle? Or at the brooding Dakota, the chilling destiny created for Rosemary's baby within those fortresslike walls? In the mind's eye, Audrey Hepburn is eternally pairing diamonds and a doughnut as she wends her swank way down 5th Avenue to have breakfast at Tiffany's. And the miniature park on Sutton Place will always be where Woody Allen and Diane Keaton began their angst-ridden *Manhattan* love affair, with the 59th Street bridge gleaming beyond and Gershwin music swelling in the background.

THERE'S A MOMENT OF sudden magic when a New York stereotype, seen so often on screen that it seems a joke, suddenly comes to life: when a gum-cracking waitress calls you "hon" or a stogie-sucking cabbie asks, "How 'bout them Yankees, Mac?" There's also the thrill of discovering one of New York's cities-within-the-city: Mulberry Street in Little Italy; Mott Street in Chinatown; Park Avenue's enclave of wealth and privilege; SoHo and TriBeCa, with their artistic types dressed in black from head to toe; or Sheridan Square, the nexus of the city's prominent lesbian and gay communities. The first glimpse of a landmark could excite the visitor's infatuation, too: frenetic Grand Central Station, abustle with suburban commuters; the concrete caverns of Wall Street, throbbing with power and ambition; or the Statue of Liberty, which neither cliché nor cheap souvenir can render common.

As you ready yourself to take on New York's contradictions, prepare to wonder and to exult. Here, on a single day, you might catch a glimpse of John Kennedy Jr., or Rollerena, the gloriously tacky drag-queen-cum-fairy-godmother on roller skates, who waves her magic wand to bestow blessings on select public events. Here you can eat sumptuously at a hot-dog stand or at a world-celebrated gourmet shrine.

Excess and deprivation mingle here: As a limousine crawls lazily to take its pampered passengers to their luxe destination, it rolls past a beggar seeking the warmth that steams from the city's belly through an iron grate. It's a ludicrously bright cartoon and a sobering documentary, New York—almost too much for one city to be. It's maddening and it's thrilling; monstrous, yet beautiful beyond parallel.

And I envy anyone their first taste of it.

— Michael Adams

Writer Michael Adams finally moved to his hometown, New York City, 17 years ago.

WHAT'S WHERE

Rockefeller Center and Midtown

Apart from sweeping panoramas from the Hudson River or the New York Bay, no other city scene so clearly says "New York" than this 19-building complex known as Rockefeller Center. These 22 acres of prime real estate (between 5th and 7th avenues and 47th and 52nd streets) with the Channel Gardens; the GE, Time & Life, and Associated Press buildings; and plazas, concourses, and street-level shops form a city within a city. St. Patrick's Cathedral, Saks Fifth Avenue, and the rest of midtown's gleaming skyscrapers are just steps away.

5th Avenue and 57th Street

One of the world's great shopping districts, 5th Avenue north of Rockefeller Center and 57th Street between Lexington Avenue and 7th Avenue is where you'll find some of the biggest names in New York retailing as well as the crème de la crème of designer boutiques. Fifty-seventh Street also is home to several theme restaurants, such as the Motown Cafe, Planet Hollywood, and the Hard Rock Cafe.

Times Square, 42nd Street, and the Theater District

The place where the ball drops on New Year's Eve, Times Square is still one of the city's principal energy centers. The Times Tower itself, from which the neighborhood took its name, is at the intersection of Broadway, 7th Avenue, and 42nd Street. Thirty or so major Broadway theaters are all nearby, in an area bounded roughly by 41st and 53rd streets between 6th and 9th avenues. Also just a short walk away are Theater Row, a string of intimate Off-Broadway houses on the south side of 42nd Street between 9th and 10th avenues, and Restaurant Row (46th Street between 8th and 9th avenues), where critics, actors, directors, playwrights, and spectators come to dine before and after the show. Going much farther east on 42nd Street, past 5th Avenue, you'll discover the Beaux Arts beauty of Grand Central Terminal, with its main entrance between Vanderbilt and Lexington avenues. East of Grand Central is the United Nations complex on a lushly landscaped riverside tract just east of 1st Avenue between 42nd and 48th streets.

Murray Hill to Union Square

Three distinct neighborhoods east of 5th Avenue between 20th and 40th streets—Murray Hill, Madison Square, and Gramercy Park—have preserved some of the historic charm of 19th-century New York: brownstone mansions and town houses, the city's earliest "skyscrapers," shady parks, and, yes, even in New York, some quiet streets. South of Gramercy Park lies Union Square, with its restored park, wonderful Greenmarket, and trend-setting restaurants.

Museum Mile and the Upper East Side

Once Manhattan's Millionaire's Row, the stretch of 5th Avenue between 79th and 104th streets has been renamed Museum Mile because of the startling number of world-class collections of art and artifacts scattered along its length (some housed in the former mansions of some of the Upper East Side's more illustrious industrialists and philanthropists). Whatever you do, don't leave New York without visiting at least one or two galleries in the largest art museum in the Western Hemisphere, the Metropolitan Museum of Art, on the Central Park side of 5th Avenue at 82nd Street.

Central Park

This 843-acre patch of rolling countryside is where Manhattanites go to escape from the urban jungle and reconnect with nature. Named a National Historic Landmark in 1965, Central Park offers the city's most soothing vistas and opportunities for just about any activity that a city dweller might engage in outdoors. All this right in the heart of the city: The park is bordered by 59th Street (called Central Park South between 5th and 8th avenues), 5th Avenue, 110th Street, and Central Park West.

The Upper West Side

The ornate prewar buildings that line the boulevards of Broadway, West End Avenue, Riverside Drive, and Central Park West provide a stately backdrop for glitzy boutiques and the scads of wanna-be soap actors hustling off to their auditions at ABC-TV and hopeful performers and aficionados making the pilgrimage to Lincoln Center. A stroll up tony Columbus Avenue should stretch at least as far as the Museum of Natural History, whose lavish grounds and pink-granite corner towers occupy a four-block tract. Farther uptown in Morningside Heights are the ivied buildings of Columbia University and the Cathedral of St. John the Divine, a magnificent Episcopal church.

Harlem

An important influence on American culture, this once-quiet country village grew into a suburb of apartment houses and brownstones for succeeding waves of German, Irish, Jewish, and Italian immigrants. For nearly a hundred years now it has been a mecca for African-American and Hispanic-American culture and life. Harlem extends north from 110th Street to about 145th Street (the border of Manhattanville); the most interesting sights on the tourist trail fall roughly between 116th Street and 135th Street.

Chelsea

Like its London district namesake, New York's Chelsea maintains a villagelike personality, with a number of quiet streets graced by lovingly renovated town houses. The neighborhood stretches from 5th Avenue west to the Hudson River, and from 14th to 23rd Street (and above). Chelsea has always been congenial to writers and artists, and it has also embraced a multicultural population for decades; it now includes an active gay community that frequents the lively stores and restaurants on 8th Avenue. In recent years, the area has witnessed an economic boost with the opening of 6th Avenue superstores and the Chelsea Piers Sports and Entertainment Complex on the Hudson. The gallery scene thrives west of 10th Avenue from 20th to 29th streets.

Greenwich Village

Extending from 14th Street south to Houston Street and from the piers of the Hudson River to 5th Avenue, the crazy-quilt pattern of narrow, tree-lined streets known to New Yorkers simply as "the Village" remains true to its 19th-century heritage as a haven for immigrants, bohemians, students, artists, actors, carousers, and tourists. It's one of the best parts of the city to wander for hours. The Village is still home to one of the largest gay communities in the country (centered on Sheridan Square and Christopher Street).

The East Village

Many regard the East Village—an area bounded by 14th Street on the north, 4th Avenue or the Bowery on the west, Houston Street on the south, and the East River—as the island's most colorful neighborhood. Here holdouts from the 1960s coexist with a deeply entrenched Eastern European community. Artists, punks, and account executives move freely between the Polish and Ukrainian coffee shops, galleries, trendy pasta bars, offbeat shops, and St. Mark's Place—a local thoroughfare for sidewalk vendors.

SoHo and TriBeCa

SoHo (*So*uth of *Ho*uston Street) is bounded on the other four sides by Broadway, Canal Street, and 6th Avenue. TriBeCa (the *Tri*angle *Be*low *Ca*nal Street) extends roughly as far south as Murray Street and east to West Broadway. Over the past 20 years both neighborhoods have gradually been transformed into lively realms of loft dwellers, galleries, and very trendy shops and cafés.

Little Italy and Chinatown

Little Italy—a few blocks south of Houston Street between Broadway and the Bowery—is today not as Italian as it used to be. Still, Mulberry Street and its famous—and, in some cases, infamous—eateries are rife with atmosphere. If you head east along Canal Street (the southern border of Little Italy), you will run into the ever-expanding and frenetic Chinatown (the area south of Canal on the east side), which has over the years spilled over into much of the Lower East Side's Jewish neighborhood and into Little Italy as well. One of the biggest attractions in Chinatown is simply the carnival-like atmosphere on the small streets, which are packed with shoppers and purveyors of untold varieties of pungent fish and exotic vegetables.

Wall Street and the Battery

The synonymous financial nexus and thoroughfare called Wall Street, which clusters downtown around the New York and American stock exchanges, wears its wealth on its architecturally stunning sleeve. At the bottom of the island, Battery Park is one of the few Manhattan locales that bring you the waterfront where in the past commerce poured in to build New York City. You also get fabulous views of the Statue of Liberty and Ellis Island.

The Seaport and the Courts

New York's days as a great 19th-century haven for clipper ships are preserved in lower Manhattan at South Street Seaport, centered on Fulton Street at the East River and crowned by the Brooklyn Bridge. Just blocks away, you can take in another slice of New York history by walking the streets of the City Hall district, with its majestic court edifices.

PLEASURES AND PASTIMES

Fine Dining

The old reliable four-star French restaurants, steak houses, delis, and diners are of course still doing what they've been doing best for years (and in some cases, decades), but there's plenty new afoot. For one thing, the bistro-trattoria mania that broke out a few years ago is going strong: The French are downtown, the Italians on the Upper East Side. The mix of small ethnic eating spots reflects shifting immigration patterns, and the newest national cuisines to make their mark are Austrian, Afghan, Brazilian, Thai, Turkish, and Jamaican. Chinatown, not to be undone, is extending its borders, and noodle shops, complete with hanging ducks, heaping bowls of fried rice, and low prices, are sprouting up everywhere.

Nightlife

New York's vibrant nightlife has something to please everyone. Much of the club life is concentrated downtown—in one night you can go to a grungy East Village dance dive, a classic West Village jazz joint, a sleekly decorated TriBeCa celebrity trap, or a preppy Wall Street hangout. Uptown's the place to go to listen to a romantic singer in a sophisticated setting like the Algonquin's Oak Room, the Cafe Carlyle, or Rainbow and Stars, with its awesome backdrop of Manhattan lights. If you just want a drink, you can frequent an unpretentious neighborhood saloon in jeans or a vintage hotel bar in your tux.

You can also write your novel in a coffee bar or laugh yourself silly at a comedy club.

Shopping

Whether you're planning to run your credit cards up to the max or just window-shop, New York offers a veritable orgy of options. Try the South Street Seaport for its unique combination of upscale, high-tech, and kitsch retail shops (and a spectacular view of the Brooklyn Bridge); the Lower East Side for inexpensive clothing and shoes; SoHo for art and antiques, avant-garde gifts and decorative items, gourmet foods, and funky clothes; 5th and Madison avenues for haute couture; Herald Square for the biggest department stores; Chelsea for hip, superstore bargains; Columbus Avenue for some of the city's glitziest upscale if not top-of-the-line shops (and one of the biggest flea markets in the city); and the Upper East Side for unique and stylish items for the home, fine antiques, and designer clothing.

Summer Arts

In summer the open spaces of the city become outdoor concert halls. Lincoln Center's Out-of-Doors and Lincoln Center Festival transform Manhattan's performing-arts centerpiece into a virtual state fair of the arts; while the theaters fill up with music, dance, and theater productions, stages set up in the plaza accommodate jazz dancers, chamber orchestras, Broadway lyricists and composers, mimes, dance bands, children's theater, and more. Metropolitan Opera in the Parks works its way throughout the five boroughs. In Central Park, the New York Shakespeare Festival stages two plays every summer, while SummerStage fills the Naumberg Bandshell with free programs ranging from grand opera to polka to experimental rock. To escape the heat, head to an indoor concert at the World Financial Center near Battery Park.

Walking

New York is a walker's city. It's hard to get lost, except in the Village, where New York's rigid grid pattern of streets falls apart. So step into your best walking shoes, choose any avenue or street, and follow it from one end to the other or from river to river, observing how the neighborhoods shade gradually into one another. Or hike across one of the city's many bridges for a fresh look at scenery that usually speeds by in a blur. Some of our favorite walks are 5th Avenue from 40th Street to Central Park; the path through Central Park from Grand Army Plaza to the Bethesda Fountain; Broadway on the Upper West Side from Lincoln Center to 86th Street; east to west on Bleecker Street in Greenwich Village; the Brooklyn Bridge from Manhattan to Brooklyn Heights and its Promenade.

GREAT ITINERARIES

Though it's difficult to substantiate the oft-touted claim that New York City is the "capital of the world," New York truly has something for everyone. For exactly that reason, prescribing visitor itineraries is a challenge. A theater buff may be content to spend days without leaving the vicinity of Times Square, the more historic minded may be equally swept away by the impressive architecture of old buildings in Lower Manhattan, and art lovers will want to spend their time darting between uptown and downtown museums and galleries. And then there are the ever-changing restaurants and shops, and the approximately 8 million characters, many of them walking the streets, that give the city its vitality. The following suggestions are merely that; when planning your own trip, be sure to consider the weather, the time of year, the day of the week, and of course your own interests. Consult Chapters 2 and 3 for more information about individual sights.

If You Have 3 Days

Begin Day 1 at **Castle Clinton** in **Battery Park** to catch the ferries to the **Statue of Liberty** and **Ellis Island.** Arrive early to minimize the wait, and if you only have the morning to spare, choose just one of these two destinations as your goal. Upon your return, walk northeast from Battery Park on Water Street, passing the **Wall Street** area on the way toward bustling **South Street Seaport,** where you can have lunch, shop, and get a feel for New York's maritime past. For more great views, head east to the **Brooklyn Bridge** or west to the **World Trade Center** observation deck. A great way to end the day is with a feast

in **Chinatown** or **Little Italy,** both in Lower Manhattan.

On Day 2 work your way north to midtown's **Grand Central Terminal,** one of the busiest places around. From here it's an easy walk or bus ride east on 42nd Street to the **United Nations** (on the East River) or west to **Times Square;** on the way you'll pass the **New York Public Library** main building, with the lions out front, and **Bryant Park.** At the United Nations, your best bet is a guided tour, but at Times Square, you're better off just observing life buzz around you, in theaters, restaurants, and shops. After lunch (you won't have any trouble finding nourishment in midtown), head over to **Fifth Avenue** and walk north to **Rockefeller Center.** If you're a shopper, Fifth Avenue will fill your afternoon. If not, visit the **Museum of Modern Art** or the **Museum of Television and Radio,** both near Rockefeller Center. At sunset, if you missed the World Trade Center the day before, head downtown on Fifth to the top of the **Empire State Building.** Otherwise, a Broadway show, preceded or followed by dinner in the theater district, will suitably end the day.

On Day 3, head out early for upper Fifth Avenue's **Museum Mile,** though which museum (or group of museums) to visit can be a hard decision. Make sure you spend some time at the **Metropolitan Museum of Art,** one of the biggest and greatest art institutions in the world. The **Guggenheim Museum** and the **Whitney Museum of American Art** (technically not on Museum Mile, but close enough) offer new and different perspectives on 20th-century art; the **Museum of the City of New York** makes Gotham's history come alive; and the **Jewish Museum** and the **Cooper-Hewitt Museum,** both quartered in former private mansions right near one another, look at Jewish culture and design, respectively, as well as the lifestyles of rich, famous, and generous New Yorkers. Break up the day with a picnic lunch and a walk in **Central Park,** conveniently steps away from the museums. If you feel that you've exhausted exhibition possibilities on the Upper East Side, or if they've exhausted you, walk west across the park (79th Street is a convenient place to enter the park, or take the 79th Street crosstown bus); a whole new world awaits on the Upper West Side, including the **American Museum of Natural History** and the **New-**

York Historical Society. Cap your day with a musical or theatrical performance at **Carnegie Hall** or **Lincoln Center**—perhaps something outside if it's summer.

If You Have 5 to 7 Days

Start Day 1 with the city's most famous three-hour tour, a circumnavigation of Manhattan on the Circle Line. This cruise begins and ends at Pier 83 at West 42nd Street, close enough for you to eat lunch in **Times Square** and then follow the second half of Day 2 as described in If You Have 3 Days, *above*. On Day 2, spend time in Lower Manhattan visiting the **New York Stock Exchange** and taking the ferries from **Castle Clinton** in **Battery Park** to the **Statue of Liberty** and **Ellis Island.** It's a tough call, but you'll have to choose between getting to the ferries early and looking at the New York Stock Exchange first-thing. Both the Statue of Liberty and the Stock Exchange limit the number of visitors per day, and waiting times increase as the day goes on. The exhibits at Ellis Island, on the other hand, are usually wait-free once you arrive. You can eat at the Statue or Ellis Island, but be sure to squeeze in time for the obligatory stop at **South Street Seaport** before the day ends.

On Day 3, follow the third-day itinerary outlined in If You Have 3 Days, *above*. Devote Day 4 to the cool and trendy—the streets of **Greenwich Village,** the **East Village,** and **SoHo.** Start at **Union Square,** preferable on a **Greenmarket** day, when you can load up on snacks. From here, there's good, varied shopping if you walk south down **Broadway** all the way though SoHo—with **Grace Church** and a few museums and galleries along the way—into **Chinatown** with its ubiquitous restaurants. If you don't wish to venture down to Lower Manhattan, spend time west of Broadway in Greenwich Village (from 14th to Houston streets); the area is full of curvy lanes and charming, low-rise historical buildings. The East Village (east of 4th Avenue between 14th and Houston streets) is where tomorrow's trends emerge, and it spills into the perpetually crowded and evolving Lower East Side, heart of immigrant New York. Bargains and tenements still define the neighborhood; for background, stop at the **Lower East Side Tenement Museum** on Orchard Street. No matter where you go downtown, you

won't want for food or diversions. Greenwich Village, the East Village, and SoHo have a number of small theaters that stage more innovative performances than the midtown showplaces.

Begin Day 5 with a leisurely breakfast in one of the quaint restaurants along **Irving Place** (east of Union Square), dining at an outdoor café if possible so you can watch the pedestrian traffic. From there, you can work your way north through **Gramercy Park,** then up Madison Avenue and across 34th Street past the **Empire State Building,** and on over to **Herald Square** (synonymous with Macy's). Otherwise, from Irving Place head over to Union Square and continue west to explore **Chelsea,** with its numerous superstores, boutiques, restaurants, and galleries. All the way west is **Chelsea Piers** (at 23rd Street on the Hudson River), which has places to walk by the water and a number of restaurants. The sunsets over the river are often quite lovely. At night, if you haven't already made it to a Broadway show, it's time (or if you have, how about a second performance?).

On Day 6, as long as the weather cooperates, there's no better place than **Central Park.** The Loop Road will be full of skaters, bikers, and runners, so join the crowd. In summer, the lawns have picnickers, sunbathers, and Frisbee players; in winter, the Wollman Skating Rink is full. And there's always the zoo, the carriage rides, and the landscaped beauty of the park. Different areas of Central Park are convenient to the **Upper East Side** and **Museum Mile** (5th Avenue), the **Upper West Side,** and **57th Street.** If you happen to be in the park on a summer day when there is a free evening performance of Shakespeare, the Metropolitan Opera, the New York Philharmonic, or music at SummerStage (☞ Chapter 5), precede the show with a picnic dinner, which can be procured from the many gourmet delis and take-out restaurants east and west of the park.

On Day 7, there's still so much to keep you amused, but rather than planning the day ahead of time leave it open to indulge a newfound fancy, or in case you missed something earlier. Check out a different Manhattan neighborhood, such as **Harlem** (the **Apollo Theater, Studio Museum,** and **Schomburg Center**), **Morningside**

Heights (**Columbia University,** the **Cathedral of St. John the Divine,** and **Riverside Park**), or Yorkville (**Gracie Mansion, Carl Schurz Park,** and old German butcher shops). Or, impress your Manhattan friends by investigating an outer borough by subway. Visit, for example, the **Brooklyn Museum of Art** and **Prospect Park** in **Brooklyn,** the **Bronx Zoo** and the **New York Botanical Garden** in the **Bronx,** or the **American Museum of the Moving Image** in **Queens,** to name just a few options.

FODOR'S CHOICE

Views to Remember

★**The lower Manhattan skyline seen from the Brooklyn Heights Promenade.** This quiet, 3-mi-long sliver of park hanging over the ferry district offers both a respite from the urban din and one of the most stunning urban panoramas: the Brooklyn Bridge, South Street Seaport, and the glittering skyscrapers of lower Manhattan, which seem to float on the water.

★**Midtown Manhattan and New York Bay from the observation deck of the World Trade Center.** Elevators glide a quarter of a mile into the sky (107 stories) to the world's highest outdoor observation platform, where, on a clear day, you can see as far as 55 mi.

★**The vista of skyscrapers ringing Central Park.** Perhaps the best spot from which to admire this picture-postcard view (Midtown's jumble of high-rises looks like a surreal two-dimensional stage set rising from the trees) is the reservoir's northwest corner or the second-floor outdoor sculpture court at the Metropolitan Museum. Gapstow Bridge by the Pond in the park is another good vantage point.

★**A moonlit look at the harbor from the Staten Island Ferry.** This ride—free as of 1997—is even more breathtaking at night with the billions of lights of Manhattan twinkling in the distance.

★**The Hudson River from the tower at Riverside Church.** Just 21 stories above street level, this perch nevertheless affords a dramatic unobstructed view of the river, the George Washington Bridge, and the Palisades of New Jersey to the west.

Architecture

★**Woolworth Building, Flatiron Building, Empire State Building, and the World Trade Center's twin towers.** Each is noteworthy for its own style and architectural features, and each, in its time, was the world's tallest building.

★**Chrysler Building.** One of the most graceful of the city's skyscrapers, this stainless-steel tower is famous for its Art Deco pinnacle, its radiator-cap ornaments and gargoyles, and its graceful African marble lobby.

★**Rockefeller Center.** A 22-acre city within the city, this complex is as remarkable for its smooth limestone structures as for its plazas, concourses, and public spaces.

★**The Dakota.** The grande dame of New York apartment houses, this brick-and-stone urban castle outclasses all the other residences of Central Park West.

★**The unbroken front of cast-iron beauties along Greene Street in SoHo.** The architectural rage of the second half of the 19th century, these facades are as functional as they are attractive.

★**The graceful town houses along St. Luke's Place in the West Village.** These brownstones from the 1850s still rank among the most successful ensembles of urban residential architecture anywhere.

★**Cathedral of St. John the Divine.** This immense limestone-and-granite Gothic house of worship supported entirely by stonemasonry is still a work in progress.

Museums

★**American Museum of Natural History.** There's something for everyone in this collection of more than 30 million artifacts. The lifelike dioramas and newly restored dinosaur collection are especially popular with children.

★**The Cloisters.** The Metropolitan Museum's medieval collection is housed in an annex on a peaceful wooded hilltop in Washington Heights, near Manhattan's northernmost tip. Don't miss the unicorn tapestries.

★**Guggenheim Museum.** Since the opening of the new Tower Galleries annex in 1992, the Guggenheim has been able to display some of the extraordinarily large pieces from its phenomenal collection of modern art.

★ **Metropolitan Museum of Art.** This is simply one of the world's greatest museums. Select one or two galleries, but don't leave without visiting the European Sculpture Court.

★ **National Museum of the American Indian.** Opened in fall 1994, this is the first national museum dedicated to Native American culture, housed in the astonishing Alexander Hamilton Custom House in lower Manhattan.

★ **Pierpont Morgan Library.** Here you'll find the repository of one of the world's finest collections of rare books, prints, and incunabula. Don't miss J.P.'s own study and library within.

Restaurants

★ **Daniel.** At Daniel Boulud's $1.9 million haven, the celebrity clientele is as dazzling as the exquisite French cuisine. $$$$

★ **Ben Benson's.** A first-rate steak house, this is the place in Midtown for chops and prime rib, Maryland crab cakes, and oversize cocktails. $$$–$$$$

★ **Palio.** You'll experience authentic Italian cuisine elevated to greatness at this high-toned restaurant named after the 800-year-old Italian horse race. $$$–$$$$

★ **Windows on the World.** "The Greatest Bar on Earth," the intimate 60-seat "Cellar in the Sky," and the dramatic 240-seat main dining room are grand enough, but don't forget those million-dollar views. $$$–$$$$

★ **American Place.** Executive chef Larry Forgione celebrates new American cooking in this stylish dining spot with kindly service; it just may be the country's finest regional American restaurant. $$$

★ **Trattoria Dell'Arte.** Across 7th Avenue from Carnegie Hall, this upbeat restaurant attracts lively crowds with its quirky, controversial decor and its creative take on traditional Italian recipes. $$–$$$

★ **Follonico.** At this Chelsea charmer, unusual pastas change with the seasons. $$

★ **Boca Chica.** Come to this East Village hot spot for a (spicy) sampling of Latin America. $

★ **Joe's Shanghai.** Chefs study years to perfect the secret of the house specialty: dumplings filled with boiling broth and pork or crab. $

★ **Takahachi.** Experience fine Japanese food in the hip East Village at giveaway prices. $

★ **Turkish Kitchen.** Manhattan's best Turkish restaurant has a striking, brightly colored multilevel dining room where you can sample delicate, authentic cuisine. $

Hotels

★ **The Carlyle.** One of New York's swankiest hotels, the Carlyle combines old-school elegance with a modern sense of fun—its legendary cabaret and bar stay packed until the wee hours. $$$$

★ **The Four Seasons.** Its I. M. Pei–designed limestone spire has earned this hotel as much fame as its sky-high prices—but luxuries such as English sycamore walk-in closets, 10-ft-high ceilings, and tubs that fill in 60 seconds make it worth the price. $$$$

★ **The Mark.** This classy but friendly baby grand hotel is just a few steps from Central Park. $$$$

★ **The Ritz-Carlton.** Presiding over Central Park South like a grand old dame, this distinguished long-timer has extravagantly appointed guest rooms with breathtaking views of the park. $$$$

★ **St. Regis.** This 5th Avenue Beaux Arts landmark bespeaks a bygone era of wealth and luxury with its ultrachic public spaces and butler-serviced guest rooms. $$$$

★ **The Fitzpatrick.** Good value and charm are what this amiable Irish boutique is all about. $$$

★ **The Paramount.** For the forever young and arty, this theater-district oddity (from French designer Philippe Starck) is definitely not for those who want their hotels to resemble English manor houses. $$$

★ **SoHo Grand.** Its monumental design pays homage to the 19th-century cast-iron buildings of SoHo; aesthetics are everything here. $$$

★ **Broadway Bed & Breakfast.** Friendly and comfortable, this bargain B&B is just steps from the theaters and Restaurant Row. $

★ **The Larchmont.** This West Village Beaux Arts brownstone offers quirky, safari-style rooms with shared bathrooms at rock-bottom prices. $

FESTIVALS AND SEASONAL EVENTS

WINTER

EARLY DEC.➤ One of the tallest Christmas trees in the country is mounted in Rockefeller Center, just above the golden Prometheus statue. Thousands of people gather to watch the ceremonial **tree lighting** (☎ 212/632–3975).

NEW YEAR'S EVE➤ The famous **Ball Drop in Times Square** (☎ 212/768–1560) is televised all over the country. In Central Park, a festive **Midnight Run** sponsored by the New York Road Runners Club (☎ 212/860–4455) starts off at Tavern on the Green.

EARLY JAN.➤ The **New York National Boat Show** at the Jacob K. Javits Convention Center (☎ 212/216–2000) exhibits the latest in boats, yachts, and other seaworthy equipment.

EARLY FEB.➤ Yankee fans will have their day at the **New York Yankees Fan Festival** (☎ 212/293–4300), where you can meet current and former players, test your swing, and bid in a memorabilia auction. **Chinese New Year** (☎ 212/373–1800) sets off a flurry of firecrackers in downtown Chinatown.

FEB. 14➤ During the **Valentine's Day Marriage Marathon,** couples marry atop the Empire State Building.

FEB.➤ Well-bred canines take over Madison Square Garden for the **Westminster Kennel Club Dog Show** (☎ 212/465–6000). In the invitational **Annual Empire State Building Run-Up** (☎ 212/736–3100), 125 runners scramble up the 1,576 stairs from the lobby of the Empire State Building to the 86th floor observation deck.

SPRING

EARLY MAR.➤ The **Triple Pier Expo** (☎ 212/255–0020) lures over 600 antiques dealers to Piers 88, 90, and 92, offering everything from art glass to furniture.

MAR. 17➤ The boisterous **St. Patrick's Day Parade** heads down 5th Avenue.

LATE MAR.–EARLY APR.➤ The **Spring Flower Show** (☎ 212/494–2922) transforms Macy's department store. Exquisite flower arrangements are also on display in Rockefeller Center.

APR.➤ The **Antiquarian Book Fair** (☎ 212/777–5218), held every year in the Upper East Side Armoury, is a book-lover's jackpot of rare volumes, famous first editions, autographs, and correspondence.

APR. 12➤ As in the classic Fred Astaire movie, you can don an extravagant hat and join the **Easter Parade** up 5th Avenue.

APR.–SEPT.➤ The **Major League baseball season** sees the New York Yankees (☎ 718/293–6000) drawing huge crowds to Yankee Stadium in the Bronx, while the Mets (☎ 718/507–8499) play at Shea Stadium in Queens.

EARLY MAY➤ The **Cherry Blossom Festival** (☎ 718/622–4433) is held at the Brooklyn Botanic Garden. **Bike New York: The Great Five Boro Bike Tour** (☎ 212/932–0778) starts off its 42-mi trail in Battery Park, winding up on Staten Island.

LATE MAY➤ Some of the world's best hoofers join the **Tap Dance Extravaganza** (☎ 718/597–4613); events are held in varying venues in Manhattan. You can stroll around the **Washington Square Outdoor Art Exhibit** beginning Memorial Day weekend.

SUMMER

JUNE➤ **Lesbian and Gay Pride Week** (☎ 212/807–7433) includes a parade, a film festival, and other activities. The **National Puerto Rican Day Parade** (☎ 212/374–5176 or 718/401–0404) along 5th Avenue includes plenty of energetic bands.

LATE JUNE➤ **New York Jazz Festival** (☎ 212/219–3006), the largest New York jazz event, spreads more than 200 groups in venues all over town. Besides classic acts, you'll find acid jazz, Latin jazz, and avant garde.

LATE JUNE–EARLY JULY➤ The **Washington Square Music Festival** (☎ 212/431–1088) is a series of free outdoor classical and jazz concerts.

JUNE–AUG.➤ Behind the main 42nd Street building of the public library, the **Bryant Park Film Festival** (☎ 212/391–4248) screens classic films on Monday nights; the lawn turns into a picnic ground. In Central Park, **SummerStage** (☎ 212/360–2777) presents free music, dance, and theater performances. **Shakespeare in the Park** (☎ 212/539–8500), sponsored by the Joseph Papp Public Theater at Central Park's Delacorte Theater, tackles the Bard. The **New York Philharmonic** (☎ 212/875–5656) chips in with free concerts in various city parks.

JULY 4➤ On **Independence Day** you can see fireworks in various locations throughout the city, especially by the waterfront.

JULY➤ **Lincoln Center Festival** (☎ 212/875–5000), an international summer performance event lasting several weeks, includes classical music concerts, contemporary music and dance presentations, stage works, and non-Western arts.

JULY–AUG.➤ **Midsummer Night Swing** (☎ 212/875–5400) fills the Fountain Plaza of Lincoln Center with swinging couples and live music; swing lessons are given before the dance.

LATE JULY➤ The **Celebrate Brooklyn Festival** (☎ 718/875–4047), New York's longest-running, free, performing arts festival, presents music, dance, theater, and film in Prospect Park.

AUG.➤ **Lincoln Center Out-of-Doors** (☎ 212/875–5108) is a series of international concerts and dance performances lasting almost the entire month. **Harlem Week** (☎ 212/427–7200) includes concerts, gospel events, and more.

LATE AUG.➤ **Brooklyn's County Fair** (☎ 718/689–8600) goes the old-fashioned route with watermelon-eating contests, pony rides, and the like.

LATE AUG.–EARLY SEPT.➤ The **U.S. Open Tennis Tournament** (☎ 800/524–8440), in Queens, is one of the premier annual sport events.

AUTUMN

SEPT.➤ The **Feast of San Gennaro** (☎ 212/226–9546) brings hordes of tourists and residents alike into Little Italy for sausage and cannoli. The **New York Armory Antiques Show** (☎ 212/472–1180) is one of the most distinguished events of the year.

MID-SEPT.➤ **New York Is Book Country** (☎ 212/207–7242) is a massive literary festival, culminating with a street fair on 5th Avenue.

SEPT.–OCT.➤ With its impressive reputation, the **New York Film Festival** (☎ 212/875–5610) makes Lincoln Center a magnet for movie aficionados.

OCT. 31➤ The **Greenwich Village Halloween Parade** (☎ 914/758–5519) conjures up a feisty crowd of costumed onlookers.

OCT.–APR.➤ **New York Rangers Hockey** (☎ 212/465–6741) attracts passionate fans at Madison Square Garden. The ever-popular **New York Knickerbockers** (☎ 212/465–5867) basketball team continues to fill up Madison Square Garden during their home games.

EARLY NOV.➤ The **New York City Marathon** (☎ 212/860–4455) is the world's largest; it goes through all five boroughs of the city and finishes at Tavern on the Green in Central Park.

NOV. 11➤ On **Veteran's Day,** an annual parade marches down 5th Avenue to the United War Veterans Council of New York County.

NOV. 26➤ The **Macy's Thanksgiving Day Parade** (☎ 212/494–5432) is a New York tradition; huge balloons float down Central Park West at 77th Street to Broadway and Herald Square.

NOV.–JAN.➤ The **Christmas Spectacular** with the fabulous Rockettes is a holiday classic at Radio City Music Hall (☎ 212/247–4777).

LATE NOV.–EARLY JAN.➤ Animated **Christmas window displays** are on view at Saks Fifth Avenue and Lord & Taylor.

2 Exploring Manhattan

Around the next corner, a visitor to New York always has something new to discover uptown and down—world-class museums and unusual galleries, breathtaking skyscrapers, historic town houses, churches and synagogues, indoor plazas, outdoor parks and gardens. From the Battery in the south to Harlem in the north, this chapter uncovers the essential places to see in each neighborhood, as well as worthwhile sights off the tourist track. Be sure to stop and rest along the way so that you can observe the fabulous street life that makes this city so unique.

MANHATTAN IS, ABOVE ALL, A WALKER'S CITY. Along its busy streets there's something else to look at every few yards. Attractions, many of them world-famous, are crowded close together on this narrow island, and because it has to grow up, not out, new layers are simply piled on top of the old. The city's character changes every few blocks, with quaint town houses shouldering sleek glass towers, gleaming gourmet supermarkets sitting around the corner from dusty thrift shops, and soot-smudged warehouses inhabited at street level by trendy neon-lit bistros. Many a visitor has been beguiled into walking a little farther, then a little farther still—"Let's just see what that copper dome and steeple belongs to. . . ."

Revised by Hannah Borgeson, David Low, and Stephen Wolf

Our walking tours cover a great deal of ground, yet they only scratch the surface. If you plod dutifully from point to point, nose buried in this book, you'll miss half the fun. Look up at the tops of skyscrapers and you'll see a riot of mosaics, carvings, and ornaments. Go inside an intriguing office building and study its lobby decor; read the directory to find out what sorts of firms have their offices there. Peep around corners, even in crowded midtown, and you may find fountains, greenery, and sudden bursts of flowers. Find a bench or ledge to perch on, and take time just to watch the people passing by. New York has so many faces that every visitor can discover a different one.

Orientation

The map of Manhattan has a Jekyll-and-Hyde aspect. The rational, Dr. Jekyll part prevails above 14th Street, where the streets form a regular grid pattern imposed in 1811. Consecutively numbered streets run east and west (crosstown), while broad avenues, most of them also numbered, run north (uptown) and south (downtown). The chief exceptions are Broadway (which runs on a diagonal from East 14th to West 79th Street) and the thoroughfares that hug the shores of the Hudson and East rivers.

Fifth Avenue is the east–west dividing line for street addresses: In both directions, numbers increase in regular increments from there. For example, on 55th Street, the addresses 1–99 East 55th Street run from 5th, past Madison, to Park (the equivalent of 4th) Avenue, 100–199 East 55th would be between Park and 3rd avenues, and so on; the addresses 1–99 West 55th Street are between 5th and 6th avenues, 100–199 West 55th would be between 6th and 7th avenues, and so forth. Above 59th Street, where Central Park interrupts the grid, West Side addresses start numbering at Central Park West, an extension of 8th Avenue. Avenue addresses are much less regular, for the numbers begin wherever each avenue begins and increase at different increments. An address at 552 3rd Avenue, for example, will not necessarily be anywhere near 552 2nd Avenue. Many New Yorkers themselves cannot master the complexities of this system, so in their daily dealings they usually include cross-street references along with avenue addresses and rely on the handy Manhattan Address Locator found in the front of the local phone book.

Below 14th Street—the area that was already settled before the 1811 grid was decreed—Manhattan streets reflect the disordered personality of Mr. Hyde. They may be aligned with the shoreline or they may twist along the route of an ancient cow path. Below 14th Street you'll find West 4th Street intersecting West 11th Street, Greenwich Street running roughly parallel to Greenwich Avenue, Leroy Street turning

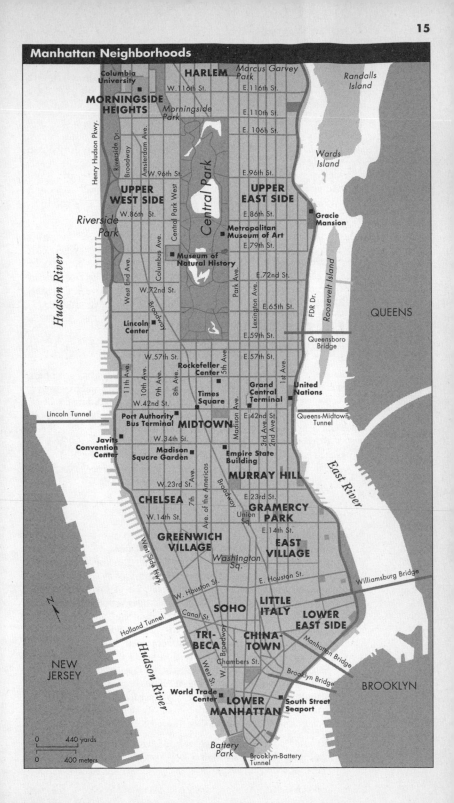

Manhattan Neighborhoods

into St. Luke's Place for one block and then becoming Leroy again. There's an East Broadway and a West Broadway, both of which run north–south and neither of which is an extension of plain old Broadway. Logic won't help you below 14th Street; only a good street map and good directions will.

You may also be confused by the way New Yorkers use "uptown" and "downtown." These terms refer both to locations and to directions. Uptown means north of wherever you are at the moment; downtown means to the south. But Uptown and Downtown are also specific parts of the city (and, some would add, two very distinct states of mind). Unfortunately, there is no consensus about where these areas are: Downtown may mean anyplace from the tip of lower Manhattan through Chelsea; it depends on the orientation of the speaker.

A similar situation exists with "East Side" and "West Side." Someone may refer to a location as "on the east side," meaning somewhere east of 5th Avenue. A hotel described as being "on the west side" may be on West 42nd Street. But when New Yorkers speak of the East Side or the West Side, they usually mean the respective areas above 59th Street, on either side of Central Park. Be prepared for misunderstandings.

ROCKEFELLER CENTER AND MIDTOWN SKYSCRAPERS

Athens has its Parthenon and Rome its Coliseum. New York's temples, which you see along this mile-long tour along six avenues and five streets, are its concrete-and-glass skyscrapers. Many of them, including the Lever House and the Seagram Building, have been pivotal in the history of modern architecture, and the 19 warm-hued limestone and aluminum buildings of Rockefeller Center are world-renowned. When movies and TV shows are set in Manhattan, they often start with a panning shot of this amazing architectural complex, because no other city scene—except perhaps the downtown skyline—so clearly says "New York."

Numbers in the text correspond to numbers in the margin and on the Midtown map.

A Good Walk

The heart of midtown Manhattan is **Rockefeller Center,** one of the greatest achievements in 20th-century urban planning. A fun way to navigate among its myriad buildings is to move from east to west following a trail punctuated by three famous statues from Greek mythology. Atlas stands sentry outside the classically inspired **International Building** ①, on 5th Avenue between 50th and 51st streets. Head one block south on 5th Avenue and turn west to walk along the **Channel Gardens** ②, a complex of rock pools and seasonally replanted flower beds. Below these is the **Lower Plaza** ③ and, towering heroically over it from an eternal ledge, the famous gold-leaf statue of Prometheus. The backdrop to this scene is the 70-story **GE Building** ④, originally known as the RCA Building, whose entrance is guarded by a striking statue of Prometheus. Straight across bustling 50th Street is America's largest indoor theater, the titanic **Radio City Music Hall** ⑤.

Two other notable Rockefeller Center buildings on the west side of 6th Avenue are the **McGraw-Hill Building** ⑥, between 48th and 50th streets, and the Time & Life Building, between 50th and 51st streets.

Continue north on 6th Avenue, leaving Rockefeller Center. On the east side of 6th Avenue between 52nd and 53rd streets, the monolithic black **CBS Building** ⑦ (a.k.a. Black Rock) stands out from the crowd. From here, it's a short stroll to three museums enshrining contemporary culture. Go east on 52nd Street to the **Museum of Television and Radio** ⑧, devoted to the two key mediums of the modern era; here, you can screen favorite television shows from your childhood from the museum's huge library. Right next door is the **"21" Club,** a famous and popular restaurant. A shortcut through the outdoor public space close to the CBS Building or through a shopping arcade farther east, at 666 5th Avenue, takes you to 53rd Street's other museums: on the south side, the **American Craft Museum** ⑨, which mounts changing exhibits of contemporary crafts from the 50 states and around the world, and, on the north side, the **Museum of Modern Art (MoMA)** ⑩, home of one of the world's most important collections of 20th-century art. Not far from MoMA, across 5th Avenue at 3 East 53rd Street, is **Paley Park,** a small "vest-pocket park" with a waterfall.

The true muse of midtown is not art but business, however, as you'll see on a brisk walk east on 53rd Street across 5th Avenue, where you'll encounter four office towers named after their corporate owners. First head north on Madison Avenue to 55th Street and the elegant rose granite tower known as the **Sony Building** ⑪, immediately recognizable from afar by its Chippendale-style pediment. Farther east and a little south on Park Avenue stand two prime examples of the functionalist International Style: **Lever House** ⑫ (between 53rd and 54th streets) and the **Seagram Building** ⑬ (between 52nd and 53rd streets), the only New York building by the celebrated Ludwig Mies van der Rohe. Finally, go one block east to Lexington Avenue where, between 53rd and 54th streets, the luminous white shaft of the **Citicorp Center** ⑭ houses thousands more New Yorkers engaged in the daily ritual that built the city—commerce. To end your walk on a less material note, return to Park Avenue and turn south to 51st Street and **St. Bartholomew's Church** ⑮, an intricate Byzantine temple struggling to be heard in the home of the skyscraper.

TIMING

To see only the buildings, block out an hour and a half. Expand your allotment depending on your interest in the museums en route. At minimum, you might spend 45 minutes in the American Craft Museum (depending on your interest in the exhibit); the same in the Museum of Television and Radio (depending on how many vintage TV shows you screen); and 3½ hours in the Museum of Modern Art (and even then you'll only dip briefly into the collections—it would be easy to pass an entire day there, ending with a movie in the museum's theater). Keep in mind that some parts of Rockefeller Center are only open during the week.

Start early in order to arrive at the Museum of Television and Radio when it opens, so that you won't have to wait for a TV console to watch your shows on; break up your MoMA visit with lunch in its café.

Sights to See

⑨ **American Craft Museum.** Distinctions between "craft" and "high art" become irrelevant here, for much of this work created by contemporary American and international artisans is provocative and fun to look at. You may see works in clay, glass, fabric, wood, metal, paper, or even chocolate. ✉ *40 W. 53rd St.,* ☎ *212/956–3535.* ✆ *$5.* ☉ *Tues.–Sun. 10–6, Thurs. 10–8.*

OFF THE
BEATEN PATH

BEEKMAN PLACE – This secluded and exclusive East Side two-block-long enclave has an aura of unperturbably elegant calm. Residents of its refined town houses have included the Rockefellers, Alfred Lunt and Lynn Fontanne, Ethel Barrymore, Irving Berlin, and, of course, Auntie Mame,

Midtown

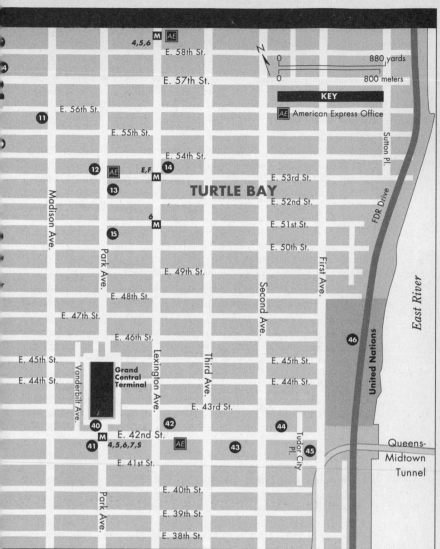

4,5,6

E. 58th St.

E. 57th St.

E. 56th St.

E. 55th St.

E. 54th St.

E,F

TURTLE BAY

E. 53rd St.

E. 52nd St.

E. 51st St.

E. 50th St.

E. 49th St.

E. 48th St.

E. 47th St.

E. 46th St.

E. 45th St.

E. 44th St.

E. 43rd St.

E. 45th St.

E. 44th St.

Grand Central Terminal

E. 42nd St.

4,5,6,7,S

E. 41st St.

E. 40th St.

E. 39th St.

E. 38th St.

Madison Ave.

Park Ave.

Vanderbilt Ave.

Lexington Ave.

Third Ave.

Second Ave.

First Ave.

Sutton Pl.

FDR Drive

East River

United Nations

Tudor City Pl.

Queens-Midtown Tunnel

N

0   880 yards

0   800 meters

KEY

AE   American Express Office

11 12 13 14 15 40 41 42 43 44 45 46

a character in the well-known Patrick Dennis play of the same name. Go down the steps at 51st Street to reach a walkway along the East River. ⊠ *East of 1st Ave., between 49th and 51st Sts.*

⑦ CBS Building. Designed by Eero Saarinen, this 38-story building has a concrete frame covered with dark gray granite. The so-called Black Rock, built in 1965, towers over the cluster of museums in the neighborhood: the Museum of Television and Radio, the American Craft Museum, and the Museum of Modern Art. ⊠ *6th Ave. between 52nd and 53rd Sts.*

② Channel Gardens. This Rockefeller Center promenade, leading from 5th Avenue to a stair connected to the ☞ **Lower Plaza,** has six pools surrounded by flower beds filled with seasonal plantings and was conceived by artists, floral designers, and sculptors—10 shows a season. The area, called the Channel Gardens, separates the British building to the north from the French building to the south (above each building's entrance is a national coat of arms). The French building contains among other shops the Metropolitan Museum of Art gift shop and, of course, **Librairie de France,** which sells French-language books, periodicals, tapes, and recordings; its surprisingly large basement contains a Spanish bookstore and a foreign-language dictionary store. ⊠ *5th Ave. between 49th and 50th Sts.*

⑭ Citicorp Center. The most striking feature of this 1977 design of architect Hugh Stubbins & Associates is the angled top. The immense solar-energy collector it was designed to carry was never installed, but the building's unique profile forever changed the New York City skyline; closer to the ground, the subway entrance at 53rd Street mimics the top of the building. At the base of Citicorp Center is a pleasant atrium mall of restaurants and shops, where occasionally there's music at lunchtime. **St. Peter's Church,** whose angled roof is tucked under the Citicorp shadow, is known for its Sunday afternoon jazz vespers at 5; below the church is a theater where various acting troupes perform. ⊠ *Lexington Ave. between 53rd and 54th Sts.,* ☎ *212/935–2200 for St. Peter's.*

OFF THE
BEATEN PATH

CORPORATE-SPONSORED EXHIBITS – Though it's not Museum Mile, midtown does benefit from companies who use part of their space to present free public exhibits. The Paine Webber Gallery (⊠ 1285 6th Ave., at 51st St.), open weekdays 8–6, hosts four exhibits a year in the base of its building. The Equitable Center (⊠ 787 7th Ave., at 51st St.) has an enormous Roy Lichtenstein work in its lobby and a gallery with changing exhibits; it is open weekdays 11–6, Saturday noon–5.

DIAMOND DISTRICT – The relatively unglitzy jewelry shops at street level on 47th Street between 5th and 6th avenues are just the tip of the iceberg; upstairs, millions of dollars' worth of gems are traded, and skilled craftsmen cut precious stones. Wheeling and dealing goes on at fever pitch, all rendered strangely exotic by the presence of a host of Hasidic Jews in severe black dress, beards, and curled side locks. During the day, this street becomes one of the slowest to navigate by foot in Manhattan because of all the people.

④ GE Building. The backdrop to the ☞ **Channel Gardens, Prometheus,** and the ☞ **Lower Plaza,** this 70-story building is the tallest tower in ☞ **Rockefeller Center.** It was known as the RCA Building until GE acquired its namesake company in 1986. The block-long street called Rockefeller Plaza, which runs between the GE Building and the Lower Plaza, is officially a private street (to maintain that status, it closes to all traffic on one day a year); each year it is the site of the ever-popular Rockefeller Christmas tree. The thoroughfare is often choked with celebrities' black limousines, for this is the headquarters of the NBC television network. From this building emanated some of the first TV programs ever, including the *Today* show. It's now broadcast from a ground-floor, glass-enclosed studio on the southwest corner of 49th Street and Rockefeller Plaza, so if you're in the area between 7 and 9 AM, your face may show up on TV behind the *Today* show hosts. To see what goes on inside, sign up for a one-hour tour of the NBC Studios. ✉ *30 Rockefeller Plaza,* ☎ *212/664–7174.* ✉ *Tour $10. Children under 6 not permitted.* ☉ *Tour departs from street level of GE Bldg. every 15 mins Easter–Labor Day weekdays, 9:30–6; Sat. 9:30–7; Sun. 9:30–4:45; Thanksgiving–New Year's Day, weekdays 9:30–5; Sat. 9:30–4:30; Sun. 9:30–4:45. Other times of yr, tour departs every ½ hr, weekdays 9:30–4:30, every 15 mins Sat. 9:30–4:30.*

As you enter the GE Building from Rockefeller Plaza, look up at the striking sculpture of Zeus above the entrance doors, executed in limestone cast in glass by Lee Lawrie, the same artist who sculpted the big Atlas in front of the ☞ **International Building** on 5th Avenue. Inside, crane your neck to see the dramatic ceiling mural entitled *Time,* by José Maria Sert.

Take some time to wander around the marble catacombs that connect the various components of Rockefeller Center. There's a lot to see: restaurants in all price ranges, from the chic American Festival Café to McDonald's; a post office and clean public rest rooms (scarce in midtown); and just about every kind of store. To find your way around, consult the strategically placed directories or obtain the free brochure, "Walking Tour of Rockefeller Center" at the GE Building information desk. Before leaving the GE Building lobby, you might also take an elevator to the 65th floor to enjoy the spectacular view with drinks or a meal at the **Rainbow Room.** When you've seen all there is to see, leave the GE Building on 6th Avenue to view the allegorical mosaics above that entrance. ✉ *Bounded by Rockefeller Plaza, 6th Ave., and 49th and 50th Sts.*

NEED A BREAK?   **Dean & Deluca** (✉ 1 Rockefeller Plaza, at 49th St., ☎ 212/664–1363) is near the GE Building. You can relax here with a cup of coffee, tea, or hot chocolate, and cookies, cakes, and small sandwiches.

❶ International Building. A huge statue of Atlas supporting the world stands sentry before this heavily visited ☞ **Rockefeller Center** structure, which houses many foreign consulates, international airlines, and a U.S. passport office. The lobby is fitted with Grecian marble. ✉ *5th Ave. between 50th and 51st Sts.*

⑫ Lever House. Architect Gordon Bunshaft, of Skidmore, Owings & Merrill, created this seminal skyscraper, a sheer, slim glass box resting on one end of a one-story-thick shelf that is balanced on square chrome columns and seems to float above the street. Because the tower occupies only half of the space above the lower floors, a great deal of airspace is left open, and the tower's side wall displays a reflection of its neighbors. It was built in 1952 to house the offices of the Lever Brothers soap company. ✉ *390 Park Ave., between 53rd and 54th Sts.*

❸ Lower Plaza. Sprawled on his ledge above this ☞ **Rockefeller Center** plaza, you will see one of the most famous sights in the complex (if not all of New York): the great gold-leaf statue of the fire-stealing Greek hero **Prometheus.** A quotation from Aeschylus is carved into the red granite wall behind. The plaza's trademark ice-skating rink is open from October through April; the rest of the year, it becomes an open-air café.

In December an enormous live Christmas tree towers above this area. On the Esplanade above the plaza, flags of the United Nations' members alternate with flags of the states. ✉ *Between 5th and 6th Aves. and 49th and 50th Sts.,* ☎ *212/332–7654 rink.*

⬤ McGraw-Hill Building. Built in 1972 to relocate McGraw-Hill from its West 42nd Street building, this ☞ **Rockefeller Center** skyscraper is notable for its street-level plaza with a 50-ft steel sun triangle that points to the seasonal positions of the sun at noon. ✉ *6th Ave. between 48th and 49th Sts.*

★ ⑩ Museum of Modern Art (MoMA). In its second- and third-floor galleries of painting and sculpture, MoMA displays some of the world's most famous modern paintings: Van Gogh's *Starry Night,* Picasso's *Les Demoiselles d'Avignon,* Matisse's *Dance.* The bright and airy six-story structure, built around a secluded sculpture garden, also includes photography, architecture, decorative arts, drawings, prints, illustrated books, and films. Afternoon and evening film shows, mostly of foreign productions and classics, are free with the price of admission; tickets, distributed in the lobby on the day of the performance, often go fast. Programs change daily; call for a schedule. Free jazz concerts are given in the café on Friday evenings. And leave time to sit outside in that wonderful Sculpture Garden, which hosts contemporary music concerts during the summer. ✉ *11 W. 53rd St.,* ☎ *212/708–9480; 212/708–9491 for jazz program.* ▦ *$8.50; pay what you wish Fri. 4:30–8:30.* ☉ *Sat.–Tues. and Thurs. 10:30–6, Fri. 10:30–8:30.*

⑧ Museum of Television and Radio. Three galleries of photographs and artifacts document the history of broadcasting in this new limestone building by Philip Johnson and John Burgee. But most visitors come here to sit at the museum consoles and watch TV: The collection includes more than 60,000 television shows and radio programs, as well as several thousand commercials. ✉ *25 W. 52nd St.,* ☎ *212/621–6800 for general information and daily events; 212/621–6600 for other information.* ▦ *$6 (suggested donation).* ☉ *Tues.–Sun. noon–6, Thurs. noon–8.*

Paley Park. A boon to midtown's weary, this memorial to former CBS executive Samuel Paley was the first of New York's "vest-pocket parks" to be inserted among the high-rise behemoths, placed on the site of the former society night spot the Stork Club. A waterfall blocks out traffic noise, and feathery honey locust trees provide shade. There's a snack bar that opens when weather permits. ✉ *3 E. 53rd St.*

⑤ Radio City Music Hall. Part of ☞ **Rockefeller Center,** this 6,000-seat Art Deco masterpiece is America's largest indoor theater, with a 60-ft-high foyer and 2-ton chandeliers. Home of the fabled Rockettes chorus line (which actually started out in St. Louis in 1925), Radio City was built as a movie theater with a stage suitable for live shows as well. Its days as a first-run movie house are long over, but after an announced closing in 1978, Radio City has had an amazing comeback, producing concerts, awards presentations, and special events, along with its own Christmas and Easter extravaganzas. On most days you can take a one-hour tour of the premises. ✉ *1260 6th Ave., at 50th St.,* ☎ *212/247–4777 or 212/632–4041 for tour information.* ▦ *Tour $13.75.* ☉ *Tours usually leave from main lobby every 30 mins Mon.–Sat. 10–5, Sun. 11–5.*

Rockefeller Center. Begun during the Great Depression of the 1930s by John D. Rockefeller, this 19-building complex occupies nearly 22 acres of prime real estate between 5th and 7th avenues and 47th and 52nd streets. Its central cluster of buildings consist of smooth shafts of warm-hued limestone, streamlined with glistening aluminum. The real genius of the complex's design was its intelligent use of public space: Its plazas, concourses, and street-level shops create a sense of community for the nearly quarter of a million human beings who use it daily. Restaurants, shoe-repair shops, doctors' offices, barbershops, banks, a post office, bookstores, clothing shops, variety stores—all are accommodated within the center, and all parts of the complex are linked by underground passageways.

Rockefeller Center helped turn midtown into New York City's second "downtown" area, which now rivals the Wall Street area in the number of its prestigious tenants. The center itself is a capital of the communications industry, containing the headquarters of a TV network (NBC), several major publishing companies (Time-Warner, McGraw-Hill), and the world's largest news-gathering organization, the Associated Press. Some of the complex's major sights include ☞ **Radio City Music Hall,** the ☞ **International Building,** the ☞ **Channel Gardens,** the ☞ **Lower Plaza,** and the ☞ **GE Building.** *☎ 212/632–3975 for Rockefeller Center information.*

★ ⑮ **St. Bartholomew's Church.** Church fathers have been eager to sell the airspace over this 1919 structure with rounded arches and an intricately tiled Byzantine dome, to take advantage of the stratospheric property values in this part of town. So far, fortunately, landmark forces have prevented any such move. ⊠ *Park Ave. between 50th and 51st Sts.*

⑬ **Seagram Building.** Architect Ludwig Mies van der Rohe, a leading interpreter of the International Style, built this simple bronze and glass boxlike tower in 1958. Its ground-level plaza, an innovation at the time, has since become a common element in urban skyscraper design due partly to a 1961 New York City resolution encouraging such land use. Inside is one of New York's most venerated restaurants, the **Four Seasons Grill and Pool Room.** ⊠ *375 Park Ave., between 52nd and 53rd Sts.,* ☎ *212/572–7000.* ☞ *Free.* ☉ *Tours Tues. at 3.*

⑪ **Sony Building.** Unlike the sterile ice-cube-tray buildings of 6th Avenue, Sony's rose granite columns, its regilded statue of the winged *Golden Boy* in the lobby, and its peculiar "Chippendale" roof have made this design of architect Philip Johnson an instant landmark for New Yorkers, who consider it the first postmodern skyscraper. Former tenant AT&T has moved to New Jersey. The first floor, Sony Plaza, includes a public seating area, cafés, a newsstand, a music store where you can purchase recordings, and the new **Sony Wonder Technology Lab,** outfitted with tremendously entertaining interactive exhibits such as a recording studio, a video-game production studio, and a TV production studio. ⊠ *550 Madison Ave., between 55th and 56th Sts.,* ☎ *212/833– 8830 for Sony Wonder Technology Lab.* ☞ *Free.* ☉ *Technology Lab Tues.–Sat. 10–6, Sun. noon–6 (last entrance 5:30); Sony Plaza daily 7 AM–11 PM.*

"21" Club. A trademark row of jockey statuettes parades along the wrought-iron balcony of this landmark restaurant, which has a burnished men's-club atmosphere, a great downstairs bar, and a power-broker clientele. In the movie *The Sweet Smell of Success,* Burt Lancaster as a powerful Broadway columnist held court at his regular table here, besieged by Tony Curtis as a pushy young publicist. ⊠ *21 W. 52nd St.,* ☎ *212/582–7200.*

5TH AVENUE AND 57TH STREET

For better or for worse, there's an increasingly fine line between retail, restaurants, and entertainment along much of the stretch of 5th Avenue upward from Rockefeller Center. This is still one of the world's great shopping districts, as evidenced by its many elegant shops as well as the international fashion firms that try to muscle in on this turf, and the rents are even higher along East 57th Street, where there's a parade of very exclusive smaller stores and upscale art galleries. But in the past few years the area's character has begun to change as brand-name stores engaged in shameless self-promotion have moved in, each one's grand opening more spectacular than the last, and each one trying to draw people in with novel decoration and entertainment schemes. Hype aside, these stores can be fun even if you don't want to buy anything. This tour mentions all the obvious stores, both new and established, but for more information about what they sell and how much it will cost, *see* Chapter 10.

Theme restaurants, another fairly recent addition to the neighborhood, dominate 57th Street west of 5th Avenue (☞ Chapter 6).

Numbers in the text correspond to numbers in the margin and on the Midtown map.

A Good Walk

Start right across the street from Rockefeller Center's Channel Gardens (☞ Rockefeller Center and Midtown Skyscrapers, *above*), at renowned **Saks Fifth Avenue** ⑯, the flagship of the national department store chain. Across 50th Street is Gothic-style **St. Patrick's** ⑰, the Roman Catholic Cathedral of New York. From outside, catch one of the city's most photographed views: the ornate white spires of St. Pat's against the black-glass curtain of Olympic Tower, a multiuse building of shops, offices, and luxury apartments.

Cartier, Inc., displays its wares in a jewel-box, turn-of-the-century mansion on the southeast corner of 52nd Street and 5th Avenue; similar houses used to line this street, and many of their residents were parishioners of **St. Thomas Church** ⑱, an Episcopal institution that has occupied the site at the northwest corner of 53rd Street and 5th Avenue since 1911. Continuing north, you'll see the imposing bulk of the **University Club** ⑲ at the northwest corner of 5th Avenue and 54th Street; this granite palace was built by New York's leading turn-of-the-century architects, McKim, Mead & White. It shares the block with the Peninsula, one of the city's fanciest hotels. Across the street is **Takashimaya New York** ⑳ (✉ 593 5th Ave.), a branch of Japan's largest department store chain.

Fifth Avenue Presbyterian Church, a grand brownstone church (1875), sits on the northwest corner of 5th Avenue and 55th Street. On the same block is **Henri Bendel** ㉑, a bustling fashion store organized like a little tower of intimate boutiques. Next door is Harry Winston (✉ 718 5th Ave.), with a spectacular selection of fine jewelry. Across the street, on the northeast corner of 5th Avenue and 55th Street, is the Disney Store (✉ 711 5th Ave.), where you can buy everything Disney, from key chains and earrings to clothes and even vacations. The Coca-Cola Store (✉ 711 5th Ave.) next door seems modest by comparison.

Trump Tower ㉒, on the east side of 5th Avenue between 56th and 57th streets, is an exclusive 68-story apartment and office building named for its developer, Donald Trump. Just north of it, the intersection of 5th Avenue and 57th Street is ground zero for high-class shopping. And what more fitting resident for this spot than **Tiffany & Co.** ㉓, the renowned jewelers. Around the corner on 57th Street, Niketown is a shrine to sports; it even has TVs and scoreboards on the first floor, so you can check on how your team is doing. It's next to 590 Madison, which to some is still the IBM Building (though the company sold it in 1996), a five-sided, 20-story sheath of dark gray-green granite and glass by Edward Larrabee Barnes. In the atrium off Madison Avenue, you can relax with a snack and enjoy the Alexander Calder sculptures.

Cross 57th Street and head back toward 5th Avenue on the north side of the street, with its stellar lineup of boutiques: the French shop Hermès (⊠ 11 E. 57th St.), the English shop Burberrys Ltd. (⊠ 9 E. 57th St.), the German shop Escada (⊠ 7 E. 57th St.), and the French classic Chanel (⊠ 5 E. 57th St.). Regular folk are less likely to feel outclassed at the newer additions to the block: Swatch (⊠ 5 E. 57th); the Original Levi's Store (⊠ 3 E. 57th St.), with the usual jeans; and Warner Brothers Studio Store (⊠ 1 E. 57th St.). The last recently expanded six floors upward, with tons of movie, television, and cartoon paraphernalia as well as interactive displays, movies, and even a café. From outside the Warner Brothers store, you can watch a larger-than-life Superman pushing up the elevator. Across 5th Avenue (at 754, to be exact), you can visit the elegant **Bergdorf Goodman** ㉔. The extravagant women's boutiques are on the west side of the avenue and the men's store on the east side, both between 57th and 58th streets. Van Cleef & Arpels jewelers is located within Bergdorf's 57th Street corner.

Cross 58th Street to **Grand Army Plaza** ㉕, the open space along 5th Avenue between 58th and 60th streets. Appropriately named the **Plaza** ㉖, the famous hotel at the western edge of this square is a registered historical landmark built in 1907. Across the street, on the southeast corner of 58th Street and 5th Avenue, is the legendary **F.A.O. Schwarz** ㉗ toy store ensconced in the General Motors Building.

Now return to 57th Street and head west, where the glamour eases off a bit. The large red No. 9 on the sidewalk, in front of the sloping headquarters of Chanel, was designed by Ivan Chermayeff, noted for saying, "If it's big and ugly, it's not big enough." You'll also pass the excellent Rizzoli bookstore (⊠ 31 W. 57th St.), and beyond that is arguably the handsomest McDonald's in the land, with an elegant blue-neon decorating scheme that's definitely not standard issue for the burger chain. From the corner of 57th Street and 5th Avenue you can see the sleek Harley-Davidson Cafe (⊠ 1370 6th Ave., at 56th St.), one of many contenders in the trendy burger-joint olympics, and the playfully menacing Jekyll and Hyde Club (⊠ 1409 6th Ave., at 57th St.).

Across 6th Avenue (remember, New Yorkers *don't* call it Avenue of the Americas, despite the street signs), you'll know you're in classical-music territory when you peer through the showroom windows at Steinway (⊠ 109 W. 57th St.). But before you get to Carnegie Hall, grab a bite (or at least steal a peek) at the Motown Cafe (⊠ 104 W. 57th St.) or Planet Hollywood (⊠ 140 W. 57th St.), where you'll find everything from Humphrey Bogart's Maltese Falcon to *Star Wars*' R2D2 and C-3PO robots; outside you can compare the size of your hand against celebrity handprints in the building's facade. On the next block is the unpretentious but nonetheless contrived Brooklyn Diner (⊠ 212 W. 57th St.).

An old joke says it all: A tourist asks an old guy with a violin case, "How do you get to Carnegie Hall?" His reply: "Practice, practice, practice." Presiding over the southeast corner of 7th Avenue and 57th

Street, **Carnegie Hall** ㉘ has been considered a premier international concert hall for decades. A small museum illuminates the site's role in musical history. Devotees of classical music may want to head from here up to nearby Lincoln Center (☞ The Upper West Side, *below*). If rock-and-roll music is more to your liking, head west one more block to the Hard Rock Cafe (✉ 221 W. 57th St.), New York City's outpost of the restaurant chain.

A few blocks south and west is the old Ed Sullivan Theater (✉ 1697 Broadway, between 53rd and 54th Sts.), now home to the *David Letterman Show.* Many shopkeepers and restaurateurs on this block have become minor late-night celebrities as a result of the talk-show host's habit of wandering out onto the street to harass his neighbors. Standby tickets become available at the box office weekdays at noon.

TIMING

This walk isn't long and can be completed in about 1½ hours. Add at least an hour for basic browsing around stores, and several more hours for serious shopping. Make sure the stores are open beforehand. If you want to eat at your favorite memorabilia-decked restaurant, plan on waiting up to an hour just for a table. Fifth Avenue is jam-packed from before Thanksgiving until New Year's.

Sights to See

㉔ **Bergdorf Goodman.** Good taste reigns supreme in this understated department store with dependable service—at a price. The Home Department has room after exquisite room of wonderful linens, tabletop items, and gifts. The men's store across the street is the place to go for that special gift. ✉ *754 5th Ave., between 57th and 58th Sts.,* ☎ *212/753–7300.*

NEED A
BREAK?
    Mangia (✉ 50 W. 57th St., ☎ 212/582-3061), an Italian and American food shop, is a great place to stop for coffee and a snack. The salad bar is exceptional. *Closed Sun.*

★ ㉘ **Carnegie Hall.** Musical headliners have been playing here since 1891, when its first concert was conducted by no less than Tchaikovsky. Outside it's a stout, square brown building with a few Moorish-style arches added, almost as an afterthought, to the facade. Inside, however, is a simply decorated 2,804-seat auditorium that is considered one of the finest in the world. It was extensively restored before its gala 1990–91 centennial season, but something was wrong with the main auditorium's acoustics. In 1995 the culprit was identified—concrete was found filling what should have been a hollow space under the stage's wood floor. The concrete was removed and the floor underpinnings were restored to what they should have been all along. The restoration also increased the size of the lobby, and a museum has been added just east of the main auditorium, displaying such memorabilia from the hall's illustrious history as a Benny Goodman clarinet and Beatles concert recordings. Guided tours of Carnegie Hall are available (they last about 45 minutes). ✉ *Carnegie Hall Rose Museum:* ✉ *881 7th Ave.,* ☎ *212/903–9629.* ▣ *Free.* ☉ *Mon.–Tues. and Thurs.–Sun. 11– 4:30. Guided tours:* ☎ *212/247–7800.* ▣ *$6.* ☉ *Tours Mon.–Tues., Thurs.–Fri. at 11:30, 2, and 3 (performance schedule permitting).*

OFF THE
BEATEN PATH
    DAHESH MUSEUM – This small exhibition space is the only U.S. museum dedicated exclusively to the European academic tradition, which encompasses the most influential and popular art of the 19th century. Bonheur, Bouguereau, Gérôme, and Troyon are among the well-known painters

represented here. ⊠ *601 5th Ave.,* ☎ *212/759–0606.* 🖃 *Free.* ⊙ *Tues.–Sat. 11–6.*

⊙ **㉗** **F.A.O. Schwarz.** The famous toy emporium has its fantastic mechanical clock right inside the front doors. Bigger than it looks from the outside, the toy-o-rama offers a vast, wondrously fun selection, although it definitely tends toward expensive imports. Browsing here brings out the child in everyone, as it did in the movie *Big,* when Tom Hanks and his boss got caught up in tap dancing on a giant keyboard. If the line to get in looks impossibly long, try walking around the block to the Madison Avenue entrance, where the wait may be shorter. ⊠ *767 5th Ave., at 58th St.,* ☎ *212/644–9410.*

㉕ **Grand Army Plaza.** Just before you get to Central Park, you'll reach this open space along 5th Avenue between 58th and 60th streets. The southern block features the **Pulitzer Fountain,** donated by publisher Joseph Pulitzer of Pulitzer prize fame. Appropriately enough for this ritzy area, the fountain is crowned by a female figure representing Abundance. The block to the north holds a gilded (some say *too* gilded) equestrian statue of Civil War general William Tecumseh Sherman; beyond it is a grand entrance to Central Park (☞ Central Park, *below*). ☞ **The Plaza,** an internationally famous hotel, is at the western edge of the square. East of Grand Army Plaza on 5th Avenue at 58th Street stands the **General Motors Building,** a 50-story tower of Georgia marble. One section of the main floor is the flagship of the legendary ☞ F.A.O. Schwarz toy store.

㉑ **Henri Bendel.** Shoppers always seem to have a good time at this beautiful store, which continues to delight with its inventive displays and sophisticated boutiques. The facade's René Lalique art-glass windows from 1912 can be viewed at close range from balconies ringing the four-story atrium. The second-floor café is particularly charming. ⊠ *712 5th Ave., between 55th and 56th Sts.,* ☎ *212/247–1100.*

㉖ **The Plaza.** This world-famous hotel is a registered historical landmark built in 1907. Its architect, Henry Hardenbergh, was the same man who designed the Dakota apartment building (☞ The Upper West Side, *below*); here he achieved a sprightly birthday-cake effect with white-glazed brick busily decorated and topped off with a copper-and-slate mansard roof. The hotel is home to the fictional children's-book star Eloise and has been featured in many movies, from Alfred Hitchcock's *North by Northwest* to more recent films such as *Arthur, Crocodile Dundee, Home Alone 2,* and, of course, *Plaza Suite.* Among the many upper-crust parties that have taken place in the Plaza's ballroom was Truman Capote's Black and White Ball of 1966, attended by everyone who was anyone—all dressed, naturally, in black and white. ⊠ *5th Ave. at 59th St.,* ☎ *212/759–3000.*

★ **⑰** **St. Patrick's Cathedral.** The Gothic-style house of worship is the Roman Catholic Cathedral of New York. Dedicated to the patron saint of the Irish—then and now one of New York's principal ethnic groups—the white marble and stone structure was begun in 1858, consecrated in 1879, and completed in 1906. The congregation purposely chose the 5th Avenue location for their church, claiming a prestigious spot for themselves at least on Sundays—otherwise they would be in the neighborhood largely as employees of the wealthy. Among the statues in the alcoves around the nave is a modern interpretation of the first American-born saint, Mother Elizabeth Seton. ⊠ *5th Ave. at 50th St.,* ☎ *212/753–2261 rectory.*

⑱ **St. Thomas Church.** This Episcopal institution with a striking French Gothic interior has occupied its present site since 1911. The impressive huge stone reredos behind the altar holds the statues of more than 50 apostles, saints, martyrs, missionaries, and other church figures; these were designed by Lee Lawrie. Christmas Eve services here have become a seasonal star. ✉ *5th Ave. at 53rd St.,* ☎ *212/757–7013.*

⑯ **Saks Fifth Avenue.** The flagship of the national department store chain moved here in 1926, solidifying midtown 5th Avenue's new status as an upscale shopping mecca. At the time, this branch's name was meant to distinguish it from its earlier incarnation on Broadway. It remains a civilized favorite among New York shoppers. ✉ *611 5th Ave., between 49th and 50th Sts.,* ☎ *212/753–4000.*

⑳ **Takashimaya New York.** This elegant yet somewhat austere branch of Japan's largest department store chain features a garden atrium, a two-floor gallery, and a tearoom. It has four floors of men's and women's clothing, gifts, and accessories and also carries household items that combine Eastern and Western styles. ✉ *693 5th Ave., between 54th and 55th Sts.,* ☎ *212/350–0100.*

㉓ **Tiffany & Co.** The renowned jewelers, with the Fort Knox–like Art Deco entrance and dramatic miniature window displays, moved uptown from Herald Square at the beginning of the century, helping to set the standard for what this neighborhood was to become. The store's signature aqua bags arouse great anticipation. A quintessential New York movie, *Breakfast at Tiffany's,* opens with Audrey Hepburn dressed in a Givenchy evening gown and emerging from a yellow cab at dawn to stand here window-shopping with a coffee and Danish. ✉ *727 5th Ave., at 57th St.,* ☎ *212/755–8000.*

㉒ **Trump Tower.** As he has done with other projects, developer Donald Trump named this exclusive 68-story apartment and office building after himself. The grand 5th Avenue entrance leads into a glitzy six-story shopping atrium paneled in pinkish-orange marble and trimmed with lustrous brass. A fountain cascades against one wall, drowning out the clamor of the city. ✉ *5th Ave. between 56th and 57th Sts.*

⑲ **University Club.** New York's leading turn-of-the-century architects, McKim, Mead & White, designed this 1899 granite palace for an exclusive midtown men's club, one of several that only recently have begun accepting women members. Pick out the crests of various prestigious universities above its windows. ✉ *1 W. 54th St.*

42ND STREET

As midtown Manhattan's central axis, 42nd Street ties together several major points of interest, passing by Times Square to Grand Central Terminal to the United Nations on the East River. Despite being on one of the world's busiest streets, some of its blocks fell upon hard times over the years. Revitalization began in the late 1980s, however, with the help of city agencies and business improvement districts, or BIDs, that tax local businesses and residents in order to provide greater levels of sanitation, security, and tourist services, among others. Bryant Park has been touted as the success of one such organization, and the blocks of 42nd Street west of Times Square are next.

Having acquired a reputation as a den of pickpockets, porno houses, prostitutes, and destitutes, the area is working to reclaim its fame as the metaphorical Broadway. After years of talks, plans, and proposals, there is finally action, and now it's hard to keep up with the pace of change. Several old theaters are in different stages of being readied for reopening. New stores, hotels, and restaurants, many with entertainment themes, are moving in as well, sure to capitalize on the tourists who can't seem to get enough of the area. In Times Square itself, the neon lights shine brighter than ever, and the ads become as creative, and even interactive, as technology allows. Some critics decry the Disney-fication of this part of town, but really, what area is more appropriate for this over-the-top treatment?

Numbers in the text correspond to numbers in the margin and on the Midtown map.

A Good Walk

The block of 42nd Street between 9th and 10th avenues is home to a string of thriving Off-Broadway playhouses, called Theatre Row (☞ Chapter 5). The monolithic Port Authority Bus Terminal, itself much improved over the last few years, sits on the next block. At No. 330, between 8th and 9th avenues, you should peek in. Originally the McGraw-Hill Building, it was designed in 1931 by Raymond Hood, who later worked on Rockefeller Center. The lobby is an Art Deco wonder of opaque glass and stainless steel, and a storefront is now used by Floating the Apple (☎ 212/564–5412), a unique environmental organization devoted to boats and the water.

The block just east of Port Authority is one of those that are most obviously being improved. Many of its buildings stood unused for years, and many others were functional only as X-rated bookstores, peep shows, or movie theaters. All this is changing, however. The Selwyn Theater (⊠ 229 W. 42nd St.) is the temporary home of a tourist information center and an exhibit about the area's past, present, and future; the office may move as buildings are renovated and the Times Square redevelopment project continues. The currently dark **Times Square Theater** is next door. Just east of this theater are the new **Ford Center for the Performing Arts** ㉙ and the **New Victory** ㉚, a rehabilitated treasure that specializes in theatrical productions for children. If you still can't erase the image of 42nd Street as a sleazy strip, look across the street and consider the new tenant of the **New Amsterdam** ㉛—the Walt Disney Company. The city claimed victory when the company agreed to rehabilitate this site (across the street from the New Victory), and it is probably Disney's presence that convinced other developers and retailers that the neighborhood really was changing. Just west of the New Amsterdam, the old Empire, Liberty, and Harris theaters are in the process of being transformed into a movie house and a Madame Tussaud's exhibit.

Although it may not exactly be the Crossroads of the World, as it is often called, **Times Square** ㉜ is one of New York's principal energy centers, not least because of its dazzling billboards. Heading east from Times Square on 42nd Street, you'll pass **Hotaling's News,** a little shop where you can buy print news from around the world. The triangle north of Times Square between 46th and 47th streets is named **Duffy Square** ㉝ after World War I hero Father Francis P. Duffy, the "Fighting Chaplain," who later was pastor of Holy Cross Church on West 42nd Street. At the intersection of 42nd Street and 6th Avenue, look north to see, on the side of a low 43rd Street building, the National Debt Clock, an electronic display established by the late real-estate developer Seymour Durst to remind passersby of how much deeper in debt the United States gets every second. At 6th Avenue and 43rd Street you can visit a branch of the International Center of Photography (☞ Museum Mile, *below*), **ICP Midtown** ㉞.

A block north of that is a rather clubby section of 44th Street that you might want to peek into before returning to 42nd Street. First, you'll see the surprisingly unpretentious **Algonquin Hotel** ㉟, a celebrity haunt. Next door is the more humble (and cheaper) Iroquois Hotel (✉ 49 W. 44th St.), where struggling actor James Dean lived in the early 1950s. Across the street from them is the **Royalton Hotel** ㊱, where, unless your clothes are suitably trendy, you'll be eyed suspiciously by the staff. Its neighbor, at 42 West 44th Street, is the Association of the Bar of the City of New York, with a neoclassical facade resembling the courthouses where its members spend so much of their time. Back on the north side of the street, at 37 West 44th Street, is the **New York Yacht Club,** and at No. 27, the redbrick Harvard Club. The newer Penn Club (✉ 30 W. 44th St.), with its elegant blue awning, is on the other side of the street. And yes, something on this block is open to the general public: the **Mechanics' and Tradesmen's Institute Building** ㊲.

At the southwest corner of 5th Avenue and 44th Street, notice the large sidewalk clock on a pedestal set in the 5th Avenue sidewalk, a relic of an era when only rich people could afford watches.

At 42nd Street at 6th Avenue, steps rise into the shrubbery and trees of the handsomely renovated **Bryant Park** ㊳, named for the poet and editor William Cullen Bryant (1794–1878). Full of benches and lawn chairs, this is a perfect place to relax for a few minutes. Though the park has been adopted as the backyard of all midtown workers, it's directly behind the magnificent Beaux Arts central research building of the **New York Public Library** ㊴, and the library houses part of its collections under the green lawn.

Continue east on 42nd Street to **Grand Central Terminal** ㊵. This Manhattan landmark was saved from the wrecking ball in a precedent-setting case that established the legality of New York's landmark preservation law. Stop on the south side of 42nd Street to admire the three huge windows separated by columns, and the Beaux Arts clock and sculpture (*Transportation*) crowning the facade above the elevated roadway (Park Avenue is routed around Grand Central's upper story). Go in the side doors on Vanderbilt Avenue to enter the cavernous main concourse, currently undergoing major renovations.

On the southwest corner of Park Avenue and 42nd Street, directly opposite Grand Central, the **Whitney Museum of American Art at Philip Morris** ㊶ occupies the ground floor of the Philip Morris Building. The museum abuts Pershing Square, the block of Park Avenue east of the viaduct. There have been various attempts to make this area more pleasant, including turning it into a pedestrian zone during the day. The southeast corner of 42nd and Park is a major departure point for buses to the three New York area airports, and upstairs at 100 East 42nd Street is the Satellite Airlines Terminal, where you'll find ticket counters for most major U.S. airlines. Next door is Green Point Savings Bank, in what's known as the Bowery Savings Bank building (✉ 110 E. 42nd St.), whose massive arches and 70-ft-high marble columns give it a commanding presence; it more closely resembles a church than a bank. At the end of the block is the Chanin Building (✉ 122 E. 42nd St.), notable for the Art Deco patterns that adorn its facade. Across the street you'll see the Grand Hyatt (✉ Park Ave. at Grand Central Terminal), which was created by wrapping a new black-glass exterior around the former Commodore Hotel.

Ask New Yorkers to name their favorite skyscraper and most will choose the Art Deco **Chrysler Building** ㊷ at 42nd Street and Lexington Avenue. Although the Chrysler Corporation itself moved out a long time ago, this graceful shaft culminating in a stainless-steel spire still captivates the eye and the imagination. On the south side of 42nd Street and east one block, the **Daily News Building** ㊸, where the newspaper was produced until spring 1995, is another art deco tower with a lobby worth visiting. The **Ford Foundation Building** ㊹, on the next block, is more modern and encloses a 12-story, ⅓-acre greenhouse.

Climb the steps along 42nd Street between 1st and 2nd avenues to enter **Tudor City** ㊺, a self-contained complex of a dozen buildings featuring half-timbering and lots of stained glass. From it, you have a great view of the **United Nations Headquarters** ㊻, which occupies a lushly landscaped 18-acre riverside tract just east of 1st Avenue between 42nd and 48th streets.

TIMING

This long walk covers vastly different types of sights, from frenzied Times Square to bucolic Bryant Park to majestic Grand Central Terminal to the inspiring United Nations. Make sure you allow ample time to see it all—more than half a day. Do this tour during daylight hours, but return to Times Square at night, perhaps for a meal or a show, to truly appreciate the neon spectacle.

Sights to See

㉟ **Algonquin Hotel.** Considering its history as a haunt of well-known writers and actors, this hotel is surprisingly unpretentious. Its most famous association is with a witty group of literary Manhattanites who gathered in its lobby and dining rooms in the 1920s—a clique that included short-story writer and critic Dorothy Parker, humorist Robert Benchley, playwright George S. Kaufman, and actress Tallulah Bankhead. One reason they met here was the hotel's proximity to the former offices of the *New Yorker* magazine at 28 West 44th (now at 20 West 43rd Street). Come here for tea in the lobby, a drink at the bar, or dinner and cabaret performances in the intimate Oak Room. ⊠ *59 W. 44th St.,* ☎ *212/840–6800.*

★ ㊳ **Bryant Park.** The New York Public Library keeps an incredible stash of books underneath this lovely stretch of green. The park, a haven for the unseemly just several years ago, now teems with well-dressed professionals who snatch up the lawn chairs for their brown-bag power lunches. Named for the poet and editor William Cullen Bryant (1794–1878), this was the site of America's first World's Fair, the Crystal Palace Exhibition of 1853–54. The park also has an elegant restaurant and a café.

★ ㊷ **Chrysler Building.** It'd be a shame to make New Yorkers pick one favorite skyscraper, but if they had to, this Art Deco masterpiece (1928–30) would probably be it. The Chrysler Corporation moved out a long time ago, but the building still has its name and many details from the company's cars—check out the elevator cabs, for example. The stainless-steel spire (polished in late 1995 to shine even brighter) was kept secret during the building's construction so other builders wouldn't know what height to try to top. The building held the world's-tallest title only briefly, and architectural spies knew about its spire before it was hoisted up to crown the building, but it still captivates the eye and the imagination, glistening in the sun during the day, glowing geometrically at night. The Chrysler Building has no observation deck, but you can go into its elegant dark lobby, which is faced with African marble and covered with a ceiling mural that salutes transportation and human endeavor. ⊠ *405 Lexington Ave., at 42nd St.*

㊸ **Daily News Building.** This Raymond Hood–designed Art Deco tower has brown-brick spandrels and windows to make it seem loftier than its 37 stories. The newspaper moved out in spring 1995, but the famous illuminated globe, 12 ft in diameter, is still there. The floor is laid out as a gigantic compass, with bronze lines indicating air mileage from principal world cities to New York. ⊠ *220 E. 42nd St.*

③③ **Duffy Square.** This triangle north of 42nd Street is named after World War I hero Father Francis P. Duffy, the "Fighting Chaplain," who later was pastor of a theater district church on West 42nd Street. Besides the suitably military statue of Father Duffy, there's also one of George M. Cohan, the indomitable trouper who wrote "Yankee Doodle Dandy." Today Duffy Square is an important place to visit for the **TKTS discount ticket booth,** which sells half-price and 25%-off tickets to Broadway and Off-Broadway shows (☞ Chapter 5). ⊠ *Between 46th and 47th Sts.*

㉙ **Ford Center for the Performing Arts.** Built by the Canadian production company Livent Inc. on the site of two classic 42nd Street legitimate theaters, the Lyric (1903) and the Apollo (1910), this spectacular $22.5 million theater was scheduled at press time to open at the end of December 1997 with a musical production of E. L. Doctorow's novel *Ragtime.* The design incorporates a landmark 43rd Street exterior wall from the Lyric and architectural elements from the Apollo, including its stage, proscenium, and dome. The theater has a 1,119-seat orchestra, two 360-seat balconies, a huge stage perfect for large-scale musical productions, and an orchestra pit big enough for 80 musicians. A 1,200-square-ft dance studio may be used for musical theater workshops.

In the early part of this century, the Lyric and the Apollo attracted such top talents to their stages as the Marx Brothers, Fred Astaire, Ethel Merman, and W. C. Fields. After going into a decline during the depression, the theaters became movie houses. In 1979 the Apollo became a legitimate theater once again with productions of *On Golden Pond* and *The Fifth of July*; afterwards it was used for rock concerts. The interiors of both houses were almost completely demolished to make way for the new theater, named for the U.S. automobile company. ⊠ *213–215 42nd St.*

㊹ **Ford Foundation Building.** A 12-story, ⅓-acre greenhouse is this building's lobby and its claim to fame. With a terraced garden, a still pool, and a couple of dozen full-grown trees, the Ford atrium is open to the public—for tranquil strolling, not for picnics—weekdays from 9 to 5. ⊠ *320 E. 43rd St., with an entrance on 42nd St.*

★ ㊵ **Grand Central Terminal.** Stop on the south side of 42nd Street to admire the three huge windows separated by columns, and the Beaux Arts clock and sculpture, *Transportation,* crowning the facade above the elevated roadway (Park Avenue is routed around Grand Central's upper story). Go in the side doors on Vanderbilt Avenue to enter the cavernous main concourse, with its 12-story-high ceiling displaying the constellations of the zodiac. Grand Central is enormous but not intimidating, bustling but calming. Constructed between 1903 and 1913, this Manhattan landmark was originally designed by a Minnesota architectural firm and later gussied up with Beaux Arts ornamentation. Neglected for a time in the 1970s and 1980s, the building is now being renovated to become a destination in its own right, with more shops and restaurants (à la Union Station in Washington, D.C.). The ceiling is being scrubbed, the marble walls cleaned, and a new staircase built in the main concourse. It's visually frustrating that so much of the interior is covered by scaffolding or behind curtains, but let's hope the renovation is worth it! The waiting room by the 42nd Street entrance, temporarily given over to food vendors ousted due to the renovation, hosts exhibits and seasonal markets, and musicians often play in the concourse. The best time to visit is at rush hour, when this room crackles with the frenzy of scurrying commuters, dashing every which way. (Remember the scene in the movie *The Fisher King,* when the crowd stopped running for trains, turned to each other, and waltzed instead?) ⊠ *Main entrance: E. 42nd St. at Park Ave.,* ☎ *212/935–3960. Tours Wed. at 12:30* PM *(meet in front of Chemical Bank inside terminal on main level).* ▣ *Tour free (donations to the Municipal Art Society accepted).*

Hotaling's News. This bustling little shop carries more than 220 daily newspapers from throughout the United States, most issues only a day or two old. ⊠ *142 W. 42nd St.,* ☎ *212/840–1868.*

㉞ ICP Midtown. The midtown branch of the International Center of Photography uptown presents several photography shows a year in an ultracontemporary, multilevel space. ⊠ *1133 6th Ave.,* ☎ *212/768–4680.* ▣ *$4; Tues. 6–8 pay as you wish.* ⊙ *Tues. 11–8, Wed.–Sun. 11–6.*

OFF THE BEATEN PATH — **JAPAN SOCIETY GALLERY –** This wonderfully serene setting holds exhibitions from well-known Japanese and American museums, as well as private collections. Also offered are movies, lectures, classes, concerts, and dramatic performances. Its newly renovated gallery was scheduled to reopen in May 1997. ⊠ *333 E. 47th St.,* ☎ *212/832-1155.* ▣ *$3 (suggested donation).* ⊙ *Tues.–Sun. 11–5.*

㊲ Mechanics' and Tradesmen's Institute Building. In its turn-of-the-century prep-school building, this institute has a wonderful library in a three-story-high hall. You can also look at displays of ancient trunks, Civil War paraphernalia, and locks and keys as old as the United States. ⊠ *20 W. 44th St.,* ☎ *212/840–1840.* ▣ *Free.* ⊙ *Weekdays 10–5.*

㉛ New Amsterdam. Starting in 1903, the likes of Eddie Cantor, Will Rogers, Fanny Brice, and the Ziegfeld Follies packed the crowds into this wonderful Art Nouveau theater. Like the rest of 42nd Street between 7th and 8th avenues, the theater and its glamour were long forgotten until the area was rejuvenated, and the unlikely new tenant here is the Walt Disney Company, which completely renovated the remarkable theater to serve as a venue for its own productions. The New Amsterdam reopened in May 1997 with the concert premiere of *King David,* a new biblical musical by Alan Menken and Tim Rice, who both worked previously on the scores of Disney animated films. ⊠ *214 W. 42nd St.*

★ **㉚ New Victory.** Previously known as the Theater Republic and the Belasco Theater, this is the oldest surviving theater in New York (it opened in 1899), but its lovely Georgian facade was buried under smut and then scaffolding for so long that people nearly forgot the treasure that was underneath. After a superb restoration job and modernization, this jewel reopened in late 1995 as the only Big Apple theater for kids; the magical interior will take you back to the beginning of this century. ⊠ *209 W. 42nd St.,* ☎ *212/239–6255.*

★ **㊴ New York Public Library (NYPL).** This 1911 masterpiece of Beaux Arts design, officially the NYPL's Center for the Humanities, was financed largely by John Jacob Astor, whose previous library building downtown has since been turned into the Joseph Papp Public Theater (☞ East Village, *below*). Its grand front steps are guarded by two crouching marble lions—dubbed "Patience" and "Fortitude" by Mayor Fiorello La Guardia, who said he visited the facility to "read between the lions." After admiring the white marble neoclassical facade (crammed with statues, as is typical of Beaux Arts buildings), walk through the bronze front doors into the grand marble lobby with its sweeping double staircase. Turn left and peek into the DeWitt Wallace Periodicals Room, decorated with trompe l'oeil paintings by Richard Haas to commemorate New York's importance as a publishing center. Then take a (quiet) look upstairs at the huge, high-ceilinged main reading room, a haven of scholarly calm, or visit changing exhibitions and the art gallery. Among the treasures you might see are Gilbert Stuart's portrait of George Washington, Charles Dickens's desk, and Thomas Jefferson's own handwritten copy of the Declaration of Independence. Free one-hour tours, each as individual as the library volunteer who leads it, leave from the lobby Monday–Saturday at 11 AM and 2 PM. ⊠ *5th Ave. between 40th and 42nd Sts.,* ☎ *212/930–0800.* ☉ *Mon. and Thurs.–Sat. 10–6, Tues.–Wed. 11–7:30 (exhibitions until 6).*

New York Yacht Club. Former longtime home of the America's Cup trophy, this Beaux Arts building is appropriately nautical. Notice its swelling window fronts, looking just like the sterns of ships, complete with stone-carved water splashing over the sill. ⊠ *37 W. 44th St.*

㊱ Royalton Hotel. Chicly redone to resemble a Deco dungeon by French designer Philippe Starck, this hotel is a midtown hot spot. You may want to step into its lobby for a peek, but you'll feel more comfortable if you're well dressed. ⊠ *44 W. 44th St.,* ☎ *212/869–4400.*

★ ㉜ **Times Square.** Love it or hate it, you can't deny that this is one of New York's principal energy centers. Like many New York City "squares," it's actually triangles formed by the angle of Broadway slashing across a major avenue—in this case, crossing 7th Avenue at 42nd Street. In exchange for having its name grace the area, the *New York Times,* then a less prestigious paper, moved into what had been a relatively quiet area known as Longacre Square when the subway opened. It erected the Times Tower and opened its headquarters here on December 31, 1904, publicizing the event with a fireworks show at midnight and thereby starting a New Year's Eve tradition. The building, bought in 1996 by Warner Brothers, is now resheathed in white marble and called **One Times Square Plaza.** Each December 31, a 200-pound ball is lowered down the building's flagpole—a tradition since 1908. The huge intersection below is mobbed with revelers, and when the ball hits bottom on the stroke of midnight, pandemonium ensues.

The present headquarters of the *New York Times* (⊠ 229 W. 43rd St.) occupies much of the block between 7th and 8th avenues; look for the blue delivery vans lined up along 43rd Street. From 44th to 51st streets, the cross streets west of Broadway are lined with some 30 major theaters. This has been the city's main theater district since the turn of the century; movie theaters joined the fray beginning in the 1920s. As the theaters drew crowds of people in the evenings, advertisers began to mount huge electric signs here, which gave the intersection its distinctive nighttime glitter. Even the developers who want to change this area intend to preserve the signs, and the current zoning actually requires buildings to have enormous ads. The ads themselves only get bigger and brighter with new technology. One of the newer ones, which features a 42-ft-tall bottle of Coca-Cola hanging over Broadway and 47th Street, uses 60 mi of optical tubing.

The triangle north of 42nd Street between 46th and 47th streets is named ☞ **Duffy Square.** A free walking tour of the area starts from the Times Square Visitor Center in the Selwyn Theater (⊠ 229 W. 42nd St.) on Friday at noon.

Times Square Theater. For two decades after its 1920 opening, the Times Square, now dark, staged top hits such as *Gentlemen Prefer Blondes, The Front Page,* and *Strike Up the Band*; Noël Coward's *Private Lives* opened here with Gertrude Lawrence, Laurence Olivier, and the author himself. ⊠ *215 W. 42nd St.*

㊺ Tudor City. A dozen buildings featuring half-timbering and lots of stained glass compose this self-contained complex. Constructed between 1925 and 1928, two of the apartment buildings of this residential enclave originally had no east-side windows, lest the tenants be forced to gaze at the slaughterhouses, breweries, and glue factories then located along the East River. Today, however, they're missing a wonderful view of the United Nations Headquarters; you'll have to walk to the terrace at the end of 43rd Street to overlook the United Nations. This will place you at the head of the **Sharansky Steps** (named for Natan—formerly Anatoly—Sharansky, the Soviet dissident), which run along the **Isaiah Wall** (inscribed "They Shall Beat Their Swords Into Plowshares"); you'll also look down into **Ralph J. Bunche Park** (named for the African-American former UN undersecretary) and **Raoul Wallenberg Walk** (named for the Swedish diplomat and World War II hero who saved many Hungarian Jews from the Nazis). ⊠ *40th to 43rd Sts., between 1st and 2nd Aves.*

★ ㊻ United Nations Headquarters. Now more than 50 years old, this symbol of global cooperation occupies a lushly landscaped 18-acre riverside tract—officially an "international zone" and not part of the United States—just east of 1st Avenue between 42nd and 48th streets. Its rose garden is especially pleasant to stroll in, although picnicking is strictly forbidden. A line of flagpoles with flags arranged in alphabetical order representing the current roster of member nations stands before the striking 550-ft-high slab of the Secretariat Building, with the domed General Assembly Building nestled at its side. The headquarters were designed in 1947–53 by an international team of architects led by Wallace Harrison. You can enter the General Assembly Building at the 46th Street door; the interior corridors overflow with imaginatively diverse artwork donated by member nations. Free tickets to assemblies are sometimes available on a first-come, first-served basis before sessions begin; pick them up in the General Assembly lobby. (The full General Assembly is in session from mid-September to mid-December.) Visitors can take lunch in the Delegates Dining Room (jackets required for men) or eat from 9 to 4:30 in the public coffee shop. The public concourse, one level down from the visitor entrance, has gift shops, a bookstore, and a post office where you can mail letters with U.N. stamps. ⊠ *Visitor entrance: 1st Ave. and 46th St.,* ☎ *212/963–7713.* ⊠ *Tour $6.50.* ☉ *Tours offered daily 9:15–4:45 (weekdays only Jan.–Feb.); 45-min tours in English leave the General Assembly lobby every 20 mins. Children under 5 not permitted.*

㊶ Whitney Museum of American Art at Philip Morris. Each year this free branch of the Upper East Side Whitney Museum, on the ground floor of the Philip Morris Building, presents five successive exhibitions of 20th-century painting and sculpture. An espresso bar and seating areas make it an agreeable place to rest. ⊠ *120 Park Ave.,* ☎ *212/878–2550.* ⊠ *Free.* ☉ *Sculpture court Mon.–Sat. 7:30 AM–9:30 PM, Sun. 11–7; gallery Mon.–Wed. and Fri. 11–6, Thurs. 11–7:30.*

OFF THE
BEATEN PATH

WORLDWIDE PLAZA – This massive, rose-colored multiuse complex sits on the former site of the second Madison Square Garden. An impressive office tower on 8th Avenue is followed by a pleasing midblock plaza with a fountain; lower-scaled residential units and movie theaters (Cineplex

Odeon Worldwide, ☎ 212/505–2463, showing films for $3) fill the block through to 9th Avenue. It was built in 1989 following a design by Skidmore, Owings & Merrill and Frank Williams. ⊠ *50th and 51st Sts. between 8th and 9th Aves.*

MURRAY HILL TO UNION SQUARE

As the city grew progressively north throughout the 19th century, one neighborhood after another had its fashionable heyday, only to fade from glory. But three neighborhoods, east of 5th Avenue roughly between 20th and 40th streets, have preserved much of their historic charm: Murray Hill's brownstone mansions and town houses; Madison Square's classic turn-of-the-century skyscrapers; and Gramercy Park's London-like leafy square. The only "must-see" along this route is the Empire State Building, but the walk as a whole is worth taking for the many moments en route when you may feel as if you've stepped back in time.

Numbers in the text correspond to numbers in the margin and on the Murray Hill to Union Square map.

A Good Walk

Begin on East 36th Street, between Madison and Park avenues, at the **Pierpont Morgan Library** ①, known as much for its incredible interior as for its contents—Old Master drawings, medieval manuscripts, illuminated books, and original music scores. As you proceed south on Madison Avenue, at 35th Street you'll pass the **Church of the Incarnation** ②, a broodingly dark brownstone version of a Gothic chapel. Across the street and taking up the entire next block is the landmark **B. Altman Building** ③, home of the famous department store from 1906 to 1989 and now site of the New York Public Library's newest research center, the **Science, Industry, and Business Library.**

At 5th Avenue and 34th Street, you can't miss the **Empire State Building** ④. It may no longer be the world's tallest building, but it is certainly one of the world's best-loved skyscrapers, and you'll understand why when you see the view from its upper decks. Leaving the Empire State Building, continue south on 5th Avenue to 29th Street and the **Marble Collegiate Church** ⑤ (1854), a marble-fronted Romanesque Revival structure. Cross the street and head east on 29th Street to the **Church of the Transfiguration** ⑥, better known as the Little Church Around the Corner. Continuing south along Madison Avenue now, you'll come to the **New York Life Insurance Building** ⑦, which occupies the block between 26th and 27th streets on the east side of Madison, its distinctive gold top visible from afar. The limestone Beaux Arts courthouse next door, at 25th Street, is the **Appellate Division of the State Supreme Court** ⑧. The **Metropolitan Life Insurance Tower** ⑨, between 23rd and 24th streets, is another lovely, classical-inspired insurance-company tower.

The park along which you've been walking for a few blocks, bordered by 5th Avenue, Broadway, Madison Avenue, and 23rd and 26th streets, is **Madison Square** ⑩, no longer the site of Madison Square Garden. You can walk through it to get to one of New York's most photographed buildings—the Renaissance-style **Flatiron Building** ⑪, by architect Daniel Burnham. This distinguished building has lent its name to the once seedy, now trendy Flatiron district, which lies to the south between 5th Avenue and Park Avenue South. The neighborhood's massive buildings, the last of the pre-skyscraper era, have had their ornate Romanesque facades gleamingly restored; hip boutiques and

Murray Hill to Union Square

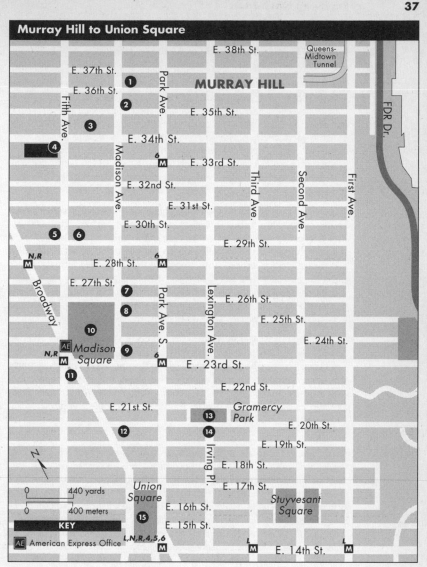

E. 38th St.

Queens-Midtown Tunnel

E. 37th St. ❶

Park Ave.

MURRAY HILL

E. 36th St. ❷

Fifth Ave.

E. 35th St.

❸

E. 34th St.

Madison Ave.

6 Ⓜ

E. 33rd St.

❹

E. 32nd St.

E. 31st St.

Third Ave.

Second Ave.

First Ave.

FDR Dr.

E. 30th St.

❺ ❻

E. 29th St.

N,R Ⓜ

E. 28th St.

6 Ⓜ

Broadway

E. 27th St. ❼

❽

Park Ave. S.

Lexington Ave.

E. 26th St.

E. 25th St.

❿

E. 24th St.

AE Madison ❾
Square

N,R Ⓜ

6 Ⓜ

E. 23rd St.

⓫

E. 22nd St.

E. 21st St.

⓭

Gramercy Park

N

⓬

⓮

E. 20th St.

Irving Pl.

E. 19th St.

E. 18th St.

E. 17th St.

0   440 yards

0   400 meters

KEY

AE American Express Office

Union Square

⓯

E. 16th St.

E. 15th St.

Stuyvesant Square

L,N,R,4,5,6 Ⓜ

L Ⓜ

E. 14th St.

L Ⓜ

Appellate Division of
the State Supreme
Court, **8**

B. Altman Building, **3**

Church of the
Incarnation, **2**

Church of the
Transfiguration, **6**

Empire State
Building, **4**

Flatiron Building, **11**

Gramercy Park, **13**

Irving Place, **14**

Madison Square, **10**

Marble Collegiate
Church, **5**

Metropolitan Life
Insurance Tower, **9**

New York Life
Insurance Building, **7**

Pierpont Morgan
Library, **1**

Theodore Roosevelt
Birthplace, **12**

Union Square, **15**

restaurants occupy their street levels, while advertising agencies, publishing houses, architects' offices, graphic design firms, residential lofts, and multimedia companies fill the upper stories.

Continue south on Broadway and turn east on 20th Street to the **Theodore Roosevelt Birthplace** ⑫, a reconstruction of the Victorian brownstone where Teddy lived until he was 15 years old. What is probably the prettiest part of this residential district lies farther east, at the top of Irving Place, between 20th and 21st streets—**Gramercy Park** ⑬, a picture-perfect city park complete with flower beds, bird feeders, sundials, and cozy benches. Wander the streets around the park (you can't get in without a key, which is available only to residents) and continue down **Irving Place** ⑭, taking time to admire the charming brownstones here, too.

Another option is to make a detour east, to the **Police Academy Museum,** predictably full of law-enforcement memorabilia. If you're really energetic, wander up to Lexington Avenue in the high 20s, a neighborhood affectionately known as Little India, where Indian restaurants, spice shops, imported-video stores, and clothing stores abound. The area also plays host to Middle Eastern, Indonesian, and Vietnamese restaurants. In this multicultural part of town, better seen during the day, don't be surprised to find a Spanish-language playhouse across the street from an Islamic bookstore.

Our walk ends at **Union Square** ⑮, which lies between Park Avenue South and Broadway and 14th and 17th streets, one block west of Irving Plaza. The neighborhood around it has improved so much recently that it now has several fashionable restaurants and stores. If possible, visit the Greenmarket on Monday, Wednesday, Friday, or Saturday, when the north side of the park bustles with friendly people and good, fresh, locally grown food.

TIMING

This tour will take about half a day. Allow 1½ hours each for the Empire State Building and the Morgan Library. Some of the office buildings included in the walk are open only during the week, so if you want to peek inside you should keep that in mind. Additionally, the Union Square Greenmarket really shouldn't be missed; it's open all day every Monday, Wednesday, Friday, and Saturday. The weather, and how it affects visibility from the Empire State Building, is something else you may want to consider. Sunsets from the top of the building are spectacular, so you may want to end your day there (but be sure to include time for the line you'll have to wait in to get to the top).

Sights to See

8 **Appellate Division of the State Supreme Court.** The roof balustrade of this imposing Corinthian structure depicts great lawmakers of the past: Moses, Justinian, Confucius, and others, although a statue of Muhammad had to be removed because it offended the Islamic religion. Rooms inside are furnished with pieces designed by Herter Brothers. ☒ *35 E. 25th St., at Madison Ave.*

3 **B. Altman Building.** One of New York's grand old department stores moved here in 1906, doing much to transform the then residential neighborhood into a shopping district. What you see from Madison Avenue was the store's office tower; along 34th Street and 5th Avenue, elaborate entrances are graced by green canopies reminiscent of old subway kiosks. After the B. Altman chain declared bankruptcy in August 1989, the landmark building sat vacant for a few years. It is now occupied by nonprofit educational agencies as well as the ☞ **Science, Industry, and Business Library.** City University is slated to move into the building's 5th Avenue side. ⊠ *34th and 35th Sts., between Madison and 5th Aves.*

② **Church of the Incarnation.** Outside, this Episcopal church is a broodingly dark brownstone version of a Gothic chapel. Inside, however, there's enough jewellike stained glass to counteract the dour effect. Look especially for the north aisle's 23rd Psalm Window, by the Tiffany Glass works, or the south aisle's two Angel windows dedicated to infants, which are by the 19th-century English writer-designer William Morris. ⊠ *205 Madison Ave., at 35th St.*

⑥ **Church of the Transfiguration.** Known as the Little Church Around the Corner, this Gothic Revival church complex is set back in a shrub-filled New York version of an old English churchyard. It won its memorable appellation in 1870 when other area churches refused to bury actor George Holland, a colleague of well-known thespian Joseph Jefferson. Jefferson was directed to the "little church around the corner" to accomplish the burial, and the Episcopal institution has welcomed literary and theater types ever since. Go inside to see the south transept's stained-glass window, by John LaFarge, depicting 19th-century superstar actor Edwin Booth as Hamlet, his famous role. ⊠ *1 E. 29th St.*

★ **④** **Empire State Building.** It may no longer be the world's tallest building, but it is certainly one of the world's best-loved skyscrapers, its pencil-slim silhouette a symbol for New York City. The Art Deco playground for King Kong opened in 1931 after only about a year and a half of construction—many floors were completely unfinished, however, so that tenants could have them custom-designed. The depression delayed this process and critics deemed it the "Empty State Building." The crowning spire was originally designed as a mooring mast for dirigibles, but none ever docked here; in 1951, a TV transmittal tower was added to the top, raising the total height to 1,472 ft. Today more than 16,000 people work in the building, and more than 2½ million people a year visit the 86th- and 102nd-floor observatories. In 1956 revolving beacons named the Freedom Lights were installed. These lights are illuminated from dusk to midnight. Ever since the 1964–65 World Fair, the top 30 stories have been spotlighted at night with colors appropriate to the season (green for St. Pat's Day, red and green around Christmas; orange and brown for Halloween).

Pass beneath the stainless-steel canopy on 34th Street to enter the three-story-high marbled lobby, where illuminated panels depicting the Seven Wonders of the World brazenly add the Empire State as number eight. Go to the concourse level to buy a ticket for the observation decks. The 102nd-floor spot is glassed in; the 86th floor is open to the air. In the movie *An Affair to Remember,* Cary Grant waited here impatiently for his rendezvous with Deborah Kerr, an event around which Nora Ephron built the entire screenplay of her 1993 hit, *Sleepless in Seattle.*

Another attraction in the building (second floor) is the **New York Skyride.** It consists of a three-minute Comedy Central TV presentation on the virtues of New York, followed by a seven-minute motion-simulator ride above and around some of New York's top attractions projected on a screen in the front of the room—you'll actually feel as if you're swooping between the twin towers of the World Trade Center. The show leaves you feeling a little dizzy and disoriented: It's not recommended for anyone who has trouble with motion sickness, and pregnant women are not admitted. ⊠ *350 5th Ave., at 34th St. Observation decks:* ☎ *212/736–3100.* 🎫 *$4.50.* ☼ *Daily 9:30 AM–mid-*

night; last elevator up leaves at 11:30 PM. New York Skyride: ☏ *212/279–9777.* ✉ *$9.* ☉ *Daily 10–10.*

★ ⓫ **Flatiron Building.** Like the Empire State Building and a host of other structures in the city, this was the tallest building in the world when it opened (1902). Architect Daniel Burnham is responsible for the design, which made ingenious use of the triangular plot of land and created very nontraditional office spaces inside—its rounded front point is only 6 ft wide, but gentle waves built into the molded limestone-and-terra-cotta side walls soften the wedge effect. Winds invariably swooped down its 20-story, 286-ft height, billowing up the skirts of women pedestrians on 23rd Street, and local traffic cops had to shoo away male gawkers—coining the phrase "23 Skiddoo." Originally named the Fuller Building, it was instantly rechristened by the public because of its resemblance to a flatiron, and eventually the nickname became official. ✉ *175 5th Ave., bordered by 22nd and 23rd Sts., 5th Ave., and Broadway.*

NEED A BREAK?   A good stop for coffee, hearty soups, salads, or wonderful sandwiches on thick, crusty bread is **La Boulangère** (✉ 49 E. 21st St., ☏ 212/475–8582), just 2½ blocks from the Flatiron Building. You can either sit at one of the tiny tables or order take-out (enjoy a picnic on a bench in Madison Square or Union Square to the south).

⓭ **Gramercy Park.** This picture-perfect park complete with flower beds, bird feeders, sundials, and cozy benches looks too good to be true, and in many ways it is—it stays pristine largely because of the locked cast-iron fence that surrounds it. Only residents of the property around the park can obtain keys. Laid out in 1831 according to a design inspired by London's residential squares, Gramercy Park is surrounded by interesting buildings.

On the south side of the square, peek inside the park and you'll see a statue of actor Edwin Booth playing Hamlet. Booth lived at No. 16, which he remodeled in the early 1880s to serve as an actors' club, the **Players Club.** Stanford White, the architect for the renovation, was a member of the club, as were many other nonactors. Members over the years have included Mark Twain, Booth Tarkington, John and Lionel Barrymore, Irving Berlin, Winston Churchill, Lord Laurence Olivier, Frank Sinatra, Walter Cronkite, Jack Lemmon, and Richard Gere.

The **National Arts Club** (15 Gramercy Park S) was once the home of Samuel Tilden, a governor of New York and the Democratic presidential candidate who, in 1876, received more popular votes than Rutherford B. Hayes, who won more electoral college votes—and the election. Calvert Vaux, codesigner of Central Park, remodeled this building in 1874, conjoining two houses. Among its Victorian Gothic decorations are medallions portraying Goethe, Dante, Milton, and Benjamin Franklin; early club members included Woodrow Wilson and Theodore Roosevelt. The Club now houses the Poetry Society of America, which sponsors poetry readings (☞ Chapter 5).

On the west end of the square, note the row of redbrick Greek Revival town houses, with their fanciful cast-iron verandas looking like something out of New Orleans's French Quarter. Mayor James Harper (elected in 1888) lived at No. 4, behind the pair of street lanterns. The actor John Garfield died in 1952 while staying at No. 3.

At the northeast corner, the ornate white terra-cotta apartment building at **36 Gramercy Park East** is guarded by concrete knights in silver-paint armor. The turreted redbrick building at **34 Gramercy Park East** was one of the city's first cooperative apartment houses; its tenants have included actors James Cagney, John Carradine, and Margaret Hamilton, who played the Wicked Witch in *The Wizard of Oz*. The austere gray-brown Friends Meeting House at 28 Gramercy Park South became the **Brotherhood Synagogue** in 1974, and a narrow plaza just east of the synagogue contains a Holocaust memorial. No. **19 Gramercy Park South** was the home in the 1880s of society doyenne Mrs. Stuyvesant Fish, a fearless iconoclast who shocked Mrs. Astor and Mrs. Vanderbilt when she reduced the time of formal dinner parties from several hours to 50 minutes, thus ushering in the modern social era.

⓮ Irving Place. Like the neighboring Gramercy Park, this short street is lined with charming row houses. **Pete's Tavern** (⊠ 18th St. and Irving Pl.) claims that O. Henry (pseudonym of William Sidney Porter), wrote "The Gift of the Magi" while sitting in the second booth to the right. It also claims to be the oldest saloon in New York (1864); both facts are disputed, but stop here anyway for a casual drink and absorb the atmosphere of the Gaslight Era. O. Henry lived at 55 Irving Place, in a building long ago demolished.

The street takes its name from another famous New York chronicler, Washington Irving (1783–1859), who wrote *The Legend of Sleepy Hollow* more than a century before O. Henry was there. A plaque on the redbrick house at 17th Street and Irving Place proclaims it the home of Washington Irving, but it was actually his nephew's house; however, the famous writer did visit there often. Walk south to 40 Irving Place, where you'll see a huge bust of the writer outside **Washington Irving High School,** alma mater of Claudette Colbert and Whoopi Goldberg.

⓾ Madison Square. New York's first baseball games were played here circa 1845. On the north end, an imposing 1881 statue by Augustus Saint-Gaudens memorializes Civil War naval hero Admiral Farragut. A statue of William Henry Seward (the Seward of the phrase "Seward's folly"—as Alaska was originally known) sits in the park's southwestern corner, though it's rumored that the sculptor placed the statesman's head on Abraham Lincoln's body. ⊠ *23rd to 26th Sts., between 5th and Madison Aves.*

❺ Marble Collegiate Church. Built in 1854 for the Reformed Protestant Dutch Congregation first organized in 1628 by Peter Minuit, the canny Dutchman who bought Manhattan from the Native Americans for $24, this impressive limestone church takes its name from the Tuckahoe marble that covers it. Dr. Norman Vincent Peale (*The Power of Positive Thinking*) was Marble Collegiate's pastor from 1932 to 1984. ⊠ *1 W. 29th St., at 5th Ave.*

❾ Metropolitan Life Insurance Tower. The tower made this building the world's tallest when it was added in 1909. At 700 ft, it re-creates the campanile of St. Mark's in Venice. The four dials of its clock are each three stories high, and their minute hands weigh half a ton each; wait for the quarter hour to hear it chime. Met Life's North Building, between 24th and 25th streets, is connected by a skywalk. Its Art Deco loggias have attracted many film crews—it appeared in such films as *After Hours, Radio Days,* and *The Fisher King.* ⊠ *1 Madison Ave., between 23rd and 24th Sts.*

❼ New York Life Insurance Building. Cass Gilbert, better known for the Woolworth Building (☞ The Seaport and the Courts, *below*), designed this in 1928. Its birthday-cake top is capped by a gilded pyramid that is stunning when lit at night. Go inside to admire the soaring lobby's coffered ceilings and ornate bronze doors. This was formerly the site of P. T. Barnum's Hippodrome, and after that (1890–1925) Madison Square Garden, designed by architect and playboy Stanford White. White was shot in the Garden's roof garden by Harry K. Thaw, the jealous husband of actress Evelyn Nesbit—a lurid episode more or less accurately depicted in E. L. Doctorow's book *Ragtime* (which was made into a movie). ⊠ *51 Madison Ave., between 26th and 27th Sts.*

★ ❶ **Pierpont Morgan Library.** The core of this small, patrician museum is the famous banker's own study and library, completed in 1905 by McKim, Mead & White. If you walk east past the museum's main entrance on 36th Street, you'll see the original library's neoclassical facade, with what is believed to be Charles McKim's face on the sphinx in the right-hand sculptured panel. Around the corner, at 37th Street and Madison Avenue, is the latest addition to the library, an 1852 Italianate brownstone that was once the home of Morgan's son, J. P. Morgan Jr. It's connected to the rest of the property by a lovely glass-roofed garden café court where lunch and afternoon tea are served. The elder Morgan's own house stood at 36th Street and Madison Avenue; it was torn down after his death and replaced with the simple neoclassical annex that today holds the library's main exhibition space. Go inside and visit the galleries for rotating exhibitions; go straight to see items from the permanent collection, principally drawings, prints, manuscripts, and rare books, and to pass through the atrium to the fine bookstore. Turn right just past the entrance and go down a long cloister corridor for the library's most impressive rooms: the elder Morgan's personal study, its red-damask-lined walls hung with first-rate paintings, and his majestic personal library with its dizzying tiers of handsomely bound rare books, letters, and illuminated manuscripts. It's hard to say which is more spectacular—the museum's collections or its interiors. ⊠ *29 E. 36th St.,* ☎ *212/685–0008.* ⊠ *$5 (suggested donation).* ⊙ *Tues.–Fri. 10:30–5, Sat. 10:30–6, Sun. noon–6.*

Police Academy Museum. The second floor of the city's police academy is full of law-enforcement memorabilia—uniforms, firearms, batons, badges, even counterfeit money—dating back to the time of the Dutch. ⊠ *235 E. 20th St.,* ☎ *212/477–9753.* ⊠ *Free.* ⊙ *Weekdays 9–3.*

Science, Industry, and Business Library. The New York Public Library raided its main building (called the Center for the Humanities since the scientific material left) and its 41st Street branch and brought all the technology-oriented material to its newest facility, which opened in 1996 in the ☞ **B. Altman Building.** SIBL, as it's called, is modern as befits its holdings but unfortunately not its location—staring out the huge windows at the busy corner, you feel as if you're in a fishbowl. The main research collections are one level below the entrance, and just at the base of the stairs is a wall of TVs tuned to business news stations. The hottest attraction, however, seems to be the hundreds of computers that are wired to the Internet and research databases. ⊠ *188 Madison Ave., at 34th St.,* ☎ *212/592–7000.* ⊙ *Mon., Fri., and Sat. 10–6, Tues.–Thurs. 11–7.*

OFF THE BEATEN PATH   **SNIFFEN COURT –** Just two blocks from the Morgan Library, this is an easily overlooked cul-de-sac of 19th-century brick stables converted into town houses, with an atmosphere that's equal parts old London and New Orleans. Peer through the locked gate to admire the lovely buildings. ⊠ *Off 36th St. between Lexington and 3rd Aves. on south side of street.*

⓬ **Theodore Roosevelt Birthplace.** The original brownstone was torn down, but this is a near-perfect reconstruction of the Victorian brownstone where Teddy lived until he was 15 years old. Before becoming president, Roosevelt was New York City's police commissioner and the governor of New York State. He's still the only president from New York City. The house contains Victorian period rooms and Roosevelt memorabilia; a selection of videos about the namesake of the teddy bear can be seen on request. Saturday-afternoon chamber-music concerts are offered each fall, winter, and spring. ⊠ *28 E. 20th St.,* ☎ *212/260–1616.* ⊠ *$2.* ⊙ *Wed.–Sun. 9–5; guided tours every hr until 4.*

⑮ Union Square. Its name, originally signifying the fact that two main roads merged here, proved doubly apt in the early 20th century when the square became a rallying spot for labor protests and mass demonstrations; many unions, as well as fringe political parties, moved their headquarters nearby. Over the years the area deteriorated into a habitat of drug dealers and kindred undesirables, until a massive renewal program in the 1980s transformed it. If possible, visit on **Greenmarket** day (Monday, Wednesday, Friday, and Saturday), when farmers from all over the Northeast, including some Pennsylvania Dutch and latter-day hippies, bring their goods to the big town: fresh produce, homemade bakery goods, cheeses, cider, New York State wines, even fish and meat.

The trendy, Warhol-founded *Interview* has its offices here, while the most recent developments have included renovation of the 1932 **Pavilion,** now flanked by playgrounds and an open-air café run by the Coffee Shop, and much new restaurant and retail activity. The handsome **Century Building** (built in 1881, ⊠ 33 E. 17th St.) has been beautifully restored and brought back to life as a Barnes & Noble bookstore; go inside to admire its cast-iron columns and the view over Union Square. The building at 17th Street and Union Square East, now housing the New York Film Academy and the Union Square Theatre, was the final home of **Tammany Hall.** This organization, famous for its days as a fairly corrupt yet effective political machine, moved here just at the height of its power in 1929, but by 1943 it had to sell the building due to bankruptcy.

MUSEUM MILE

Once known as Millionaire's Row, the stretch of 5th Avenue between 79th and 104th streets has been fittingly renamed Museum Mile, for it now contains an impressive cluster of cultural institutions. The connection is more than coincidental: Many museums are housed in what used to be the great mansions of merchant princes and wealthy industrialists. A large percentage of these buildings were constructed of limestone (it's cheaper than marble) and reflect the Beaux Arts style, which was very popular among the wealthy at the turn of the century.

Numbers in the text correspond to numbers in the margin and on the Museum Mile, Upper East Side map.

A Good Walk

You won't need a map for this tour; it's a simple, straight walk up 5th Avenue, from 70th Street to 105th. Walking the Museum Mile actually covers closer to 2 mi. If you walk up the west side of the street (crossing over to visit museums, of course), you'll be under the canopy of Central Park and have a good view of the mansions and apartments across the street. If you're not sure whether you're interested in a particular museum, stop in its gift store; museum shops are usually good indicators of what's in the rest of the building. A brochure called "Museum Mile" is available at most institutions listed below; it provides brief descriptions of the various museums along the route as well as their opening hours.

Begin at 5th Avenue and 70th Street with the **Frick Collection** ①, housed in an ornate, imposing Beaux Arts mansion built in 1914 for coke-and-steel baron Henry Clay Frick. It's a few blocks north before you get to the next stop. On your way, be sure to admire the former mansions, some of them now converted into multiple-family dwellings, among them the Gothic Revival facade of what's now on the southeast corner of 5th Avenue at 79th Street. One block north is the **American Irish Historical Society** ②, another fine example of the French-influenced Beaux Arts style that was so popular at the turn of the century.

From here, you can't miss the **Metropolitan Museum of Art** ③, the largest art museum in the Western Hemisphere, encroaching on Central Park's turf. The goings on around the steps that sweep you up into the museum are worthy of at least casual observation—its a favorite spot for performance artists and musicians as well as sophisticated souvenir sellers.

Across from the Met, between 82nd and 83rd streets, one Beaux Arts town house stands its ground amid newer apartment blocks. It now belongs to the Federal Republic of Germany, which has installed a branch of the Goethe Institute here—called **Goethe House** ④. At the corner of 85th Street is 1040 5th Avenue, former home of Jacqueline Kennedy Onassis, from which she could easily walk into Central Park and to the reservoir that now bears her name. Up at 86th Street and 5th Avenue, a brightly embellished limestone-and-redbrick mansion, designed by Carrère and Hastings to echo the buildings on the Place des Vosges in Paris, was once the home of Mrs. Cornelius Vanderbilt III.

Frank Lloyd Wright's **Guggenheim Museum** ⑤ (opened in 1959) is a controversial piece of architecture—even many of those who like its assertive six-story spiral rotunda will admit that it does not result in the best space in which to view art. A block north stands the **National Academy of Design** ⑥, housed in a stately 19th-century mansion and a pair of town houses on 89th Street. At 91st Street you'll find the former residence of industrialist Andrew Carnegie, now a museum named after him that's devoted to contemporary and historic design—the **Cooper-Hewitt Museum** ⑦. Across 91st Street, the **Convent of the Sacred Heart** is in a huge Italianate mansion originally built in 1918 for financier Otto Kahn, a noted patron of the arts.

As you continue north, the next museum you'll come to is at 92nd Street, the **Jewish Museum** ⑧, which opened its expanded and renovated facilities in 1993. The handsome, well-proportioned Georgian-style mansion on the corner of 5th Avenue and 94th Street was built in 1914 for Willard Straight, founder of the *New Republic* magazine. Today it is the home of the **International Center of Photography** ⑨. As you proceed north on 5th Avenue, for architectural variety you may want to walk a few paces east on 97th Street to see the onion-domed tower of the **Russian Orthodox Cathedral of St. Nicholas,** built in 1902.

Between 98th and 101st streets, 5th Avenue is dominated by the various buildings of **Mount Sinai Hospital,** which was originally founded in 1852 by a group of wealthy Jewish citizens and moved here in 1904. The 1976 addition, the Annenberg Building, is a looming tower of Cor-Ten steel that has deliberately been allowed to develop a patina of rust.

The **Museum of the City of New York** ⑩, which has permanent and changing exhibits related to Big Apple history, is one of the homier muse-

American Irish
Historical Society, **2**

Americas Society, **16**

Asia Society, **17**

Asphalt Green, **24**

Bloomingdale's, **13**

Carl Schurz Park, **22**

Carlyle Hotel, **20**

Conservatory
Garden, **12**

Cooper-Hewitt
Museum, **7**

El Museo del
Barrio, **11**

Frick Collection, **1**

Goethe House, **4**

Gracie Mansion, **23**

Guggenheim
Museum, **5**

Henderson Place
Historic District, **21**

International Center of
Photography, **9**

Jewish Museum, **8**

Metropolitan Museum
of Art, **3**

Museum of the City of
New York, **10**

National Academy of
Design, **6**

Ralph Lauren, **18**

Seventh Regiment
Armory, **15**

Temple Emanu-El, **14**

Whitney Museum of
American Art, **19**

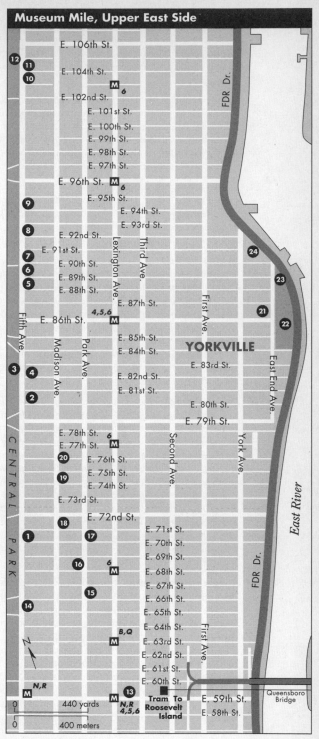

Museum Mile, Upper East Side

ums on this tour. Another is **El Museo del Barrio** ⑪, founded in 1969, concentrating on Latin culture in general, with a particular emphasis on Puerto Rican art. Having completed this long walk, you may want to reward yourself by crossing the street to Central Park's **Conservatory Garden** ⑫, a formal, enclosed tract in the otherwise rambling park.

TIMING

It would be impossible to do justice to all these collections in one outing; the Metropolitan Museum alone contains too much to see in a day. You may want to select one or two museums or exhibits to linger in and simply walk past the others, appreciating their exteriors (this in itself constitutes a minicourse in modern architecture). Save the rest for another day—or for your next trip to New York.

Do be sure to pick the right day of the week for this tour: Most of these museums are closed at least one day of the week, usually on Monday, but a few have free admission during extended hours on Tuesday or Thursday evening. Others have drinks, snacks, and/or music during late weekend hours. The Jewish Museum is closed Saturday.

Sights to See

❷ **American Irish Historical Society.** U.S. Steel president William Ellis Corey, who scandalized his social class by marrying musical comedy star Mabelle Gilman, once owned this Beaux Arts town house with its ornamentation and mansard roof. The society's library holdings chronicle people of Irish descent who became successful in the United States, and the society hosts talks of interest to this contingency approximately once a week in the summer. Tours of the mansion are usually available on request. ✉ *991 5th Ave., at 80th St.,* ☎ *212/288–2263.* ✉ *Free.* ☽ *Weekdays 10:30–5:30.*

★ ⑫ **Conservatory Garden.** The entrance, at 105th Street, leads through elaborate wrought-iron gates that once graced the mansion of Cornelius Vanderbilt II. In contrast to the deliberately rustic effect of the rest of the park, these 6 acres compose a symmetrical, formal garden. The central lawn is bordered by yew hedges and flowering crab-apple trees, leading to a reflecting pool flanked by a large wisteria arbor. To the south is a high-hedged flower garden named after Frances Hodgson Burnett, author of the children's classic *The Secret Garden.* To the north is the Untermeyer Fountain, with its three spirited girls dancing at the heart of a huge circular bed where 20,000 tulips bloom in the spring and 5,000 chrysanthemums in the fall. Many a New York wedding party stops here for photos. ✉ *Entrance at 105th St. and 5th Ave.* ☽ *Daily 8 AM–dusk.*

❼ **Cooper-Hewitt Museum** (officially called the Smithsonian Institution's National Design Museum). Andrew Carnegie sought comfort more than show when he built this 64-room house on what were the outskirts of town in 1901; he administered his extensive philanthropic projects from the first-floor study. (Note the low doorways—Carnegie was only 5 ft 2 inches tall.) The core of the museum's collection was begun in 1897 by the three Hewitt sisters, granddaughters of inventor and industrialist Peter Cooper; major holdings include drawings, prints, textiles, furniture, metalwork, ceramics, glass, woodwork, and wall coverings. The Smithsonian rescued the museum from financial ruin in 1963, and the Carnegie Corporation donated the mansion in 1972. The museum, which closed for renovations for about a year in 1995, is now open again, and in fall 1997 a new building was scheduled to open, housing a Design Resource Center and a terrace garden. A café is also being added. The changing exhibitions, which focus on various aspects of contemporary or historical design, are invariably well researched, enlightening, and often amusing. ⊠ *2 E. 91st St.,* ☎ *212/860–6868.* ☜ *$3; free Tues. 5–9.* ☼ *Tues. 10–9, Wed.–Sat. 10–5, Sun. noon–5.*

⑪ **El Museo del Barrio.** *El barrio* is Spanish for "the neighborhood," and the museum is positioned on the edge of Spanish Harlem, a largely Puerto Rican neighborhood. Though the museum focuses on Latin American and Latino culture, and has objects from the Caribbean and Central and South America, its collection of Puerto Rican art is particularly strong. The 8,000-object permanent collection includes numerous pre-Columbian artifacts. ⊠ *1230 5th Ave., at 104th St.,* ☎ *212/831–7272.* ☜ *$4 (suggested donation).* ☼ *Wed.–Sun. 11–5; May–Sept., Thurs. until 8.*

★ ❶ **Frick Collection.** Coke-and-steel baron Henry Clay Frick found a home for the superb art collection he was amassing far from the soot and smoke of Pittsburgh, where he'd made his fortune. The mansion was designed by architects Carrère and Hastings (also responsible for the New York Public Library on 5th Avenue at 42nd Street) and built in 1914. Opened as a public museum in 1935 and expanded in 1977, it still resembles a gracious private home, albeit one with a bona fide masterpiece or two in almost every room. Strolling through the mansion, one can imagine how it felt to live with Vermeers by the front stairs, Gainsborough and Reynolds portraits in the dining room, canvases by Constable and Turner in the library, and Titians, Holbeins, a Giovanni Bellini, and an El Greco in the living room. Some of the collection's best pieces include Rembrandt's *The Polish Rider* and Jean-Honoré Fragonard's series *The Progress of Love.* You can rest in the tranquil indoor court with a fountain and glass ceiling. ⊠ *1 E. 70th St.,* ☎ *212/288–0700.* ☜ *$5. Children under 10 not admitted.* ☼ *Tues.–Sat. 10–6, Sun. 1–6.*

❹ **Goethe House.** This institute, which doubles as a German cultural center, offers art exhibitions as well as lectures, films, and workshops; its extensive library includes current issues of German newspapers and periodicals. ⊠ *1014 5th Ave., at 82nd St.,* ☎ *212/439–8700.* ☜ *Exhibitions free.* ☼ *Tues. and Thurs. 10–7, Wed., Fri., and Sun. 10–5, Sat. noon–5.*

❺ **Guggenheim Museum.** Frank Lloyd Wright eschewed cities, and this building of his (opened in 1959, shortly after he died) is a controversial work of architecture that is either praised as his crowning achievement or criticized as looking like a giant toilet. You can't help admiring his attention to detail, however, evident in the circular pattern of the sidewalk outside the museum, for example, and the porthole-like windows on its south side. Inside, the assertive six-story spiral rotunda makes for challenging viewing: Under a 92-ft-high glass dome, a ¼-mi-long ramp spirals down past changing exhibitions of modern art. The museum has especially strong holdings in Wassily Kandinsky, Paul Klee, and Pablo Picasso; the oldest pieces are by the French Impressionists. The Tower Galleries opened in 1992, creating additional gallery space to display the recently acquired Panza di Buomo collection of minimalist art, among other works. The 10-story annex designed by Gwathmey Siegel and based on Wright's original designs offers four spacious galleries that can accommodate the extraordinarily large art pieces that the Guggenheim owns but previously had no room to display. In 1992 the museum also received a gift from the Robert Mapplethorpe Foundation of more than 200 of the photographer's works, some of which are on view in the Guggenheim's SoHo branch (☞ SoHo and TriBeCa, *below*). ⊠ *1071 5th Ave., at 88th St.,* ☎ *212/423–3500.* ☜ *$8, Fri.*

6–8 pay as you wish; joint admission to both Guggenheim branches
$10. ☉ Sun.–Wed. 10–6, Fri.–Sat. 10–8.

❾ **International Center of Photography** (ICP). A relatively young institution—founded in 1974—ICP is building a strong collection of 20th-
century photography. Its changing exhibitions, both here and at its
midtown branch (☞ 42nd Street, *above*), often focus on the work of
a single prominent photographer or one photographic genre (portraits, architecture, etc.). The bookstore carries an impressive array of
photography-oriented books, prints, and postcards. The imposing
Georgian Revival exterior here belies the quaintness (meant in the
best possible sense) of the museum inside. ✉ *1130 5th Ave., at 94th
St.,* ☎ *212/860–1777.* 💲 *$4; Tues. 6–8 pay as you wish.* ☉ *Tues. 11–
8, Wed.–Sun. 11–6.*

❽ **Jewish Museum.** The permanent two-floor exhibition, which complements temporary shows, traces the development of Jewish culture and
identity over 4,000 years. The exhibition draws on the museum's enormous collection of artwork, ceremonial objects, and electronic media.
An expansion completed in 1993 preserved the gray-stone Gothic-style
1908 mansion occupied by the museum since 1947 and enlarged the
1963 addition; a café and a larger shop were also added. At the same
time, the mansion facade was extended, giving the museum the appearance of a late–French Gothic château. This museum sometimes has
a line to get in that extends down the block, so try to arrive early in
the day. ✉ *1109 5th Ave., at 92nd St.,* ☎ *212/423–3230.* 💲 *$7; Tues.
after 5 pay as you wish.* ☉ *Sun.–Mon. and Wed.–Thurs. 11–5:45, Tues.
11–8.*

★ ❸ **Metropolitan Museum of Art.** Billing itself as "New York's number one
tourist attraction," the Met may be selling itself short: The quality and
range of its holdings make it one of the world's greatest museums. It's
the largest art museum in the Western Hemisphere (1.6 million square
ft), and its permanent collection of more than 2 million works of art
from all over the world includes objects from prehistoric to modern
times. The museum, founded in 1870, moved to this location in 1880,
but the original redbrick building by Calvert Vaux has since been encased in other architecture, which in turn has been encased in other
architecture. The majestic 5th Avenue facade, designed by Richard Morris Hunt, was built in 1902 of gray Indiana limestone; later additions
eventually surrounded the original building on the sides and back. (On
a side wall of the new ground-floor European Sculpture Court, you
can glimpse the museum's original redbrick facade.)

The 5th Avenue entrance leads into the Great Hall, a soaring neoclassical chamber that has been designated a landmark. Past the admission booths, a vast marble staircase leads up to the European painting
galleries, whose highlights include Botticelli's *The Last Communion
of St. Jerome,* Pieter Brueghel's *The Harvesters,* El Greco's *View of
Toledo,* Johannes Vermeer's *Young Woman with a Water Jug,* and Rembrandt's *Aristotle with a Bust of Homer.* The arcaded European Sculpture Court includes Auguste Rodin's massive bronze *The Burghers of
Calais.*

American art has its own wing, back in the northwest corner; the best
approach is on the first floor, where you enter through a refreshingly
light and airy garden court graced with Tiffany stained-glass windows, cast-iron staircases by Louis Sullivan, and a marble Federal-style
facade taken from the Wall Street branch of the United States Bank.
Take the elevator to the third floor and begin working your way down
through the rooms decorated in period furniture—everything from a

Shaker retiring room to a Federal-era ballroom to the living room of a Frank Lloyd Wright house—and the excellent galleries of American painting.

In the realm of 20th-century art, the Met was a latecomer, allowing the Museum of Modern Art and the Whitney to build their collections with little competition until the Metropolitan's contemporary art department was finally established in 1967. The big museum has been trying to make up for lost time, however, and in 1987 it opened the three-story Lila Acheson Wallace Wing, in the southwest corner. Pablo Picasso's 1906 portrait of Gertrude Stein is the centerpiece of this collection.

There is much more to the Met than paintings, however. Visitors with a taste for classical art should go immediately to the left of the Great Hall on the first floor to see the Greek and Roman statuary, not to mention a large collection of rare Roman wall paintings excavated from the lava of Mount Vesuvius. Directly above these galleries, on the second floor, you'll find room after room of Grecian urns and other classical vases. The Met's awesome Egyptian collection, spanning some 3,000 years, is on the first floor, directly to the right of the Great Hall. Its centerpiece is the Temple of Dendur, an entire Roman-period temple (circa 15 BC) donated by the Egyptian government in thanks for U.S. help in saving ancient monuments. Placed in a specially built gallery with views of Central Park to refresh the eye, the temple faces east, as it did in its original location, and a pool of water has been installed at the same distance from it as the river Nile once stood. Another spot suitable for contemplation is directly above the Egyptian treasures, in the Asian galleries: The Astor Court Chinese garden reproduces a Ming Dynasty (1368–1644) scholar's courtyard, complete with water splashing over artfully positioned rocks.

The Armana Art Galleries are right near the Temple of Dendur, on the first floor past the staircase in the Great Hall. Armana was an Egyptian city founded during the reign of King Akhenaton on the east bank of the Nile, and the galleries contain works from 1353 BC–1295 BC, including reliefs, sculpture, and paintings. There's also a fine arms-and-armor exhibit on the first floor (go through the medieval tapestries, just behind the main staircase, and turn right). The Met's medieval collection here is lovely, but to see the real medieval treasures, don't miss a trip to the **Cloisters**, the Met's annex in Washington Heights (☞ Morningside Heights, *below*). Keep going straight from the medieval galleries until you enter the cool skylit white space of the Lehman Pavilion, where the small but exquisite personal collection of the late donor, investment banker Robert Lehman, is displayed in rooms resembling those of his West 54th Street town house. This is one of the lesser-known wings of the Met (perhaps because it's tucked away behind so many other galleries), so it's a good place to go when the other galleries begin to feel crowded. The Costume Institute, one level below the main floor's Egyptian Art exhibit, has changing but always extremely well-done displays of clothing and fashion. A rooftop sculpture garden, open during the summer, provides a unique view of Central Park.

Although it exhibits only a portion of its vast holdings, the Met offers more than can reasonably be seen in one visit. The best advice for tackling the museum itself is to take it in manageable chunks, and know that somewhere, in some wing, there's an empty exhibit that just might be more interesting than the one you can't see for all the people. Walking tours and lectures are free with your admission contribution. Tours covering various sections of the museum begin about every 15 minutes on weekdays, less frequently on weekends; they depart from the

Tour Board in the Great Hall. Self-guided audio tours can also be rented at a desk in the Great Hall. Lectures, often related to temporary exhibitions, are given frequently. ⊠ *5th Ave. at 82nd St.,* ☎ *212/879–5500.* ⊠ *$8 (suggested donation).* ⊙ *Tues.–Thurs. and Sun. 9:30–5:15, Fri.–Sat. 9:30–8:45.*

NEED A   Although the Metropolitan has a good museum café, only a block away
BREAK?   is a friendly, sparkling-clean coffee shop: **Nectar of 82nd** (⊠ 1090
                Madison Ave., at 82nd St., ☎ 212/772–0916), where you can stop
                for a quick refreshment. If you're looking for something more substantial,
                the menu has omelets, salads, soups, burgers—the portions are gener-
                ous and the prices quite reasonable.

★ ⑩ **Museum of the City of New York.** From the Dutch settlers of Nieuw Amsterdam to the present day, with period rooms, dioramas, slide shows, films, prints, paintings, sculpture, and clever displays of memorabilia, this museum's got it all. An exhibit on the Port of New York illuminates the role of the harbor in New York's rise to greatness; the noteworthy Toy Gallery has several meticulously detailed dollhouses. Weekend programs appeal especially to children. Currently undergoing a $36 million renovation, and contemplating a merger with the New-York Historical Society across town, the massive Georgian mansion that houses the museum should be considerably brightened by the year 2000. ⊠ *1220 5th Ave., at 103rd St.,* ☎ *212/534–1672.* ⊠ *$5 (suggested donation).* ⊙ *Wed.–Sat. 10–5, Sun. 1–5.*

⑥ **National Academy of Design.** The academy, which was founded in 1825, has always required each elected member to donate a representative work of art, which has resulted in a strong collection of 19th- and 20th-century American art. Members have included Mary Cassatt, Samuel F. B. Morse, Winslow Homer, John Singer Sargent, Frank Lloyd Wright, Jacob Lawrence, and Robert Rauschenberg. Changing shows of American art and architecture, some curated by member artists, are drawn from the permanent collection. The collection's home is a stately 19th-century mansion and a pair of town houses. The Academy also schedules exhibits that have originated elsewhere. ⊠ *1083 5th Ave., at 89th St.,* ☎ *212/369–4880.* ⊠ *$5; free Fri. 5–8.* ⊙ *Wed.–Sun. noon–5, Fri. until 8.*

THE UPPER EAST SIDE

The words "Upper East Side" leave a bad taste in the mouths of many New Yorkers, connoting old money, conservative values, and snobbery. For others, those same qualities make this neighborhood the epitome of the high-style, high-society way of life often associated with the Big Apple. It is true that between 5th and Lexington avenues, up to about 96th Street or so, the trappings of wealth are apparent: well-kept buildings, children in private school uniforms, nannies wheeling grand baby carriages, dog walkers, limousines, doormen in braided livery. This is the territory where Sherman McCoy, protagonist of Tom Wolfe's *The Bonfire of the Vanities,* lived in pride before his fall, and where the heroine of Woody Allen's movie *Alice* felt suffocated despite her money.

But like all other New York neighborhoods, this one is diverse, and plenty of local residents live modestly. The northeast section particularly, which is known as **Yorkville,** is more affordable and ethnic, a jumbled mix of high and low buildings, old and young people. Until the 1830s, when the New York & Harlem Railroad and a stagecoach line began racing through, this was a quiet, remote hamlet with a large German population. Over the years it has also welcomed waves of immigrants from Austria, Hungary, and Czechoslovakia, and local shops and restaurants still bear reminders of this European heritage.

Numbers in the text correspond to numbers in the margin and on the Museum Mile, Upper East Side map.

A Good Walk

A fitting place to begin your exploration of the moneyed Upper East Side is that infamous shrine to conspicuous consumption, **Bloomingdale's** ⑬, at 59th Street between Lexington and 3rd avenues. Serious shoppers can get a lot accomplished here, while others may have more fun just watching. Leaving Bloomingdale's, head west on 60th Street toward 5th Avenue. As you cross Park Avenue, stop for a moment on the wide, neatly planted median strip. Railroad tracks once ran above ground here; they were covered with a roadway just after World War I, and the grand, sweeping street that resulted became a distinguished residential address. Look south toward midtown and you'll see the Met Life Building; squished up against it, the Helmsley Building looks small and frilly by comparison. Then turn to look uptown, and you'll see a thoroughfare lined with massive buildings that are more like mansions stacked atop one another than apartment complexes. Decorations such as colorful tulips in the spring and lighted pine trees in December in the "park" proclaimed by the street's name are paid for by residents.

On the northwest corner of 60th Street and Park Avenue is Christ Church United Methodist Church, built during the depression but designed to look centuries old, with its random pattern of limestone blocks. Inside, the Byzantine-style sanctuary (open Sundays and holidays) glitters with golden handmade mosaics. Continue west on 60th Street to pass a grouping of clubs, membership-only societies that cater to the privileged. Their admirable architecture, on the other hand, is there for all to see. Ornate grillwork curls over the doorway of the scholarly **Grolier Club,** on the north side of 60th Street. On the block right before the park is the **Harmonie Club,** one of several private men's clubs (many of which now admit women) in this area. Across the street is the even more lordly **Metropolitan Club.**

Take a right at 5th Avenue. At 61st Street you'll pass the Pierre, a hotel that opened in 1930; notice its lovely mansard roof and tower. At 800 5th Avenue is an innocuous office with a little sign letting you know that dermatologist Dr. Zizmor practices here. There are many doctors in the area, but take note: He's famous for his ads ("Tired of that tatoo?") that plaster the city's public-transit system, and they bring him patients by the dozen. As you cross 62nd Street, look at the elegant brick-and-limestone mansion at 2 East 62nd, the home of the Knickerbocker Club, another private social club.

Across the street is the Fifth Avenue Synagogue, a limestone temple built in 1959. Its pointed oval windows are filled with stained glass in striking abstract designs. You may want to detour down this elegant block of town houses; take special note of No. 11, which has elaborate Corinthian pilasters and an impressive wrought-iron entryway. Farther up 5th Avenue, at 65th Street, is another notable Jewish house of worship: **Temple Emanu-El** ⑭, the world's largest Reform Jewish synagogue. If you walk east from 5th Avenue on 65th Street, you'll reach the **China House Gallery** (⊠ 125 E. 65th St.), which houses displays of Chinese art.

Turn right on 66th Street, past the site of the house (⊠ 3 E. 66th St.) where Ulysses S. Grant spent his final years, before moving permanently up to Grant's Tomb (☞ Morningside Heights, *below*). (If you are interested in presidential homes, you may want to detour over to 65th Street between Madison and Park avenues to Nos. 45 and 47 East 65th Street, a pair of town houses built in 1910 for Sara Delano Roosevelt and her son, Franklin; FDR once lay recovering from polio at No. 47.) Next door, at 5 East 66th Street, is the **Lotos Club,** a private club whose members are devoted to arts and literature.

Continue east across Madison Avenue to Park Avenue. The large apartment building on the northeast corner of Madison Avenue and 66th Street was built from 1906 to 1908 with lovely Gothic-style detail. The red Victorian castle-fortress at 66th Street and Park Avenue is the **Seventh Regiment Armory** ⑮, now used as a meeting and exhibition space.

Though houses have generally been replaced by apartment buildings along Park Avenue, a few surviving mansions give you an idea of how the neighborhood once looked. The grandly simple silvery limestone palace on the southwest corner of 68th Street, built in 1920, now houses the prestigious Council on Foreign Relations (✉ 58 E. 68th St.). The dark-red brick town house on the northwest corner was built for Percy Pyne in 1909–11 by McKim, Mead & White and is now the **Americas Society** ⑯, which has an art gallery that is open to the public. The three houses to the north—built during the following decade and designed by three different architects—carried on the Pyne mansion's Georgian design to create a unified block. Today these buildings hold the Spanish Institute (✉ 684 Park Ave.), the Italian Cultural Institute (✉ 686 Park Ave.), and the Italian Consulate (✉ 690 Park Ave.). Two blocks north, on the east side of Park Avenue, is the **Asia Society** ⑰, a museum and educational center.

At this point shoppers may want to get down to business back on Madison Avenue. The catchphrase "Madison Avenue" no longer refers to the midtown advertising district (most major agencies have moved away from there anyway) but instead to uptown's fashion district, between 59th and 79th streets, an exclusive area of haute-couture designer boutiques, patrician art galleries, and unique specialty stores. Many of these shops are small, intimate, expensive—and almost invariably closed on Sunday, but new, larger brand-name stores such as Calvin Klein (at 60th St.) and the Giorgio Armani Boutique (at 66th St.) are flocking to the prestigious neighborhood. Even if you're just window-shopping, it's fun to step inside the tony digs of **Ralph Lauren** ⑱ at 72nd Street, which hardly seems like a store at all. The **Whitney Museum of American Art** ⑲, a striking building whose base is smaller than its upper floors, looms on the right at 75th Street, its collection well worth seeing. At Madison Avenue and 76th Street is the **Carlyle Hotel** ⑳, one of the city's most elite and discreet properties.

The final leg of this tour is several blocks away. How you get through Yorkville is up to you, but we suggest walking east on 78th Street, then north on 2nd Avenue, and east again on 86th. The blocks of 78th between Park and 2nd avenues are home to rows of well-maintained Italianate town houses from the mid-1800s. On 2nd Avenue there are plenty of shops and restaurants at street level to entertain you, some of them reflecting the area's Eastern European heritage. At 81st Street, for example, is the Hungarian Meat Market (1560 2nd Ave.), and at 86th, the German store Schaller & Weber (1654 2nd Ave.), recognizable by the array of sausages hanging in the window. There are also a lot of secondhand stores that sell all sorts of odds and ends discarded by the privileged, including the Irvington Institute Thrift Shop, at the southeast corner of 80th Street and 2nd Avenue, which uses its merchandise to create especially entertaining window displays.

On 86th Street at East End Avenue, the **Henderson Place Historic District** ㉑ includes 24 small-scale town houses built in the 1880s in the Queen Anne style, which was developed in England by Richard Norman Shaw. As if these beautiful dwellings weren't enough, residents here are doubly blessed by the view of and easy access to **Carl Schurz Park** ㉒, across the street and overlooking the East River. **Gracie Mansion** ㉓, the mayor's house, sits at its northern end. The park comes to a narrow stop at 90th Street, but the greenery continues at **Asphalt Green** ㉔, a concrete parabolic former asphalt plant that's now protected by landmark status and part of a fitness center.

TIMING

This tour covers a lot of ground, but many of the sights require looking, not stopping. Allow about three leisurely hours for the walk. The art institutions—the Americas Society, Asia Society, and the Whitney Museum—may take more of your time, if you'd like them to, so watch their opening hours.

Sights to See

OFF THE
BEATEN PATH

ABIGAIL ADAMS SMITH MUSEUM – Once the converted carriage house of the home of President John Adams's daughter Abigail and her husband, Colonel William Stephen Smith, this 18th-century treasure is now owned by the Colonial Dames of America and largely restored to its early 19th-century use as a day hotel. Nine rooms display furniture and articles of the Federal and Empire periods, and an adjoining garden is designed in 18th-century style. This stone house, complete with a lawn, is hidden among newer, taller structures a few blocks east of Bloomingdale's. ✉ *421 E. 61st St.,* ☎ *212/838–6878.* ⊠ *$3.* ☉ *Tues.–Sun. 11–4, Tues. until 9 June–July; closed Aug.*

⑯ **Americas Society.** This McKim, Mead & White–designed town house was among the first on this part of Park Avenue (built 1909–11). It was commissioned by Percy Pyne, the grandson of noted financier Moses Taylor and a notable financier himself. From 1948 to 1963, the mansion was the Soviet Mission to the United Nations; when the Russians moved out, developers wanted to raze the town house, but in 1965 the Marquesa de Cuevas (a Rockefeller descendant) acquired the property and presented it to the Center for Inter-American Relations, now called the Americas Society, whose mission is to educate U.S. citizens about the rest of the Western Hemisphere. It has an art gallery that's open to the public. ✉ *680 Park Ave.,* ☎ *212/249–8950.* ⊠ *$3 (suggested gallery donation).* ☉ *Tues.–Sun. noon–6.*

⑰ **Asia Society.** The eight-story red granite building that houses this museum and educational center pleasantly complements the older, more traditional architecture of Park Avenue. This nonprofit educational society, founded in 1956 and headquartered here, offers a regular program of lectures, films, and performances, in addition to exhibitions. These feature Asian art, including South Asian stone and bronze sculptures; art from India, Nepal, Pakistan, and Afghanistan; bronze vessels, ceramics, sculpture, and paintings from China; Korean ceramics; and paintings, wood sculptures, and ceramics from Japan. ✉ *725 Park Ave., at 70th St.,* ☎ *212/288–6400.* ⊠ *$3; free Thurs. 6–8.* ☉ *Tues.–Wed. and Fri.–Sat. 11–6, Thurs. 11–8, Sun. noon–5.*

㉔ **Asphalt Green.** You probably won't think this building is beautiful, but the design was rather unique considering its original, unglorious tenant—an asphalt plant. When it was built in 1941–44, it was the country's first reinforced concrete arch, and it will be here for the ages thanks to landmark status. The plant is now part of a fitness complex—there are often games on the bright green lawn out front, and the natatorium (Aquacenter) next door houses the city's largest pool. ⊠ *90th St. between York Ave. and FDR Dr.*

⑬ Bloomingdale's. This block-long behemoth is noisy, trendy, and crowded; you'll find everything from designer clothes to high-tech teakettles in slick, sophisticated displays. Most selections are high quality, and sale prices on designer goods can be extremely satisfying. Not one to shrink from the limelight, Bloomie's has appeared in more than a few Manhattan movies. Diane Keaton and Michael Murphy shared a perfume-counter encounter here in Woody Allen's *Manhattan*; Robin Williams, playing a Russian musician, defected to the West in *Moscow on the Hudson*; and mermaid Darryl Hannah, in *Splash,* took a crash course in human culture in front of a bank of TVs in the electronics department. ⊠ *59th St. between Lexington and 3rd Aves.,* ☎ *212/705–2000.*

㉒ Carl Schurz Park. During the American Revolution, a house on this promontory was used as a fortification by the Continental Army, then was taken over as a British outpost. In more peaceful times, the land became known as East End Park. It was renamed in 1911 to honor Carl Schurz (1829–1906), a famous 19th-century German immigrant who eventually served the United States as a minister to Spain, a major general in the Union Army, and a senator of Missouri. During the Hayes administration, Schurz was Secretary of the Interior; he later moved back to Yorkville and worked as editor of the *New York Evening Post* and *Harper's Weekly.*

A curved stone staircase leads up to the wrought-iron railings at the edge of John Finley walk, which overlooks the churning East River—actually just an estuary connecting the Long Island Sound with the harbor. You can see the Triborough, Hell's Gate, and Queensboro bridges, Ward's, Randall's, and Roosevelt islands, and, on the other side of the river, Astoria, Queens. The view is so tranquil that you'd never guess you're directly above the FDR Drive. Behind you, along the walk, are raised flower beds planted with all sorts of interesting blooms; there are also a few recreation areas and a playground in the park. Though it doesn't compare in size with the West Side's Riverside Park, this area is a treasure to Upper East Siders.

Stroll up Carl Schurz Park to reach one of the city's most famous residences, ☞ **Gracie Mansion,** where the mayor of New York resides. The park tapers to an end at 90th Street, where there is a dock from which ferry boats depart to lower Manhattan. ⊠ *E. 84th to E. 90th St., between East End Ave. and the East River.*

⑳ Carlyle Hotel. The mood here is English manor house. The hotel has the elegant Cafe Carlyle, where top performers such as Bobby Short appear regularly, and the more relaxed Bemelmans Bar, with murals by Ludwig Bemelmans, the famed illustrator of the Madeline children's books. Stargazers, take note: This elite and discreet hotel's roster of rich-and-famous guests has included Elizabeth Taylor, George C. Scott, Steve Martin, and Warren Beatty and Annette Bening. In the early 1960s President John F. Kennedy frequently stayed here; rumor has it that he entertained Marilyn Monroe in his rooms. ⊠ *35 E. 76th St., at Madison Ave.,* ☎ *212/744–1600.*

China House Gallery (China Institute). A pair of fierce, fat stone lions guards the doorway of this pleasant redbrick town house, where changing public exhibitions of Chinese art are held. ⊠ *125 E. 65th St.,* ☎ *212/744–8181.* ▨ *$5 (suggested donation).* ☉ *Mon. and Wed.–Sat. 10–5, Tues. 10–8, Sun. 1–5.*

㉓ Gracie Mansion. This is the official home of the mayor of New York. Surrounded by a small lawn and flower beds, this Federal-style yellow frame residence still feels like a country manor house, which is what it was built as in 1779 by wealthy merchant Archibald Gracie. The Gracie family entertained many notable guests at the mansion, including Louis Philippe (later king of France), President John Quincy Adams, the Marquis de Lafayette, Alexander Hamilton, James Fenimore Cooper, Washington Irving, and John Jacob Astor. The city purchased Gracie Mansion in 1887, and, after a period of use as the Museum of the City of New York, Mayor Fiorello H. La Guardia made it the official mayor's residence. ⊠ *Carl Schurz Park, East End Ave., opposite 88th St.,* ☎ *212/570–4751.* ⊡ *$4. Guided tours mid-Mar.–mid-Nov., Wed.; all tours by advance reservation only.*

Grolier Club. Founded in 1884, this private club is named after the 16th-century French bibliophile Jean Grolier. Its members are devoted to the bookmaking crafts; one of them, Bertram Grosvenor Goodhue, designed this neatly proportioned redbrick building in 1917. The club presents public exhibitions and has a specialized reference library that is open by appointment only. ⊠ *47 E. 60th St.,* ☎ *212/838–6690.* ⊡ *Free.* ☉ *Gallery Mon.–Sat. 10–5.*

Harmonie Club. One of several private men's clubs (many of which now admit women) in this area, this was built in 1905 by McKim, Mead & White. The building, a pseudo-Renaissance palace stretched to high-rise proportions, is closely guarded by a doorman, so it's best to admire it from afar. ⊠ *4 E. 60th St.*

㉑ Henderson Place Historic District. Originally consisting of 32 small-scale town houses, Henderson Place still has 24 stone-and-brick buildings. They were built in the 1880s in the Queen Anne style, which was developed in England by Richard Norman Shaw. Designed to be comfortable yet romantic dwellings, they combine elements of the Elizabethan manor house with classic Flemish details. Note, especially, the lovely bay windows, the turrets marking the corner of each block, and the symmetrical roof gables, pediments, parapets, chimneys, and dormer windows. ⊠ *East End Ave. between 86th and 87th Sts.*

NEED A BREAK? **Rush'n Express** (⊠ 306 E. 86th St., ☎ 212/517–4949), two blocks from Henderson Place, has unbeatable Russian food and real Russian tea, served from a samovar. You can indulge in wonderfully squishy blini, tart *kissel* (cranberry puree), borscht, and all sorts of other inexpensive items.

Lotos Club. Founded in 1870, this private club has members devoted to the arts and literature. Its current home is a handsomely ornate French Renaissance mansion originally designed as a private residence by Richard Howland Hunt. ⊠ *5 E. 66th St.*

Metropolitan Club. A lordly neoclassical edifice, this was built in 1891 by the grandest producers of such structures—McKim, Mead & White. Ironically, this exclusive club was established by J. P. Morgan when a friend of his was refused membership in the Union League Club; its members today include leaders of foreign countries and presidents of major corporations. ⊠ *1 E. 60th St.*

⑱ Ralph Lauren. This store seems more like a private home. In fact, it's in the landmark Rhinelander Mansion and has preserved the grand house's walnut fittings, Oriental carpets, and family portraits as an aristocratic setting in which to display high-style preppy clothing (which is draped about casually, as though waiting to be put away). In the fourth-floor home-furnishings section, merchandise is arrayed in to-the-manor-born dream suites. ⊠ *867 Madison Ave., at 72nd St.,* ☎ *212/606–2100.*

OFF THE
BEATEN PATH

ROOSEVELT ISLAND – This 2½-mi-long East River island was taken over by a completely self-sufficient residential complex in the 1970s, although only half of the high-rise buildings originally planned have been built. Some fragments remain of the asylums, hospitals, and jails once clustered here, when it was known as Welfare Island and before that Blackwell's Island (Mae West and William "Boss" Tweed are among those who served time here). Walkways along the edge of the island provide fine river views, and it's surprisingly quiet, considering that the city is so close. The real treat, however, is the 3½-minute ride over on an aerial tram; the entrance is at 2nd Avenue and 60th Street, a few blocks east from Bloomingdale's. The one-way fare is $1.50. ⊠ *East River, from 48th to 85th St.*

⓯ Seventh Regiment Armory. This huge structure is no longer used as a military headquarters, but it has plenty of meeting and social space, which is used for a tennis club, a restaurant, a shelter for homeless people, and an exhibit hall that hosts, among other events, two posh annual antiques shows. Both Louis Comfort Tiffany and Stanford White helped design its surprisingly residential interior; go up the front stairs into the wood-paneled lobby and take a look around. Tours are available by appointment. ⊠ *643 Park Ave.,* ☎ *212/744–2968 curator's office.*

⓮ Temple Emanu-El. The world's largest Reform Jewish synagogue seats 2,500 worshipers. Built in 1929 of limestone, it is covered with mosaics and designed in the Romanesque style with Byzantine influences; the building features Moorish and Art Deco ornamentation. ⊠ *1 E. 65th St.,* ☎ *212/744–1400.* ☉ *Services Fri. 5 PM, Sat. 10:30 AM; weekday services Sun.–Thurs. 5:30 PM; guided group tours of synagogue by appointment.*

⓳ Whitney Museum of American Art. This museum grew out of a gallery in the studio of the sculptor and collector Gertrude Vanderbilt Whitney, whose talent and taste were fortuitously accompanied by the wealth of two prominent families. The current building, opened in 1966, is a minimalist gray granite vault separated from Madison Avenue by a dry moat; it was designed by Marcel Breuer, a member of the Bauhaus school, which prized functionality in architecture. Though part of the building is devoted to office space, the museum is planning to move these quarters to neighboring town houses to create more exhibit space. The monolithic exterior is much more forbidding than the interior, where changing exhibitions offer an intelligent survey of 20th-century American works; the second-floor shows, among other exhibits, hosts daring new work from American video artists and filmmakers, and the third-floor gallery features a sample of the permanent collection, including Edward Hopper's haunting *Early Sunday Morning* (1930), Georgia O'Keeffe's *White Calico Flower* (1931), and Jasper Johns's *Three Flags* (1958). The Whitney also has a branch across from Grand Central Terminal (☞ *42nd Street, above*). ⊠ *945 Madison Ave., at 75th St.,* ☎ *212/570–3676.* ☎ *$8; free Thurs. 6–8.* ☉ *Wed. and Fri.–Sun. 11–6, Thurs. 1–8.*

CENTRAL PARK

Many people consider Central Park the greatest—and most indispensable—part of New York City. Without the park's 843 acres of meandering paths, tranquil lakes, ponds, and open meadows, New Yorkers might be a lot less sane. Every day, thousands of joggers, cyclists, in-line skaters, and walkers make their daily jaunts around "the loop," the Reservoir, and various other parts of the park. Come summertime the park serves as Manhattan's Riviera, with sunseekers crowding every available patch of grass. Throughout the year, pleasure-seekers of all ages come to enjoy horseback riding, softball, ice skating or roller-skating, rock climbing, croquet, tennis, bird-watching, boating, chess, checkers, theater, concerts, skateboarding, folk dancing, and more, or simply to escape from the rumble of traffic, walk through the trees, and feel—at least for a moment—far from the urban realities of the city.

Although it appears to be nothing more than a swath of rolling countryside exempted from urban development, Central Park was in fact the first artificially landscaped park in the United States. The design for the park was conceived in 1857 by park superintendent Frederick Law Olmsted and Calvert Vaux, one of the founders of the landscape architecture profession in the United States. Their design was one of 33 submitted in a contest arranged by the Central Park Commission—the first such contest in the country. The Greensward Plan, as it was called, combined pastoral, picturesque, and formal elements: Open rolling meadows complement fanciful landscapes and grand, formal walkways. The southern portion of the park features many formal elements, while the northern end is deliberately more rustic. Four transverse roads—at 66th, 79th, 86th, and 96th streets—were designed to carry crosstown traffic beneath the park's hills and tunnels so that park goers would not be disturbed, and 40 bridges were conceived—each with its own unique design and name—to give people easy access to various areas.

The task of constructing the park was monumental. Hundreds of residents of shantytowns were displaced, swamps were drained, and great walls of Manhattan schist were blasted. Thousands of workers were employed to remove some 5 million cubic yards of soil and plant thousands of trees and shrubs in a project that lasted 16 years and cost $14 million.

In the years following the park's opening in 1857, more than half of its visitors arrived by carriage. Today, with a little imagination, you can still experience the park as they did, by hiring a horse-drawn carriage at Grand Army Plaza or any other major intersection of Central Park South (59th St., between 5th and 8th Aves.). Official rates are $34 for the first half hour, and $10 for every ¼ additional hour.

Numbers in the text correspond to numbers in the margin and on the Central Park map.

A Good Walk

If you want to explore the park on foot, begin at the southeast corner at Grand Army Plaza (at 59th St.). The first path off the main road (East Drive) leads to the **Pond** ①, where Gapstow Bridge provides a great vantage point for the oft-photographed midtown skyscrapers. Heading north on the road, you'll come to **Wollman Memorial Rink** ②, whose popularity is second only to that of the rink at Rockefeller Center. Turn your back to the rink and you'll see the historic **Dairy** ③, which now serves as the park's visitor center. As you walk up the hill to the

Dairy, you'll pass the Chess and Checkers House to your left, where gamesters gather on weekends. (Playing pieces are available at the Dairy on Saturdays and Sundays, 11:30 AM–3 PM.) Inside the Dairy, Central Park's history is explained through exhibits, models, and videos.

As you leave the Dairy, to your right (west) is the Playmates Arch— aptly named, since it leads to a large area of ball fields and play-grounds. Coming through the arch, you'll hear the jaunty music of the antique **Carousel** ④, the second oldest on the East Coast.

Turning your back to the Carousel, climb the slope to the left of the Playmates Arch and walk beside the Center Drive, which veers to the right. Stop for a look at **Sheep Meadow** ⑤, a 15-acre expanse that was used for grazing sheep until 1934, and the neighboring **Mineral Springs Pavilion** ⑥, one of the park's original refreshment stands. The grand, formal walkway east of Sheep Meadow is the **Mall** ⑦, whose "Liter-ary Walk" is lined with statues of famous writers.

As you stroll up the Mall, note the contrast between the peaceful Sheep Meadow, to your left, and the buzzing path ahead, where jog-gers, rollerbladers, and cyclists speed by. This path is the 72nd Street transverse, the only crosstown street that connects with the East, Cen-ter, and West drives. The transverse cuts across the park at the west end of the Mall; you can either cross it or pass beneath it through a lovely tiled arcade—note the elaborately carved birds and fruit trees that adorn the upper parts of both staircases—to reach **Bethesda Foun-tain** ⑧, set on an elaborately patterned paved terrace on the edge of the Lake.

If you're in the mood for recreation, take the path east from the ter-race to **Loeb Boathouse** ⑨, where in season you can rent rowboats and bicycles. The path to the west of the terrace leads to **Bow Bridge** ⑩, a splendid cast-iron bridge arching over a neck of the Lake. Across the bridge is the **Ramble** ⑪, a heavily wooded, wild area laced with 37 acres of twisting, climbing paths. Then recross Bow Bridge and continue west along the lakeside path for a view of the Lake from **Cherry Hill** ⑫.

Turn your back to the Lake and follow the path back to the 72nd Street transverse; on the rocky outcrop across the road, you'll see a statue of a falconer gracefully lofting his bird. Turn to the right and you'll see a more prosaic statue, the pompous bronze figure of Daniel Webster with his hand thrust into his coat. Cross Center Drive behind Webster, being careful to watch for traffic coming around the corner. You've now come to **Strawberry Fields** ⑬, a lush, English-style garden memo-rializing John Lennon.

At the top of Strawberry Fields' hill, turn right through a rustic wood arbor thickly hung with wisteria vines. From here, follow the down-hill path to Eaglevale Arch, the southern portal to **Naturalists' Walk** ⑭. After you've explored the varied landscapes of the walk, head back to-ward the Park Drive, where directly across the street you will see the quaint wood **Swedish Cottage** ⑮, scene of marionette shows. Staying on the west side of the Drive, continue north along the path to Sum-mit Rock, the highest natural point in the park. After you've enjoyed the view here, head down the other side of the promontory; a path will lead you back toward the Park Drive.

Cross the Park Drive and you'll find yourself at the north end of the Great Lawn (☞ *below*), at the Arthur Ross Pinetum, a collection of pine trees and evergreens from around the world. Follow the path south along the Great Lawn to the open-air **Delacorte Theater** ⑯, where the

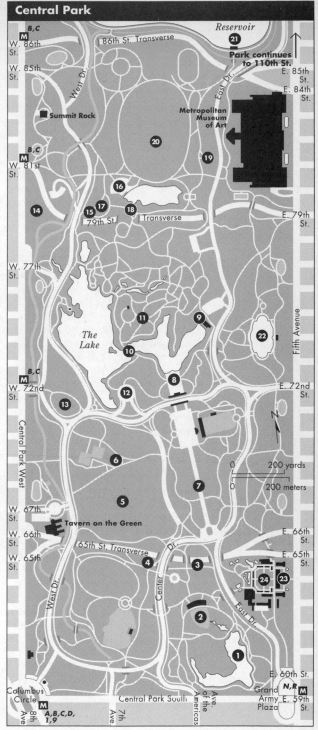

Central Park

Joseph Papp Shakespeare Theater Company performs each summer. Just south of the theater is **Shakespeare Garden** ⑰, a lush, landscaped hill covered with flowers and plants that have figured in the writings of the Bard. From the top of the hill you can follow a path to the aptly named Vista Rock, which is dominated by the circa 1872 **Belvedere Castle** ⑱. The castle is now used as a measurement station of the U.S. Weather Bureau; inside is a nature center.

From the castle's plaza, follow the downhill path east along Turtle Pond, populated by fish, ducks, and dragonflies, in addition to turtles, of course. At the east end of the pond you'll pass a statue of King Jagiello of Poland; groups gather here for folk-dancing on weekends. Follow the path north to **Cleopatra's Needle** ⑲, an Egyptian obelisk just east of the **Great Lawn** ⑳. Vigorous walkers may want to continue north to the **Jacqueline Kennedy Onassis Reservoir** ㉑ for a glimpse of one of the most popular and scenic jogging paths in the city. Others can return south from Cleopatra's Needle, following the path to the left under Greywacke Arch, which leads around the back corner of the Metropolitan Museum.

Continuing south on the path that runs along the east side of the park, you'll come to one of the park's most formal areas: the symmetrical stone basin of the **Conservatory Water** ㉒, which is usually crowded with remote-control model sailboats. Climb the hill at the far end of the water, cross the 72nd Street transverse, and follow the path south to the Children's Zoo; you'll pass under the Denesmouth Arch to the elaborately designed **Delacorte Clock.** A path to the left will take you around to the front entrance of the **Arsenal** ㉓, which houses various exhibits and some great WPA-era murals. Just past the clock is the **Central Park Zoo** ㉔, home to polar bears, sea lions, monkeys, and more.

TIMING

The walk described above takes you through many of the park's landmarks, but it may also wear you out. If you begin to tire, don't feel compelled to continue—sit down and enjoy the park the way many New Yorkers do—as a place to rest.

Allow three to four hours for this route so that you can enjoy its pastoral pleasures in an appropriately leisurely mood. Those who wish to stroll unharassed by traffic should bear in mind that the circular drive through the park is closed to auto traffic on weekdays 10 AM–3 PM (excepting the southeastern portion of the road, up to 72nd Street) and 7–10 PM, and on weekends and holidays. Nonautomotive traffic is often heavy, and sometimes fast-moving, so always be careful when you're crossing the road, and stay toward the inside when you're walking. Weekends are the liveliest time in the park—free entertainment is on tap, and the entire social microcosm is on parade. Weekend crowds make it safe to go into virtually any area of the park, although even on weekdays you should be safe anywhere along this tour. However, you're advised to take this walk during the day, since the park is fairly empty after dark. Despite its bad reputation, Central Park has the lowest crime rate of any precinct in the city—although the spectacularly ugly and frightening attacks on women in April 1989, September 1995, and June 1996 have reminded New Yorkers that the wisest course is to stay where the crowds are. The Ramble, a densely wooded, isolated section of the park, is best visited with a friend.

We've done our best to provide opening hours for the various park attractions, but schedules fluctuate according to the seasons, the weather, and special events schedules. If there's something you don't want to miss, call ahead to confirm the schedule before you set out for the park;

you may also want to find out about scheduled events or ranger-led walks and talks. For park information and events, call 212/360–3444. For a schedule of weekend walks and talks led by Urban Park Rangers, call 212/427–4040 or 800/201–7275. Information booths are scattered about the park to help you find your way.

Food for thought: Although there are cafés connected with several attractions, as well as food stands near many entrances, most of the food choices are limited and predictable; a picnic lunch is usually a good idea. The Boathouse Cafe at the Loeb Boathouse (☞ *below*), however, is pleasant.

Sights to See

㉓ **The Arsenal.** The park's oldest building, the Arsenal dates from 1857, before Central Park was even created. It occupies a pre–Civil War arsenal and now serves as headquarters of the Parks and Recreation Department. At one time, it was the home of the American Museum of Natural History, which is now on Central Park West at 79th Street (☞ The Upper West Side, *below*). The downstairs lobby has some great WPA-era murals; an upstairs gallery features changing exhibitions relating to urban design and natural and organic themes; and a third-floor conference room houses the rendering of the Greensward Plan—the design that Olmsted and Vaux conceived for the park. ☎ *212/360–8111.* ⊙ *Weekdays 9–4:30.*

⑱ **Belvedere Castle.** Standing regally atop Vista Rock, Belvedere Castle was built in 1872 of the same gray Manhattan schist that thrusts out of the soil in dramatic outcrops throughout the park. If you step through the pavilion out onto the lip of the rock, you can examine some of this schist, polished and striated by Ice Age glaciers. From here you can look down directly upon the stage of the Delacorte; you can also observe the picnickers and softball players on the Great Lawn.

The castle itself, a typically 19th-century mishmash of styles—Gothic with Romanesque, Chinese, Moorish, and Egyptian motifs—was deliberately kept small so that when it was viewed from across the Lake, the Lake would seem bigger. (The Ramble's forest now obscures the Lake's castle view.) Since 1919 it has been a measurement station of the U.S. Weather Bureau; look up to see the twirling meteorological instruments atop the tower. Climb out onto its balconies for a dramatic view. On the ground floor, the Henry Luce Nature Observatory has nature exhibits, children's workshops, and educational programs. ☎ *212/772–0210.* ▦ *Free.* ⊙ *Mid-Feb.–mid-Oct., Tues.–Sun. 11–5; mid-Oct.–mid-Feb., Tues.–Sun. 11–4.*

★ ⑧ **Bethesda Fountain.** Built in 1863 to commemorate the soldiers who died at sea during the Civil War, the ornate, three-tiered Bethesda Fountain was named after the biblical Bethesda pool in Jerusalem, which was supposedly given healing powers by an angel—hence the statue of an angel rising from the center. This statue, called *The Angel of the Waters,* figured prominently in Tony Kushner's epic drama *Angels in America.* Perch on the low terrace wall or the edge of the fountain and watch the rowboaters stroke past on the Lake.

⑩ **Bow Bridge.** This splendid cast-iron bridge arches over a neck of the Lake to the ☞ **Ramble.** Stand here to take in the picture-postcard view of the water reflecting a quintessentially New York image of vintage apartment buildings peeping above the treetops.

★ ☾ ④ **Carousel.** Remarkable for the size of its hand-carved steeds—all 57 of them are three-quarters the size of real horses—this carousel was built in 1903 and later moved here from Coney Island. Today it's considered one of the best examples of turn-of-the-century folk art. The organ plays a variety of tunes, new and old. ☎ 212/879–0244. 🖼 90¢. ☉ *Summer, daily 10:30–8, weekends 10:30–6:30; winter, weekends 10–4, weather permitting.*

🖐 ㉔ **Central Park Zoo.** Recently renamed the Central Park Wildlife Center, the zoo is a small but delightful menagerie. Clustered around the central Sea Lion Pool are separate exhibits for each of the earth's major environments; the Polar Circle features a huge penguin tank and polar-bear floe; the open-air Temperate Territory is highlighted by a pit of chattering monkeys; and the Tropic Zone contains the flora and fauna of a miniature rain forest. This is a good zoo for children and adults who like to take time to watch the animals; even a leisurely visit will take only about an hour, for there are only about 100 species on display. Go to the Bronx Zoo (☞ Chapter 3) if you need tigers, giraffes, and elephants—the biggest specimens here are the polar bears. The Children's Zoo, on the north side of Denesmouth Arch, is closed at present. ⊠ *Entrance at 5th Ave. and 64th St.,* ☎ *212/439–6500.* 🖼 *$2.50. No children under 16 admitted without adult.* ☉ *Apr.–Oct., weekdays 10–5, weekends 10:30–5:30; Nov.–Mar., daily 10–4:30.*

⑫ **Cherry Hill.** Originally a watering area for horses, this circular plaza with a small wrought-iron-and-gilt fountain is a great vantage point for the Lake and the west-side skyline.

⑲ **Cleopatra's Needle.** This exotic, hieroglyphic-covered obelisk was a gift to the city in 1881 from the khedive of Egypt. The copper crabs supporting the huge stone at each corner almost seem squashed by its weight. The Needle is, appropriately, near the glass-enclosed wing of the Metropolitan Museum (☞ Museum Mile, *above*), which houses the Egyptian Temple of Dendur.

Conservatory Garden. ☞ Museum Mile, *above.*

🖐 ㉒ **Conservatory Water.** At the symmetrical stone basin of this neo-Renaissance-style concrete basin you can watch some very sophisticated model boats being raced each Saturday morning at 10. (Model boats are occasionally for rent here.) At the north end is one of the park's most beloved statues, José de Creeft's 1960 bronze sculpture of **Alice in Wonderland,** sitting on a giant mushroom with the Mad Hatter, White Rabbit, and leering Cheshire Cat in attendance. Children are encouraged to clamber all over it. On the west side of the pond, a bronze statue of **Hans Christian Andersen,** the Ugly Duckling at his feet, is the site of storytelling hours on summer weekends.

❸ **The Dairy.** As its name implies, this was originally an actual dairy built in the 19th century, when cows grazed in the area. In those days, toys could be rented and milk purchased at the Dairy, which lay within the so-called children's district—the area below 65th Street where fanciful rustic shelters, the Carousel, and the Dairy attracted youngsters.

Today the Dairy's painted, pointed eaves, steeple, and high-pitched slate roof harbor the park's visitor center, offering informative exhibits and interactive videos on the history and construction of the park. Here you can buy maps and souvenirs, and a small research library lends out books about the park. ☎ *212/794–6565.* ☉ *Winter, Tues.–Sun. 11–4; summer, Tues.–Sun. 11–5.*

🖐 **Delacorte Clock.** Set above a redbrick arch near the Central Park Zoo, this delightful glockenspiel was dedicated to the city by philanthropist George T. Delacorte. Its fanciful bronze face is decorated with a menagerie of mechanical animals, including a dancing bear, a kangaroo, a penguin, and monkeys that rotate and hammer their bells when the clock chimes its tune every half hour.

⑯ **Delacorte Theater.** Some of the best plays in New York take place at this open-air theater-in-the-round, where the Joseph Papp Shakespeare Theater Company (☞ Chapter 5) performs each summer. Tickets are free, but expect a wait in line (sometimes a few hours) to pick them up. ☎ 212/861–7277.

⑳ **Great Lawn.** This newly sodded 15-acre expanse of green was scheduled to reopen in 1997 after a two-year, $18 million restoration. The area hums with action on weekends and most summer evenings, when its softball fields and picnicking grounds provide a much-needed outlet for city dwellers of all ages.

OFF THE
BEATEN PATH
HARLEM MEER – Those who never venture beyond 96th Street miss out on one of the park's most unusual attractions: Harlem Meer, where as many as 100 people fish for stocked largemouth bass, catfish, golden shiners, and bluegills every day. The upper park's other main attraction is the Charles A. Dana Discovery Center, at the north end of the meer. Here you can learn about geography, orienteering, ecology, and the history of the upper park. Within walking distance of the center are fortifications from the American Revolution and other historic sites, as well as woodlands, meadows, rocky bluffs, lakes, and streams. ⌖ 5th Ave. and 110th St., ☎ 212/860–1370. ☉ Tues.–Sun. 11–4.

㉑ **Jacqueline Kennedy Onassis Reservoir.** Quite possibly the most popular jogging path in all of New York City, this 1.58-mi track is also one of the most beautiful places to be come fall and spring, when the hundreds of trees around it burst into color. The reservoir itself is more or less a holding tank; the city's main reservoirs are upstate. The body of water was named in honor of one of its most famous users after her death in 1994.

❾ **Loeb Boathouse.** At the brick neo-Victorian boathouse you can rent bicycles as well as boats. Loeb also has a better-than-average restaurant, the Boathouse Cafe, where the characters dined in the movies *Three Men and a Little Lady, Postcards from the Edge,* and *The Manchurian Candidate.* The cafeteria end has a good cheap breakfast, including freshly made scones, and lunch. ⌖ Boat rental $10 per hr, $30 deposit; ☎ 212/517–4723. ⌖ Bicycle rental $8–$10 per hr, tandems $14 per hr, deposit required; ☎ 212/861–4137. ☉ Mar.–Nov., weekdays 10–6, weekends 9–6, weather permitting. Boathouse Cafe: ☎ 212/517–2233. ☉ Mar.-Sept., Tues.–Fri. noon–4, weekends 11:30–dusk.

❼ **The Mall.** A broad, formal walkway where fashionable ladies and men used to gather to see and be seen around the turn of the century, the Mall looks as grand as ever. The southern end of its main path, the "Literary Walk," is covered by the canopy of the largest group of American elms in the Northeast and lined by statues of famous men of letters, including Shakespeare, Robert Burns, and Sir Walter Scott. East of the Mall, behind the Naumburg Bandshell, is the site of free summertime concerts, SummerStage.

❻ **Mineral Springs Pavilion.** The Moorish-style palace at the northern end of ☞ **Sheep Meadow** was designed by Calvert Vaux and J. Wrey Mould, who also designed Bethesda Terrace. Built as one of the park's four refreshment stands in the late 1860s, the pavilion still has a snack bar today.

Behind the pavilion are the **Croquet Grounds** and **Lawn Bowling Greens.** During the season (May–November) you can peer through gaps in the high hedges to watch the players, usually dressed in crisp white.

⑭ **Naturalists' Walk.** Starting at the new 79th Street entrance to the park across from the Museum of Natural History, this recently created nature walk is one of the best places to learn about local wildlife, bird life, flora, fauna, and geology. As you wind your way toward ☞ **Belvedere Castle** you'll find the spectacular rock outcrops of Geology Walk, a stream that attracts countless species of birds, a woodland area with various native trees, stepping-stone trails that lead over rocky bluffs, and a sitting area.

❶ **The Pond.** Swans and ducks can sometimes be spotted on the calm waters of the Pond. For an unbeatable view of the city skyline, walk along the shore to **Gapstow Bridge.** From left to right, you'll see the peak-roofed brown Sherry-Netherland hotel, the black-and-white General Motors Building, the rose-colored "Chippendale" top of the Sony Building, the black-glass shaft of Trump Tower, and in front the green gables of the Plaza hotel.

⑪ **The Ramble.** Across the Bow Bridge from the Lake, the Ramble is a heavily wooded, wild 37-acre area laced with twisting, climbing paths, designed to resemble upstate New York's Adirondack Mountain region. This is prime bird-watching territory; a rest stop along a major migratory route, it shelters many of the more than 260 species of birds that have been sighted in the park. Because it is so dense and isolated, however, it is not a good place to wander alone.

⑰ **Shakespeare Garden.** One of the park's few formal flower plantings, this lushly landscaped, terraced hill is one of the more hidden spots in the park. Literary types may recognize some of the flowers that have figured in various plays.

❺ **Sheep Meadow.** Used as a sheep grazing area until 1934, this grassy 15-acre meadow is now a favorite of picnickers, sunbathers, and people seeking relaxation. It's an officially designated quiet zone; the most vigorous sports allowed are kite-flying and Frisbee-tossing.

Just west of the meadow, the famous **Tavern on the Green,** originally the sheepfold, was erected by Boss Tweed in 1870 and is now considered one of the glitziest, kitschiest restaurants in Manhattan.

★ ⑬ **Strawberry Fields.** Called the "international peace garden," this memorial to John Lennon is one of the most visited sights in the park. Climbing up a hill, its curving paths, shrubs, trees, and flower beds—all donated from nearly every country of the world—create a deliberately informal pastoral landscape, reminiscent of the English parks Lennon may have been thinking of when he wrote the Beatles song "Strawberry Fields Forever" in 1967. A black-and-white mosaic set into one of the sidewalks contains the word "Imagine," another Lennon song title, and is a popular site for flowers and tributes left for Lennon and other dead musicians. Just beyond the trees, at 72nd Street and Central Park West, is the Dakota (☞ The Upper West Side, *below*), where Lennon lived at the time of his death in 1980.

☾ ⑮ **Swedish Cottage.** Looking like something straight out of Germany's Black Forest, this dark-wood chalet is used for marionette shows. ☎ *212/988–9093. ✄ $5. ☺ Shows Tues.–Fri. 10:30 and noon; Sat. noon and 3; call for reservations.*

☾ ❷ **Wollman Memorial Rink.** Now a beloved recreational facility, this was once a symbol of municipal inefficiency to New Yorkers. Fruitless and costly attempts by the city to repair the deteriorated rink kept it closed for years, until real-estate mogul Donald Trump adopted the project and quickly completed it in 1986. Even if you don't want to join in, you can stand on the terrace here to watch ice-skaters throughout the winter, and roller skaters in the summer. ☏ *212/396–1010.* ⌧ *$7, skate rentals and lockers extra.* ☉ *Mid-Oct.–Mar., Mon. 10–4, Tues.–Thurs. 10–9:30, Fri. 10 AM–11 PM, weekends 10–9 for ice-skating; late Apr.–Sept., hrs are approximately the same for in-line skating. Call to confirm prices and hrs, as dates are subject to change due to weather.*

THE UPPER WEST SIDE

The Upper West Side has never been as fashionable as the East Side. It has always had an earthier appeal, even though it, too, has had many famous residents, past and present, along with a similar mix of real estate—large apartment buildings along Central Park West, West End Avenue, and Riverside Drive, and town houses on the shady, quiet cross streets—much of which is now protected by landmark status. Unlike that of the East Side, this neighborhood's development largely followed the routes of mass transit, with an elevated train pioneering the way (1879) and subways coming around the turn of the century.

Once a haven for the Jewish intelligentsia, and still a liberal stronghold, the West Side in the 1960s had become a rather grungy multiethnic community. A slow process of gentrification began in the 1970s, when actors, writers, and gays began to move into the area. Today this neighborhood is quite desirable, with lots of restored brownstones and high-priced co-op apartments. Young professionals gravitate to its small apartments and graduate to its larger ones when they become young families. On weekends they cram the sidewalks as they push babies around in their imported strollers, but in the evenings the action moves inside, where singles from the city and suburbs mingle in bars and restaurants. Columbus Avenue is one such boutique-and-restaurant strip; Amsterdam Avenue is slowly following suit, its shop fronts a mix of bodegas and boutiques. Along upper Broadway, new luxury apartment towers are slowly blocking in the horizon. Many longtime West Siders decry the "yuppification" of their neighborhoods that began about 15 years ago, but now the good news is that small businesses thrive on blocks that a decade ago were not safe to walk on.

Part of the popularity of the neighborhood—which is, of course, enhanced by being Jerry Seinfeld country—is its two parks, Central and Riverside, that form its eastern and western boundaries, respectively. Between them, the American Museum of Natural History, Columbus Avenue, and Lincoln Center always attract big crowds.

Numbers in the text correspond to numbers in the margin and on the Upper West Side, Morningside Heights map.

A Good Walk

The West Side story begins at **Columbus Circle** ①, the unsightly intersection of Broadway, 8th Avenue, Central Park West, and Central Park South. This is a good place to start any tour of the city, for it is the headquarters of the **New York Convention and Visitors Bureau.**

For a tour of the Upper West Side, however, turn your back on the circle and walk up Central Park West: With its parade of elegant, monumental buildings on one side and Central Park on the other, this is one of the city's grandest avenues. In the 1930s, it was quite the rage to have your home address at the block-long Century (⌧ 25 Central Park W), which went up in 1931, taking with it one of the last large

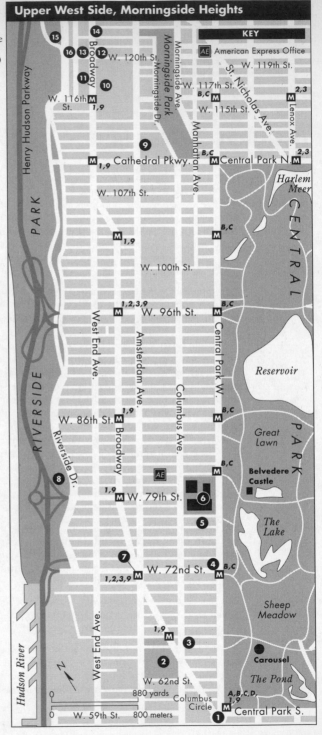

Upper West Side, Morningside Heights

lots below 96th Street—only two buildings have gone up on this stretch since then.

Continue past the solid brick-and-limestone New York Society for Ethical Culture buildings (✉ 33 Central Park W), where lectures and concerts are held periodically, to 64th Street. The view up the avenue from here is particularly handsome. Turn west on 64th and you will pass the back of the West Side YMCA on the left. As you approach Broadway, New York's premier performing arts venue, **Lincoln Center** ②, will widen into view. This quintet of travertine-marble buildings, designed by five different architects, contains some of the city's most distinctive public spaces. Summer nights, the fountain in the central plaza with the Metropolitan Opera House behind is a lovely sight.

Across the busy three-way intersection, on the east side of Columbus Avenue just below 66th Street, the appreciation of culture continues at the **Museum of American Folk Art** ③. Around the corner on 66th Street is the headquarters of the ABC television network; ABC owns several buildings along Columbus Avenue as well, including some studios where news shows and soap operas are filmed, so keep an eye out for your favorite daytime doctors, tycoons, and temptresses.

Turn right from Columbus Avenue onto **West 67th Street** and head toward Central Park along this handsome block of former artists' studios. Midway down the block on the left is the Elizabethan front of the Hotel des Artistes, also home of the spirited Café des Artistes. Just inside Central Park is Tavern on the Green, a restaurant and cabaret that is very popular with tourists.

Walk north on the east (park) side of Central Park West for the best view of the stately apartment buildings that line the avenue. Mixed among them is the Spanish & Portuguese Synagogue, Shearith Israel at 70th Street, thought to be the first synagogue built in the classical style of the Second Temple in Jerusalem. At 72nd Street, cross back over Central Park West to get a close view of the **Dakota** ④, the apartment building–cum–château that presides over the block. Its neighbors to the north include several other famous apartment buildings and their famous residents: the Langham (✉ 135 Central Park W), an Italian Renaissance–style high-rise designed by leading apartment architect Emery Roth in 1929–30; the twin-towered San Remo (✉ 145–146 Central Park W), also designed by Roth and over the years home to Rita Hayworth, Dustin Hoffman, Raquel Welch, Paul Simon, Barry Manilow, Tony Randall, and Diane Keaton—but not to Madonna, whose application was rejected; and the Kenilworth (✉ 151 Central Park W), with its immense pair of ornate front columns, once the address of Basil Rathbone (film's quintessential Sherlock Holmes) and Michael Douglas. The final beauty is the cubic Beresford (✉ 211 Central Park W, at 81st St.), also by Emery Roth, whose lighted towers romantically haunt the night sky.

The buildings of Central Park West fold back at 77th and 81st streets to make room for the Museum of Natural History—the reason many people visit the neighborhood. Before dashing off to fight the crowds there, however, you can learn more about your host city inside the starchy neoclassical building on Central Park West between 76th and 77th streets (entrance on 77th), the headquarters of the **New-York Historical Society** ⑤. Then, at the **American Museum of Natural History** ⑥, past and present inhabitants of the entire world are the order of the day. Along with the surrounding grounds, the museum occupies a four-block tract bounded by Central Park West, Columbus Avenue, and 77th and 81st streets.

At this point you've covered the mandatory itinerary for the neighborhood. If you've had enough sightseeing, you could forsake the rest of this tour for boutique shopping along Columbus Avenue (☞ Chapter 10), which is directly behind the museum. If you're here on a Sunday, check out the flea market at the southwest corner of 77th Street and Columbus Avenue.

If you continue with this tour, you'll snake through the neighborhood past some institutions that figure prominently in the daily lives of New Yorkers. On the west side of Broadway, choose among four shrines to which you'd like to make a pilgrimage: There's Zabar's (between 80th and 81st Sts.), where shoppers have to muscle for elbow room while trying to secure bargain prices on exquisite delicatessen items, prepared foods, gourmet groceries, coffee, and cheeses as well as cookware, dishes, and small appliances; H & H Bagels (at 80th St., southwest corner), which sells (and ships around the world) several varieties of huge, chewy bagels hot from the oven; Citarella's store (at 75th St., southwest corner), with its intricate, often absurd arrangements of seafood on shaved ice in the front window; and the bountiful but unpretentious Fairway Market (2127 Broadway, at 74th St.), where baby carriages bevy for space with snack food, cheeses, and produce that practically bursts onto the street. You can go to one of these places to assemble a picnic to take to either Central or Riverside Park.

At 73rd Street and Broadway on the west side of the street, look up at the white facade and fairy-castle turrets of the **Ansonia Hotel,** a turn-of-the-century luxury building. Here, where Broadway cuts across Amsterdam Avenue, the triangle north of 72nd is Verdi Square (named for Italian opera composer Giuseppe Verdi). In the 1970s this square was better known as Needle Park because of the drug addicts who hung out here. Now, elderly West Siders kibitz on the wood benches. The triangle south of 72nd Street is Sherman Square (named for Union Civil War general William Tecumseh Sherman); the charming **subway kiosk** ⑦ here is an official city landmark.

There are other alternative walks in the neighborhood as well—strolling blocks like West 71st or West 74th Street between Broadway and Central Park West, or winding your way up Riverside Drive to 116th Street and Columbia University in Morningside Heights. The latter would take you past the park that many neighborhood residents consider their private backyard: **Riverside Park** ⑧, a long, slender green space along the Hudson River—yet another landscaped by Central Park architects Olmsted and Vaux. Its finest stretches are between 79th Street and Grant's Tomb (☞ Morningside Heights, *below*) at 122nd Street.

TIMING

Part of this neighborhood's charm is its tree-lined park blocks and the buildings that line them, and just walking the ones on this tour would easily take two or three hours. To see some of what's inside the buildings lengthens the journey to the better part of a day. Plan according to which museums you'd like to visit, which days they're open, and how long you'd like to spend there. The exhibits at both the Museum of American Folk Art and the New-York Historical Society shouldn't take more than an hour or so to view. The American Museum of Natural History, on the other hand, is mammoth and often quite crowded. In bad weather, you might want to limit your itinerary to what's covered between Lincoln Center and the Museum of Natural History. If you're in town in late November, come to the delightful Macy's Thanksgiving Day Parade or the night-before-Thanksgiving inflation of aerial floats. The parade begins at the Museum of Natural History at 9 AM Thanksgiving morning and heads down Central Park West.

Sights to See

American Bible Society. A swirling staircase takes you to a little-known second-floor library that displays, among other things, Helen Keller's massive 10-volume Braille Bible, a replica of the original Gutenberg press, and a Torah (Jewish scriptures) from China. ✉ *1865 Broadway, at 61st St.,* ☎ *212/408–1200.* ⊙ *Bookstore weekdays 9:30–5, library 9:30–4:30.*

★ ❻ **American Museum of Natural History.** Approaching from the south, you can see the structure's original architecture in the pink granite corner towers, with their beehive crowns. Though the lines may be shorter at the south-side entrance, you should brave the crowds pouring in off Central Park West. Here, a neoclassical facade was added, its centerpiece an enormous equestrian statue of President Theodore Roosevelt, naturalist and explorer. Even if you don't want to visit the museum, you should look into **Theodore Roosevelt Rotunda,** a massive marble-laden, barrel-vaulted space where a five-story-tall cast of Barosaurus rears on its hind legs, protecting its fossilized baby from a fossil allosaurus.

With a collection of more than 30 million artifacts, the museum displays something for every taste, from a 94-ft blue whale to the 563-carat Star of India sapphire. Among the most enduringly popular exhibits are the wondrously detailed dioramas of animal habitat groups, on the first and second floors just behind the rotunda, and the fourth-floor halls full of dinosaur skeletons. These two halls—of Saurischian and Ornithischian dinosaurs—use real fossils and interactive computer stations to present the most recent interpretations of how dinosaurs might have behaved. The Hall of Human Biology and Evolution investigates the workings of the human body and features a computerized archaeological dig and an electronic newspaper about human evolution. An IMAX Theater projects films on a four-story screen. The **Hayden Planetarium** is closed for replacement by a new building, which will not be completed until 1999. ✉ *Central Park West at 79th St.,* ☎ *212/769–5200 for museum tickets and programs, 212/769–5100 for museum general information, 212/769–5034 for IMAX Theater show times.* ✉ *Museum $8 (suggested donation), IMAX Theater $12; combination tickets available.* ⊙ *Sun.–Thurs. 10–5:45; Fri.–Sat. 10–8:45.*

NEED A BREAK?	For a diner-style cheeseburger or just a banana split, stop by **EJ's Luncheonette** (✉ 447 Amsterdam Ave., between 81st and 82nd Sts., ☎ 212/873-3444).

Ansonia Hotel. This 1904 Beaux Arts masterpiece commands its corner of Broadway with as much architectural detail as good taste can stand. It was built as an apartment hotel, with suites without kitchens (and separate quarters for a staff who took care of the food). Designed to be fireproof, it has thick, soundproof walls that make it attractive to musicians; famous denizens of the past include Enrico Caruso, Igor Stravinsky, Arturo Toscanini, Florenz Ziegfeld, Theodore Dreiser, and Babe Ruth. The Ansonia is now a condominium apartment building. ✉ *2019 Broadway, between 73rd and 74th Sts.*

❶ **Columbus Circle.** This confusing intersection has never had the grandeur or the definition of Broadway's major intersections to the south, but it does have a 700-ton monument capped by a statue of Christopher himself in the middle of a traffic island; it had to be elaborately supported when the land underneath was torn up during the construction of the Columbus Circle subway station in the early 1900s. The city perpetually tries to improve traffic conditions here, but it has yet to approve a concrete plan for all this concrete.

On the southwest quadrant of the circle is the **New York Coliseum,** a blank, functional-looking, white brick building that served as the city's chief convention and trade-show venue before the Jacob Javits Center opened farther south on 11th Avenue. A soaring multiuse complex proposed for the site was bitterly opposed by New Yorkers determined not to let its huge shadow be cast across Central Park; the site continues to be embroiled in suits and countersuits. On the northeast corner of the circle, the *Maine Monument* stands as a pleasantly civic entrance to Central Park, with its florid bronze figures perched atop a stocky limestone pedestal. The wedge of land between Central Park West and Broadway recently became the site of the hideous, worst-of-the-'80s-style ☞ **Trump International Hotel and Tower.**

★ ❹ **The Dakota.** People once thought this building was so far from the city that it might as well have been in the Dakotas; that's how the structure got its name. Indeed, the picturesque gables here housed some of the West Side's first residents, and their remarkable home (built 1880–84) set a high standard for apartment building that followed. A sort of buff-color château, with copper turrets, the Dakota is often depicted in scenes of Old New York, and it was by looking out of a window here that Si Morley was able to travel back in time in Jack Finney's *Time and Again*. Its slightly spooky appearance was played up in the movie *Rosemary's Baby,* which was filmed here.

The building's entrance is on 72nd Street, and you should look beyond the guard's station there into the surprisingly spacious, lovely courtyard. At this gate, in December 1980, a deranged fan shot John Lennon as he came home from a recording session. Other celebrity tenants have included Boris Karloff, Rudolf Nureyev, José Ferrer and Rosemary Clooney, Lauren Bacall, Rex Reed, and Gilda Radner. ⊠ *1 W. 72nd St., at Central Park W.*

★ ❷ **Lincoln Center.** A neighborhood was razed when Lincoln Center was built during the 1960s (*West Side Story* was filmed on the slum's gritty, deserted streets just before the demolition crews moved in), but that has long been forgotten by the artists who've since moved to the area, as well as their patrons. A unified complex of pale travertine marble, Lincoln Center can seat nearly 18,000 spectators at one time in its various halls.

Stand on Broadway, facing the central court with its huge fountain. The three concert halls on this plaza, designed by three different architects, clearly relate to one another, with their rhythmical bilevel facades, yet each has different lines and details. On the left, huge honeycomb lights hang on the portico of Philip Johnson's **New York State Theater,** home to the New York City Ballet and the New York City Opera. Straight ahead, at the rear of the plaza, is Wallace Harrison's **Metropolitan Opera House,** its brilliant-colored Chagall murals visible through the arched lobby windows; the Metropolitan Opera and American Ballet Theatre perform here. To your right, abstract bronze sculptures distinguish Max Abramovitz's **Avery Fisher Hall,** host to the New York Philharmonic Orchestra.

Wander through the plaza, and then angle to your left between the New York State Theater and the Metropolitan Opera House into **Damrosch Park,** where summer open-air festivals are often accompanied by free concerts at the **Guggenheim Bandshell.** Angle to your right from the plaza, between the Metropolitan and Avery Fisher, and you'll come to the North Plaza—the best of Lincoln Center's spaces—with a massive

Henry Moore sculpture reclining in a reflecting pool. The long lines and glass wall of Eero Saarinen's **Vivian Beaumont Theater** stand behind the pool. It is officially considered a Broadway house, in spite of being far removed from the theater district. Below it is the smaller **Mitzi E. Newhouse Theater,** where many award-winning plays originated. To the rear is the **New York Public Library for the Performing Arts,** a branch library with an extensive collection of books, records, and scores on music, theater, and dance; visitors can listen to any of 50,000 records and tapes, or check out its four galleries.

An overpass leads from this plaza across 65th Street to the world-renowned **Juilliard School** for music and theater. Check here to see if there's a concert or a play going on (often they are free); actors Kevin Kline and Patti LuPone once performed here. Turn right for an elevator down to street level and **Alice Tully Hall,** home of the Chamber Music Society of Lincoln Center and the New York Film Festival. Or turn left from the overpass and follow the walkway west to Lincoln Center's **Walter Reade Theater,** one of the finest places in the city to watch films (☞ Chapter 5).

You can wander freely through the lobbies of all these buildings. One-hour guided "Introduction to Lincoln Center" tours, given daily, cover the center's history and wealth of artwork and usually visit the three principal theaters, performance schedules permitting. ☎ *212/875–5000 for general information, 212/875–5350 for tour schedule and reservations.* ☎ *Tour $8.25.*

| NEED A BREAK? | Before or after a Lincoln Center performance, the pleasant **Cafe Mozart** (✉ 154 W. 70th St., ☎ 212/595-9797) is the closest place to stop for conversation with a friend. The operatic atmosphere and espresso at **Cafe La Fortuna** (✉ 69 W. 71st St., ☎ 212/724-5846) are just right. |

❸ **Museum of American Folk Art.** Changing exhibits here can be fascinating, and the museum is small enough to absorb in a short period of time. Its collection includes arts and crafts from all over the Americas: native paintings, quilts, carvings, dolls, trade signs, painted wood carousel horses, and a giant Indian-chief copper weather vane. The gift shop has some craft items, books, and great cards. ✉ *2 Lincoln Sq. (Columbus Ave. between 65th and 66th Sts.),* ☎ *212/595–9533.* ☎ *$3 (suggested donation).* ☉ *Tues.–Sun. 11:30–7:30.*

New York Convention and Visitors Bureau. This weird pseudo-Byzantine structure was ostensibly modeled after the Doge's Palace in Venice but is locally nicknamed the Lollipop Building. Count on the bureau for brochures; bus and subway maps; hotel, restaurant, and shopping guides; a seasonal calendar of events; free TV-show tickets (sometimes) and discounts on Broadway theater; and sound advice. ✉ *2 Columbus Circle,* ☎ *212/397–8200.* ☉ *Weekdays 9–6, weekends 10–3.*

❺ **New-York Historical Society.** Founded back when New York was undistinguished enough to have to hyphenate its name (1804), this is the city's oldest museum; it moved to this site in 1908. Its collections and changing exhibits shed light on America's decorative art, history, and everyday life, with a special focus on New York—perhaps you'll see 18th-century roach traps, high-society punch bowls, or Tiffany lamps. The research library, which contains the original watercolors for Audubon's *Birds of America* and the architectural files of McKim, Mead & White, is renowned in scholarly circles. Sadly, lack of funding closed the museum for a couple years, and despite the money raised by auctioning off some of its treasures, it has continued to struggle financially since reopening in spring 1995. ✉ 2 W. 77th St., ☎ 212/873–3400. 🎟 *Museum $5 (suggested donation).* ☉ *Museum Wed.–Sun. noon–5, library Wed.–Fri. noon–5.*

⑧ Riverside Park. Long and narrow, Riverside Park runs along the Hudson all the way from 72nd Street to 159th Street. The **Promenade,** a broad formal walkway with a stone parapet looking out over the river, extends from 80th Street to a few blocks north. Descend the steps here and go through the underpass beneath Riverside Drive to reach the **79th Street Boat Basin,** a rare spot in Manhattan where you can walk right along the river's edge, smell the salt air, and watch a flotilla of houseboats bobbing in the water. Yes, these boats do actually sail—at least once a year when they have to prove their seaworthiness.

If you walk to the end of the Promenade, you'll see a patch of its median strip exploding with flowers tended by nearby residents. Look up to your right, where the Civil War **Soldiers' and Sailors' Monument,** an imposing circle of white marble columns, crests a hill along Riverside Drive. Climb to its base for a refreshing view of Riverside Park, the Hudson River, and the New Jersey waterfront.

Spanish & Portuguese Synagogue, Shearith Israel (Orthodox Jewish). Built in 1897, this is the fifth home of the oldest Jewish congregation in the United States, founded in 1654. The adjoining "Little Synagogue" is a replica of Shearith Israel's Georgian-style first synagogue. ✉ *8 W. 70th St.,* ☎ *212/873–0300.*

❼ Subway kiosk. This brick and terra-cotta building with rounded neo-Dutch molding is one of two remaining control houses from the original subway line (the other is at Bowling Green). Built in 1904–05, this was the first express station north of 42nd Street. ✉ *72nd and Broadway.*

Trump International Hotel and Tower. The former headquarters of Paramount Communications, and before that the Gulf and Western Building, no longer resembles its previous selves, alas. To the tune of $250 million, the formerly marble-clad tower has been gutted and rewrapped in a lamentable brown-glass and metallic-gold curtain wall—a style that should have died with the eighties—making it a fitting addition to Donald Trump's real-estate collection. ✉ *106 Central Park S,* ☎ *212/299–1000.*

West 67th Street. Between Columbus Avenue and Central Park West, many of the apartment buildings on West 67th Street were designed as "studio buildings," with high ceilings and immense windows that make them ideal for artists—these were the days when "studio apartment" allowed far more space than one room barely big enough for a futon. Look up at the facades and imagine the spaces within. Also notice the Gothic motifs, carved in white stone or wrought in iron, that decorate several of these buildings at street level. Perhaps the finest apartment building on the block is the **Hotel des Artistes,** built in 1918 on the corner of Central Park West, with its elaborate mock-Elizabethan lobby. Its tenants have included Isadora Duncan, Rudolph Valentino, Norman Rockwell, Noël Coward, Fannie Hurst, and contemporary actors Joel Grey and Richard Thomas and artist Leroy Neiman; another tenant, Howard Chandler Christy, designed the lush, soft-toned murals in the excellent ground-floor restaurant, **Café des Artistes,** where Louis Malle's *My Dinner with André* was filmed.

MORNINGSIDE HEIGHTS

On the high ridge just north and west of Central Park, a cultural out-post grew up at the end of the 19th century, spearheaded by a triad of institutions: the relocated Columbia University, which developed the mind; St. Luke's Hospital, which cared for the body; and the Cathedral of St. John the Divine, which tended the soul. Idealistically conceived of as an American Acropolis, the cluster of academic and religious institutions that developed here managed to keep these blocks stable during years when neighborhoods on all sides were collapsing. More recently, West Side gentrification has reclaimed the area to the south, while the areas north and east of here haven't changed as much. Yet within the gates of the Columbia or Barnard campus, or inside the hush of the cathedral or Riverside Church, the pace of life seems slower, more contemplative. Being a student neighborhood, the area has a casual atmosphere that is hip, friendly, and fun.

Numbers in the text correspond to numbers in the margin and on the Upper West Side, Morningside Heights map.

A Good Walk

Broadway is the undeniable heartbeat of Morningside Heights, but many of its most remarkable sights will take you east and west of the main thoroughfare. Walk east from Broadway on grungy 112th Street to see the massive **Cathedral of St. John the Divine** ⑨ loom up before you. You could easily spend an hour wandering through the church, inspecting its architecture, noticing different characters in its stained-glass windows, looking at its tapestry and art exhibits, and in its gift store. Don't miss a stroll on the driveway just south of the nave. It doesn't look like much, but it leads back past a neoclassical building to the delightful Biblical Garden—an utter escape from the urban crush. Just south of the upper drive, the Peace Fountain sits in a circular plaza off Amsterdam at 111th Street.

From here, swing east on 113th Street to secluded Morningside Drive. You'll pass the Beaux Arts–baroque 1896 core of St. Luke's Hospital, which has grown rather awkwardly into a jumble of newer buildings. On Morningside Drive at 114th Street, the **Church of Notre Dame** nestles into its corner with as much personality but far less bulk than the other churches on this tour. At 116th Street, catercorner from Columbia's President's House, you may want to pause on the overlook on the right to gaze out at the skyline and down into Morningside Park, tumbling precipitously into a wooded gorge. Designed by Olmsted and Vaux, of Central Park fame, the park has a lovely landscape, but since it is bordered by some rough blocks of Harlem, it would be safest not to get any closer.

Turn back toward Amsterdam Avenue on 116th Street, and walk past the Law School's streamlined Greene Hall to the eastern gates of **Columbia University** ⑩. Its quadrangle is hardly a respite from the urban activity around it, but it does have its share of collegiate grandeur. The university's renowned Journalism School, founded by Joseph Pulitzer (and the reason Columbia bestows Pulitzer Prizes each spring), holds classes in the building just south of the campus's west gates. The official college bookstore is at 115th Street and Broadway. Across Broadway from Columbia proper is its sister institution, **Barnard College** ⑪, another green oasis.

Institutes of higher learning abound as you follow Broadway on the east side of the street north to 120th Street, where on your right is **Teach-**

ers College ⑫, a part of Columbia, and on your left, on the west side of the street, is the interdenominational **Union Theological Seminary** ⑬. At the northeast corner of 122nd Street and Broadway, behind a large blank-walled redbrick tower that fronts the intersection at an angle, is the **Jewish Theological Seminary** ⑭. Walk west on 122nd Street; between Claremont Avenue and Broadway, you'll see the prestigious Manhattan School of Music on your right, with musical instruments carved into the stone beneath its upper-story windows. Between Claremont and Riverside Drive, you may want to sit for a moment in Sakura Park, a quiet formal garden.

Across Riverside Drive at West 122nd Street, in Riverside Park, you can see for yourself who's buried in the stolid, immense General Grant Memorial, commonly known as **Grant's Tomb** ⑮. Just to the south, on Riverside Drive at 120th Street, our tour ends at **Riverside Church** ⑯.

TIMING

To get the true flavor of the neighborhood, which is often student-dominated, you'll want to visit during the week, when classes are in session. You'll be able to visit campus buildings, sample café life as it's meant to be, and because the major churches on the tour are active weeklong, you won't miss seeing them in action. If you visit on a Sunday, however, you could attend church services and ascend the tower at Riverside Church. Allow yourself about two hours to leisurely walk the tour, stopping for at least a few minutes to look at the sights covered. To take any guided tours, allow longer.

Sights to See

⓫ **Barnard College.** Established in 1889 and one of the former Seven Sisters of women's colleges, Barnard has steadfastly remained single-sex and independent from Columbia, although its students can take classes there (and vice versa). Note the bear (the college's mascot) on the shield above the main gates at 117th Street. Through the gates is **Barnard Hall,** which houses classrooms, offices, a pool, and dance studios. Its brick-and-limestone design echoes the design of Columbia University's buildings. To the right of Barnard Hall, a path leads through the narrow but neatly landscaped campus; to the left from the main gate is a quiet residential quadrangle. ☎ *212/854–2014 to arrange tours.* ☉ *Tours Mon.–Sat. 10:30 and 2:30.*

★ ❾ **Cathedral of St. John the Divine.** When New York's major Episcopal church is completed, it will be the world's largest Gothic cathedral; until then, you can have a rare, fascinating look at a cathedral in progress. Work on this immense limestone-and-granite church has progressed in spurts. Its first cornerstone was laid in 1892 and its second in 1925, but with the United States' entry into World War II, construction came to a "temporary" halt that lasted until 1982. St. John's follows traditional Gothic engineering—it is supported by stonemasonry rather than by a steel skeleton—so new stonecutters, many of them youngsters from nearby Harlem neighborhoods, had to be trained before work could proceed. That had to be abandoned, however, in 1993 due to lack of funding. The masons found other work, and the two front towers, transept, and great central tower remain unfinished. The proposed south transept is a radical conception: a "bioshelter" with branching columns, a glass roof, and an upper-level arboretum where sunlight will filter down through lush greenery, echoing the effect of stained glass. A model in the **gift shop** shows what the cathedral might look like when completed, probably quite a few years into the future. The superb shop (on the cathedral's north side), open daily 9–5, is known for its fine selection of international crafts, jewelry, religious artifacts, world music, and ecological literature.

On the wide steps climbing to the Amsterdam Avenue entrance, five portals arch over the entrance doors; the central one shows St. John having his vision of the Lord. The bronze doors he presides over open only twice a year—on Easter and in October for the Feast of St. Francis, so animals as large as an elephant and a camel can come in along with cats and dogs and be blessed. Looking at the doors, you can see scenes from the Old Testament on the left, the New Testament on the right. Statuary, much of it still not finished, is on the doorjambs, and this is currently the only part of the cathedral with "building" going on—during weekdays from approximately April to October, you can watch masons carving. Look closely at the pedestal of the third statue from the inside on the right-hand side of this center portal for a modern-day interpretation of Revelations: It's New York City's skyline under clouds resulting from a nuclear explosion.

The vast nave, the length of two football fields (601 ft, actually), can hold 6,000 worshipers. As is traditional in cathedrals, nothing inside is permanently fixed, except the pulpit. The small chapels that are separated from the nave by side aisles have a surprisingly contemporary outlook. The first bay on your left is devoted to sports; the second, the arts. Its **Poet's Corner** is modeled on the one in Westminster Abbey. One of the chapels of the right-hand aisle movingly mourns the spread of AIDS.

Beneath the 155-ft-high central dome, tall enough even to give the Statue of Liberty and her torch some breathing room, you can see another quirk of the cathedral: Its original Romanesque-Byzantine design was scrapped by 1911, when architect Ralph Adams Cram took over and instated what he felt to be a proper French-Gothic style. Here, where the transept will someday cross the nave, note the rough granite walls of the original scheme (they will eventually be covered with limestone); note also that the side nearer the entrance has a pointed Gothic arch, while the rounded arch near the altar is Romanesque. The altar area itself expresses the cathedral's interfaith tradition and international mission—with menorahs, Shinto vases, golden chests presented by the king of Siam, and in the ring of chapels behind the altar, dedications to various ethnic groups. The **Saint Saviour Chapel** contains a three-panel plaster altar with religious scenes by New York artist Keith Haring. (This was his last work; he died of AIDS in 1990.) The **Baptistry,** to the left of the altar, is an exquisite octagonal chapel with a 15-ft-high marble font and a polychrome sculpted frieze commemorating New York's Dutch heritage.

A peaceful precinct of Gothic-style châteaus that includes the Bishop's House, the Deanery, and the Cathedral School, known as the **cathedral close,** lies to the south of the cathedral. The subject of the **Peace Fountain** is the struggle of good versus evil. The forces of good, embodied in the figure of the archangel Michael, triumph by decapitating Satan, whose head hangs from one side. The fountain is encircled by small, whimsical animal figures sculpted by children and also cast in bronze.

Nestled at the southeast corner of the grounds by the Cathedral School, the **Biblical Garden** is a delightful spot. Perennials, roses, herbs, and an arbor are planted in and around the stone border of a Greek cross, all within the compass of the cathedral, a low stone wall, and a hedge. Stone benches provide a place to rest your feet. Around the bend from this garden, a small rose garden will thrill your nose with its spicy scents.

Along with Sunday services (8, 9, 9:30, 11 AM, and 1 and 7 PM), the cathedral operates a score of community outreach programs, has changing museum and art gallery displays, supports artists-in-residence and an early-music consortium, generates income through a tapestry works, and presents a full calendar of nonreligious (classical, folk, solstice) concerts. Christmas-week programs are especially worth looking into if you are in town. ⊠ *1047 Amsterdam Ave., at 112th St.,* ☎ *212/316–7540 or 212/662–2133 for box office; 212/932–7347 to arrange tours.* ◔ *Mon.–Sat. 7–6, Sun. 7 AM–8 PM; tours Tues.–Sat. at 11, Sun. at 1; vertical tours 1st and 3rd Sat. of month at noon and 2.* ▦ *Tours $3 (suggested donation), vertical tours $10 (suggested donation).*

| NEED A BREAK? | If your spiritual side has had enough and your stomach is crying out for its share, head for the **Hungarian Pastry Shop** (⊠ 1030 Amsterdam Ave., ☎ 212/866–4230) for luscious desserts and coffees. |

Church of Notre Dame. A French neoclassical landmark building, this Roman Catholic church has a replica of the French grotto of Lourdes behind its altar. It once served a predominantly French community of immigrants, but like the neighborhood, today's congregation is more diverse ethnically, with Irish, German, Italian, African-American, Hispanic, and Filipino members. The building is open 15 minutes before masses, which are held mornings at 8, Sundays at 8:30, 10 (in Spanish), 11:30, and 5 PM. ⊠ *405 W. 114th St.,* ☎ *212/866–1500.*

⑩ Columbia University. This wealthy, private, coed Ivy League school was New York's first college when it was founded in 1754. Back then, before American independence, it was called King's College—note the gilded crowns on the black wrought-iron gates at the Amsterdam Avenue entrance. The herringbone-patterned brick paths of College Walk lead into the refreshingly green main quadrangle, dominated by massive neoclassical **Butler Library** to the south and the rotunda-topped **Low Memorial Library** to the north. Butler, built in 1934, holds the bulk of the university's 5 million books; Low, built in 1895–97 by McKim, Mead & White (who laid out the general campus plan when the college moved here in 1897) and modeled on the Roman Pantheon, is now mostly offices, but on weekdays you can go inside to see its domed, templelike former Reading Room. Low Library also houses the visitor center, where you can pick up a campus guide or arrange a tour. The steps of Low Library, presided over by Daniel Chester French's statue *Alma Mater,* have been a focal point for campus life, not least during the student riots of 1968. ⊠ *Visitor Center, north of W. 116th St., between Amsterdam Ave. and Broadway,* ☎ *212/854–4900.* ◔ *Weekdays 9–5. Tours begin Sat. at 10 AM from Room 213, Low Library.*

Before Columbia moved here, this land was occupied by the Bloomingdale Insane Asylum; the sole survivor of those days is **Buell Hall,** the gabled orange-red brick house just east of Low Library. Just north is **St. Paul's Chapel** (1907), an exquisite little Byzantine-style domed church laid out in the shape of a cross. Step inside to admire the tiled vaulting. ☎ *212/854–3574 for chapel.* ◔ *Sept.–May, Sun.–Thurs. 10–10, Fri. 10–1 AM, Sat. noon–1 AM; Sun. services 10:30–2:30 and 7–10. Greatly reduced hrs June–Aug. and during winter intersession, so call ahead for Sun. schedule. Free organ recitals selected Thurs. noon.*

| NEED A BREAK? | The exterior of **Tom's Restaurant** (⊠ 2880 Broadway, at 112th St., ☎ 212/864–6137) frequently appears on the TV show *Seinfeld,* and the place also figures in Suzanne Vega's song *Solitude Standing.* Whether |

or not you care about its fame, this diner is still a good place to unwind with a refreshment or a snack.

⓯ **Grant's Tomb.** Civil War general and two-term president Ulysses S. Grant and his wife, Julia Dent Grant, are buried here. The white mausoleum, constructed of more than 8,000 tons of granite, with imposing columns and a classical pediment, is modeled on a number of other famous mausoleums. It opened in 1897, almost 12 years after Grant's death—his remains sat in a temporary brick vault until the monument was completed. Under a small white dome, the Grants' twin black marble sarcophagi are sunk into a deep circular chamber visible from above; minigalleries to the sides display photographs and Grant memorabilia. You can walk downstairs to get a closer view of the tombs as well as busts of some of Grant's best generals, an added courtesy of the WPA. In contrast to this austere monument, the surrounding plaza features colorful 1960s-era mosaic benches designed by local schoolchildren. ⊠ *Riverside Dr. and 122nd St.,* ☏ *212/666–1640.* ⛫ *Free.* ☉ *Daily 9–5, 15- to 20-min tours free on request.*

⓮ **Jewish Theological Seminary.** The seminary was founded in 1887 as a training ground for rabbis, cantors, and scholars of Conservative Judaism, but this complex wasn't built until 1930. The tower, which housed part of the seminary's excellent library, was extensively renovated after a fire in 1966. ⊠ *3080 Broadway, at 122nd St.*

OFF THE BEATEN PATH

NICHOLAS ROERICH MUSEUM – Housed in an Upper West Side town house (built in 1898), this small, eccentric museum displays the work of the Russian artist who, among many other things, designed sets for Diaghilev ballets. Vast paintings of the Himalayas are a focal point of the collection. ⊠ *319 W. 107th St.,* ☏ *212/864-7752.* ⛫ *Free.* ☉ *Tues.–Sun. 2-5.*

★ ⓰ **Riverside Church.** In this modern (1930) Gothic-style edifice, the smooth, pale limestone walls seem the antithesis of the Cathedral of St. John the Divine's rough gray hulk. Although most of the building is refined and restrained, the main entrance, on Riverside Drive, explodes with elaborate stone carvings (modeled on the French cathedral of Chartres, as are many other decorative details here). Inside, look at the handsomely ornamented main sanctuary, which seats only half as many people as St. John the Divine does; if you're here on Sunday, take the elevator to the top of the 22-story, 356-ft **tower,** with its 74-bell carillon, the largest in the world. Although it is affiliated with the Baptist church and the United Church of Christ, Riverside is basically nondenominational, interracial, international, extremely political, and socially conscious. Its calendar includes political and community events, dance and theater programs, and concerts, along with regular Sunday services. ⊠ *Riverside Dr. and 122nd St.,* ☏ *212/870–6700.* ☉ *Mon.-Sat. 9–5, Sun. noon–4; service each Sun. 10:45. Tower Tues.–Sat. 11–4, Sun. noon–6.* ⛫ *Church free, tower $1.*

⓬ **Teachers College.** Redbrick Victorian buildings house Columbia University's Teachers College, founded in 1887 and still the world's largest graduate school in the field of education. Names of famous teachers throughout history line the band of stone along the Broadway facade. ⊠ *525 W. 120th St.*

⓭ **Union Theological Seminary.** Founded in 1836, the seminary moved here, to its rough gray collegiate Gothic quadrangle, in 1910; it has one of the world's finest theological libraries. Step inside the main entrance, on Broadway at 121st Street, and ask to look around the serene central quadrangle. ⊠ *W. 120th to W. 122nd Sts., between Broadway and Claremont Ave.*

HARLEM

Harlem has been the mecca for African-American culture and life for nearly a century. Originally called Nieuw Haarlem and settled by Dutch farmers, Harlem was a well-to-do suburb in the 19th century; black New Yorkers began settling here in large numbers in about 1900, moving into a surplus of fine apartment buildings and town houses built by real-estate developers for a middle-class white market that never materialized. By the 1920s, Harlem (with one "a") had become the most famous black community in the United States, perhaps in the world. In an astonishing confluence of talent known as the Harlem Renaissance, black novelists, playwrights, musicians, and artists, many of them seeking to escape discrimination and worse in other parts of the country, gathered here. Black performers starred in chic Harlem jazz clubs—which, ironically, only whites could attend. Throughout the Roaring '20s, while whites flocked here for the infamous parties and nightlife, blacks settled in for the opportunity this self-sustaining community represented. But the depression hit Harlem hard. By the late 1930s it was no longer a popular social spot for downtown New Yorkers, and many successful African-American families began moving out to houses in the suburbs of Queens and New Jersey.

By the 1960s Harlem's population had dropped dramatically, and many of those who remained were disillusioned enough to join in civil rights riots. A vicious cycle of crowded housing, poverty, and crime was choking the neighborhood, turning it into a simmering ghetto. Today, however, Harlem is well on its way to restoring itself. Mixed in with some of the seedy remains of the past are old jewels such as the refurbished Apollo Theatre and such newer attractions as the Studio Museum. A great number of Harlem's classic brownstones and limestone buildings are being restored and lived in by young families, bringing new life to the community.

Deserted buildings, burned-out shop fronts, and yards of rubble still scar certain parts; although a few whites live here, some white visitors may feel conspicuous in what is still a largely black neighborhood. But Harlemites are accustomed to seeing tourists—white and otherwise—on their streets; only common traveler's caution is necessary during daytime excursions to any of the places highlighted. For nighttime outings it's smart to take a taxi, as in many other parts of the city. Bus tours may be a good way to see Harlem, because they cover more areas than the central Harlem walk outlined below (☞ Sightseeing *in* the Gold Guide).

Note that the city's north–south avenues acquire different names up here, commemorating heroes of black history: 6th Avenue becomes Lenox Avenue or Malcolm X Boulevard, 7th Avenue is Adam Clayton Powell Jr. Boulevard, and 8th Avenue is Frederick Douglass Boulevard; 125th Street, the major east–west street, is now Martin Luther King Jr. Boulevard. Many people still use the streets' former names, but the street signs use only the new ones.

Numbers in the text correspond to numbers in the margin and on the Harlem map.

A Good Walk

Beginning on West 115th Street and Adam Clayton Powell Jr. Boulevard, head west on the north side of the block to admire the facade of this branch of the **New York Public Library** ①. It's sufficiently interesting for you to make the trip even on Sundays, when the library is closed. The next two stops, however, are most worthwhile on Sundays, because church is in session and gospel singers are singing. Soulful, moving, often joyous gospel music blends elements from African songs and chants, American spirituals, and rhythm and blues. Memorial Baptist Church (✉ 141 W. 115th St., ☎ 212/663–8830) welcomes visitors at its soulful two-hour service, which begins at 10:45. Gospel fans and visitors are also welcome at the 10:45 Sunday service at Canaan Baptist Church of Christ (✉ 132 W. 116th St., ☎ 212/866–0301), where Rev. Dr. Wyatt Tee Walker is pastor.

On the southwest corner of 116th Street and Lenox Avenue, notice the aluminum onion dome topping the Malcolm Shabazz Mosque (✉ 102 W. 116th St.), a former casino that was converted in the mid-1960s to a black Muslim temple (Malcolm X once preached here). Several Muslim stores are located nearby. Continuing north along Lenox Avenue and then east on 120th Street brings you to **Marcus Garvey Park** ②, which interrupts 5th Avenue between 120th and 124th streets. Stay outside the park, but be sure to notice its watchtower and the pretty row houses as you skirt its west side.

Harlem's main thoroughfare is 125th Street, the chief artery of its cultural, retail, and economic life. Real-estate values here have never come close to those downtown along 5th Avenue or even Broadway, and many of the commercial buildings rise only a few stories. But never fear—Harlem isn't missing out on the malling of America, as new businesses—many of them branches of national chains—have moved in of late, bringing new shop fronts along a retail row that used to see many "For Rent" signs. There's even a bona fide mall planned for the street—Harlem USA. Above the street-level stores is the home of the National Black Theatre (✉ 2033 5th Ave., between 125th and 126th Sts., ☎ 212/722–3800), which produces new works by contemporary African-American writers. One block west, on Lenox Avenue between 126th and 127th streets, is **Sylvia's Soul Food Restaurant,** owned by Sylvia Woods, the self-proclaimed Queen of Soul Food in New York.

Continuing west along 125th Street, you can't help but notice the lovely **Theresa Towers** office building, formerly the Hotel Theresa, at the southwest corner of Adam Clayton Powell Jr. Boulevard, and the modern, hulking State Office Building across the street, the latter temporarily housing the **Afro Arts Cultural Centre.** Both of these buildings tower over their neighbors. Farther down the street is another community showplace, the **Studio Museum in Harlem** ③, and on the next block across the street, the famous **Apollo Theatre** ④. One of Harlem's greatest landmarks, it was fantastically restored and brought back to life in 1986.

Return to Adam Clayton Powell Jr. Boulevard and head north. At 126th Street, the **Black Fashion Museum** ⑤ is housed in a brownstone. As you continue north, between 131st and 132nd streets you'll pass what is today the Williams Institutional (Christian Methodist Episcopal) Church. Once this was the Lafayette Theater, which presented black revues in the 1920s and housed the WPA's Federal Negro Theater in the 1930s. A tree outside the theater was considered a lucky charm for black actors to touch; having fallen victim to exhaust fumes, it has been replaced by the colorful, abstract metal "tree" on the traffic island in the center of the street.

At 135th Street, cross back to Lenox Avenue, where you'll find the **Schomburg Center for Research in Black Culture** ⑥, a research branch

80

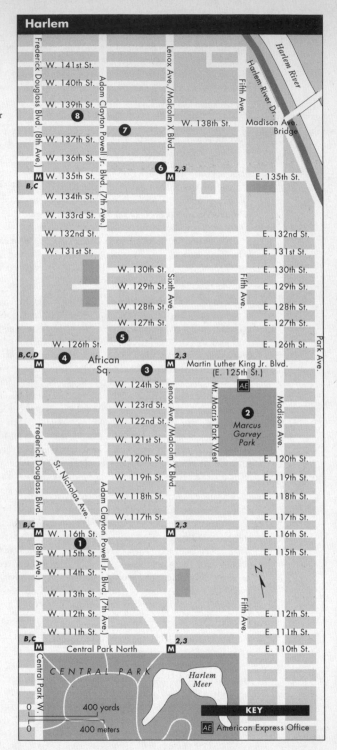

of the New York Public Library that also functions as a community center of sorts. Another neighborhood landmark, the **Abyssinian Baptist Church** ⑦, was one of the first black institutions to settle in Harlem when it moved here in the 1920s; it was founded downtown in 1808. Across 7th Avenue from the church is St. Nicholas Historic District, a handsome set of town houses known as **Strivers' Row** ⑧.

TIMING

The walk takes about four hours, including stops at the Studio Museum and the Schomburg Center. Sunday is a good time to tour Harlem if you'd like to listen to gospel music at one of the area's many churches, and weekends in general are the liveliest time for walking around in this neighborhood. If you do attend a church service, remember that most other people are there to worship and that they may not think of themselves or their church as tourist attractions. Be respectful of ushers, who may ask you to sit in a special section, don't take pictures, make a contribution when the collection comes around, and stay for the full service. The Apollo tour and the Black Fashion Museum are by appointment only, so be sure to make those arrangements in advance if you're interested.

Sights to See

⑦ **Abyssinian Baptist Church.** The Gothic-style bluestone church, which moved here in the 1920s, is further distinguished by its famous family of ministers—Adam Clayton Powell Sr. and his son, Adam Clayton Powell Jr., the first black U.S. congressman. Stop in on Sunday to hear the gospel choir and the fiery sermon of its present activist minister, the Reverend Calvin Butts. The baptismal font's Coptic Cross was a gift from Haile Selassie. ⊠ *132 Odell Clark Pl. (W. 138th St.),* ☎ *212/862–7474.* ⊙ *Sun. services 9 and 11 AM.*

Afro Arts Cultural Centre. Artifacts from East, West, North, and Central Africa are on exhibit. The center is currently housed in the State Office Building while the permanent space at 2191 Adam Clayton Powell Jr. Boulevard undergoes renovation—call before you go to confirm its location. ⊠ *163 W. 125th St., Room 913,* ☎ *212/749–0827.* ⊠ *$3.75 (suggested donation).* ⊙ *Daily 9–5.*

OFF THE
BEATEN PATH **AMERICAN NUMISMATIC SOCIETY –** The society, founded in 1858, displays its vast collection of coins and medals, including many that date back to ancient civilizations, in one of several museums in the Audubon Terrace complex. ⊠ *Broadway at 155th St.,* ☎ *212/234–3130.* ⊠ *Free (donations accepted).* ⊙ *Tues.–Sat. 9–4:30, Sun. 1–4.*

④ **Apollo Theatre.** When it opened in 1913 it was a burlesque hall for white audiences only, but after 1934, music greats such as Billie Holiday, Ella Fitzgerald, Duke Ellington, Count Basie, and Aretha Franklin performed at the Apollo. The theater fell on hard times and closed for a while in the early 1970s but has been renovated and in use again since 1986. The current Apollo's roster of stars isn't as consistent as it was in the past, but its regular Wednesday-night amateur performances at 7:30 PM are as wild and raucous as they were in the theater's heyday. You can see the theater, its backstage, soundstage, TV control room, recording studio, and dressing rooms on a guided tour. ⊠ *253 W. 125th St.,* ☎ *212/749–5838 for performance schedules, 212/222–0992, ext. 205, to arrange tours.* ⊠ *60-min tours $6 weekdays, $8 weekends; 30-min tours $3 weekdays, $4 weekends.*

⑤ **Black Fashion Museum.** Costumes from black theater and films are displayed, and the work of black fashion designers of the past century is highlighted. ⊠ *155 W. 126th St.,* ☎ *212/666–1320.* ☜ *$3 (suggested donation).* ⊘ *By appointment only.*

OFF THE BEATEN PATH

CLOISTERS – Perched atop a wooded hilltop near Manhattan's northernmost tip, the Cloisters houses the Metropolitan Museum of Art's medieval European collection in the style of a medieval monastery. Colonnaded walks connect authentic French and Spanish monastic cloisters, a French Romanesque chapel, a 12th-century chapter house, and a Romanesque apse. An entire room is devoted to a superb set of 15th- and 16th-century tapestries depicting a unicorn hunt. The view of the Hudson River and the New Jersey Palisades (an undeveloped Rockefeller family preserve) enhances the experience. From Harlem, the Cloisters is easily accessible by public transportation. The M4 "Cloisters–Fort Tryon Park" bus provides a lengthy but scenic ride; catch it along Broadway, or take Subway A to 190th Street. If you're traveling from below 110th Street, Bus M4 runs along Madison Avenue. ⊠ *Fort Tryon Park,* ☎ *212/923–3700.* ☜ *$8 (suggested donation).* ⊘ *Tues.–Sun. 9:30–5:15; closes at 4:45 Nov.–Feb.*

❷ Marcus Garvey Park. Originally Mount Morris Park, this rocky plot of land was renamed in 1973 after Marcus Garvey (1887–1940), who led the back-to-Africa movement. It's not known for being safe, so you should stay outside the park itself. From the street on its southern side, however, you can see its three-tiered, cast-iron fire **watchtower** (1856), the only remaining part of a now defunct citywide network useful in the days before the telephone. The handsome neoclassical row houses of the **Mount Morris Park Historic District** front the west side of the park and line side streets. ⊠ *Interrupts 5th Ave. between 120th and 124th Sts., Madison Ave. to Mt. Morris Park W.*

❶ New York Public Library 115th Street Branch. This bubbly Beaux Arts row house was designed by McKim, Mead & White in 1903–05. The money for the construction of this and more than 60 other branch libraries was donated by Andrew Carnegie in 1901, and almost all of these were narrow, midblock structures—because Manhattan real estate is so expensive. ⊠ *203 W. 115th St.,* ☎ *212/666–9393.* ⊘ *Mon. and Wed.–Thurs. 10–6, Tues. 1–8, Fri. 1–6, Sat. 1–5.*

★ ❻ Schomburg Center for Research in Black Culture. In 1926 the New York Public Library's Division of Negro History acquired the vast collection of Arturo Alfonso Schomburg, a scholar of black and Puerto Rican descent. In 1940, after Schomburg died, this collection, which included more than 10,000 books, documents, and photographs recording black history, was named after him. In 1972 the ever-growing collection was designated a research library, and in 1980 it moved into this modern redbrick building from the handsome Victorian one next door (designed by McKim, Mead & White and paid for by Andrew Carnegie), which is now a branch library. Today more than 5,000,000 items compose the collection. The expansion and renovation of the original Schomburg building was completed in 1991 and includes the refurbished **American Negro Theatre** and increased gallery space. Just past the main entrance is an airy lobby, also the entrance to the **Langston Hughes Auditorium.** Inlaid in the floor is the artistic work *Rivers,* a memorial tribute to Hughes, whose remains are interred here. The center's resources include rare manuscripts, art and artifacts, motion pictures, records, and videotapes. Regular exhibits, performing-arts programs, and lectures continue to contribute to Harlem culture. ⊠ *515 Lenox Ave., at 135th St.,* ☎ *212/491–2200.* ☜ *Free.* ⊘

Mon.–Wed. noon–8, Thurs.–Sat. 10–6. Exhibits Mon.–Wed. noon–6; Fri.–Sat. 10–6, Sun. 1–5.

NEED A
BREAK?

A good place for coffee and maybe a bite to eat, whether it's grits, a delicious dessert, or even a fried chicken meal, is **Pan Pan Restaurant** (✉ 500 Lenox Ave., at 135th St., ☎ 212/926–4900), catercorner from the Schomburg Center. Sit at the curved counter and watch the busy intersection through the window.

8 Strivers' Row. Since 1919 African-American doctors, lawyers, and other middle-class professionals have owned these elegant homes, designed by famous period architects such as Stanford White (his contributions are on the north side of 139th Street). Behind each row are service alleys, a rare luxury in Manhattan. Musicians W. C. Handy ("The St. Louis Blues") and Eubie Blake ("I'm Just Wild About Harry") were among the residents here. The area, now officially known as the **St. Nicholas Historic District,** got its nickname because less affluent Harlemites felt that its residents were "striving" to become well-to-do. These quiet, tree-lined streets are a remarkable reminder of the Harlem that used to be. ✉ *W. 138th and W. 139th Sts., between 7th and 8th Aves.*

3 Studio Museum in Harlem. One of the community's showplaces, this small art museum houses a large collection of paintings, sculpture, and photographs (including historic photographs of Harlem by James Van DerZee, popular in the 1930s). The museum often offers special lectures and programs, and its gift shop is full of black American and African-inspired books, posters, and jewelry. ✉ *144 W. 125th St.,* ☎ *212/864–4500.* ✎ *$5; sculpture garden free.* ⊙ *Wed.–Fri. 10–5, weekends 1–6.*

Sylvia's Soul Food Restaurant. Sylvia Woods remains most nights until 10 chatting with her customers, contributing to her restaurant's popularity among residents and tourists alike. Southern specialties and cordiality are the rule here. ✉ *328 Lenox Ave., between 126th and 127th Sts.,* ☎ *212/996–0660.*

Theresa Towers. Its former incarnation as Harlem's poshest place to stay, the Hotel Theresa, is still evident from the HT crests under some windows and a sign painted on its west side, which towers over the neighboring buildings. Fidel Castro left his midtown accommodations to stay here during his 1960 visit to the United Nations. Now an office building, Theresa Towers is home to several community organizations. ✉ *2090 Adam Clayton Powell Jr. Blvd., at 125th St.*

CHELSEA

Like the London district of the same name, New York's Chelsea has preserved its villagelike personality. Both have their quiet nooks where the 19th century seems to live on; both have been havens for artists, writers, and bohemians. Although London's Chelsea is a much more upscale chunk of real estate, New York's Chelsea is catching up, with town-house renovations reclaiming block after block of the side streets. Within the past few years, several historic cast-iron buildings on 6th Avenue have also been restored, attracting superstore tenants that have revitalized the area. Although 7th, 8th, and 9th avenues may never equal the shopping mecca of King's Road in London's Chelsea, they have plenty of hip, one-of-a-kind boutiques sprinkled among unassuming grocery stores and other remnants of the neighborhood's immigrant past.

Precisely speaking, the New York neighborhood was named not after Chelsea itself but after London's Chelsea Royal Hospital, an old soldiers' home. Running from 14th to 24th Street, from 8th Avenue west, it was one family's country estate until the 1830s, when Clement Clarke Moore saw the city moving north and decided to divide his land into lots. With an instinctive gift for urban planning, he dictated a pattern of development that ensured street after street of graceful row houses. A clergyman and classics professor, Moore is probably best known for his 1822 poem "A Visit from St. Nicholas," which he composed while bringing a sleigh full of Christmas treats from lower Manhattan to his Chelsea home.

Today's Chelsea extends from 5th Avenue west, and from 14th Street to 23rd. Eighth Avenue now rivals Christopher Street in the West Village as a gay concourse: Several bookstores, shops, fitness clubs, and restaurants cater to a gay clientele on both sides of the street. Yet the thriving neighborhood also accommodates a multicultural population that has lived here for decades as well as a burgeoning art community west of 10th Avenue. Locals anticipate an economic boost as a result of the opening of the Chelsea Piers Sports and Entertainment Complex on the Hudson.

Numbers in the text correspond to numbers in the margin and on the Chelsea map.

A Good Walk

Begin your Chelsea tour on the corner of 6th Avenue and 18th Street. Sixth Avenue was once known as Ladies' Mile for its concentration of major department stores. After the stores moved uptown in the early 1900s, the neighborhood declined and the grand old store buildings stood empty and dilapidated. The 1990s, however, brought the renaissance of the Flatiron district to the east (☞ Murray Hill to Union Square, *above*), and several old buildings have been renovated all along 6th Avenue. Stand at 6th Avenue and 18th Street and imagine it in the latter part of the 19th century, when the elevated tracks of the 6th Avenue El train still cast their shadow along this street.

From the west side of the avenue you can look across at the embellished, glazed terra-cotta building between 18th and 19th streets. Originally constructed in 1896 as the **Siegel-Cooper Dry Goods Store** ①, it encompasses 15½ acres of space. Today its main tenants are Bed, Bath & Beyond, Filene's Basement, and T. J. Maxx.

Between 18th and 19th streets on the west side of the avenue is the original, cast-iron **B. Altman Dry Goods Store** ②, built in 1877 and now home to Today's Man, a discount menswear store. Continue walking north to 20th Street. The Church of the Holy Communion, a former Gothic-style Episcopal house of worship dating from 1846, is on the northeast corner of the avenue. To the horror of some preservationists, it was converted a few years ago into Limelight, a popular nightclub, now closed. On the west side of the avenue between 20th and 21st streets stands another former cast-iron retail palace, the **Hugh O'Neill Dry Goods Store** ③, a renovated structure housing a publishing company.

If you're here on a weekend, you might like to take a flea-market break: 6th Avenue between 24th and 27th streets is the site of the city's longest-running outdoor market. Three hundred vendors sell antiques and memorabilia here from 9 to 5 on weekends.

Next, turn left from 6th Avenue onto 21st Street (on the south side of the street) for a look at the Third Cemetery of the Spanish & Portuguese

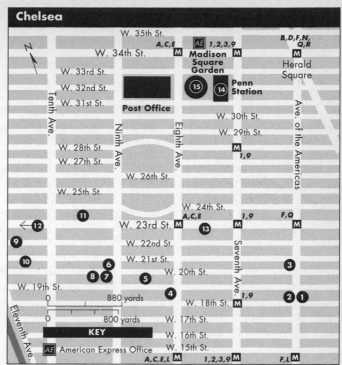

Synagogue, Shearith Israel, a private green oasis with a hardy old ailanthus tree. In use from 1829 to 1851, it is one of three graveyards created in Manhattan by this congregation (☞ Greenwich Village *and* Little Italy and Chinatown, *below*).

Continue west on 21st Street to 8th Avenue, where the Chelsea Historic District officially begins. Between 19th and 23rd streets, from 8th to 10th Avenue, you'll find examples of all of Chelsea's architectural periods: Greek and Gothic Revival, Italianate, and 1890s apartment buildings. But before you start prowling around there, you may want to head down to 19th Street and 8th Avenue to see the Art Deco **Joyce Theater** ④, primarily a dance venue. Its presence has helped to attract several good, moderately priced restaurants to 8th Avenue.

On 20th Street, between 8th and 9th avenues, you'll find the 19th-century **St. Peter's Episcopal Church** ⑤, which has three buildings: a rectory, a fieldstone church, and a brick parish hall. Next, head west on 20th Street to 9th Avenue; on the west side of the avenue, between 20th and 21st streets, is the **General Theological Seminary** ⑥, the oldest Episcopal seminary in the United States.

Across the street from the seminary, at **404 West 20th Street** ⑦, is the oldest house in the historic district. The residences next door, from 406 to 418 West 20th, are called **Cushman Row** ⑧ and are excellent examples of Greek Revival town houses. Farther down West 20th Street, stop to look at the fine Italianate houses at Nos. 446 to 450. The arched windows and doorways are hallmarks of this style, which prized circular forms—not least because, being expensive to build, they showed off the owner's wealth.

West 22nd Street has a string of handsome old row houses just east of 10th Avenue. No. 435 was the longtime residence of actors Geraldine Page and Rip Torn; they nicknamed this Chelsea town house the Torn Page. In 1987, a year after winning an Oscar for *The Trip to Bountiful,* Page suffered a fatal heart attack here.

Between 10th and 11th avenues, stretching from 20th to 29th Street, you can explore the **Chelsea galleries.** A good place to start your investigation is 22nd Street, where you'll find the anchor of Chelsea's renaissance as an art community, the **Dia Center for the Arts** ⑨, which is dedicated to contemporary art. On the same street you can visit seven other smaller galleries. Other major Chelsea exhibition spaces include the **Paula Cooper Gallery** ⑩ on 21st Street and three galleries on 24th Street: Metro Pictures, Barbara Gladstone, and Matthew Marks.

From the galleries, return to 10th Avenue and walk to 23rd Street. On the block spanning 23rd and 24th streets, between 9th and 10th avenues on the north side of the street, you can't miss the **London Terrace Apartments** ⑪, a vast 1930 complex containing 1,670 apartments. As you walk along 23rd Street, notice the lions on the arched entrances; from the side they look as if they're snarling, but from the front they display wide grins.

If you walk west on 23rd Street as far as you can go, you'll reach the mammoth new **Chelsea Piers Sports and Entertainment Complex** ⑫, extending from 17th to 23rd Street along the Hudson River waterfront; it has an entrance at 23rd Street.

Otherwise, continue east on 23rd Street. During the 1880s and Gay '90s, the street was the heart of the entertainment district, lined with theaters, music halls, and beer gardens. Today it is an undistinguished, even run-down, commercial thoroughfare, but there is one relic of its once-proud past: the **Chelsea Hotel** ⑬, between 7th and 8th avenues, which opened in 1884 as a cooperative apartment house and became a hotel in 1905.

Go back to 7th Avenue and walk uptown a few blocks—you'll be leaving Chelsea and entering the garment district, where wheeled racks of clothing add to the traffic volume, and you may well stumble upon your dream designer sale (accept all flyers). Officially, the clothing quarter begins at 28th Street, but the bulk of the ateliers is farther up in the 30s, past **Penn Station** ⑭, stretching between 31st and 33rd streets. Manhattan's other Amtrak/LIRR station lies beneath the two-square-block Penn Plaza. Behind Penn Station on 8th Avenue stands the concrete-clad cylinder that is **Madison Square Garden** ⑮, host to numerous sporting events and major concerts.

TIMING

Allow yourself at least three to four hours to explore Chelsea. If your schedule permits, plan to spend the day so you have ample time to browse the stores and galleries.

Sights to See

❷ **B. Altman Dry Goods Store.** Built in 1877 with additions in 1887 and 1910, this ornate cast-iron giant originally housed B. Altman Dry Goods until the business moved in 1906 to set up shop in its imposing quarters at 5th Avenue and 34th Street. The latter store closed in late 1989. ✉ *621 6th Ave., between 18th and 19th Sts.*

Chelsea galleries. Extending from 20th to 29th Street between 10th and 11th avenues, the Chelsea art scene expanded significantly in late 1996 and 1997. Several of the most recent additions are large, upscale places, featuring a contemporary industrial look popularized by architects such as Richard Gluckman and William Katz: white-painted open exhibition spaces without columns, garage-door facades, and concrete floors. Still, a few smaller, quirkier low-budget galleries may be found in the neighborhood as well. Perhaps begin your peregrination on 22nd Street, which has the **Dia Center for the Arts** (☞ *below*) and seven other galleries. You'll probably want to stop at **Matthew Marks Gallery** (✉ 522 W. 22nd St., ☎ 212/861−9455) and three spaces at 530 West 22nd Street: **Morris-Healy** (☎ 212/243−3753), **Pat Hearn Gallery** (☎ 212/727−7366), and **Annina Nosei** (☎ 212/741−8695). At 504 22nd Street, you'll find three spaces that opened in late 1996: **Jessica Fredericks Gallery** (☎ 212/633−6555), **Xavier LaBoulbenne** (☎ 212/462−4111), and **Linda Kirkland Gallery** (☎ 212/627−3930), all featuring younger artists; the same building also houses **Art Resources Transfer** (☎ 212/691−5956), which publishes books based on conversations with artists and sponsors art-related video screenings and readings.

Contemporary art mavens will also want to visit the SoHo transplant ☞ **Paula Cooper Gallery** on 20th Street and, on 24th Street, **Barbara Gladstone** (✉ 515 W. 24th St. ☎ 212/206−9300), **Metro Pictures** (✉ 519 W. 24th St., ☎ 212/206−7100), and **Matthew Marks's** second Chelsea gallery space (✉ 523 W. 24th St., ☎ 212/243−0200); the latter three major players, known collectively as M.G.M., all represent high-profile creators. Among the smaller, no-frills operations in the area are **Clementine Gallery** (✉ 526 W. 26th St., 2nd floor, ☎ 212/243−5937) in a building overflowing with artists' and photographers' studios and **Viewing Room Exhibitions** (✉ 515 W. 29th St., 3rd floor, ☎ 212/290−8117), run by two painters.

Because each gallery keeps its own particular hours, it's best to call ahead about openings and closings.

🔞 **Chelsea Hotel.** Constructed of red brick with lacy wrought-iron balconies and a mansard roof, this neighborhood landmark opened in 1884 as a cooperative apartment house and became a hotel in 1905, although it has always catered to long-term tenants, with a tradition of broadmindedness that has attracted many creative types. Its literary roll call of former live-ins includes Mark Twain, Eugene O'Neill, O. Henry, Thomas Wolfe, Tennessee Williams, Vladimir Nabokov, Mary McCarthy, Brendan Behan, Arthur Miller, Dylan Thomas, William S. Burroughs, and Arthur C. Clarke (who wrote the script for *2001: A Space Odyssey* while living here). In 1966 Andy Warhol filmed artist Brigid Polk in her Chelsea Hotel room, which eventually became *The Chelsea Girls*, considered by many to be Warhol's best film. More recently, the hotel was seen on screen in *Sid and Nancy* (1986), a dramatization of a true-life Chelsea Hotel murder, when drugged punk rocker Sid Vicious allegedly stabbed his girlfriend Nancy Spungen to death. The shabby, seedy aura of the Chelsea Hotel is part of its allure. Read the commemorative plaques outside and then step into the lobby to look at the unusual artwork, some of it donated in lieu of rent by residents down on their luck. ✉ *222 W. 23rd St., between 7th and 8th Aves.,* ☎ *212/243−3700.*

🔞 **Chelsea Piers Sports and Entertainment Complex.** Beginning in 1910, the Chelsea Piers was the launching point for a new generation of big ocean liners; it was also the destination of the *Titanic,* which never arrived, and the departure point for the last sailing of the *Lusitania.* During the past few decades, the piers were grimy, gloomy, and practically abandoned. All that has changed with the transformation of the old pier buildings along the Hudson River into this splendid 1.7-million-square-ft state-of-the-art facility, which opened in 1995, providing an amazing selection of activities to the sports enthusiast. The $100 million complex has two year-round indoor ice-skating rinks for public skating, ice hockey and lessons; a field house accommodating gymnastics, indoor soccer, field hockey, lacrosse, basketball courts, and batting cages; two outdoor regulation-size in-line and rollerskating rinks; and the city's only year-round outdoor golf driving range, with four levels of heated stalls overlooking a 200-yard fairway by the river. The 150,000 square-ft Sports Center encompasses the world's longest indoor running track, the largest rock-climbing wall in the Northeast, three basketball courts, a sand volleyball court, a huge weight training area, a 25-yard pool, a boxing ring, and a sports medicine center.

From the Maritime Center, the city's largest marina, with a 1.2-mi esplanade, Spirit Cruises runs three boats providing food, musical entertainment, dancing, and sightseeing around New York Harbor. Small boats dock at the 70-slip Surfside 3 Marina. Silver Screen Studios, an active film and television production center located on two levels in the Chelsea Piers, provides a home to the network television series *Law and Order* and *Spin City*. The complex also has a wall of historical photographs, sporting goods shops, and several restaurants with river views, including the Crab House and the Chelsea Brewing Company. ⊠ *Piers 59–62 on the Hudson River from 17th to 23rd Sts.; entrance at 23rd St.,* ☎ *212/336–6666.*

⑧ Cushman Row. Built by dry-goods merchant Don Alonzo Cushman, a friend of Clement Clarke Moore, who made a fortune developing Chelsea, this group of homes between 9th and 10th avenues represents some of the country's most perfect examples of Greek Revival town houses. The residences retain such original details as small wreath-encircled attic windows, deeply recessed doorways with brownstone frames, and striking iron balustrades and fences. Notice, too, the pineapples, a traditional symbol of welcome, atop the newels in front of Nos. 416 and 418. ⊠ *406–418 W. 20th St.*

★ ⑨ Dia Center for the Arts. This facility provides contemporary artists with the chance to develop new work or to mount an organized exhibit on a full floor for extended time periods, usually an entire year. Besides installations by diverse artists, you might find an exhibit from Dia's permanent collection, which includes creations by Joseph Beuys, Walter De Maria, Dan Flavin, Blinky Palermo, Cy Twombly, and Andy Warhol, among others. Outside on the roof there's a fascinating exhibition designed by Dan Graham, which consists of a two-way mirror glass cylinder inside a cube. ⊠ *548 W. 22nd St.,* ☎ *212/989–5912.* ▣ *$3 (suggested donation).* ☉ *Thurs.–Sun. noon–6.*

NEED A BREAK?	If you're ready for a steaming cup of coffee and some apple pie, you'll be glad to see the shiny **Empire Diner** (⊠ 210 10th Ave., ☎ 212/243-2736) gleefully lighting up the corner of 22nd Street and 10th Avenue. Though the food is somewhat overpriced, the authentic diner atmosphere here is cheerful and friendly, and it's open 24 hours.

❼ 404 West 20th Street. The oldest house in the historic district was built between 1829 and 1830 in the Federal style. It still has one clapboard side wall; over the years it acquired a Greek Revival doorway and Italianate windows on the parlor floor, and the roof was raised one story.

OFF THE BEATEN PATH	**GARMENT DISTRICT –** This district teems with warehouses, workshops, and showrooms that manufacture and finish mostly women's and children's clothing. On weekdays the streets are crowded with trucks and the sidewalks swarm with daredevil deliverymen wheeling garment racks between factories and specialized subcontractors. ⊠ *7th Ave. between 31st and 41st Sts., also called Fashion Avenue.*

6 **General Theological Seminary.** When Chelsea developer Clement Clarke Moore divided up his estate, he began by deeding a large section to this Episcopal seminary, where he taught Hebrew and Greek. At 9th Avenue and 20th Street, the religious oasis still occupies a block-long stretch. The stoutly fenced campus is accessible through the modern building on 9th Avenue; during off hours you can view the grounds from West 20th Street. The **West Building** (1836) is another early example of Gothic Revival architecture in the city. Most of the rest of the complex was completed in 1883–1902, when Eugene Augustus Hoffman, the school's third dean, hired architect Charles Coolidge Haight to design a campus that would rival those of most other American colleges of the day, in the style known as English Collegiate Gothic, which Haight had pioneered. The general campus plan is in an "E" shape, with the spine facing 21st Street. In the center is the **Chapel of the Good Shepherd,** with its 161-ft-high bell tower. **Sherred Hall,** a three-story classroom building flanked by dormitories, expresses beautifully the simple quality and uniform look Haight strove for. **Hoffman Hall,** the refectory-gymnasium, has an enormous dining hall that resembles a medieval knight's council chamber. A 1960s-era building facing 9th Avenue houses administrative offices, a bookstore, and the 210,000-volume **St. Mark's Library,** generally considered the nation's greatest ecclesiastical library; it has the world's largest collection of Latin bibles. ☒ *175 9th Ave.,* ☎ *212/243–5150.* ☉ *Grounds weekdays noon–3; call for information to use the library.*

3 **Hugh O'Neill Dry Goods Store.** Constructed in 1875, this cast-iron building, originally an emporium, features Corinthian columns and pilasters; its corner towers were once topped off with huge bulbous domes. Look up at the pediment and you'll see the name of the original tenant proudly displayed. The renovated structure now houses the Elsevier Science Publishing Company and Goldman's Treasures, an antiques store. ☒ *655–671 6th Ave., between 20th and 21st Sts.*

4 **Joyce Theater.** The former Elgin movie house built in 1942 was gutted and in 1982 transformed into this sleek modern theater that pays tribute to its Art Deco origins. If you have any interest in modern dance, it's well worth checking out who is performing at the Joyce during your stay. ☒ *175 8th Ave., at 19th St.,* ☎ *212/242–0800.*

NEED A BREAK?
The Big Cup (☒ 228 8th Ave., between 21st and 22nd Sts., ☎ 212/206–0059), a lively neighborhood meeting spot, serves good coffee, tea, and pastries.

11 **London Terrace Apartments.** When this huge brick complex first opened in 1930, the doormen dressed as London bobbies. London Terrace is actually made up of two rows of interconnected buildings, which enclose a block-long private garden. The complex contains 1,670 apartments with shops along the avenues it borders. ☒ *W. 23rd to W. 24th Sts., between 9th and 10th Aves.*

15 **Madison Square Garden.** A concrete-clad cylinder serves as the 20,000-seat home of the New York Knicks and Rangers and also accommodates other sporting events and major concerts. Behind-the-scenes tours, from locker rooms to stage, are available. Much to the dismay of architects and preservationists, the ponderous Madison Square Garden was constructed on the site of the original vast Pennsylvania Station, which possessed a soaring Beaux Arts majesty until it was demolished in 1962. ☒ *31st to 33rd Sts., between 7th and 8th Aves.,* ☎ *212/465–5801.* ☟ *Tours $8.* ☉ *Tours weekdays 10, 11, noon, 1, 2, and 3; Sat. 10, 11, noon, 1, and 2; Sun. 11, noon, 1, and 2.*

⑩ **Paula Cooper Gallery.** In 1996, after 28 years in SoHo, Paula Cooper moved her respected gallery to Chelsea, to a glorious 5,000-square-ft exhibition and office space, allowing for multiple exhibitions, historical presentations, large-scale sculpture shows, and site-specific installations. The main gallery has 2,500 square ft of columnless space, an immaculate concrete floor, a 27-ft high beamed vaulted ceiling, and skylights, while the second more intimate, 500-square-ft space can be opened to the street. Exhibitions have been devoted to such international artists as Carl Andre, Andres Serrano, and Tony Smith. ⊠ *534 W. 21st St.,* ☎ *212/255–1105.* ▢ *Free.* ☉ *Tues.–Sat. 10–6.*

⑭ **Penn Station.** The original Pennsylvania Station contained a grand iron-and-glass train shed and an enormous Roman Revival waiting room, designed by McKim, Mead & White. Sadly destroyed in 1962, the widely admired terminal was replaced by the undistinguished (some call it ugly) Amtrak/LIRR station, which lies beneath the two-square-block Penn Plaza office building and Madison Square Garden. ⊠ *W. 31st to 33rd Sts., between 7th and 8th Aves.*

⑤ **St. Peter's Episcopal Church.** Built between 1836 and 1838, St. Peter's has been hidden behind scaffolding for several years. The Greek Revival–style **rectory** (1832), to the right of the main church, originally served as the sanctuary. Four years after it was built, the congregation had already laid foundations for a bigger church when, it is said, a vestryman returned from England bursting with excitement over the Gothic Revival that had just taken hold there. The fieldstone **church** that resulted ranks as one of New York's earliest examples of Gothic Revival architecture. The church "welcomes all faiths and uncertain faiths." To the left of the church, the brick **parish hall** is an example of the so-called Victorian Gothic style; its churchlike front was added in 1871. It's now the home of the Atlantic Theater Company, founded by playwright David Mamet. The company stages small productions by emerging writers. The wrought-iron fence framing the three buildings once enclosed St. Paul's Chapel downtown (☞ The Seaport and the Courts, *below*). ⊠ *344 W. 20th St.,* ☎ *212/929–2390.*

① **Siegel-Cooper Dry Goods Store.** Built much later than its neighbors in 1896, this impressive building adorned with glazed terra-cotta encompasses 15½ acres of space, yet it was built in only five months. In its retail heyday, the store's main floor featured an immense fountain— a circular marble terrace with an enormous white-marble-and-brass replica of *The Republic,* the statue Daniel Chester French displayed at the 1883 Chicago World's Fair—which became a favorite rendezvous point for New Yorkers. During World War I, the building was a military hospital. The structure was recently renovated, bringing attention to its splendid ornamentation: round wreathed windows, Corinthian and Doric pilasters, Romanesque rounded arches, lion heads, and more. Today one of its main tenants is **Bed, Bath & Beyond,** an impressive emporium with 11 sections of household items at discounted prices. Bed, Bath & Beyond has received a good share of the credit for revitalizing retail business in this area; it was the first superstore to open in Chelsea. **Filene's Basement** and **T. J. Maxx** are more recent retail additions to the building. ⊠ *620 6th Ave., between 18th and 19th Sts.*

NEED A
BREAK?

Flatiron Diner and Baking Company (⊠ 18 W. 18th St., ☎ 212/989–7700) serves coffee, tea, sandwiches, and homebaked goods for a quick snack in the front of the restaurant, which is cheerfully decorated with antique signs, bicycles, radios, and appliances.

GREENWICH VILLAGE

Greenwich Village, which New Yorkers almost invariably speak of simply as "the Village," enjoyed a raffish reputation for years. Originally a rural outpost of the city—a haven for New Yorkers during early 19th-century smallpox and yellow fever epidemics—many of its blocks still look somewhat pastoral, with brick town houses and low rises, tiny green parks and hidden courtyards, and a crazy-quilt pattern of narrow, tree-lined streets. In the mid-19th century, however, as the city spread north of 14th Street, the Village became the province of immigrants, bohemians, and students (New York University, today the nation's largest private university, was planted next to Washington Square in 1831). Its politics were radical and its attitudes tolerant, which is one reason it remains a home to such a large gay community.

Several generations of writers and artists have lived and worked here: in the 19th century, Henry James, Edgar Allan Poe, Mark Twain, Walt Whitman, and Stephen Crane; at the turn of the century, O. Henry, Edith Wharton, Theodore Dreiser, and Hart Crane; and during the 1920s and '30s, John Dos Passos, Norman Rockwell, Sinclair Lewis, John Reed, Eugene O'Neill, Edward Hopper, and Edna St. Vincent Millay. In the late 1940s and early 1950s, the Abstract Expressionist painters Franz Kline, Jackson Pollock, Mark Rothko, and Willem de Kooning congregated here, as did the Beat writers Jack Kerouac, Allen Ginsberg, and Lawrence Ferlinghetti. The 1960s brought folk musicians and poets, notably Bob Dylan and Peter, Paul, and Mary.

Today Village apartments and town houses go for high rents, and several posh restaurants have put down roots there. Except for the isolated western fringe, where a string of tough gay bars along West Street attract some drug traffic and prostitution, the Village is about as safe and clean as the Upper East Side. Nevertheless, something about the tangled street plan and the small buildings encourages anarchy. Shabby shop fronts, hole-in-the-wall restaurants, and nonmainstream arts groups persist and thrive here. There's still a large student population, and several longtime residents remain, paying cheap rents thanks to rent-control laws. The Village is no longer dangerous, but it still feels bohemian.

Numbers in the text correspond to numbers in the margin and on the Greenwich Village and the East Village map.

A Good Walk

Begin your tour of Greenwich Village at the foot of 5th Avenue at Washington Arch in **Washington Square** ①, a hugely popular, 9½-acre park that provides a neighborhood oasis for locals and tourists alike. Most of the buildings bordering Washington Square belong to New York University (NYU). On Washington Square North, between University Place and MacDougal Street, stretches the **Row** ②, composed of two blocks of lovingly preserved Greek Revival and Federal-style town houses.

On the east side of the square, you can take in a contemporary art exhibit at **Grey Art Gallery** ③, housed in NYU's main building (✉ 100 Washington Square E). If you walk to the south side of the square, a trio of red sandstone hulks represents an abortive 1960s attempt to create a unified campus look for NYU, as envisioned by architects Philip Johnson and Richard Foster. At one time, plans called for all of the Washington Square buildings to be refaced in this red stone; fortunately, the cost proved prohibitive. At La Guardia Place and Washington Square South, the undistinguished modern Loeb Student Center stands on the site of a famous boardinghouse that had been nicknamed the

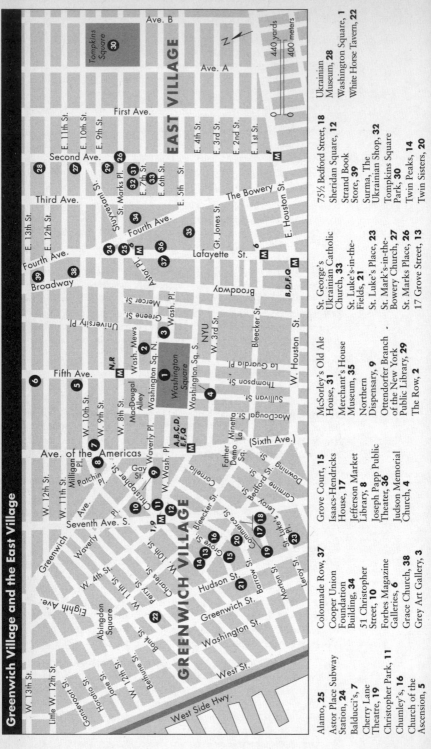

Greenwich Village and the East Village

House of Genius for the talented writers who lived there over the years: Theodore Dreiser, John Dos Passos, and Eugene O'Neill, among others. A block west of the Student Center, at the corner of Washington Square South and Thompson Street, is the square-towered **Judson Memorial Church** ④.

From Washington Square Arch and the park, cross Washington Square North to the east side of 5th Avenue. On your right, at the northeast corner of Washington Square North and 5th Avenue, you'll see the portico entrance to 7–13 Washington Square North. Beyond the white columns of this entrance is the small, attractive Willy's Garden. A statue of Miguel de Cervantes, the author of *Don Quixote,* stands at the far end. The likeness, cast in 1724, was a gift from the mayor of Madrid to former New York City mayor Ed Koch. It stood in Bryant Park for several years and was donated to NYU in 1989.

Another half a block north on the east side of 5th Avenue is **Washington Mews,** a cobblestone private street. A similar Village mews, Mac-Dougal Alley, can be found between 8th Street and the square just off MacDougal Street, one block west.

Continue up the west side of 5th Avenue; you'll pass the **Church of the Ascension** ⑤ (✉ 5th Ave. and W. 10th St.), a Gothic Revival brownstone building. At 5th Avenue and 12th Street, you can stop in the **Forbes Magazine Galleries** ⑥, which house the late publisher Malcolm Forbes's unusual personal collection.

Backtrack on 5th Avenue to West 11th Street and turn right to see one of the best examples of a Village town-house block. One exception to the general 19th-century redbrick look is the modern, angled front window of 18 West 11th Street, usually occupied by a stuffed bear whose outfit changes from day to day. This house was built after the original was destroyed in a 1970 explosion; members of the radical Weathermen Underground faction had started a bomb factory in the basement. At the end of the block, behind a low gray stone wall on the south side of the street, is the Second Shearith Israel graveyard, used by the country's oldest Jewish congregation after the cemetery in Chinatown (☞ Little Italy and Chinatown, *below*) and before the one in Chelsea (☞ Chelsea, *above*).

On Avenue of the Americas (6th Avenue), turn left to sample the wares at **Balducci's** ⑦ (✉ 424 6th Ave., at 9th St.), a popular gourmet food store. Directly opposite, the triangle formed by West 10th Street, 6th Avenue, and Greenwich Avenue originally held a market, a jail, and the magnificent towered courthouse that is now the **Jefferson Market Library** ⑧.

Just west of 6th Avenue on 10th Street is the wrought-iron gateway to a tiny courtyard called **Patchin Place**; around the corner, on 6th Avenue just north of 10th Street, is a similar cul-de-sac, Milligan Place, which few New Yorkers even know is there.

Next, proceed to Christopher Street, which veers off from the southern end of the library triangle. Christopher Street has long been the symbolic heart of New York's gay and lesbian community. Before you proceed just a few steps, you'll see **Gay Street** on your left. This quiet curved thoroughfare of early 19th-century row houses was immortalized in Ruth McKinney's book *My Sister Eileen.*

Continue west on Christopher Street, crossing Waverly Place; on your left, you'll pass the 1831 brick **Northern Dispensary** ⑨ building, which at one time provided health care to poor neighborhood residents. Across the street is **51 Christopher Street** ⑩, which used to be the site of a bar named the Stonewall Inn. At this address, a historic clash in 1969 between city police and gay men marked the beginning of the gay rights movement. Right across from 51 Christopher Street is a green triangle named **Christopher Park** ⑪, which is sometimes confused with another landscaped triangle to the south (between Washington Place, Barrow Street, and 7th Avenue) called **Sheridan Square** ⑫.

Across the busy intersection of 7th Avenue, Christopher Street has many bars and stores; several of them cater to a gay clientele, but the street is by no means off-limits to other people. Two shops worth a visit are McNulty's Tea and Coffee Co. (✉ 109 Christopher St.), with a large variety of tea and coffee blends, and Li-Lac Chocolate Shop (✉ 120 Christopher St.), a longtime favorite in the area for its homemade chocolate and butter crunch.

West of 7th Avenue, the Village turns into a picture-book town of twisting tree-lined streets, quaint houses, and tiny restaurants. Follow Grove Street from Sheridan Square west past the house where Thomas Paine died (✉ 59 Grove St.)—now the site of Marie's Crisis Cafe—and the boyhood home of poet Hart Crane (✉ 45 Grove St.).

At this point you'll be close to the intersection of Grove and Bleecker streets. You may now choose to take a leisurely stroll along the portion of Bleecker Street that extends west of 7th Avenue from Grove to Bank Street, heading in the direction of Abingdon Square. This section of Bleecker Street is full of crafts and antiques shops, coffee-houses, and small restaurants.

If you choose to forego Bleecker Street, continue your walk west on Grove Street. The secluded intersection of Grove and Bedford streets seems to have fallen through a time warp into the 19th century. On the northeast corner stands **17 Grove Street** ⑬, one of the few remaining clapboard structures in the city. Behind it, at 102 Bedford Street, is **Twin Peaks** ⑭, an early 19th-century house that resembles a Swiss chalet. Heading west, Grove Street curves in front of the iron gate of **Grove Court** ⑮, a group of mid-19th-century brick-front residences.

Take a left from Grove Street and walk down Bedford Street until you get to No. 86. Behind the unmarked door is **Chumley's** ⑯, a former speakeasy. Walk a couple of blocks further down to the **Isaacs-Hendricks House** ⑰ (✉ 77 Bedford St.), the oldest house in the Village. The place next door, **75½ Bedford Street** ⑱, at 9½ ft wide, is New York's narrowest house.

Heading west from Grove Street onto Commerce Street, you soon reach the historic **Cherry Lane Theater** ⑲ (✉ 38 Commerce St.). Across the street stand two nearly identical brick houses (✉ 39 and 41 Commerce St.) separated by a garden and popularly known as the **Twin Sisters** ⑳. Across the street, Grange Hall (✉ 50 Commerce St.) serves comfort food in an intriguing restored speakeasy.

Follow Barrow Street to Hudson Street, so named because this was originally the bank of the Hudson River. The block to the northwest is owned by **St. Luke's-in-the-Fields** ㉑, built in 1822 as a country chapel for downtown's Trinity Church. Writer Bret Harte once lived at 487 Hudson Street, at the end of the row. If your feet are getting tired, you can head north on Hudson Street for four blocks and take a rest at the legendary **White Horse Tavern** ㉒ at 11th Street.

If you choose to continue, head south on Hudson Street for two blocks until you reach Leroy Street. East of Hudson Street, for the length of a block, Leroy Street becomes **St. Luke's Place** ㉓, a row of classic 1860s town houses shaded by graceful gingko trees. Across 7th Avenue, St. Luke's Place becomes Leroy Street again, which terminates in an old Italian neighborhood at Bleecker Street. Amazingly unchanged amid all the Village gentrification, Bleecker between 6th and 7th avenues seems more vital these days than Little Italy does. For authentic Italian ambience, stop into one of the fragrant Italian bakeries, such as A. Zito & Sons (⊠ 259 Bleecker St.) and Rocco's (⊠ 243 Bleecker St.), or look inside the old-style butcher shops, such as Ottomanelli & Sons (⊠ 285 Bleecker St.) and Faicco's (⊠ 260 Bleecker St.). John's Pizzeria (⊠ 278 Bleecker St.) is one of those places that locals swear by. Be forewarned, however: no slices; whole pies only.

Head east on Bleecker and you'll come to Father Demo Square (Bleecker St. and 6th Ave.). Across Bleecker Street you'll see the Church of Our Lady of Pompeii, where Mother Cabrini, a naturalized Italian immigrant who became the first American saint, often prayed.

Head up 6th Avenue to 3rd Street and check out the playground caged there within a chain-link fence. NBA stars of tomorrow learn their moves on this patch of asphalt, where city-style basketball is played all afternoon and evening in all but the very coldest weather.

Return along Washington Square South to MacDougal Street and turn right. The Provincetown Playhouse (⊠ 133 MacDougal St.) premiered many of Eugene O'Neill's plays. Louisa May Alcott wrote *Little Women* while living at 130–132 MacDougal Street. The two houses at 127 and 129 MacDougal Street were built for Aaron Burr in 1829; notice the pineapple newel posts, a symbol of hospitality.

At Minetta Tavern (⊠ 113 MacDougal St.), a venerable Village watering hole, turn right onto Minetta Lane, which leads to narrow Minetta Street, another former speakeasy alley. Both streets follow the course of Minetta Brook, which once flowed through this neighborhood and still bubbles deep beneath the pavement.

The foot of Minetta Street returns you to the corner of 6th Avenue and Bleecker Street, where you will have reached the stomping grounds of 1960s-era folksingers (many of them performed at the now-defunct Folk City, one block north on West 3rd Street). This area still attracts a young crowd—partly because of the proximity of NYU—to its cafés, bars, jazz clubs, coffeehouses, theaters, and cabarets (☞ Chapter 8), not to mention its long row of unpretentious ethnic restaurants.

TIMING

Allow yourself a full day to take this walk. Greenwich Village moves at a slower pace than the rest of city, and you'll want to take your time exploring back streets and stopping at shops and cafés.

Sights to See

❼ Balducci's. From the vegetable stand of the late Louis Balducci Sr. sprouted this full-service gourmet food store. Along with more than 80 Italian cheeses and 50 kinds of bread, the family-owned enterprise features imported Italian specialties, first-rate takeout foods, and a prodigious selection of fresh seafood. ⊠ *424 6th Ave., at 9th St.,* ☎ *212/673–2600.*

⓳ Cherry Lane Theatre. One of the original Off-Broadway houses, this 1817 building was converted into a theater in 1923, thanks to Edna St. Vincent Millay and a group of theater artists. Over the years it was the site of American premieres of works by O'Neill, Beckett, Ionesco, Albee, Pinter, and Mamet. The playhouse was modernized in 1996, but it still contains the original audience seats. Just a few steps away from the theater at 48 Commerce Street stands a handsome renovated Greek-revival building originally constructed in 1844 for merchant prince

Alexander T. Stewart on land leased from downtown Trinity Church. ⊠ *38 Commerce St.,* ☎ *212/989–2020.*

⑪ Christopher Park. Sometimes mistaken for Sheridan Square, this pleasant triangular oasis contains a bronze statue of Civil War general Philip Sheridan and striking sculptures designed by George Segal of a lesbian couple sitting on a bench and gay male partners standing near them; both couples appear to be having a conversation. ⊠ *Bordered by Washington Pl. and Grove and Christopher Sts.*

⑯ Chumley's. Behind an unmarked door on Bedford Street lies a welcoming tavern that was once a speakeasy during the Prohibition era. At the time, the unmarked entrance provided a quick getaway for customers when the local police arrived. Ever popular with local residents, Chumley's has another "secret" entrance in Pamela Court, accessed at 58 Barrow Street around the corner. The former speakeasy maintains much of its original ambience, with oak booths, a fireplace once used by a blacksmith, and subdued lighting. For years Chumley's attracted a literary clientele, and the bookcovers of their publications were proudly displayed (and still appear) on the walls. John Steinbeck, Ernest Hemingway, Edna Ferber, Simone de Beauvoir, Jack Kerouac, and Horton Foote are just a few of the many writers who once spent time here. ⊠ *86 Bedford St., near Barrow St.,* ☎ *212/675–4449.*

⑤ Church of the Ascension. Inside this 1841 Gothic Revival–style brownstone designed by Richard Upjohn, you can admire a mural depicting the Ascension of Jesus and stained-glass windows by John LaFarge, as well as a marble altar sculpture by Louis Saint-Gaudens. In 1844 President John Tyler married Julia Gardiner here. ⊠ *36–38 5th Ave., at W. 10th St.*

⑩ 51 Christopher Street. On June 27, 1969, a gay bar at this address named the Stonewall Inn was the site of a clash between gay men (some in drag) and the New York City police. As these men were being forced into paddy wagons, sympathetic gay onlookers protested and started fighting back, throwing beer bottles and garbage cans. The Stonewall Riot is now commemorated each year in several American cities at the end of June with parades and celebrations that honor the gay rights movement. A clothing store now occupies the site of the event; a more recent bar named Stonewall is next door at No. 53.

NEED A BREAK?

If you're yearning for a *pain au chocolat* or a madeleine, stop by **Marquet Patisserie** (⊠ 15 E. 12th St., ☎ 212/243-7752), a sleek, friendly café that serves irresistible French pastries, great coffee, and satisfying sandwiches, salads, and quiches.

★ ⑥ Forbes Magazine Galleries. The late publisher Malcolm Forbes's idiosyncratic personal collection fills the ground floor of the limestone Forbes Magazine Building, once the home of Macmillan Publishing. Exhibits change in the large painting gallery and one of two autograph galleries, while permanent highlights include U.S. presidential papers, more than 500 intricate model boats, 12,000 toy soldiers, and some of the oldest Monopoly game sets ever made. Perhaps the most memorable permanent display contains exquisite items created by the House of Fabergé, including 12 jeweled eggs designed for the last of the Russian czars. ⊠ *62 5th Ave., at 12th St.,* ☎ *212/206–5548.* ⛶ *Free.* ☾ *Tues.–Wed. and Fri.–Sat. 10–4.*

OFF THE BEATEN PATH

GANSEVOORT MARKET – Each morning otherwise undistinguished warehouse buildings become the meat market for the city's retailers and restaurants. Racks of carcasses make a fascinating, if not very pretty, sight. Action peaks on weekdays from 5 to 9 AM. ✉ *Between 9th Ave. and the Hudson River, from Gansevoort St. north to 14th St.*

Gay Street. A curved lane lined with small row houses circa 1810, one-block-long Gay Street was originally a black neighborhood and later a strip of speakeasies. In the 1930s the short thoroughfare and nearby Christopher Street became famous nationwide when Ruth McKinney published her autobiographical stories in the *New Yorker,* based on what happened when she and her sister moved to Greenwich Village from Ohio. McKinney created her somewhat zany tales in the basement of No. 14, and they appeared in book form as *My Sister Eileen* in 1938. Also on Gay Street, Howdy Doody was designed in the basement of No. 12. ✉ *Between Christopher St. and Waverly Pl.*

③ Grey Art Gallery. On the east side of Washington Square, New York University's main building contains a welcoming street-level space with changing exhibitions usually focusing on contemporary art. ✉ *100 Washington Sq. E,* ☎ *212/998–6780.* 🎟 *$2.50 (suggested donation).* ☉ *Sept.–July, Tues. and Thurs.–Fri. 11–6, Wed. 11–8:30, Sat. 11–5.*

⑮ Grove Court. This enclave of brick-front town houses was built between 1853 and 1854. Intended originally as apartments for employees at neighborhood hotels, Grove Court used to be called Mixed Ale Alley because of the residents' propensity to pool beverages brought from work. It now houses a more affluent crowd. ✉ *10–12 Grove St.*

⑰ Isaacs-Hendricks House. Originally built as a Federal-style wood-frame residence in 1799, this immaculate structure is the oldest remaining house in Greenwich Village. Its first owner, Joshua Issacs, a wholesale merchant, lost the farmhouse to creditors; the building then belonged to copper supplier Harmon Hendricks. The village landmark was remodeled twice; it received its brick face in 1836, and the third floor was added in 1928. ✉ *77 Bedford St., at Commerce St.*

⑧ Jefferson Market Library. Critics variously termed this magnificent towered courthouse's hodgepodge of styles Venetian, Victorian, or Italian; Villagers, noting the alternating wide bands of red brick and narrow strips of granite, dubbed it the Lean Bacon Style. Over the years, the structure has housed a number of government agencies (public works, civil defense, census bureau, police academy); it was on the verge of demolition when public-spirited citizens saved it and turned it into a public library in 1967. Note the fountain at the corner of West 10th Street and 6th Avenue, and the seal of the City of New York on the east front; inside, look at the handsome interior doorways and climb the graceful circular stairway. If the gate is open, visit the flower garden behind the library, a project run by local green thumbs. ✉ *425 6th Ave., at 10th St.,* ☎ *212/243–4334.*

④ Judson Memorial Church. Designed by celebrated architect Stanford White, this Italian Roman-Renaissance church has long attracted a congregation interested in the arts and community activism. Funded by the Astor family and John D. Rockefeller and constructed in 1892, the yellow brick and limestone building was the brainchild of Edward Judson, who hoped to reach out to the poor immigrants in adjacent Little Italy. The church has stained-glass windows designed by John LaFarge and a 10-story campanile. ✉ *51–54 Washington Sq. S, at Thompson St.,* ☎ *212/477–0351.*

⑨ Northern Dispensary. Constructed for $4,700 in 1831, this triangular Georgian brick building originally served as a health-care clinic for indigent Villagers. Edgar Allan Poe was a frequent patient. In more recent times, the structure has housed a dental clinic and a nursing home for AIDS patients. While the Dispensary has one side on two streets (Grove and Christopher where they meet), it has two sides facing one street—Waverly Place, which splits in two directions. ⊠ *165 Waverly Pl.*

Patchin Place. This charming cul-de-sac off 10th Street (between Greenwich and 6th Aves.) has 10 miniature row houses dating from 1848. Around the corner on 6th Avenue is a similar dead-end street, **Milligan Place,** consisting of four small homes completed in 1852. The houses in both quiet enclaves were originally built for the waiters (mostly Basques) who worked at the high-society Brevoort Hotel, long ago demolished, on 5th Avenue. Patchin Place later became home to several writers, including Theodore Dreiser, e.e. cummings, Jane Bowles, and Djuna Barnes. John Reed and Louise Bryant also lived there. Milligan Place eventually became the address for several playwrights, including Eugene O'Neill.

★ ❷ **The Row.** Built from 1829 through 1839, this series of beautifully preserved Greek Revival town houses along Washington Square North (on the two blocks between University Pl. and MacDougal St.) once belonged to merchants and bankers; now the buildings serve as New York University offices and faculty housing. Developers were not so tactful when they demolished 18 Washington Square North, once the home of Henry James's grandmother, which he later used as the setting for his novel *Washington Square* (Henry himself was born just off the square, in a long-gone house on Washington Place). The oldest building on the block, 20 Washington Square North, was constructed in 1829 in the Federal style. Notice its Flemish bond brickwork—alternate bricks inserted with the smaller surface (headers) facing out—which before 1830 was considered the best way to build stable walls. ⊠ *1–13 Washington Sq. N, between University Pl. and 5th Ave.; 19–26 Washington Sq. N, between 5th Ave. and MacDougal St.*

★ ㉑ **St. Luke's-in-the-Fields.** The first warden of St. Luke's, which was constructed in 1822 as a country chapel for downtown's Trinity Church, was Clement (" 'Twas the Night Before Christmas") Clarke Moore, who figured so largely in Chelsea's history (☞ Chelsea, *above*). An unadorned structure of soft-colored brick, the chapel was nearly destroyed by fire in 1981, but a flood of donations, many quite small, from residents of the West Village financed restoration of the square central tower. Bret Harte once lived at 487 Hudson Street (today the St. Luke's Parish House), at the end of the row. The Barrow Street Garden on the chapel grounds is worth visiting. ⊠ *485 Hudson St., between Barrow and Christopher Sts.*

★ ㉓ **St. Luke's Place.** This often peaceful street has 15 classic Italianate brownstone and brick town houses (1852–53), shaded by graceful gingko trees. Novelist Theodore Dreiser wrote *An American Tragedy* at No. 16, and poet Marianne Moore resided at No. 14. Mayor Jimmy Walker (first elected in 1926) lived at No. 6; the lampposts in front are "mayor's lamps," which were sometimes placed in front of the residences of New York mayors. This block is often used as a film location, too: No. 12 was shown as the Huxtables' home on *The Cosby Show* (although the family supposedly lived in Brooklyn), and No. 4 was the setting of the Audrey Hepburn movie *Wait Until Dark*. Before 1890 the playground on the south side of the street was a graveyard where, according to legend, the dauphin of France—the lost son of Louis XVI and Marie Antoinette—is buried. ⊠ *Between Hudson St. and 7th Ave. S.*

NEED A
BREAK?

At the corner of Hudson Street and St. Luke's Place, the **Anglers and Writers Café** (⊠ 420 Hudson St., ☎ 212/675–0810) lives up to its name with bookshelves, fishing tackle, and pictures of Door County, Wisconsin, hung on the walls. Weary wanderers may linger over a pot of tea and a slice of cake for an hour or so, absorbing the place's restful charm.

⑬ **17 Grove Street.** William Hyde, a prosperous window-sash maker, built this clapboard residence in 1822; a third floor was added in 1870. Hyde added a workshop behind the house in 1833. The building has since served many functions; it housed a brothel during the Civil War. The structure is the Village's largest remaining wood-frame house. ⊠ *17 Grove St., at Bedford St.*

⑱ **75½ Bedford Street.** Rising real-estate rates inspired the construction of New York City's narrowest house—just 9½ ft wide—in 1873. It was built on a lot that was originally a carriage entrance of the Isaacs-Hendricks House next door. Several celebrities have resided in this sliver of a building, including actor John Barrymore and poet Edna St. Vincent Millay, who wrote the Pulitzer Prize–winning *Ballad of the Harp-Weaver* during her stay here from 1923 to 1924. ⊠ *75½ Bedford St., between Commerce and Morton Sts.*

⑫ **Sheridan Square.** At one time an unused asphalt space, this lovely green triangle was recently landscaped following an extensive dig by urban archaeologists, who unearthed artifacts dating back to the Dutch and Native American eras. ⊠ *Bordered by Washington Pl. and W. 4th, Barrow, and Grove Sts.*

⑭ **Twin Peaks.** In 1925 financier Otto Kahn gave money to a Village eccentric named Clifford Daily to remodel an 1835 house for artists' use. The building was whimsically altered with stucco, half-timbers, and the addition of a pair of steep roof peaks. The result was something that might be described as an ersatz Swiss chalet. ⊠ *102 Bedford St., between Grove and Christopher Sts.*

⑳ **Twin Sisters.** These attractive Federal-style brick homes connected by a walled garden were said to have been erected by a sea captain for two daughters who loathed each other. Historical record insists that they were built in 1831 and 1832 by a milkman who needed the two houses and an open courtyard for his work. The striking mansard roofs were added in 1873. ⊠ *39 and 41 Commerce St.*

★ **Washington Arch.** Designed by Stanford White, a wood version of Washington Arch was built in 1889 to commemorate the 100th anniversary of George Washington's presidential inauguration and was originally placed about half a block north of its present location. The arch was reproduced in marble in 1892, and the statues—*Washington at War* on the left, *Washington at Peace* on the right—were added in 1916 and 1918, respectively. The civilian version of Washington was the work of Alexander Stirling Calder, father of the renowned artist Alexander Calder. Bodybuilder Charles Atlas modeled for *Peace.* The arch is certainly one of the most photographed sites in Greenwich Village. ⊠ *Washington Sq. at south end of 5th Ave.*

Washington Mews. This cobblestone private street is lined on one side with the former stables of the houses on the Row on Washington Square North. Writer Walter Lippmann and artist-patron Gertrude Vanderbilt Whitney (founder of the Whitney Museum) once had homes in the mews; today it's mostly owned by New York University. ⊠ *Between 5th Ave. and University Pl.*

★ ❶ **Washington Square.** The highly popular 9½-acre park started out as a cemetery, principally for yellow-fever victims, and an estimated 10,000–22,000 bodies lie below. In the early 1800s it was a parade ground and the site of public executions; bodies dangled from a conspicuous Hanging Elm that still stands at the northwest corner of the square. Later Washington Square became the focus of a fashionable residential neighborhood and a center of outdoor activity. By the early 1980s, Washington Square had deteriorated into a tawdry place only a drug dealer could love. Then community activism motivated a police crackdown that sent the drug traffic elsewhere and made Washington Square somewhat more comfortable again for Frisbee players, street musicians, skateboarders, jugglers, stand-up comics, sitters, strollers, chess players, and a huge outdoor art fair each spring and fall. The park figures in Henry James's novel of the same name. ✉ *At south end of 5th Ave.*

㉒ **White Horse Tavern.** Built in 1880, this amiable bar with a black-painted front is housed in one of the city's few remaining wood-frame structures. Formerly a speakeasy and a seamen's tavern, the White Horse has been popular with artists and writers for decades; its best-known customer was Welsh poet Dylan Thomas who had a room named after him here after his death in 1953. This watering hole can become crowded on weekends with tourists and suburbanites, so come here during the week to get the true Village experience. ✉ *567 Hudson St., at 11th St.,* ☎ *212/243–9260.*

THE EAST VILLAGE

The gritty tenements of the East Village—an area bounded by 14th Street on the north, 4th Avenue or the Bowery on the west, Houston Street on the south, and the East River—provided inexpensive living places for artists, writers, and actors after real estate prices in SoHo (☞ SoHo and TriBeCa, *below*) zoomed sky-high in the 1980s. New residents brought in their wake new restaurants, shops, and somewhat cleaner streets, while the old East Villagers maintained the trappings of the counterculture. Longtime bastions of the arts, such as the theaters Classic Stage Company and LaMaMa, and St. Mark's-in-the-Bowery Church were joined by newer institutions such as PS 122, and several "hot" art galleries opened in narrow East Village storefronts. But the East Village scene lasted only a couple of years—just long enough to drive up rents substantially on some blocks, but not long enough to drive out all of the neighborhood's original residents. Today an interesting mix has survived: artistic types in black leather and longtime members of various immigrant enclaves, principally Polish, Ukrainian, and Slovene. More recent arrivals come from the Dominican Republic, Japan, and the Philippines. The neighborhood also has its share of homeless people and drug addicts (more so as you head deeper east into the run-down buildings along Avenues A, B, C, and D).

Numbers in the text correspond to numbers in the margin and on the Greenwich Village and the East Village map.

A Good Walk

Begin at the intersection of East 8th Street, 4th Avenue, and Astor Place, where you'll see two traffic islands. One of these contains an ornate cast-iron kiosk, a replica of a Beaux Arts subway entrance, which provides access to the **Astor Place Subway Station** ㉔. Go down into the station to see the authentically reproduced wall tiles with a beaver motif. On the other traffic island stands the **Alamo** ㉕, a huge black cube sculpted by Bernard Rosenthal.

Go straight east from the Alamo to **St. Mark's Place** ㉖, the name given to 8th Street in the East Village. This often crowded thoroughfare has long attracted assorted fringe elements—punks, hyperkinetic club-crawlers, and washed-out counterculturists.

Second Avenue, which St. Mark's crosses after one block, was called the **Yiddish Rialto** in the early part of this century. At this time several theaters between Houston and 14th streets presented Yiddish-language dramatic and musical productions. Two survivors from that period are the Orpheum (⊠ 126 2nd Ave., at 8th St.) and the former Yiddish Arts Theatre, now the multiscreen Village East Cinemas (⊠ 189 2nd Ave., at 12th St.).

Second Avenue is also home to a neighborhood landmark, **St. Mark's-in-the-Bowery Church** ㉗, a stately Episcopal church on the corner of 10th Street that serves as a community cultural center and public meeting hall. From in front of the church, you can take a quiet detour to investigate the facades of handsome redbrick row houses on Stuyvesant Street, which stretches southwest to 9th Street. If you continue north up 2nd Avenue from St. Mark's-in-the-Bowery Church, you'll reach the **Ukrainian Museum** ㉘ (⊠ 203 2nd Ave., between 12th and 13th Sts.), a modest upstairs gallery celebrating the cultural heritage of Ukraine.

Next, walk south on 2nd Avenue to 9th Street. At 135 2nd Avenue (between 9th St. and St. Mark's Pl.) is the **Ottendorfer Branch of the New York Public Library** ㉙. A leisurely stroll east on 9th Street from 2nd Avenue to Avenue A will take you past a number of cafés and small, friendly shops selling designer and vintage clothing, housewares, toys, herbs, leather goods, recordings, and much more. Among the stores worth your while are Dinosaur Hill (⊠ 306 9th St.) for children's toys and clothes; No More Eggs (⊠ 312 9th St.) for fabrics, pillows, and curtains; Mostly Bali (⊠ 324 9th St.) for Balinese art objects and puppets; Clayworks Pottery (⊠ 332 9th St.); Hoshoni (⊠ 309 E. 9th St.) for housewares designed by American Southwest artists; and Jan Eleni (⊠ 315 E. 9th St.) for 19th-century home accessories.

At the northeast corner of 1st Avenue and 9th Street stands PS 122 (⊠ 150 1st Ave.), a former public school building transformed into a complex of spaces for avant-garde entertainment. If you continue east on 9th Street or St. Mark's Place, you're heading toward **Alphabet City,** the area's nickname; here the avenues are named A, B, C, and D. St. Mark's Place between 1st Avenue and Avenue A is lined with inexpensive cafés catering to a late-night younger crowd. Across from St. Mark's Place on Avenue A is the recently renovated **Tompkins Square Park** ㉚, a fairly peaceful haven from busy street life and sightseeing.

Next, head back west and follow 7th Street away from the southwest corner of Tompkins Square Park, studying the mix of small stores and restaurants to get a reading on the neighborhood's culture-in-flux. Walking on 7th Street west toward 3rd Avenue, you'll pass **McSorley's Old Ale House** ㉛ (⊠ 15 E. 7th St.), one of New York's oldest bars. Just past McSorley's is **Surma, the Ukrainian Shop** ㉜ (⊠ 11 E. 7th St.), selling all sorts of Ukrainian-made goods. Across the street is the somewhat jarring sight of **St. George's Ukrainian Catholic Church** ㉝ (⊠ 16–20 7th St.), with its copper dome.

Across 3rd Avenue, the massive brownstone **Cooper Union Foundation Building** ㉞, a tuition-free school for artists, architects, and engineers, overlooks Cooper Square, a large open space. Across the street from the west side of the Cooper Union Building is the enormous Carl Fischer Music Store (⊠ 62 Cooper Sq.), where musicians select from an infinitude of sheet music and confer with the knowledgeable staff. Just south of this music store are the offices of the liberal downtown *Village Voice* newspaper (⊠ 36 Cooper Sq.).

If you're here from Sunday through Thursday, walk south on Cooper Square and turn left on 4th Street to visit the **Merchant's House Museum** ㉟ (⊠ 24 E. 4th St.), where 19th-century family life can be viewed thanks to the preservation of the original furnishings and architecture.

One block west of Cooper Square, you'll find Lafayette Street. The long block between East 4th Street and Astor Place contains on its east side a grand Italian Renaissance–style structure housing the New York Shakespeare Festival's **Joseph Papp Public Theater** ㊱ (⊠ 425 Lafayette St.); in the 19th century the city's first free library opened here. Across the street note the imposing marble Corinthian columns fronting **Colonnade Row** ㊲ (⊠ 428–434 Lafayette St.), a stretch of four 19th-century Greek Revival houses, whose facades are in need of a cleaning.

Walking north on Lafayette Street, you'll be back at Astor Place and the site of the Alamo, where you began your walk. West of Astor Place, you may choose to turn left (south) on Broadway to hit a trendy downtown shopping strip, with several clothing shops (some of them selling secondhand items); chain stores such as Star Magic and the Body Shop; and Tower Records. Above street level, the old warehouses here have mostly been converted into residential lofts.

Heading north on Broadway from Astor Place, you'll catch sight of the striking marble spire of **Grace Church** ㊳, a lovely Episcopal church on the corner of Broadway and 10th Street. If you continue north on the same side of the street as the church, you'll pass a few of the many antique stores in the area. You can end your walk at the popular **Strand Book Store** ㊴ (⊠ 828 Broadway, at 12th St.), the largest secondhand bookstore in the city and an absolutely necessary stop for anyone who loves to read.

TIMING
Allow about three hours for the walk. If you plan to stop at museums, add one hour, and at least another hour to browse in shops along the way. If you end your walk at the Strand Book Store, you may want to stop somewhere for coffee before perusing the bookshelves, which can easily take yet another hour of your time.

Sights to See

㉕   **Alamo.** Created by Bernard Rosenthal in 1967, this massive black cube made of steel was originally part of a temporary citywide exhibit, but it became a permanent installation thanks to a private donor. It was one of the first abstract sculptures in New York City to be placed in a public space. Balanced on a post, the "Cube," as it is locally known, rotates slowly when pushed. ⊠ *On traffic island at Astor Pl. and Lafayette St.*

Alphabet City. If you continue east on St. Mark's Place you'll see that the avenues are labeled with letters, not numbers, after you pass 1st Avenue. Until fairly recently, this area, nicknamed Alphabet City, meant a burned-out territory of slums and drug haunts, but some blocks and buildings were gentrified during the height of the East Village art scene in the mid-'80s. The reasonably priced restaurants with their bohemian atmosphere on St. Mark's Place and Avenue A (several of them serving ethnic cuisine) attract a large number of visitors "slumming it" from other parts of the city, as well as tourists. A close-knit Puerto Rican community lies east of Avenue A, lending a Latin flavor to many of the local dining spots and businesses. You'll also find a number of grungy bars, such as **Lakeside Lounge** (✉ 162–4 Ave. B, between 10th and 11th Sts.), and trendy, cheap cafés, such as **Alejandra's Adopt** (✉ 190 Ave. B, near 12th St.) and **Kate's Joint** (58 Ave. B, between 4th and 5th Sts.) ✉ *Alphabet City extends approximately from Ave. A to the East River, between 14th and Houston Sts.*

NEED A BREAK? **Old Devil Moon** (✉ 511 E. 12th St., ☎ 212/475–4357) is a delightfully snug, dimly lit hangout with whimsical decor where you can stop for a drink, snack, or something more substantial.

㉔ **Astor Place Subway Station.** At the entrance providing access to the uptown Subway 6 line, you'll find an ornate cast-iron replica of a Beaux Arts kiosk; at the beginning of this century, almost every IRT subway entrance resembled this one. If you descend into the station, you'll see authentically reproduced ceramic wall tiles of beavers, a reference to the fur trade that contributed to John Jacob Astor's fortune. Milton Glaser, a Cooper Union graduate, designed the station's attractive abstract murals. ✉ *On traffic island at 8th St. and 4th Ave.*

㊲ **Colonnade Row.** Marble Corinthian columns front this grand sweep of four Greek Revival mansions (originally nine) constructed in 1833, with stonework accomplished by Sing Sing penitentiary prisoners. Although sadly run-down today, in their time these once-elegant homes served as residences to millionaires John Jacob Astor and Cornelius Vanderbilt until they moved uptown. Writers Washington Irving, William Makepeace Thackeray, and Charles Dickens all stayed here at one time or another. Today three houses are occupied on street level by restaurants, while the northernmost building has the Astor Place Theatre as one of its residents. ✉ *428–434 Lafayette St., between Astor Pl. and E. 4th St.*

㉞ **Cooper Union Foundation Building.** This impressive high-rise brownstone dominates **Cooper Square,** a large open space situated where 3rd and 4th avenues merge into the Bowery. A statue of industrialist Peter Cooper, by Augustus Saint-Gaudens, presides over the square. Cooper founded this college in 1859 to provide a forum for public opinion and free technical education for the working class; it still offers tuition-free education in architecture, art, and engineering. Cooper Union was the first structure to be supported by steel railroad rails—rolled in Cooper's own plant. Two galleries in the building are open to the public, presenting changing exhibitions during the academic year. ✉ *E. 7th St. to Astor Pl., 4th Ave. to the Bowery at Cooper Sq. Galleries:* ☎ *212/353–4155.* 🎫 *Free.* 🕓 *Weekdays 11–7, Sat. noon–5.*

★ ㊳ **Grace Church.** Topped by a finely ornamented octagonal marble spire, this remarkable Episcopal church, designed by James Renwick Jr., has some excellent pre-Raphaelite stained-glass windows inside. The building—a fine mid-19th-century example of an English Gothic Revival church—fronts a small green yard facing Broadway. The church has been the site of many society weddings (including that of P. T. Barnum show member Tom Thumb). ✉ *802 Broadway, at E. 10th St.,* ☎ *212/254–2000.*

㊱ **Joseph Papp Public Theater.** In 1854 John Jacob Astor opened the city's first free library in this imposing redbrick Italian Renaissance–style building, which was renovated in 1967 as the Public Theater to serve as the permanent home of the New York Shakespeare Festival. The theater opened its doors with the popular rock musical *Hair.* Under the leadership of the late Joseph Papp, the Public's five playhouses built a fine reputation for bold and innovative performances; the long-running hit

A Chorus Line had its first performances here, but so have many less commercial plays. Today director and producer George Wolfe heads the Public, which continues to present controversial modern works and imaginative Shakespeare productions. ⊠ *425 Lafayette St.,* ☎ *212/260–2400.*

31 **McSorley's Old Ale House.** One of several claimants to the distinction of being New York's oldest bar, this often-crowded saloon attracts many collegiate types enticed by McSorley's own brands of ale. The mahogany bar, gas lamps, and potbelly stove all hark back to decades past. McSorley's opened in 1854 but didn't admit women until 1970. Joseph Mitchell immortalized the spot in short stories he wrote for the *New Yorker.* ⊠ *15 E. 7th St.,* ☎ *212/473–9138.*

35 **Merchant's House Museum.** Come here for a rare glimpse of family life in the mid-19th century. Built in 1831–32, this redbrick house, combining Federal and Greek Revival styles, was purchased in 1835 by Seabury Tredwell, a retired merchant, and remained the home of the Tredwell family from 1835 to 1933, when the last of the elderly Tredwell sisters died. The original furnishings and architectural features remain intact; family memorabilia are also on display. The Greek Revival–style parlors have 13-ft ceilings with intricate plaster work, free-standing Ionic columns, a mahogany pocket-door screen, and black marble fireplaces. Self-guided tour brochures are always available, and guided tours are given on Sunday. ⊠ *29 E. 4th St.,* ☎ *212/777–1089.* ▨ *$3.* ☉ *Sun.–Thurs. 1–4.*

29 **Ottendorfer Branch of the New York Public Library.** The first Manhattan building to be constructed as a free public library, this 1884 structure designed by William Schickel incorporates elements from several late Victorian styles; the early use of molded terra-cotta interior remains untouched. The rust-colored building dates from a time when the East Village was heavily populated by German immigrants, and was a gift from Oswald Ottendorfer, a rich German philanthropist and newspaper editor. It began as the German-language branch of the Free Circulating Library (hence the words "Freie Bibliothek und Lesehalle" on its facade) and eventually became part of the city's public library system. ⊠ *135 2nd Ave., near St. Mark's Pl.,* ☎ *212/674–0947.*

33 **St. George's Ukrainian Catholic Church.** Notable for its copper dome and the three brightly colored religious murals on its facade, this ostentatious modern church serves as a central meeting place for the old local Ukrainian population. Built in 1977, it took the place of the more modest Greek Revival–style St. George's Ruthenian Church. An annual Ukrainian folk festival occurs here in the spring. ⊠ *16–20 E. 7th St.,* ☎ *212/674–1615.*

27 **St. Mark's-in-the-Bowery Church.** A Greek Revival steeple and a cast-iron front porch were added to this 1799 fieldstone country church, which occupies the former site of the family chapel of the old Dutch governor Peter Stuyvesant. St. Mark's is the city's oldest continually used Christian church building (Stuyvesant and Commodore Perry are buried here). Its interior had to be completely restored after a disastrous fire in 1978, and stained-glass windows were added to the balcony in 1982. Over the years St. Mark's has hosted much countercultural activity. In the 1920s a forward-thinking pastor injected the Episcopal ritual with Native American chants, Greek folk dancing, and Eastern mantras. William Carlos Williams, Amy Lowell, and Carl Sandburg once read here, and Isadora Duncan, Houdini, and Merce Cunningham also performed here. During the hippie era, St. Mark's welcomed avant-garde poets and playwrights, including Sam Shepard. Today dancers, poets, and performance artists cavort in the main sanctuary, where pews have been removed to accommodate them. ⊠ *Corner of 2nd Ave. and E. 10th St.,* ☎ 212/674–6377.

NEED A BREAK? Bright and bustling **Veselka** (⊠ 144 2nd Ave., at 9th St., ☎ 212/228–9682), a longtime East Village favorite, serves bagels, muffins, Italian coffee, egg creams, and Ben & Jerry's ice cream alongside good, traditional Ukrainian fare such as borscht, kielbasa, and veal goulash.

㉖ St. Mark's Place. Starting at 3rd Avenue and going east, 8th Street changes its named to St. Mark's Place, the longtime hub of the hip East Village. During the 1950s, beatniks such as Allen Ginsberg and Jack Kerouac lived and wrote in the area; the 1960s brought Bill Graham's Fillmore East concerts, the Electric Circus, and hallucinogenic drugs. The black-clad, pink-haired, or shaved-head punks followed, and some remain today. St. Mark's Place between 2nd and 3rd avenues is lined with ethnic restaurants, jewelry stalls, leather shops, and stores selling books, posters, and eccentric clothing, although the arrival of a branch of the Gap seems to signal that this street has lost its countercultural relevance.

At 80 St. Mark's Place near 1st Avenue, you'll find the former location of the Theater 80 repertory movie house, now the home of the Pearl Theatre Company, which performs classic plays from around the world. Be sure to look down at the sidewalk, where you'll find the handprints, footprints, and autographs of such past screen luminaries as Joan Crawford, Ruby Keeler, Joan Blondell, and Myrna Loy.

At 96–98 St. Mark's Place (between 1st Ave. and Ave. A), if you take a look up on your right, you may recognize these facades from the cover of Led Zeppelin's *Physical Graffiti* album. The cafés between 1st Avenue and Avenue A attract customers late into the night.

★ **㉝ Strand Book Store.** Serious book lovers from around the world make pilgrimages to this secondhand book emporium with a stock of some 2 million volumes, including thousands of collector's items. (The slogan "Eight Miles of Books" calls out from the store's sign.) Opened in 1929 by Ben Bass, the Strand was originally found on 4th Avenue's Book Row until it moved to its present four-story location on Broadway in 1956. Review copies of new books sell for 50% off, and used books are often priced at much less. Don't be surprised if you wind up buying a book you weren't looking for; that's part of the fun of shopping here. ⊠ *828 Broadway, at 12th St.,* ☎ 212/473–1452.

★ **Stuyvesant Street.** This short thoroughfare between 2nd and 3rd Avenues angles southwest back to 9th Street. The area was once Governor Stuyvesant's "bouwerie," or farm; among the handsome redbrick row houses are the Federal-style **Stuyvesant-Fish House** (⊠ 21 Stuyvesant St.), which was built in 1804 as a wedding gift for a great-great-granddaughter of the governor, and **Renwick Triangle,** an attractive group of carefully restored one- and two-story brick and brownstone residences originally constructed in 1861. At press time, the George Hecht Viewing Gardens were being constructed at 3rd Avenue and 9th Street, with one side of the gardens bordering Stuyvesant Street.

㉜ Surma, the Ukrainian Shop. The exotic stock at this charming little store includes Ukrainian books, magazines, cassettes, and greeting cards, as well as musical instruments, painted eggs, and an exhaustive collection of peasant blouses. ⊠ *11 E. 7th St.,* ☎ 212/477–0729.

㉚ Tompkins Square Park. This leafy oasis amid crowded apartment buildings received a much-needed renovation in 1992, making it a pleasant place to sit on a bench on a sunny afternoon. Several times old and new East Villagers have clashed around the park vicinity. The square's well-established tent city of homeless people provided the spark in the summers of 1988 and 1989, as police moved to rid the park of vagrants, and neighborhood residents vociferously took sides. Riots broke out, and tempers ran high. The homeless people have since moved on.

East of the park at 151 Avenue B (near 9th St.) stands an 1849 four-story white-painted brownstone, where renowned jazz musician Charlie Parker lived from 1950 to 1954. On the northwest corner of Avenue B and 10th Street is the **Life Cafe,** a frequently busy local hangout that is featured in the hit Broadway musical *Rent*. ⊠ *Tompkins Square Park: bordered by Aves. A and B and 7th and 10th Sts.*

㉘ Ukrainian Museum. At this small upstairs gallery, the cultural heritage of Ukraine is celebrated. Now that this country has become independent again, there's something especially poignant about this collection, nurtured in exile throughout the years of Soviet domination: ceramics, jewelry, hundreds of brilliantly colored Easter eggs, and an extensive collection of Ukrainian costumes and textiles. ⊠ *203 2nd Ave., between 12th and 13th Sts.,* ☏ *212/228–0110.* 🎟 *$1.* ☺ *Wed.–Sun. 1–5.*

Yiddish Rialto. Second Avenue in the East Village was known in the early part of this century as the Yiddish Rialto. Between Houston and 14th streets, eight theaters presented Yiddish-language productions of musicals, revues, and heart-wrenching melodramas. Two theaters from that golden era remain: the **Orpheum** (⊠ 126 2nd Ave.), still a legitimate playhouse, and the neo-Moorish Yiddish Arts Theatre, now the renovated multiscreen **Village East Cinemas** (⊠ 189 2nd Ave., at 12th St.), which has preserved the original ornate ceiling. Also, in front of the **Second Avenue Deli** (⊠ 2nd Ave. and 10th St.), Hollywood-style squares have been embedded in the sidewalk to commemorate Yiddish stage luminaries.

NEED A BREAK?	The East Village has some of the best Italian pastries in the city. **De Robertis Pasticceria** (⊠ 176 1st Ave., between 10th and 11th Sts., ☏ 212/674-7137) offers exceptional cheesecake and cappuccinos in its original 1904 setting, complete with glistening mosaic tiles. Opened in 1894, the popular **Veniero Pasticceria** (⊠ 342 E. 11th St., ☏ 212/674-7264) has rows and rows of incredibly fresh cannoli, fruit tarts, cheesecakes, cookies, and other desserts on display in glass cases; there's a separate café section.

SOHO AND TRIBECA

Today the names of these two downtown neighborhoods are virtually synonymous with a certain eclectic elegance—an amalgam of black-clad artists, young Wall Streeters, track-lit loft apartments, hip art galleries, and restaurants with a minimalist approach to both food and decor. It's all very urban, very cool, very now.

Twenty-five years ago, they were virtual wastelands. SoHo (so named because it is the district *S*outh of *Ho*uston Street, bounded by Broadway, Canal Street, and 6th Avenue) was regularly referred to as "Hell's Hundred Acres" because of the many fires that raged through the untended warehouses crowding the area. It was saved by two factors: (1) preservationists here discovered the world's greatest concentration of cast-iron architecture and fought to prevent demolition; and (2) artists discovered the large, cheap, well-lit spaces that cast-iron buildings provide.

All the rage between 1860 and 1890, cast-iron buildings were popular because they did not require massive walls to bear the weight of the upper stories. Since there was no need for load-bearing walls, these buildings had more interior space and larger windows. They were also versatile, with various architectural elements produced from standardized molds to mimic any style—Italianate, Victorian Gothic, neo-Grecian, to name but a few visible in SoHo. At first it was technically illegal for artists to live in their loft studios, but so many did that eventually the zoning laws were changed to permit residence.

By 1980 SoHo's galleries, trendy shops, and cafés, together with its marvelous cast-iron buildings and vintage Belgian-block pavements (the 19th-century successor to traditional cobblestones), had made SoHo such a desirable residential area that only the most successful artists could afford it. Seeking similar space, artists moved downtown to another half-abandoned industrial district, for which a new, SoHo-like name was invented: TriBeCa (the *Tri*angle *Be*low *Ca*nal Street), although in effect it goes no farther south than Murray Street and no farther east than West Broadway). The same scenario played itself out again, and TriBeCa's rising rents are already beyond the means of most artists, who have moved instead to west Chelsea, Long Island City, areas of Brooklyn, or New Jersey. But despite their gentrification, SoHo and TriBeCa retain some of their gritty bohemianism—one local store terms it shabby chic—that has come to dominate the downtown scene. In the case of SoHo, however, the arrival of large chain stores such as Pottery Barn and J. Crew has given some blocks the feeling of an outdoor suburban shopping mall.

Numbers in the text correspond to numbers in the margin and on the SoHo, TriBeCa, Little Italy, Chinatown map.

A Good Walk

Starting at Houston (pronounced *how*-ston) Street, walk south down Broadway, stopping at the many museums that crowd both sides of the street between Houston and Prince streets. The most noteworthy of these is the **Guggenheim Museum SoHo** ①, which opened in 1992—but also worthwhile are the **Alternative Museum** ②, whose political and sociopolitical themes make for lively discussion; the **Museum for African Art** ③, whose handsome two-story building complements its high-quality exhibits; and the **New Museum of Contemporary Art** ④, which is devoted exclusively to living artists. Several art galleries (☞ Chapter 10) share these blocks as well, most notably at 586 Broadway, which has 10 galleries and the trendy Armani Exchange store on the ground level.

Just south of Prince Street, 560 Broadway on the east side of the block is another popular exhibit space, home to 18 galleries. Across the street, the 1907 Singer Building (✉ 561 Broadway) shows the final flower of the cast-iron style, with wrought-iron balconies, terra-cotta panels, and broad expanses of windows. On the bottom floor of this building is Kate's Paperie, where handmade paper is elevated to a high art form.

If you have youngsters with you, take them over to the **Children's Museum of the Arts** ⑤ at 72 Spring Street between Crosby and Lafayette streets. The exhibits here are largely interactive and should provide a welcome respite from SoHo's mostly grown-up pursuits.

108

SoHo, TriBeCa, Little Italy, Chinatown

Leroy St.

Downing St.

Clarkson St.

1,9 M

Ave. of the Americas (Sixth Ave.)

MacDougal St.

Sullivan St.

**GREENWICH
VILLAGE**

W. Houston St.

Hudson St.

King St.

Varick St.

Charlton St.

C,E M

Washington St.

Vandam St.

Spring St.

Dominick St.

Broome St.

Holland Tunnel
Entrance

Thompson St.

Canal St.

1,9 M

A,C,E M

Watts St.

Holland Tunnel
Exit

Varick St.

Desbrosses St.

Greenwich St.

Vestry St.

Laight St.

Ericsson Pl.

Hubert St.

West St.

N. Moore St.

12 Franklin St.

TRIBECA

Jay St.

Staple St.

Harrison St.

11

13

14

1,2,3,9

Stuyvesant
High School ■

Chambers St. M

15

Warren St.

Murray St.

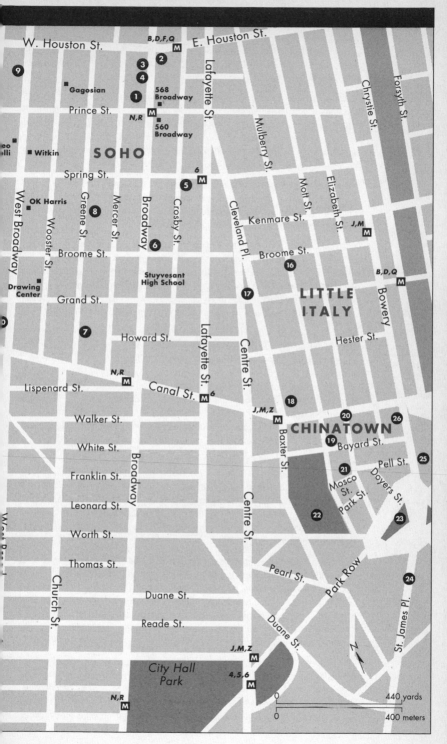

W. Houston St.

B,D,F,Q

E. Houston St.

9

3

2

4

1

Gagosian

568 Broadway

Prince St.

N,R

560 Broadway

Witkin

SOHO

Spring St.

6

5

West Broadway

OK Harris

Greene St.

8

Mercer St.

Broadway

Crosby St.

6

Broome St.

Wooster St.

Stuyvesant High School

Drawing Center

Grand St.

7

Howard St.

Lispenard St.

N,R

Canal St.

6

Walker St.

White St.

Broadway

Franklin St.

Leonard St.

Worth St.

Thomas St.

Church St.

Duane St.

Reade St.

J,M,Z

City Hall Park

4,5,6

N,R

Lafayette St.

Mulberry St.

Mott St.

Elizabeth St.

J,M

Kenmare St.

Cleveland Pl.

Broome St.

16

LITTLE ITALY

17

Hester St.

Centre St.

18

J,M,Z

CHINATOWN

20

26

19

Bayard St.

25

21

Pell St.

Mosco St.

Doyers St.

Park St.

22

23

Pearl St.

Park Row

24

Duane St.

St. James Pl.

Chrystie St.

Forsyth St.

Bowery

B,D,Q

Baxter St.

N

440 yards

0

400 meters

0

One block south (downtown) of the Singer Building, between Spring and Broome streets, a cluster of lofts that were originally part of the 1897 New Era Building (✉ 495 Broadway) boast an Art Nouveau copper mansard; La Boulangère bakery now resides on the street level. At the northeast corner of Broadway and Broome Street is the **Haughwout Building** ⑥, a restored classic of the cast-iron genre.

At the southeast corner of Broadway and Broome Street, note, at 486 Broadway, the Romanesque and Moorish Revival building with half-round brick arches; this is the former Mechanics and Traders Bank. At the northwest corner of Broadway and Grand Street, the popular SoHo Antiques Fair draws about 100 dealers to sell everything from used bicycles to vintage posters and prints on weekends from 9 to 5.

For a taste of pre-gentrified SoHo, detour west from Broadway to Mercer Street or east to Crosby Street, where Belgian street pavers, multiple loading docks, and a patchwork of fire escapes recall the days when these streets were used as service thoroughfares.

Go west from Broadway on Grand Street (passing designer Yoshi Yamamoto's store at 103 Grand Street) to **Greene Street,** where cast-iron buildings abound, such as the **Queen of Greene Street** ⑦ and the **King of Greene Street** ⑧. Also, several of SoHo's better exhibition spaces run by younger and more innovative dealers and artists are clustered on the southern end of Greene and Wooster streets near Grand Street.

Walking north on Greene Street, you can visit some of SoHo's best or soon-to-be-best galleries: David Zwirner (✉ 43 Greene St.), Laurie Wittels and Andre Zarre (✉ 48 Greene St.), Jack Tilton (✉ 49 Greene St.), and Boesky & Callery (✉ 51 Greene St.) for starters. For a look at one of the city's most artful retail stores, head to Zona (✉ 97 Greene St.); next door, Shabby Chic (✉ 97 Greene St.) defines the style so prevalent in this upscale bohemian neighborhood. Across the street, look at Arkitektura (✉ 96 Greene St.) for quality art deco reproductions, and Equator (✉ 98 Greene St.) for Indonesian and Thai furniture.

Greene Street between Prince and Spring streets is notable for the SoHo Building (✉ 104–110 Greene St.); towering 13 stories, it is SoHo's tallest building. On this block you'll also find Anna Sui (✉ 113 Greene St.), a boutique whose pricey avant-garde fashions are among New York's most cutting-edge. At Prince Street, walk one block west to Wooster Street, which, like a few other SoHo streets, still has its original Belgian pavers.

Going south on Wooster, shoppers will find a retail paradise in the blocks between Prince and Spring streets—most notably the whimsical Todd Oldham boutique (✉ 123 Wooster St.), Simon Pearce (✉ 120 Wooster St.) for fine glassware, and Comme des Garçons (✉ 116 Wooster St.), where high-style fashions are sold in a spartan setting. Also in this vicinity is one of Manhattan's finest photography galleries, Howard Greenberg (✉ 120 Wooster St.)

Proceeding even farther south on Wooster, between Broome and Grand streets and Grand and Canal streets, you'll find more art worth checking out at the Drawing Center (✉ 35 Wooster St.), Spencer Brownstone (✉ 39 Wooster St.), and Basilico Fine Arts and Friedrich Petzel (✉ 26 Wooster St.). Right nearby, between Wooster and Greene streets, also stop at Deitch Projects (✉ 76 Grand St.).

Now head back north on Wooster Street to the blocks between West Houston and Prince streets. Here you may investigate the **New York Earth Room** ⑨ and the Gagosian Gallery (✉ 136 Wooster St.), operated by prominent uptown dealer Larry Gagosian.

From Wooster Street, walk one block west on Prince Street to SoHo's main drag, West Broadway, whose range of galleries and stores puts other streets to shame. In the block between Prince and Spring streets alone, you'll find Nancy Hoffman (⊠ 429 W. Broadway); the gallery complex at 415 West Broadway, which includes the Witkin Gallery for photography; and 420 West Broadway, with six separate galleries, including two of the biggest SoHo names, Leo Castelli and the Sonnabend Gallery.

Continue south on West Broadway to the blocks between Spring and Broome streets, where you'll find Robert Lee Morris (⊠ 400 W. Broadway), carrying the designer's jewelry, handbags, and home accessories; the immense OK Harris art gallery (⊠ 383 W. Broadway); and Smith & Hawken (⊠ 392 W. Broadway), a gardener's emporium. Stay on West Broadway on the west side of the street and proceed south; between Grand and Canal streets stands the **SoHo Grand Hotel** ⑩, the first major hotel to be built in the neighborhood since the 1880s.

From here, TriBeCa is less than one block away; just follow West Broadway south to Canal Street, the neighborhood's official boundary. Stop to marvel at the life-size iron Statue of Liberty crown rising above the kitschy blue-tiled entrance to El Teddy's (⊠ 219 W. Broadway), a gourmet Mexican restaurant. Continue south to Duane Street to reach the calm, shady **Duane Park** ⑪. Two blocks north, Worth Street was once the center of the garment trade, the 19th-century equivalent of today's 7th Avenue. The area to the west, near the Hudson River docks, became the heart of the wholesale food business; a few wholesalers such as Bazzini's (☞ *below*) still remain.

Back on West Broadway, walk one block north on Hudson Street. On your right you'll see the Art Deco Western Union Building (⊠ 60 Hudson St.), where 19 subtly shaded colors of brick are laid in undulating patterns. Turn left from Hudson Street onto quiet Jay Street and pause at narrow Staple Street, whose green pedestrian walkway overhead links two warehouses. If you continue west on Jay Street you'll pass the loading docks of a 100-year-old food wholesaler, Bazzini's Nuts and Confections, where an upscale retail shop peddles nuts, coffee beans, and candies; there are also a few tables where you can enjoy a light snack.

On Greenwich Street at Franklin Street you'll find actor Robert De Niro's trendy restaurant, the Tribeca Grill; the same building houses the **Tribeca Film Center** ⑫, also owned by De Niro. As you walk south down Greenwich Street, notice on your right a surprising row of early 19th-century town houses nestled in the side of **Independence Plaza** ⑬, a huge high-rise apartment complex. Continuing south on Greenwich Street, you'll soon come to the 2½-acre **Washington Market Park** ⑭, a pleasant, landscaped oasis.

At the corner of the park, turn west on Chambers Street, heading west toward the Hudson River. A five-minute walk will bring you to the overpass across the West Side Highway. Here, behind the huge Stuyvesant High School building, you'll reach the north end of the recently landscaped **Hudson River Park** ⑮, a great place for a peaceful stroll.

TIMING

To see SoHo and TriBeCa at their liveliest, visit on a Saturday, when the fashionable art crowd is joined by smartly dressed uptowners and suburbanites who come down for a little shopping and gallery hopping. If you want to avoid crowds, take this walk during the week. Keep in mind that most galleries are closed on Sunday and Monday. If you allow time for leisurely browsing in several galleries and museums, as well as a stop for lunch, this tour can easily take up to an entire day.

Sights to See

② **Alternative Museum.** This small museum exhibits art with a sociopolitical twist, addressing issues such as homelessness, media manipulation, and gender stereotypes. ⊠ *594 Broadway, near E. Houston St.,* ☎ *212/966–4444.* ⌷ *$3 (suggested donation).* ☾ *Tues.–Sat. 11–6.*

OFF THE BEATEN PATH

CHARLTON STREET – The city's longest stretch of redbrick town houses preserved from the 1820s and 1830s runs along the north side of this street (west of 6th Ave. and south of W. Houston St.), with high stoops, paneled front doors, leaded-glass windows, and narrow dormer windows all intact. While you're here, stroll along parallel King and Vandam streets for more fine Federal houses. This quiet enclave was once an estate called Richmond Hill, whose various residents included George Washington, John and Abigail Adams, and Aaron Burr.

---

⑤ **Children's Museum of the Arts.** In a loftlike space in SoHo, children ages 1 to 10 have the chance to become actively involved in visual and performing arts. They can play with brightly colored balls, draw on a computer, read in a special corner, and have fun in an art workshop. ⊠ *72 Spring St.,* ☎ *212/941–9198.* ⌷ *$4 weekdays, $5 weekends.* ☾ *Tues.–Fri. noon–6, weekends 11–5.*

⑪ **Duane Park.** Preserved since 1800 as a calm, shady triangle, this little urban oasis is still surrounded by cheese, butter, and egg warehouses. ⊠ *Bordered by Hudson, Duane, and Staple Sts.*

NEED A BREAK?

For a real New York story, duck into the **Odeon** (⊠ 145 W. Broadway, ☎ 212/233–0507), an art deco restaurant-bar. With black-and-red banquettes, chrome mirrors, neon-lit clocks, and ceiling fans, this place has a distinctively slick atmosphere. Come for a drink at the bar or a snack anytime from noon to 2 AM.

Greene Street. Cast-iron architecture is at its finest here; the block between Canal and Grand streets (⊠ 8–34 Greene St.) represents the longest row of cast-iron buildings anywhere. Handsome as they are, these buildings were always commercial, containing stores and light manufacturing, principally textiles. Along this street notice the iron loading docks and the sidewalk vault covers that lead into basement storage areas. Two standout buildings on Greene Street are the so-called ☞ **Queen of Green Street** and the ☞ **King of Greene Street.** Even the lampposts on Greene Street are architectural gems: Note their turn-of-the-century bishop's-crook style, adorned with various cast-iron curlicues from their bases to their curved tops.

NEED A BREAK?

Space Untitled Espresso Bar (⊠ 133 Greene St., near W. Houston St., ☎ 212/260–6677) serves all kinds of coffee, tea, sweets, and lunch sandwiches, as well as wine and beer, in a minimalist gallery setting.

---

① **Guggenheim Museum SoHo.** Since it opened in 1992, this downtown branch of the uptown museum has displayed a revolving series of exhibitions, both contemporary work and pieces from the Guggenheim's permanent collection. The museum occupies space in a landmark 19th-century redbrick structure with its original cast-iron storefronts and detailed cornice. Arata Isozaki designed the two floors of stark, loftlike galleries as well as the museum store facing Broadway. ⊠ *575 Broadway, at Prince St.,* ☎ *212/423–3500.* ⌷ *$6.* ☾ *Wed.–Fri. and Sun. 11–6, Sat. 11–8.*

NEED A
BREAK? Diagonally across from the Guggenheim Museum SoHo, **Dean & DeLuca** (✉ 560 Broadway, at Prince St., ☎ 212/431–1691), the gourmet emporium, brews superb coffee and tea, but it gets crowded fast.

❻ Haughwout Building. Nicknamed the Parthenon of Cast Iron, this Venetian palazzo–style structure was built in 1857 to house Eder Haughwout's china and glassware business. Inside, the building once contained the world's first commercial passenger elevator, a steam-powered device invented by Elisha Graves Otis. ✉ *488 Broadway, at Broome St.*

★ **❶❺ Hudson River Park.** A landscaped oasis with playgrounds, promenades and walkways, handball and basketball courts, and grassy areas, this park on the river at the corner of Chambers and West streets and north of the World Financial Center is strewn with downtown residents soaking up rays on sunny days. **The Real World** sculpture garden at its north end, by Tom Otterness, playfully pokes fun at the area's capitalist ethos. The fairly new Stuyvesant High School building is also at this end of the park; on the far side of it begins the paved river promenade that extends to Gansevoort Street in the West Village. The promenade is full of skaters, joggers, and strollers at all hours, and the benches along the path are terrific spots from which to watch the sunset over New Jersey. You'll notice the small **Hudson River Sculpture Center** at Pier 25. These pieces are exhibited by local artists—unrepresented elsewhere—and are available for sale. For information about the sculpture, call Stephen Mann at 212/587–1030. The park is part of plans for an even larger park to extend north to midtown, managed by the Hudson River Park Conservancy.

❶❸ Independence Plaza. These high-rise towers at the intersection of Greenwich and Harrison streets are the fruit of a pleasant, if somewhat utilitarian, project of the mid-1970s that was supposed to be part of a wave of demolition and construction—until the preservationists stepped in. For several years Independence Plaza remained a middle-class island stranded downtown, far from stores, schools, and neighbors. With TriBeCa's increasingly chic reputation, however, plus the development of Battery Park City to the south, it has become a much more desirable address.

The three-story redbrick houses that share Harrison Street with Independence Plaza were moved here from various sites in the neighborhood when, in the early 1970s, the food wholesalers' central market nearby was razed and moved to the Bronx. ✉ *Greenwich St. between Duane and N. Moore Sts.*

❽ King of Greene Street. This five-story Renaissance-style 1873 building has a magnificent projecting porch of Corinthian columns and pilasters. Today the King (now painted ivory) houses the M-13 art gallery, Alice's Antiques, and Bennison Fabrics. ✉ *72–76 Greene St., between Spring and Broome Sts.*

❸ Museum for African Art. Dedicated to contemporary and traditional African art, this small but expertly conceived museum is housed in a handsome two-story space designed by Maya Lin, who also designed the Vietnam Veterans Memorial in Washington, D.C. Exhibits may include contemporary sculpture, ceremonial masks, architectural details, costumes, and textiles. The entertaining museum store features African crafts, clothing, and jewelry. ✉ *593 Broadway, near Houston St.*, ☎ *212/966–1313.* 🎫 *$4.* ☉ *Tues.–Fri. 10:30–5:30, weekends noon–6.*

❹ New Museum of Contemporary Art. The avant-garde exhibitions here, all by living artists, are often radically innovative and socially conscious. Past exhibitions have included "alt.youth.media," in which video-tapes, Web sites, and interactive computer projects explored issues concerning today's youths; and "A Labor of Love," in which the handmade folk and craft works of more than 40 contemporary artists were meant to question the definition of high art. ⊠ *583 Broadway, between Houston and Prince Sts.,* ☎ *212/219–1222.* ⊡ *$4; free Sat. 6 PM–8 PM.* ☉ *Wed.–Fri. and Sun. noon–6, Sat. noon–8.*

❾ New York Earth Room. Walter de Maria's 1980 avant-garde work consists of 140 tons of gently sculpted soil (22 inches deep) filling 3,600 square ft of space of a second-floor gallery. ⊠ *141 Wooster St., between Houston and Prince Sts.,* ☎ *212/473–8072.* ⊡ *Free.* ☉ *Jan.–mid-June and mid-Sept.–Dec., Wed.–Sat. noon–6.*

❼ Queen of Greene Street. The regal grace of this 1873 cast-iron beauty is exemplified by its dormers, columns, window arches, projecting central bays, and Second Empire roof. ⊠ *28–30 Greene St., between Grand and Canal Sts.*

❿ SoHo Grand Hotel. The first major hotel to appear in the area since the 1800s, the immaculate 15-story SoHo Grand opened its doors in August 1996; it has already attracted such film celebrities as Meryl Streep and Al Pacino, as well as guests who work in the fashion, advertising, design, and arts communities. The owners, Hartz Mountain Industries, hired a SoHo architect (David Helpern) and interior designer (William Sofield) to create a building that would pay tribute to the neighborhood's architectural history, particularly the cast-iron historic district.

At the entrance you encounter Manhattan's only "dog bar," a 17-century French stone basin that signals that this property welcomes pets. Enormous redbrick sculpted columns anchor the large two-level lobby. An impressive staircase—made of translucent bottle glass and iron and suspended from the ceiling by two cables—links the entryway with the second-floor, 7,000-square-ft lobby. After a long day of walking the SoHo streets, you can enjoy a refreshment as you relax on one of the oversize sofas and chairs in the lobby lounge. You're sure to admire the lobby's 16-ft-high windows covered in sheer muslin and velvet drapes, the pine tusk tables, the William Morris textiles covering the furniture, the handmade bronze and mica lanterns, and the massive stone columns supporting the paneled mercury mirror ceiling. The classy Canal Room serves memorable regional American cuisine (three meals a day), and you can also socialize in the inviting wood-paneled Grand Bar. ⊠ *310 W. Broadway, at Grand St.,* ☎ *212/965–3000.*

NEED A BREAK?

For a taste of SoHo shabby chic, head for **Scharmann's** (⊠ 386 W. Broadway, between Spring and Broome Sts., ☎ 212/219-2561), where the hip drink tea from gleaming brass pots on oversize couches, mismatched chairs, and a bean bag or two.

Staple Street. Little more than an alley, Staple Street was named for the staple products unloaded here by ships in transit that didn't want to pay duty on any extra cargo. Framed at the end of the alley is the redbrick **New York Mercantile Exchange**, its square corner tower topped by a bulbous roof. On the ground floor is the acclaimed French restaurant Chanterelle.

⑫ Tribeca Film Center. Robert De Niro created this complex of editing, screening, and production rooms, where Miramax Films, Stephen Spielberg, Quincy Jones, and De Niro himself keep offices. Like many of the other chic buildings in this area, it's inside a former factory, the old Coffee Building. On the ground floor is the trendy Tribeca Grill restaurant, also owned by Robert De Niro. ⊠ *375 Greenwich St., between Franklin and N. Moore Sts.*

⑭ **Washington Market Park.** This much-needed recreation space for TriBeCa was named after the great food market that once sprawled over the area. It is now a green, landscaped oasis with a playground and a gazebo. Just across Chambers Street from the park, **PS 234,** a public elementary school, has opened to serve TriBeCa's younger generation. At the corner, a stout little red tower resembles a lighthouse, and iron ship figures are worked into the playground fence—reminders of the neighborhood's long-gone dockside past. ⊠ *Greenwich St. between Chambers and Duane Sts.*

LITTLE ITALY AND CHINATOWN

Mulberry Street is the heart of Little Italy; in fact, at this point it's virtually the entire body. In 1932 an estimated 98% of the inhabitants of this area were of Italian birth or heritage, but since then the growth and expansion of neighboring Chinatown have encroached on the Italian neighborhood to such an extent that merchants and community leaders of the Little Italy Restoration Association (LIRA) negotiated a truce in which the Chinese agreed to let at least Mulberry remain an all-Italian street.

In the second half of the 19th century, when Italian immigration peaked, the neighborhood stretched from Houston Street to Canal Street and the Bowery to Broadway. During this time Italians founded at least three Italian parishes, including the Church of the Transfiguration (now almost wholly Chinese); they also operated an Italian-language newspaper, *Il Progresso.*

In 1926 immigrants from southern Italy celebrated the first Feast of San Gennaro along Mulberry Street—a 10-day street fair that still takes place every September. Dedicated to the patron saint of Naples, the festival transforms Mulberry Street into a virtual al fresco restaurant, as wall-to-wall vendors sell traditional fried sausages and pastries. Today the festival is one of the few reminders of Little Italy's vibrant history, as the neighborhood continues to be overwhelmed by the ever-expanding Chinatown and as Italians continue to move out of Manhattan. If you want the flavor of a complete Italian neighborhood, you'd do better to visit Carroll Gardens in Brooklyn or Arthur Avenue in the Bronx (☞ Chapter 3)—or rent a video of the Martin Scorsese movie *Mean Streets,* which was filmed in Little Italy back in the early 1970s.

Still, the neighborhood is full of enticing eateries and historical sights of interest. Note the many tenement buildings with fire escapes projecting over the sidewalks. Most of these are of the late-19th-century New York style known as railroad flats: six-story buildings on 25- by 90-ft lots, with all the rooms in each apartment placed in a straight line like railroad cars. This style was common in the densely populated immigrant neighborhoods of lower Manhattan until 1901, when the city passed an ordinance requiring air shafts in the interior of buildings.

Visibly exotic, Chinatown is a popular tourist attraction, but it is also a real, vital community where about half of the city's population of 300,000 Chinese still live. Its main businesses are restaurants and garment factories; some 55% of its residents speak little or no English. Theoretically, Chinatown is divided from Little Italy by Canal Street, the bustling artery that links the Holland Tunnel (to New Jersey) and the Manhattan Bridge (to Brooklyn). However, in recent years an influx of immigrants from the People's Republic of China, Taiwan, and especially Hong Kong has swelled Manhattan's Chinese population, and Hong Kong residents, anticipating the return of the British colony to PRC domination in 1997, have been investing their capital in Chinatown real estate. Consequently, Chinatown now spills over its traditional borders into Little Italy to the north and the formerly Jewish Lower East Side to the east.

Its prolific expansion is a relatively recent development. The first Chinese immigrants were primarily railroad workers who came from the West in the 1870s to settle in a limited section of the Lower East Side. For nearly a century, anti-immigration laws prohibited most men from having their wives and families join them; the neighborhood became known as a "bachelor society," and for years its population remained static. It was not until the end of World War II, when Chinese immigration quotas were increased, that the neighborhood began the outward expansion that is still taking place today.

As a result of its rapid growth, Chinatown has become more lively than ever. Where once there was just a handful of businesses in Chinatown, today it's a virtual marketplace, crammed with souvenir shops and restaurants in funky pagoda-style buildings and crowded with pedestrians day and night. Here you can find every imaginable type of Chinese cuisine, from fast-food noodles or dumplings to sumptuous Hunan, Szechuan, Cantonese, Mandarin, and Shanghai feasts (☞ Chapter 6). You can also stroll among countless sidewalk markets bursting with stacks of fresh seafood and strange-shaped vegetables in extraterrestrial shades of green. Food shops proudly display their wares: If America's motto is "a chicken in every pot," then Chinatown's must be "a roast duck in every window."

Numbers in the text correspond to numbers in the margin and on the SoHo, TriBeCa, Little Italy, Chinatown map.

A Good Walk

Start your tour at the intersection of Spring and Mulberry streets, which still has a residential feel. Take a moment to poke your nose into the **D & G Bakery** (⊠ 45 Spring St.), one of the last coal-oven bakeries in the United States. Walk down **Mulberry Street** ⑯ to Broome Street, a gastronomic thoroughfare.

At the southwest corner of Broome and Mulberry streets, stairs lead down through a glass entrance to what seems to be a blue-tiled cave—and, appropriately enough, it is the Grotta Azzurra (Blue Grotto) restaurant, a longtime favorite for both the hearty food and the very Italian ambience (⊠ 387 Broome St., ☎ 212/925–8775).

East of Mulberry Street, the building at 375 Broome Street is known for its sheet-metal cornice that bears the face of a distinguished, albeit anonymous, bearded man.

To see the ornate Renaissance Revival building that is the original **New York City Police Headquarters** ⑰, walk west on Broome Street to Centre Street, between Broome and Grand streets. Then work your way back to the corner of Grand and Mulberry streets and stop to get the lay of the land. Facing north (uptown), on your right you'll see a series of multistory houses from the early 19th century, built long before the great flood of immigration hit this neighborhood between 1890 and 1924. Turn and look south along the east side of Mulberry Street to see Little Italy's trademark railroad-flat-style tenement buildings.

On the southeast corner of Grand Street, E. Rossi & Co. (✉ 191 Grand St.), established in 1902, is an antiquated little shop that sells housewares, espresso makers, embroidered religious postcards, and jocular Italian T-shirts. Two doors east on Grand Street is Ferrara's (✉ 195 Grand St.), a 100-year-old pastry shop that ships its creations—cannoli, peasant pie, Italian rum cake—all over the world. Another survivor of the pre-tenement era is the two-story, dormered brick Van Rensselaer House, now Paolucci's Restaurant (✉ 149 Mulberry St.); built in 1816, it is a prime example of the Italian Federal style.

One block south of Grand Street, on the corner of Hester and Mulberry streets, you'll reach the site of what was once Umberto's Clam House (✉ 129 Mulberry St.), best known as the place where mobster Joey Gallo was munching scungilli in 1973 when he was fatally surprised by a task force of mob hit men. Turn left onto Hester Street to visit yet another Little Italy institution, Puglia (✉ 189 Hester St.), a restaurant where guests sit at long communal tables, sing along with house entertainers, and enjoy southern Italian specialties with quantities of homemade wine. (For other Little Italy restaurants, *see* Chapter 6.)

One street west, on Baxter Street about three-quarters of a block toward Canal Street, stands the **San Gennaro Church** ⑱, which each year around mid-September sponsors Little Italy's keynote event, the annual Feast of San Gennaro.

To reach Chinatown from Little Italy, cross Canal Street at Mulberry Street. A good place to get oriented is the **Museum of Chinese in the Americas** ⑲, in a century-old schoolhouse at the corner of Bayard and Mulberry streets. For a taste of Chinatown-style commercialism, walk one block north to Canal Street, where restaurants and markets abound. If Chinese food products intrigue you, stop to browse in **Kam Man** (✉ 200 Canal St.), and then head east to **Mott Street** ⑳, the principal business street of the neighborhood.

Turn right from Canal Street onto Mott Street and walk three blocks. On the corner of Mott and Mosco streets, you'll find the **Church of the Transfiguration** ㉑ (✉ 25 Mott St.), where the faithful have worshiped since 1801. From here, turn right from Mott Street onto Mosco Street, proceeding downhill to Mulberry Street, where you'll see **Columbus Park** ㉒. This peaceful spot occupies the area once known as the Five Points, a tough 19th-century slum ruled by Irish gangs.

Across Mott Street from the church, you'll see a sign for Pell Street, a narrow lane of wall-to-wall restaurants whose neon signs stretch halfway across the thoroughfare. Halfway up Pell is **Doyers Street,** the site of turn-of-the-century gang wars. At the end of Doyers you'll find the **Bowery.** Cross the street to **Chatham Square** ㉓, where the Kum Lau Arch honors Chinese casualties in American wars. From Chatham Square, cross over the east side, past Park Row. Take a sharp right turn onto St. James Place to find two remnants of this neighborhood's pre-Chinatown past. On St. James Place is the **First Shearith Israel graveyard** ㉔, the first Jewish cemetery in the United States. Walk a half block farther, turn left on James Street, and you'll see St. James Church (✉ 32 James St.), a stately 1837 Greek Revival edifice where Al Smith, who rose from this poor Irish neighborhood to become New York's governor and a 1928 Democratic presidential candidate, once served as altar boy.

Return to Chatham Square once again and walk north up the Bowery to **Confucius Plaza** ㉕, where a statue of the Chinese sage stands guard.

Then cross the Bowery back to the west side of the street; at the corner of Pell Street stands 18 Bowery, which is one of Manhattan's oldest homes—a Federal and Georgian structure built in 1785 by meat wholesaler Edward Mooney. Farther north up the Bowery, a younger side of Chinatown is shown at the **Asian American Arts Centre** ㉖ (✉ 26 Bowery), which displays current work by Asian-American artists. For some exotic shopping, duck into the Canal Arcade, a passage linking the Bowery and Elizabeth Street.

Continue north. At the intersection of the Bowery and Canal Street, a grand arch and colonnade mark the entrance to the Manhattan Bridge, which leads to Brooklyn. This corner was once the center of New York's diamond district. Today most jewelry dealers have moved uptown, but you can still find some pretty good deals at jewelers on the Bowery and the north side of Canal Street.

TIMING

Since Little Italy consists of little more than one street, a tour of the area shouldn't take more than one hour. Most attractions are food-related, so plan on visiting around lunchtime. Another fun time to visit is during the 10-day San Gennaro festival, around mid-September.

Come on a weekend to see Chinatown at its liveliest; locals crowd the streets from dawn until dusk, along with a slew of tourists. If you're looking for a more relaxed experience, opt for a weekday instead. Allowing for stops at the two local museums and a lunch break, a Chinatown tour will take about three additional hours.

Sights to See

㉖ **Asian American Arts Centre.** This place may look plain, but it does offer impressive contemporary works by Asian-American artists, annual Chinese folk-art exhibitions during the Chinese New Year, performances by the Asian American Dance Theater, and videotapes of Asian American art and events. The center also sells unique art objects from China. There's no sign out front and the door reads "KTV-City"; ring buzzer No. 1. ✉ *26 Bowery, between Bayard and Canal Sts.,* ☎ *212/233–2154.* ▣ *Free.* ☉ *Tues.–Fri. noon–6, Sat. 3–6.*

The Bowery. Now a commercial thoroughfare lined with stores selling light fixtures and secondhand restaurant equipment, in the 17th century this broad boulevard was a farming area north of the city; its name derives from *bowerij,* the Dutch word for farm. As the city's growing population moved northward the Bowery became a broad, elegant avenue lined with taverns and theaters.

In the late 1800s the placement of an elevated subway line over the Bowery and the proliferation of saloons and brothels led to its demise as an elegant commercial thoroughfare; by the early 20th century it had become infamous as a skid row full of indigents and crime. After 1970, efforts at gentrification had some effect, and the neighborhood's indigent population dispersed. Today the Bowery is a major, if forgotten, artery through lower Manhattan.

㉓ **Chatham Square.** Ten streets converge at this labyrinthine intersection, creating pandemonium for cars and a nightmare for pedestrians. A memorial, the **Kim Lau Arch,** honoring Chinese casualties in American wars, stands on an island in the eye of the storm. On the far end of the square, at the corner of Catherine Street and East Broadway, there's a **Republic Bank for Savings**—originally a branch of the Manhattan Savings Bank. It was built to resemble a pagoda.

㉑ **Church of the Transfiguration.** Built in 1801 as the Zion Episcopal Church, this is an imposing Georgian structure with Gothic windows. It is now a Chinese Catholic church distinguished by its trilingualism: Here Mass is said in Cantonese, Mandarin, and English. ✉ *25 Mott St.,* ☎ *212/962–5157.*

NEED A
BREAK? Right across from the Church of the Transfiguration, at the corner of Mott and Mosco Streets, you'll see a red shack, **Cecilia Tam's Hong Kong Egg Cake Company,** where Ms. Tam makes mouthwatering small, round egg cakes for $1 a portion, Tuesday through Sunday, from early morning until 5. At 35 Pell Street off Mott Street is **May May Chinese Gourmet Bakery** (☎ 212/267–0733), a local favorite, with Chinese pastries, rice dumplings wrapped in banana leaves, yam cakes, and other sweet treats. A colorful flag hangs outside the entrance of the **Chinatown Ice Cream Factory** (✉ 65 Bayard St., between Mott and Elizabeth Sts., ☎ 212/608–4170), where the flavors range from red bean to litchi to green tea. Prepare to eat your scoop on the run, since there's no seating here.

㉒ Columbus Park. Today this shady, paved urban space is where children play and elderly Chinese gather to reminisce about their homeland. One hundred years ago, the then-swampy area was known as the Five Points—after the intersection of Mulberry Street, Anthony (now Worth) Street, Cross (now Park) Street, Orange (now Baxter) Street, and Little Water Street (no longer in existence)—and was notoriously ruled by dangerous Irish gangs. In the 1880s a neighborhood-improvement campaign brought about the creation of the park.

㉕ Confucius Plaza. At this open area at an intersection, a bronze statue of Confucius presides in front of the redbrick high-rise apartment complex named for him. The statue was originally opposed by leftist Chinese immigrants, who considered the sage a reactionary symbol of old China. That the statue is there tells you something about Chinatown's political makeup. ✉ *Intersection of Bowery and Division St.*

Doyers Street. The "bloody angle"—an unexpected sharp turn halfway down this little alleyway—was the site of turn-of-the-century battles between Chinatown's Hip Sing and On Leon tongs, gangs who fought for control over the local gambling and opium trades. Today the street is among the most colorful in Chinatown, lined with tea parlors and barbershops.

㉔ First Shearith Israel graveyard. Consecrated in 1656 by the country's oldest Jewish congregation, this small burial ground bears the remains of Sephardic Jews (of Spanish-Portuguese extraction) who emigrated from Brazil in the mid-17th century. The second and third Shearith Israel graveyards are in Greenwich Village and Chelsea, respectively. ✉ *55 St. James Pl.*

OFF THE
BEATEN PATH **LOWER EAST SIDE TENEMENT MUSEUM –** America's first urban living-history museum preserves and interprets the life of immigrants and migrants in New York's Lower East Side. A guided tour takes you to a restored 1863 tenement building (97 Orchard St.) where you can view the apartments of Natalie Gumpertz, a German-Jewish dressmaker (dating from 1878); Adolph and Rosaria Baldizzi, Catholic immigrants from Sicily (1935); the Rogarshevsky family from Eastern Europe (1918); and the Consino family, Sephardic Jews from Kastoria, Turkey, which is now part of Greece (1915). The Consino family apartment has been reconstructed from a child's point of view, and children and adults can actually touch items in the exhibit. The museum also leads historic walking tours around Orchard Street. If you wish to forego the tours, for a reduced fee you can watch a slide show tracing the history of the tene-

ment building and the neighborhood as well as a video with interviews of Lower East Side residents past and present. The gallery (free of charge) has changing exhibits relating to Lower East Side history, in addition to a list of the former residents of 97 Orchard Street. (The museum may be reached by subway by taking the F train to Delancey Street, the B, D, Q to Grand Street, or the J, M, Z to Essex Street; or take Bus M15 to Allen and Delancey streets.) ⊠ *90 Orchard St.,* ☎ *212/431–0233.* 🎫 *Tenement tour $8, tenement and Orchard St. walking tours $14, slide show and video only $3.* 🕐 *Museum Tues.–Fri. noon–5, weekends 11–5; tenement tours Tues.–Fri. 1, 2, and 3, weekends every 45 mins 11–4:15; walking tours weekends 1:30, 2:30.*

㉑ Mott Street. The main commercial artery of Chinatown, Mott Street has appeared in innumerable movies and television as the street that exemplifies the neighborhood. It's also so well known to New Yorkers that it's been immortalized in the lyrics of "Manhattan," a song by Rodgers and Hart. Chinatown began in the late 1880s when Chinese immigrants (mostly men) settled in tenements in a small area that included the lower portion of Mott Street as well as nearby Pell and Doyer streets. Today the street is often crowded during the day and especially on weekends; it overflows with popular restaurants, bakeries, souvenir shops, and food markets.

Quong Yuen Shing & Co. (⊠ 32 Mott St.), also known as the Mott Street General Store, is one of Chinatown's oldest curio shops, with porcelain bowls, teapots, and cups for sale. Right next door is one of Chinatown's best and oldest bakeries, **Fung Wong** (⊠ 30 Mott St.), where you can stock up on almond cookies, sticky rice cakes, sweet egg tarts, roast pork buns, and other goodies you'll be pressed to find elsewhere in Manhattan. If you've never tried dim sum (Chinese dumplings and other small dishes), now's your chance; **20 Mott Street** and **Mandarin Court** (⊠ 69 Mott St.) are good bets.

⑯ Mulberry Street. Crowded with restaurants, cafés, bakeries, imported-food shops, and souvenir stores, Mulberry Street is where Little Italy lives and breathes. Especially on weekends, this is a street for strolling, gawking, and inhaling the aroma of garlic and olive oil. Some restaurants and cafés display high-tech Eurodesign; others seem dedicated to staying exactly as their old customers remember them.

<table>
<tr><td>NEED A
BREAK?</td><td>You can savor cannoli and other sweet treats at **Caffè Roma** (⊠ 385 Broome St., ☎ 212/226–8413), a traditional neighborhood favorite with wrought-iron chairs and a pounded-tin ceiling.</td></tr>
</table>

⑲ Museum of Chinese in the Americas (MCA). In a century-old school-house that once served Italian-American and Chinese-American children, MCA is the only U.S. museum devoted to preserving the history of the Chinese people throughout the Western Hemisphere. A gallery designed by Billie Tsien improves the museum. The permanent exhibit entitled "Where's Home? Chinese in the Americas" explores the Chinese-American experience by weaving together displays of artists' creations and personal and domestic artifacts with historical documentation. Among the fascinating objects on display are slippers for binding feet, Chinese musical instruments, a reversible silk gown (circa 1900) worn at a Cantonese opera performance, items from a Chinese laundry, and antique business signs. Changing exhibits fill a second room; recent shows dealt with sights round Chinatown and Brooklyn's Sunset Park Chinese community. MCA sponsors workshops, walking tours, lectures, and family events. Its archives dedicated to Chinese-American history and culture include 2,000 volumes; it's open by appointment only. ⊠

70 Mulberry St., 2nd floor, ☎ *212/619–4785.* ▣ *$3.* ⊙ *Tues.–Sun. 10:30–5.*

⑰ New York City Police Headquarters. The fabulously ornate building that served as the New York City police headquarters until 1973 was converted into a high-priced condominium complex in 1988; big-name residents have included Cindy Crawford, Winona Ryder, and Steffi Graf, among others. Notice the baroque touches that embellish its classical Renaissance Revival design. ⊠ *240 Centre St., between Broome and Grand Sts.*

⑱ San Gennaro Church. Every year around mid-September, San Gennaro Church—officially called the Most Precious Blood Church, National Shrine of San Gennaro—sponsors the feast of San Gennaro, the biggest event in Little Italy. (The community's other big festival celebrates St. Anthony of Padua in June; the church connected to the festival is at Houston and Sullivan streets, in what is now SoHo.) During the feasts, Little Italy's streets are closed to traffic, arches of tinsel span the thoroughfares, the sidewalks are lined with booths offering games and food, and the whole scene is one noisy, crowded, kitschy, delightful party. ⊠ *113 Baxter St., near Canal St.*

WALL STREET AND THE BATTERY

Island city that it is, much of Manhattan strangely turns its back on the rushing waters that surround it. Not so the Battery. From waterside walks in Battery Park, you can look out on the confluence of the Hudson and East River estuaries where bustling seaborne commerce once glutted the harbor that built the "good city of old Manhatto," Herman Melville's moniker from the second chapter of *Moby-Dick*.

It was here that the Dutch established the colony of Nieuw Amsterdam in 1625; in 1789 the first capital building of the United States found itself here. The city did not really expand beyond these precincts until the middle of the 19th century. Today this historic heart of New York is increasingly being abandoned by companies for cheaper and better-equipped buildings in midtown and the suburbs, but all sorts of tax breaks, rezonings, and incentives, including plans to convert parts of some buildings to residences, are being worked up to help the area maintain its vitality. Lower Manhattan is still in many ways dominated by Wall Street, which is both an actual street and a shorthand name for the vast, powerful financial community that clusters around the New York and American stock exchanges. A different but equally awe-inspiring type of sight can be found at the tip of the island as you gaze across the great silvery harbor to the enduring symbols of America: the Statue of Liberty and Ellis Island, port of entry for countless immigrants to a new land.

Numbers in the text correspond to numbers in the margin and on the Lower Manhattan map.

A Good Walk

The immediate vicinity of the Staten Island Ferry Terminal (for subway riders, that's just outside the South Ferry station on the 1 and 9 lines) is a little unsightly, but that doesn't detract from the pleasure of a ride on the **Staten Island Ferry** ①. It is still the best scenic ride in town—and as of 1997, it's free. The 20- to 30-minute ride across New York Harbor provides great views of the Manhattan skyline, Ellis Island, the Statue of Liberty, the Verrazano-Narrows Bridge, and the New Jersey coast—and the blue-and-orange boats are a delight.

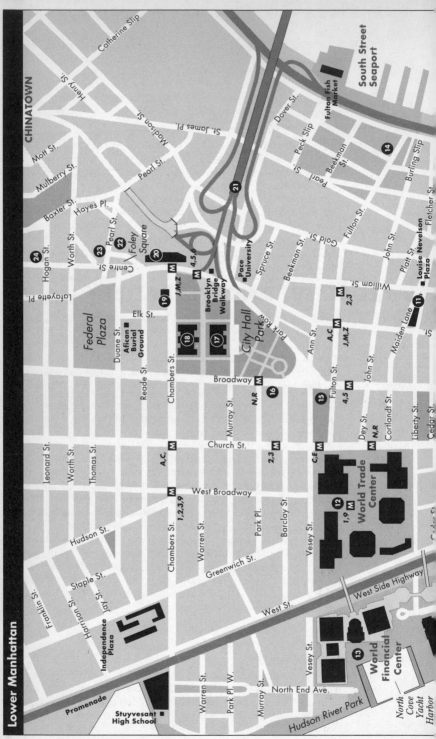

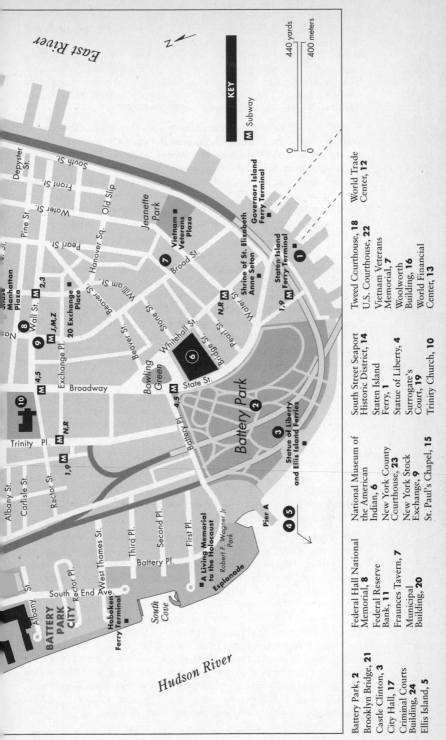

East River

KEY

M Subway

440 yards

400 meters

Depyster St.

South St.

Front St.

Water St.

Pine St.

Old Slip

Jeanette Park

Hanover Sq.

Pearl St.

Broad St.

M Vietnam Veterans Plaza

Shrine of St. Elizabeth Anne Seton

Governors Island Ferry Terminal

7

N,R M

Chase Manhattan Plaza

M 2,3

Wall St.

20 Exchange Place

Beaver St.

William St.

Stone St.

Whitehall St.

Bridge St.

State St.

Pearl St.

Staten Island Ferry Terminal

1,9

1

8

9 M J,M,Z

N M

M 4,5

Exchange Pl.

Broadway

Bowling Green

M 4,5

Battery Park

2

10

Trinity Pl.

M N,R

M

1,9

Albany St.

Carlisle St.

Rector St.

Battery Pl.

Statue of Liberty and Ellis Island Ferries

3

4 5

Pier A

South Street Seaport Historic District, **14**

Staten Island Ferry, **1**

Statue of Liberty, **4**

Surrogate's Court, **19**

Trinity Church, **10**

National Museum of the American Indian, **6**

New York County Courthouse, **23**

New York Stock Exchange, **9**

St. Paul's Chapel, **15**

Tweed Courthouse, **18**

U.S. Courthouse, **22**

Vietnam Veterans Memorial, **7**

Woolworth Building, **16**

World Financial Center, **13**

World Trade Center, **12**

Federal Hall National Memorial, **8**

Federal Reserve Bank, **11**

Fraunces Tavern, **7**

Municipal Building, **20**

Battery Park, **2**

Brooklyn Bridge, **21**

Castle Clinton, **3**

City Hall, **17**

Criminal Courts Building, **24**

Ellis Island, **5**

Albany St.

West Thames St.

Rector Pl.

South End Ave.

Third Pl.

Second Pl.

First Pl.

Battery Pl.

Battery Pl.

A Living Memorial to the Holocaust

Esplanade

Robert F. Wagner Jr. Park

BATTERY PARK CITY

Albany

Hoboken Ferry Terminal

South Cove

Hudson River

If you look north from the Staten Island Ferry Terminal, the tall white columns and curved brick front of the 1793 **Shrine of St. Elizabeth Ann Seton** are a dignified sight. The house used to be one of many mansions lining State Street. To the left of the shrine, the verdant **Battery Park** ②, Manhattan's green toe, curves up the west side of the island. It is filled with sculpture and monuments, one of which is the circular **Castle Clinton** ③. The venerable fort is where you buy tickets for the ferries to the **Statue of Liberty** ④ and **Ellis Island** ⑤.

From Castle Clinton you can head farther north to the gardens, lawns, and riverside walks of **Robert F. Wagner Jr. Park** (which contains **A Living Memorial to the Holocaust–Museum of Jewish Heritage**) or follow the rose walk to Bowling Green. Exiting the Battery Park at Bowling Green, across State Street you'll see the fabulous Beaux Arts Alexander Hamilton Custom House, home of the **National Museum of the American Indian** ⑥. The museum faces **Bowling Green,** an oval greensward at the foot of Broadway that became New York's first public park in 1733.

Next follow Whitehall Street down the east side of the American Indian museum. A left turn onto Bridge Street will bring into focus a block of early New York buildings. As you approach Broad Street, the two-tone Georgian **Fraunces Tavern** ⑦ will appear. The complex of five largely 19th-century buildings houses a museum, restaurant, and bar. Across Pearl Street, 85 Broad Street pays due homage to urban archaeology with a transparent panel in the sidewalk showing the excavated foundations of the 17th-century Stadt Huys, the Old Dutch City Hall. The course of old Dutch Stone Street is marked in the lobby with a line of brown paving stones.

Head north on Pearl Street to **Hanover Square,** a quiet tree-lined plaza. Walk inland up Hanover Square to the triangular convergences of South William and Beaver streets. On the right, 20 Exchange Place towers and adds street-level interest with weighty Art Deco doorways depicting the engines of commerce. Two blocks farther north, William Street crosses **Wall Street,** a jaw-dropping display of the money that built Manhattan—the massive arcade of 55 Wall Street alone speaks volumes. Developers' greed backfired here—they built on every inch of land only to have property values decrease once people realized how stultifying the results were.

One block west on Wall Street, where Broad Street becomes Nassau Street, you'll find on your right a regal statue of George Washington on the steps of the **Federal Hall National Memorial** ⑧. This 1883 statue, by noted sculptor and relative of the president, John Quincy Adams Ward, marks the spot where Washington was sworn in as the first U.S. president in 1789. Across the street is an investment bank built by J. P. Morgan in 1913. By building only four stories Morgan was in effect declaring himself above the pressures of Wall Street real estate values. Now **Morgan Guaranty Trust,** the building bears pockmarks near the fourth window on the Wall Street side; these were created when a bomb that had been placed in a pushcart exploded in 1920. Perhaps the heart of the area is the temple-fronted **New York Stock Exchange** ⑨ at 20 Broad Street. From its visitor center you can watch stressed-out traders gesture wildly in the name of making deals.

The focal point at the end of Wall Street is the brownstone **Trinity Church** ⑩, which was established as an Anglican parish in 1697. The present 1846 structure, by Richard Upjohn, ranked as the city's tallest building for most of the second half of the 19th century. Just north of the church is tiny Thames Street, where a pair of skyscrapers playfully called the Thames Twins—the Trinity and U.S. Realty buildings—display early 20th-century attempts to apply Gothic decoration to skyscrapers. Across the street at 120 Broadway, the 1915 Equitable Building rises 30 stories straight from its base with no setback; its overpowering shadow on the street helped persuade the city government to pass the nation's first zoning law. Large public plazas around the bases of skyscrapers have helped to alleviate this problem, at the same time creating space for public sculpture.

Four pieces of sculpture make for an interesting side tour. The first, on Broadway between Cedar and Liberty streets, where the black-glass Marine Midland Bank (1971) heightens the drama of the red-and-silver Isamu Noguchi sculpture *Cube* in its plaza. You'll see the next piece framed at the end of Cedar Lane, two blocks east. The plaza surrounding the 65-story Chase Manhattan Bank Building holds a striking black-and-white *Group of Four Trees,* by Jean Dubuffet, and an inset circular sculpture garden also by Noguchi. Just north of the Chase plaza, where Liberty Street converges with William Street and Maiden Lane under the Federal Reserve Bank, the triangular Louise Nevelson Plaza contains four pieces of her black, welded-steel abstract sculpture: three of moderate size and one 70-footer.

The massive, rusticated **Federal Reserve Bank** ⑪ (1924) directly across the street recalls Florence's Palazzo Strozzi and looks the way a bank ought to: solid, imposing, and absolutely impregnable.

Walk west back toward Broadway on Maiden Lane, which will turn into Cortland Street. The contrast between the Federal Reserve's 1924 vision of architectural power and that of the 1,350-ft-tall towers of the **World Trade Center** ⑫ couldn't be more striking. The 16-acre, 12-million-square-ft complex contains New York's tallest buildings. During the towers' construction more than a million cubic yards of rock and soil were excavated—then moved across West Street to help beget the 100-acre **Battery Park City** development, a complete neighborhood built from scratch. Take the pedestrian overpass north of 1 World Trade Center to Battery Park City's centerpiece, the **World Financial Center** ⑬, a four-tower complex designed by Cesar Pelli, with some heavy-duty corporate tenants. Just north of the basin is the terminal for ferry service to Hoboken, New Jersey. Beyond the ferry terminal is the southern end of the **Hudson River Park.** To the south, a longer riverside Esplanade accompanies the residential part of Battery Park City and connects with Robert F. Wagner Jr. Park.

TIMING

The Manhattan side of this tour takes most of a day—allow more time to ferry out to the Statue of Liberty and Ellis Island. Visit on a weekday to capture the district's true vitality—but expect to be jostled on the crowded sidewalks if you stand too long, peering at the great buildings that surge skyward on every corner. If you visit on a weekend, on the other hand, you'll feel like a lone explorer among a canyon of buildings. Either way, winds from the harbor whipping around the buildings can make this area feel markedly colder than other parts of the city—a great thing in summer—so dress accordingly. Start early, preferably making the first ferry, to try to beat the crowds to Liberty and Ellis islands. You should also get tickets by lunchtime if you plan to visit the Stock Exchange, which is open only on weekdays until 4. The best place to end the day is looking west over the Hudson for the sunset.

Sights to See

2 **Battery Park.** Jutting out as if it were Manhattan's green toe, this verdant landfill is loaded with monuments. The park's name refers to a line of cannons once mounted here to defend the shoreline (which ran along what is currently State Street). Starting near the Staten Island Ferry Terminal, head north along the water's edge to the **East Coast Memorial,** a statue of a fierce eagle that presides over eight granite slabs inscribed with the names of U.S. servicemen who died in the western Atlantic during World War II. Climb the steps of the East Coast Memorial for a fine view of the main features of **New York Harbor;** from left to right: **Governors Island,** a Coast Guard installation that is looking for a new tenant for 1998 and beyond, when the Coast Guard will leave it; hilly **Staten Island** in the distance; the **Statue of Liberty** on Liberty Island; **Ellis Island,** gateway to the New World for generations of immigrants; and the old railway terminal in **Liberty State Park,** on the mainland in Jersey City, New Jersey. On crystal-clear days, you can see all the way to Port Elizabeth's cranes, which seem to mimic the stance of Lady Liberty.

Continue north past a romantic **statue of Giovanni da Verrazano,** the Florentine merchant who piloted the ship that first sighted New York and its harbor in 1524. The **Verrazano-Narrows Bridge** between Brooklyn and Staten Island—so long that the curvature of the earth had to be figured into its dimensions—is visible from here, just beyond Governors Island.

Battery Park is also home to ☞ **Castle Clinton,** the takeoff point for ferries to the ☞ **Statue of Liberty** and ☞ **Ellis Island.**

Battery Park City. An impressive feat of urban planning, this complete 92-acre neighborhood was built from scratch on lower Manhattan landfill near the Hudson River. Its residential parts, a mix of high-rises, town houses, shops, and green squares, does a surprisingly good job of duplicating the rhythms of the rest of the city. Its commercial centerpiece is the ☞ **World Financial Center.**

Bowling Green. This oval greensward at the foot of Broadway became New York's first public park in 1733. On July 9, 1776, a few hours after citizens learned about the signing of the Declaration of Independence, rioters toppled a statue of British king George III that had occupied the spot for 11 years; much of the statue's lead was melted down into bullets. In 1783, when the occupying British forces fled the city, they defiantly hoisted a Union Jack on a greased, uncleated flagpole so it couldn't be lowered; patriot John Van Arsdale drove his own cleats into the pole to replace the flag with the Stars and Stripes. The entrance to the subway station here is original, built in 1904–05.

3 **Castle Clinton.** In Battery Park, this circular redstone fortress first stood on an island 200 ft from shore as a defense for New York Harbor. In 1824 it became Castle Garden, an entertainment and concert facility that reached its zenith in 1850 when more than 6,000 people (the capacity of Radio City Music Hall) attended the U.S. debut of the Swedish Nightingale, Jenny Lind. After landfill connected it to the city, Castle Clinton became, in succession, an immigrant processing center, an aquarium, and now a restored fort, museum, and ticket office for ferries to the ☞ **Statue of Liberty** and ☞ **Ellis Island.** The ferry ride is one loop; you can get off at Liberty Island, visit the statue, then reboard any ferry and continue on to Ellis Island, boarding another boat once you have finished exploring the historic immigration facility there.

Inside the old fort there are dioramas of lower Manhattan in 1812, 1886, and 1941. Outside the landward entrance is a statue titled *The Emigrants,* at the beginning of a broad mall that leads back across the park to the Netherlands Memorial, a quaint flagpole depicting the bead exchange that bought from the Native Americans the land to establish Fort Amsterdam in 1626. Inscriptions describe the event in English and Dutch. ⊠ *Castle Clinton:* ☎ *212/269–5755.* ☉ *Tours hourly 10:35–3:35 daily. Ferry information:* ☎ *212/269–5755;* ⊞ *$7 round-trip;* ☉ *Departures daily every 30 mins 9:30–3:30 (more departures and extended hrs in summer).*

★ ❺ **Ellis Island.** Approximately 17 million men, women, and children entered the country at this federal immigration facility between 1892 and 1954—the ancestors of more than 40% of Americans living today. After a $140 million restoration, the center opened in September 1990 to record crowds. Now a national monument, the island's main building contains the **Ellis Island Immigration Museum,** with exhibits detailing not only the island's history but the whole history of immigration to America. Perhaps the most moving exhibit is the American Immigrant Wall of Honor, where the names of nearly 400,000 immigrant Americans are inscribed along an outdoor promenade overlooking the Statue of Liberty and the Manhattan skyline. The names include Miles Standish, Priscilla Alden, George Washington's grandfather, Irving Berlin, and possibly an ancestor of yours. For ferry information, *see* Castle Clinton, *above. Ellis Island:* ☎ *212/363–3200; 212/883–1986 for Wall of Honor information.* ⊞ *Free.*

❽ **Federal Hall National Memorial.** On the steps of this Greek Revival building stands a regal statue of George Washington, who on that site—then also Federal Hall—was sworn in as the nation's first president in 1789. The likeness was made by noted sculptor and presidential relative John Quincy Adams Ward. After the capital moved to Philadelphia in 1790, the original Federal Hall became New York's City Hall, then was demolished in 1812 when the present City Hall (☞ The Seaport and the Courts, *below*) was completed. The clean and simple lines of the current structure, built as a U.S. Customs House in 1842, were modeled on the Parthenon, a potent symbol for a young nation striving to emulate classic Greek democracy. It's now a museum featuring exhibits on New York and Wall Street. Guided site tours are sometimes available on request, and you can also pick up brochures that lead you on differently themed self-guided walking tours of downtown. ⊠ *26 Wall St.,* ☎ *212/825–6888.* ⊞ *Free.* ☉ *Weekdays 9–5, and weekends in summer 9–5.*

⓫ **Federal Reserve Bank.** Gray, solid, imposing, and absolutely impregnable, this is how a bank should look. Built in 1935, this neo-Renaissance structure made of sandstone, limestone, and ironwork goes five levels underground. Vaults here reputedly contain a third of the world's gold reserves. The bank was the setting for a robbery scene in the recent movie *Die Hard II.* ⊠ *33 Liberty St.,* ☎ *212/720–6130.* ⊞ *Free.* ☉ *1-hr tour by advance (at least 5 days) reservation, weekdays at 10:30, 11:30, 1:30, and 2:30.*

❼ **Fraunces Tavern.** Redbrick along one side, cream-colored brick along the other, the main corner building is a stately Colonial house with a white marble portico and coffered frieze, built in 1719 and converted to a tavern in 1762. It was the meeting place for the Sons of Liberty up until the Revolutionary War. This was also the site where, in 1783, George Washington delivered a farewell address to his officers celebrating the British evacuation of New York. Later, the building housed some offices of the fledgling U.S. government. Today, a museum, restaurant, and bar compose this historic five-building complex. Fraunces Tavern contains two fully furnished period rooms and other displays of 18th- and 19th-century American history. The museum also offers family programs (such as a scavenger hunt), lectures, workshops, and concerts. ⊠ *54 Pearl St., at Broad St.,* ☎ *212/425–1778.* 🎫 *Museum $2.50.* ◷ *Museum weekdays 10–4:45, weekends noon–4.*

<table>
<tr><td>NEED A
BREAK?</td><td>The **brick plaza behind 85 Broad Street** is flanked by a variety of small restaurants. Order a take-out meal or snack and eat it out here on the benches, where you can watch busy office workers milling past and enjoy not being one of them.</td></tr>
</table>

Hanover Square. This quiet tree-lined plaza stood on the waterfront pre-landfill, when the East River ran past present-day Pearl Street. This was the city's original printing-house square; on the site of 81 Pearl Street, William Bradford established the first printing press in the colonies. The pirate Captain Kidd lived in the neighborhood, and the graceful brownstone **India House** (1837), a private club at No. 1, used to house the New York Cotton Exchange.

Hudson River Park. ☞ SoHo and TriBeCa, *above.*

A Living Memorial to the Holocaust–Museum of Jewish Heritage. Moored in one of the city's most enviable waterfront settings at the north end of ☞ **Robert F. Wagner Jr. Park** just below Battery Park City, this newest of downtown museums focuses on the dynamism of 20th-century Jewish culture around the globe; Hitler's war against the Jews, using firsthand recollections; and Jewish life after the Holocaust. It was scheduled to open in the second half of 1997. ⊠ *40 1st Pl., Battery Park City,* ☎ *212/687–9141.*

<table>
<tr><td>OFF THE
BEATEN PATH</td><td>**MUSEUM OF AMERICAN FINANCIAL HISTORY –** On the site of Alexander Hamilton's law office (today the Standard Oil Building), this four-room museum displays artifacts of the financial markets' history, including a vintage ticker-tape machine and an interactive kiosk. ⊠ *24 Broadway, just north of Bowling Green,* ☎ *212/908–4519.* 🎫 *Free.* ◷ *Weekdays 11:30–2:30 or by appointment.*</td></tr>
</table>

★ ❻ **National Museum of the American Indian.** This museum is the first of its kind to be dedicated to Native American culture, with well-mounted exhibits that examine the history and the current cultures of native peoples from all over the Americas through literature, dance, lectures, readings, film, and crafts. Contemporary Native Americans are also part of the life of the museum, both as part of visiting programs and at all levels of staff. George Gustav Heye, a wealthy New Yorker, amassed most of the museum's collection, which includes pottery, weaving, and basketry from the southwestern United States, painted hides from the Plains Indians of North America, carved jade from the Mexican Olmec and Maya cultures, and contemporary Native American paintings. There is a research library, a media room with interactive computer programs, and a gift shop off the main lobby.

The museum is housed in one of lower Manhattan's finest buildings. The ornate Beaux Arts (1907) gem originally functioned as the **Alexander Hamilton Custom House.** Above its base, massive granite columns rise to a pediment topped by a double row of statuary. Daniel Chester French, better known for the sculpture of Lincoln in the Lincoln Memorial in Washington, D.C., carved the lower statues, which symbolize various continents (left to right: Asia, the Americas, Europe, Africa). The upper row represents the major trading cities of the world.

Inside, the display of white and colored marble couldn't be more remarkable. The semicircular side staircases are equally breathtaking. ✉ *1 Bowling Green,* ☎ *212/668–6624.* 🎫 *Free.* ☉ *Daily 10–5, Thurs. 10–8.*

9 **New York Stock Exchange.** The stock exchange nearly bursts from this little building, constructed before modern technology came to Wall Street. Compared with the Federal Hall memorial, this neoclassical building is much more elaborately decorated, as befitted the more grandiose national image of 1901, when it was designed. Inside, after what may be a lengthy wait, you can take an elevator to the third-floor visitor center. A self-guided tour, informative slide shows, video displays, and guides may help you interpret the seeming chaos you'll see from the visitors' gallery overlooking the immense (50-ft-high) trading hall. ✉ *Tickets available at 20 Broad St.,* ☎ *212/656–5165.* 🎫 *Free tickets distributed beginning at 9; come before 1 PM to assure entrance.* ☉ *Weekdays 9:15–4.*

★ **Robert F. Wagner Jr. Park.** The link in the chain of parks that stretch from ☞ **Battery Park** to above the ☞ **World Financial Center,** this newest addition to the downtown waterfront may be the best of the bunch. Lawns, walks, gardens, and benches spill right down to the river. Behind these, a brown-brick structure rises two stories to provide river and harbor panoramas. A stream of runners and bladers flows by, making it a toss-up to say which is better: the people-watching or the views of the Statue of Liberty and Ellis Island. ✉ *Between Battery Pl. and the Hudson River.*

Shrine of St. Elizabeth Ann Seton. The rectory of the shrine is a red-brick Federal-style town house, an example of the mansions that used to line the street, with a distinctive portico shaped to fit the curving street. This house was built in 1793 as the home of the wealthy Watson family; Mother Seton and her family lived here from 1801 to 1803. She joined the Catholic Church in 1805, after the death of her husband, and went on to found the Sisters of Charity, the first American order of nuns. In 1975 she became the first American-born saint. Masses are held here daily. ✉ *7–8 State St.,* ☎ *212/269–6865.*

★ **1** **Staten Island Ferry.** The best deal in town is right here. The free 20- to 30-minute ride across New York Harbor provides great views of the Manhattan skyline, the Statue of Liberty, the Verrazano-Narrows Bridge, and the New Jersey coast. The classic blue-and-orange ferries embark on various schedules: every 15 minutes during rush hours, every 20–30 minutes most other times, and every hour after 11 PM and on weekend mornings. A word of advice, however: Although commuters love the ferry service's swift, new low-slung craft, the boats ride low in the water and have no outside deck space. Wait for one of the higher, more open old-timers. Once you're on Staten Island (☞ Chapter 3), you can, of course, stay as long as you like, though most tourists return immediately. ☎ *718/390–5253.*

★ **4** **Statue of Liberty.** After arriving on Liberty Island (*see* Castle Clinton, *above,* for ferry information), you have two ways to get from the ground-floor entrance to the monument: You can take an elevator 10 stories to the top of the 89-ft-high pedestal, or if you're strong of heart and limb, you can climb 354 steps (the equivalent of a 22-story building) to the crown. (Visitors cannot go up into the torch.) It usually takes two to three hours to walk up to the crown because of the wait beforehand. Erected in 1886 and refurbished for its centennial, the Statue of Liberty weighs 225 tons and stands 151 ft from her feet to her torch. Exhibits inside illustrate the statue's history, including videos of the view from the crown for those who don't make the climb. There is also a model of the statue's face for the blind to feel and a pleasant outdoor café. ⊠ *Liberty Island,* ☏ *212/363–3200.* ⌺ *Free.*

🔟 **Trinity Church.** Established as an Anglican parish in 1697, the present structure (1846), by Richard Upjohn, ranked as the city's tallest building for most of the second half of the 19th century. Its three huge bronze doors were designed by Richard Morris Hunt to recall Lorenzo Ghiberti's doors for the Baptistery in Florence, Italy. After the exterior sandstone was restored in 1991, New Yorkers were amazed to discover that a church they had always thought of as black was actually rosy pink—now it's faded back to a sandy color. The church's Gothic Revival interior is surprisingly light and elegant. On the church's north side is a 2½-acre graveyard: Alexander Hamilton is buried beneath a white stone pyramid, and a monument commemorates Robert Fulton, the inventor of the steamboat (he's actually buried in the Livingstone family vault, with his wife). The church, which has many theater people in its congregation, does a popular dramatic midnight Mass at Christmas. ⊠ *74 Trinity Pl. (Broadway at the head of Wall St.),* ☏ *212/602–0800.*

OFF THE
BEATEN PATH

VIETNAM VETERANS MEMORIAL – At this 14-ft-high, 70-ft-long rectangular memorial (1985), moving passages from news dispatches and the letters of servicemen and servicewomen have been etched into a wall of greenish glass. Unfortunately, the brick plaza around it may be desolate on weekends. ⊠ *At end of Coenties Slip, between Water and South Sts.*

Wall Street. The street is named after a wood wall built across the island in 1653 to defend the Dutch colony against the native Indians. Arguably the most famous thoroughfare in the world, though only a third of a mile long, Wall Street began its financial career with stock traders conducting business along the sidewalks or at tables beneath a sheltering buttonwood tree. Today it's a dizzyingly narrow canyon— look to the east and you'll glimpse a sliver of East River waterfront, look to the west and you'll see the spire of Trinity Church, tightly framed by skyscrapers at the head of the street.

To learn the difference between Ionic and Corinthian columns, look at the **Citibank Building** (⊠ 55 Wall St.). The lower stories were part of an earlier U.S. Customs House, built in 1836–42, and it was literally a bullish day on Wall Street when oxen hauled its 16 granite Ionic columns up to the site. When the National City Bank took over the building in 1899, it hired architects McKim, Mead & White to redesign the building and in 1909 added the second tier of columns but made them Corinthian.

⑬ **World Financial Center.** At this four-tower complex designed by Cesar Pelli, the heavy-duty corporate tenants include Merrill Lynch, American Express, and Dow Jones. You'll come out into the soaring **Winter Garden** atrium, its cascade of pink marble steps spilling down into a vaulted plaza with 16 giant palm trees, framed by a vast arched window overlooking the Hudson. This stunning space has become a popular venue for free performances by top-flight musicians and dancers—a great way to beat summer heat. Surrounding the atrium are several upscale shops and a skylit food court.

The outdoor plaza right behind the atrium curls around a tidy little yacht basin; take in the view of the Statue of Liberty and read the stirring quotations worked into the iron railings. Just north of the basin is the terminal for **ferry service** to Hoboken, New Jersey (☏ 908/463–3779), on the other side of the Hudson River. It's a $2, eight-minute ride to Frank Sinatra's hometown, with a spectacular view of lower Manhattan.

To the south, a longer riverside **Esplanade** begins at the residential part of Battery Park City and connects with ☞ **Robert F. Wagner Jr. Park** and **Battery Park.** Especially noteworthy among the artwork populating the Esplanade are Ned Smyth's columned plaza with chessboards and the South Cove (a collaborative effort), a romantic curved stage set of wood piers and a steel-frame lookout. ⊠ *World Financial Center, West St., Battery Park City,* ☎ *212/945–0505.*

NEED A
BREAK?

While the World Financial Center courtyard also offers several full-service restaurants, for a quick bite head for **Minters** (☎ 212/945–4455)—and be sure to leave room for great ice cream cones.

★ ⑫ **World Trade Center.** The only way to grasp just how big these buildings are is to crane your neck and look straight up at them from the base. This 16-acre, 12-million-square-ft complex contains New York's two tallest buildings (each 1,350 ft high). To reach the **Top of the World** observation deck on the 107th floor of 2 World Trade Center, elevators glide a quarter of a mile into the sky—in only 58 seconds. The view potentially extends 55 mi, although signs at the ticket window disclose how far you can see that day and whether the outdoor deck is open. In February 1993, the Center was the site of a bombing by terrorists that killed six people and caused extensive damage to the area. However, the Center has, for the most part, returned to normal operations, though security has been tightened considerably within the complex. ☎ *212/323–2340.* ▣ *$10.* ☉ *June–Aug., daily 9:30 AM–11:30 PM; Sept.–May, daily 9:30–9:30.*

Some 50,000 people work in this seven-building complex, and at street level and underground it contains more than 60 stores, services, and restaurants, the adjacent New York Marriott World Trade Center hotel, and a skating rink. There's a TKTS booth selling discount tickets to Broadway and Off-Broadway shows (☞ Chapter 5) in the mezzanine of 2 World Trade Center (it's open weekdays 11–5:30, Saturday 11–1); and on the ninth floor of 4 World Trade Center, a visitors' gallery, which you can visit by reserving two weeks in advance, overlooks the trading floor of the **Commodities Exchange** (☎ 212/748–1006). ⊠ *Church to West Sts., Liberty to Vesey Sts.*

THE SEAPORT AND THE COURTS

New York's role as a great seaport is easiest to understand downtown, with both the Hudson River and East River waterfronts within walking distance. While the deeper Hudson River came into its own in the steamship era, the more sheltered waters of the East River saw most of the action in the 19th century, during the age of clipper ships. This era is preserved in the South Street Seaport restoration, centered on Fulton Street between Water Street and the East River. Only a few blocks away, you can visit another seat of New York history: the City Hall neighborhood, which includes Manhattan's magisterial court and government buildings.

Numbers in the text correspond to numbers in the margin and on the Lower Manhattan map.

A Good Walk

Begin at the intersection of Water and Fulton streets. The latter thoroughfare was named after the ferry to Brooklyn that once docked at its foot (the ferry itself was named after its inventor, Robert Fulton), while Water Street was once the shoreline. On the 19th-century land-fill across the street is the 11-block **South Street Seaport Historic District** ⑭, which was created in 1967 to preserve the area's heritage as a port and prevent it from being completely overtaken by skyscrapers. You could easily spend a few hours here, looking at the Seaport museum, boats, shops, and restaurants.

When you're ready to leave, return to Fulton Street and walk away from the river to Broadway, to **St. Paul's Chapel** ⑮, the oldest (1766) surviving church in Manhattan. Forking off to your right is **Park Row,** which was known as Newspaper Row from the mid-19th to early 20th century, when most of the city's 20 or so daily newspapers had offices there. In tribute to that past, a statue of Benjamin Franklin (who was, after all, a printer) stands in front of Pace University farther up on Park Row. Two blocks north on Broadway is one of the finest skyscrapers in the city, the Gothic **Woolworth Building** ⑯, for which Frank Woolworth paid $13 million—in cash.

Between Broadway and Park Row is triangular **City Hall Park,** originally the town common, which gives way to a slew of government offices. **City Hall** ⑰, built between 1803 and 1812, is unexpectedly sedate, small-scale, and charming. Lurking directly behind it is the **Tweed Courthouse** ⑱, named for the notorious politician "Boss" William Marcy Tweed. It is an Anglo-Italianate gem, one of the finest designs in the City Hall area. The small plaza east of Tweed Courthouse is used as a farmers' market (Tues. Apr.–Dec. and Fri. year-round), and it contains a Big Apple novelty that just might be worth the 25¢ it costs to get in—a public toilet. The design is subject to so many stipulations—the toilet cleans itself after every use, and people who stay too long need to be kicked out, for example—that so far this is the only one in the city that's in service.

Who would think of finding an eight-story, Beaux Arts château in lower Manhattan? That's the 1911 **Surrogate's Court** ⑲, also called the Hall of Records (✉ 31 Chambers St.), directly opposite the Tweed Courthouse on the north side of Chambers Street. Across Centre Street from the château is the city government's first skyscraper, the imposing **Municipal Building** ⑳, built in 1914 by McKim, Mead & White. Just south of the Municipal Building, a ramp curves up into the pedestrian walkway over the **Brooklyn Bridge** ㉑. How romantic it would be to look out from the bridge on the docks of "mast-hemmed Manhattan" of Walt Whitman's "Crossing Brooklyn Ferry." By the time the bridge was built, Fulton Ferry was making more than 1,000 crossings per day. The East River is far quieter now, but the river-and-four-borough views from the bridge are no less wondrous.

Foley Square, a name that has become synonymous with the New York court system, opens out above the Municipal Building. On the right, the orderly progression of the Corinthian colonnades of the **U.S. Courthouse** ㉒ and the **New York County Courthouse** ㉓ is a fitting reflection of the epigraph carved in the latter's frieze: THE TRUE ADMINISTRATION OF JUSTICE IS THE FIRMEST PILLAR OF GOOD GOVERNMENT. Turn to look across Foley Square at Federal Plaza, which sprawls in front of the grid-like skyscraper of the Javits Federal Building. The black-glass box to the left houses the U.S. Court of International Trade. Just south of it, at the corner of Duane and Elk, is the site of the **African Burial Ground,** where thousands of African-Americans from the colonial period were laid to rest.

Continue north up Centre Street past neoclassical civic office buildings to 100 Centre Street, the **Criminal Courts Building** ㉔, a rather foreboding construction with Art Moderne details. In contrast, the Civil and Municipal Courthouse across the way at 111 Centre Street is an uninspired modern cube, although it, too, has held sensational trials. On the west side of this small square is the slick black-granite Family Court (⊠ 60 Lafayette St.), with its intriguing angular facade.

Turn left onto Leonard Street, which runs just south of the Family Court, and take a look at the ornate Victorian building that runs the length of the block on your left. This is the old New York Life Insurance Company headquarters (⊠ 346 Broadway), an 1870 building that was remodeled and enlarged in 1896 by McKim, Mead & White. The ornate clock tower facing Broadway is now occupied by the avant-garde Clocktower Gallery, which is currently used as rehearsal space by various artists and is therefore not open to the public. The stretch of Broadway south of here is the subject of what is believed to be the oldest photograph of New York. The picture focuses on a paving project—to historically eliminate the morass of muddy streets—that took place in 1850.

From here, a tasty day's-end meal in Chinatown (☞ Little Italy and Chinatown, *above*) is only a few blocks north and east.

TIMING

You can easily spend a half day at the Seaport, or longer if you browse in shops. The rest of the tour is just walking and takes about 1½ hours. The real Seaport opens well before the sun rises and clears out not much after, when fishmongers leave to make way for the tourists. Unless you're really interested in wholesale fish, however, you're best off visiting the Seaport when its other attractions are open. Try to do this during the week, so that the government offices will be open, too. Also, consider walking Brooklyn Bridge in the late afternoon for dramatic contrasts of light, but just to be safe, make sure other pedestrians are strolling nearby.

Sights to See

African Burial Ground. This grassy corner is part of the original local area used to inter the earliest African-Americans—an estimated 20,000 until the cemetery was closed in 1794. The site was discovered during a 1991 construction project, and by an Act of Congress it was made into a National Historical Landmark, dedicated to the people who were enslaved in the city between 1626 and Emancipation Day in New York, July 4, 1827. ⊠ *Duane and Elk Sts.*

★ ㉑ **Brooklyn Bridge.** Its Great Bridge promenade takes a half hour to walk and is a New York experience on a par with the Statue of Liberty trip or the Empire State Building ascent. Before this bridge was built, Brooklynites had to rely on the Fulton Street ferry to get to Brooklyn—a charming way to travel, surely, but unreliable in fog or ice. After some 50 years of talk about a bridge, John Augustus Roebling, a respected engineer, was handed a construction assignment in 1867. (Ironically, he was fatally injured by a ferry in 1869.) As the project to build the first steel suspension bridge slowly took shape over the next 15 years, it captured the imagination of the city; on its completion in 1883, it was called the Eighth Wonder of the World. Its twin pointed-arch towers rise 268 ft from the river below. The roadway is supported by a web of steel cables, hung from the towers and attached to block-long anchorages on either shore. It is hardly the longest suspension bridge in the world anymore, but it remains a symbol of human accomplishment. As you look south from the walkway, the pinnacles of downtown Manhattan loom on your right, Brooklyn Heights rises on your left, Governor's Island is washed by the tides, and the harbor opens toward Lady Liberty, showing herself in profile. Turn about for a fine view up the East River, spanned within sight by the Manhattan and Williamsburg bridges. You don't need binoculars to enjoy the vistas, but you'd do well to bring a hat or scarf, because the wind can whip through the cables like a dervish.

⑰ City Hall. For a city as overwhelming as New York, this main government building, built between 1803 and 1812, is unexpectedly decorous. It reflects not big-city brawn but the classical refinement and civility of Enlightenment Europe—a columned and arched little palace with a cupola crowned by a statue of Lady Justice. Originally its front and sides were clad in white marble while the back was faced in cheap brownstone, because city fathers assumed New York would never grow farther north than this. Limestone now covers all four sides. The major interior feature is a domed rotunda from which a sweeping marble double staircase leads to the second-floor public rooms. The Victorian-style City Council Chamber in the east wing is small and clubby, with mahogany detailing and ornate gilding; the Board of Estimate chamber to the west has colonial paintings and church-pew-style seating; and the Governor's Room at the head of the stairs, used for ceremonial events, is filled with historic portraits and furniture, including a writing table that George Washington used in 1789 when New York was the U.S. capital. The blue room, which was traditionally the mayor's office, is on the ground floor; it is now used for mayoral press conferences.

The building figured prominently in the 1996 film *City Hall,* starring Al Pacino and John Cusack. On either side of the edifice are free interactive video machines that dispense information/propaganda to both tourists and residents on area attractions, civic procedures, City Hall history, mass transit, and other topics. ✉ *City Hall Park,* ☎ *212/788–6879 for tour information.*

City Hall Park. Originally the town common, in its day this green spot has hosted hangings, riots, and demonstrations; it is also the finish line for ticker-tape parades up lower Broadway (though ticker tape is nowadays replaced with perforated margin strips torn off from computer paper). A bronze statue of patriot Nathan Hale, who was hanged in 1776 as a spy by the British troops occupying New York City, stands on the Broadway side of the park. ✉ *Between Broadway and Park Row/Centre St., from Vesey St./Ann St. to Chambers St.*

㉔ Criminal Courts Building. This rather grim Art Deco tower may be familiar to fans of the television show *NYPD Blue,* connecting by a skywalk (New York's Bridge of Sighs) to the detention center known as the Tombs. In *The Bonfire of the Vanities,* Tom Wolfe wrote a chilling description of this court's menacing atmosphere. ✉ *100 Centre St.*

⑳ Municipal Building. Who else but the venerable architecture firm McKim, Mead & White would the city government trust to build its first skyscraper in 1914? The roof section alone is 10 stories high, bristling with towers and peaks and topped by a gilt statue of Civic Fame. This is where New Yorkers come to pay parking fines and get marriage licenses. An immense arch straddles Chambers Street (traffic used to flow through here); the vaulted plaza in front was the site of a scene in the movie *Crocodile Dundee,* in which the Aussie hunter coolly scares off would-be muggers with his bowie knife. ✉ *1 Centre St.*

㉓ New York County Courthouse. With its stately columns, pediments, and 100-ft-wide flight of steps, this 1912 classical temple front is yet another spin-off on Rome's Pantheon. Its deviation from that high architectural standard is in its hexagonal rotunda, shaped to fit an irregular plot of land. That quintessential courtroom drama *Twelve*

Angry Men was filmed here, as was the unpopular film *Legal Eagles*. The courthouse also hosts thousands of marriages a year. ⊠ *Foley Sq.*

⑮ **St. Paul's Chapel.** The oldest (1766) surviving church in Manhattan, this Episcopal house of worship was the site of the prayer service following George Washington's inauguration as president. Built of rough Manhattan brownstone, it was modeled on London's St. Martin-in-the-Fields. It's open until 3 every day except Saturday for prayer and meditation; look in the north aisle for Washington's pew. ⊠ *Broadway and Fulton St.,* ☎ *212/602–0874.*

★ ⑭ **South Street Seaport Historic District.** Had it not been declared a historic district in 1967, this charming, cobblestone corner of the city would likely have been gobbled up by skyscrapers. The Rouse Corporation, which had already created slick so-called festival marketplaces in Boston (Quincy Market) and Baltimore (Harborplace), was hired to restore and adapt the existing historic buildings, preserving the commercial feel of centuries past.

The little white lighthouse at Water and Fulton streets is the **Titanic Memorial,** commemorating the sinking of the RMS *Titanic* in 1912. Beyond it, Fulton Street, cobbled in blocks of Belgian granite, is a pedestrian mall that swarms with visitors, especially on fine-weather weekends. Immediately to your left is the **Cannon's Walk Block,** which contains 15 restored buildings.

At 211 Water Street is **Bowne & Co.,** a reconstructed working 19th-century print shop. Around the corner, a narrow court called Cannon's Walk, lined with shops, opens onto Fulton Street; follow it around to Front Street. Directly across Front Street is the **Fulton Market Building,** a modern building, full of shops and restaurants, that updates on multiple levels the bustling atmosphere of the old victual markets that occupied this site from 1822 on. On the south side of Fulton Street is the seaport's architectural centerpiece, **Schermerhorn Row,** a redbrick terrace of Georgian- and Federal-style warehouses and countinghouses built in 1811–12. Today the ground floors are occupied by upscale shops, bars, and restaurants, and the **South Street Seaport Museum.** ⊠ *12 Fulton St.,* ☎ *212/669–9400; 212/732–7678 for events and shopping information.* ▧ *$6 (to ships, galleries, walking tours, Maritime Crafts Center, films, and other seaport events).* ☉ *Museum Apr.–Sept., daily 10–6, Thurs. 10–8; Oct.–Mar., Wed.–Mon. 10–5.*

Cross South Street under an elevated stretch of FDR Drive to **Pier 16,** where the historic ships are docked, including the *Peking,* the second-largest sailing ship in existence; the full-rigged *Wavertree*; and the lightship *Ambrose.* The Pier 16 ticket booth provides information and sells tickets to the museum, the ships, tours, and exhibits. Pier 16 also hosts frequent concerts and performances and is the departure point for the one-hour **Seaport Liberty Cruise** (☎ *212/630–8888*), which runs from late March through November. The fare is $12; combination fare for cruise and other attractions is $15.

To the north is **Pier 17,** a multilevel dockside shopping mall. Its weathered-wood rear decks make a splendid spot from which to sit and contemplate the river; look north to see the Brooklyn, Manhattan, and Williamsburg bridges, and look across to see Brooklyn Heights.

As your nose may already have surmised, the blocks along South Street north of the museum complex still house a working fish market, which has been in operation since the 1770s. Although the city has tried to relocate the hundreds of fishmongers of the **Fulton Fish Market** to the South Bronx, the area remains a beehive of activity. Get up early (or stay up late) if you want to see it: The action begins around midnight and ends by 8 AM. *Tours by reservation only*, ☎ *212/748–8590.* ✉ *$10.* ⊙ *1st and 3rd Thurs. every month May–Sept. at 6 AM.*

<table>
<tr><td>NEED A
BREAK?</td><td>The cuisine at the fast-food stalls on Pier 17's third-floor **Promenade Food Court** is nonchain eclectic: Seaport Fries, Pizza on the Pier, Wok & Roll, Simply Seafood, and Salad Experience. What's really spectacular is the view from the tables in a glass-walled atrium.</td></tr>
</table>

⑲ Surrogate's Court. Also called the **Hall of Records,** this building is the most ornate of the City Hall court trio. In true Beaux Arts fashion, sculpture and ornament seem to have been added wherever possible to the basic neoclassical structure, yet the overall effect is graceful rather than cluttered. Filmmakers sometimes use its ornate lobby in opera scenes. A courtroom here was the venue for *Johnson* v. *Johnson,* where the heirs to the Johnson & Johnson fortune waged their bitter battle. ✉ *31 Chambers St.*

⑱ Tweed Courthouse. Under the corrupt management of notorious politician "Boss" William Marcy Tweed, this building took some $12 million and nine years to build (it was finally finished in 1872, but the ensuing public outrage drove Tweed from office). Although it is imposing, with its columned classical pediment outside and seven-story rotunda inside, almost none of the boatloads of marble that Tweed had shipped from Europe made their way into this building. Today it houses municipal offices; it has also served as a location for several films, most notably *The Verdict.* ✉ *52 Chambers St.*

㉒ U.S. Courthouse. Cass Gilbert built this in 1936, convinced that it complemented the much finer nearby Woolworth Building, which he had designed earlier. Granite steps climb to a massive columned portico; above this rises a 32-story tower topped by a gilded pyramid, not unlike that with which Gilbert crowned the New York Life building uptown. This courthouse has been the site of such famous cases as the tax-evasion trial of hotel queen Leona Helmsley. ✉ *26 Foley Sq.*

★ **⑯ Woolworth Building.** Called the Cathedral of Commerce, this ornate white terra-cotta edifice was, at 792 ft, the world's tallest building when it opened in 1913; it still houses the Woolworth corporate offices. Take a peek at the **lobby:** Among its extravagant Gothic-style details are sculptures set into arches in the lobby ceiling; one of them represents an elderly F. W. Woolworth pinching his pennies, while another depicts the architect, Cass Gilbert, cradling in his arms a model of his creation. ✉ *Park Pl. and Broadway.*

3 Exploring the Other Boroughs

Many of New York's treasures await visitors who venture to the outer boroughs. The Bronx has a world-renowned zoo. In Brooklyn you can revel in the verdant majesty of a botanical garden and take in the lovely river views of the Brooklyn Heights Promenade. Queens has the lively Greek neighborhood of Astoria. And if you take the pleasant ferry ride to Staten Island, you can visit historic Richmondtown.

By Amy
McConnell
and Matthew
Lore

MANY VISITORS TO MANHATTAN notice the four outer boroughs—Brooklyn, Queens, the Bronx, and Staten Island—only from an airplane window or the deck of a Circle Line cruise, leaving those areas to remain ciphers. "Don't fall asleep on the subway," the unschooled tourist tells himself, "or you may end up in the Bronx!"

Manhattanites themselves, many driven over the river by astronomical rents, discovered the outer boroughs in the late 1970s and 1980s. They found sky, trees, and living space among the 19th-century brownstones, converted industrial lofts, Art Deco apartment palaces, and tidy bungalows. They also found fascinating ethnic enclaves and a host of museums and parks.

The reality is that Manhattan is only a small part of New York City. Its population of about 1.5 million is smaller than that of either Brooklyn (2.3 million) or Queens (2 million) and only slightly larger than that of the Bronx (1.2 million). Staten Island may be less populous (391,000), but it's 2½ times the size of Manhattan.

There are things to see and do in the outer boroughs that you simply won't find in Manhattan, and most are just a subway ride away from midtown. Manhattanites may try to put you off such a journey, but don't be daunted. After a couple of beers, those same people may rave about their favorite place for cheesecake (Junior's on Flatbush Avenue in Brooklyn) or a great outdoor barbecue they had at their sister-in-law's mock-Tudor brick house (in Forest Hills Gardens, Queens); you may even have to listen to a story about their life's peak experience—found in the bleachers of Yankee Stadium in . . . the Bronx.

THE BRONX

The only borough attached to the North American mainland, the Bronx has plenty of attractions worth your while. This is where you'll find the city's most famous botanical garden and its oldest and largest zoo. In addition, there's the friendly Italian neighborhood of Belmont; wealthy Riverdale, with its riverside estates; and of course, Yankee Stadium, the home of the New York Yankees.

Though it's hard to imagine today, in the 1920s the Bronx was a desirable place to live. The building of the elevated subway line attracted an upwardly mobile population of average but improving means; Yankee Stadium was built; and the mile-long Grand Concourse was fashioned as New York's Champs-Elysées, lined with elaborate Art Deco buildings that still stand today.

Things changed for the worse in the 1960s and '70s as immigrants and laborers poured into the city and cheap housing projects were built in the Bronx—a comfortable distance from Manhattan. Government incentives lured the rich out of their ritzy Grand Concourse apartments and rents plummeted. Crime and urban decay tore apart the community.

Over the past several years, grassroots organizations have been working hard to salvage the Bronx, and their efforts are starting to pay off. Though many areas remain threatening, especially for unfamiliar visitors, the neighborhoods and attractions mentioned in this chapter are perfectly safe.

The New York Botanical Garden, the Bronx Zoo, and Belmont

Within the 5-mi vicinity covered in this tour, you can stroll among gardens of roses (250 different kinds), peonies (58 varieties), and medicinal herbs; watch red pandas swing from tree to tree; and sample biscotti at a third-generation bakery where patrons greet customers by name.

Numbers in the text correspond to numbers in the margin and on the New York Botanical Garden and Bronx Zoo map.

A Good Walk

The most direct route to the **New York Botanical Garden** ① is via Metro North to the Botanical Garden stop, which is right across from the garden's parking lot. You cross Southern Boulevard to the garden entrance. Alternatively, take Subway D or 4 to Bedford Park Boulevard. From the subway station, continue east on Bedford Park Boulevard (a 10-minute walk) to the Southern Boulevard entrance of the garden, where you may be tempted to spend the whole day. When you're ready to leave the garden grounds, exit via the Main Gate. Turn left and walk along Southern Boulevard to Pelham Parkway; turn left onto Fordham Road and continue to the Rainey Gate entrance of the **Bronx Zoo** ② (officially called the International Wildlife Conservation Center)—another must-see sight that could easily hold you for most of the day.

Exit the zoo via Southern Boulevard, turn right, and walk two blocks to East 187th Street; this will lead you straight into the heart of **Belmont,** an Italian neighborhood. You'll know you're in the right place when you see the imposing brick structure of **Our Lady of Mt. Carmel Roman Catholic Church** ③ (at Belmont Avenue and East 187th Street), the spiritual heart of the neighborhood—but for the true Belmont experience, a walk through the **Arthur Avenue Retail Market** ④ and a dish of pasta at **Dominick's** ⑤ are essential.

Fordham University ⑥ occupies a large plot of land north of Belmont. Follow Arthur Avenue to East Fordham Road (head toward the tall Gothic tower in the distance) and turn left. For a peek at the handsome inner campus, turn right on Bathgate Avenue (look for the inconspicuous street sign on the left side of the road); this will lead you to the college gate, which is manned by a security guard. Otherwise, continue on East Fordham Road three blocks to chaotic Fordham Plaza, nicknamed the Times Square of the Bronx. To return to Manhattan, take the Metro North at East Fordham Road and Webster Avenue, or continue on East Fordham Road about four blocks up to the Fordham Road subway station (at the Grand Concourse) for the D train.

TIMING

The Bronx Zoo and the New York Botanical Garden are each vast and interesting enough to merit half a day or more. If you're planning on visiting both, start early and plan on a late lunch or early dinner in Belmont. Saturday is the best day to see the Italian neighborhood at its liveliest; on Sunday most stores are closed. The zoo and the botanical garden are less crowded on weekdays—except Wednesdays, when admission to both is free and crowds often rush to snatch up the bargain.

Sights to See

Belmont. Often called the Little Italy of the Bronx, this is where some 14,500 local families socialize, shop, work, and eat, eat, eat. On Saturday afternoons, as residents rush around buying freshly baked bread

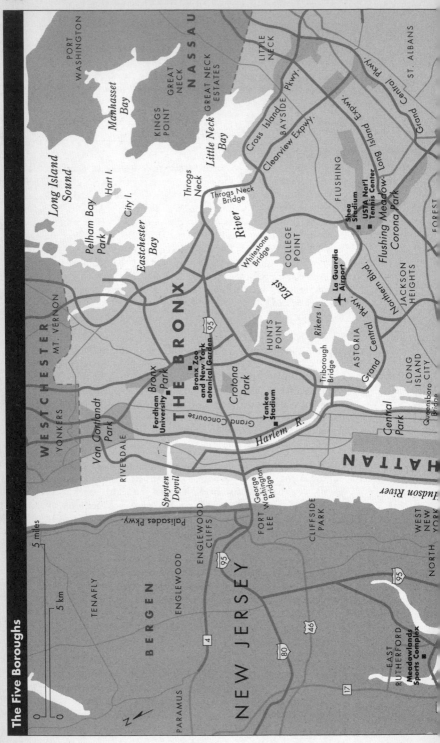

The Five Boroughs

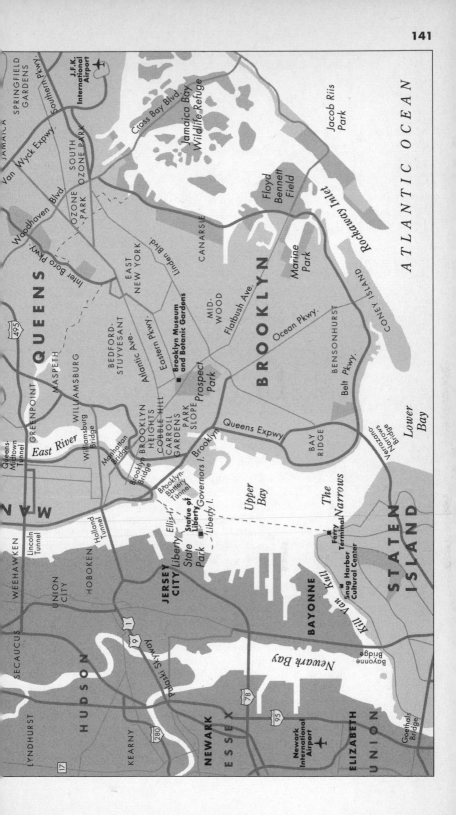

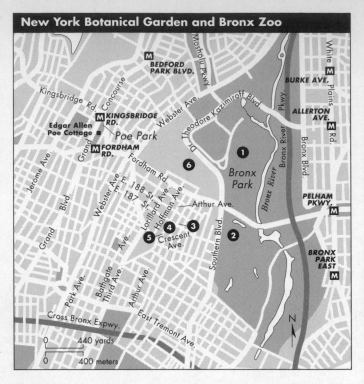

New York Botanical Garden and Bronx Zoo

and homemade salami, you may as well be in a small market town in
Italy. Don't be surprised to hear people speaking Italian in the neighborhood's tidy streets.

Across from Our Lady of Mt. Carmel Roman Catholic Church (☞
below), the **Catholic Goods Center** (✉ 630 E. 187th St.) sells multilingual Bibles and greeting cards as well as religious art. Next to the
Catholic Goods Center, **Borgatti's Ravioli & Egg Noodles** (✉ 632 E.
187th St.) is known for its homemade pastas, and **Danny's Pork Store**
(✉ 626 E. 187th St.) has homemade sausages. One block down, **Mount
Carmel Wines & Spirits** has a tremendous selection of Italian wines
and grappas in beautiful bottles. On Arthur Avenue, the gastronomic
temptations continue: Don't miss **Madonia Bros. Bakery** (✉ 2348 Arthur
Ave.), whose brick ovens have been turning out golden-brown loaves
since 1918.

★ ❷ **Bronx Zoo.** Opened in 1899, this zoo is one of the nation's largest, with
265 acres and more than 4,000 animals representing more than 600
species. One of the first zoos to use naturalistic, parklike settings instead of caged enclosures, it's full of fascinating exhibits such as "Jungle World," an indoor tropical rain forest complete with five waterfalls,
millipedes, flowering orchids, and pythons; "Wild Asia," where tigers
and elephants roam free on nearly 40 acres of open meadows and dark
forests; and "World of Birds," a huge, glassed-in aviary where birds
cozy up to visitors. Three different rides, including a shuttle bus, a mono-
rail, and a tram, offer various perspectives of the grounds during summer.

The **Children's Zoo** has many hands-on learning activities, as well as a large petting zoo. At the **Zoo Center,** visitors will find a rare black rhino.

To get to the Bronx Zoo, take Subway 2 to Pelham Parkway and walk three blocks west to the zoo. You can also take the Metro North train (☎ 212/532–4900) from Grand Central Terminal (☞ 42nd Street *in* Chapter 2) or catch the Liberty Line Bx M11 express bus (☎ 718/652– 8400) from mid-Manhattan. ⊠ *Bronx River Pkwy. and Fordham Rd.,* ☎ *718/367–1010.* ☎ *Apr.–Oct., Thurs.–Tues. $6.75; Nov.–Mar., Thurs.–Tues. $3; free Wed.* ☉ *Mar.–Oct., weekdays 10–5, weekends 10–5:30; Nov.–Feb., daily 10–4:30. Children's Zoo:* ☎ *$2;* ☉ *Apr.–Oct.*

⑤ **Dominick's.** There are no menus and no wine lists at this neighborhood favorite, where the question "What do you have?" is most often answered with "What do you want?" What you'll want is a heaping dish of traditional spaghetti with meatballs—some of the best you'll find in New York City—along with crusty bread and wine poured from a jug. The same family has been cooking at Dominick's since the 1940s, serving loyal fans at congested communal tables with red-and-white checked cloths. Expect to pay about $50 for two people. ⊠ *2335 Arthur Ave.,* ☎ *718/733–2807. Closed Tues.*

OFF THE
BEATEN PATH

EDGAR ALLAN POE COTTAGE – If you finish your tour while it's still light out, venture up Fordham Road to Kingsbridge Road, turn right, and walk the short block to Poe Park, where the Bronx County Historical Society maintains the Edgar Allan Poe Cottage, open weekends only. It was here that Poe and his sickly wife, Virginia, sought refuge from Manhattan and from the vicissitudes of the writerly life between 1846 and 1849. He wandered the countryside on foot and listened to the sound of the church bells at nearby St. John's College Church (now Fordham University); word has it that these bells inspired one of his most famous poems, "The Bells." At night the park attracts loiterers; visit only by day. ⊠ *E. Kingsbridge Rd. and Grand Concourse,* ☎ *718/881–8900.* ☎ *$2.* ☉ *Mid-Jan.–mid-Dec., Sat. 10–4, Sun. 1–5.*

⑥ **Fordham University.** A small enclave of distinguished Collegiate Gothic architecture in the midst of urban sprawl, this university opened in 1841 as a Jesuit college and was, for a time, one of the country's preeminent schools. Fordham now has an undergraduate enrollment of nearly 6,000 and a second campus near Lincoln Center. Enter the grounds via Bathgate Avenue, a few blocks west of Arthur Avenue (the security guard may require you to show ID), to see **Old Rose Hill Manor Dig;** the **University Church,** whose stained glass was donated by King Louis Philippe of France (1773–1850); the pleasant **Edward's Parade** quadrangle in the center of campus; and **Keating Hall,** sitting like a Gothic fortress in the center of things. Maps are posted around the campus and are available in the security office on your left inside the gate.

★ ① **New York Botanical Garden.** Considered one of the leading botany centers of the world, this 250-acre garden built around the dramatic gorge of the Bronx River is one of the best reasons to make a trip to the Bronx. The garden was founded by Dr. Nathaniel Lord Britton and his wife, Elizabeth. After visiting England's Kew Gardens in 1889, they returned full of fervor to create a similar haven in New York. In 1991 the New York Botanical Garden celebrated its centennial.

On the botanical garden grounds is the historic **Lorillard Snuff Mill,** built by two French Huguenot manufacturers in 1840 to power the grinding of tobacco for snuff. Nearby, the Lorillards grew roses to supply fragrance for their blend.

A walk along the Bronx River from the mill leads the visitor to the garden's 40-acre **Forest,** the largest remnant of the forest that once covered New York City. Outdoor plant collections include the **Peggy Rockefeller Rose Garden,** with 230 different kinds of roses. At the **Museum Building** there's a gardening shop, a library, and a world-renowned herbarium holding 6 million dried plant specimens.

After a four-year renovation was completed in 1997, the historic **Enid A. Haupt Conservatory** once again displays rain forests, deserts, and special exhibitions. An even newer attraction is the **Everett Children's Adventure Garden,** 8 acres of plant and science exhibits for children, including a boulder maze, giant animal topiaries, a wild wetland trail, and a plant discovery center.

To get to the Botanical Garden, take the Metro North train (☎ 212/532–4900) to the garden from Grand Central Terminal (☞ 42nd Street *in* Chapter 2); or take Subway D or 4 to the Bedford Park Boulevard stop and walk eight blocks east to the entrance on Bedford Park Boulevard. ⊠ *200th St. and Southern Blvd.,* ☎ *718/817–8700.* ⊠ *$3; free Sat. 10–noon and Wed. Parking $4.* ۞ *Nov.–Mar., Tues.–Sun. 10–4; Apr.–Oct., Tues.–Sun. 10–6.*

❸ **Our Lady of Mt. Carmel Roman Catholic Church.** Rising like a beacon of faith above all the neighboring food stores and restaurants, this is the spiritual center of Belmont. In 1907, when an Irish priest who spoke Italian successfully petitioned the archdiocese for an Italian church to serve the new immigrant community, many Italian residents of the neighborhood volunteered to help build the church in order to keep the costs down. Step inside the church and you'll find many plaques indicating donated pews and other gifts. ⊠ *627 E. 187th St.*

NEED A   At **Egidio's Pastry Shop** (⊠ 622 E. 187th St., ☎ 718/295–6077), a
BREAK?   neighborhood favorite, you can sample handmade Italian pastries, washed down with a strong shot of espresso. The homemade gelatos next door are top-notch.

Wave Hill

Perhaps the poshest neighborhood in the Bronx, Riverdale is the place to go for a glimpse of the lifestyles of rich and famous commuters. In the early part of this century, Manhattan millionaires, including the Kennedy family, built summer homes here, with stirring views of the New Jersey Palisades across the Hudson River. Wave Hill is the only one open to the public; its gardens and landscaped grounds provide a splendid place to spend a morning or afternoon.

A Good Tour

Riverdale and Wave Hill are best visited by car. From Manhattan take Exit 21 and follow the signs to Wave Hill. If you don't have a car, take the Metro North train to the Riverdale stop and walk up West 254th Street to Sycamore, turn right, and continue to Independence Avenue. Here, between 248th and 254th streets, you'll find some of Riverdale's handsomest mansions, including **Wave Hill.** The 28-acre estate was built in 1843, then lavishly expanded by J.P. Morgan's partner George Perkins. Mark Twain rented Wave Hill, and Theodore Roosevelt summered here until the property was acquired by the City of New York. Today, world-renowned gardens attract green thumbs from afar (free garden tours take place Sundays at 2:15), grand beech and oak trees adorn wide lawns, and the rugged cliffs known as the Palisades loom across the Hudson, by turns framed by elegant pergolas and hidden

along curving pathways. Additional draws are a greenhouse and conservatory, gardening and crafts workshops, a summertime dance series, and changing art exhibits. ⊠ *W. 249th St. and Independence Ave.,*
☎ *718/549–2055.* ☒ *Mid-Mar.–mid-Nov. $4; Sat.* AM *and Tues. free;*
mid-Nov.–mid-Mar. free. ☉ *Mid-May–mid-Oct., Tues.–Thurs. and*
weekends 10–5:30, Fri. 10–dusk; mid-Oct.–mid-May, Tues.–Sun. 10–
4:30.

TIMING
Allow half a day for an unhurried tour of Riverdale. Spring and fall
are ideal times to see Wave Hill's gardens at their best; the estate is closed
in winter.

BROOKLYN

New York City's most populous borough is also its most popular—
aside from Manhattan, that is. More people visit Brooklyn than any
of the other outer boroughs; and several Brooklyn neighborhoods, particularly Brooklyn Heights, Park Slope, Cobble Hill, and Carroll Gardens, are consistently desirable as places to live, with dignified
brownstone- and tree-lined streets, water views, handsome parks, and
small businesses.

Brooklyn Heights, Cobble Hill, and Carroll Gardens

"All the advantages of the country, with most of the conveniences of
the city." So ran the ads for a real-estate development that sprang up
in the 1820s just across the East River from downtown Manhattan.
Brooklyn Heights—named for its enviable hilltop position—was New
York's first suburb, linked to the city originally by ferry and later by
the Brooklyn Bridge. Feverish construction led by wealthy industrialists and shipping magnates quickly transformed the airy heights into
a fashionable upper-middle-class community.

The Heights deteriorated in the 1930s. In the 1940s and 1950s, the
area became an alternative to the bohemian haven of Greenwich Village—home to writers including Carson McCullers, W. H. Auden,
Arthur Miller, Truman Capote, Richard Wright, Alfred Kazin, Norman Mailer, and Hart Crane. Given the neighborhood's European feel
and convenient setting, it's not hard to imagine why they came.

Thanks to the vigorous efforts of preservationists in the 1960s, much
of the Heights was designated as New York's first historic district. Some
600 buildings more than 100 years old, representing a wide range of
American building styles, are in excellent condition today.

Cranberry and Pineapple are just two of the unusual street names
around here. Word has it that these names were created by a certain
Miss Sarah Middagh, who despised the practice of naming streets for
the town fathers and instead named them after various fruits.

A short hop across Atlantic Avenue from Brooklyn Heights, Cobble
Hill is another quiet residential area of leafy streets lined with notable
town houses built, like those in the Heights, by 19th-century New York's
upper middle class. The neighborhood is popular with young professionals and their children; on weekends, the sidewalks are busy with
residents pushing strollers, walking dogs, or chatting with their neighbors. A bit farther south, around President Street, Cobble Hill turns
into the historically Italian, working-class section of Carroll Gardens,
a neighborhood distinguished by deep blocks that allow for front
yards that are unusually large, at least by New York standards. On nice

days, residents can be found tending their front-yard gardens or sitting on their stoops as they watch life go by.

Numbers in the text correspond to numbers in the margin and on the Brooklyn Heights, Cobble Hill, and Carroll Gardens map.

A Good Walk

Take Subway 2 or 3 from Manhattan to Clark Street, or Subway 6 to Borough Hall and walk up Court Street to Clark Street. From Clark, turn left on Henry Street toward Pineapple Street. From here you'll be able to see the blue towers of the Manhattan Bridge, linking Brooklyn to Manhattan; you'll have a view of the Brooklyn Bridge itself in a few minutes.

Turn left onto Orange Street. On the north side of the block (the right-hand side of the street) between Henry and Hicks streets is a formidable institution, the **Plymouth Church of the Pilgrims** ①, the vortex of abolitionist sentiment in the years before the Civil War. Turn right on Hicks Street and follow it to Middagh Street (pronounced *mid*-awe). At its intersection with Willow Street is **24 Middagh Street** ②, the oldest home in the neighborhood. Venture a few steps west on Middagh to watch neighborhood children and their parents playing at the pleasant Harry Chapin Playground, named after the late singer-songwriter.

Backtrack on **Willow Street** and observe the outstanding architecture between Clark and Pierrepont streets (Nos. 149, 155, 157, and 159 are especially notable). As you turn right on Pierrepont heading toward the river, glance down Columbia Heights to your right, where the brownstones are particularly elegant.

Pierrepont Street ends at the **Brooklyn Heights Promenade** ③, one of the most famous vista points in all of New York City. This is a great place for a picnic, with take-out food from one of the many Montague Street restaurants or provisions from the exotic food stores on nearby Atlantic Avenue; try Sahadi Importing (✉ 187–189 Atlantic Ave., ☎ 718/624–4550) in particular. As you leave the Promenade (via Montague Street), look left to see Nos. 2 and 3 Pierrepont Place, two brick-and-brownstone palaces built in the 1850s by a China trader and philanthropist and used as a location for John Huston's film *Prizzi's Honor.* On your right lies Montague Terrace, where Thomas Wolfe lived when he finished *You Can't Go Home Again.*

After you've soaked in the views from the Promenade, leave it via Montague Street, the commercial spine of the Heights, heading east past restaurants representing a multitude of ethnic cuisines. At the northeast corner of Montague and Clinton streets is **St. Ann's and the Holy Trinity Church** ④, known for its historic stained-glass windows and performing-arts center.

Beyond Clinton on the north side of Montague Street, note an interesting row of banks: Chase (✉ 177 Montague St.), a copy of the Palazzo della Gran Guardia in Verona, Italy; a Citibank (✉ 181 Montague St.) that looks like a latter-day Roman temple; and the Art Deco Municipal Credit Union (✉ 185 Montague St.). Continue east on Montague if you wish to visit the historic **Brooklyn Borough Hall** ⑤ or detour a block north up Clinton Street to the elegant redbrick **Brooklyn Historical Society** ⑥, slated to be closed for renovation throughout 1998.

Return south along Clinton Street, and then turn right onto Remsen Street. At the corner of Remsen and Henry streets, stop to take in the Romanesque Revival **Our Lady of Lebanon Maronite Church** ⑦. Continue west on Remsen Street and then turn left onto Hicks Street to

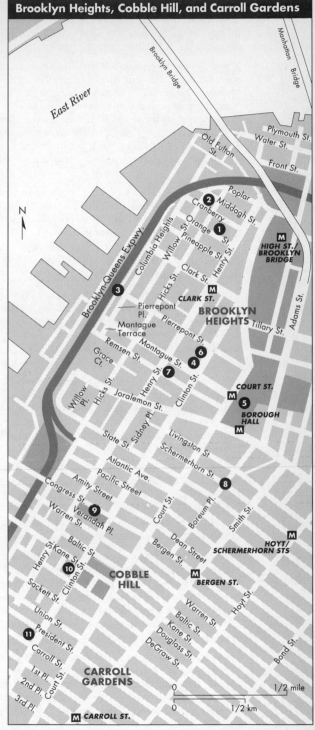

Brooklyn Heights, Cobble Hill, and Carroll Gardens

visit the 1847 Gothic Revival Grace Church at No. 254. Across Hicks Street is Grace Court Alley, a traditional mews with a score of beautifully restored redbrick carriage houses, which were once stables for the mansions on Remsen and Joralemon streets.

Just a few more steps down Hicks Street, turn right and stroll down cobblestoned Joralemon Street, noting Nos. 29–75, a row of modest brick row houses that delicately sidestep their way down the hill toward the river and the piers beyond the expressway. Follow Willow Place south along the peaceful block between Joralemon and State streets. Watch for the quietly elegant former Willow Place Chapel, built in 1876, and Nos. 43–49, four redbrick houses linked by a majestic two-story colonnade that looks transplanted from an antebellum southern mansion.

At the end of Willow Place, turn left on State Street and follow it past Hicks and Henry streets back to Clinton. If you're so inclined, make a left on Clinton and then the next right on Schermerhorn Street to visit the **New York City Transit Museum** ⑧. Otherwise turn right down Clinton to Atlantic Avenue, a busy thoroughfare crowded with Middle Eastern restaurants and, a few blocks farther east (to your left), a dozen antique furniture stores.

Atlantic Avenue is the official dividing line between the neighborhoods of Brooklyn Heights and Cobble Hill. For a taste of the latter, go two blocks south down Clinton Street to Amity. You may want to turn left to **197 Amity Street,** where Jennie Jerome, the mother of Winston Churchill, was born in 1854.

Return to Clinton and go one more block south, where on the west side of the street you'll find **Cobble Hill Park** ⑨, bordered by Verandah Place, a charming row of converted stable buildings where Thomas Wolfe once lived. Proceed south down Clinton Street to observe block after block of distinguished row houses, ranging from Romanesque Revival to neoclassical to Italianate brownstone. Three blocks south of the park, at 320 Clinton Street, is the Episcopal **Christ Church** ⑩, designed by Richard Upjohn.

About four blocks farther down Clinton, toward President Street, Cobble Hill gives way to the largely Italian Carroll Gardens. Wander down President, Carroll, and 1st and 2nd places to see the lovingly tended gardens; notice the abundance of religious statuary that attests to the largely Catholic makeup of the neighborhood.

Before leaving Clinton Street, stop for a look at the **Guido Funeral Home** ⑪ (on the northwest corner of Carroll and Clinton streets), one of the city's finest examples of a Greek Revival town house. Turn left (east) on Carroll Street to Court Street, the main commercial thoroughfare of the neighborhood. Carroll Gardens peters out about five blocks south (to the right); from here it's about 10 blocks back to Atlantic Avenue, to the north.

If you have the stamina to continue on to the Park Slope tour, take the F train from the Carroll Street subway station (at the intersection of Carroll and Smith streets) three more stops, in the direction of Coney Island, to the 7th Avenue stop. Alternatively, you can return to Manhattan via the F train.

TIMING

Allow three to four hours for a leisurely tour of these three neighborhoods, more if you plan on stopping for a picnic along the Promenade or a meal along Montague Street. Try to come on a clear, sunny day, when the view from the Promenade is most spectacular.

Sights to See

★ ❺ **Brooklyn Borough Hall.** Built in 1848 and thoroughly restored in the late 1980s, this Greek Revival landmark is arguably Brooklyn's most handsome building. The hammered-brass top of the cast-iron cupola (a successor to the original wooden one, which burned in 1895) was restored by the same French craftsmen who restored the Statue of Liberty. The stately building boasts Tuccahoe marble both inside and out; other highlights are the square rotunda and the two-story, Beaux Art courtroom with plaster columns painted to look like wood. Today the hall serves as the office of Brooklyn's borough president. On Tuesday and Saturday, a city Greenmarket sets up on the flagstone plaza in front, where bundles of fresh flowers and produce tempt shoppers from the Heights. ✉ 209 Joralemon St., ☎ 718/875–4047. ⚏ Free. ☉ Tours Tues. 1–2:30. Groups should telephone ahead.

★ ❸ **Brooklyn Heights Promenade.** East–west streets—from Orange on the north to Remsen on the south—end at this ⅓-mi-long sliver of park, which hangs over Brooklyn's industrial waterfront like one of Babylon's fabled gardens. Cantilevered over two lanes of the Brooklyn–Queens Expressway and a service road, the esplanade has benches offering some of the most enthralling views anywhere of the Manhattan skyline. Circling gulls squawk, tugboats honk, and the city seems like a magical place. This is a terrific vantage point from which to admire the Brooklyn Bridge, the historic steel suspension bridge designed by John Augustus Roebling and completed in 1883 (☞ The Seaport and the Courts in Chapter 2). The small island to your left is Governors Island, a military installation, the future of which is now being hotly debated.

❻ **Brooklyn Historical Society.** Erected in 1878–80, this elegant redbrick museum and library was the first major structure in New York to feature terra-cotta ornamentation, which includes lifelike busts, capitals, and friezes. The building is undergoing a major renovation and will be shrouded in scaffolding through the first half of 1998 and entirely closed. Neither its exhibits on Brooklyn history nor its impressive library will be accessible during the renovation, but to compensate for the closure, the society will be offering frequent Saturday walking tours of different Brooklyn neighborhoods. ✉ 128 Pierrepont St., ☎ 718/624–0890. ☉ Closed for renovations. Call for information about walking tours.

❿ **Christ Church.** This sandstone Episcopal church, with its lean tower-dominated facade, was designed by the prolific architect Richard Upjohn, who lived nearby at 296 Clinton Street. (He also designed Grace Church, at 254 Hicks Street.) The pulpit, lectern, and altar are the work of Louis Comfort Tiffany. The setting, on a tree-embowered patch of green enclosed by a wrought-iron fence, has the tranquil air of an English churchyard. ✉ 320 Clinton St., at Kane St.

❾ **Cobble Hill Park.** This lovely green oasis, one of the first "vest-pocket" parks in the city, has marble columns at its entrances, antique benches and tables, and a playground at one end. Bordering the park's south side is **Verandah Place**, a charming row of converted stable buildings where Thomas Wolfe once resided (one of his many residences in the borough). ✉ Congress St. between Clinton and Henry Sts.

NEED A BREAK? Between Court and Clinton streets on Atlantic Avenue are a half-dozen Middle Eastern gourmet markets and eateries. The best of these is 45-year-old **Sahadi Importing** (✉ 187–189 Atlantic Ave., ☎ 718/624–4550), where serious cooks stock up on astonishingly cheap and

delicious dried fruits, nuts, oils, olives, and spices, among other things.
Damascus Bread & Pastry (✉ 195 Atlantic Ave., ☎ 718/625–7070) is
a take-out joint with stellar spinach pie and baklava.

Columbia Heights. Among the majestic residences on this street, **Nos.
210–220** compose a brownstone grouping often cited as the most graceful in New York. Norman Mailer lives on this street, and from a rear
window in **No. 111**, John Roebling's son Washington, who in 1869
succeeded his father as chief engineer for the Brooklyn Bridge, directed the building of the bridge from his sickbed.

Court Street. The main commercial thoroughfare of Cobble Hill and
Carroll Gardens, Court Street overflows with activity, with its cafés,
restaurants, bookstores, old-fashioned bakeries, and a multiplex movie
theater. Before you head back to Manhattan, gather some of Carroll
Gardens' Italian specialties. Fresh pasta, mozzarella, sausages, olives,
and prepared dishes are available at a number of shops, including **Pas-
tosa Ravioli** (✉ 347 Court St., ☎ 718/625–9482), where the gnocchi
is particularly good, and **Caputo's Dairy** (✉ 460 Court St., ☎ 718/855–
8852), with a wide selection of homemade pastas and sauces.

NEED A
BREAK?
With its whirring ceiling fans, painted tin ceiling, and old wooden tables, **Roberto Cappuccino Caffè and Tea Room** (✉ 221 Court St., at
Wycoff St., ☎ 718/858–7693) is a charming spot for soup, sandwiches, coffee, and tea. At **Shakespeare's Sister** (✉ 270 Court St., at
Kane St., ☎ 718/694–0084) you can soothe yourself with any one of
a great variety of teas and light snacks while viewing art exhibits—usually featuring work by women.

⑪ F. G. Guido Funeral Home. Once the John Rankin Residence, this free-
standing three-story redbrick building, built in 1840, is considered one
of the city's finest examples of a Greek Revival town house. Its recessed
portal, bordered by limestone and topped with a fanlight, is particularly distinguished. ✉ *440 Clinton St.*

⑧ New York City Transit Museum. If you've always wanted to know
what an old-fashioned subway car looked like, here's your chance to
find out. Located inside a converted 1930s subway station, the museum displays 18 restored classic subway cars and has an operating
signal tower. ✉ *Boerum Pl. at Schermerhorn St.,* ☎ *718/243–3060.*
$3. ⊙ Tues.–Fri. 10–4, weekends noon–5.

197 Amity St. Jennie Jerome, the mother of Winston Churchill, was
born in this modest house in 1854. (Perversely, a plaque at 426 Henry
Street, southwest of here, identifies *that* building as the famous woman's
birthplace. The Henry Street address is actually where Jennie's parents
lived before she was born.)

❼ Our Lady of Lebanon Maronite Church. One of the oldest Romanesque
Revival buildings in the country, this Congregational church was designed by Richard Upjohn in 1844. Its doors, which depict Norman
churches, were salvaged from the 1943 wreck of the ocean liner *Nor-
mandie.* ✉ *113 Remsen St., at Henry St.*

❶ Plymouth Church of the Pilgrims. Thanks to the stirring oratory of Brooklyn's most eminent theologian, Henry Ward Beecher, this house of worship was the vortex of abolitionist sentiment in the years before the
Civil War. Because it provided refuge to American slaves, the church
is known as the Grand Central Terminal of the Underground Railroad.
Like those of many other neighborhood churches, its windows were
designed by Louis Comfort Tiffany. Beside the church is a courtyard

(locked, alas) with a statue of Beecher, which you can see through the gate. Nearby, at 22 Willow Street, Beecher's house still stands—a prim Greek Revival brownstone. ⊠ *Orange St. between Henry and Hicks Sts.*

4 **St. Ann's and the Holy Trinity Church.** The church, a national historic landmark, claims 60 of the first stained-glass windows made in the United States. More than half have been restored to date; through the **St. Ann's Center for Restoration and the Arts,** visitors can see the restoration process up close (call the box office to arrange a visit). In 1980 the church created its own performing-arts center, Arts at St. Ann's, referred to in *Rolling Stone* as "New York's hippest hall." A wide variety of non-classical music—jazz, blues, world and new music, musical theater, and experimental opera—is performed March through May and October through December. The church is open only for performances and Sunday at 11 AM for Episcopal worship services. ⊠ *157 Montague St., at Clinton St.,* ☎ *718/858–2424.* ☺ *Box office Tues.–Sat. noon–6.*

2 **24 Middagh Street.** This 1824 Federal-style clapboard residence with a mansard roof is the oldest home in the neighborhood. Peer through a door in the wall on the Willow Street side for a glimpse of the cottage garden and carriage house in the rear.

Willow Street. One of the prettiest and most architecturally varied blocks in Brooklyn Heights is Willow Street between Clark and Pierrepont streets. **Nos. 155–159** are three distinguished brick Federal row houses that were allegedly stops on the Underground Railroad.

Coney Island

Named Konijn Eiland (Rabbit Island) by the Dutch for its wild rabbit population, Coney Island has a boardwalk, a 2½-mi-long beach, a huge amusement park, the city's only aquarium, and easy proximity to Brighton Beach, a Russian enclave drenched in old-world atmosphere. Although Coney Island may have declined from its glory days early in this century—when visitors lunched at an ocean-side hotel built in the shape of an elephant, glided across the nation's biggest dance floor at Dreamland, or toured a replica of old Baghdad called Luna Park—it's still a great place to experience the sounds, smells, and sights of summer: hot dogs, suntan lotion, crowds, fried clams, girls and boys necking under the boardwalk, and old men staring vacantly out to sea, not to mention the heart-stopping roll of the king of roller coasters, the Cyclone, and the Wonder Wheel.

A Good Walk

Coney Island is the last stop on the B and F trains heading toward Brooklyn. The Coney Island boardwalk still remains the hub of the action; amble along it to take in the local color. For a taste of times gone by, stop at the **Sideshows by the Seashore and the Coney Island Museum,** where fire-eaters and sword swallowers carry on the traditions of what was once billed as the "World's Largest Playground." Entertainment of a more natural sort can be had at the **Aquarium for Wildlife Conservation,** where five beluga whales and some 10,000 other creatures of the sea make their home. From here, so-called Little Odessa is just a short walk away. To get there, take Surf Avenue to Brighton Beach Avenue, where a community of some 90,000 Russian, Ukrainian, and Georgian emigrés operate countless inexpensive restaurants. This is the place to find borscht and blinis, not to mention caviar, at prices that put Petrossian to shame.

TIMING

Coney Island is at its liveliest on weekends, when crowds come out to play, and in summer. Brighton Beach is a vibrant neighborhood year-round. Allow a full day for this trip, since the subway ride from Manhattan (one-way) takes at least an hour.

Sights to See

★ ☉ **Aquarium for Wildlife Conservation.** Moved to Coney Island in 1955 from its former digs at Battery Park, New York City's only aquarium is worth a trip in itself. Here otters, walruses, penguins, and seals lounge on a replicated Pacific coast; a 180,000-gallon sea-water complex hosts beluga whales; and dolphins and sea lions perform in the Aquatheater. ⊠ *W. 8th St. and Surf Ave.,* ☎ *718/265–3474.* ☜ *$7.75.* ☉ *Daily 10–4:45.*

☉ **Sideshows by the Seashore and the Coney Island Museum.** A lively traditional circus sideshow, complete with a fire-eater, sword swallower, snake charmer, and contortionist, can be seen here. On the first Saturday after summer solstice, the cast of the sideshow and an amazing array of local legends take part in the increasingly renowned Mermaid Parade, in which 50 antique cars, six marching bands, and artistic floats with a mermaid theme throng the Boardwalk and Surf Avenue. Upstairs from Sideshows, the Coney Island Museum has historic Coney Island memorabilia and a wealth of tourist information. ⊠ *Sideshows: W. 12th St. and Surf Ave.; museum:* ⊠ *1208 Surf Ave.;* ☎ *718/372–5159 for both.* ☜ *Sideshows $3, museum 99¢.* ☉ *Memorial Day–Labor Day, Wed.–Sun. noon–midnight; Labor Day–Memorial Day, weekends noon–5.*

Park Slope and Prospect Park

Park Slope grew up in the late 1800s and is today one of Brooklyn's most sought-after places to live. The largely residential neighborhood has row after row of dazzlingly well-maintained brownstones dating from the turn of the century. The "Park" in Park Slope refers to Prospect Park, one of New York's most revered green spaces, encompassing 526 acres of meadow, woodland, and water, miles of drives and paths, and home to a zoo, skating rink, concert bandshell, and much more. Just beyond the park's borders are the outsized Grand Army Plaza, with its Arc de Triomphe–style Soldiers' and Sailors' Memorial Arch; the stately Brooklyn Museum and Brooklyn Library; and the scenic Brooklyn Botanic Garden, a worthwhile destination virtually any time of year.

Numbers in the text correspond to numbers in the margin and on the Park Slope and Prospect Park map.

A Good Walk

Start your tour at **Seventh Avenue,** the neighborhood's commercial center, accessible by Subways D and F (7th Ave. stop) and by Subways 2 and 3 (Grand Army Plaza stop). The beginning of this walk is closer to Subway D, 2, or 3. Turn east from 7th Avenue onto Lincoln Place to find the **Montauk Club** ① (⊠ 25 8th Ave.), whose sumptuous Venetian-palace style belies its standing as one of Brooklyn's most prestigious men's clubs. Make your way south along 8th Avenue, sampling the brownstones on various streets along the way (President and Carroll streets are especially handsome), until you reach **Montgomery Place** ②, with its remarkable row of Romanesque Revival brownstones.

From Montgomery Place, walk one block east along Prospect Park West to **Grand Army Plaza** ③, whose center is dominated by the Soldiers'

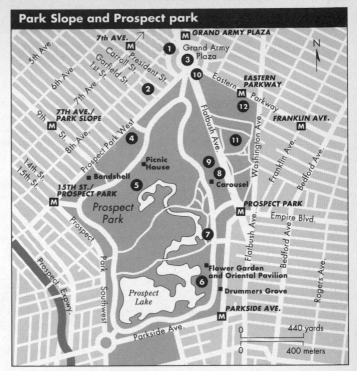

Park Slope and Prospect park

and Sailors' Memorial Arch, patterned on the Arc de Triomphe in Paris. Southeast of the plaza is the main entrance to the 526-acre **Prospect Park,** designed by Frederick Law Olmsted and Calvert Vaux, who also created Manhattan's Central Park. The best way to experience the park is to walk the entirety of its 3.3-mi circular drive and make detours off of it as you wish. On summer evenings and weekends year-round, when the drive is closed to vehicular traffic, joggers, skaters, and bicyclists have it to themselves and make a high-energy parade. Immediately upon entering the park, veer right on the circular drive. Take a moment to admire the 75-acre Long Meadow, one of New York's greatest open spaces and a haven for picnickers, kite fliers, and dog lovers on nice weekends. Remarkably, more than 130 years after the park's construction, the view down the Long Meadow from here still takes in no buildings—only grass, trees, and sky. A short distance down the drive, just beyond a circular playground on your right, a small access road leads you around to the **Litchfield Villa** ④, an elaborate Italianate mansion and home of the park's administrative offices.

Continuing on the circular drive from the villa, you'll next come to two popular park structures on your left—the Picnic House, frequently rented for weddings, and, a moment later, the **Tennis House** ⑤, home to the Brooklyn Center for Urban Education. Off to the right, just a few steps farther, is the bandshell, site of the park's enormously popular free summer performing-arts series. Continue around the circular drive, which makes a big turn to the left as it curves around the park's half-dozen baseball diamonds, in continuous use by local leagues between Memorial Day and Labor Day; the diamonds mark the far southern end of the Long Meadow. You'll soon glimpse on your left the glorious 60-acre Prospect Lake, a refuge for waterfowl, including a few resident swans. Beyond the Ocean Parkway/Coney Island Avenue park entrance, as you reach the lake's outer reaches, in swift succession you'll come upon the **Drummers Grove** on the right, and, on the left, the **Wollman Memorial Rink** ⑥, Flower Garden, Oriental Pavilion, and **Boathouse** ⑦.

Not far beyond the Boathouse, off on the eastern edge of the park (to your right) are the carousel, and beyond that the **Lefferts Homestead Children's Museum** ⑧ and the **Prospect Park Wildlife Conservation Center** ⑨, a small zoo. From here, you're just a short walk up the last of the circular drive back to Grand Army Plaza, at which point you've come full circle around the park. To the east of the park's main entrance, you will find the main branch of the **Brooklyn Public Library** ⑩. A couple hundred yards east on the grand **Eastern Parkway** lie the entrances to two of Brooklyn's most important cultural offerings: the beautifully tended **Brooklyn Botanic Garden** ⑪, which occupies 52 acres across Flatbush Avenue from Prospect Park, and the world-class **Brooklyn Museum of Art** ⑫. To return to Manhattan, you can take Subway 2 or 3 from the station right in front of the museum.

TIMING

You could very well spend a whole day at the Brooklyn Museum alone—and another day exploring Prospect Park and the Brooklyn Botanic Garden. If you do choose to fit everything into one trip, break up your wanderings with a visit to 7th Avenue, where restaurants and cafés abound. Weekends are the best time to observe local life along 7th Avenue and to enjoy the park, when it's closed to vehicles. The Botanic Garden reaches its prime during spring, when the cherry blossoms bloom like pink snow, although its gardens and greenhouses have been designed to offer year-round pleasures.

Sights to See

❼ **Boathouse.** Styled after Sansovino's 16th-century Library at St. Mark's in Venice, this 1905 lakefront structure in Prospect Park, built about 40 years after the park was first created, sits opposite the **Lullwater Bridge**, which affords a lovely view of it, particularly on evenings when the light is just right and the lake reflects an exact image of the building. Unfortunately, its white-glazed terra-cotta facade has been heavily water-damaged; the building has been unattractively fenced off and will be closed at least through 1998. Just steps from the boathouse (on the left as you face the Cleft Ridge Span) and unaffected by its closure is the lovely **Camperdown Elm,** immortalized by the poet Marianne Moore, who in the 1960s was an early park preservationist.

★ ⑪ **Brooklyn Botanic Garden.** A major attraction at this 52-acre botanic garden, one of the finest in the country, is the beguiling **Japanese Garden**—complete with a blazing red *torii* gate and a pond laid out in the shape of the Chinese character for "heart." The Japanese cherry arbor in the Japanese Garden turns into a heart-stopping cloud of pink every spring. You can also wander through the **Cranford Rose Garden** (5,000 bushes, 1,200 varieties); the **Fragrance Garden,** designed especially for the blind; the **Shakespeare Garden,** featuring more than 80 plants immortalized by the Bard (including many kinds of roses); and **Celebrity Path,** Brooklyn's answer to Hollywood's Walk of Fame, with the names of homegrown stars—including Mel Brooks, Woody Allen, Mary Tyler Moore, Barbra Streisand, Mae West, and Maurice Sendak—inscribed on stepping-stones. A complex of handsome greenhouses called the **Steinhardt Conservatory** holds thriving desert, tropical, temperate, and aquatic vegetation, as well as a display charting the evolution of plants over the past 140 million years. The extraordinary **C.V. Starr**

Bonsai Museum in the Conservatory exhibits about 80 miniature Japanese specimens. Free tours are given weekends at 1 PM, except for holiday weekends. ✉ *1000 Washington Ave., between Empire Blvd. and south side of Brooklyn Museum,* ☎ *718/622–4433.* ▧ *$3; free Tues.* ☉ *Garden Apr.–Sept., Tues.–Fri. 8–6, weekends 10–6; Oct.–Mar., Tues.–Fri. 8–4:30, weekends 10–4:30. Steinhardt Conservatory Apr.–Sept., Tues.–Sun. 10–5:30; Oct.–Mar., Tues.–Sun. 10–4.*

★ ⑫ **Brooklyn Museum of Art.** Housed in a massive, regal building designed by McKim, Mead & White in 1893, this world-class museum welcomes visitors to its Eastern Parkway entrance (from which a grand staircase was removed in 1934) with allegorical figures of Brooklyn and Manhattan, originally carved by Daniel Chester French for the Manhattan Bridge. With approximately 1.5 million objects, the Brooklyn collection is the second-largest art museum in New York. Look especially for its **Egyptian Art** collection (third floor), considered one of the best of its kind, or the **African and Pre-Columbian Art** collection (first floor), another one recognized worldwide. In the gallery of **American painting and sculpture** (fifth floor) you'll find *Brooklyn Bridge* by Georgia O'Keeffe, as well as striking works by Winslow Homer, John Singer Sargent, Stuart Davis, and Gilbert Stuart. The **Period Rooms** (fourth floor) include the complete interior of the Jan Martense Schenck House, built in the Brooklyn Flatlands section in 1675, as well as a Moorish-style room from the 54th Street mansion of John D. Rockefeller. The museum's 1993 renovation by Japanese architect Arata Isozaki and New York firm James Stewart Polshek includes a new auditorium with a wavelike ceiling, and new galleries in the oldest part of the building, adding 30,000 square ft of exhibition space. Outdoors, the **Frieda Schiff Warburg Memorial Sculpture Garden** showcases architectural fragments from demolished New York buildings, including Penn Station. The museum also has excellent special exhibitions and dramatic views of Manhattan from its Eastern Parkway–Washington Avenue corner. ✉ *200 Eastern Pkwy.,* ☎ *718/638–5000.* ▧ *$4 (suggested donation).* ☉ *Wed.–Fri. 10–5, Sat. 11–9, Sun. 11–6.*

⑩ **Brooklyn Public Library.** This grand neoclassical edifice has held its post near the Brooklyn Museum since 1941. Designed to resemble an open book, with a gilt-inscribed spine on Grand Army Plaza that opens out to Eastern Parkway and Flatbush Avenue, it remains an architectural wonder, touted for its bright limestone walls, perfect proportions, and ornate decorative details. The 15 bronze figures over the entrance represent favorite characters in American literature; they were sculpted by Thomas Hudson Jones, who also designed the Tomb of the Unknown Soldier in Arlington National Cemetery. ✉ *Grand Army Plaza at intersection of Flatbush Ave. and Eastern Pkwy.,* ☎ *718/780–7700.* ☉ *Tues.–Thurs. 9–8; Mon., Fri., and Sat. 10–6; Sun. 1–5.*

Drummers Grove. Designated as an official ☞ **Prospect Park** site in 1996, this area has long been a popular informal weekend gathering spot for Caribbean and African-American musicians, many of whom live in the neighborhood bordering the eastern side of the park. Sunday afternoons, especially during seasonable months, you'll find dozens of drummers, chanters, dancers, and other revelers getting down, joined by an audience of stalled bicyclists, joggers, and skaters lulled by the mesmerizing beat, beat, beat of the tom-tom.

Eastern Parkway. The first six-lane parkway in the world, this major boulevard mimics the grand sweep of the boulevards of Paris and Vienna; it originates at Grand Army Plaza. Frederick Law Olmsted and Calvert Vaux conceived the design in 1866, in tandem with their plans for the park; at that time the parkway ended at Ralph Avenue, then the border of Brooklyn. Today Eastern Parkway continues to play an important role in Brooklyn culture: Every Labor Day weekend it hosts the biggest and liveliest carnival outside the Caribbean—a cacophony of calypso, steel band, and reggae music, with plenty of conch curry, spice bread, and meat patties to go around.

❸ Grand Army Plaza. Prospect Park West, Eastern Parkway, and Flatbush and Vanderbilt avenues radiate outward from this geographic star. At the center stands the **Soldiers' and Sailors' Memorial Arch,** honoring Civil War veterans and patterned on the Arc de Triomphe in Paris. Three heroic sculptural groupings adorn the arch: atop, a four-horsed chariot by Frederick MacMonnies, so dynamic that it almost seems on the verge of catapulting off the arch; to the sides, the victorious Union Army and Navy of the Civil War. Inside are bas-reliefs of presidents Abraham Lincoln and Ulysses S. Grant, sculpted by Thomas Eakins and William O'Donovan, respectively. Crossing the broad streets around here can be hazardous; beware.

To the northwest of the arch, Neptune and a passel of debauched Tritons leer over the edges of the **Bailey Fountain,** where tulle-drenched brides and grooms in technicolor tuxes pose after exchanging vows. On Saturdays year-round, the second-largest of the city's Greenmarkets (after Union Square's in downtown Manhattan) sets up shop in the plaza; heaps of locally grown produce, flowers and plants, baked goods, and other foodstuffs attract throngs of neighborhood residents.

✋ ❽ Lefferts Homestead Children's Museum. Built in 1783 and moved to ☞ Prospect Park in 1918, this gambrel-roofed Dutch colonial farmhouse contains a historic house museum for children. Adults will enjoy the two period rooms furnished with antiques, while children love playing in the four rooms with period reproduction furniture. Nearby is a restored 1912 **carousel.** *Museum:* ☎ *718/965–6505.* ✉ *Free.* ☉ *Mid-Apr.–mid-Dec., weekends 1–4:30; weekdays and mid-Dec.–Mar. by appointment. Hrs vary, so call ahead. Carousel:* ☎ *50¢ per ride on weekends.* ☉ *Closed mid-Oct.–early Apr.*

❹ Litchfield Villa. The most important sight on the western border of ☞ Prospect Park, this Italianate mansion built in 1857 was designed by Alexander Jackson Davis, considered the foremost architect of his day, for a prominent railroad magnate. It has housed the park's headquarters since 1883, but visitors are welcome to step inside and view the domed octagonal rotunda. Not far from the Litchfield Villa on the park's circular drive is the **Picnic House,** one of the park's less architecturally distinguished buildings, used mostly for private functions. ✉ *Prospect Park W and 3rd St.,* ☎ *718/965–8999 for park hot line.*

❶ Montauk Club. The home of a venerable men's club, this 1891 mansion designed by Francis H. Kimball is modeled on Venice's Ca' d'Oro and other Gothic Venetian palaces. It is Park Slope's most impressive building and easily rivals the showcase mansions with more prestigious addresses on Manhattan's Upper East Side. Notice the friezes of Montauk Indians and the 19th-century private side entrance for members' wives. ✉ *25 8th Ave.*

❷ Montgomery Place. This block-long street between 8th Avenue and Prospect Park West is considered to be one of Park Slope's finest thoroughfares; it's filled with a picturesque variety of town houses designed by the Romanesque Revival genius C.P.H. Gilbert.

Prospect Park. When they initiated construction of this 526-acre park in 1866, Frederick Law Olmsted and Calvert Vaux considered their plan superior to that of Central Park (☞ Chapter 2)—which was being completed as they started work here—because no streets divided it and no bordering skyscrapers infringed on its borders. It is regarded by Olmsted aficionados as among his very best creations, and although its fortunes have risen and fallen over the last 130 years, a large number of restoration projects now planned or in progress are helping to revitalize the park. The largest of these involves the **Ravine,** the wooded core of the park. Though just steps from the Long Meadow (the main path from the park's 9th Street entrance leads right down to it), it vividly conveys a sense of wilderness and demonstrates Olmsted's genius at juxtaposing vastly different landscapes. Currently undergoing a monumental multiphase restoration, the Ravine is scheduled to be closed through 2000, although park administrators hope to have a few paths that run through it open by mid-1998.

A rewarding visit to the park need not involve any specific destination, as the park's winding paths and drives, undulating hills, unexpected vistas, and astonishing variety of open spaces serve up unanticipated pleasures at every turn. But visitors desiring specific destinations won't be disappointed; key attractions include the ☞ **Tennis House,** the ☞ **Wollman Memorial Skating Rink,** the ☞ **Prospect Park Wildlife Conservation Center,** and the **bandshell.** Located at the Park's 9th Street entrance (at Prospect Park West), the bandshell is home of the annual Celebrate Brooklyn Festival, which from mid-June through Labor Day sponsors free performances—with an emphasis on music—to please every taste, from African-Caribbean jazz to Kurt Weill, the Brooklyn Philharmonic playing Duke Ellington to bluegrass and zydeco groups. A performance here on a glorious summer evening is *the* best way to enjoy the park and the Slope at their finest. ⊠ *Bandshell, Prospect Park W and 9th St.,* ☎ *718/855–7882, ext. 52.* ⊠ *Free.* ☉ *Concerts mid-June–Labor Day, Fri.–Sat. 7 PM, some Sun. 2 PM, plus additional times. Call for details.*

NEED A
BREAK?

The Living Room Café (⊠ 188 Prospect Park W, at 14th St., ☎ 718/369–0824), in the historic, recently renovated Pavilion Theater (once a single-screen grande dame and now a five-plex cinema), is just a short walk from the bandshell and has quickly become a favorite neighborhood hangout. You can gaze out the oversize windows overlooking the park and soak in the zany decor as you nibble on crepes, sandwiches, a sundae, or an egg cream from the Ben & Jerry's Ice Cream Parlour.

☺ ❾ **Prospect Park Wildlife Conservation Center.** Small, friendly, and educational, this children's zoo off the main road of ☞ **Prospect Park** has just the right combination of indoor and outdoor exhibits along with a number of unusual and endangered species among its 160 inhabitants. The central sea-lion pool is a hit with youngsters, as are the indoor exhibits—"Animal Lifestyles," which explains habitats and adaptations, and "Animals in Our Lives," showcasing animals that make good pets and animals used on the farm. There's also an outdoor discovery trail with a simulated prairie-dog burrow and a naturalistic pond. The zoo is run by the Wildlife Conservation Society, which also oversees the Bronx Zoo (☞ The Bronx, *above*). ☎ 718/399–7339. ⊠ *$2.50.* ☉ *Nov.–Mar., daily 10–4:30; Apr.–Oct., weekdays 10–5, weekends 10–5:30.*

Seventh Avenue. Restaurants, groceries, bookstores, cafés, bakeries, churches, and many other neighborhood businesses stretch continuously down Park Slope's commercial spine from Flatbush Avenue roughly to 14th Street, where things peter out. A leisurely stroll will yield finds for browsers and buyers of all interests, but a few choice spots—beginning at the north (Flatbush) end and moving south—include the **New Prospect** (⌧ 52 7th Ave.), the best place to pick up some ready-made food; **Prints Charming** (⌧ 54 7th Ave.), offering a good selection of both framed and unframed prints; **Cousin John's Bakery** (⌧ 70 7th Ave.), one of the neighborhood's best; **Leaf 'n Bean** (⌧ 83 7th Ave.), a charming tea and coffee shop with lots of hard-to-find paraphernalia; **Leon Paley Ltd. Wines & Spirits** (⌧ 88 7th Ave.), a wine store of real distinction; the **Clay Pot** (⌧ 162 7th Ave.), which sells a distinctive array of handmade crafts and jewelry; and **Connecticut Muffin** (⌧ 171 7th Ave.), one of the neighborhood's most popular people-watching spots.

A bit farther down, closer to 9th Street (where the F train stops), be sure not to miss **Cheese in the Park** (⌧ 446 9th St., at 7th Ave.), with a fine selection of imported cheeses and locally made breads; another branch of **Cousin John's Bakery** (⌧ 343 7th Ave.); and the funkiest store in the Slope, **Scouting Party** (⌧ 349 7th Ave., at 10th St.), a riotous mix of toys and doodads that will appeal to kids and adults alike, plus a small but well-chosen selection of jewelry, crafts, cards, and used books.

NEED A BREAK?

Second Street Café (⌧ 189 7th Ave., at 2nd St., ☎ 718/369–6928) is a homey restaurant and coffee bar with lunch on weekdays, brunch on weekends, and counter-service coffee-bar fare in late afternoons and evenings. Try the raisin-studded bread pudding or heart-warming soups such as curry pumpkin. The coffee house of choice around here is **Ozzie's Coffee & Tea** (⌧ 57 7th Ave., at Lincoln Pl., ☎ 718/398–6695), a converted drugstore with its apothecary cases still intact.

⑤ Tennis House. The most prominent of several neoclassical structures in the park, this 1910 limestone and yellow brick building postdates by 40 years the more rustic structures favored by Olmsted and Vaux, few of which survive. The Tennis House's most elegant features are the triple-bay Palladian arches on both its north and south facade, and its airy terra-cotta barrel-vaulted arcade on the south side. The building's large tiled central court has amazing acoustics—shout "hello" and listen to your voice bounce back at you. The house sits atop a modest knoll overlooking the south end of the Long Meadow, where spring through fall you can almost always catch a baseball or softball game at one of the nearby diamonds. In the basement is the **Brooklyn Center for the Urban Environment,** which houses rotating exhibits about urban issues. ☎ *718/788–8500.* ⌧ *Free.* ☉ *Weekdays 8:30–5 (Tennis House only) and weekends noon–4 (Tennis House and BCUE gallery, when an exhibit is up).*

⑥ Wollman Memorial Rink. A cousin to Wollman Rink in Central Park (☞ Chapter 2), this is one of ☞ **Prospect Park**'s most popular destinations. Besides skating in the winter, boat rentals are available here weekends and holidays from April through the end of October (☎ 718/282–7789); the cost is $10 per hour. The rink is directly across the circular drive from the ☞ **Drummers Grove** and adjacent to the **Flower Garden,** the most formally laid-out area of the park. Unfortunately, the construction of the Wollman Rink destroyed this area's original close connection with the lake. In the early days, an orchestra would play on an island just off the shore while spectators strolled along the terraces and radial pathways among the busts of composers including Mozart and Beethoven or sat beneath the beautiful **Oriental Pavilion,** an open shelter supported by eight hand-painted wrought-iron columns and illuminated within by a central stained-glass skylight. Today this area of the park tends to attract teenagers from the adjacent neighborhood, who don't make visitors feel especially welcome, and during the winter music blares from the rink. ☎ *718/287–5538.* ☜ *$3.50 skate rental.* ☉ *Mid-Nov.–early Mar., Wed.–Sun. 10 AM–closing times vary.*

QUEENS

Home of the La Guardia and John F. Kennedy International airports and many of Manhattan's bedroom communities, Queens is perhaps New York City's most underappreciated borough. Here are countless ethnic neighborhoods (with some of the city's tastiest—and cheapest—restaurants) and little-known historic sites, most of them less than 10 minutes by subway from Grand Central Terminal.

Astoria

Home to a vital community of some 35,000 Greeks, Astoria is a place where people socialize on their front lawns at dusk and where mom-and-pop businesses thrive. Here you can buy Cypriot cured olives and feta cheese from store owners who will tell you where to go for the best spinach pie; or you can sit outside at one of the many *xaxaroplasteion* (pastry shops), eating baklava and watching the elevated subways speed by.

Originally German, then Italian, Astoria earned the nickname Little Athens in the late 1960s; by the early 1990s, Greeks accounted for slightly less than half the population. Today there are also substantial numbers of Asians, Eastern Europeans, Irish, and Hispanic immigrants in Astoria, not to mention an ever-growing contingent of former Manhattan residents in search of cheaper rents and a safer, friendlier atmosphere.

It may seem ironic that such a melting pot made history as the center of one of America's most traditionally white-bread industries—namely, show business. Before Hollywood, in the 1920s, such stars as Gloria Swanson, Rudolph Valentino, and the Marx Brothers came to this neighborhood to work at "the Big House," Paramount's moviemaking center in the east. At that time the Kaufman-Astoria studios were the largest and most important filmmaking studios in the country; today they remain the largest in the East, and they're still used for major films and television shows.

Numbers in the text correspond to numbers in the margin and on the Astoria map.

A Good Tour

By subway, take the N train from Manhattan to the Broadway stop. Walk five blocks along Broadway to 36th Street; turn right and walk two blocks to 35th Avenue (bear with the confusion of intersecting streets, drives, and avenues). Here you'll find the American Museum of the **Moving Image** ①, the reason most people come to Astoria; you may spend hours studying its exhibits on film production and catching bits of the regularly scheduled film series and directors' talks. Next door, the 13-acre Kaufman-Astoria Studios, a former powerhouse in the American movie industry, has been used for the filming of *The Cotton Club* and *Sabrina* and television series such as *Cosby* and *Sesame Street*.

Head for the heart of the Greek community by wandering along Broadway between 31st and 36th streets. Here Greek pastry shops and coffeehouses abound, and the elevated subway brings a constant stream

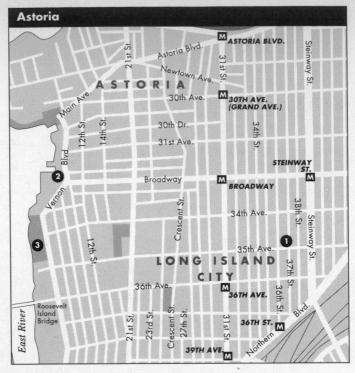

of activity. Farther up, 30th Avenue has every kind of food store imaginable; between 35th and 36th streets alone you'll find a *salumeria*, a meat market, a bakery, a wholesale international-food store, and more. The largest Orthodox community outside Greece worships at St. Demetrios Cathedral (✉ 30-11 30th Dr.), just off 30th Avenue.

Anyone interested in sculpture won't want to miss the funky **Socrates Sculpture Park** ② and the more refined **Isamu Noguchi Sculpture Museum** ③. From the Broadway subway station, walk eight blocks (about 15 minutes) toward the river. At Vernon and Broadway, the Socrates Sculpture Park at first almost appears to be an urban hallucination, with its large, abstract artwork framed by the Manhattan skyline. Three blocks to the left on Vernon Boulevard, with its entrance on 33rd Road, the Isamu Noguchi Sculpture Museum has hundreds of Noguchi's works displayed in an indoor-outdoor setting that evokes the tranquillity of a Zen garden.

TIMING

To see Greek Astoria at its finest, visit on a Saturday, when sidewalk culture comes to life. Weekdays are also pleasant, as the neighborhood's quiet pace offers a welcome alternative to frenetic Manhattan. Allow at least three hours for a leisurely visit to the American Museum of the Moving Image and a tour of Greek Astoria; add another hour or two if you plan to visit the more distant Socrates Sculpture Park and Isamu Noguchi Sculpture Museum (the latter is closed in winter).

Sights to See

★ ❶ **American Museum of the Moving Image.** Learn what goes into producing, directing, and editing films and TV by trying your hand at all three. Newly expanded and redesigned to the tune of $3 million, the museum's core exhibit, "Behind the Screen," invites you to produce and play back your own animated shorts, replace a line of dialogue from a TV show or movie with your own voice, watch a director call the camera shots for a televised baseball game, or create a video flip book of stop-motion images of yourself (which you can then buy in the souvenir shop). Frequent workshops and demonstrations address more complex topics like flatbed and nonlinear editing, and helpful "educators" are on hand to answer questions. The museum's collection of movie memorabilia includes 70,000 items; in the costume display you might find outfits worn by Marlene Dietrich and Robin Williams, among others. More than 300 screenings per year are held in the Riklis Theater—among them tributes to Hollywood directors, cinematographers, writers, and stars. Check out one of the shorts or vintage film serials shown every hour in Tut's Fever Movie Palace, a garish re-creation of an Egyptian-style picture palace of the 1930s, designed by Red Grooms and Lysiane Luong. ⊠ *35th Ave. between 36th and 37th Sts.,* ☎ *718/784–0077.* 🎟 *$7.* ⊙ *Tues.–Fri. noon–5, weekends 11–6.*

NEED A BREAK?
At the **Omonia Café** (⊠ 32–20 Broadway, ☎ 718/274–6650) you can watch the constant activity on Broadway while nursing coffee and honey-sweet pastries. At Broadway and 34th Street, **Uncle George's** (⊠ 33–19 Broadway, ☎ 718/626–0593) is a 24-hour Greek diner where rotisserie-roasted lamb and other Greek classics can be had for a song.

★ ❸ **Isamu Noguchi Sculpture Museum.** Some 30 years ago, Japanese sculptor Isamu Noguchi took studio space here in what was a photo engraver's factory. Part of it now holds 12 galleries showcasing the sculptor's evocative work in stone and stage-set designs, with videos documenting his long career. A small sculpture garden adjoins the museum. Weekend bus service to Noguchi Museum leaves every hour on the half hour, 11:30–3:30, from the Asia Society, at Park Avenue and 70th Street, in Manhattan. ⊠ *32–61 Vernon Blvd., entrance on 33rd Rd.,* ☎ *718/204–7088.* 🎟 *$4 (suggested donation).* ⊙ *Apr.–Oct., Wed.–Fri. 10–5, weekends 11–6.*

❷ **Socrates Sculpture Park.** The ancient Greeks excelled in the art of sculpture, which was often displayed in outdoor temples. It is appropriate, then, that Astoria should have an outdoor sculpture park. At the end of Vernon Boulevard, down the street from the Isamu Noguchi Sculpture Museum where it meets the East River, this 4.2-acre park was once an illegal dump site; in 1985 locals rallied to transform it into a public art space. Today a view of the river and the Manhattan skyline beyond frames huge works of art made of scrap metal, old tires, and other recycled products. ⊠ *Vernon Blvd. at Broadway,* ☎ *718/956–1819.* ⊙ *Daily 10 AM–sunset.*

STATEN ISLAND

Even though Staten Island (SI) is officially a borough of New York City, many Staten Islanders refer to Manhattan as "the City." Perhaps that's because farms and vast woodlands have distinguished it from the more crowded and developed Manhattan since 1661, when it was permanently settled as a farming community by the Dutch. Today Staten Island still feels provincial and even old-fashioned compared with New York City; indeed, time stands still in the two re-created villages of Richmondtown and Snug Harbor. Although it's less convenient to get to Staten Island than the other boroughs, the 20-minute ferry ride across the New York Harbor affords phenomenal views of Lower Manhattan and the Statue of Liberty—and it's free. On weekend mornings (until 11:30 AM), ferries leave the southern tip of Manhattan every hour; on weekdays and weekend afternoons you can catch one at least every half hour. Call 718/815–2628 for schedules and directions.

Snug Harbor and Beyond

Just 2 mi from the ferry terminal, the restored sailor's community of Snug Harbor is by far the most popular of Staten Island's attractions. For a highly enjoyable daytime outing, take the scenic ferry ride from Manhattan and visit Snug Harbor and two small but engaging nearby museums; then stop perhaps for a meal at Adobe Blues.

Numbers in the text correspond to numbers in the margin and on the Staten Island map.

A Good Tour

From the Staten Island ferry terminal, a seven-minute (2-mi) ride on the S40 bus will take you to the **Snug Harbor Cultural Center** ①, an 83-acre complex with an art gallery, a botanical garden, a children's museum, and a colorful history. Signal the driver as soon as you glimpse the beginning of the black iron fence along the edge of the property.

If the day is still young, return to the ferry terminal and catch the S51–Bay Street bus for the 15-minute ride to Hylan Boulevard to see the turn-of-the-century photographs displayed in the picturesque **Alice Austen House** ②. Italian history buffs should head to the **Garibaldi-Meucci Museum** ③, where war general Giuseppe Garibaldi lived in exile with his friend Antonio Meucci—the true inventor of the telephone.

TIMING
The Snug Harbor Cultural Center alone will take at least half a day, including the ferry commute; add to that the Alice Austen House and the Garibaldi-Meucci Museum and you're in for a whole-day adventure. If you're interested in visiting all three attractions, plan your visit toward the end of the week, when both the museums are open. The Garibaldi-Meucci Museum is closed in winter.

Sights to See

❷ **Alice Austen House.** Photographer Alice Austen (1866–1952) defied tradition when, as a girl of 10, she received her first camera as a gift from an uncle and promptly began taking pictures of everything around her. Austen went on to make photography her lifetime avocation, recording on film a vivid social history of Staten Island in the early part of the century; one of the local ferries is actually named for her. The cozy, ivy-covered Dutch-style cottage known as Clear Comfort, where she lived almost all her life, has been restored, and many of her photographs are on display. ✉ *2 Hylan Blvd.,* ☎ *718/816–4506.* ☞ *$3 (suggested donation).* ◷ *Mar.–Dec., Thurs.–Sun. noon–5.*

❸ **Garibaldi-Meucci Museum.** Housed in an altered Federal farmhouse, this small museum is full of letters and photographs from the life of fiery Italian patriot Giuseppe Garibaldi; it also documents Antonio Meucci's claim that he invented the telephone before Alexander Graham Bell did. Appropriately, the museum is in the heart of the Italian neighborhood of Rosebank; the colorful, if kitschy, **Our Lady of Mount Saint Carmel Society Shrine** is just around the corner, at 36 Amity Street. Ask the curator for directions. ✉ *420 Tompkins Ave.,* ☎ *718/442–1608.* ☞ *Free; donations accepted.* ◷ *Apr.–Nov., weekends 1–5; other times by appointment.*

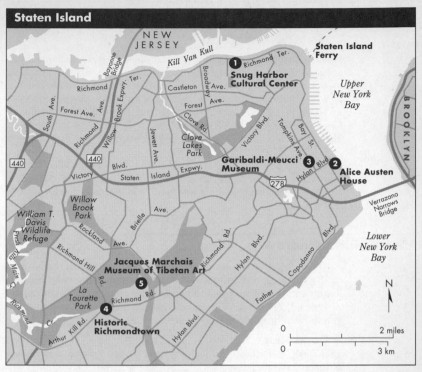

Staten Island

NEW JERSEY

Kill Van Kull

Bayonne Bridge

Richmond

Castleton Ave.

Broadway

Forest Ave.

1 Richmond Ter.

Snug Harbor Cultural Center

Staten Island Ferry

Upper New York Bay

B R O O K L Y N

South Ave.

Forest Ave.

Willow Brook Expwy.

Richmond

Jewett Ave.

Forest Ave.

Clove Rd.

Clove Lakes Park

Victory Blvd.

Tompkins Ave.

Bay St.

440

440

Blvd.

Victory

Staten Island Expwy.

Garibaldi-Meucci Museum **3**

278

Hylan Blvd.

2 **Alice Austen House**

Verrazano Narrows Bridge

Willow Brook Park

Ave.

Brielle

Rockland Ave.

William T. Davis Wildlife Refuge

Fresh Kills

Richmond Hill

Richmond Rd.

Hylan Blvd.

Capodanno Blvd.

Lower New York Bay

Jacques Marchais Museum of Tibetan Art

5

La Tourette Park

Richmond Rd.

4

Historic Richmondtown

Father

N

Arthur Kill Rd.

Hylan Blvd.

0 — 2 miles

0 — 3 km

★ **1** **Snug Harbor Cultural Center.** Once part of a sprawling farm, then a home for "aged, decrepit, and worn-out sailors," this 83-acre property is based around a row of five columned Greek Revival temples, built between 1831 and 1880, and consists of 28 historic buildings, most of which have been restored. Its newly renovated **Music Hall,** the second-oldest hall in the city (after Carnegie), now offers frequent performances; and the former chapel now houses the 210-seat **Veterans Memorial Hall,** site of many indoor concerts and gatherings, including an annual music festival.

Snug Harbor's Main Hall—the oldest building on the property, dating from 1833—holds the **Newhouse Center for Contemporary Art,** which features changing exhibitions. The building next door to the Newhouse Center houses the **John A. Noble Collection** of maritime art, with paintings, lithographs, photographs, and drawings. The complex has a gift shop and a cafeteria. The ☞ **Staten Island Botanical Gardens** and the ☞ **Staten Island Children's Museum** are also on the grounds. ✉ *1000 Richmond Terr.,* ☎ *718/448–2500,* ☎ *718/447–6490 for John A. Noble Collection.* 🎫 *Cultural Center grounds free, Newhouse Center $1 (suggested donation), John A. Noble Collection $2 (various charges for special events), free guided tours weekends 2* PM. ☉ *Grounds 8 AM–dusk, Newhouse Center Wed.–Sun. 10–5, John A. Noble Collection Wed.–Sat. 11–4 and by appointment.*

Staten Island Botanical Gardens. On the grounds of the ☞ **Snug Harbor Cultural Center,** this 83-acre haven includes a perennial garden, a greenhouse, a vineyard, 10 acres of natural marsh habitat, a fragrance garden for the physically challenged, and a rose garden. An authentic

Chinese Scholar's Garden, with a meditation area and a water garden, is in progress. ✉ *1000 Richmond Terr.,* ☎ *718/273–8200.* ✆ *Free.* ☾ *Dawn–dusk.*

☾ **Staten Island Children's Museum.** Five galleries at this popular museum are devoted to revolving hands-on exhibitions that introduce children to such diverse topics as news and media, storytelling, and insects. Portia's Playhouse, an interactive children's theater, invites tykes to step up to the stage and even try on costumes. ✉ *Snug Harbor Cultural Center, 1000 Richmond Terr.,* ☎ *718/273–2060.* ✆ *$4.* ☾ *July–Aug., Tues.–Sun. 11–5; Oct.–June, Tues.–Sun. noon–5.*

NEED A BREAK? | Those with a powerful thirst should head straight to **Adobe Blues** (✉ 63 Lafayette St., just off Richmond Terr., ☎ 718/720–2583), a southwestern-style saloon and restaurant with more than 200 beers and a killer chili con carne.

Historic Richmondtown

Hilly and full of green space, the scenic southern part of the island is far from the ferry terminal but worth the trip. Sprawling Historic Richmondtown takes you on a vivid journey into Staten Island's past, and the hilltop Jacques Marchais Museum of Tibetan Art transports you to the hilltop mountains of the Far East.

A Good Tour

Take the S74–Richmond Road bus from the ferry terminal to **Historic Richmondtown** ④ (about 25 minutes), whose 27 historic buildings date from the 17th, 18th, and 19th centuries. Afterward, grab lunch at **M. Bennet Café** or the **Parsonage** restaurant, both housed in historic buildings; or walk about a half-mile east on Richmond Road and up steep Lighthouse Avenue to the **Jacques Marchais Museum of Tibetan Art** ⑤, which has the largest collection of such art outside Tibet.

TIMING

Set aside the better part of a day for a trip to Historic Richmondtown, which is on the opposite end of the island from the ferry terminal; add on a couple of hours for the Tibetan Museum. The latter is closed Monday and Tuesday; in winter it's open by appointment only, so call ahead. Historic Richmondtown hosts a variety of seasonal celebrations, including an autumn crafts fair and a Christmas celebration; in summer some of the staff dresses in old-fashioned costumes.

Sights to See

★ ❹ **Historic Richmondtown.** These 27 buildings constructed as early as 1685 are situated in a 100-acre complex that was the site of Staten Island's original county seat. The buildings have been restored inside and out; some were here originally, whereas others were relocated from other spots on the island. Many of the buildings, such as the Greek Revival courthouse, which serves as the **visitor center,** date from the 19th century; other architectural styles on site range from Dutch colonial to Victorian Gothic Revival. During the warmer months, costumed staff demonstrate Early American crafts and trades such as printing, tinsmithing, and baking.

The **Voorlezer's House,** built in 1695, is the oldest elementary schoolhouse still standing in the United States; it looks like the mold from which all little red schoolhouses were cast.

The **Staten Island Historical Society Museum,** built in 1848 as the second county clerk's and surrogate's office, now has in its archives American china, furniture, toys, and tools, plus a collection of Staten Island photographs.

During a summer visit, you might want to make reservations for the 19th-century dinner, cooked outdoors and served with utensils of the period. The Autumn Celebration shows off craftspeople demonstrating their skills; the annual Encampment in July is a reenactment of a Civil War battle; and December brings a monthlong Christmas celebration. Richmondtown regularly hosts other fairs, flea markets, and tours of the historic buildings. A tavern on the grounds of the historic village hosts a Saturday-night concert series showcasing ethnic and folk music; call the visitor center for details. ⊠ *441 Clarke Ave.,* ☎ *718/351–1611.* ▣ *$4.* ⊙ *Sept.–June, Wed.–Sun. 10–5; July–Aug., Wed.–Fri. 10–5, weekends 1–5.*

NEED A BREAK? For a taste of Richmondtown cuisine, head to **M. Bennet Café** (⊠ 3730 Richmond Rd., ☎ 718/980–3410), which serves excellent American food in a 19th-century building.

❺ **Jacques Marchais Museum of Tibetan Art.** One of the largest private, nonprofit collections of Tibetan sculpture, scrolls, and paintings outside of Tibet is displayed in a museum resembling a Tibetan temple. Try to visit on a day when the monks bless the temple—and you. ⊠ *338 Lighthouse Ave.,* ☎ *718/987–3500.* ▣ *$3; occasionally an additional $3 charge for special Sun. programs.* ⊙ *Apr.–Nov., Wed.–Sun. 1–5; Dec.–Mar., by appointment only.*

4 Exploring New York City with Children

New York is as magical a place for children as it is for adults. Although hotels and restaurants tend to be geared firmly to the grown-ups, when provision has been made for children, it is usually accomplished in a grand way. The world's best and largest toy shop, the biggest dinosaur skeletons, the biggest and best park, the nicest city seaport, the best burgers, and, of course, some of the world's tallest buildings are here.

BESIDES NEW YORK'S CHILD-PLEASING SIGHTS, there are rare ambient treats to stumble upon—from brightly colored pictograms in Chinatown to the spectacular four-story-high neon signs in Times Square, from Central Park squirrels to Greenwich Village street musicians good enough to appear on television (and sometimes they do).

By Kate Sekules

Updated by Margaret Mittelbach

To get children psyched up for a New York trip, give them *Eloise,* by Kay Thompson; *A Cricket in Times Square,* by George Selden; *From the Mixed-up Files of Mrs. Basil E. Frankweiler,* by E. L. Konigsburg; *My New York,* by Kathy Jakobsen; or *Stuart Little,* by E. B. White.

SIGHTSEEING

As far as outdoors sights are concerned, there is plenty to please; surprising pockets of street sculpture, graffiti art, strange building facades, and quirky shop windows may be found on almost every block. In no other city are you more likely to entertain offspring simply by wandering. Children get a kick from taking in the sheer size of the buildings, and from riding cabs, or even buses and subways (especially the first or last car, with a view of the track and tunnels). You can also try taking more exotic transportation. To get a feeling for turn-of-the-century New York, try riding in a **horse-drawn carriage** around Central Park (⊠ Grand Army Plaza or intersections of Central Park S, between 5th and 7th Aves.). Rides cost $34 for about 20 minutes.

Set sail on the restored 19th-century schooner *The Pioneer* (⊠ South Street Seaport, ☎ 212/748–8786). The cost is $16 for adults, $6 for children under 12, for two hours; reservations are required. For an aerial view of the city, take an **Island Helicopter** tour (⊠ 34th St. and East River, ☎ 212/683–4575) for $44–$129.

For little more than the price of a subway token, the **Roosevelt Island Aerial Tramway** (⊠ 2nd Ave. at 60th St., ☎ 212/832–4543) across the East River is a sure hit. Trams run every 15 minutes during regular hours and every 7½ minutes during rush hours.

Ferry rides are great fun. For a close-up view of the boats, islands, and other sights of New York Harbor, try the free ride on the **Staten Island Ferry** (⊠ Terminal in Battery Park). Or, for $2 ($1 for kids 6–11) take the scenic **Port Imperial Ferry** (⊠ Terminal at World Financial Center, ☎ 212/564–8846) across the Hudson River and catch a free shuttle bus to the Liberty Science Center (☞ Museums, *below*).

Kids also enjoy New York's opportunities for vertical travel. Take the elevator to the 107th floor of the **World Trade Center** (⊠ 1 World Trade Center, ☎ 212/323–2340) for a panoramic view, 1,350 ft above the city (☞ Wall Street and the Battery *in* Chapter 2). The favorite midtown high-level view is from the 102nd floor of the **Empire State Building** (⊠ 350 5th Ave., at 34th St., ☎ 212/736–3100) (☞ Murray Hill to Union Square *in* Chapter 2).

Museums

Although just about every major museum in New York City has something to interest children, certain ones hold special appeal. At the top of the list is the **American Museum of Natural History** (⊠ Central Park W at W. 79th St., ☎ 212/769–5100), with its lifelike dioramas and collection of giant dinosaurs, including a huge Tyrannosaurus rex (☞ The Upper West Side *in* Chapter 2).

The **Children's Museum of Manhattan** is a kind of indoor playground for kids 1–10, where they can climb, crawl, paint, make collages, try on costumes, and even film their own newscasts. Daily workshops are included in the admission price. ✉ *212 W. 83rd St.,* ☎ *212/721–1234.* 🎟 *$5 adults and children.* ☉ *Mon. and Wed.–Thurs. 1:30–5:30, Fri.–Sun. 10–5.*

The **Children's Museum of the Arts,** in a loftlike space in SoHo, allows children ages 18 months to 10 to become actively involved in visual and performing arts. Highlights include the Monet Ball Pond, where children can play with brightly colored balls near a water-lily mural; the Music Garden and Wonder Theater, where performances are held; a reading nook with cushions and futons; and daily art activities. ✉ *72 Spring St.,* ☎ *212/941–9198.* 🎟 *$4 weekdays and $5 weekends for adults under 65 and children over 18 months.* ☉ *Tues.–Fri. noon–6, weekends 11–5.*

A big favorite—literally—with the younger generation is the **Intrepid Sea-Air-Space Museum,** an immense World War II aircraft carrier. On deck is a startling array of aircraft; inside there are aviation and military exhibits, as well as skinny hallways, winding staircases, and dozens of knobs, buttons, and wheels to manipulate. ✉ *Pier 86, at 12th Ave. and W. 46th St.,* ☎ *212/245–0072.* 🎟 *$10 adults, $5 children 6–11.* ☉ *May–Sept., Mon.–Sat. 10–5, Sun. 10–6; Oct.–Apr., Wed.–Sun. 10–5.*

In the nautical vein, the **South Street Seaport Museum** is an 11-square-block "museum without walls" with a fleet of historic sailing ships, cobblestone streets, 19th-century architecture, an old print shop, a maritime crafts center, and a children's center with hands-on exhibits about the history of ships and the sea. *Museum Visitors' Center:* ✉ *12 Fulton St.,* ☎ *212/748–8600.* 🎟 *$6 adults, $3 children under 12.* ☉ *Apr.–Sept., daily 10–6; Oct.–Mar., Wed.–Mon. 10–5.*

Aspiring heroes appreciate the **New York City Fire Museum** (✉ 278 Spring St., ☎ 212/691–1303), with its comprehensive collection of authentic fire-fighting tools from the 18th, 19th, and 20th centuries. Hand-pulled and horse-drawn apparatus, engines, sliding poles, uniforms, and fireboat equipment are all on display; tours are given by real fire-fighters. ✉ *278 Spring St., near Varick St.,* ☎ *212/691–1303.* 🎟 *$4 (suggested donation).* ☉ *Tues.–Sun. 10–4.*

Kids tend to like the **Forbes Magazine Galleries** (✉ 62 5th Ave., at 12th St., ☎ 212/206–5548) for the collections of toy soldiers and boats, and rooms with the bejeweled Fabergé eggs (☞ Greenwich Village *in* Chapter 2).

For children eight and older, the **Sony Wonder Technology Lab** is an interactive science and communications technology exhibit that allows kids to log on computers, play sound engineer, and be on TV. ✉ *550 Madison Ave., at 56th St.,* ☎ *212/833–8100.* 🎟 *Free.* ☉ *Tues.–Sat. 10–6, Sun. noon–6.*

Many "adult" museums in Manhattan offer special programs for kids. Meanwhile, don't ignore the city's outer boroughs and environs, which can be easily reached by mass transit.

For children who like hands-on involvement, the place to go is the **Brooklyn Children's Museum,** considered one of the best in the world. This interactive museum is full of tunnels to crawl through and animals to pet. ✉ *145 Brooklyn Ave.,* ☎ *718/735–4432.* 🎟 *$3 (suggested donation).* ☉ *June–Aug., Mon. and Wed.–Sun. noon–5; Sept.–May, Wed.–Fri. 2–5, weekends noon–5.*

Located underground in an old subway station in downtown Brooklyn, the **Transit Museum** houses full-size, turn-of-the-century and modern subway cars and working miniature subway trains. ⊠ *Boerum and Schermerhorn Sts.,* ☎ *718/243–3063.* ☞ *$3 adults, $1.50 children.* ◷ *Tues. and Thurs.–Fri. 10–4, Wed. 10–6, weekends noon–5.*

In Queens, the **New York Hall of Science** in Flushing Meadows–Corona Park allows budding researchers to access 160 exhibits (many of them touchable) on subjects ranging from microbes to lasers. ⊠ *111th St. at 46th Ave.,* ☎ *718/699–0005.* ☞ *$4.50 adults, $3 children; free Wed. and Thurs. 2–5.* ◷ *Wed.–Sun. 10–5.*

The hands-on exhibits of the **Staten Island Children's Museum** (⊠ 1000 Richmond Terr., ☎ 718/273–2060), on everything from the five senses to high technology, will particularly enthrall younger kids (☞ Staten Island *in* Chapter 3). Children with a strong sense of the past may enjoy **Historic Richmondtown** (441 Clarke Ave., ☎ 718/351–1611), which has a Museum of Childhood with displays of antique dolls, toys, and children's furniture (☞ Staten Island *in* Chapter 3).

Just across the Hudson River in Liberty State Park, New Jersey, the **Liberty Science Center** is the largest science museum in the New York metropolitan area. Highlights include an insect zoo, a 100-ft touch tunnel, an amazing 700-pound geodesic globe, the Kodak OMNI Theater for viewing IMAX movies on a gigantic screen, and "Brain Trek," a 3-D laser show. ⊠ *Liberty State Park, 251 Philip St., Jersey City, NJ,* ☎ *201/200–1000.* ☞ *$9.50 adults, $6.50 children 2–12; OMNI Theater $7 adults, $5 children under 12; Williams Theater ("Brain Trek") $2; combined admission to exhibits and theaters $15 adults, $11 children 2–12; pay what you wish 1st Wed. of month 1 PM–closing.* ◷ *Apr.–Aug., daily 9:30–5:30; Sept.–Mar., Tues.–Sun. 9:30–5:30. Call center for directions by car, the PATH train, or ferry.*

Parks and Playgrounds

New York's great outdoors sounds like a contradiction in terms, especially when you add children to the equation. But in **Central Park,** children can ride bicycles, row boats, go horseback riding, ice-skate, rollerblade, skateboard, fly kites, throw Frisbees, and much more (☞ Central Park *in* Chapter 2). Favorite destinations include the **Conservatory Water,** which attracts owners of large, remote-controlled model boats; it is near the statues of Alice in Wonderland and Hans Christian Andersen. Younger children enjoy the hands-on activities at the park's fairy-tale-like **Belvedere Castle** (☎ 212/772–0210). The antique **Carousel** (⊠ Central Park at 65th St., ☎ 212/879–0244), complete with painted steeds that prance to jaunty organ music, costs only 90¢ a ride. The pretty **Wollman Rink** (☎ 212/396–1010) has outdoor rollerblading classes and sessions—ice-skating in winter (☞ Chapter 9). At the beautifully restored **Harlem Meer,** kids of all ages are encouraged to fish along the shore for bass and sunfish. Free fishing poles and bait are given out at the **Charles A. Dana Discovery Center** (☎ 212/860–1370).

At Brooklyn's 536-acre **Prospect Park,** kids enjoy kite flying and picnicking on the 90-acre Long Meadow (☞ Brooklyn *in* Chapter 3). The cherry trees, giant glass greenhouses, and spicy herbs at the **Brooklyn Botanic Garden** (⊠ 1000 Washington Ave., ☎ 718/622–4433) will please both kids and parents (☞ Brooklyn *in* Chapter 3).

In the Bronx, adjacent to the Bronx Zoo, the **New York Botanical Garden** (⊠ 200th St. and Southern Blvd., ☎ 718/817–8700) is one of the world's largest botanical gardens, with a large conservatory, 12 outdoor gardens, walking trails, and 40 acres of forest (☞ The Bronx *in* Chapter 3).

Manhattan has wonderful state-of-the-art playgrounds. **Central Park**'s 21 playgrounds are full of slides, bridges, bars, swings, towers, and tunnels; they're carpeted with sand or soft rubber matting and often cooled in summer by sprinklers, fountains, or running water. Good ones can be found along 5th Avenue at 67th Street near the zoo, at 71st and 77th streets, at 85th Street near the Metropolitan Museum, and at 96th Street. Along Central Park West, the best ones are at 68th, 82nd, 85th, 93rd (with a Wild West theme), and 96th streets. The **Hecksher Playground,** in Central Park at 62nd Street, is the park's largest—and a favorite with local schoolchildren.

Top-rated by Manhattan kids is the playground at **Hudson River Park** (⊠ West St. south of Vesey St.), which offers kid-size bronze sculptures of people and animals integrated into the parkscape. Not far from the financial district, **Washington Market Park** (⊠ Greenwich St. between Chambers and Duane Sts.) features a pretty tree-filled layout and great play equipment. **Washington Square Park** (⊠ Southern end of 5th Ave., between Waverly Pl. and W. 4th St.) has a popular and shady playground, as well as live jugglers and magicians in summertime. In **Riverside Park,** west of Riverside Drive, the best playgrounds are at 77th and 91st streets; the one at 77th Street has a circle of spouting elephant fountains. The **Asser Levy Playground** (⊠ 23rd St., 1 block from East River) is the first in Manhattan to cater fully to children with disabilities, with giant, multicolored mazelike structures; helter-skelter slides with wheelchair stations; and textured pavement for children who are blind.

At indoor playgrounds, kids can burn up energy no matter what the weather. **Playspace** (⊠ 2473 Broadway, at 92nd St., ☎ 212/769–2300) provides sandboxes, toys, games, and room to run for youngsters six months–six years; the cost is $4.50 per person (including parents). **Kidmazeum** (⊠ 80 East End Ave., at 83rd St., ☎ 212/327–4800) offers a sprawling maze, children's village, Lego room, and computer lab for children 12 and under; entry costs $8 per child and is free for adults. For kids aged 1–10, **WonderCamp** (⊠ 27 W. 23rd St., ☎ 212/243–1111) features a jungle gym, giant bouncing balls, organized games, and drama classes for $6.50 per visitor.

Zoos

Central Park Zoo (⊠ Off 5th Ave. at 64th St., ☎ 212/861–6030), officially called the **Central Park Wildlife Conservation Center,** is of a very manageable size, even for toddlers (☞ Central Park *in* Chapter 2). The antics of the Japanese snow monkeys—which live here on their own private island—are endlessly fascinating. But the diving and swimming polar bears steal the show.

The **Bronx Zoo** (⊠ 2300 Southern Blvd., ☎ 718/367–1010), officially called the **International Wildlife Conservation Park** (☞ The Bronx *in* Chapter 3), is the largest zoo in the United States. Most of the animals here live in replicas of their natural habitats.

Brooklyn's **Prospect Park Wildlife Conservation Center** (⊠ Flatbush Ave. at Empire Blvd., ☎ 718/399–7339) (☞ Brooklyn *in* Chapter 3) focuses on small animals, such as prairie dogs and red pandas.

The **Queens Wildlife Conservation Center** shows North American animals in approximations of their natural habitat. The inhabitants include black bears, mountain lions, sea lions, bobcats, coyotes, bison, and elk. ⊠ 53–51 111th St., Flushing Meadows Park, ☎ 718/271–

7761. 🖾 *$2.50 adults, 50¢ children 3–12.* ⊙ *Weekdays 10–5, weekends 10–5:30.*

The **Staten Island Zoo** is small but of high quality and features one of the world's finest collections of snakes, as well as a separate Children's Zoo. 🖾 *Barrett Park, 614 Broadway, Staten Island,* ☎ *718/442–3100.* 🖾 *$3 adults, $2 children 3–11; pay as you wish Wed. 2–4:45.* ⊙ *Daily 10–4:45.*

In Brooklyn, the **Aquarium for Wildlife Conservation** (🖾 Surf Ave. at W. 8th St., Coney Island, ☎ 718/265–3474) has nearly 300 different marine creatures, including dolphins, sharks, walruses, and whales (☞ Brooklyn *in* Chapter 3).

THE ARTS AND ENTERTAINMENT

In New York, theater groups exist just for children, art museums organize special programs, and kids can choose among art classes, summer courses, the circus, music concerts, storytelling, parades, and puppet shows.

Madison Square Garden (🖾 7th Ave. between 31st and 33rd Sts., ☎ 212/465–6000) offers, besides sports events (☞ Chapter 9), some Disney and Sesame Street extravaganzas that appeal especially to children. There are major ice shows in winter, and each spring brings the **Ringling Bros. and Barnum & Bailey Circus** (check local newspapers for dates, times, and ticket information). The **Big Apple Circus** (🖾 35 W. 35th St., ☎ 212/268–0055) charms the toughest New Yorkers in locations all over the city during spring and summer and is in residence at Lincoln Center from October through January.

Film

Several museums sponsor special film programs aimed at families and children, including the Museum of Modern Art, the Museum of Television and Radio (☞ Rockefeller Center *in* Chapter 2), and the American Museum of the Moving Image (☞ Queens *in* Chapter 3). At the **Sony IMAX Theater** (🖾 1998 Broadway, at 68th St., ☎ 212/336–5000) audience members strap on high-tech headgear that makes nature and specially created feature films appear in 3-D. To experience the **Cinema Ride** (🖾 1481 Broadway, at 42nd St., ☎ 212/391–6550) in Times Square, movie-goers slip on 3-D glasses and enter a "motion simulation" capsule that rocks and rolls with such films as the "Atlantis Submarine Race" and "Galactic Flight." Kids thrill at the amazing nature films shown on the huge screen in the **IMAX Theater** (🖾 Central Park W and 79th St., ☎ 212/769–5650) at the American Museum of Natural History. The **Walter Reade Theater** (🖾 165 W. 65th St., ☎ 212/875–5600) shows feature films for children on weekends and sponsors children's film festivals.

Music

The **Little Orchestra Society** (🖾 220 W. 42nd St., ☎ 212/704–2100) organizes concert series that introduce classical music to children ages 3–5 at Florence Gould Hall (🖾 55 E. 59th St.) and ages 5–12 at Lincoln Center. The **Metropolitan Opera** offers its **Growing Up with Opera** program (☎ 212/769–7008) and also sponsors an out-of-doors summer arts program, with plenty in it for children. To introduce parents and their kids to jazz music, **Jazz at Lincoln Center** (🖾 140 W. 65th St., ☎ 212/875–5299) hosts an annual **Jazz for Young People** concert series hosted by Wynton Marsalis.

Puppet Shows

Marionette Theater (✉ Swedish Cottage, Central Park at W. 81st St., ☎ 212/988–9093) features programs Tuesday–Saturday. **Puppet Playhouse** (✉ Asphalt Green, 555 E. 90th St., ☎ 212/369–8890) offers weekend shows with puppets and marionettes. **Puppetworks** (✉ 338 6th Ave., Park Slope, Brooklyn, ☎ 718/965–3391) presents marionettes performing classic children's stories.

Storytelling

Books of Wonder (✉ 16 W. 18th St., ☎ 212/989–3270) has storytelling on Sunday morning. **Barnes & Noble** (✉ 1280 Lexington Ave., at 86th St., ☎ 212/423–9900; ✉ Citicorp Bldg., 54th St. at 3rd. Ave., ☎ 212/750–8033; ✉ 2289 Broadway at 82nd St., ☎ 212/362–8835; ✉ 1972 Broadway, at 66th St., ☎ 212/595–6859; ✉ 600 5th Ave., at 48th St., ☎ 212/765–0590; ✉ 675 6th Ave., at 22nd St., ☎ 212/727–1227; ✉ 33 E. 17th St., ☎ 212/253–0810; ✉ 4 Astor Pl., between Broadway and Lafayette, ☎ 212/420–1322) hosts readings for kids.

Theater

Miss Majesty's Lollipop Playhouse (✉ Grove Street Playhouse, 39 Grove St., between W. 4th St. and 7th Ave., ☎ 212/741–6436) brings fairy tales and nursery rhymes to life on weekend afternoons. **New York Children's Theater** (✉ Lincoln Square Theater, 250 W. 65th St., ☎ 212/496–8009) is determinedly realistic in style and explores topics such as literacy and aging. **New Victory Theater** (✉ 209 W. 42nd St., ☎ 212/239–6255), the oldest surviving theater in New York, now presents a variety of plays and performances devoted solely to families. **Paper Bag Players** (✉ Sylvia and Danny Kaye Playhouse, 68th St. between Park and Lexington Aves., ☎ 212/772–4448) is the longest-running children's theater group in the nation. **Tada!** (✉ 120 W. 28th St., ☎ 212/627–1732) is a popular children's group with a multiethnic perspective. **Theaterworks/USA** (✉ Promenade Theater, Broadway at 76th St., ☎ 212/677–5959) mounts classic stories and original musicals based on well-known children's books. The **13th Street Theater** (✉ 50 W. 13th St., ☎ 212/675–6677) presents its children's offerings on weekends. **West End Kids Productions** (✉ The Knitting Factory, 74 Leonard St.; ✉ The West End Gate Children's Theater, 2911 Broadway; ☎ 212/877–6115) stages whimsical weekend performances for young audiences.

DINING

If you're looking for a low-key place to park the kids for a quick bite, the city's ubiquitous diners (also known locally as coffee shops) are probably your best bets. Usually featuring comfy booths and lunch counters with stools that swivel, diners don't offer gourmet food, but with their ready supply of hamburgers and pancakes served 24 hours a day, they may end up being your kids' favorite culinary moments. For more exotic fare, try the following eateries that appeal to young appetites.

Lower Manhattan and Chinatown

The younger ones should enjoy **Minter's Fun Food and Drink** (✉ 250 Vesey St., at 4 World Financial Center, ☎ 212/945–4455) for chocolate beverages. The surprising charms of the only **McDonald's** branch with doorman and pianist (✉ 160 Broadway, between Maiden La. and Liberty St., ☎ 212/385–2063) are obvious. In Chinatown, don't miss the green-tea or red-bean ice cream at the **Chinatown Ice Cream Factory** (⊠ 65 Bayard St., between Mott and Elizabeth Sts., ☎ 212/608–4170). Chinatown is also a good place to take the whole family for lunch or dinner at reasonable prices. **Mandarin Court** (⊠ 61 Mott St., ☎ 212/608–3838) serves dim sum every day until 3.

SoHo and TriBeCa

In SoHo, the airy decor at **Jerry's** (⊠ 101 Prince St., ☎ 212/966–9464) is popular with local artists and their young protégés. The **Cupping Room Café** (⊠ 359 W. Broadway, near Broome St., ☎ 212/925–2898) provides waffles throughout the day. In TriBeCa, **Bubby's** (⊠ 120 Hudson St., at N. Moore, ☎ 212/219–0666) has casual dining and great baked goods.

Greenwich Village and the East Village

In the West Village, **Arturo's** (⊠ 106 W. Houston St., at Thompson St., ☎ 212/677–3820) serves coal-fired pizza with child-friendly aplomb. **Aggie's** (⊠ 146 W. Houston St., at MacDougal St., ☎ 212/673–8994) is a funky coffee shop with sprightly soups and sandwiches. **Elephant and Castle** (⊠ 68 Greenwich Ave., near W. 11th St., ☎ 212/243–1400) has burgers and great french fries. For huge Cal-Tex servings at low prices, try **Benny's Burritos** (⊠ 113 Greenwich Ave., at Jane St., ☎ 212/727–0584). The **Cowgirl Hall of Fame** (⊠ 519 Hudson St., at W. 10th St., ☎ 212/633–1133) dishes up both Cajun cooking and cowgirl memorabilia.

In the East Village, the **Time Cafe** (⊠ 380 Lafayette St., below E. 4th St., ☎ 212/533–7000) is sunny, relaxed, and fantastic for brunch when it serves heavenly southern-style biscuits. Kids will love **Stingy Lulus** (⊠ 129 St. Mark's Pl., between 1st Ave. and Ave. A, ☎ 212/674–3545), a raucous diner that raided the middle America truck stops for its blue-plate-special decor. **Two Boots** (⊠ 37 Ave. A, between 2nd and 3rd Sts., ☎ 212/505–2276), which refers to the geographical "boots" of Italy and Louisiana, serves both pizza and jambalaya.

Gramercy Park and Chelsea

Just off Union Square is **America** (⊠ 9 E. 18th St., ☎ 212/505–2110), where everything is huge—menu, portions, spaces—except your check. The **Royal Canadian Pancake House** (⊠ 180 3rd Ave., between 16th and 17th Sts., ☎ 212/777–9288) has more than 50 flavors, including peanut-butter pancakes with real maple syrup. On Chelsea's bustling 6th Avenue, the 1940s-style **Hot Tomato** (⊠ 676 6th Ave., at 21st St., ☎ 212/691–3535) serves up tomato soup, meat loaf, and mashed potatoes.

Midtown

The **American Festival Café** (⊠ Rockefeller Center, 20 W. 50th St., ☎ 212/332–7620) is the essential NYC family dining experience. With its displays of famous designer gowns, the **Fashion Cafe** (⊠ 51st St. between 5th and 6th Aves., in Rockefeller Plaza, ☎ 212/765–3131) will enthrall would-be supermodels. **Television City** (⊠ 1258 6th Ave., at 50th St., ☎ 212/246–4234) is designed like a working TV studio, so kids can play weather forecasters and be interviewed by "newscasters" while waiting for their french fries.

In the theater district, the **Stage Delicatessen** (⊠ 834 7th Ave., at 54th St., ☎ 212/245–7850) will wow kids with its enormous piles of corned beef. As you move west, prepare yourself for the "restaurant-as-theme park" district near Carnegie Hall. Young music fans will be impressed by the **Hard Rock Cafe** (✉ 221 W. 57th St., ☎ 212/459–9320), **Planet Hollywood** (✉ 140 W. 57th St., ☎ 212/333–7827), and **Motown Cafe** (✉ 104 W. 57th St., ☎ 212/581–8030). The motorcycle-oriented **Harley-Davidson Cafe** (✉ 1370 6th Ave., at 56th St., ☎ 212/245–6000) bills itself as the "newest American legend." **Mickey Mantle's** (✉ 42 Central Park S, near 6th Ave., ☎ 212/688–7777) excites ball-crazy kids.

Upper West Side

A good bet near Lincoln Center is the **Saloon** (✉ 1920 Broadway, at 64th St., ☎ 212/874–1500), with a long menu and an occasional skating waiter. **Fiorello's Roman Café** (✉ 1900 Broadway, near 63rd St., ☎ 212/595–5330) has individual pizzas and outside seating. Fun, messy ribs and chicken entice youngsters at **Dallas BBQ** (✉ 27 W. 72nd St., ☎ 212/873–2004). **Big Nick's** pizza joint (✉ 2175 Broadway, at 77th St., ☎ 212/724–2010) gives out balloons that say "Big Nick Loves Me." **Mad Fish** (✉ 2182 Broadway, at 77th St., ☎ 212/787–0202) serves up high-quality seafood as well as fish-and-chips. Very child-friendly, the **Popover Cafe** (✉ 551 Amsterdam Ave., at 87th St., ☎ 212/595–8555) has comfortable booths, hearty food, and teddy bears lurking in odd corners. At the brasserie-style **Boulevard** (✉ 2398 Broadway, at 88th St., ☎ 212/874–7400), kids can eat spaghetti and draw on the tablecloths.

Upper East Side

Serendipity 3 (✉ 225 E. 60th St., ☎ 212/838–3531), "the ice cream parlor to the stars," is perfect for a light meal or dessert. **Jackson Hole** (✉ 232 E. 64th St., ☎ 212/371–7187) is a reliable, pleasant burger joint with other branches around town. **China Fun** (✉ 250 E. 65th St., ☎ 212/752–0810) has an extensive Chinese menu to satisfy the most picky child. **EJ's Luncheonette** (✉ 1271 3rd Ave., ☎ 212/472–0600) serves good meat loaf and other blue-plate specials. Central Park's **Boathouse Café** (✉ Near E. 72nd St., ☎ 212/517–3623) can be somewhat pricey, but it's wonderfully soothing. **Barking Dog Luncheonette** (✉ 1678 3rd Ave., at 94th St., ☎ 212/831–1800) has a festive menu of sandwiches, burgers, salads, and shakes as well as a special drinking fountain for dogs.

LODGING

Since the vast majority of hotels are in midtown Manhattan, your choice of which neighborhood to pick for a family stay is limited. However, some hotels are better prepared for families than others, and a few even have playrooms for young guests. Generally speaking, as in any other big city, most Manhattan hotels will provide an extra bed, baby-sitting, and stroller rental—all the common requirements of families traveling with young children—but call ahead.

Good bets for families, at the top end of the scale, include the following. Kids like the **Holiday Inn–Crown Plaza** (✉ 1605 Broadway, ☎ 212/977–4000) for its swimming pool, and parents will like it for its lifeguard. Also good choices, thanks to their child-pleasing swimming pools, are the Sheraton Manhattan, the Vista, and the UN Plaza–Park Hyatt. The **Doubletree Guest Suites** (✉ 1563 Broadway, at 47th St., ☎ 212/403–6300) has a "Kids Quarters" playroom with toys and games. Any of the **Manhattan East Suite Hotels** (☎ 212/465–3690) properties would make an excellent choice, since they resemble tiny apartments. At the **San Carlos** (✉ 150 E. 50th St., ☎ 212/755–1800), the large suites have kitchen facilities. On the far Upper West Side, near Columbia University, **International House** (✉ 500 Riverside Dr., ☎ 212/316–8436), formerly for students only, has several family-size apartments for $115–125 per night. The **Vanderbilt Y** (✉ 224 E. 47th St., ☎ 212/756–9600) in midtown has some family rooms with two bunk beds apiece for $110 per night.

SHOPPING

Adults and children alike find shopping nirvana in New York. One of the world's best toy stores, **F.A.O. Schwarz** (✉ 5th Ave. at 58th St., ☎ 212/644–9400) is probably highlight number one for young consumers (☞ Toys *in* Chapter 10). With two seemingly endless floors of toys, your kids may not know where to start—but a talking bear located near the escalator will be glad to assist them.

For stores featuring toys, games, magic, and general gizmos, *see* Fun and Games *in* Chapter 10. **Dollhouse Antics** (✉ 1343 Madison Ave., at 94th St., ☎ 212/876–2288) stocks miniature furnishings at 1-inch scale. Children should like the **Big City Kite Co.** (✉ 1210 Lexington Ave., at 82nd St., ☎ 212/472–2623), which has one of the best kite selections anywhere. **Children's General Store** (✉ 2473 Broadway, at 92nd St., ☎ 212/580–2723), located beneath the indoor playground Playspace, sells a new breed of "educational" toys for infants and preteens; they're so fun and colorful, kids will actually enjoy them. It's easy to lose yourself in SoHo's **Enchanted Forest** (✉ 85 Mercer St., ☎ 212/925–6677), where the often handmade and always original games, toys, and stuffed animals will charm kids and parents alike. For older kids, **Forbidden Planet** (✉ 840 Broadway, at 13th St., ☎ 212/473–1576) stocks everything relating to science fiction and fantasy, such as comic books and monster masks. **Little Rickie** (✉ 49½ 1st Ave., at 3rd St., ☎ 212/505–6467) specializes in kitschy, oddball merchandise, from snowdomes and balloon modeling kits to legitimate folk art. At the **Pull Cart** ceramics studio (✉ 31 W. 21st St., 7th floor, ☎ 212/727–7089), kids can pick out and paint their own tablewares. **Quest Toys** (✉ 225 Liberty St., at 2 World Financial Center, ☎ 212/945–9330), near Hudson River Park and Battery Park City, has wooden toys and trains that will intrigue both kids and adults.

In addition to the stores listed under Children's Clothing in Chapter 10, try the following. On the Upper West Side, which is without a doubt the most kid-friendly neighborhood in Manhattan, **Monkeys & Bears** (✉ 506 Amsterdam Ave., between 84th and 85th Sts., ☎ 212/873–2673) stocks all-age clothes, both hip and traditional. **Kids Are Magic** (✉ 2293 Broadway, between 82nd and 83rd Sts., ☎ 212/875–9240) sports two stories of reasonably priced clothes and toys. **Shoofly** (✉ 465 Amsterdam Ave., between 82nd and 83rd Sts., ☎ 212/580–4390) sells designer footwear, hats, knapsacks, and a huge assortment of hair ribbons. On the Upper East Side, Madison Avenue's boutiques offer an array of choices for dressing the well-heeled child. **Chocolate Soup** (✉ 946 Madison Ave., between 74th and 75th Sts., ☎ 212/861–2210) sells hand-sewn and imported clothes for kids. **Jacadi** (✉ 787 Madison Ave., at 67th St., ☎ 212/535–3200; ✉ 1281 Madison Ave., at 91st St., ☎ 212/369–1616) stocks toddler-size clothes from Paris, as well as fashions for older children and stuffed animals. For the more radical child in your life, check out the avant-garde children's stores that have recently popped up in the East Village. **Dinosaur Hill** (✉ 306 E. 9th St., ☎ 212/473–5850) sells unusual handmade clothes for newborns to eight-year-olds, as well as discovery toys. **Meki Kids** (✉ 149 Ave. A, ☎ 212/995–2884) makes colorful, fashion-forward clothing—such as bell bottoms and Judy Jetson vinyl dresses—for both babies and kids.

It's worth visiting the clothing and toy sections of **department stores.** Visit **Macy's** for the thrill of size and **Stern's** for the cool atrium plaza. Go to Macy's during the holiday season between Thanksgiving and Christmas, and enjoy the enchanting Christmas window displays for free. Don't miss the animated windows at **Lord & Taylor** and **Saks Fifth Avenue,** either; the elegant ones at **Bergdorf Goodman, Bloomingdale's,** and **Barneys New York** tend to be aimed squarely at adults, but kids usually enjoy them, too (☞ Department Stores *in* Chapter 10).

Babies have their own shopping needs, though they don't know it. On the Upper West Side, the comprehensively stocked **Albee's** (⊠ 715 Amsterdam Ave., at 95th St., ☎ 212/662–5740) has clothes, cribs, and snappy-looking strollers. The very upscale **Bellini** (⊠ 110 W. 86th St., between Columbus and Amsterdam Aves., ☎ 212/580–3801; ⊠ 1305 2nd Ave., at 68th St., ☎ 212/517–9233) specializes in both infant fashions and baby-pleasing home furnishings. **Hush-A-Bye** (⊠ 1459 1st Ave., at 76th St., ☎ 212/988–4500) caters to the Upper East Side small-fry with a mix of clothes, furniture, and toys. **Schneider's** (⊠ 20 Ave. A, at 2nd St., ☎ 212/228–3540) is a very well stocked store for downtown infants and discount hunters. **Z'Baby Company** (⊠ 100 W. 72nd St., at Columbus Ave., ☎ 212/579–2229) specializes in funky designer clothing and accessories, from dalmatian-print jumpers to velvet-lined rockers.

For children's books, **Books of Wonder** (⊠ 16 W. 18th St., ☎ 212/989–3270) has an extensive stock and a friendly staff that can help select gifts for all reading levels; Oziana is a specialty. **Bank Street College Bookstore** (⊠ 2875 Broadway, at 112th St., ☎ 212/678–1654) carries politically correct kids books, among its 40,000-odd titles. In the West Village, **Tootsie's Children's Bookstore** (⊠ 554 Hudson St., ☎ 212/242–0182) has hardbacks and softbacks for kids up to 14, and **Tootsie's Baby,** across the street (⊠ 543 Hudson St., ☎ 212/462–2618), sells books, handmade puppets, and toys for the under-2½ crowd. **Barnes & Noble**'s several branches around town all have large children's books sections (☞ Storytelling *in* The Arts and Entertainment, *above*).

For comics, try **Village Comics** (⊠ 214 Sullivan St., ☎ 212/777–2770) for its enormous selection of new comic books, as well as T-shirts, trading cards, and model kits. **Funny Business Comics** (⊠ 660-B Amsterdam Ave., at 92nd St., ☎ 212/799–9477) carries a delightful stock of old and new issues.

5 The Arts

For lovers of the arts, New York is close to paradise. Theater fans can choose among big Broadway productions, stellar revivals of classics, and works by emerging playwrights Off-Broadway. Music devotees have the chance to see the world's top performers, appearing in premier showcases such as Carnegie Hall and the Metropolitan Opera House. For dance aficionados, there are two first-rate ballet troupes and a fine selection of modern-dance venues. Film fanatics can indulge in recent Hollywood releases, classics, foreign movies, and independent works.

■ N A CITY AS LARGE AS NEW YORK, urban hassles sometimes appear insurmountable. When it's pouring rain,
every cab seems engaged or off-duty. Waiting at the post

By David Low   office, supermarket, and even the cash machine almost always takes
longer than you expected. Even buying a pair of socks can become a
chore when a store is busy, which is usually the case. But in the end,
New Yorkers put up with all the stress for at least one obvious reason:
the city's unrivaled artistic life. Despite the immense competition and
the threat of cuts in city aid to the arts, artists from all disciplines continue to come to the city to find their peers and to produce their work.
Audiences benefit greatly.

New York has somewhere between 200 and 250 legitimate theaters,
and many more ad hoc venues—parks, churches, universities, museums, lofts, galleries, streets, and rooftops—where performances ranging from Shakespeare to sword-dancing take place. The city is, as well,
a revolving door of festivals and special events: Summer jazz, one-act-
play marathons, international film series, and musical celebrations
from the classical to the avant-garde are just a few.

Arts Centers

New York's most renowned centers for the arts are tourist attractions
in themselves.

Carnegie Hall (⊠ 881 7th Ave., at 57th St., ☎ 212/247–7800) is
world famous as a premier hall for concerts, attracting great orchestras from around the world and music masters such as Arturo Toscanini,
Leonard Bernstein, Isaac Stern, Yo-Yo Ma, Kathleen Battle, Frank
Sinatra, and the Beatles. Performances are held in both its main auditorium (opened in 1891 with a concert conducted by Tchaikovsky) and
in Weill Recital Hall, where rising young talents often make their first
New York debuts. Although the emphasis is on classical music, Carnegie
Hall also hosts jazz, cabaret, and folk-music series.

City Center (⊠ 131 W. 55th St., ☎ 212/581–1212; mailing address
for ticket orders: ⊠ CityTix, 130 W. 56th St., 4th floor, New York,
NY 10019), under its eccentric, tiled Spanish dome (built in 1923 by
the Ancient and Accepted Order of the Mystic Shrine and saved from
demolition in 1943 by Mayor Fiorello La Guardia), presents dance
troupes such as Alvin Ailey and Paul Taylor, as well as concert versions
of American musicals. The Manhattan Theatre Club (☞ Theater,
below) also resides here, with its highly regarded program of innovative contemporary drama.

Lincoln Center (⊠ W. 62nd to 66th Sts., Columbus to Amsterdam
Aves., ☎ 212/875–5000) is a 14-acre complex that houses the Metropolitan Opera, the New York Philharmonic, the Juilliard School, the New
York City Ballet, the American Ballet Theatre, the New York City Opera,
the Film Society of Lincoln Center, the Chamber Music Society of Lincoln Center, the Lincoln Center Theater, the School of American Ballet, and the New York Public Library's Library and Museum of the
Performing Arts. Tours of Lincoln Center are available (☎ 212/875–
5350; ☞ The Upper West Side *in* Chapter 2).

In 1996 the complex inaugurated the **Lincoln Center Festival,** an international summer performance event under the direction of arts
critic and writer John Rockwell. The program includes classical music
concerts, contemporary music and dance presentations, stage works,
and non-Western arts.

Madison Square Garden (⊠ W. 31st to W. 33rd Sts. on 7th Ave., ☎ 212/465–6741), camped atop Penn Station, includes a renovated 20,000-seat arena and the sleek 5,600-seat Paramount Theater. In addition to sports events such as basketball, ice hockey, tennis, and boxing, the complex draws large crowds to pop music concerts by stars as diverse as Barbra Streisand, Paul Simon, and Elton John. If your favorite rock band isn't appearing at Madison Square Garden, check out its suburban sister halls, **Nassau Veterans Memorial Coliseum** (⊠ Uniondale, Long Island, ☎ 516/794–9300) and **Continental Airlines Sports Arena** (⊠ East Rutherford, NJ, ☎ 201/935–3900).

Radio City Music Hall (⊠ 1260 6th Ave., at 50th St., ☎ 212/247–4777), an Art Deco gem, opened in 1932; it has 6,000 seats, a 60-ft-high foyer, 2-ton chandeliers, and a powerful Wurlitzer organ. On this vast stage you'll find everything from rock and pop concerts to Christmas and Easter extravaganzas (featuring the perennial Rockettes kick line), and star-studded TV specials. Tours (☎ 212/632–4041) are conducted daily (☞ Rockefeller Center and Midtown Skyscrapers *in* Chapter 2).

Brooklyn Academy of Music (BAM; ⊠ 30 Lafayette Ave., Brooklyn, ☎ 718/636–4100), America's oldest performing arts center, began in 1859, but its reputation today is far from stodgy thanks to its daring and innovative dance, music, opera, and theater productions. The main performance spaces are the 2,000-seat Opera House, a white Renaissance Revival palace built in 1908, and the 900-seat Majestic Theatre, a partly restored vaudeville house around the corner. Thanks to a $20 million renovation that began in late 1996 (to be completed by early 1998), BAM gained a multiplex movie theater, a café, and a bookstore.

Manhattan has several small-scale yet important arts centers:

The Kitchen (⊠ 512 W. 19th St., ☎ 212/255–5793) showcases avantgarde videos, music, performance art, and dance.
Merkin Concert Hall (⊠ 129 W. 67th St., ☎ 212/501–3330) mainly features chamber-music concerts.
92nd Street Y (⊠ 1395 Lexington Ave., ☎ 212/996–1100), known for its classical-music concerts, also sponsors readings by famous writers, and the Lyrics and Lyricists series.
Sylvia and Danny Kaye Playhouse (⊠ Hunter College, 68th St. between Park and Lexington Aves., ☎ 212/772–4448), a lovely concert hall, has a varied calendar of music, dance, opera, and theater events.
Symphony Space (⊠ 2537 Broadway, at 95th St., ☎ 212/864–5400), a cavernous converted movie theater, schedules an eclectic offering that ranges from folk music to short stories read by celebrities.
Town Hall (⊠ 123 W. 43rd St., ☎ 212/840–2824) hosts a diverse program of chamber and popular music, cabaret performances, and standup comedy.
Tribeca Performing Arts Center (⊠ 199 Chambers St., ☎ 212/346–8510) presents a lively and eclectic program of theater, dance, and music events.

Getting Tickets

Prices for **tickets** in New York, especially for Broadway shows, never seem to stop rising. Major concerts and recitals, however, can be equally expensive. The top Broadway ticket prices for musicals are $75; the best seats for nonmusicals can cost as much as $65.

On the positive side, tickets for New York City's arts events usually aren't too hard to come by—unless, of course, you're dead set on seeing the season's hottest sold-out show. Generally, a theater or concert hall's box office is the best place to buy tickets, since in-house ticket sellers make it their business to know about their theaters and shows and don't mind pointing out (on a chart) where you'll be seated. It's always a good idea to purchase tickets in advance to avoid disappointment, especially if you're traveling a long distance. For advance purchase, send the theater or hall a certified check or money order, several alternate dates, and a self-addressed, stamped envelope.

You can also pull out a credit card and call **Tele-charge** (☎ 212/239–6200) or **TicketMaster** (☎ 212/307–4100) to reserve tickets for Broadway and Off-Broadway shows—newspaper ads generally will specify which you should use for any given event. Both services will give you seat locations over the phone upon request. A surcharge ($2–$5.50 per ticket) will be added to the total in addition to a $2.50 handling fee. You can arrange to have your tickets mailed to you or have them waiting for you at the theater.

For those willing to pay top dollar to see that show or concert everyone's talking about but no one can get tickets for, try a ticket broker. Recently, some brokers charged $100–$150 for tickets to *Rent*; had the same seat been available at the box office, it would have sold for $70. Among the brokers to try are **Continental/Golden and Leblangs Theatre Tickets** (☎ 212/944–8910 or 800/299–8587) and **West Side Ticket Agency** (☎ 212/719–2566). Also, check the lobbies of major hotels for ticket-broker outlets.

You may be tempted to buy from ticket scalpers. But beware: They have reportedly sold tickets to the big hits for up to $200, when seats were still available at the box office for much less. Bear in mind that ticket scalping is against the law in New York. Also, these scalpers may even sell you phony tickets.

Off- and Off-Off-Broadway theaters have their own joint box office called **Ticket Central** (✉ 416 W. 42nd St., ☎ 212/279–4200). It's open daily between 1 and 8 PM. Although there are no discounts here, tickets to performances in these theaters are usually less expensive than Broadway tickets, and they cover an array of events, including legitimate theater, performance art, and dance.

Discount Tickets

The **TKTS booth** in Duffy Square (✉ 47th St. and Broadway, ☎ 212/768–1818) is New York's best-known discount source. TKTS sells day-of-performance tickets for Broadway and Off-Broadway plays at discounts that, depending on a show's popularity, often go as low as 50% to 75% of the usual price, plus a $2.50 surcharge per ticket. The names of shows available on that day are posted on electronic boards in front of the booth. If you're interested in a Wednesday or Saturday matinee, go to the booth between 10 and 2, check out what's offered, and then wait in line. For evening performances, the booth is open 3–8; for Sunday matinee and evening performances, noon–8. *Note: TKTS accepts only cash or traveler's checks—no credit cards.*

The wait is generally pleasant (weather permitting), as the bright lights and babble of Broadway surround you. (Lines, however, can be particularly long on weekends.) You're likely to meet friendly theater lovers in line eager to share opinions about shows they've recently seen; often you'll even meet struggling actors who can give you the inside scoop. By the time you get to the booth, you may be willing to take a gamble on a show you would otherwise never have picked, and it just might be more memorable than one of the long-running hits.

So successful has TKTS proved that an auxiliary booth operates in the Wall Street area (✉ 2 World Trade Center mezzanine). The World Trade Center branch is open weekdays 11–5:30, Saturday 11–3:30. For matinees and Sundays, you have to purchase tickets the day before the performance. The lines at the downtown TKTS booth are usually shorter than those at Duffy Square, though the uptown booth usually has a larger selection of plays.

Discounts on big-name, long-running shows (such as *Miss Saigon* and *Les Misérables*) are often available if you can lay your hands on a couple of **"twofers"**—discount ticket coupons found on various cash registers around town, near the lines at TKTS, at the Times Square visitor information office (at the northwest corner of 7th Ave. and 42nd St.), at the New York Visitors and Convention Bureau (at 2 Columbus Circle), and at the office of their producer, the **Hit Show Club** (✉ 630 9th Ave., 8th floor, ☎ 212/581–4211), open weekdays 9–4.

Some theaters, such as **Classic Stage Company** (✉ 136 E. 13th St., ☎ 212/677–4210) and the **Joseph Papp Public Theater** (✉ 425 Lafayette St., ☎ 212/260–2400), offer reduced rates on unsold tickets the day of the performance, usually a half hour before curtain time. Other shows have front-row orchestra seats available at a reduced price (about $20) the day of the performance. These special discounts are sometimes noted in the newspaper theater listings or ads. Occasionally, box offices offer same-day standing-room tickets ($10–$20) for sold-out shows; check with the particular theater for more information.

Some Broadway and Off-Broadway shows sell reduced-priced tickets for performances scheduled before opening night. Look at newspaper ads for discounted previews, or consult the box office. Tickets may cost less at matinees, particularly on Wednesday.

Finding Out What's On

To find out who or what's playing where, your first stop should be the newsstand. The *New York Times* isn't a prerequisite for finding out what's going on around town, but it comes in pretty handy, especially on Friday, with its "Weekend" section. The Sunday "Arts and Leisure" section features longer articles on everything from opera to soap opera—and a lot more theater ads, plus a full, detailed survey of cultural events for the upcoming week.

The *New Yorker* magazine has long been known for its discerning and often witty listings called "Goings On About Town"—a section at the front of the magazine that contains ruthlessly succinct reviews of theater, dance, art, music, film, and nightlife. *New York* magazine's "Cue" listings are extremely helpful, covering everything from art to the written word.

For adventurous, more unconventional tastes, consult *Time Out New York,* a comprehensive guide to all kinds of entertainment happenings around town, with particularly good coverage of the downtown scene. The free weekly newspaper the *Village Voice* is a lively information source; its club listings and "Choices" section are both reliable. *Metro Source, Next, HomoExtra, Sappho's Isle, Time Out New York, Paper,* and the *Village Voice* illuminate the gay and lesbian scene.

The League of New York Theatres and Producers and *Playbill* magazine publish a twice-monthly *Broadway Theatre Guide,* available in hotels and theaters around town. For information on the lower Manhattan cultural scene, write for a *Downtown Arts Activities Calendar* (✉

Lower Manhattan Cultural Council, 15 World Trade Center, Suite 9325, 10048, ☏ 212/432–0900).

NYC/ON STAGE (☏ 212/768–1818) is the Theatre Development Fund's 24-hour information service.

THEATER

The theater—not the Statue of Liberty or South Street Seaport—is the city's number one tourist attraction, and uptown or downtown you can spot theater folk pursuing their work with customary passion and panache. Delicate little ladies tottering about in their pillbox hats are really theatrical grande dames with fast answers to the flashers on 8th Avenue; shifty-looking guys toting battered briefcases turn out to be famous directors; and the girls and boys scuttling through stage doors are chorus members rushing to exchange their Nikes for tap shoes.

Broadway Theater District
To most people, New York theater means **Broadway,** that region bounded by 42nd and 53rd streets, between 6th and 9th avenues, where bright, transforming lights shine upon porn theaters and jewel-box playhouses alike. Although the area's busy sidewalks contain more than their share of hustlers and pickpockets, visitors brave them for the playhouses' plentiful delights. Extravagant plans for redevelopment of the Times Square area continue to ricochet from marquee to marquee. With every thud of the wrecker's ball, theater devotees pray for the survival of the essence of Broadway—as Paul Goldberger put it in the *New York Times,* "the world of memory, the magical Times Square of old, the lively, glittering district of theaters, restaurants, cabarets, hotels, and neon signs that was in many ways the city's symbolic heart."

Some of the old playhouses are as interesting for their history as for their current offerings. The **St. James** (✉ 246 W. 44th St.), for instance, is where Lauren Bacall served as an usherette in the '40s and where a sleeper of a musical called *Oklahoma!* woke up as a hit. At the **Shubert Theatre** (✉ 225 W. 44th St.), Barbra Streisand made her 1962 Broadway debut in *I Can Get It for You Wholesale,* and the long-run record breaker, *A Chorus Line,* played for 15 years. The **Martin Beck Theatre** (✉ 302 W. 45th St.), built in 1924 in Byzantine style, is the stage that served up premieres of Eugene O'Neill's *The Iceman Cometh,* Arthur Miller's *The Crucible,* and Tennessee Williams's *Sweet Bird of Youth.* Theater names read like a roll call of American theater history: **Booth, Ethel Barrymore, Eugene O'Neill, Gershwin, Lunt-Fontanne, Richard Rodgers,** and **Neil Simon,** among others.

As you stroll around the theater district, you may also see **Shubert Alley,** a shortcut between 44th and 45th streets where theater moguls used to park their limousines, today the site of a jam-packed Great White Way memorabilia store called One Shubert Alley; and **Restaurant Row** (✉ 46th St., between 8th and 9th Aves.), which offers plenty of choices.

Within the past three years, several **42nd Street houses** have come back to life. The **New Victory** (✉ 209 W. 42nd St.), previously known as the Theater Republic and the Belasco Theater, is the oldest surviving playhouse in New York, with a lovely Georgian facade; reopened in 1995 and now completely modernized, it stages exciting productions for kids. The **Ford Center for the Performing Arts** (✉ 213–215 42nd St.), a lavish 1,839-seat theater constructed on the site of two classic houses, the Lyric and the Apollo, incorporates original architectural elements from both theaters, along with state-of-the-art facilities to ac-

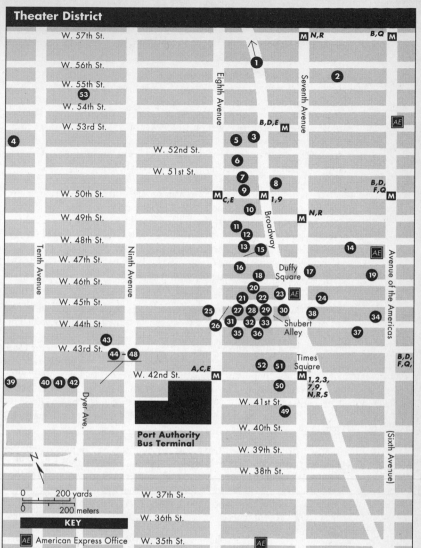

commodate grand-scale musical shows. Across the street, the Walt Disney Company has refurbished the Art Nouveau **New Amsterdam** (✉ 214 W. 42nd St.); Eddie Cantor, Will Rogers, Fanny Brice, and the Ziegfeld Follies once drew crowds here.

Beyond Broadway

Not all that long ago it was relatively simple to categorize the New York stage beyond Broadway. It was divided into **Off-Broadway** and **Off-Off-Broadway,** depending on a variety of factors that included theatrical contract type, location, and ticket price. Today such distinctions seem strained, as Off-Broadway prices have risen and the quality of some Off-Off-Broadway productions has decidedly improved. Off- and Off-Off-Broadway is where Eric Bogosian, Ann Magnuson, John Leguizamo, Danny Hoch, and Laurie Anderson make their home and where *Driving Miss Daisy, Steel Magnolias,* and *Jeffrey* were first conceived. Attendance and ticket sales remain relatively healthy, proving how vital this segment of the theater world is to New York culture. Recent long-running hits have included the surreal *Blue Man Group*; *Stomp,* a percussion performance piece; and *Forbidden Broadway Strikes Back!,* an evening of parodies of Broadway shows. Off-Broadway is also still home to the romantic musical *The Fantasticks,* the longest-running play in U.S. theater history.

One of the major Off-Broadway enclaves is **Theatre Row,** a collection of small houses (100 seats or fewer)—such as the **John Houseman Theatre** (✉ 450 W. 42nd St., ☎ 212/967–9077), the **Douglas Fairbanks Theatre** (✉ 432 W. 42nd St., ☎ 212/239–4321), and **Playwrights Horizons** (✉ 416 W. 42nd St., ☎ 212/279–4200)—on the downtown side of 42nd Street between 9th and 10th avenues. A block east of Theatre Row is the **Westside Theatre** (✉ 407 W. 43rd St., ☎ 212/307–4100). Other small playhouses west of Broadway include **Theatre Four** (✉ 424 W. 55th St., ☎ 212/757–3900) and the **47th Street Theatre** (✉ 212/239–6200).

Name actors appear in top-flight productions at the two theaters at **Lincoln Center:** the **Vivian Beaumont** (actually considered a Broadway playhouse) and the more intimate **Mitzi E. Newhouse** (✉ 65th St. and Broadway, ☎ 212/239–6200 for both), which has scored some startling successes, including John Guare's *Six Degrees of Separation,* Tom Stoppard's *Arcadia,* and acclaimed revivals of *Carousel, The Heiress,* and *A Delicate Balance.*

Downtown in the East Village, at the **Joseph Papp Public Theater** (✉ 425 Lafayette St., ☎ 212/260–2400), renamed in 1992 to honor its late founder and longtime guiding genius, producer George C. Wolfe continues the tradition of innovative theater, mounting new and classic plays, along with dance concerts, literary readings, and musical events. In the summertime, the Public raises its sets in Central Park's open-air **Delacorte Theater** for Shakespeare in the Park. Free tickets for evening performances are handed out to those who have waited in line beforehand at around 1 PM downtown at the Public and uptown at the Delacorte.

Greenwich Village, around Sheridan Square, is another Off-Broadway neighborhood. Its theaters include the **Actors Playhouse** (✉ 100 7th Ave. S, ☎ 212/239–6200); the **Cherry Lane Theatre** (✉ 38 Commerce St., ☎ 212/989–2020); the **Lucille Lortel Theatre** (✉ 121 Christopher St., ☎ 212/239–6200); the **Minetta Lane Theatre** (✉ 18 Minetta La., ☎ 212/420–8000); the **Players Theater** (✉ 115 MacDougal St., ☎ 212/254–5076); and the **Sullivan Street Playhouse** (✉ 181 Sullivan St., ☎ 212/674–3838).

Many estimable **Off-Broadway theaters** are flung across the Manhattan map: the **Astor Place Theatre** (✉ 434 Lafayette St., ☎ 212/254–4370); the **Orpheum Theatre** (✉ 126 2nd Ave., at 8th St., ☎ 212/477–2477); the **Variety Arts Theatre** (✉ 110 3rd Ave., at 14th St., ☎ 212/239–6200); the **Union Square Theatre** (✉ 100 E. 17th St., ☎ 212/505–0700); the **American Place Theatre** (✉ 111 W. 46th St., ☎ 239–6200); the **Lamb's Theatre** (✉ 130 W. 44th St., ☎ 212/997–1780); the **Triad Theatre** (✉ 158 W. 72nd St., ☎ 212/799–4599); and the **Promenade Theatre** (✉ Broadway at 76th St., ☎ 212/580–1313).

THEATER COMPANIES
Several Off- and Off-Off-Broadway theater groups are worth keeping your eye on:

American Jewish Theatre (✉ 307 W. 26th St., ☎ 212/633–9797) stages contemporary plays and revivals of musicals, more often than not with a Jewish theme.

Atlantic Theater Company (✉ 33 W. 20th St., ☎ 212/645–1242), founded by playwright David Mamet and actor William H. Macy, is dedicated to producing controversial new plays.

Drama Dept. (✉ Administrative office: 450 W. 42nd St., ☎ 212/629–3014) doesn't have a permanent home, but the energetic company of young actors, playwrights, and other theater artists has won high acclaim for its lively, imaginative revivals of overlooked plays.

Classic Stage Company (CSC; ✉ 136 E. 13th St., ☎ 212/677–4210) provides a showcase for the classics—some arcane, others European—in new translations and adaptations.

Ensemble Studio Theatre (✉ 549 W. 52nd St., ☎ 212/247–3405), with its tried-and-true roster of players, stresses new dramatic works. It also presents an annual one-act-play marathon.

Irish Repertory Theatre (✉ 132 W. 22nd St., ☎ 212/727–2737) stages classic and contemporary Irish plays.

Jean Cocteau Repertory (✉ Bouwerie Lane Theatre, 330 Bowery, ☎ 212/677–0060), founded in 1971, reinvents international classics, intelligently performed by its resident acting troupe.

Jewish Repertory Theatre (✉ Playhouse 91, 316 E. 91st St., ☎ 212/831–2000), begun in 1972, produces plays and musicals about Jewish life such as *Crossing Delancey,* the basis for the hit film.

Manhattan Theatre Club (✉ At City Center, 131 W. 55th St., ☎ 212/581–1212) stages some of the most talked-about new plays and musicals in town; Terrence McNally, Athol Fugard, and Stephen Sondheim have all had their work produced here.

New York Theater Workshop (✉ 79 E. 4th St., ☎ 212/460–5475) produces challenging new theater by American and international playwrights like Tony Kushner and Caryl Churchill.

Pan Asian Repertory Theatre (✉ Playhouse 46 in St. Clement's Church, 423 W. 46th St., ☎ 212/245–2660), a center for Asian and Asian-American artists, focuses on new works or adapted Western plays.

Pearl Theatre Company (✉ 80 St. Mark's Pl., ☎ 212/598–9802) is the intimate home of a troupe of resident players who concentrate on classics from around the globe; the works of such masters as Molière, Ibsen, Shakespeare, and Sophocles have found a new life here.

Primary Stages (✉ 354 W. 45th St., ☎ 212/333–4052) puts the spotlight on new work by American playwrights, such as David Ives and Donald Margulies.

Repertorio Español (✉ Gramercy Arts Theatre, 138 E. 27th St., ☎ 212/889–2850) is an Obie award–winning Spanish-arts repertory theater; performances are in Spanish.

Second Stage (✉ McGinn/Cazale Theatre, 2162 Broadway, at W. 76th St., ☎ 212/873–6103) is committed to new works and recent plays that may not have been given a fair chance their first time around.
Signature Theatre Company (✉ Administrative office: 422 W. 42nd St., ☎ 212/967–1913) devotes each season to the sensitive productions of the works of one American playwright; past seasons have recognized the plays of Edward Albee, Horton Foote, Adrienne Kennedy, and Sam Shepard. In 1998 Arthur Miller's plays will be performed.
Vineyard Theater (✉ 108 E. 15th St., ☎ 212/353–3366) features innovative new plays and musicals by established and emerging artists.
WPA Theatre (✉ 519 W. 23rd St., ☎ 212/206–0523) showcases new works by American playwrights, such as Paul Rudnick and Charles Busch.
York Theatre Company (✉ Theatre at St. Peter's Church, 54th St. at Lexington Ave., ☎ 212/935–5820) presents acclaimed revivals of plays and musicals in addition to new theater works.

Avant-Garde

Last, but not at all least, is New York's fabled theatrical **avant-garde.** The experimental theater movement's founders may no longer be the long-haired hippies they were when they first started doing mixed-media productions and promoting off-center playwrights (such as Sam Shepard and John Guare) in the '60s, but they continue at the forefront.

Ellen Stewart, also known, simply and elegantly, as La Mama, started the theater complex **La MaMa E.T.C.** (✉ 74A E. 4th St., ☎ 212/475–7710) in 1961. Over the past three decades, her East Village organization has branched out to import European innovators and has grown physically as well. It now encompasses a First Floor Theater, an Annex Theater, and a club. Productions include everything from African fables to new-wave opera to reinterpretations of the Greek classics; past triumphs have included the original performances of *Godspell* and *Torch Song Trilogy*.

A four-theater cultural complex is home to the experimentalist **Theater for the New City** (✉ 155 1st Ave., between 9th and 10th Sts., ☎ 212/254–1109), which devotes its productions to new playwrights. The complex also sponsors a free street-theater program, arts festivals, and Christmas and Halloween spectacles.

Hailed by the *New York Times* as "a first-class magician of the avant-garde," Richard Foreman oversees the **Ontological-Hysteric Theater** (✉ St. Mark's-in-the-Bowery Church, 10th St. and 2nd Ave., ☎ 212/533–4650), whose daring and unconventional productions illuminate the human condition, often exploring the realm of dreams and nightmares. During the summer, the theater sponsors the Blueprint Series, which allows novice directors to test their skills in front of an audience.

Performance Art

Intentionally difficult to categorize, performance art is a curious mélange of artistic disciplines blending music and sound, dance, video and lights, words, and whatever else comes to the performance artist's mind, to produce events of erratic success—sometimes fascinating, sometimes deadening. Performance art is almost exclusively a downtown endeavor, though it is also showcased in the outer boroughs, especially Brooklyn, where the **Brooklyn Academy of Music** (✉ 30 Lafayette Ave., Brooklyn, ☎ 718/636–4100) has built its considerable reputation on its annual Next Wave Festival, which features many performance works.

Manhattan has a few notable performance-art showcases:

Dixon Place (✉ 258 Bowery, between Houston and Prince Sts., ☏ 212/219–3088) presents an eccentric, eclectic schedule, including comedy acts, musicians, and readings.

The Kitchen (✉ 512 W. 19th St., ☏ 212/255–5793) is perhaps *the* Manhattan center for performance art, although video, dance, and music have their moments here, too.

PS 122 (✉ 150 1st Ave., at 9th St., ☏ 212/477–5288) occupies a former public school that was comedian George Burns's alma mater. This vibrant East Village venue presents exhibitions and productions that come and go quickly, and they're never boring. Look especially for its annual marathon in February, in which scores of dazzling downtowners take part.

DANCE

Ballet

Visiting balletomanes live out their dreams in New York, where two powerhouse companies—the New York City Ballet and the American Ballet Theatre—continue to please and astonish.

The **New York City Ballet (NYCB),** a hallmark troupe for nearly 50 years, recently marked its 106th season with compelling examples of exceptional dances from the company's vast repertory, including works by George Balanchine, Jerome Robbins, Ballet Master-in-Chief Peter Martins, and others. NYCB performs in Lincoln Center's **New York State Theater** (☏ 212/870–5570). Its winter season runs from mid-November through February—with the beloved annual production of *George Balanchine's The Nutcracker* ushering in the December holiday season—while its spring season lasts from late April through June.

Founded by Lincoln Kirstein and Balanchine in 1948, NYCB continues to stress dance as a whole above individual ballet stars, though that hasn't stopped a number of principal dancers (such as Kyra Nichols, Darci Kistler, Damian Woetzel, and Jock Soto) from standing out. The company has more than 80 dancers and performs and maintains an active repertoire of 20th-century works unmatched in the world.

Across the plaza at Lincoln Center, the **Metropolitan Opera House** (☏ 212/362–6000) is home to **American Ballet Theatre,** renowned for its brilliant renditions of the great 19th-century classics (*Swan Lake, Giselle, The Sleeping Beauty,* and *La Bayardère*) as well as for the unique scope of its eclectic contemporary repertoire (including works by all the 20th-century masters—Balanchine, Tudor, Robbins, and de Mille, among others). Since its inception in 1940, the company has included some of the greatest dancers of the century, such as Mikhail Baryshnikov, Natalia Makarova, Rudolf Nureyev, Gelsey Kirkland, and Cynthia Gregory. Since 1992, American Ballet Theatre has been directed by Kevin McKenzie, one of the company's leading male dancers in the 1980s. Its New York season runs from April to June.

Part of Lincoln Center's dance vitality is accounted for by the presence of the **School of American Ballet** (✉ 70 Lincoln Center Plaza), the focus for the dreams of young dancers across the country. Some 2,000 of them vie for spots in SAB's summer session, and a talented handful of the 200 who make it into the summer group go on to join the school. Here the Balanchine legacy lives on, and soulful-eyed baby dancers are molded into professional performers. You can see SAB students dashing across 66th and Broadway with leotard-stuffed bags slung over their shoulders.

The varied bill at **City Center** (✉ 131 W. 55th St., ☎ 212/581–1212) often includes touring ballet companies.

Modern Dance

At **City Center** (✉ 131 W. 55th St., ☎ 212/581–1212), the moderns hold sway. In seasons past, the **Alvin Ailey Dance Company, Twyla Tharp and Dancers,** the **Martha Graham Dance Company,** the **Paul Taylor Dance Company,** the **Dance Theater of Harlem,** and the **Merce Cunningham Dance Company** have performed here. The **Brooklyn Academy of Music** (✉ 30 Lafayette Ave., ☎ 718/636–4100) features both American and foreign contemporary dance troupes as part of its **Next Wave Festival** every fall.

A growing international modern-dance center is the **Joyce Theater** (✉ 175 8th Ave., ☎ 212/242–0800), housed in a former Art Deco movie theater. The Joyce is the permanent home of **Feld Ballets/NY,** founded in 1974 by an upstart ABT dancer who went on to become a principal fixture on the dance scene. Recent featured companies have included the startling **Parsons Dance Company,** the lyrical **Lar Lubovitch Dance Company,** the passionate **Ballet Hispanico,** and the fantastical **Momix** troupe. The Joyce has an eclectic program, including tap, jazz, ballroom, and ethnic dance, and it often showcases emerging choreographers. It has another space downtown, the **Joyce Soho** (✉ 155 Mercer St., ☎ 212/431–9233), which hosts a number of performances by highly talented local dancers.

Manhattan has several other small-scale, mostly experimental and avant-garde dance forums:

Dance Theater Workshop (✉ 219 W. 19th St., ☎ 212/924–0077) serves as one of New York's most successful laboratories for new dance.

Danspace Project (✉ St. Mark's-in-the-Bowery Church, 10th St. and 2nd Ave., ☎ 212/674–8194) sponsors a series of avant-garde choreography that runs from September through June.

Merce Cunningham Studio (✉ 55 Bethune St., ☎ 212/691–9751) showcases performances by cutting-edge modern dance companies.

92nd St. Y Harkness Dance Project (✉ 1395 Lexington Ave., ☎ 212/996–1100) presents emerging dance troupes with discussion following performances.

PS 122 (✉ 150 1st Ave., at 9th St., ☎ 212/477–5288) programs dance events that often border on performance art.

Repertorio Español (✉ 138 E. 27th St., ☎ 212/889–2850) is often visited by the famed Spanish stylist Pilar Rioja.

Sylvia and Danny Kaye Playhouse (✉ Hunter College, 68th St., between Park and Lexington Aves., ☎ 212/772–4448) hosts up-and-coming dance companies.

Symphony Space (✉ 2537 Broadway, at 95th St., ☎ 212/864–5400) often focuses on ethnic dance.

Tribeca Performing Arts Center (✉ 199 Chambers St., ☎ 212/346–8510) presents dance troupes from around the world.

MUSIC

"Gentlemen," conductor Serge Koussevitzky once told the assembled Boston Symphony Orchestra, "maybe it's good enough for Cleveland or Cincinnati, but it's not good enough for New York." That's New York's place in the musical world, in a nutshell.

New York possesses not only the country's oldest symphony, the New York Philharmonic, but also three renowned conservatories—the

Juilliard School, the Manhattan School of Music, and Mannes College of Music—plus myriad other musical performance groups. Since the turn of the century, the world's great orchestras and soloists have made Manhattan a principal stopping point.

If you're visiting the city for its music, New York has an overwhelming number of happenings to keep you busy. In an average week, between 50 and 150 events—everything from zydeco to Debussy, Cole Porter, Kurt Weill, and reggae—appear in newspaper and magazine listings, and weekly concert calendars are published in all of the major newspapers. Record and music shops serve as music information centers. These shops include the cavernous **Tower Records** (⊠ 692 Broadway, at 4th St., ☎ 212/505–1500), **Trump Tower** (⊠ 725 5th Ave., at 57th St., ☎ 212/838–8110; ⊠ 1961 Broadway, at 66th St., ☎ 212/799–2500), **HMV** (⊠ 2081 Broadway, at 72nd St., ☎ 212/721–5900; ⊠ 1280 Lexington Ave., at 86th St., ☎ 212/348–0800; ⊠ 565 5th Ave., at 46th St., ☎ 212/681–6700; ⊠ 59 W. 34th St., ☎ 212/629–6900), **J & R Music World** (⊠ 15–33 Park Row, across from City Hall, ☎ 212/238–9000), the reliable **Bleecker Bob's Golden Oldies** (⊠ 118 W. 3rd St., ☎ 212/475–9677), and the classy **Joseph Patelson Music House** (⊠ 160 W. 56th St., ☎ 212/582–5840).

Classical Music

Lincoln Center (⊠ W. 62nd St. to 66th Sts., Columbus to Amsterdam Aves.) remains the city's musical nerve center, especially when it comes to the classics.

Avery Fisher Hall (☎ 212/875–5030), designed by Max Abramovitz, opened at Lincoln Center in 1961 as Philharmonic Hall but underwent drastic renovation in 1976 to improve the acoustics (at a price tag of $5 million). The result is an auditorium that follows the classic European rectangular pattern. To its stage come the world's great musicians; to its boxes, the black-tie-and-diamond-tiara set.

The **New York Philharmonic** (☎ 212/875–5656), led by Music Director Kurt Masur, performs at Avery Fisher Hall from late September to early June. In addition to its magical concerts showcasing exceptional guest artists and the works of specific composers, the Philharmonic also schedules weeknight Rush Hour Concerts at 6:45 PM and Casual Saturdays Concerts at 2 PM; these special events, offered throughout the season, last one hour and are priced lower than the regular subscription concerts. Rush Hour Concerts are followed by receptions with the conductor on the Grand Promenade, and Casual Saturdays Concerts feature discussions after the performances.

A note for New York Philharmonic devotees: In season, and when conductors and soloists are amenable, weekday orchestra rehearsals at 9:45 AM are open to the public for $10.

During the summer at Avery Fisher Hall, the popular **Mostly Mozart** (☎ 212/875–5135) concert series presents an impressive roster of classical performers.

Near Avery Fisher is **Alice Tully Hall** (⊠ Broadway at 65th St., ☎ 212/875–5050), an intimate "little white box," considered as acoustically perfect as concert houses get. Here you can listen to the **Chamber Music Society of Lincoln Center,** promising Juilliard students, chamber music ensembles, music on period instruments, choral music, famous soloists, and concert groups. Lincoln Center's outdoor **Damrosch Park** and nearby **Bruno Walter Auditorium** (in the Library of the Performing Arts, ☎ 212/870–1630) often offer free concerts.

While Lincoln Center is only some 30 years old, another famous classical music palace—**Carnegie Hall** (✉ W. 57th St. at 7th Ave., ☎ 212/247–7800)—recently celebrated its 100th birthday. This is the place where the great pianist Paderewski was attacked by ebullient crowds (who claimed kisses and locks of his hair) after a performance in 1891; where young Leonard Bernstein, standing in for New York Philharmonic conductor Bruno Walter, made his triumphant debut in 1943; where Jack Benny and Isaac Stern fiddled together; and where the Beatles played one of their first U.S. concerts. When threats of the wrecker's ball loomed large in 1960, a consortium of Carnegie loyalists (headed by Isaac Stern) rose to save it; an eventual multimillion-dollar renovation in 1986 worked cosmetic wonders.

In addition to Lincoln Center and Carnegie Hall, the city has many other prime classical music locales around the city:

Aaron Davis Hall at City College (✉ W. 133rd St. at Convent Ave., ☎ 212/650–6900) is an uptown venue for world music events and a variety of classical concerts and dance programs.

Bargemusic at the Fulton Ferry Landing in Brooklyn (☎ 718/624–4061) keeps chamber-music groups busy year-round on an old barge with a fabulous skyline view.

Brooklyn Academy of Music (✉ 30 Lafayette Ave., ☎ 718/636–4100) continues to experiment with new and old musical styles, and it's still a showcase for the Brooklyn Philharmonic.

Grace Rainey Rogers Auditorium at the Metropolitan Museum of Art (✉ 5th Ave. at 82nd St., ☎ 212/570–3949) offers performances of classical music in stately surroundings.

Merkin Concert Hall at the Abraham Goodman House (✉ 129 W. 67th St., ☎ 212/550–3330) is almost as prestigious for performers as the concert halls at Lincoln Center.

Miller Theatre (✉ Columbia University, Broadway at 116th St., ☎ 212/854–7799) features a varied program of classical performers, such as the New York Virtuosi Chamber Symphony.

92nd St. Y (✉ 1395 Lexington Ave., ☎ 212/996–1100) showcases star recitalists and chamber music groups.

Sylvia and Danny Kaye Playhouse (✉ Hunter College, 68th St. between Park and Lexington Aves., ☎ 212/772–4448) presents a varied program of events, including distinguished soloists and chamber music groups, in a small state-of-the-art concert hall.

Outdoor Concerts

Weather permitting, the city presents myriad musical events in the great outdoors. Each August, the plaza around Lincoln Center explodes with the **Lincoln Center Out-of-Doors** (☎ 212/875–5108) series. In the summertime, both the **Metropolitan Opera** and the **New York Philharmonic** appear in municipal parks to play free concerts, filling verdant spaces with the haunting strains of *La Bohème* or the thunder of the *1812 Overture* (for information call Lincoln Center, ☎ 212/875–5400, or the City Parks Special Events Hotline, ☎ 212/360–3456). **Central Park SummerStage** (✉ Rumsey Playfield, Central Park at 72nd St., ☎ 212/360–2777 or 800/201–7275) presents free music programs, ranging from world music to alternative rock, generally on Saturday and Sunday afternoons from June through August. The **Museum of Modern Art** hosts free Friday and Saturday evening concerts of 20th-century music in its sculpture garden as part of the **Summergarden** series (☎ 212/708–9480), held from mid-June through August. A **Jazzmobile** (☎ 212/866–4900) transports jazz and Latin music to parks throughout the five boroughs in July and August; Wednesday evening concerts are held at Grant's Tomb (✉ Riverside Dr. and 122nd

St.). **Prospect Park** comes alive with the sounds of its annual **Celebrate Brooklyn Concert Series** (✉ 9th Street Bandshell, 9th St. and Prospect Park W, Park Slope, Brooklyn, ☎ 718/965–8969). **Pier 16 at South Street Seaport** (☎ 212/732–7678) becomes the setting for a cornucopia of musical entertainment Thursday through Saturday evening from Memorial Day to Labor Day; it also sponsors holiday music concerts from late November through January 1 on weekday evenings and weekend afternoons.

Lunchtime Concerts

During the workweek, **lunchtime concerts** provide musical midday breaks at public atriums all over the city. Events are generally free, and bag-lunching is encouraged. Check out the **World Financial Center's Winter Garden Atrium** (across the West Side Highway from the World Trade Center). Of course, everywhere—in parks, on street corners, and down under in the subway—aspiring musicians of all kinds hold forth, with their instrument cases thrown open for contributions. True, some are hacks, but others are bona fide professionals: moonlighting violinists, Broadway chorus members indulging their love of the barbershop quartet, or horn players prowling up from clubs.

A midtown music break can be found at **St. Peter's Lutheran Church** (✉ 619 Lexington Ave., at the Citicorp Center, ☎ 212/935–2200), with its Wednesday series of lunchtime jazz at 12:30 and organ concerts on Friday at 12:45.

Downtown, the venerable **St. Paul's Chapel** (✉ Fulton St. and Broadway, ☎ 212/602–0874) presents lunchtime concerts on Monday at noon. **Trinity Church** (✉ 74 Trinity Pl., ☎ 212/602–0873) also has concerts on Thursday at 1 PM. Programs at both churches may include classical or contemporary music. A $2 contribution is suggested.

OPERA

Recent decades have sharply intensified the public's appreciation of grand opera—partly because of the charismatic personalities of such great singers as Luciano Pavarotti, Placido Domingo, and Cecilia Bartoli and partly because of the efforts of New York's magnetic **Metropolitan Opera** (☎ 212/362–6000). A Met premiere draws the rich and famous, the critics, and the connoisseurs. At the Met's elegant Lincoln Center home, with its Marc Chagall murals and weighty Austrian-crystal chandeliers, the supercharged atmosphere gives audiences a sense that something special is going to happen, even before the curtain goes up. Luciano Pavarotti put it best: "When it comes to classical music, New York can truly be called a beacon of light—with that special quality that makes it *unico in mondo,* unique in the world."

The Metropolitan Opera performs its vaunted repertoire from October to mid-April, and though tickets can cost more than $100, many less expensive seats and standing room are available. The top-priced tickets are the center box seats, which are actually few in number and almost never available without a subscription. Unlike Broadway theaters, the Metropolitan Opera House has several different price levels, with some 600 seats sold at $24; bear in mind that weekday prices are slightly lower than weekend prices. Standing-room tickets for the week's performances go on sale on Saturday.

The **New York City Opera,** which performs from September through November and in March and April at Lincoln Center's **New York State Theater** (☎ 212/870–5570), continues its tradition of offering a diverse repertoire, consisting of adventurous and rarely seen works as well as beloved classic opera and operetta favorites. City Opera has widened its program to include several time-honored musicals, such as *A Little Night Music, The Most Happy Fella, Brigadoon,* and *Cinderella.* The company has a reputation for nurturing the talent of young American stars-to-be. (A surprising number of the world's finest singers, such as Placido Domingo, Frederica von Stade, and Beverly Sills, began their careers at City Opera.) The company maintains its ingenious practice of "supertitling"—electronically displaying, above the stage, line-by-line English translations of foreign-language operas. Recent seasons have included such old favorites as *Carmen, Madama Butterfly,* and *La Traviata* as well as premieres of challenging new works such as *The Times of Harvey Milk.*

Opera aficionados should also keep track of the **Carnegie Hall** (☎ 212/247–7800) schedule for debuting singers and performances by the **Opera Orchestra of New York,** (✉ Box 1226, 10023, ☎ 212/799–1982), which specializes in presenting rarely performed operas in concert form, often with star soloists. Pay close attention to provocative opera offerings at the **Brooklyn Academy of Music** (☎ 718/636–4100), which often premieres avant-garde works difficult to see elsewhere.

The city has a few lesser-known opera groups:

Amato Opera Theatre (✉ 319 Bowery, ☎ 212/228–8200) is an intimate showcase for rising singers.
New York Gilbert and Sullivan Players (✉ 302 W. 91st St., ☎ 212/769–1000 or 212/864–5400 for box office) presents lively productions of G & S classics, usually at Symphony Space (✉ 95th and Broadway).
New York Grand Opera (✉ 154 W. 57th St., Suite 125, ☎ 212/245–8837) mounts free summer performances of Verdi operas—with a full orchestra and professional singers—at Central Park SummerStage at Rumsey Playfield (Central Park at 72nd St.).

FILM AND VIDEO

On any given week, New York City might be described as a kind of film archive featuring all the major new releases, classics renowned and obscure, unusual foreign offerings, small independent flicks, and cutting-edge experimental works. Because you don't usually need to buy tickets in advance, except on Friday and Saturday evenings, moviegoing is a great spur-of-the-moment way to rest from sightseeing. You may have to stand awhile in a line that winds around the block, but even that can be entertaining—conversations overheard in such queues are generally just as good as the previews of coming attractions. Note, however, that these lines are generally for people who have already bought their tickets; be sure, as you approach the theater, to ask if there are separate lines for ticket *holders* and ticket *buyers.*

For information on first-run movie schedules and theaters, dial 212/777–3456, the **MovieFone** sponsored by WNEW 102.7 FM and the *New York Times.* You can also call this number to order tickets in advance with a credit card; not all movie theaters participate, however, and the surcharge is $1.50 per ticket.

Festivals

New York's numero uno film program remains the **New York Film Festival,** conducted by the Film Society of Lincoln Center every September and October at Alice Tully and Avery Fisher halls (☎ 212/875–5600). Its program includes exceptional movies, most of them never seen before in the United States; the festival's hits usually make their way into local movie houses over the following couple of months. This festival

Pick up the phone.
Pick up the miles.

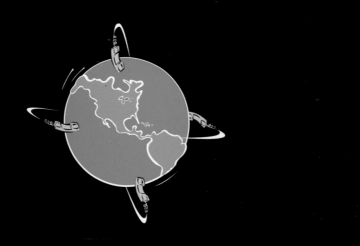

1-800-FLY-FREE

Is this a great time, or what? :-)

Now when you sign up with MCI you can receive up to 8,000 bonus frequent flyer miles on one of seven major airlines.

Then earn another 5 miles for every dollar you spend on a variety of MCI services, including MCI Card® calls from virtually anywhere in the world.*

You're going to use these services anyway. Why not rack up the miles while you're doing it?

has presented the U.S. premieres of such memorable movies as Martin Scorsese's *Mean Streets,* François Truffaut's *Day for Night,* Quentin Tarantino's *Pulp Fiction,* and Mike Leigh's *Secrets and Lies.* Each March the Film Society joins forces with the Museum of Modern Art to produce a **New Directors/New Films** series, where the best works by up-and-coming directors get their moment to flicker. Several movies included in this festival have gone on to become box-office successes. The series is held at MoMA's Roy and Niuta Titus theaters (✉ 11 W. 53rd St., ☎ 212/708–9480).

Museums

The **American Museum of the Moving Image** (✉ 35th Ave. at 36th St., Astoria, Queens, ☎ 718/784–0077) is the only museum in the nation devoted to motion pictures, video, and digital media. Its core exhibition, "Behind the Screen," takes visitors step by step through the process of producing, marketing, and exhibiting moving images through a combination of artifacts, texts, live demonstrations, and video screenings. Visitors can make their own video flipbook, edit sound effects, dub dialogue, and create their own animation through 13 computer-based interactive experiences. Located on the site of the historic Kaufman-Astoria Studios, the museum presents changing exhibits, lectures, and provocative film programs, including major artist-oriented retrospectives, Hollywood classics, experimental videos, and TV documentaries. Screenings are held in the intimate 195-seat Riklis Theatre.

In midtown Manhattan, the **Museum of Television & Radio** (✉ 25 W. 52nd St., ☎ 212/621–6800) has a gigantic collection of 75,000 radio and TV shows, from the golden past to the present. The museum's library provides 96 consoles where you can watch or listen to whatever you wish for up to two hours at a time. The museum presents scheduled theater screenings, gallery exhibits, and series for children.

First-Run Houses

New suburban-style **multiscreen complexes** have sprung up all over town, even in such hip urban neighborhoods as SoHo (Houston and Mercer Sts.), the East Village (2nd Ave. at 12th St. and 3rd Ave. at 11th St.), the Flatiron district (890 Broadway, at 19th St.), and Hell's Kitchen (Worldwide Plaza, 320 W. 50th St.). Although the increase in the number of screens seems to have eased lines at the box office somewhat, these cinemas often show the same mainstream commercial movies, so long lines still snake around the corner at the few theaters that show more offbeat fare. Manhattan's most impressive multiplex movie house, **Sony Theatres Lincoln Square** (✉ Broadway and 68th St., ☎ 212/336–5000), has 12 state-of-the-art theaters designed to recall grand old movie palaces and an eight-story, 600-seat IMAX Theatre that is equipped not only for large-scale formatted films but also for 3-D imagery. *Across the Sea of Time,* an exciting journey back into New York's past, is one of several short films on view at the IMAX Theatre.

Besides the Lincoln Square, two other New York theaters preserve the size and allure of the great movie houses of the past. The **Ziegfeld** (✉ 141 W. 54th St., west of 6th Ave., ☎ 212/765–7600) has a huge screen, brilliant red decor, and an awesome sound system. **Radio City Music Hall** (✉ 1260 6th Ave., at 50th St., ☎ 212/247–4777) with its art-deco setting, 34-ft-high screen, and 4,500-watt projector, is occasionally used for movie screenings.

Revival Houses

One of the best places to see old films in Manhattan is the **Walter Reade Theater** at Lincoln Center (✉ 70 Lincoln Center Plaza, Broadway at

65th St., ☎ 212/875–5600), operated by the Film Society of Lincoln Center. This comfortable movie house presents several fascinating series that run concurrently, devoted to specific themes or a certain director's body of work; movies for kids are featured on Saturday morning. The auditorium is a little gem with excellent sight lines, and tickets can be purchased at the box office weeks in advance.

Revivals can also be found at:

American Museum of the Moving Image (✉ 35th Ave. at 36th St., Astoria, Queens, ☎ 718/784–0077) offers American film series, often in historical contexts. Programs also honor overlooked artists, such as cinematographers and screenwriters.

Anthology Film Archives (✉ 32 2nd Ave., at 2nd St., ☎ 212/505–5181) shows movies that have made a significant contribution to film history.

Film Forum (✉ 209 W. Houston St., ☎ 212/727–8110) has three screens showing often quirky series based on movie genres, directors, and other film artists.

The Museum of Modern Art (✉ 11 W. 53rd St., ☎ 212/708–9480) includes rare classic films in its many excellent revival series.

Foreign and Independent Films

Between the interest generated by the New York Film Festival, the city's population of foreign executives and diplomats, a resident corps of independent filmmakers, and a large contingent of cosmopolitan cinemaniacs, there's always an audience here for foreign films and for innovative new American films and videos that buck the Hollywood currents. New York has several cinemas that more or less specialize in such films.

Angelika 57 (✉ 225 W. 57th St., ☎ 212/586–1900) shows film programs similar to those of its downtown sister theater, the Angelika Film Center.

Angelika Film Center (✉ W. Houston and Mercer Sts., ☎ 212/995–2000) offers several screens devoted to offbeat independent and foreign films, as well as a lively café catering to a youthful crowd.

Anthology Film Archives (✉ 32 2nd Ave., at 2nd St., ☎ 212/505–5181) presents esoteric independent fare seldom shown elsewhere.

Carnegie Hall Cinemas (✉ 887 7th Ave., between 56th and 57th Sts., ☎ 212/265–2520) screens intriguing new films in two small theaters.

Cinema Village (✉ 12th St. between 5th Ave. and University Pl., ☎ 212/924–3363) schedules innovative independent features and occasional animation festivals. Programs concentrating on movies produced in Hong Kong are particularly popular.

Eastside Playhouse (✉ 3rd Ave. between 55th and 56th Sts., ☎ 212/755–3020) usually shows first-run art films.

Film Forum (✉ 209 W. Houston St., ☎ 212/727–8110) presents some of the best new independent films and hard-to-see foreign movies.

Lincoln Plaza (✉ Broadway between 62nd and 63rd Sts., ☎ 212/757–2280) has six subterranean cinemas playing long-run foreign and independent hits.

Millennium (✉ 66 E. 4th St., ☎ 212/673–0090) focuses on the avant-garde.

Quad Cinema (✉ 13th St. between 5th and 6th Aves., ☎ 212/255–8800) plays first-run art and foreign films on very small screens.

Screening Room (✉ 54 Varick St., ☎ 212/334-2100) screens provocative independent movies in a theater that adjoins a restaurant.

68th Street Playhouse (✉ 3rd Ave. at 68th St., ☎ 212/734–0302) has exclusive extended runs of critically acclaimed films.

Sony Paris (✉ 58th St. between 5th and 6th Aves., ☎ 212/980–5656) is an exquisite showcase for much-talked-about new American and foreign entries.
Village East Cinemas (✉ 2nd Ave. at 12th St., ☎ 212/529–6799) presents cutting-edge independent features alongside mainstream Hollywood productions.

Foreign and independent films and videos frequently run at cultural societies and museums around town, including the following:

Asia Society (✉ 725 Park Ave., at 70th St., ☎ 212/288–6400) shows excellent films from countries all over Asia.
French Institute (✉ Florence Gould Hall, 55 E. 59th St., ☎ 212/355–6160) programs retrospectives of French movies, often devoted to a particular theme or director.
Goethe House (✉ 1014 5th Ave., between 82nd and 83rd Sts., ☎ 212/439–8700) screens movies by leading German filmmakers.
Japan Society (✉ 333 47th St., ☎ 212/752–3015) focuses on Japanese films rarely available in other parts of the city.
The Museum of Modern Art (✉ 11 W. 53rd St., ☎ 212/708–9480) frequently shows foreign classics and hard-to-see independent films.
Whitney Museum of American Art (✉ Madison Ave. at 75th St., ☎ 212/570–3676) is a reliable forum for experimental and independent films.

READINGS AND LECTURES

New York is the center of American publishing, and as a result many writers from around the world—however reclusive—eventually find reason to come here, either to visit or to live. If you're interested in seeing the written word and catching a glimpse of the people who create books, a New York prose or poetry reading can be a lot of fun and often inspirational. Readings unfold all over the city—in bookstores, libraries, museums, bars, and legitimate theaters—attracting debuting talents and some of the top names in contemporary literature, writers such as E. L. Doctorow, Nadine Gordimer, Toni Morrison, Edna O'Brien, Seamus Heaney, Philip Roth, Kazuo Ishiguro, and many others.

Poetry Calendar (✉ 611 Broadway, Suite 905, 10012, ☎ 212/260–7097), published monthly September through June, provides extensive listings of prose and poetry readings around the city. The calendar is available by subscription or for free at several Manhattan bookstores. Check also listings for readings in *New York* magazine, the *New Yorker, Time Out New York,* and the *Village Voice.*

Authors, poets, lyricists, and playwrights take the stage at the **92nd St. Y** (✉ 1395 Lexington Ave., ☎ 212/996–1100). **Symphony Space** (✉ Broadway at 95th St., ☎ 212/864–5400) holds a number of readings, including the Selected Shorts series of stories read by prominent actors. Manhattan Theatre Club sponsors **Writers in Performance** (✉ 131 W. 55th St., ☎ 212/645–5848), a provocative program of dramatic readings and roundtable discussions that showcase novelists, poets, and playwrights from the United States and abroad.

Downtown, rising young scribes appear at **Limbo** (✉ 47 Ave. A, between 3rd and 4th Sts., ☎ 212/477–5271), a coffee bar. **Dixon Place** (✉ 258 Bowery, between Houston and Prince Sts., ☎ 212/219–3088) and the **Kitchen** (✉ 512 W. 19th St., ☎ 212/255–5793) both sponsor readings regularly, some of which border on performance art.

Distinguished series of **poetry readings** are sponsored by several organizations in Manhattan, including the **Academy of American Poets** (⊠ 580 Broadway, ☎ 212/274–0343), **Dia Center for the Arts** (⊠ 548 W. 22nd St., ☎ 212/989–5566), the **Poetry Project** (⊠ St. Mark's-in-the-Bowery Church, E. 10th St. and 2nd Ave., ☎ 212/674–0910), **Poetry Society of America** (⊠ 15 Gramercy Park S, ☎ 212/254–9628), and **Poets House** (⊠ 72 Spring St., ☎ 212/431–7920).

Informal poetry readings, sometimes with an "open-mike" policy that allows audience members to read their own work, continue to crop up with frequency in New York City clubs and bars. These events are fairly popular, particularly with a younger crowd. There may be a low cover charge ($2–$5), and food and drink are usually available. Some reliable spots include **Biblio's** (⊠ 317 Church St., ☎ 212/334–6990); **Ear Inn** (⊠ 326 Spring St., ☎ 212/226–9060), on Saturday afternoons; **Cornelia Street Café** (⊠ 29 Cornelia St., ☎ 212/989–9319); the **Knitting Factory** (⊠ 74 Leonard St., ☎ 212/219–3055); and **Nuyorican Poets Cafe** (⊠ 236 E. 3rd St., ☎ 212/505–8183), with a variety of multicultural poets scheduled weekly and a Poetry Slam competition each Friday.

Many **Manhattan bookstores** organize evening readings by authors of recently published books. Best bets are **Barnes & Noble** (⊠ 1280 Lexington Ave., at 86th St., ☎ 212/423–9900; ⊠ Citicorp Bldg., 54th St. at 3rd. Ave., ☎ 212/750–8033; ⊠ 2289 Broadway, at 82nd St., ☎ 212/362–8835; ⊠ 1972 Broadway, at 66th St., ☎ 212/595–6859; ⊠ 605 5th Ave., at 48th St., ☎ 212/765–0590; ⊠ 675 6th Ave., at 22nd St., ☎ 212/727–1227; ⊠ 33 Union Sq., ☎ 212/253–0810; ⊠ 4 Astor Pl., ☎ 212/420–1322); **Borders** (⊠ 5 World Trade Center, ☎ 212/839–8049); **Posman Books** (⊠ 1 University Pl., between Waverly Pl. and 8th St., ☎ 212/533–2665); **Rizzoli Bookstore** (⊠ 454 W. Broadway, between Prince and Houston Sts., ☎ 212/674–1616); **Shakespeare and Co.** (⊠ 739 Lexington Ave., between 68th and 69th Sts., ☎ 212/570–0201); **Three Lives and Co.** (⊠ 154 W. 10th St., ☎ 212/741–2069); and **Tower Books** (⊠ 383 Lafayette St., at 4th St., ☎ 212/228–5100). For readings by gay and lesbian authors, try **A Different Light** (⊠ 151 W. 19th St., ☎ 212/989–4850).

A major reading and talk series held at the **Lincoln Center Library for the Performing Arts** (☎ 212/870–1630) specializes in musicians, directors, singers, and actors. Several branches of the **New York Public Library** (NYPL) present lectures and reading events. A monthly calendar of free library readings is available at each branch.

At the **Metropolitan Museum of Art** (⊠ 5th Ave. at 82nd St., ☎ 212/570–3949), seasonal lectures regularly draw sellout crowds. Artists and world-eminent art historians speak here.

6 Dining

Dining out is one of New York's greatest pleasures. Because of the city's prominence as an international financial and cultural center, you can easily sample a multitude of foreign cuisines in the span of a week as well as regional dishes from around the United States. Manhattan has a restaurant to match any taste or pocketbook—from extravagant caviar and sushi bars to trendsetting TriBeCa haunts to affordable bistros, trattorias, coffee shops, and delis. If you're looking for innovative cuisine, you'll discover it prepared by some of the best chefs anywhere, and you can find places that serve traditional meals as well.

THAT INTERNATIONAL APPENDAGE to the United States known as the Big Apple supports more good restaurants, and more kinds of them, than any other city in the world. And while it's possible to spend big bucks and eat badly, it's equally possible to dine like a king for a pittance. Food is one of the city's joys. Its restaurant mix also has an idiosyncratic charm. Hotel dining rooms—which have the resources to provide the professional service staff, fine china, comprehensive wine cellar, and top-flight kitchen required for serious dining—are increasingly common, with a life and often an entrance of their own. New York bistros and trattorias are as excellent as they are inexpensive and abundant, and the city is dotted with outstanding steak houses (meat has apparently made a comeback). Star chefs such as Larry Forgione, Daniel Boulud, David Burke, and Gray Kunz have given the city a coterie of innovative kitchens whose graduates have assured that even neighborhood eateries serve more than usually interesting fare.

By J. Walman

French, Italian, and international restaurants improve each year and frequently compare favorably to their counterparts abroad. Seafood dining spots are improving—indeed, there are even a few outstanding ones, and New York is finally beginning to utilize its waterfront. Despite the prevalence of small Indian restaurants, their menus and spicing usually tend to be similar. Spanish cooking has finally taken flight, but as for Brazilian fare, an authentic *feijoada* (the stew of black beans with smoked meats) is hard to find.

New York's best breakfasts are not limited to so-called tablecloth restaurants. Dozens of Greek-owned coffee shops pride themselves on perfectly scrambled eggs, savory hash browns, and that New York institution, the toasted bagel. Chinatown's tea houses go nonstop from 8 AM till 5 PM, and "Little Korea," a string of amazingly inexpensive possibilities centered on West 32nd Street, between 5th and 7th avenues, is open around the clock. The coffeehouse explosion offers a civilized respite from Manhattan frenzy: Most offer restorative snacks in addition to a long list of java drinks (with or without caffeine), and the bounty of breweries, wine/champagne/cigar bars and club lounges caters to appetites of all dimensions. (Some bars will even allow you to "order in" from neighboring take-out emporiums—so inquire).

Such small ethnic eating spots are legion in New York, their mix constantly changing with shifting immigration patterns; countries like Afghanistan, Thailand, Turkey, Senegal, and Jamaica are currently adding culinary breadth to the dining scene. There are more Chinese options than ever, and you are no longer obliged to endure rude service and dingy surroundings: Brightening today's Chinatowns (which thrive in Brooklyn and Queens as well as Manhattan) are noisy, gaudy eating emporiums in the Hong Kong style, and Asian-inspired fare is available in modish spots, from Aja to Zoe (Lespinasse, one of Manhattan's best haute kitchens, has made a trademark of it). Szechuan may be out, but Cantonese home cooking, with its fresh ingredients and simple cooking, is in. The Chinese tea lunch known as dim (touch) sum (heart, thus "to touch one's heart")—consisting of various dumplings, small cooked dishes, rice, noodles, puffs, balls, claws, you name it—holds strong. (At a dim sum lunch or brunch, point to what you want as trolleys bearing these delicacies wheel past your table.) The next wave? Caribbean cuisine is currently popular. Malaysian, Burmese, Vietnamese, Korean, Spanish, Middle Eastern, and African cuisines may gain a stronghold, not to mention African-American cooking and some of the little-known regional foods of Italy and other European nations.

Bottom line? Take a chance. Not every venture will be a success. But the whole experience will be rewarding. That's a promise.

Planning Your Culinary Itinerary

In most great restaurant towns, there is generally one best restaurant; New York generously offers a variety of candidates. Times being what they are, top restaurants have short lives, chefs play musical kitchens, and today's star is often tomorrow's laggard. As in France, it's prudent to seek out restaurants on their way up and to approach celebrities with caution. Temper your visits to famous restaurants with informed selections from among lesser-knowns. Can a famous restaurant produce a really spectacular dinner? Probably. Will an unknown diner receive a great meal on the first visit to a fashionable restaurant? Probably not. Even in these recessionary times, the snob snub is not dead.

Our Selections

We firmly believe that everybody should be treated like somebody, and our recommendations take into account the reception as well as the food, decor, service, and wines. When there are several restaurants within a genre, we choose the most interesting. Some famous restaurants, elsewhere held in high regard, have not captured our accolades; others are omitted because they treat guests shabbily or are poor value. To familiarize you with the kitchen's style, we also mention dishes we have sampled. Menus change often (sometimes daily); signature dishes are becoming a thing of the past. It's the kitchen's style that counts, so look for similar preparations or ingredients.

Wine

New York won't disappoint on this score. Generally, the most expensive wines have the smallest markup, the mid-price spectrum offers the best values, and the least-expensive offerings are poor values. Half bottles are hard to find. Increasingly common instead is wine by the glass; younger restaurants as well as a number of old-timers offer serious vintages at sensible prices this way. If the wine list is large, have an aperitif and take your time in ordering. Remember: You're the buyer. Note that many restaurants allow you to bring your own bottle, charging a service fee ranging from $5 to about $25.

Tipping

Rules are simple. Never tip the maître d' unless you're out to impress your companion. In most restaurants, tip the waiter at least 15% to 20%. (To figure the amount quickly, just double the tax noted on the check—it's 8¼% of your bill—and round up or slightly down.)

In stylish establishments, give 5% to the captain, even if he did most of the work, and 15% to the waiter. To a busboy, a couple of dollars is appreciated but hardly expected. Give wine stewards about $5 per bottle, more if you order important wines that require decanting or other special services. Give the captain or sommelier his or her tip, palmed in your hand, with a friendly shake and a smile. Tip at least $1 per coat checked.

Prices

New York gets a bum rap. Of course, you can order caviar and champagne or Bordeaux of great years; you will pay accordingly. But you will also do that in Nashville and Los Angeles. Our point is that each price stratum has its own equilibrium. Translation: $20 is only inexpensive if you get $20 worth of value, and $100 may be a bargain. Visitors from abroad will find New York is the world's least expensive international center in terms of food.

CATEGORY	COST*
$$$$	over $60
$$$	$40–$59
$$	$20–$39
$	under $20

per person for a three-course meal, excluding drinks, service, and 8¼% sales tax

Restaurants marked with two prices ($–$$, for example) include modest restaurants where choosing the most expensive dishes can push your check into the next category and also pricier restaurants where you can lower your tab by opting for the less-expensive fare or choosing a prix-fixe meal such as $19.98 lunches or dinners found in many New York restaurants. Brunches are also price-wise. Most prix-fixe menus don't include coffee or drinks.

If you're watching your budget, always ask the price of the specials. Rather than being sensibly attached to the menu, European-style, specials are often recited by the waiter with no mention of cost. Ask.

Finally, always go over your bill. Mistakes do occur (and not always in the restaurant's favor).

Dress

Use common sense. Dress up for grand restaurants, and wear neat but casual clothes for casual spots. Midtown is more conservative than residential neighborhoods, SoHo and TriBeCa trendier than the Upper East and Upper West sides. Shorts are appropriate only in summer and in the most casual spots. When in doubt, call ahead.

Reservations

Make a reservation. If you change your mind, cancel—it's only courteous. Tables can be hard to come by between 7 and 9; if a restaurant tells you that it can seat you only before 6 or after 10, you may decide that it doesn't need you. Or you may be persuaded that eating early or late is okay. Eating after a play or concert is quite common in New York, and there's no shortage of options. And don't be afraid to speak up if you prefer to sit in a certain area or if you want a special table.

Smoking

New York is no longer smoker-friendly. Only restaurants with fewer than 35 seats legally allow smoking. Establishments may allow you to smoke at the bar or at a table outdoors, if such seating is available. A recent phenomenon, however, is the rise of the cigar bar. Many restaurants have added areas for smoking cigars, and some establishments are devoted solely to this pastime. Cigar bars often stock a superb selection of single-malt scotches, cognacs, wines, and champagnes along with elegant snacking (sandwiches, salads, tapas, and caviar).

MANHATTAN RESTAURANTS

Lower Manhattan

American

$$ ✕ **Fraunces Tavern.** Opened as a tavern in 1762 by Samuel Fraunces, George Washington's steward, this Georgian brick landmark dates back to 1719; George Washington delivered his farewell address here when the British evacuated New York. Today the place has a clubby bar and faithful Colonial decor; it's a nice spot for cocktails (they're rather good) and for basic eggs-bacon-and-oatmeal breakfasts. Any other time, stick to steaks or, Wednesday, pot roast. ✉ *54 Pearl St., at Broad St.,* ☎ *212/269–0144. Reservations essential. AE, DC, MC, V. Closed weekends.*

Chinese

$$$ ✕ **Au Mandarin.** One of the best bets in Manhattan for haute Chinese, this World Financial Center restaurant has a courtyard-like setting, an exotic fish tank, and classy furnishings. The dining experience combines a polished atmosphere with careful service. You might start with vegetarian dumplings or Shanghai buns, then move on to Shanghai prawns, followed by Peking duck, tangerine beef, and delicate rice noodles with julienne vegetables. ✉ *200–250 Vesey St. (World Financial Center),* ☎ *212/385–0313. AE, DC, MC, V.*

Contemporary

$$$–$$$$ ✕ **Hudson River Club.** This distinguished restaurant has spacious wood-paneled rooms with paisley-print banquettes, spectacular views of the Hudson River and the Statue of Liberty, and a spirited bar with piano music. The kitchen celebrates Hudson River valley produce in such hallmark dishes as mint cured apple-smoked salmon Napoleon and veal shank with horseradish mashed potatoes. Desserts—like the signature tower of chocolate (combining brownie, mousse, and meringue)—are edible sculptures, while the New York State cheese plate with walnut bread and nut muffins serves as a perfect foil to the magnificent wines from the regional American wine list. ✉ *4 World Financial Center,* ☎ *212/786–1500. Reservations essential. AE, DC, MC, V. No lunch Sat.*

$$$–$$$$ ✕ **Windows on the World.** This monumental restaurant on the World
★ Trade Center's 107th floor reopened in 1996 after a $25 million makeover. When you step off the elevator, you encounter an impressive 38-ft-wide curtain of beads as you're welcomed by pages dressed in rainbow colors. The complex now includes The Greatest Bar on Earth (actually three bars) with a full, multiethnic menu, and dancing after 10 PM; the adjacent Skybox, a cigar-smoking oasis; and the intimate, 60-seat Cellar in the Sky, where a seven-course dinner is served, accompanied by five wines. The 240-seat main dining room has artwork by Milton Glaser, apricot-fabric banquettes, origami fabric-wrapped ceilings, and panoramic windows with stunning Manhattan views; meals are served on whimsical china with designs of stars, moons, and clouds. Don't miss the whole seared foie gras, roasted in Sauternes and grapes, served with a galette of pear and potatoes. Follow this with a whole veal shank, roasted with cumin, garlic, and Mexican aromatics. ✉ *1 World Trade Center, 107th floor,* ☎ *212/524–7011; 212/938–0030 for Cellar in the Sky. Reservations essential. Jacket required. AE, DC, MC, V.*

Downtown Manhattan Dining

Acme Bar and Grill, **23**
Agrotikon, **8**
Arturo's, **26**
Au Mandarin, **62**
Ballatos, **28**
Boca Chica, **20**
Brothers Bar-B-Q, **24**
Cafe Fes, **12**
Caffè Lure, **27**
Capsouto Frères, **38**
Casa La Femme, **31**
Cendrillon
  Asian Grill and
  Mamba Bar, **40**
Chanterelle, **53**
Chez Jacqueline, **25**
Da Nico, **36**
Dix et Sept, **2**

Duane Park Café, **57**
El Pollo, **37**
El Teddy's, **50**
Erizo Latino, **32**
Felix, **39**
First, **19**
Fraunces Tavern, **59**
French Roast, **4**
Global 33, **21**
Gianni's, **60**
Golden Unicorn, **56**
Gotham Bar & Grill, **6**
Grand Ticino, **22**
Hudson River Club, **61**
Il Cortile, **45**
Indochine, **14**
James Beard House, **3**
Joe's Shanghai, **42**

Lanza Restaurant, **10**
L'Auberge Du Midi, **1**
Layla, **52**
Le Jardin Bistro, **29**
Lucky Strike, **41**
Manila Garden, **7**
Match, **30**
Mirezi, **5**
Montrachet, **51**
New York
  Noodletown, **54**
Nobu, **49**
Odeon, **58**
Pacifica, **46**
Penang Soho, **34**
Pisces, **17**
Roettelle A. G., **16**
Second Avenue Deli, **11**

S.P.Q.R., **43**
Spring Street Natural
  Restaurant & Bar, **35**
Sweet 'n' Tart Cafe, **44**
Takahachi, **18**
Teresa's, **15**
13 Barrow, **13**
Tribeca Grill, **48**
20 Mott, **55**
Windows On The
  World, **63**
Xunta, **9**
Zeppole (Tribakery
  Cafe), **47**
Zoë, **33**

Seafood

$$ ✕ **Gianni's.** This is the most earnest restaurant near South Street Seaport, an area not noted for gastronomic excellence. Pastas, salads, and seafood work best. Or try an out-of-the-ordinary sandwich. There's an outdoor café during the summer. ⊠ *15 Fulton St., ☎ 212/608–7300. AE, DC, MC, V.*

SoHo and TriBeCa

American Casual

$ ✕ **Lucky Strike.** One of Manhattan's funkiest small restaurants, this unadorned SoHo boîte doesn't look like much. In the crowded back room, specials and available wines are written on mirrors on the walls. You can have a terrific steak and *pommes frites* (french fries) at a bargain price, good burgers, and great bread pudding; the homemade bread is also worth the trip. The crowd mobbing the bar is young and hip. ⊠ *59 Grand St., between Wooster St. and W. Broadway, ☎ 212/941–0479 or 212/941–0772. Reservations not accepted. AE, DC, MC, V.*

Contemporary

$$$$ ✕ **Chanterelle.** Soft peach walls, luxuriously spaced tables, towering
★ ceilings, and glorious displays of flowers set the stage for what is arguably New York's finest new-American restaurant. The unassuming, flawless service complements chef David Waltuck's inventions, which are carefully prepared and beautifully presented. Although the signature seafood sausage, charred on the outside and succulent within, and the Japanese-style raw seafood are both always available, other dishes on the menu are changeable, dictated by the bounty of the seasons. Trust your exceptional sommelier to find value in the discriminating, beautifully chosen wine list. Lunch and dinner are prix fixe. ⊠ *2 Harrison St., near Hudson St., ☎ 212/966–6960. Reservations essential. AE, DC, MC, V. Closed Sun.–Mon. No lunch.*

$$–$$$ ✕ **Tribeca Grill.** This cavernous brick-walled restaurant, subtly lighted and anchored by the bar from the old Maxwell's Plum, displays art by the late Robert De Niro Sr., father of the actor, who opened it with various celebrity partners and now owns it with Montrachet's Drew Nieporent. The best dishes are the simple ones, such as crisp fried oysters with anchovy aïoli and herb-crusted rack of lamb with oven-roasted vegetables; desserts are amicable (try banana tart with milk-chocolate ice cream), as is the staff. ⊠ *375 Greenwich St., near Franklin St., ☎ 212/941–3900. Reservations essential. AE, DC, MC, V. No lunch Sat.*

$$–$$$ ✕ **Zoë.** Thalia and Stephen Loffredo's colorful, high-ceilinged SoHo eatery with terra-cotta columns and floor has an open kitchen that produces impressive food, such as grilled yellowfin tuna on wok-charred vegetables. Zoë also has an exceptionally well organized wine list and a fine group of carefully tended wines by the glass. This is one of Manhattan's better places to have weekend brunch. ⊠ *90 Prince St., between Broadway and Mercer St., ☎ 212/966–6722. Reservations essential. AE, DC, MC, V.*

$$ ✕ **Duane Park Café.** This quiet TriBeCa find is owned by its Japanese chef, Seiji Maeda. It can spoil you with its comfortable seating, excellent service, serious but fairly priced wines, and international menu. Look for marinated duck and arugula salad as well as crispy skate with the Japanese-inspired *ponzu* sauce. The pleasing design incorporates dark columns, a salmon color scheme, maple-veneered walls, and an abundance of cherry wood. ⊠ *157 Duane St., between W. Broadway and Hudson St., ☎ 212/732–5555. AE, D, DC, MC, V. Closed Sun. No lunch Sat.*

$$ ✕ **Match.** This bilevel restaurant-lounge is hot enough to scorch the heels of a seasoned fire walker. Open beams and machine fixtures, blond-wood paneling, and old-world booths hugging the wall preserve the memory of the building's industrial past (Match is housed in the former home of New York's oldest electrical company). Check out the raw bar, which teems with fabulous presentations of fresh shellfish, sushi, sashimi, and caviar, or go for the dim-sum platter. There's also a Match Uptown (✉ 33 E. 60th St., ☎ 212/906–9173.) ✉ *160 Mercer St., between Houston and Prince Sts.,* ☎ *212/343–0020. AE, MC, V.*

$–$$ ✕ **Odeon.** Established in 1980, this was downtown's first "trendy" restaurant, and it's still one of the neighborhood's best. The art deco cafeteria setting includes plentiful neon, vinyl banquettes, and Formica tables, and the pleasant service, low prices, and well-chosen wine list are all pluses. But let's not neglect the food: crab and potato fritters with soy-daikon sauce, and grilled lamb and leek sandwich on country bread are equally tantalizing. ✉ *145 W. Broadway at Thomas St.,* ☎ *212/233–0507. AE, DC, MC, V.*

French

$$$–$$$$ ✕ **Montrachet.** This TriBeCa trendsetter, owned by Tribeca Grill's
★   Drew Nieporent, is unpretentious in its decor: pastel walls, plush mauve banquettes, and engaging works of art. There's a choice of two three-course menus as well as a five-course tasting affair. A satisfying dinner might include the signature truffle-crusted salmon in red-wine fumé and the banana-chocolate gratin (a pudding-like dessert, quickly finished under the grill). There's an interesting selection of wines from diminutive regional vineyards. ✉ *239 W. Broadway, between Walker and White Sts.,* ☎ *212/219–2777. Reservations essential. AE. Closed Sun. No lunch Mon.–Thurs. or Sat.*

$$–$$$ ✕ **Capsouto Frères.** You'd never guess this romantic spot with ex-
★   posed brick walls, tall columns, and wooden floors was once a warehouse. With its top-notch service, classical music, and reasonable prices, this 1891 TriBeCa landmark is also a winner. Chef Charles Tutino prepares classics with a solid, contemporary touch—for instance, terrine Provençale and Peking duck in cassis-ginger sauce. Dessert soufflés around town pale against the light, delicious versions here. ✉ *451 Washington St., near Watts St.,* ☎ *212/966–4900. Reservations essential. AE, DC, MC, V. No lunch Mon.*

$–$$ ✕ **Caffè Lure.** Owner Jean Claude Iacovelli earned his stripes at Bouley.
★   The room is small, rough, and raffish with its tin ceiling, tables topped with brown paper and flacons of water, and walls festooned with vintage advertising signs and fishing lures—hence the name. The culinary emphasis here is on seafood; try baby lobster with spinach and port sauce or roast monkfish with black-olive pureed potatoes and mushrooms. You can also play it simple and enjoy some of the best brick-oven-fired pizza imaginable. ✉ *169 Sullivan St., between Houston and Bleecker Sts.,* ☎ *212/473–2642. No credit cards.*

$–$$ ✕ **Felix.** No, you haven't traveled 3,000 mi to Paris's Left Bank; this charming bistro is in SoHo, a taxi ride from midtown. Whether you dine inside or alfresco, the service is friendly and the contemporary bistro fare is attractively presented. Try the steak with thin, crunchy french fries. ✉ *340 W. Broadway, at Grand St.,* ☎ *212/431–0021. AE. No lunch Mon.*

$ ✕ **Le Jardin Bistro.** Gerard and Pamela Maurice's welcoming house with a lovely garden and grape arbor really belongs in a small French village. There's no pretension—just hearty portions of French food. The small, charming interior has a tin ceiling, ceiling fans, an antique mirror, and lace café curtains. The fine steak tartare comes with light and grease-free pommes frîtes. You can't go wrong with any of the pleasant house wines or the homemade desserts. ⊠ *25 Cleveland Pl., near Spring St.,* ☎ *212/343–9599. Reservations essential. AE, DC, MC, V.*

Health

$–$$ ✕ **Spring Street Natural Restaurant and Bar.** The big open room has ceiling fans, overhead globe lights, wood floors, and a long comfortable bar; in warm weather, there are also tables outside. Two vegetarian dishes are standouts: corn-fried organic *seitan* (a sort of wheat gluten), in two dipping sauces, and a crispy tempeh. You can't go wrong with any of the healthy yet heavenly desserts. ⊠ *62 Spring St., at Lafayette St.,* ☎ *212/966–0290. AE, DC, MC, V.*

Italian

$–$$ ✕ **Zeppole (Tribakery Cafe).** Owned by Drew Nieporent and Robert De Niro, this rustic Italian restaurant with exposed brick walls and comfy banquettes is named for the fried sugared Neapolitan puffs, popular at Italian street fairs. You can't go wrong with any of the pasta, but also consider the grilled chicken *diavalo,* coated with mustard and bread crumbs. Desserts are dandy, especially the nut-filled carrot cake. During the day, come here for some of New York's best bread and cold antipasti. ⊠ *186 Franklin St., between Greenwich and Hudson Sts.,* ☎ *212/431–1114. Reservations essential. AE, DC, MC, V. Closed Sun. No lunch Sat.*

Japanese

$$$–$$$$ ✕ **Nobu.** A curved wall of river-worn black pebbles, a 12-seat onyx-
★ faced sushi bar (perfect for single diners), bare-wood tables, birch trees, and a hand-painted beech floor create drama as well as conversation. Sake is the drink of choice, and the clientele is as interesting as the kitchen, which is ruled by celebrity chef Nobu Matsuhisa, of Los Angeles. It's difficult to decide which direction to go on his menu: rock-shrimp tempura; black cod with miso; new-style sashimi—all are tours de force. ⊠ *105 Hudson St., off Franklin St.,* ☎ *212/219–0500 or 212/219–8095 for same-day reservations. Reservations essential. AE, DC, MC, V. Closed Sun. No lunch.*

Latin

$$–$$$ ✕ **Erizo Latino.** The wood-beamed trellis and decorative iron chandeliers with flickering candles contribute to the romantic ambience of this pan-Latino restaurant. You might start with a classic *mojito,* the Cuban cocktail of rum, mint, sugar, and lime juice. Owner-chef Alex Garcia's menu includes *erizo* (sea urchins) served in their shell, with three piquant vinegar-based sauces, tamales (Cuban or Puerto Rican), and a standout all-seafood mixed grill, plus some kicky desserts such as *quesillo de coco* (caramelized coconut cream). ⊠ *422 W. Broadway, near Prince St.,* ☎ *212/941–5811. AE, DC, MC, V.*

$ ✕ **El Pollo.** This trilevel SoHo restaurant has a soaring ceiling, Mission-style tables and chairs, and walls decorated with Peruvian carvings and oil paintings. The menu provides a good introduction to Peruvian cuisine. The specialty—whole chicken, marinated in garlic, wine, pepper, lemon, oregano, vinegar, and spices—is rotisserie roasted and a bargain. For an appetizer, try the traditional cold potatoes, prepared in a zesty cheese sauce. El Pollo has an unassuming uptown counterpart (1746 1st Ave., between 90th and 91st Sts., ☎ 212/996–7810). ⊠ *482 Broome St., at Wooster St.,* ☎ *212/431–5666. AE, DC, MC, V.*

Malaysian

$–$$ ✕ **Penang SoHo.** This is a Technicolor fantasy, with a dramatic waterfall, palm trees, tropical flowers, bar seats with backs made of hoe handles, and individual little huts for small groups. The menu includes relatively authentic culinary masterpieces, such as *sarang burung,* a ring of fried taro filled with scallops, squid, shrimp, and vegetables. For dessert have a pancake filled with ground peanuts and sweet corn and an iced Malaysian coffee. ✉ *109 Spring St., between Greene and Mercer Sts.,* ☎ *212/274–8883. AE, MC, V.*

Mexican

$$ ✕ **El Teddy's.** The margaritas get high marks and the food is mostly wonderful, revealing both authentic Mexican subtleties and contemporary creativity, from the smoked chicken and goat-cheese quesadilla to the grilled rare yellowfin tuna. The roster of inventive desserts includes almond flan and flourless chocolate cake. This is a Mexican restaurant like no other, with its mirrors, tiles, glitter, and grotesque use of colors. ✉ *219 W. Broadway, between Franklin and White Sts.,* ☎ *212/941–7070. Reservations essential. AE, MC, V. No lunch weekends.*

Middle Eastern

$$$ ✕ **Layla.** Mosaics made of pottery shards form exotic collages within this leviathan space. Owned by Drew Nieporent (of Tribeca Grill, Nobu, and Montrachet fame) and actor Robert De Niro, this campy takeoff on the Middle East comes complete with live belly dancers and lifelike mannequins of water-pipe smokers. The "chef's feast" consists of various hot and cold Middle Eastern appetizers, including stuffed baby calamari and delicious sardines, wrapped in phyllo to dip in black-olive oil. ✉ *211 W. Broadway, at Franklin St.,* ☎ *212/431–0700. Reservations essential. AE, DC, MC, V. No lunch weekends.*

$$–$$$ ✕ **Casa La Femme.** This enterprising restaurant changes its entire decor every six months. Currently the theme is Egyptian, with burgundy banquettes and tables under flowing white tents. In season, there's a sidewalk café. Standout dishes include meze, the Middle Eastern equivalent of mixed hors d'oeuvres, and Moroccan vegetarian *tagine,* which is a spicy stew. ✉ *150 Wooster St., between Houston and Prince Sts.,* ☎ *212/505–0005. AE, DC, MC, V.*

Philippine

$$–$$$ ✕ **Cendrillon Asian Grill and Marimba Bar.** Cendrillon means Cinderella
★ in French, so the slipper-shape bar is apropos. The all-exposed redbrick dining room has beautiful wood tables with delicate inlay designs. Don't miss the spring rolls, Asian barbecues (duck, spareribs, chicken), black rice salad, and adobo—the national dish of the Philippines, prepared here with quail and rabbit in the traditional vinegar and garlic sauce. ✉ *45 Mercer St., between Broome and Grand Sts.,* ☎ *212/343–9012. AE, DC, MC, V. Closed Sun.*

Chinatown, Little Italy, and Lower East Side

Chinese

$$ ✕ **Golden Unicorn.** This Hong Kong–style restaurant has an outstanding 12-course banquet (which must be ordered three days in advance), a real bargain if shared by 10. Served in a small private room, it may include such dishes as roast suckling pig, scallops and seafood in a noodle nest, whole steamed fish, fried rice with raisins, lobster with ginger, and unusual desserts based on warm or chilled fruit or rice soups. If you're seeking something less elaborate, sit in the regular dining room and order à la carte. ✉ *18 E. Broadway, at Catherine St.,* ☎ *212/941–0911. AE, MC, V.*

$$ ✕ **Pacifica.** Holiday Inn houses this elegant Chinatown restaurant. Take the escalator to the second floor and pass through the tasteful lobby to a well-appointed room in shades of gold, salmon, and soft green. Ignore the pastas and order simple and classic dishes such as salt-baked triple delight, consisting of shrimp, scallops, and calamari,

or steamed fish with ginger and scallions. ⊠ *138 Lafayette St., between Canal and Howard Sts.,* ☎ *212/941–4168. AE, DC, MC, V.*

$–$$ ✕ **New York Noodletown.** This unassuming place with a window full of hanging cooked ducks remains one of the best small Chinatown restaurants. Single diners may have to sit at communal round tables, and if you're not careful, you can spend more than the no-nonsense coffee-shop decor suggests. Soup and noodles are the things to order here, and you'll find none better elsewhere; treat yourself to delicious shrimp, Chinese greens, and soft egg noodles served in a remarkably cultivated seafood broth. ⊠ *28½ Bowery, at Bayard St.,* ☎ *212/349–0923. Reservations not accepted. No credit cards.*

$–$$ ✕ **20 Mott.** This three-story restaurant, an excellent choice for dim sum,
★ is neat if nondescript, and the service rates a notch above average. To get food that's authentic, you must insist on it (look around and point), and when you do, you may be served fabulous steamed dumplings; deep-fried eel with orange peel and spicy XO sauce (a Hong Kong specialty that's rare here)—or different but equally novel dishes. ⊠ *20 Mott St., between Bowery and Pell Sts.,* ☎ *212/964–0380. AE, MC, V.*

$ ✕ **Joe's Shanghai.** At this modern, clean, and unadorned dining spot,
★ you'll find a staff eager to please. The specialty here, known as "bun," is a delicious dumpling containing not only ground pork or crab but also piping-hot broth. Also recommended are the Shanghai fried flat noodles—long, winding doughy miracles served in an intense brown sauce—and stewed pork balls, big puffy blobs of meats embellished with steamed baby Chinese cabbage. ⊠ *9 Pell St.,* ☎ *212/233–8888. No credit cards.*

$ ✕ **Sweet'n'Tart Cafe.** You step down into what looks like the inside of a pink sea shell, furnished with Formica tables and a counter to the right. The menu has some 20 curative soups: little white bowls composed of such exotica as quail eggs, almonds and Asian pears, snow fungi, and spooky-sounding herbs, which actually taste wonderful. This is the place to sample *congee,* that porridge-like concoction eaten for breakfast in Hong Kong. The friendly waiters may advise you to accompany the congee with a sugarless cruller; follow their advice, because the crullers are terrific. Less adventurous souls can enjoy dim sum or fresh fruit shakes. ⊠ *76 Mott St., at Canal St.,* ☎ *212/334–8088. No credit cards.*

Italian

$$–$$$ ✕ **Il Cortile.** The setting resembles an Italian palazzo with statues, a Roman brick wall, sprays of fresh flowers, plants, trees, and a skylit courtyard. Rack of veal De Georgio, made with sausage, herbs, and prosciutto sauce, is the house specialty. ⊠ *125 Mulberry St., between Canal and Hester Sts.,* ☎ *212/226–6060. Reservations essential. AE, DC, MC, V.*

$$ ✕ **S.P.Q.R.** This inviting spot with spacious tables, brickwork, and lots of fresh flowers is one of the few earnest restaurants in Little Italy, an area noted more for fun than food. In addition to the good pasta, there's a terrific veal chop and a phenomenal cheesecake. ⊠ *133 Mulberry St., between Hester and Grand Sts.,* ☎ *212/925–3120. AE, DC, MC, V.*

$ ✕ **Ballato's.** This old-timer has been attractively revamped with a Kostabi painting, red-oak floors, and an enclosed garden. The menu has inexpensive pastas and good daily specials; if you've never sampled tripe, Ballato's version, prepared in a superb marinara sauce, is worth investigating. ⊠ *55 E. Houston St., between Mott and Mulberry Sts.,* ☎ *212/274–8881. AE, DC, MC, V. Closed weekends. No lunch.*

Pizza

$–$$ ✕ **Da Nico.** This Little Italy restaurant deserves praise for its outstanding rotisserie grills and thin-crusted, charred, coal-oven pizza. The roast chicken is delicious, the roast suckling pig soul-stirring. You can dine up front by the marble bar or in a comfortable back room with a skylight. ✉ *164 Mulberry St., between Grand and Broome Sts.,* ☎ *212/343–1212. AE, DC, MC, V.*

East Village

American

$–$$ ✕ **First.** Come here for inner-city flavor, late-night dining, and intriguing food. The decor features an open kitchen, hammered-metal tables against silk horseshoe-shape banquettes, and a bar graced with a lovely display of photographs by local photographers. The wine list is carefully chosen (several fine vintages are available by the glass). On Sunday, there's a fun brunch and a one-of-a-kind roast suckling pig dinner. ✉ *87 1st Ave., between 5th and 6th Sts.,* ☎ *212/674–3823. Reservations essential. AE, MC, V. No lunch.*

$ ✕ **Acme Bar and Grill.** At this friendly eatery, the vintage-shack decor is incredibly kitschy, including shelves filled with innumerable bottles of hot sauce. The sound system blasts Chicago blues and jazz. The Cajun-influenced menu embraces chicken, ribs, crab cakes, catfish, and shrimp—steamed in Old Bay spice, barbecued, or blackened. The coleslaw (coarsely cut and a mix of different colored cabbages, onions, and mayo) is worth a detour. ✉ *9 Great Jones St., between Broadway and Lafayette St.,* ☎ *212/420–1934. DC, MC, V.*

Asian

$$ ✕ **Indochine.** Palm leafs painted on cream-colored walls, black-and-
★   white tile floors, mirrors, leather banquettes, and live palm trees team up with some of the most fascinating food this side of Saigon. Select from among such savory soups as *pho* (sliced fillet of beef, rice noodles, bean sprouts) and *noum protchok namya* (fish, scallops, shrimp, coconut milk, rice vermicelli). The *banh cuon* (steamed Vietnamese ravioli filled with chicken, shiitake, bean sprouts) is celestial. ✉ *430 Lafayette St., between 4th St. and Astor Pl.,* ☎ *212/505–5111. Reservations essential. AE, DC, MC, V. No lunch.*

Contemporary

$$ ✕ **Global 33.** It looks like an airport lounge furnished by Bloomingdale's, with vinyl, pewter, Lucite, and cast-concrete decor. In this hip space, would-be jet-setters can enjoy generous retro cocktails and tapas-size goodies. Even the blasting music becomes tolerable when you try the luscious herbed rack of lamb with mashed potatoes, followed by chocolate espresso torte. ✉ *93 2nd Ave., between 5th and 6th Sts.,* ☎ *212/477–8427. AE. No lunch.*

Deli

$–$$ ✕ **Second Avenue Deli.** The menu here has a bevy of Eastern European Jewish classics, including chicken in the pot, matzo-ball soup, chopped liver, Romanian tenderloin, and *cholent* (a central European Jewish dish of meat, bean, and grain)—they're alive and well and accompanied by humor-filled New York Jewish service from days of yore, as well as interesting memorabilia from the Yiddish theater. ✉ *156 2nd Ave., at 10th St.,* ☎ *212/677–0606. AE.*

Eastern European

$ ✕ **Teresa's.** Homesick Poles mix with cost-conscious students at this Polish luncheonette. Comfort your tummy with *bigos,* the Polish national stew—sauerkraut layered with fresh and smoked meats and sausage—and the hearty, stick-to-the-ribs dumplings known as pierogi, filled with meat, fish, cheese, or mushrooms, boiled or fried and served with sour cream. ⊠ *103 1st Ave., between 6th and 7th Sts.,* ☎ *212/228–0604. No credit cards.*

Greek

$–$$ ✕ **Agrotikon.** Designed by artist Anna Lascari, this immaculate white,
★ blue, and green dining room with two fireplaces has been whimsically decorated with decals of fruit and tiny blue fish. Owner and executive chef Kostis Tsingas oversees the most inventive Greek restaurant in town. Don't miss the meatballs of baby calamari. Also worth your while is the whole red snapper, accompanied by delightfully crunchy dandelion greens. ⊠ *322 E. 14th St., between 1st and 2nd Aves.,* ☎ *212/473–2602. AE, DC, MC, V. Closed Mon.*

Italian

$ ✕ **Lanza Restaurant.** Ceiling fans, paintings of Italian scenes, and an inviting garden create the feel of an authentic trattoria. The good classic food offers one of Manhattan's greatest restaurant bargains, which explains the crowds of hungry New Yorkers. ⊠ *168 1st Ave., between 10th and 11th Sts.,* ☎ *212/674–7014. AE, DC, MC, V.*

Japanese

$ ✕ **Takahachi.** One of the best small Japanese restaurants in Manhat-
★ tan, it's neat and amazingly inexpensive, offering such unusual dishes as fried shiitake filled with ground salmon and seared tuna with black pepper and mustard sauce. There's also a good early-bird special, served until 7 PM. ⊠ *85 Ave. A, between 5th and 6th Sts.,* ☎ *212/505–6524. AE, MC, V. No lunch.*

Latin

$ ✕ **Boca Chica.** At this raffish East Villager start with a potent *caipir-*
★ *inha* (Brazilian rum, lime juice, and sugar). Assertively seasoned food from several Latin American nations at giveaway prices is Boca Chica's forte. Check out the plantains, served as croquettes or filled with spicy meat; soupy Puerto Rican chicken-rice stew; or Cuban sandwiches blending roast pork, ham, and pickles. Lively music and dancing have their way on weekends, and watch your step—there's often an equally lively boa constrictor by the bar. ⊠ *13 1st Ave., near 1st St.,* ☎ *212/473–0108. AE, DC, MC, V. No lunch Mon.–Sat.*

Philippine

$ ✕ **Manila Garden.** Authentic Philippine cuisine, combining Asian and Spanish flavors, may be savored at this lovely spot, with a white grand piano, a seasonal garden, and fresh orchids on each table. Tuesdays, you can take advantage of the bargain buffet at lunch and dinner. Other times, enjoy wonderful *lechon* (roasted pig), *lumpia Shanghai* (a delicious pork egg roll), and chicken adobo. For dessert, order the flan, which is richer than its Spanish counterpart, and *halo halo* (ice cream topped with fruit). ⊠ *325 E. 14th St., between 1st and 2nd Aves.,* ☎ *212/777–6314. AE, DC, MC, V.*

Seafood

$–$$ ✕ **Pisces.** This striking restaurant, where tables near the open windows seem to spill out into Alphabet City, as this neighborhood of lettered avenues is called, has fallen victim to the quick-change-chef syndrome. But a sophisticated menu combined with reasonable prices still make it worthwhile. Brunch is served on weekends. ⊠ *95 Ave. A, at 6th St.,* ☎ *212/260–6660. AE, MC, V. No lunch weekdays.*

Spanish

$ ✕ **Xunta.** The dining room has wine barrels for tables, high stools (watch your balance), fish nets covering the ceiling, and a brick bar with over-hanging dried peppers. Of the 32 tapas, don't miss the tortilla *española con cebola* (classic potato omelet with onions)—it is superb. Other recommended dishes include grilled shrimp, tuna or codfish empanadas, and sautéed *cigalas* (a typical shellfish in white wine and cherry-tomato sauce). ⊠ *174 1st Ave., between 10th and 11th Sts.,* ☎ *212/614–0620. AE, DC, MC, V.*

Swiss

$ ✕ **Roettelle A. G.** If you hanker for hearty European cooking, you'll
★ love this charming East Village town house, where you can sit in a hidden nook in one of the several dining rooms, in the cozy bar, or under an arbor in the garden sipping Swiss wine and eating *viande de Grisons* (Swiss dried beef) or raclette (mild melted cheese served with boiled potatoes and tiny pickles). Sauerbraten with spaetzle and red cabbage is delicious, and it's rare to taste apple strudel and linzer torte this good. Prices are low, and there's also a bargain two-course fixed-price dinner. ⊠ *126 E. 7th St., between 1st Ave. and Ave. A,* ☎ *212/674–4140. Reservations essential. MC, V. Closed Sun.*

Greenwich Village

Asian

$$ ✕ **Mirezi.** This cutting-edge Pan-Asian bistro and grill (whose name means "future land" in Korean) has two levels; the stark and simple downstairs area includes a few tables and a sake/Asian-tapas-bar. The walls in the striking, dimly lit main dining room are rimmed with banquettes and decorated with miniature TV screens. You'll want to try *bibimbap,* a Korean dish served in a clay pot brimming with rice, beef, and Asian vegetables. Warm apple sesame tart with green coconut ice cream makes a satisfying dessert. ⊠ *59 5th Ave., between 12th and 13th Sts.,* ☎ *212/242–9710. AE, DC, MC, V. No lunch Mon.–Sat.*

Barbecue

$ ✕ **Brothers Bar-B-Q.** This huge, barnlike space on two levels has a lounge area decorated in the offbeat style of the American South, with hair dryers, tacky period-plastic furniture circa 1949, Texaco, Esso, and Shell oil signs, and even a garage door. Monday nights, it's all-you-can-eat; sample puffy hush puppies with hot sauce, smoked sausage over black-eyed peas, fried wings and smoked rib tips in bourbon sauce, shrimp po'boy sandwiches, and terrific chicken and ribs. There's enough of a selection of tequila shots to satisfy Pancho Villa, 11 bottled beers and seven on tap. ⊠ *225 Varick St., at Clarkston St.,* ☎ *212/727–2775. AE.*

Contemporary

$$$$ ✕ **James Beard House.** One of America's great cooks and an icon of American cuisine, cookbook author and bon vivant James Beard is no longer with us, but his generous spirit lives on in his Greenwich Village brownstone, now owned by a foundation that bears his name. In addition to nurturing the culinary arts with awards and scholarships, the foundation invites the world's most creative chefs to the house to

cook in Beard's kitchen. For them, this is a performance of a lifetime, for which they pull out all stops. For the assembled diners, who include New York's food-loving movers and shakers, it's a chance to sample the work of top chefs without leaving the city. All of these events—dinner nightly and luncheon on most Fridays—are warm and festive affairs. ⊠ *167 W. 12th St., off 6th Ave.,* ☏ *212/627–2308. Reservations essential (about 1 month in advance). AE, DC, MC, V.*

$$$–$$$$ ✕ **Gotham Bar and Grill.** Chef Alfred Portale originated the vertical
★ style of food presentation here, which turns each plate into an artful edible tower. Rack of lamb is always dependable, and the Gotham chocolate cake, served with toasted almond ice cream, should not be ignored. The lofty, multilevel space was the prototype of the new-style New York restaurant, with its warm salmon-and-green color scheme, diffused lighting from shirred-fabric fixtures, and large window overlooking a courtyard. ⊠ *12 E. 12th St.,* ☏ *212/620–4020. Reservations essential. AE, DC, MC, V. No lunch weekends.*

$$ ✕ **13 Barrow.** This dimly lit, romantic storefront restaurant has a 15-ft redbrick ceiling; deep green upholstered banquettes with comfy, patterned throw pillows; and an open kitchen. A good way to start your meal is with one of the superb pizzas—favorites include Peking duck or Yukon gold potato with rosemary and truffle oil. A standout entrée is the double-thick pork chop with ginger-plum barbecue sauce and *moo shu* pancakes. Top it all off with a hot-butterscotch sundae with candied pecans. ⊠ *13 Barrow St., between 7th Ave. S and W. 4th St.,* ☏ *212/727–1300. Reservations essential. AE, DC, MC, V. Closed Sun. No lunch.*

French

$–$$ ✕ **Chez Jacqueline.** This charming bistro feels just like France with its specials written on the blackboard outside and cast of regulars at the bar. Owner Jacqueline Zini greets you like an old friend, and you'll want to become part of her family after sampling the delectable Provençale dishes, such as *soupe de poisson,* a creamy puree of seafood and vegetables; *jarret de veau,* or veal shank braised with tomatoes, potatoes, zucchini, garlic, endive, and olives in marrow sauce; veal kid neys; and the celebrated upside-down apple tart. The prix-fixe dinner is a good buy. ⊠ *72 MacDougal St., between W. Houston and Bleecker Sts.,* ☏ *212/505–0727. Reservations essential. AE, MC, V. No lunch weekends.*

$–$$ ✕ **Dix et Sept.** Named for its location at West 10th Street and 7th Avenue, this spot has a warm neighborhood feel, a cozy bar area, a comfortable back room with exposed brick walls and framed prints, and another, more formal room upstairs. Start with something simple like asparagus-and-leek vinaigrette. Then select from one of the interesting daily specials such as cassoulet of preserved duck, sausage, and smoked ham. ⊠ *181 W. 10th St.,* ☏ *212/645–8023. Reservations essential. AE, DC, MC, V. No lunch.*

$–$$ ✕ **L'Auberge Du Midi.** If you want the "perfect Greenwich Village
★ restaurant," look no further than this seductive bistro, with its French country atmosphere combining exposed brick, copper pots, and stone floors. Try the unblemished roast rack of lamb with fresh thyme and *gratin chaud de pommes au Calvados* (glazed hot apples and almond paste, flavored with apple brandy). There's a charming sidewalk café, weather permitting. ⊠ *310 W. 4th St., between W. 12th and Bank Sts.,*

☎ *212/242–4705. Reservations essential. AE, MC, V. Closed Mon. Nov.–Mar. No lunch.*

$ ✕ **French Roast.** This casual, around-the-clock spot with a Left Bank ambience charges bargain prices for some very good bistro dishes rarely encountered, such as poached beef marrow finished with bread crumbs and served in broth. The *croque monsieur* (melted cheese sandwich, done in the style of French toast) is first-rate. Or just stop for coffee and dessert. ✉ *458 6th Ave., at 11th St.,* ☎ *212/533–2233. AE, MC, V.*

Italian

$–$$ ✕ **Grand Ticino.** Walk down a few stairs to enter this agreeable little restaurant, with its hunter-green walls and romantic lighting. It's named after the Swiss Canton of Ticino and served its first meal in 1919. Home to artists and writers (Eugene O'Neill and Edna St. Vincent Millay were regulars), the Grand Ticino even made a cameo appearance in the movie *Moonstruck.* The menu includes excellent pasta, a wonderfully simple broiled chicken, and very good calves' liver. ✉ *228 Thompson St., between W. 3rd and Bleecker Sts.,* ☎ *212/777–5922. Reservations essential. AE, DC, MC, V. Closed Sun.*

Moroccan

$–$$ ✕ **Cafe Fes.** This amiable Moroccan restaurant, situated on one of Greenwich Village's most charming streets, is named after co-owner and chef Drissa Rafael's hometown. She and husband Jean Roger have created a perfect setting with peach walls, Moroccan lanterns, a tin ceiling, and a small fountain. The cold mixed salad, made with pureed eggplant and spinach, is a delectable beginning. The menu also includes the classic couscous, served in three variations, and *tajine,* a stewlike entrée made of lamb with prunes or artichokes and fava beans. ✉ *246 W. 4th St., at Charles St.,* ☎ *212/924–7653. AE, DC, MC, V. No lunch.*

Pizza

$ ✕ **Arturo's.** Few guidebooks list this brick-walled Village landmark, but the body-to-body crowds teetering on the wobbly wooden chairs suggest good things. The pizza is terrific, cooked in a coal-fired oven. Basic pastas as well as seafood, veal, and chicken concoctions with mozzarella and lots of tomato sauce come at giveaway prices. ✉ *106 W. Houston St., off Thompson St.,* ☎ *212/677–3820. AE, MC, V.*

Gramercy Park, Murray Hill, Chelsea, and the Flatiron District

American

$$$–$$$$ ✕ **Gramercy Tavern.** A 91-ft-long mural of fruit and vegetables wraps around the bar. Although the look is reminiscent of an English tavern, the food is decidedly new American. The "Tavern," as opposed to the main dining room, does not take reservations and offers some terrific plates from the wood-burning grill (hanger steak sandwich, for one). An appealing selection of cheese and a stellar wine list are offered here and in the main room with its smooth service and unrivaled media hype, making Gramercy Tavern a hard-to-get reservation. ✉ *42 E. 20th St., between Park Ave. S and Broadway,* ☎ *212/477–0777. Reservations essential. AE, DC, MC, V. No lunch Sun.*

$$$–$$$$ ✕ **Union Square Cafe.** In this spiffy restaurant where mahogany moldings outline white walls hung with bright modern paintings, the disposition is unpretentious, the service friendly, and the atmosphere pleasant. Breads are delicious and appetizers sparkle; we heartily endorse the iced oysters on the half shell, shucked to order, with shallot vinaigrette. While dinner entrées are conscientious, the sandwiches served

at lunch—for example, fresh tuna club on Tom Cat white bread with slab bacon, arugula, and homemade herb-potato chips—approach the divine. ⊠ *21 E. 16th St.,* ☎ *212/243–4020. Reservations essential. AE, DC, MC, V. No lunch Sun.*

$$$ ✕ **American Place.** This stylish establishment with kindly service gets
★ our vote as the country's finest regional American restaurant. Executive chef Larry Forgione is a leading supporter of new American cooking. His seasonal menu ranges from fresh Maine deviled-crab spring roll to cedar-planked salmon with seasonal vegetables. The high-ceilinged room with its Art Deco brasserie-style light fixtures, colorful Mikasa china, generously spaced tables, and Frank Stella paintings represents luxury at its most effortless. ⊠ *2 Park Ave., at 32nd St.,* ☎ *212/684–2122. Reservations essential. AE, DC, MC, V. No lunch weekends.*

$$$ ✕ **Verbena.** In this small, cunning restaurant in the historic Inn at Irving Place, windows are dotted with small pots of herbs, and there are two small rooms with fireplaces and an engaging garden. An olive, beige, and mustard color scheme plays backdrop to executive chef Diane Foley's inventive yet severely simple style, as evidenced in chopped endive salad with melted Taleggio cheese tart, beer-braised ribs of beef with horseradish dumplings, and bittersweet chocolate soufflé. ⊠ *54 Irving Pl., at 17th St.,* ☎ *212/260–5454. Reservations essential. AE, DC, MC, V. No lunch Mon.–Sat.*

$$–$$$ ✕ **Granville.** The decor—wrought-iron chandeliers, Asian carpets, and mahogany and leather furniture—brings to mind an English men's club. Nonsmokers are obliged to dine downstairs. Upstairs you'll find individual humidor lockers, a large bar with a different DJ every night, a superlative cigar lounge with overstuffed chairs and couches, and a dining room with a red-and-green tin ceiling. The savory entrées include cured sea bass on a sheet of nori, with ponzu sauce, and roasted monkfish in green curry. You may also indulge in an exotic cocktail, such as a ginger-lemongrass martini. ⊠ *40 E. 20th St., between Broadway and Park Ave.,* ☎ *212/253–9088. AE, DC, MC, V. No lunch weekends.*

$$ ✕ **Blue Water Grill.** This popular restaurant, housed in what was once
★ a bank, retains the original 1904 molded ceiling and marble. A copper-and-tile raw bar anchors one end of the sweeping room with its warm hues of indigo blue, sienna, and yellow. The menu is strong on seafood, served neat (chilled whole lobster; shrimp in the rough); in the au courant "global" style (Moroccan-spiced red snapper, Maryland crab cakes, warm shrimp cocktail in bamboo steamers with Japanese and Shanghai sauces); or in simple preparations from a wood-burning oven. For dessert, go for the brownie ice cream sundae. ⊠ *31 Union Sq. W, at 16th St.,* ☎ *212/675–9500. Reservations essential. AE, DC, MC, V.*

American Casual

$$ ✕ **Park Avalon.** The flagship restaurant of Steven Hanson (owner of Isabella's and Blue Water Grill) has two dining levels, huge alabaster-shaded light fixtures, massive mirrors, and a bar area with floor-to-ceiling wine cases and a dramatic display of lit candles. The trendy menu includes good pasta creations, such as homemade cracked black-pepper fettuccine with grilled portobello mushrooms, spinach, and cheese; another highlight is grilled free-range chicken with roasted garlic crust, sautéed broccoli rabe, and rosemary mashed potatoes. There are several low-fat desserts as well as marvelously intense sorbets. ⊠ *255 Park Ave. S, between 18th and 19th Sts.,* ☎ *212/533–2500. AE, DC, MC, V.*

Asian

$–$$ ✕ **Republic.** Downtown epicureans on the run flock to this innovative Asian noodle emporium. At one of the two long bluestone bars, you can simultaneously dine and enjoy the spectacle of chefs scurrying amid clouds of steam in the open kitchen. The menu contains chiefly rice dishes or noodles, stir-fried with hints of ginger, peanuts, and coriander or served in savory broths, made with coconut milk, lemongrass, Asian basil, and lime leaf. There's also an uptown branch (✉ 2290 Broadway, between 82nd and 83rd Sts., ☎ 212/579–5959). ✉ *37A Union Sq. W, between 16th and 17th Sts., ☎ 212/627–7172. AE, DC, MC, V.*

Contemporary

$$$ ✕ **Aja.** The mix of new American, southwestern, Thai, Vietnamese, Korean, and classic French cuisine is positively futuristic. Witness the tuna tartare with a blend of sesame, avocado, and daikon; and the steamed lobster–Penang curry, with roasted eggplant and grilled pineapple. The decor is almost as quirky as the menu: distressed finishes and natural woods, bold color combinations (brilliant chartreuse, deep brick, and pale gold), and sofas and chairs covered in lush damask. ✉ *937 Broadway, at 22nd St., ☎ 212/473–8388. Reservations essential. AE, DC, MC, V. Closed Sun.*

$$$ ✕ **Water Club.** This glass-enclosed barge in the East River is decidedly
★ dramatic, with its long wood-paneled bar, blazing fireplace, appetizing shellfish display, and panoramic water views. Food is ingeniously presented. Tuna tartare with marinated shiitake mushrooms, wasabi, spicy ocean salad, and flying-fish roe arrives on a porthole with a tiny anchor supporting a jar of caviar. Or order the exemplary sautéed red snapper fillet with lobster dumpling fennel and saffron bouillon. Sample any dessert your conscience desires: Chocolate flourless cake with peppermint-stick ice cream will sweeten even the sourest disposition. Sunday brunch is winsome. ✉ *500 E. 30th St., ☎ 212/683–3333. Reservations essential. Jacket required. AE, DC, MC, V.*

$$–$$$ ✕ **Flowers.** The intimate Tuscan-style dining room resembles a coun-
★ try-barn interior. Baskets of dried flowers adorn the walls, and copper light-fixtures exude a comforting glow that dims as the evening progresses. Executive chef and co-owner Marc Salonsky incorporates such influences as Asian (crispy shrimp roll with soy-ginger vinaigrette and spaghetti vegetables), Caribbean (roasted baby lamb chops with Jamaican spices), and Italian (risotto of seasonal wild mushrooms, asparagus, rosemary, and white truffle oil). Desserts are lovely—especially baked Alaska. ✉ *21 W. 17th St., between 5th and 6th Aves., ☎ 212/691– 8888. AE, DC, MC, V. Closed Sun. No lunch Sat.*

$$–$$$ ✕ **Lola.** Here, beautiful people dance to loud music when they're not sipping wine at the bar or languishing romantically on striped banquettes in the main dining room with bouquets of fresh flowers. Perhaps start with a stack of ribbon onion rings, and then follow with the signature Lola fried chicken and Cuban-style black beans. ✉ *30 W. 22nd St., between 5th and 6th Aves., ☎ 212/675–6700. AE, DC, MC, V. No lunch Sat.*

French

$$ ✕ **Les Halles.** Strikingly unpretentious, this French-American steak
★ house has a homey interior, with posters plastered on antique walls, a tin ceiling, and a windowed kitchen. This is the place to go for crispy duck-leg confit and frisée salad, warm sausages with lentils, and heaping plates of garlicky cold cuts. A good bet is the extraordinary *côte de boeuf,* with béarnaise sauce, a massive rib steak for two served from

a wooden board. ⊠ *411 Park Ave. S, between 28th and 29th Sts.,* ☎ *212/679–4111. AE, DC, MC, V.*

Indian

$–$$ ✕ **Mavalli Palace.** Service may be a bit slow here, but the gentle prices and marvelous dishes more than compensate. Magnificent crepes made with lentils and rice flour are wrapped around potatoes and a fiery chutney. Fresh onions top *uttappam,* a rice and lentil pancake. This pretty place has exposed brick walls and blond wood chairs. ⊠ *46 E. 29th St.,* ☎ *212/679–5535. AE, DC, MC, V. Closed Mon.*

Italian

$$$ ✕ **Le Madri.** The Tuscan-style space with a vaulted ceiling and wood-burning pizza oven is the creation of Pino Luongo (of Coco Pazzo). Fried calamari and zucchini with spicy roast-pepper tomato sauce might be a prelude to braised veal shank with portobello mushrooms and saffron risotto. You're bound to enjoy the impeccable desserts, such as *tortino* (a warm chocolate-hazelnut cake), and the top-flight service. ⊠ *168 W. 18th St.,* ☎ *212/727–8022. Reservations essential. AE, DC, MC, V.*

$$–$$$ ✕ **Follonico.** You'll like the vintage wainscoting, muted Tuscan colors,
★ open kitchen, and wood-burning oven—but most of all, you will like the food, chef-owner Alan Tardi's personal interpretation of regional cuisine from Tuscany. The deep-fried oysters crowned with horseradish cream and *osetra* caviar are so good you'll want to overindulge. But save room for one of the unusual pastas. *Fazzoletto,* a handkerchief pasta imprinted with fresh herbs, is sauced differently with each visit— but it's always inspired. Follow this with a whole red snapper, baked in a rock-salt crust. Fresh fruit granita is refreshing, but it would be a shame to leave without submerging a *biscotti* into a compatible dessert wine and some bracing espresso. ⊠ *6 W. 24th St.,* ☎ *212/691–6359. Reservations essential. AE, DC, MC, V. Closed Sun. No lunch Sat.*

$$–$$$ ✕ **I Trulli.** Nicola Marzovilla of Tempo, a successful Italian restaurant, created this intimate space with rough-hewn gold walls, a glass-enclosed fireplace, a garden for summer dining, and a whitewashed open grill with the traditional beehive shape of early Pugliese houses. Start your dinner with an out-of-the-ordinary glass of wine from a little-known producer and one of the enticing appetizers, such as baked oysters with pancetta, Tallegio cheese, and bread crumbs. Specialties use game, meat, and fish cooked in the wood-fired oven. ⊠ *122 E. 27th St., between Lexington and Park Ave. S,* ☎ *212/481–7372. Reservations essential. AE, DC, MC, V. Closed Sun. No lunch Sat.*

$$ ✕ **Sal Anthony's.** Of the many Italian restaurants in this historic area, this town-house dining room is one of the best and most pleasant. Opened in 1966, long before a pasta palace anchored every other corner, Sal Anthony's has attracted a loyal cadre with its deferential service, superior wine list, thick veal chops, and pretty decor—oil paintings on brick walls, huge bouquets, and crisp white cloths on well-spaced tables. ⊠ *55 Irving Pl.,* ☎ *212/982–9030. Reservations essential. AE, DC, MC, V.*

$–$$ ✕ **Caffe Bondi Ristorante.** This fascinating small restaurant with a
★ garden boasts one of Manhattan's most authentic menus (a food historian helped re-create the cooking of southern Italy in the 18th and 19th centuries): artichokes braised in almond sauce, ravioli filled with pumpkin and ricotta, oven roasted boar chops, quail stuffed with grapes, and a chocolate almond torte you'll remember for a lifetime. The wine list is short, excellent, and fairly priced. ⊠ *7 W. 20th St.,* ☎ *212/691–8136. AE, MC, V. Closed Sun.*

Latin

$$$ ✕ **Patria.** Owned by Philip Suarez (of Vong and Jo Jo), this trendy trilevel
★   Caribbean café, painted in striking earth tones, has handsome mosaics
and an open grill. The fluctuating menu offers variations of several eth-
nic entrées such as meat, vegetable, or seafood empanadas as well as
soups and seafood (look for the crispy red snapper with coconut-
conch rice). Even nonsmokers will want to indulge in the signature
dessert, a chocolate cigar with edible matches. The wine list focuses
on Spain, Argentina, and California. ⊠ *250 Park Ave. S, at 20th St.,*
☎ *212/777–6211. Reservations essential. AE, MC, V.*

Seafood

$-$$ ✕ **Crab House.** Part of a national chain, this large restaurant with 650
seats at Chelsea Piers has knotty-pine walls, waterfront dining, and spec-
tacular views of the Statue of Liberty and the Verrazano-Narrows
Bridge. You can't go wrong with the all-you-can-eat salad bar or the
tender cod, fried in a crispy beer-batter, served with fries. The Crab
House has a sports bar called Madison Square Garden, where you can
sample fine locally brewed beers. ⊠ *Chelsea Pier 61, 23rd St. near the
Hudson River,* ☎ *212/366–4111. AE, DC, MC, V.*

Senegalese

$ ✕ **Ngone.** At this pleasant dining spot, colorful African-patterned
cloths cover the tables, and the walls display tapestries and painted scenes
of the countryside, filled with elephants and wild game. Among the
appealingly hot dishes are traditional *boulettes* (appetizers of boneless
fish, seasoned with parsley and spices), chicken *yassa* (cooked with lemon,
ginger, carrots, and potatoes), and lamb in a creamy peanut sauce. The
Senegalese version of French toast provides a comforting conclusion
to your meal. Although the Muslim staff abstains from liquor, you may
bring your own wine or beer. ⊠ *823 6th Ave., between 28th and 29th
Sts.,* ☎ *212/967–7899. No credit cards. BYOB. Closed Sun.*

Southwestern

$$$ ✕ **Mesa Grill.** Chef Bobby Flay and owner Jerome Kretchmer have Man-
hattan foodies in the palms of their hands in this former bank, now
done up with vinyl banquettes, green-and-yellow walls, and industrial
fans. You can't go wrong with the small menu. Try the shrimp with a
roasted garlic and corn tamale, the pumpkin soup with chili cream, or
the chili-crusted rabbit with sweet-potato polenta and caramelized
mango sauce. Chocolate–peanut butter ice cream cake with roasted
marshmallows is just one of the unbeatable desserts. ⊠ *102 5th Ave.,
between 15th and 16th Sts.,* ☎ *212/807–7400. Reservations essen-
tial. AE, MC, V.*

Spanish

$$ ✕ **Bolo.** With its tile-edged brick oven, vivid gold–red-cobalt color
scheme, state-of-the-art open kitchen, and polished wood bar, the de-
sign here fuses Manhattan and Spain. The food aims at New York palates:
Oven-roasted baby shrimp with toasted garlic is garnished with fragrant sprigs of thyme, and curried shellfish paella unites bivalves with
sausage, chicken, and rice. If you're not in the mood for the perfect
house sangria, choose from the well-chosen and well-priced wine list.
⊠ *23 E. 22nd St.,* ☎ *212/228–2200. Reservations essential. AE, MC,
V. Closed Sun. No lunch Sat.*

Turkish

$ ✕ **Turkish Kitchen.** Manhattan's best Turkish restaurant is housed in
★   a striking multilevel room with lipstick-red walls, chairs with skirted
slipcovers, framed prints, and kilims covering the walls and floor. The
young staff dressed in long white chefs' aprons serves delicate and au-

thentic food. For appetizers, choose from such delectable offerings as velvety char-grilled eggplant salad, pan-fried calves' liver, and fried calamari. The stuffed cabbage and bulgur-wheat patties, filled with ground lamb, pine nuts, and currants, are both highly recommended. ⊠ *386 3rd Ave., between 27th and 28th Sts.,* ☎ *212/679–1810. AE, DC, MC, V. No lunch weekends.*

Vegetarian

$–$$ ✕ **Zen Palate.** In this remarkable vegetarian restaurant, walls are made from squares of fragile rice paper, and there are wooden beams and bamboo chairs. The resplendent appetizers include taro spring rolls, Vietnamese-style autumn rolls, and marinated seaweed. Entrées have poetic names like "Festival on a Roll" (seasoned spinach in soybean crepes with a spicy sauce) and "Dreamland" (layers of spinach linguine, bean sprouts, and shredded black mushrooms). ⊠ *34 Union Sq. E, at 16th St.,* ☎ *212/614–9291;* ⊠ *663 9th Ave.,* ☎ *212/582–1669;* ⊠ *2170 Broadway,* ☎ *212/501–7768. AE, MC, V. No lunch Sun.*

Midtown

Afghan

$ ✕ **Pamir.** Afghan cuisine might be loosely described as a combination
★ of Italian, Chinese, and Middle Eastern cooking; for New Yorkers, it's exotic, healthy, and delicious. This attractive two-level restaurant has gold-leaf chandeliers, hanging brass pots, Asian rugs, and brass sconces. It serves such memorable dishes as delicate, deep-fried turnovers with stuffing of pumpkin or carrot; scallion-filled dumplings topped with yogurt and meat sauce; and a mélange of seasoned lamb garnished with pistachio nuts, almonds, orange strips, cardamom, and rose water. ⊠ *1065 1st Ave., at 58th St.,* ☎ *212/644–9258;* ⊠ *1437 2nd Ave., between 74th and 75th Sts.,* ☎ *212/734–3791. AE, DC, MC, V. No lunch Sat.–Mon.*

American

$$$$ ✕ **Rainbow Room.** This $25 million dinner-and-dancing room on the 65th floor remains a monument to glamour and fantasy with its state-of-the-art sound and lighting systems and colored lights beaming across a domed ceiling. Tables clad in silver lamé rise in tiers around a revolving dance floor lit by an immense chandelier; aubergine walls frame panoramic 50-mi views through floor-to-ceiling windows. Revamped retro dishes including lobster Thermidor and oysters Rockefeller contrast with specialties utilizing Hudson River valley produce (such as local cheeses, game, and New York State foie gras), all prepared by executive chef Waldy Malouf, formerly of the Hudson River Club. ⊠ *30 Rockefeller Plaza,* ☎ *212/632–5000 or 212/632–5100. Reservations essential. Jacket and tie. AE, DC, MC, V. Closed Mon. (Sun.–Mon. in summer).*

$$$$ ✕ **"21" Club.** Not all are treated equally in this four-story brownstone
★ landmark, a former speakeasy, purchased in 1995 by the Orient Express Hotels Group. If you're not known, the greeting can be indifferent, even chilly. Once you're inside, though, service is seamless, and it's exciting to hobnob with celebrities and tycoons and sip a well-made cocktail in the lounge before dinner. Here is one of the world's great wine cellars, with some 50,000 bottles (restored in 1996 and available for special tasting dinners). The Grill Room is *the* place to be, with its banquettes, red-checked tablecloths, and a ceiling hung with toys; it serves such standbys as the signature "21" burger. ⊠ *21 W. 52nd St.,* ☎ *212/582–7200. Reservations essential. Jacket and tie. AE, DC, MC, V. Closed Sun. No lunch Sat.*

218

Midtown Manhattan Dining

$$$–$$$$ ✕ **Fifty Seven Fifty Seven.** Designed by I. M. Pei, the Four Seasons Hotel, which houses this room, is strikingly sleek, and its 22-ft coffered ceilings, inlaid maple floors, and onyx-studded bronze chandeliers set the tone for urbane food served superbly. Imaginative appetizers like lobster Caesar salad are exceptional, and it's hard to choose between the perfectly timed herb-roasted rack of lamb and the moist rack of veal with its crispy onion garnish. ⊠ *57 E. 57th St.,* ☎ *212/758–5757. AE, DC, MC, V.*

$$–$$$ ✕ **Judson Grill.** Another venture of Jerome Kretchmer (of Gotham Bar
★ and Grill fame), the airy space with a bar and balcony has red velour banquettes, mirrored walls, lofty ceilings, engaging John Parks murals, and immense gold vases. The open kitchen produces sumptuous dishes like seared New York State foie gras and inventive fish entrées, yet the more down-to-earth preparations—salads, sandwiches, and steaks— are equally well executed. The wine list is beautifully organized and eminently agreeable. ⊠ *152 W. 52nd St.,* ☎ *212/582–5252. AE, DC, MC, V. Closed Sun. No lunch Sat.*

$$–$$$ ✕ **Maloney and Porcelli.** Pictures of eagles and a large fish suspended from the ceiling brighten up this lively two-level space, decorated in a green-and-beige color scheme with wood accents. A large, square bar marks the center of the room. The definitive dish is a crackling pork shank with firecracker apple sauce. It's huge, juicy, and served on a bed of poppy-seed sauerkraut, with a mason jar of tangy, homemade apple sauce. Among the fun desserts, try the drunken doughnuts, served with three little pots of liqueur-flavored jam. The wine list is inventive (40 wines, for example, priced under $40). ⊠ *37 E. 50th St., between Madison and Park Aves.,* ☎ *212/750–2233. AE, DC, MC, V.*

$$ ✕ **Ambassador Grill.** If it's Sunday, head for the Park Hyatt Hotel, which
★ houses this greenhouse-inspired model of modern elegance with black-and-white tile floors, pink tablecloths, abundant plants, and an open kitchen. The brunch buffet is one of the finest in the city. But then the dining experience here is always first-class (and at less than first-class prices). There's also an amazing prix-fixe dinner. ⊠ *1 United Nations Plaza, at 44th St.,* ☎ *212/702–5014. Reservations essential. AE, DC, MC, V.*

$$ ✕ **Billy's.** In this quintessential New York neighborhood restaurant, established in 1870, straightforward burgers, steaks, fish, and pasta dishes take second place to such down-home specials as chicken potpie, turkey with real mashed potatoes, and corned beef and cabbage. Billy's neighborhood is unusually moneyed (it's the home of the exclusive River House and the kind of people who are written up in *Fortune* magazine and the society pages), so the people-watching is often as satisfying as the comfort food and vintage setting. ⊠ *948 1st Ave., between 52nd and 53rd Sts.,* ☎ *212/753–1870. AE, DC, MC, V.*

Basque

$$$ ✕ **Marichu.** Natural brick, old beams from Connecticut, and a lovely garden grace New York's only Basque restaurant. As prepared here, Basque cuisine is refined and elegant, with notable seafood offerings. There's no better way to start than with Rioja peppers, stuffed with a puree of cod. Order one of the changing house specials—you won't be disappointed. And do explore the fascinating list of Spanish wines. ⊠ *342 E. 46th St., between 1st and 2nd Aves.,* ☎ *212/370–1866. AE, DC, MC, V. No lunch weekends.*

Brewery

$–$$ ✕ **Commonwealth Brewing Company.** This energetic spot sports a clean, modern look with blond wood floors, huge beer vats behind a glass wall, maroon padded booths, and black wood tables. Come here for the fabulous European-style ales and lagers—we suggest tasting them all, including Rockefeller Red, Hudson River Porter, Gotham City Gold, Lady Liberty Lager, and a wheat brew, enhanced by a twist of lemon. The ambitious menu should satisfy the hardiest of appetites. Go for the sampler, served on a multitiered rack; its contents change daily, but it may include German beer and cheese dip, tuna tartare, Asian chicken sticks, or crab cakes. There are also sausage specials and a fabulous herb-crusted five-grain vegetable chop. Sure to please is the terrific Hudson River Porter cheesecake with sugar crunch dipping crackers for dessert. ⊠ *10 Rockefeller Plaza, at 48th St.,* ☎ *212/977–2269. AE, DC, MC, V. No lunch weekends.*

$–$$ ✕ **Typhoon Brewery.** Downstairs, there's a satay bar serving raw and cooked appetizers and a long brew bar offering six beers (including India pale ale, nut brown ale, and American amber) and 30 wines, all by the glass. Upstairs in a brick-walled area with exposed pipes, you dine at galvanized-steel tabletops in wonderful circular booths surrounded by industrial metal cages. The excellent Thai dishes include shell-on shrimp with garlic and pepper and seasonal Thai vegetables in green curry. For dessert, don't miss the banana fritters with banana ice cream. ⊠ *22 E. 54th St., between Madison and 5th Aves.,* ☎ *212/754–9006. AE, DC, MC, V. No lunch weekends.*

Chinese

$$$–$$$$ ✕ **Tse Yang.** There are Tse Yangs in Paris, Geneva, and Beverly Hills, but this one is perhaps the most dramatic, with its dark polished wood, dim lighting, elegant tableware, and exotic fish tank. One of the joys of dining here is experimenting with wine and food combinations. Try the crisp whole sea bass with an equally crisp sauvignon blanc or the Peking duck, served traditionally with doilies (thin pancakes) and skin, with a spicy gewürztraminer. ⊠ *34 E. 51st St.,* ☎ *212/688–5447. Reservations essential. AE, DC, MC, V.*

$$–$$$ ✕ **Chiam.** Although purists argue that the only worthy Chinese eateries are in Chinatown, such venues as this, with its polished service, make a persuasive case for the more westernized uptown experience. The stylish setting includes natural wood, an understated white-and-black motif, and a courtyard view. The wine list is extraordinary for a Chinese restaurant (inquire about special wine-tasting dinners). Enlist the services of your congenial captain, who will select from such diverse menu options as squab *soon* (minced pigeon in lettuce leaves) and steamed lotus-wrapped chicken. ⊠ *160 E. 48th St.,* ☎ *212/371–2323. AE, DC, MC, V.*

$$–$$$ ✕ **Jimmy Sung's.** Four dramatic peacock-fountain chandeliers cast off restrained lighting at this elegant Chinese restaurant with rich carpeting, patterned wallpaper, gleaming cherry-wood paneling, and ornately carved wood arches. The menu concentrates on Manchurian, Shanghai, and Mandarin cuisine, all discreetly served on lovely china. Begin your dinner auspiciously with vegetarian pie with house pancake—crisp sheets of bean curd are stuffed in a puffy pancake, accompanied by plum sauce and scallions. Next, choose among such well-prepared entrées as salt-baked fresh cuttlefish, shrimp or scallops with chili pepper (a dish rarely encountered uptown), or sliced prawn, barely cooked, and served with an ethereal egg white sauce. ⊠ *219 E. 44th St., between 2nd and 3rd Aves.,* ☎ *212/682–5678. AE, DC, MC, V.*

$$–$$$ ✕ **Tang Pavillion.** Outside of Chinatown, this is the most authentic Chi-
   ★   nese restaurant in Manhattan, featuring the cuisine of Shanghai and
        Soo Chow. Request the Shanghai menu, which is presented in English
        as well as Chinese. Go with a group on your first visit so you may share
        the crisp baby eel, drunken chicken, Tung-Po pork stuffed in incredi-
        bly light doughy buns, jumbo shrimp with walnuts in a slightly sweet,
        slightly spicy sauce, and green beans and tofu sheets (reminiscent of
        pasta). ✉ *65 W. 55th St.,* ☎ *212/956–6888. Reservations essential.
        AE, DC, MC, V.*

Contemporary

$$$$ ✕ **Lespinasse.** The pulchritudinous (some call it stuffy) Louis XV
   ★   decor of this St. Regis Sheraton dining room, with its oil paintings and
        commodious seating in satin chairs, is an ideal setting for the refined
        cuisine of Gray Kunz, who honed his craft under Switzerland's cele-
        brated Frédy Girardet. Kunz's Singapore past as chef of Hong Kong's
        Regent Hotel dining room is evident in some of the entrées with Asian
        accents. A less adventurous repast might begin with herbed risotto and
        mushroom fricassee, move on to rack of lamb on curried eggplant tart,
        and conclude with warm chocolate tartlet with orange-grapefruit
        coulis. ✉ *2 E. 55th St.,* ☎ *212/339–6719. Jacket required. AE, DC,
        MC, V. Closed Sun.*

$$$–$$$$ ✕ **Four Seasons Grill and Pool Room.** The two unique dining areas in
   ★   the Mies van der Rohe–designed Seagram building feature architect Philip
        Johnson's timeless contemporary design. The Grill Room, bastion of
        the power lunch, also offers an affordable prix-fixe dinner. Starkly mas-
        culine, it has inviting leather banquettes, rosewood walls, a renowned
        floating sculpture, and one of the best bars in New York. A short stroll
        through the marble corridor leads to the celebrated Pool Room, with
        its illuminated trees, Carrera marble gurgling pool, and undulating chain
        curtains. The eclectic international menu changes often, and you'll ap-
        preciate the aristocratic wine list and smooth service. ✉ *99 E. 52nd
        St.,* ☎ *212/754–9494. Reservations essential. Jacket required. AE, DC,
        MC, V. Closed Sun. No lunch Sat.*

$$$–$$$$ ✕ **March.** With its travertine floor, working fireplace, and burled teak
   ★   and English elm wainscoting, this singular restaurant is elegantly un-
        derstated. Co-owner Joseph Salice supervises the polished and incon-
        spicuous service, and the cuisine of chef Wayne Nish is at once restrained
        and inspired, demonstrating a mastery of classical technique coupled
        with artful contemporary presentations. Dishes include Japanese-in-
        fluenced sashimi of Japanese yellowfin tuna with olive oil and soy sauce
        and luxury offerings, such as the whimsical "Beggar's Purses," filled
        with lobster and truffles. ✉ *405 E. 58th St.,* ☎ *212/754–6272. Reser-
        vations essential. AE, DC, MC, V. Closed Sun. No lunch.*

$$$ ✕ **China Grill.** This huge restaurant has jade-color walls, cloudlike light
        fixtures, and an open kitchen. The Asian-inspired cuisine may make
        you overlook the noise: lobster or duck pancakes, sake-cured salmon
        rolls, duck in caramelized black vinegar, and, for dessert, coconut
        crème brûlée or chocolate hazelnut bombe. The wine list is full of plea-
        sures; the dessert wines are perfect as aperitifs and with vinegar-based
        and sweet-and-sour sauces. Check out the flavored sakes. ✉ *60 W. 53rd
        St.,* ☎ *212/333–7788. AE, DC, MC, V. No lunch weekends.*

$$$ ✕ **Monkey Bar.** Cobalt-blue bread plates and glasses, etched-glass
   ★   panels of the Manhattan skyline, velvet banquettes with a colorful palm-
        tree design, and cute little monkeys hanging from the lighting fixtures
        all contribute to the lively atmosphere of this fashionable restaurant.
        You can bypass the mobbed bar scene by entering through the sub-
        dued Hotel Elysée. There's no monkey business going on with the food;
        perfectly roasted cod with silky mashed potatoes, carrots, and celery-

root chips as well as the baked Alaska for dessert are both recommended. ⊠ *60 E. 54th St.,* ☎ *212/838–2600. Reservations essential. Jacket required. AE, DC, MC, V. No lunch weekends.*

$$–$$$ ✕ **Bryant Park Grill, Roof Restaurant and BP Cafe.** Stone fountains, Parisian chairs, and a 200-seat outdoor garden precede the more formal Grill area, graced with rare lacquered woods, slate floors, and velvet leaf-patterned banquettes. Food is reasonably good, considering the volume demand on the kitchen. A typical dinner: calamari salad, Joe's special (scrambled eggs, sautéed spinach, ground sirloin, and mushrooms), and chocolate soufflé. ⊠ *25 W. 40th St., between 5th and 6th Aves.,* ☎ *212/840–6500. AE, DC, MC, V.*

$$ ✕ **Vong.** Jean-Georges Vongerichten's stint at Bangkok's Oriental Hotel inspired this radiant restaurant with its potted palms and gold-leaf ceiling. While the menu changes often, reliable standbys include the lobster and daikon roll with rosemary-ginger dip; lobster in Thai spices; and the distinctive rabbit curry braised with carrots and cumin seed. Prices, though not bad, can be kept down by ordering a second appetizer in lieu of an entrée. Wines are well chosen, but you may favor beer. ⊠ *200 E. 54th St.,* ☎ *212/486–9592. Reservations essential. AE, DC, MC, V. No lunch weekends.*

French

$$$$ ✕ **La Côte Basque.** A landmark in French dining has found a new home.
★ Practically all the elements of the original restaurant have been imported, including the dark wooden cross beams, signature murals by Bernard Lamotte, faux windows, and even the revolving door. Executive chef-owner Jean-Jacques Rachou has lightened the cuisine but retained the generous portions. Customers can partake of a reasonable (for such quality) fixed-price, three-course dinner, with very few surcharges. Begin with the trio of patés or one of the gossamer soufflés. If two select the signature roast duckling with honey, Grand Marnier, and black-cherry sauce, your waiter will deliver it whole for inspection and then carve it before you. Allow plenty of time to survey the extraordinary wine list. ⊠ *60 W. 55th St., between 5th and 6th Aves.,* ☎ *212/688–6525. Reservations essential. Jacket and tie. AE, DC, MC, V. No lunch Sun.*

$$$$ ✕ **Lutèce.** One of New York's most prestigious restaurants, Lutèce was sold in 1994 to the Ark Group (owner of B. Smith's, Ernie's, Jim McMullen, American Place, and others). The service ranges from friendly to somewhat distant; the menu retains signature dishes (the onion tart, for example) and favorites of the old regime alongside more contemporary creations. You can still savor the classic soufflés. ⊠ *249 E. 50th St.,* ☎ *212/752–2225. Reservations essential. Jacket required. AE, DC, MC, V. Closed Sun. and Aug. No lunch Mon. and Sat.*

$$$–$$$$ ✕ **La Reserve.** This luxurious, exceedingly beautiful restaurant can be an excellent value if you go for the prix-fixe lunch. Lighting is soft, the flowers and murals lovely, the service smooth, and the wine list replete with great bottles from great châteaux in great years. The cuisine represents a contemporary side of the classical French kitchen; lobster salad, smoked salmon, saddle of rabbit, poached Dover sole with an artichoke mousse, and *panier Pompadour,* a basket of fresh raspberries and white and dark chocolate mousse, are all artfully presented. ⊠ *4 W. 49th St.,* ☎ *212/247–2993. Reservations essential. Jacket and tie. AF, DC, MC, V. Closed Sun. No lunch Sat.*

$$$–$$$$ ✕ **Peacock Alley.** This luxurious Waldorf-Astoria salon offers the pro-
★ fessional service, fine china, and comprehensive wine cellar that distinguish many of today's hotel restaurants. It also has tranquil lighting, lovely murals with a peacock motif, and cushy seating at banquettes and roomy tables. Chef de cuisine Laurent Manrique makes certain

the kitchen lives up to the surroundings. Look for superlative game specials (including hare, pheasant, and wood pigeon) and dishes from Manrique's native Gascony: an assortment of cold foie gras pâté. ⊠ *301 Park Ave., between 49th and 50th Sts., ☎ 212/872–4895. Reservations essential. AE, DC, MC, V. Closed Sun. No lunch Sat.*

$$$ ✕ **Adrienne.** The graceful restaurant of the Peninsula Hotel offers extravagant comfort. The Belle Epoque decor, subdued lighting, spacious seating, and attention to detail afford a rare respite from the trendy at one extreme and tired at the other. Service is extraordinary. The kitchen is dependable, if not adventurous, and Sunday brunch is elegance itself, an elaborate buffet with harp music. ⊠ *700 5th Ave., at 55th St., ☎ 212/903–3918. AE, DC, MC, V. Reservations essential. No lunch Sat., no dinner Sun.–Mon.*

$$$ ✕ **Bouterin.** Baskets of apples and copper pans adorn the walls, adding a warm touch to the new home of chef-owner Antoine Bouterin, formerly of Le Périgord. The mix-and-match feel of the decor arises from Monsieur Bouterin's interest in antiques collecting. The short menu of unpretentious dishes specializes in the cuisine of Provence and includes an old-fashioned lamb stew, cooked for seven hours and best eaten with a spoon. ⊠ *420 E. 59th St., off 1st Ave., ☎ 212/758–0323. Reservations essential. Jacket required. AE, DC, MC, V. Closed Sun. No lunch.*

$$$ ✕ **La Caravelle.** Rita and André Jammet's celebration of the good life is New York's most Parisian restaurant. The appealing main dining room comes alive with Jean Pagès murals, its colors spilling over to the pink-peach banquettes. Mirrors, flowers, and the Caravelle coat of arms add to the scene, as does the most professional service staff in town. Enjoy truffled pike dumplings in lobster sauce; the perfectly roasted chicken in a delicate bath of champagne and cream; and one of the irresistible cloudlike soufflés (which must be requested at the beginning of the meal). ⊠ *33 W. 55th St., ☎ 212/586–4252. Reservations essential. Jacket and tie. AE, DC, MC, V. Closed Sun. No lunch Sat.*

$$$ ✕ **Le Périgord.** When you enter this luxurious restaurant, you're greeted with dusty rose walls, well-spaced tables, and an inviting display of hors d'oeuvres and desserts. The international clientele demands first-class food at a fair price, and that's what owner–maître d'hôtel Georges Briguet provides. As in southwestern France, begin with fresh foie gras, which is worth the modest surcharge on the prix-fixe dinner. There's a juicy sautéed beef fillet in red wine and bone marrow sauce. The Lyonnaise dessert cart is tempting with homemade tarts and cakes. ⊠ *405 E. 52nd St., ☎ 212/755–6244. Reservations essential. Jacket and tie. AE, DC, MC, V. Closed Sun. No lunch Sat.*

$$ ✕ **Cafe Centro.** Reminiscent of a French brasserie with terrazzo floors, interior columns accented with gold leaf, and a glass-enclosed kitchen, this pleasant café has an eclectic menu, including a good three-pound T-bone steak and some compelling desserts. The wine list is admirable, while the separate beer bar offers more than 30 selections and has its own attractively priced menu with fun snacks. ⊠ *200 Park Ave., between 45th St. and Vanderbilt Ave., in the Met Life Bldg., ☎ 212/818–1222. AE, DC, MC, V. Closed Sun. No lunch Sat.*

$$ ✕ **Cité.** Alan Stillman (of Smith and Wollensky, Manhattan Ocean Club, Post House, and Park Avenue Café fame) offers an incredible deal. His Art Deco Parisian-style brasserie with crystal chandeliers and imported grillwork (not to be confused with the more casual adjoining bistro) pours four wines with dinner free of charge. The wines change, but they're always top-drawer. An excellent three-course dinner is served from 8 PM to midnight. The food ranges from American steak house to Mediterranean, and since there's a real chef in the kitchen, you needn't stick to the excellent roast beef and sparkling shrimp or

In case you want to see the world.

At American Express, we're here to make your journey a smooth one. So we have over 1,700 travel service locations in over 120 countries ready to help. What else would you expect from the world's largest travel agency?

do more

AMERICAN EXPRESS

http://www.americanexpress.com/travel

Travel

In case you want to be welcomed there.

We're here to see that you're always welcomed at establishments everywhere. That's why millions of people carry the American Express® Card – for peace of mind, confidence, and security, around the world or just around the corner.

do more

Cards

In case you're running low.

We're here to help with more than 118,000 Express Cash locations around the world. In order to enroll, just call American Express before you start your vacation.

do more

And just in case.

We're here with American Express® Travelers Cheques and Cheques *for Two.*® They're the safest way to carry money on your vacation and the surest way to get a refund, practically anywhere, anytime.

Another way we help you...

do more

AMERICAN EXPRESS

Travelers Cheques

lobster cocktail. ⊠ *120 W. 51st St.,* ☎ *212/956–7100. AE, DC, MC, V.*

Indian

$$–$$$ ✕ **Dawat.** One of the city's finest Indian restaurants, this classy, un-
★ derstated spot has roomy tables and consultant Madhur Jaffrey's creative cuisine. Provocative choices include shrimp in mustard seeds
with curry leaves, and Parsi-style salmon, steamed in a banana leaf with
coriander chutney. The *kulcha,* an onion-stuffed bread flavored with
fresh coriander, is particularly good. Dawat demonstrates the charms
of Indian sweets; try the pudding-like carrot halvah, the *kheer* (rice pudding) with pistachios, and *kulfi,* a delicate frozen dessert. ⊠ *210 E.
58th St.,* ☎ *212/355–7555. Reservations essential. AE, DC, MC, V.
No lunch Sun.*

$$ ✕ **Jewel of India.** Since its opening in 1990, this glittering restau-
rant—with its attractive lounge and bar area and popular luncheon buf-
fet—has had a loyal following. The main dining room shimmers with
hammered silver, mother of pearl, and brass and overflows with wall
hangings, exotic sculptures, and carved rosewood screens. In the sub-
continent's exotic cookery, each dish must exhibit its distinct flavor;
spice plays against spice. Jewel of India specializes in the fare of the
north, which trades in the south's vegetarian dishes for subtle meat prepa-
rations. The marvelous herb-scented breads and knockout tandoori show
off the kitchen's prowess. ⊠ *15 W. 44th St.,* ☎ *212/869–5544. Reser-
vations essential. AE, DC, MC, V.*

Italian

$$$$ ✕ **Felidia.** Manhattanites frequent this celebrated bilevel *ristorante* as
★ much for the winning enthusiasm of Lidia Bastianich, who owns it with
her husband, Felix, as for the food, whose style is evidenced in an array
of regional and seasonal masterpieces, including dishes featuring white
truffles and some exceptional game preparations in the fall. Fresh
homemade pasta, roasted whole fish of the day, and an elite wine list
composed of Italy's finest vineyards can always be counted on. Guests
dine in an attractive front room with a wooden bar, in the rustic room
beyond, and in a skylit balcony with terra-cotta floor, hanging tapestry,
and lovely plants. ⊠ *243 E. 58th St.,* ☎ *212/758–1479. Reservations
essential. Jacket and tie. AE, DC, MC, V. Closed Sun. No lunch Sat.*

$$$–$$$$ ✕ **Il Nido.** This fashionable restaurant, with wood beams set in rough
plaster walls, strives to create the interior of a Tuscan farmhouse.
Hands-on restaurateur Adi Giovanetti finishes pastas, whisks zabaglione,
and prepares the masterful blend of Gorgonzola and cognac to spread
on toast. Dishes will please traditionalists: salmon carpaccio, *malfatti*
(a raviolilike pasta), baked red snapper. Be prepared to wait for your
table. ⊠ *251 E. 53rd St.,* ☎ *212/753–8450. Reservations essential.
AE, DC, MC, V. Closed Sun. No lunch Sat.*

$$$ ✕ **Girafe.** This Italian restaurant, with its name spelled in French, has
a 20-ft-high metal statue of its namesake waiting outside to greet you.
Inside, you can sample a northern Italian traditional meal: hay and straw
(green and white vermicelli) in a bath of cream, prosciutto, and peas,
served with a thick, juicy veal chop. The house tiramisu definitely qual-
ifies as one of Manhattan's best. ⊠ *208 E. 58th St., between 2nd and
3rd Aves.,* ☎ *212/752–3054. Reservations essential. Jacket required.
AE, DC, MC, V. Closed Sun. No lunch Sat.*

$$ ✕ **Anche Vivolo.** Austrian shades and big clay pots of fresh flowers help
create the feel of an enclosed garden. This is one of the best deals in
an expensive part of town. Huge portions of such well-prepared dishes
as linguine *Francesco* (with garlic, anchovies, basil, tomatoes, and
oregano) would cost at least 50% more at most of the other restau-

rants on this Italianate block. The best entrée is often a special. ⊠ *222 E. 58th St., between 2nd and 3rd Aves.,* ☎ *212/308–0112. AE, DC, MC, V. Closed Sun. No lunch Sat.*

$–$$ ✕ **Naples Ristorante e Pizzeria.** The main dining room with three pizza ovens named after volcanoes is brightened by shelves of appetizing take-out items and gleaming white tiles softened by bands of terracotta. Equally tempting are the risotto cake, stuffed with meat ragu and boiled egg, and pizza, served by the half "metre" or as a whole pie for four or more. The long bar serves terrific wines by the glass and an interesting selection of antipasti and other appetizers. There's also a colorful outdoor patio. ⊠ *Met Life Bldg., 200 Park Ave., at E. 45th St.,* ☎ *212/972–7001. AE, DC, MC, V. Closed weekends.*

Japanese

$$$$ ✕ **Otabe.** The sleek dining room has attractive wall prints and spacious seating. Among the appealing appetizers, try grilled eel on a bed of cucumber with a bouquet of fresh ginger or deep-fried tofu and eggplant. Adventurous souls will love the sparkling slices of raw tuna sashimi brushed with garlic-flavored soy sauce. Traditional Kyoto cuisine (a tasting menu of several small dishes) can be ordered, and in a room in back, you can experience superbly authentic *teppan* (barbecue-style grill) cooking. Here, you can spoil yourself with Kobe beef, so tender knives are unnecessary. ⊠ *68 E. 56th St.,* ☎ *212/223–7575. AE, DC, MC, V. Closed Sun. No lunch Sat.*

$$$$ ✕ **Seryna.** This lovely restaurant vividly evokes Tokyo with its digni-
★   fied air, earth tones, and comfortable seating at big wooden tables. Although the sushi is superbly fresh, the specialty is steak *ishiyaki,* cooked table-side on a smoldering rock. In the six-course *wagyu* dinner, you can choose between it and *shabu shabu,* another mealtime dish-cum-event: You begin with a broth to which you add meat (which you then eat), then vegetables, then noodles, and conclude by sipping the bracing soup. Cocktails are served in small carafes that come buried in crushed ice. Service is superb. ⊠ *11 E. 53rd St.,* ☎ *212/980–9393. Reservations essential. AE, DC, MC, V. Closed Sun. No lunch Sat.*

$$–$$$ ✕ **Haikara Grill.** Haikara means "high-class" in Japanese, and Manhattan's first kosher sushi has an opulent ambience. The main dining room with its wall of mirrors features framed Japanese prints and a striking framed kimono. You'll enjoy the traditional *bento* (Japanese dinner box), partitioned with a bowl of soup, raw-fish rolls, steak, blanched vegetables, and sesame noodles. Desserts are simple, such as fresh fruit, attractively presented in edible chocolate cups. ⊠ *1016 2nd Ave., between 53rd and 54th Sts.,* ☎ *212/355–7000. AE, DC, MC, V. Closed Fri. No dinner, no lunch Sat.*

Korean

$ ✕ **New York Kom Tang Soot Bul House.** Specializing in barbecue, this
★   is one of the best Korean restaurants on a street jammed with them, and dinner is a show. So come ready for charades (little English is spoken); wear clothes you don't mind getting smoky (from the hibachis in the center of the communal tables); and insist on the attractive second floor. Dinner starts with 10 delicious side dishes, including kimchi (peppery Korean pickle). Afterward there's soup, then the main event: You cook thin slices of beef or chicken over red-hot coals, top them with hot chilies and raw garlic, and wrap it all up with lettuce. ⊠ *32 W. 32nd St.,* ☎ *212/947–8482. AE, MC, V.*

Latin

$ ✕ **Ipanema.** This snug, modern restaurant has white and peach-colored walls covered with vivid oil paintings of Rio and Bahia. It's a comfortable place to sample Brazil's exotic cuisine. Feijoada, the national meal—black beans with smoked meats, collard greens, oranges, chili peppers, and a comforting grain called *farofa*—is good here. And don't miss the great drinks made with *cachaça* (Brazilian rum)—*batidas* (with coconut milk) and caipirinhas. ⊠ *13 W. 46th St.,* ☎ *212/730–5848. AE, DC, MC, V.*

Mexican

$$–$$$ ✕ **Rosa Mexicano.** Owner Josefina Howard is serious about her profession, and her authentic restaurant is a delight. The food is carefully executed, including guacamole prepared table-side and a cold seafood platter. There are a number of interesting regional dishes, including duck enchiladas and chicken steamed in beer. The chocolate chili-mousse cake has a real kick. ⊠ *1063 1st Ave., at 58th St.,* ☎ *212/753–7407. Reservations essential. AE, DC, MC, V. No lunch.*

$ ✕ **Alamo.** The facade mimics the entrance to a ranch, but the scene inside is cosmopolitan. There's an unpretentious main dining room a few steps up, decorated with piñatas and colorful Mexican posters, and an even more comfortable second level, with a brass railing and big comfy booths. You'll enjoy creative riffs on Mexican and Texas-style cooking. Guacamole is chunky and made to order at your table. Several vegetarian dishes stand out, such as *chili relleno* (green chili pepper stuffed with cheese and batter fried). ⊠ *304 E. 48th St.,* ☎ *212/759–0590. AE, DC, MC, V. Closed Sun. No lunch Sat.*

Scandinavian

$$$ ✕ **Aquavit.** Although you can dine in the delightful café upstairs for half the price, the striking downstairs room in the late Nelson Rockefeller's town house—with its atrium, Roger Smith kites, and waterfall—*is* Aquavit. Swedish fare has been stripped of its homeyness and decked out in contemporary garb, with impressive results. Order roasted-lobster salad or the more traditional herring plate as appetizers. Then explore cherry-crusted rack of lamb or an uncommon tea-smoked duck breast. Triangles of gingerbread with mascarpone ice cream or an out-of-the-ordinary cheese plate make stellar desserts. New York's largest selection of aquavits keeps company with the standout wine list. ⊠ *13 W. 54th St.,* ☎ *212/307–7311. Reservations essential downstairs. AE, DC, MC, V. No lunch Sat., no dinner Sun.*

Seafood

$$$–$$$$ ✕ **Manhattan Ocean Club.** This sophisticated bilevel restaurant with comfortable seating is embellished with Picasso ceramics from the collection of owner Alan Stillman. Shellfish by the piece, a good starter, is impeccably fresh. Tuna arrives seared and rare inside, with lattice potatoes and a green salsa. Other admirable entrées may include roasted blackfish with shiitake mushrooms, shallots, and penne pasta, or perfectly grilled swordfish. The warm chocolate tart is luscious. ⊠ *57 W. 58th St.,* ☎ *212/371–7777. Reservations essential. AE, DC, MC, V. No lunch weekends.*

$$$–$$$$ ✕ **Oceana.** Seafood for the civilized. Neither trendy nor snobby,
★ Oceana is also pretty, with its warm wood decor, contemporary lighting, bright murals, and posters of luxury oceanliners. You can dine upstairs and down as well as in the wine cellar; service is smooth. The kitchen gets high marks for salmon tartare wrapped in smoked salmon, crab cakes, lobster ravioli, and bouillabaisse. The wine list (with more than 100 whites) is first-rate; the white Bordeaux are recommended. The three-course dinner offers good value, as does the six-course tasting menu. ⊠ *55 E. 54th St.,* ☎ *212/759–5941. Reservations essential. Jacket required. AE, DC, MC, V. Closed Sun. No lunch Sat.*

$$$–$$$$ ✕ **Sea Grill.** Famous restaurants with extraordinary views are often
★   suspect when it comes to the food. But *this* famous restaurant, with a
      spectacular view of the Rockefeller Center ice rink in winter and cap-
      tivating patio dining in summer, can stand tall. The kitchen, under the
      direction of one of Manhattan's master chefs, Ed Brown (of Tropica
      and Judson Grill), creates some of Manhattan's best seafood dishes.
      Charred, moist sugarcane shrimp on skewers with buttery rice is a sim-
      ple composition, prepared with complementing fresh herbs, spices, and
      a subtle sauce. We applaud the best lime pie this side of the Keys. ✉
      19 W. 49th St., ☎ *212/332–7610. Reservations essential. AE, DC, MC,
      V. Closed Sun. No lunch Sat.*

$$ ✕ **Docks.** The large brass-trimmed bar of this striking, high-ceilinged,
      art deco bilevel brasserie displays scrupulously fresh shellfish pre-
      sented on tiered platters. Cooked preparations run the gamut from tra-
      ditional American to inventive-eclectic. Steamers in beer broth and
      Maryland crab cakes are generally available as appetizers. For the
      main course, you can order grilled or fried wolffish, monkfish, snap-
      per, and other seafood, depending on what's fresh that day. Lobster is
      as good as it gets in Manhattan. ✉ *633 3rd Ave., at 40th St.,* ☎
      212/986–8080; ✉ *2427 Broadway, at 89th St.,* ☎ *212/724–5588.
      Reservations essential. AE, DC, MC, V. No lunch Sat.*

Steak

$$$–$$$$ ✕ **Morton's.** Although famous for its steaks, New York has never seen
      anything like this branch of Chicago's famous steak house, in a mas-
      culine, dimly lit room that's easy on the spirit. Service is enthusiastic,
      the bar knows how to make a drink, and oh, those steaks and chops,
      that double-cut prime rib, and those 4½-pound lobsters! Hash browns
      and fresh asparagus are also terrific; for dessert, go straight to the cheese-
      cake or the rich chocolate-velvet cake. The wine list offers hundreds
      of extraordinary reds, and there is an excellent single-malt Scotch list.
      ✉ *551 5th Ave., at 45th St.,* ☎ *212/972–3315;* ✉ *90 West St.,* ☎
      *212/732–5665. Reservations essential. AE, DC, MC, V. No lunch
      weekends.*

$$$–$$$$ ✕ **Pen and Pencil.** It's hard to beat this civilized and thoroughly pleas-
      ant restaurant with its comfortable bar area, fitted out with leather ban-
      quettes, and intimate main dining room, recalling a private club—lunch
      is particularly pleasant. Here's a steak house where grilled swordfish
      and sole stand out, and from time to time there's a special menu fea-
      turing low-cholesterol buffalo meat. ✉ *205 E. 45th St.,* ☎ *212/682–
      8660. Reservations essential. AE, DC, MC, V. No lunch weekends.*

$$$–$$$$ ✕ **Smith and Wollensky.** This archetypal New York–style steak house,
      with its bold and unabashedly masculine setting, gargantuan portions,
      and lofty list of wines (strong in red Bordeaux and California caber-
      nets), is one of the best. Meat is dry-aged in-house, and sirloin, porter-
      house, and double sirloin arrive cooked to a turn. Order a side of hash
      browns or cottage fries and creamed or sautéed spinach, but skip the
      perfunctory appetizers and desserts. There is a generous selection of
      single-malt Scotch. The bustling, less-pricey Wollensky's Grill next
      door has pleasant sidewalk seating in summer. ✉ *201 E. 49th St.,* ☎
      *212/753–1530; 212/753–0444 for Grill. Reservations essential. AE,
      DC, MC, V. No lunch weekends at restaurant.*

Vietnamese

$$–$$$ ✕ **Le Colonial.** The dining room here comes straight out of Somerset
      Maugham, with its rattan chairs, potted palms, ceiling fans, shutters,
      and period photographs. The food, although Westernized, is usually
      well prepared; start with the superb *bahn cuon*—steamed Vietnamese
      ravioli with chicken, shrimp, and mushrooms—and move on to crisp-

seared whole snapper with spicy and sour sauce. The sorbets, ice creams, and fruit-based puddings are right on. Don't miss the Vietnamese coffee—strong black brew over a layer of condensed milk. Nirvana in a cup! ⊠ *149 E. 57th St.,* ☎ *212/752–0808. Reservations essential. AE, DC, MC, V.*

Theater District and Carnegie Hall

American Casual

$–$$ ✕ **Hard Rock Cafe.** This restaurant with the fins of a vintage Cadillac as a marquee is best known for its loud rock music, rock-star memorabilia, and teenyboppers. Truth be told, the food is quite tasty. The pork barbecue, listed as pig sandwich, is as good as you often find in North Carolina. Or try the club sandwich—crispy bacon, roast chicken, lettuce, tomato, and mayo between huge slabs of ice-box bread. Because portions are huge, everything can be split. To avoid waits, go at opening hours and avoid school holidays. ⊠ *221 W. 57th St.,* ☎ *212/489–6565. AE, MC, V.*

$–$$ ✕ **Joe Allen.** With its brick walls, dark wood bar, and showbiz posters, it looks like a pub, but the food warrants the smart white tablecloths. The menu has several satisfying offerings: a marvelous meat-loaf sandwich and an exceptional grilled calves' liver, thinly cut and served with creamy mashed potatoes. You might even glimpse a celebrity or two. ⊠ *26 W. 46th St.,* ☎ *212/581–6464. Reservations essential. MC, V.*

$–$$ ✕ **Official All Star Cafe.** Athletic memorabilia pervades this theme restaurant. You can admire Andre Agassi's ponytail and a room devoted to actor Charlie Sheen's baseball collection, including Babe Ruth's 1927 World Series ring. The stadium-like dining room has a 60-ft ceiling, circled by a miniature blimp on a track, and around its perimeter are some 30 giant video screens playing memorable moments in sports. The huge circular booths may make you feel as if you're sitting inside oversize catchers' mitts. The menu is strictly standard American fare: T-bone steak, homemade corned-beef hash, and burgers (beef, turkey, or vegetable) with a choice of 17 toppings. ⊠ *1540 Broadway, at 45th St.,* ☎ *212/840–8326. AE, MC, V.*

$ ✕ **Film Center Cafe.** Customers dine at vintage Formica tables and in cozy booths, surrounded by authentic Art Deco decor, pink neon lights, old radios, film reels, and wall murals of 20th Century Fox, Paramount, and MGM logos. For dinner, your friendly waiter will bring you good diner food, such as chili or meat loaf with soothing mashed potatoes. From 11 AM to 4 PM on Sundays, a limited retro-price menu offers unlimited cocktails, home-style brunch, and a hot cup of java. ⊠ *635 9th Ave., between 44th and 45th Sts.,* ☎ *212/262–2525. AE, DC, MC, V. No lunch Sat.*

$ ✕ **Motown Cafe.** On three floors, you're surrounded by the history of musical recording. You'll also see the biggest record in the world: a classic 45 that is 27 ft in diameter and revolves on the ceiling. The stairway to the mezzanine is actually a ladder of gold records honoring Motown singers. While the food isn't Grammy material, desserts really rock and roll—the homemade ice cream sandwich plays lead, while a fabulous peach cobbler and sweet potato–pecan pie do great backup. ⊠ *104 W. 57th St., near 6th Ave.,* ☎ *212/581–8030. AE, DC, MC, V.*

$ ✕ **Planet Hollywood.** This café is fun; its owners and shareholders include Bruce Willis, Demi Moore, Sylvester Stallone, Keith Barish, and Arnold Schwarzenegger. The walls are full of celebrity handprints outside and movie memorabilia inside; check out the gremlin. Who cares that the place rates a 10 on the decibel scale? The food is adequate; you'll be happiest if you stick with the southwestern-style nachos, the fajitas, and the playful pizzas. ⊠ *140 W. 57th St.*, ☎ *212/333–7827. AE, DC, MC, V.*

Barbecue

$ ✕ **Virgil's.** This massive roadhouse in the theater district has clever neon and Formica decor. Start perhaps with stuffed jalapeños or buttermilk onion rings with blue-cheese dip. Then go for the "pig out"—a rack of pork ribs, Texas hot links, pulled pork, rack of lamb, chicken, and more. Wash it all down with beer from a good list. ⊠ *152 W. 44th St.*, ☎ *212/921–9494. Reservations essential. AE, MC, V.*

Caribbean

$ ✕ **Island Spice.** This spotless and altogether delightful spot, with green
★   walls and plastic tablecloths, serves some of New York's best Caribbean fare. The kitchen's gastronomic reggae shows up in such dishes as the zesty jerk pork and chicken curry; delicious whole red snapper, pan-fried and then steamed with peppers, onions, and tomatoes; and the tender, curried goat, which you stuff into Indian flat bread—what a terrific sandwich. Brunch is served on Sunday. ⊠ *402 W. 44th St.*, ☎ *212/765–1737. Reservations essential. AE, DC, MC, V.*

Contemporary

$$$ ✕ **Halcyon.** Peacock-green banquettes line the perimeter of the room, dominated by a domed ceiling painted to resemble the sky; looking up, you'll see gold star bursts and an antique brass chandelier. Despite the elaborate setting, the food is refreshingly simple, including such standards as hearts of romaine Caesar salad and roasted rack of lamb. Sunday brunch in the Marketplace in the Sky on the 53rd floor offers one of the best views (and buffets) in town. ⊠ *151 W. 54th St., in the Rihga Royal Hotel*, ☎ *212/468–8888. AE, DC, MC, V.*

Deli

$ ✕ **Carnegie Deli.** Although not what it was, this no-nonsense spot is still one of midtown's two best delis, a species distinguished by crowds, noise, impatient service, and jumbo sandwiches. Ask the counterman to hand-slice your corned beef or pastrami; the extra juiciness and superior texture warrant the extra charge. To drink? Try cream soda or celery tonic. ⊠ *854 7th Ave., between 54th and 55th Sts.*, ☎ *212/757–2245. No credit cards.*

$ ✕ **Stage Deli.** One taste of its chopped liver and pickles and you'll know why this monument to corned beef and pastrami, founded in 1936 by Max Asnas, a Russian immigrant, transcends the tourist-trap syndrome. It personifies the New York theater culture. Bossy waiters and regular guests like Milton Berle and Eddie Cantor were legion. Today the waitpersons seem almost genteel, but the sandwiches are more gargantuan than ever. ⊠ *834 7th Ave., between 53rd and 54th Sts.*, ☎ *212/245–7850. AE, DC, MC, V. No lunch Sat.*

Ethiopian

$ ✕ **Meskerem Ethiopian Restaurant.** This simple Hell's Kitchen storefront restaurant, named for the month of September, has 25 tables and yellow walls adorned with Ethiopian art. Among the tasty Ethiopian delicacies are *Kitfo*, similar to steak tartare, which can be ordered raw, rare or well done, and *Yebeg Alecha*, which consists of tender pieces of lamb, marinated in Ethiopian butter (flavored with curry, rosemary, and a special herb called *kosart*) and then sautéed with fresh ginger and a bit more curry. ⊠ *468 W. 47th St., off 10th Ave.*, ☎ *212/664–0520. AE, DC, MC, V.*

French

$$$$ ✕ **Le Bernardin.** Since 1986, this French seafood restaurant has been
★ a trendsetter with inventive fish creations carefully prepared. The
plush, expansive, and softly lit teak-paneled room—with its well-
spaced tables, huge bouquets of flowers, late-19th-century French oil
paintings, and low noise level—is as popular as ever. Service is impeccable,
and the food can still dazzle, with such recommended offerings as Spanish mackerel tartare with osetra caviar, red snapper in sherry-wine vinaigrette, and some of the finest desserts in town. The wine list is strong
on white Burgundies. ✉ *155 W. 51st St.,* ☎ *212/489–1515. Reservations essential. Jacket required. AE, DC, MC, V. Closed Sun. No lunch
Sat.*

$$$$ ✕ **Les Célébrités.** From the moon-shaped banquettes and the plush red
carpets to the careful lighting and paintings by celebrity artists, this
intimate restaurant in the Essex House hotel is definitely lavish. The
glassed-in kitchen, discretely hidden by a painting on canvas (of the
fabled French ocean liner the *Normandy*), opens occasionally to re-
veal executive chef Christian Delouvrier busily preparing such specialties
as a playful foie-gras burger, in which Granny Smith apple slices replace bread and elegant goose-liver subs for beef. The six-item tasting
dinner showcases his strengths. The wine list is extensive (and expensive), but there is also a good selection by the glass. ✉ *160 Central
Park S,* ☎ *212/484–5113. Reservations essential. Jacket and tie. AE,
DC, MC, V. Closed Sun.–Mon. No lunch.*

$$$–$$$$ ✕ **Petrossian.** This Art Deco caviar bar and restaurant is like no other
★ New York dining spot, with its fur-trimmed banquettes, granite bar,
profusion of marble, and contributions of Erté and Lalique. You'll prob-
ably want to start with gobs of fresh caviar: beluga (the largest egg and
most popular with Americans), Sevruga (smaller and a favorite of the
British), or osetra (yellowish and highly prized by Russians on buttered
toast or blini, a puffy pancake), with no competing garnishes. Petrossian
offers an outstanding prix-fixe dinner (one of the world's great bar-
gains in luxury dining) all evening; the supplement for 30 grams of
sevruga is relatively small. You may drink vodka with the caviar or
champagne throughout. ✉ *182 W. 58th St.,* ☎ *212/245–2214. Reser-
vations essential. AE, DC, MC, V.*

$$ ✕ **Café Botanica.** With its high ceilings, wicker chairs, soft-green tablecloths, and ravishing views of Central Park, this glorious café, airy as
a country garden, serves inventive and elegant food. The pretheater dinner is an exceptional value. You'll find the service neither intimidating nor overbearing, and the wine list is priced fairly. If you can't make
it for dinner, try the equally splendid fixed-price lunch or Sunday
brunch. ✉ *160 Central Park S,* ☎ *212/484–5120. Reservations essential. AE, DC, MC. V.*

$$ ✕ **Jean Lafitte.** Owned by Eric Demarchelier (of the successful Le Se-
lect and Demarchelier), this popular spot has an attractively priced prix-
fixe menu. The à la carte menu also lists Creole dishes, in deference to
the Jean Lafitte–New Orleans connection. The ambience and decor,
with lots of wood, mirrors, brass railings, and Art Nouveau tulip-shaped
lighting fixtures, is straight out of Paris. You'll also welcome the
sprightly bar scene. ✉ *68 W. 58th St.,* ☎ *212/751–2323. Reservations
essential. AE, DC, MC, V. No lunch weekends.*

Greek

$ ✕ **Uncle Nick's.** At this inexpensive taberna, you dine in a long room,
★ with a navy-blue pipe-lined tin ceiling, an exposed kitchen, and a
wood floor. Note the appetizing displays of whole red snapper, porgy,
and striped bass. Uncle Nick's owners, Tony and Mike Vanatakis,
prepare each fish selection with simplicity and care. Be sure to try as

many of the excellent appetizers as your tummy can handle, including crispy fried smelts, tender grilled baby octopus, marvelous sweetbreads, and giant lima beans with tomatoes and herbs. ⊠ *747 9th Ave., between 50th and 51st Sts.,* ☎ *212/245–7992. MC, V.*

Indian

$$–$$$ ✕ **Shaan.** The name of this restaurant means "pride" in Hindi, and owners Victor Khubani and Bhushan Arora have good reason to be proud of their elegant palace with a deep-burgundy marquee, hand-carved doors, Italian and Portuguese marble, hand-embroidered tapestries, and roomy banquettes. The spicing in the unusual dishes ranges from subtle to fiery. The Bengali-born chef prepares splendid tandoori lobster, rack of lamb, or quail, which are marinated in yogurt and spices and cooked in a clay oven. ⊠ *57 W. 48th St.,* ☎ *212/977–8400. AE, DC, MC, V.*

Italian

$$$–$$$$ ✕ **Barbetta.** New York's oldest restaurant (opened in 1906) still operated by its founding family was one of the first to produce northern ★ Italian food in America, and it retains its simplicity and fidelity to tradition. This island of civility in two distinguished, antiques-furnished town houses has an enchanting garden, verdant with century-old trees. The *carne cruda* (hand-chopped raw veal with lemon juice and olive oil) and handmade *agnolotti* (pasta cut into small round pieces, stuffed with meat or vegetables, and folded in half like turnovers) are superb. Besides the well-priced, carefully selected short wine list, there is a long version with many bottles dating from 1880. ⊠ *321 W. 46th St.,* ☎ *212/246–9171. Reservations essential. AE, DC, MC, V. Closed Sun. No lunch Mon.*

$$$–$$$$ ✕ **Palio.** Named after the 800-year-old Italian horse race that celebrates ★ the Assumption of the Virgin, this exceptional restaurant has an impressive 13-ft mural by Sandro Chia. Your name is discreetly requested as you're ushered to an elevator and the second-floor dining room with light oak paneling and luxuriously spaced tables set with Frette linen and Riedel crystal. Food and service to match such a high tone must be unblemished, and Palio meets the challenge. Here you'll experience authentic Italian cuisine, from a regional six-course menu from Siena to one based on aged balsamic vinegar. The wine selection and service are commensurate with the posh setting. ⊠ *151 W. 51st St.,* ☎ *212/245–4850. Reservations essential. Jacket and tie. AE, DC, MC, V. Closed Sun. No lunch Sat.*

$$$–$$$$ ✕ **San Domenico.** Owner Tony May has raised America's consciousness of the Italian *cucina.* Soft egg ravioli with truffle butter in addi- ★ tion to loin of veal in smoked-bacon cream sauce and polenta *nera* (chocolate hazelnut dessert soufflé) are hardly run of the mill offerings, and the private villa-like setting, with terra-cotta floors, sumptuous leather chairs, and lots of warm, earthy hues, is understated and elegant. The huge wine list showcases Italy's great vintages. Your tab drops if you stick to prix-fixe dinners, especially on Sunday; throw caution to the wind, and you may have to thumb a ride home. ⊠ *240 Central Park S,* ☎ *212/265–5959. Reservations essential. Jacket and tie required except on Sun. AE, MC, DC, V. No lunch weekends.*

$$$ ✕ **Osteria del Circo.** A monumental polished wood bar dominates the entrance to this festive restaurant, run by the Maccioni family (owners of Le Cirque). A circus atmosphere has been created by architect Adam Tihany, thanks to the center pillar with large monkeys doing tricks, orange and red flags suspended from the high ceiling alongside a ropelike ladder, and large metallic statues floating over the $2 million open mosaic kitchen. The signature Pizza Pazza Circo (Crazy Pizza) has a delicate layer of mascarpone cheese and tomato, topped with thin prosciutto di Parma. Mama Egi's Ravioli is filled with herbed spinach in a delicate sage sauce. Don't miss the Circo Cappuccino Cup, which is actually espresso mousse served in a coffee cup. ⊠ *120 W. 55th St., off 6th Ave.,* ☎ *212/265–3636. Reservations essential. AE, DC, MC, V. No lunch Sun.*

\$\$\$ ✕ **Remi.** This stylish Italian restaurant—designed by architect Adam Tihany, who co-owns it with chef Francesco Antonucci—is striking with its nautical decor, skylighted open atrium-garden, blue-and-white-striped banquettes, Venetian-glass chandeliers, and soaring room-length mural of Venice by Paulin Paris. The accompanying contemporary Venetian cuisine is beautifully presented. Fresh sardines make a lovely beginning with their contrasting sweet-and-sour onion garnish, and you can't go wrong with the expertly prepared rack of lamb or any of the wonderful desserts. ⊠ *145 W. 53rd St.,* ☎ *212/581–4242. Reservations essential. AE, DC, MC, V. No lunch weekends.*

\$\$–\$\$\$ ✕ **Lattanzi Ristorante.** Although not kosher, the cuisine here derives from the Jewish ghetto with such dishes as baby artichokes flattened like a pancake and parchment-fried, so that even the leaves are edible. Noteworthy pastas include homemade noodles with artichoke sauce and Pecorino cheese. Breads are remarkable, especially a huge, flat un-leavened sheet of homemade matzo and the garlicky bread sticks. Don't ignore the homemade napoleon. You'll dine in an elegant town house with several exposed-brick rooms, candles, flowers, and one of Manhattan's most romantic gardens. ⊠ *361 W. 46th St.,* ☎ *212/315–0980. Reservations essential. AE, DC, MC, V. Closed Sun. No lunch Sat.*

\$\$–\$\$\$ ✕ **Trattoria Dell'Arte.** This popular trattoria near Carnegie Hall still ★ displays the controversial oversize renderings of body parts, alongside portraits of Italian artists, in its three dining rooms. But you'll proba-bly be more interested in the mouthwatering antipasti on the bar and the tasty pasta, pizza, hot focaccia sandwiches, and grilled double veal chop, served with a mountain of shoestring potatoes. The cannoli is wonderful. Check out the great wine list and flavored grappas. ⊠ *900 7th Ave., between 56th and 57th Sts.,* ☎ *212/245–9800. Reservations essential. AE, DC, MC, V.*

\$–\$\$ ✕ **Frico Bar.** Owned by Lidia Bastianich of Felidia and son Joseph of Becco, this casual place serves an array of tempting snacks ranging from thin-crust pizza to the house specialty, *frico,* a crustless pizza of grid-dle-crisped cheese stuffed with potatoes and vegetables. As in the Friu-lian countryside, wine comes on tap, along with 10 excellent beers. The restaurant has an engaging decor: tile floors and a moon and star logo displayed on the attractive wooden tables. ⊠ *402 W. 43rd St., off 9th Ave.,* ☎ *212/564–7272. AE, DC, MC, V.*

\$–\$\$ ✕ **Osteria al Droge.** Warm yellow walls and a two-tiered room with a charming balcony, long mahogany bar, colorful framed posters, and bare oak family tables conjure Tuscany in Times Square. You are bound to enjoy thin-crusted pizza with mozzarella, fresh tomatoes, arugula, and prosciutto and marvelous risottos. Leave room for warm pecan tart and cinnamon ice cream. ⊠ *142 W. 44th St.,* ☎ *212/944–3643. Reservations essential. AE, DC, MC, V.*

\$ ✕ **Mangia e Bevi.** This down-to-earth slice of Naples features murals of Italy, ceiling fans, checkered tablecloths, an open kitchen, and a wood-burning oven. Pizza fans are kept happy (try the white four-cheese pizza), and there's also good bread to smear with virgin olive oil and focac-cia with herb-marinated Mediterranean olives. Among the bargain-priced pasta, perhaps try rigatoni *Amatriciana*—brimming with homemade tomato sauce, Italian bacon, and spices. Waiters in T-shirts are help-ful as the music blares and customers slap tambourines and join in the fun. ⊠ *800 9th Ave., at 53rd St.,* ☎ *212/956–3976. AE, DC, MC, V.*

Latin

$$ ✕ **Victor's Café 52.** This Technicolor Cuban restaurant has big high-back booths, a tile floor, and a raised back room with skylight. The blasting Latin American music and an atmosphere harking back to movie musicals set in old Havana seem not to bode well for serious dining. But fear not—the food is often fine, a contemporary transcription of Cuban, Puerto Rican, and Latino signature dishes. ⊠ 236 W. 52nd St., ☎ 212/586–7714. AE, DC, MC, V.

$ ✕ **Pomaire.** Named after a small village renowned for its pottery (in which many of the dishes are served), this uncommon restaurant with exposed brick, handmade rugs, a faux skylight, and attractive paintings sometimes offers live music. The menu lists several intriguing dinner options, such as *pastel de choclo*, a casserole of beef, olives, chicken, onions, and egg that is covered with a corn puree, dusted with sugar, and baked in a clay pot. Leave room for *torta de mil hojas*—leaves of pastry layered with caramel. ⊠ 371 W. 46th St., off 9th Ave., ☎ 212/956–3056. AE, DC, MC, V. No lunch.

Southwestern

$$ ✕ **Tapika.** The design of the relaxed dining room by architect David Rockwell pays a fanciful tribute to the American West: adobe-brown walls, colored picket fencing around the windows, faux pony-skin bar stools, branded wood, and steel light fixtures with Native American cutout designs. Chef David Walzog expertly reinvents southwestern cuisine with such dishes as barbecued short ribs falling off the bone, wild-mushroom tamale, and incendiary yet scrumptious ground-vegetable chili rellenos served with smoked tomato salsa and crumpled cheese. The margaritas are terrific. ⊠ 950 8th Ave., at 56th St., ☎ 212/397–3737. DC, MC, V.

Steak

$$$–$$$$ ✕ **Ben Benson's.** Not only are steaks, chops, and accompaniments first-★ rate here, there is also a real chef in the kitchen. Witness such contemporary steak-house fare as cold lobster cocktail and Maryland crab cakes, steaks, chops, and the fabulous prime rib, as well as such excellent daily specials as Friday's crusted fish hash. Don't miss the horseradish mashed potatoes or the excellent home fries. The wine list improves with each visit. This convivial spot has a masculine interior—brass plaques inscribed with names of celebrities, framed pictures of animals and game birds. ⊠ 123 W. 52nd St., ☎ 212/581–8888. Reservations essential. AE, DC, MC, V. No lunch weekends.

$$$–$$$$ ✕ **Gallagher's.** The most casual of New York steak houses, with checkered tablecloths and photos of sports greats on the walls, Gallagher's has almost no pretensions and nothing to hide. Look for the meat-aging room, visible through the window. You won't be disappointed with the famous aged sirloin steaks, oversize lobsters, or any of the fabulous potato dishes (try the O'Brien with its sweet pepper and onion flavor). Don't miss the creamy rice pudding. ⊠ 228 W. 52nd St., ☎ 212/245–5336. Reservations essential. AE, DC, MC, V.

$$$–$$$$ ✕ **Le Marais.** The appetizing display of raw meats and terrines at the ★ entrance and the bare wood floors may remind you of a Parisian bistro. Tables covered with butcher paper, French wall posters, and maroon banquettes reinforce that image. Yet the clientele (mostly male) is strictly kosher. A cold *terrine de boeuf en gelée façon pot au feu* (marinated short ribs) starts the meal on the right note, and rib steak for two is cooked to a turn, tender, and juicy. The accompanying fries are perfect. ⊠ 150 W. 46th St., ☎ 212/869–0900. AE, DC, MC, V. No dinner Fri., no lunch Sat.

$$$–$$$$ ✕ **Ruth's Chris.** Manhattan's genteel addition to this group of more than 40 so-named restaurants around the world is giving other steak houses around town a run for their money. With its impressionistic oil paintings, dark red walls, and crisp white napery on well-spaced tables, it's much more inviting than its location at the base of a nondescript office tower might suggest. Moreover, the steaks and chops, served sizzling in butter unless you specify otherwise, are tops. The menu defines degrees of doneness according to temperature and color, and the kitchen gives you just what you request. ⊠ *148 W. 51st St.,* ☎ *212/245–9600. Reservations essential. AE, DC, MC, V. No lunch weekends.*

Upper East Side

American Casual

$$–$$$ ✕ **Lobster Club.** This two-story town-house restaurant resembles a New England inn with its bleached-wood beamed ceilings, inlaid mosaic floors, and more formal second floor with a fireplace, vaulted ceiling, and chandelier with flickering candles. Celebrity-chef Anne Rosenzweig has created an appealing menu; for instance, the signature lobster club sandwich, a luxurious play on a classic dish, is accompanied by plantain chips. The wine list has a choice of 9 to 12 bottles in various price ranges. ⊠ *24 E. 80th St.,* ☎ *212/249–6500. Reservations essential. AE, MC, V. No lunch Sun.*

$ ✕ **Hi-Life Restaurant and Lounge.** Young East Siders wait in line to sit
★ down at one of the spacious half-moon-shaped booths at this bilevel Art Deco café. The draw? Soothing prices, huge portions, and some of the best martinis in town. Join the crowd and polish off sushi, or something from the raw bar, before you proceed to the filet mignon, sliced and served with potato salad or heaping bowls of pad thai noodles with chicken or shrimp. Hi-Life's West Side location serves similar fare (⊠ 477 Amsterdam Ave., at 83rd St., ☎ 212/787–7199). ⊠ *1340 1st Ave., at 72nd St.,* ☎ *212/249–3600. AE, DC, MC, V.*

$ ✕ **Serendipity 3.** This whimsical store-cum-café has been producing excellent burgers, sandwiches, salads, and other interesting if overly complicated plates since 1954. But most people come for the fantasy sundaes—huge, naughty, and decadent. You'll love the thick frozen hot chocolate. ⊠ *225 E. 60th St.,* ☎ *212/838–3531. AE, DC, MC, V. BYOB.*

$ ✕ **Seventh Regiment Mess and Bar.** The fourth floor of the historic Seventh Regiment Armory is home to this unusual restaurant with high ceilings, wooden beams, and appropriately militaristic motifs. You won't find fancy cooking—just homey food, such as chicken à la king, pork chops, roast beef, and mustardy deviled beef bones—at rock-bottom prices. ⊠ *643 Park Ave., at 66th St.,* ☎ *212/744–4107. AE, MC, V. Closed Sun.–Mon. No lunch.*

Chinese

$–$$ ✕ **Evergreen Cafe.** Come here for the Chinatown-style dumplings (try asparagus or seafood fillings) and the full range of noodle and rice dishes, such as Singapore-style curry-flavored noodles or diced chicken in salted fish-flavor fried rice. This attractive restaurant has blond wood tables, ceiling fans, and an illuminated emerald sculpture; the back dining room tends to be more quiet. ⊠ *1288 1st Ave., at 69th St.,* ☎ *212/744–3266. AE, DC, MC, V.*

Contemporary

$$$$ ✕ **Aureole.** Charles Palmer's fashionable restaurant, with its alluring bas-reliefs, baskets of dried flowers, and swank town-house location, is one of the town's toughest reservations. Appetizers are generally trustworthy; desserts are visual masterpieces. Wine prices are high, and the

Uptown Manhattan Dining

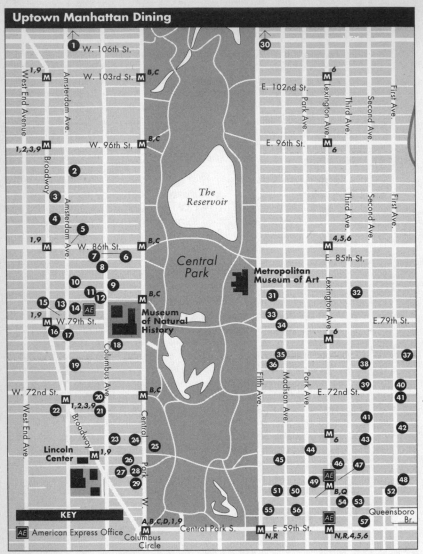

Afgan Kebob
House #2, **41**

Arcadia, **51**

Arizona 206, **57**

Aureole, **56**

Boonthai, **39**

Café des Artistes, **24**

Café Luxembourg, **22**

Café Pierre, **55**

Carmine's, **3**

China Fun, **20**

Coco Pazzo, **36**

Daniel, **35**

Emily's, **30**

Evergreen Cafe, **42**

Ferrier, **45**

Firehouse, **7**

Fujiyama Mama, **9**

Gabriela's, **2**

Isabella's, **18**

Hi-Life Restaurant
and Lounge, **10**

Jo Jo, **47**

Joe's Fish Shack, **6**

L'Absinthe, **43**

Le Select, **8**

Lincoln Tavern, **27**

The Lobster Club, **33**

Mad Fish, **17**

Main Street, **12**

Manhattan Café, **48**

Matthew's, **54**

Montien, **52**

Nino's, **40**

Parioli
Romanissimo, **31**

Park Avenue Cafe, **49**

Penang Columbus, **21**

Persepolis, **38**

Picholine, **28**

Popover Café, **5**

Post House, **50**

Rain, **11**

Red Tulip, **37**

Sarabeth's Kitchen, **14**

Savaan, **15**

The Savannah Club, **4**

Serendipity 3, **53**

Seventh Regiment
Mess and Bar, **44**

Shark Bar, **19**

Shun Lee West, **26**

Sign of the Dove, **46**

Sofia Fabulous Pizza, **34**

Stingray, **13**

Tavern on
the Green, **25**

Terrace, **1**

Two Two Two, **16**

Vince & Eddie's, **23**

West 63rd Street
Steakhouse, **29**

Zocalo, **32**

ventilation and ambience upstairs are sub-par. ✉ *34 E. 61st St.,* ☎ *212/319–1660. Reservations essential. AE, DC, MC, V. Closed Sun. No lunch Sat.*

$$$ ✕ **Jo Jo.** New York's most fashionable bistro has an upstairs dining
★ area with burgundy banquettes, a black-and-white tile floor, and the obligatory etched-glass and gilt-edge mirrors. Celebrity-chef Jean-Georges Vongerichten follows a culinary approach that is personal (French with Asian accents), healthy (infused oils, juices, and reduction rather than heavy sauces), and classic (hardy bistro dishes freely updated). Goat-cheese-and-potato terrine is typical of Vongerichten's culinary range, as are the signature shrimp in spiced-carrot juice and Thai lime leaves, and the simple chicken roasted with ginger, green olives, and ginger juice, accompanied by chickpea-tahini fritters. ✉ *160 E. 64th St.,* ☎ *212/223–5656. Reservations essential. AE, MC, V. Closed Sun. No lunch Sat.*

$$$ ✕ **Park Avenue Cafe.** American folk art, antique toys, and sheaves of dried wheat decorate this unpretentious pacesetter. The Flag Room, to the left of the bar, is more sedate. David Burke's imaginative presentations are often whimsical. Salmon is cured like pastrami and arrives on a marble slab, with warm corn blini (pancakes), while the signature swordfish "chop" comes dressed with a numbered tag (save the tag, sign the book, and you may win an all-inclusive holiday). The pastry chef's masterpieces include a milk-chocolate crème brûlée and "opera in the park," a cake decorated to mimic Central Park. ✉ *100 E. 63rd St.,* ☎ *212/644–1900. Reservations essential. AE, DC, MC, V. No lunch Sat.*

$$$ ✕ **Sign of the Dove.** Skylights, stunning floral arrangements, brick arches,
★ and piano music lend a distinctive character to each of the dining rooms here, some of the prettiest in town. From Andrew D'Amico's distinguished kitchen, don't miss the singular preparations of tuna (at times in aromatic broth with Asian vegetables), the low-cholesterol venison dish, or the omnipresent warm chocolate soufflé cake with housemade vanilla ice cream. Prix-fixe menus put this place squarely among the city's best famous-restaurant values. ✉ *1110 3rd Ave., at 65th St.,* ☎ *212/861–8080. Reservations essential. AE, DC, MC, V. No lunch Mon.*

$$–$$$ ✕ **Matthew's.** This popular café is airy and attractive with its white shutters, ceiling fans, rattan chairs, jumbo potted plants, and warm colors. Young chef Matthew Kenney has an eclectic contemporary style. You'll relish the tuna tartare (more coarsely chopped here than in most other new American restaurants), served with a Mediterranean-green-olive condiment. There's also a terrific Moroccan-spiced lamb shank with dried fruits and couscous, and a soft-centered chocolate hazelnut cake that makes life worth living. ✉ *1030 3rd Ave., at 61st St.,* ☎ *212/838–4343. Reservations essential. AE, DC, MC, V.*

Eastern European
$–$$ ✕ **Red Tulip.** With the gypsy violins and high-back wooden booths, the atmosphere is early Budapest (via MGM), heavy on the gemütlichkeit. The food is a bit more contemporary; try the celebrated chicken paprika with egg dumplings, the crispy roast goose, the stuffed cabbage, or the sausage with onions, green peppers, and tomato sauce. *Palacsinta* (crepes) with assorted fillings are a graceful example of this time-honored dessert. ✉ *439 E. 75th St.,* ☎ *212/734–4893. AE, DC, MC, V. Closed Mon.–Tues. No lunch.*

French

$$$$ ✕ **Café Pierre.** The long room is a jewel, with its ornate mirrors, overhead cloud murals, and tables fitted with gold lamé skirts under crisp white cloths. The cosmopolitan cuisine gets high marks as does the selection of glass wines. You can have coffee or an after-dinner drink at the sophisticated piano bar, where there's dancing Thursday, Friday, and Saturday nights. ⊠ *2 E. 61st St.,* ☎ *212/940–8195. Reservations essential. Jacket and tie. AE, DC, MC, V.*

$$$$ ✕ **Daniel.** At Daniel Boulud's $1.9 million restaurant, lavish flower ar-
★ rangements, antique mirrors, and wall-to-wall celebrities adorn the main dining room, with its exquisite table settings by Limoges, gold-tinted walls, and red-checked banquettes. The cuisine (at once contemporary and classic) is among the best in New York. Note the uncommon tuna tartare, with a touch of curry, and the signature black sea bass, wrapped in a crispy potato shell. Spoil yourself with the all-chocolate or all-fruit dessert menu. ⊠ *20 E. 76th St.,* ☎ *212/288–0033. Reservations essential. Jacket required. AE, D, DC, MC, V. Closed Sun. No lunch Mon.*

$$$ ✕ **Arcadia.** Owned by celebrity chef Anne Rosenzweig, a small bar pre-
★ cedes the main dining room, which is small and romantic with its soft lighting, plum banquettes, chair backs outfitted in patterned slipcovers, and a mural devoted to the seasons. Service is first-rate. Signature dishes include a delicious appetizer of four corn cakes with crème fraîche and caviars (yellow and black); house-smoked lobster cooked with tarragon butter; and a warm chocolate brioche-based bread pudding with brandy custard sauce. The wine list is excellent, if expensive, and there's a special reserve list with "historic bottles" of old California. ⊠ *21 E. 62nd St., off Madison Ave.,* ☎ *212/223–2900. Reservations essential. AE, MC, V. Closed Sun. No lunch Sat.*

$$–$$$ ✕ **L'Absinthe.** The wonderful Art Nouveau bistro decor features etched
★ glass, huge gilt-framed mirrors, tile floors, and a few sidewalk tables. Chef-owner Jean-Michel Bergougnoux takes shellfish and cheese seriously, and they are both beautifully presented. Highlights on the menu include a fine foie gras terrine, slow-braised beef with carrots, poached free-range chicken in truffle broth, and a thin, crisp apple tart or warm chocolate cake. ⊠ *227 E. 67th St.,* ☎ *212/794–4950. Reservations essential. AE, MC, V.*

$$ ✕ **Ferrier.** There are a few tables at its sidewalk café in the summer, but any time of the year, this very popular bistro will give you some idea of how tinned sardines must feel. So tuck in your tummy and turn up your hearing aid (the noise level tests one's tolerance for audio excess). The service and reception are so friendly and the food so delicious and copious you won't even mind the relatively high prices. Savor steak au poivre, grilled tuna Ferrier, and profiteroles. Alas, the wine list is not up to par. ⊠ *29 E. 65th St.,* ☎ *212/772–9000. Reservations essential. AE, DC, MC, V.*

Italian

$$$$ ✕ **Parioli Romanissimo.** In a splendid town house, this special restaurant is one of Manhattan's last bastions of civility. You enter through a small bar and make your way down a long corridor, where you'll see one of New York's most astounding selections of imported cheese. The exquisite main dining area overlooking an enclosed garden room features a marble fireplace, the original plaster-molded ceiling, and spacious tables. Pasta is always wonderful here, as are such graceful offerings as sautéed sea scallops seared in peppercorns, in a discreet watercress sauce, and roasted rack of young lamb, marinated in spicy oil, herbs, and garlic. The wine list showcases jewels from Italy, France, and California, and 12 kinds of tea are available, presented in apothecary jars. ⊠ *24 E. 81st St.,* ☎ *212/288–2391. Reservations essential. Jacket required. AE, DC, MC, V. Closed Sun. No lunch.*

$$–$$$ ✕ **Coco Pazzo.** In one of New York's celebrity-spotting restaurants, the main dining room is aglow with ecru walls, yellow tablecloths, colorful murals, and huge urns of flowers. All pastas and risottos are splendid, and it's hard to resist the *maccheroncini al pepolino*—rectangles of fresh egg pasta in a rich tomato sauce with thyme and grated aged Pecorino cheese. If push comes to shove (or waistline challenges impulse), the entrée of choice is the roasted whole fish of the day. *Cros ta di frutta fresca* (open-faced fruit tart) changes its face often but never disappoints. ⊠ *23 E. 74th St.,* ☎ *212/794–0205. Reservations essential. AE, MC, V. Closed Sun. No lunch.*

$$–$$$ ✕ **Nino's.** Lobster *fra diablo,* finished in the old-world style in a chafing dish and served on a bed of perfect linguini, is a specialty at this popular Italian restaurant with its lively piano bar, sienna walls hung with large framed paintings, and breathtaking floral arrangements. And even fresh fruit becomes an uncommon dessert when it's artistically arranged on an ice sculpture, preceding beautiful *espresso-macchiato.* ⊠ *1354 1st Ave., between 72nd and 73rd Sts.,* ☎ *212/988–0002. Reservations essential. AE, MC, V. No lunch.*

Mexican

$–$$ ✕ **Zocalo.** Come here for fabulous margaritas, lovely dips of warm *tomatillo* (green tomato), tomato *chipotle* (smoked chili), *pico de gallo* (raw onion-tomato salsa), and a chunky guacamole beautifully presented in the traditional *molcajete* (lava-rock utensil). This attractive Mexican restaurant has an inviting bar area and a long main dining room with burnt-orange and blue walls. Among the surprising dishes are grilled clams in a banana-leaf wrapping with a peanut-tomato sauce and chocolate sorbet laced with jalapeño peppers. ⊠ *174 82nd St., off 3rd Ave.,* ☎ *212/717–7772. AE, DC, MC, V.*

Middle Eastern

$ ✕ **Afghan Kebab House #2.** At this cavelike Afghan restaurant, scenic posters, copper platters, and Afghan rugs cover the walls. Newcomers to this cuisine should enjoy the *aushak* or boiled dumplings, filled with scallions, herbs, and spices and topped with yogurt; the spiced half-chicken, marinated in fresh grated spices and hot peppers; and the vegetable combination plate. ⊠ *1345 2nd Ave., between 70th and 71st Sts.,* ☎ *212/517–2776. AE, DC, MC, V. BYOB.*

$ ✕ **Persepolis.** Manhattan's only authentic Persian restaurant has been artfully decorated with smoked-glass mirrors, huge globe light fixtures, and carpeted banquettes. Make an effort to order as many appetizers as you can handle, and don't omit baba ghanoush, *torshi* (pickled carrots, eggplant, celery, garlic, and parsley), and the olive salad. The Persepolis kebab (filet mignon, chopped steak, and chicken) on skewers is a good example of this delicate and choice cuisine. ⊠ *1423 2nd Ave., between 74th and 75th Sts.,* ☎ *212/535–1100. AE, DC, MC, V.*

Pizza

$ ✕ **Sofia Fabulous Pizza.** Mediterranean-colored friezes grace this
★ trendy café with wine racks, a vaulted ceiling, and wall sconces made of Japanese paper. Here you'll sample the best pizza and variations on focaccia in Manhattan. In the breathtaking thin-crust pizza, prepared with filtered water to resemble the dough of Naples, Sofia uses mozzarella made daily with fresh milk. For a singular treat, try the mashed potatoes slathered with homemade tomato sauce and Parmesan cheese and then baked in the oven. ⊠ *1022 Madison Ave., near 79th St.,* ☎ *212/734–2676. AE, DC, MC, V.*

Southwestern

$$–$$$ ✕ **Arizona 206.** Santa Fe meets Manhattan at this seemingly casual eatery, which also incorporates the less-expensive adjacent Arizona Café. There's a cozy nook with a working fireplace as you enter and an inviting bar with superb margaritas, 18 premium tequilas, 22 microbrewery beers, and 11 wines by the glass. Stucco walls mimic an adobe hut, and colorful Native American prints cover the chair cushions. But no Mojave truck stop aspired to serving cuisine so urbane and inventive, such as the lipstick chili relleno, a seasonal chili of crab, fresh corn, carrot-ginger butter, black beans, and habanera sauce, which bursts with flavor. The lobster tamale stuffed with diced meat, wild mushrooms, chili, and cactus is another wonder. ✉ *206 E. 60th St.,* ☎ *212/838–0440. AE, DC, MC, V. No lunch Sun.*

Steak

$$$–$$$$ ✕ **Manhattan Café.** You enter this steak house through a bronze door-
★ way that belonged to the old Biltmore hotel. Cut flowers, Art Deco chandeliers, Persian carpets, and deep hunter-green upholstery are a far cry from the rush-and-crush atmosphere of most of its competitors. Steaks are among the best in town. And don't overlook the well-prepared seafood dishes, Lyonnaise potatoes, and some savory Italian specialties. Sunday brunch is a pleasure. ✉ *1161 1st Ave., between 63rd and 64th Sts.,* ☎ *212/888–6556. AE, DC, MC, V. No lunch Sat.*

$$$–$$$$ ✕ **Post House.** Superior grilling and first-rate ingredients are only half the appeal. Good service, inventive daily specials, and the inordinately comfortable main dining room, with leather armchairs, capacious tables, and parquet floor, complete the story. Triple lamb chops are prima, Caesar salad perfection. The signature chocolate box—Belgian chocolate filled with white and dark chocolate mousse—may be copied by others but not duplicated. The wine list is vast and beautifully organized, including the "Wine Library" (wines at least 10 years old) and "California Cache" (California wines unavailable elsewhere). ✉ *28 E. 63rd St.,* ☎ *212/935–2888. Reservations essential. Jacket required. AE, DC, MC, V. Closed Sun. No lunch Sat.*

Thai

$–$$ ✕ **Boonthai.** At this mirrored, softly lit charmer with its pretty paintings, crisply set tables, and handsome breakfront, Julie, the owner, greets you warmly. Your dining experience can be tempered to your taste. If you like your food hot, sample the deep-fried whole fish with chili sauce. Or order the chicken in not-so-spicy *masman* (red Muslim curry) sauce, the pad thai, or the obliging deep-fried duck. ✉ *1393A 2nd Ave., between 72nd and 73rd Sts.,* ☎ *212/249–8484. Reservations essential. AE, MC, V. No lunch weekends.*

$–$$ ✕ **Montien.** Not only will you find the Thai cuisine extremely fresh, flavorful, and impeccably prepared and presented, you'll also dine in a lovely room with mirrors, flowers, and wood carvings of exotic birds. Choose a remarkable salad of roasted duck, cashews, apple, chilis, and lemon juice or a red, green, or yellow chicken curry. Dining with a group of at least four makes prices wondrously affordable. ✉ *1134 1st Ave., between 62nd and 63rd Sts.,* ☎ *212/421–4433. AE, DC, MC, V.*

Lincoln Center

American Casual

$$ ✕ **Vince and Eddie's.** This bucolic restaurant offers realistic prices, generous portions, and friendly service. It encompasses a series of small rooms and a seasonal garden patterned on a country inn. Executive chef Scott Campbell's new-American fare is always a pleasure. Lamb

shank with dried cherries and mashed turnips has deservedly become a classic. Save room for the magnificent desserts: Sorbets, ice creams, and even humble cobblers take on a new dimension. ⊠ *70 W. 68th St., ☎ 212/721–0068. Reservations essential. AE, DC, MC, V.*

$–$$ ✕ **Lincoln Tavern.** At this classic pub with high ceilings, wood walls, leather banquettes, and vintage black-and-white photographs, you have a good choice of American entrées, typified by chicken quesadilla with fresh roasted corn and jalapeño jack cheese, braised lamb shank with seasonal vegetables, and a chocolate macadamia-nut brownie for dessert. ⊠ *51 W. 64th St., ☎ 212/721–8271. AE, DC, MC, V.*

Chinese

$$–$$$ ✕ **Shun Lee West.** It's a dramatically lighted study in black, accented by white dragons and monkeys. Service is good, and considering the number of people the restaurant serves, the food can be excellent. Shanghai steamed dumplings and giant prawns make stellar starters. Then try the Peking duck, sweetbreads with hot peppers and scallions, or rack of lamb Szechuan style. Fresh fruit makes an ideal dessert. The food at Shun Lee Palace (⊠ *155 E. 55th St., ☎ 212/371–8844), under the same management, is equally good. ⊠ 43 W. 65th St., ☎ 212/595–8895. Reservations essential. AE, DC, MC, V.*

Contemporary

$$$ ✕ **Tavern on the Green.** The reception can be perfunctory and the service polite but inept. Nevertheless, Warner LeRoy's lavish restaurant is a visual fantasy, and careful selection can yield a satisfying meal. There's also jazz, dancing, and cabaret. Request the brilliant Crystal Room, for its view of the twinkle-lighted trees, or opt for alfresco dining in the engaging garden. Prix-fixe menus lower the tab. ⊠ *In Central Park at 67th St., ☎ 212/873–3200. Reservations essential. AE, DC, MC, V.*

Continental

$$$–$$$$ ✕ **Café des Artistes.** Writer–restaurant consultant George Lang's mas-
★ terpiece, this most European of cafés provides a snug and beautiful ambience with its polished oak woodwork and rosy Howard Chandler Christy murals of nymphs at play. The cuisine is as refined as the setting. Four-way salmon, with tidbits of the fish that are smoked, poached, dill-marinated, or raw, is a perfect introduction, and it would be hard to find a better pot-au-feu, a French variation on pot roast, here beautifully presented with bone marrow and traditional accompaniments. Desserts are appealing: request the mocha *dacquoise* (layers of hazelnut meringue, sandwiched together with French buttercream). For wines, go with the George Lang selections, *Gundel* wines from Hungary, or the special basket wines. Customers adore the especially festive brunch. ⊠ *1 W. 67th St., ☎ 212/877–3500. Reservations essential. Jacket required. AE, DC, MC, V.*

French

$$ ✕ **Café Luxembourg.** With its well-heeled clientele, this bustling, sophisticated bistro with airy arched windows, a zinc-top bar, and racks of newspapers is a bit of SoHo on the Upper West Side. Here's the place for steak frîtes, soothing roasted free-range chicken with mashed potatoes, or a robust cassoulet. Desserts are mostly fine, especially the mouthwatering profiteroles. Several prix-fixe menus lower the tab. There is a very good selection of wines. ⊠ *200 W. 70th St., ☎ 212/873–7411. Reservations essential. AE, DC, MC, V. No lunch Mon.*

Mediterranean

$$$-$$$$ ✕ **Picholine.** Named for a small green Mediterranean olive, this mel-
★   low restaurant is patterned on a Provençal farmhouse, with soft col-
ors, wood floors, and dried flowers. Chef-proprietor Terrance Brennan's
food is among the finest in Manhattan. Top dishes include the signa-
ture grilled octopus with fennel, potato, and lemon-pepper dressing;
Moroccan-spiced loin of lamb with vegetable couscous and mint-yo-
gurt sauce; and tournedos of salmon with horseradish crust, cucum-
bers, and salmon caviar. A cheese selection of some 30 varieties, in prime
condition and served at room temperature, is indicative of Brennan's
commitment to quality. The wine list offers outstanding wines by the
glass; there's also a small wine area seating up to eight that offers spe-
cial tasting menus. ✉ *35 W. 64th St., off Broadway,* ☎ *212/724–8585.*
Reservations essential. AE, DC, MC, V. Closed Sun. No lunch Mon.

Steak

$$-$$$ ✕ **West 63rd Street Steakhouse.** An elevator takes you to the mezza-
nine of this sumptuous steak house, located in the Radisson Empire
hotel. The leopard carpeting extends to the main dining room, which
is lined with floral banquettes. A prime porterhouse for two is always
a test of the management's commitment to first-rate preparation, and
the kitchen triumphs in the art of grilling: Steaks are charred, pink,
juicy, warm, sliced on the bone, and delicious. ✉ *44 W. 63rd St.,* ☎
212/246–6363. Reservations essential. AE, DC, MC, V.

Upper West Side

American Casual

$$ ✕ **Main Street.** Bring kids, friends, and an appetite—everything is
served family style. Picture a whole roast chicken and a really good
meat loaf. This American-as-apple-pie restaurant prepares them all well.
Since every order comes large enough to split four ways, don't let the
prices turn you off (just divide by four). Check out the terrific puddings and stupendous pies. The lighting is a bit uncharitable, and the
decibel level can be unfortunate. ✉ *446 Columbus Ave., between 81st
and 82nd Sts.,* ☎ *212/873–5025. AE, DC, MC, V. No lunch weekdays.*

$-$$ ✕ **Popover Café.** There's a certain captivating, innocent quality to the
honest American food in this vintage West Side tearoom-cum-restau-
rant full of teddy bears. Besides the superb popover, you'll admire the
terrific soups and the delectable sandwiches. Sunday brunch packs them
in. ✉ *551 Amsterdam Ave., between 86th and 87th Sts.,* ☎ *212/595–
8555. Reservations essential. AE, MC, V.*

$-$$ ✕ **Sarabeth's Kitchen.** Despite the bric-a-brac and homespun charm,
this is more than a tearoom, with a menu that embraces Italianate
smoked-salmon bruschetta, homespun American chicken potpie, and
pan-seared salmon on wild rice. Desserts such as cranberry-pear bread
pudding and homemade ice creams and sorbets are worthwhile. This
is a fine place for breakfast and brunch. ✉ *423 Amsterdam Ave., between 80th and 81st Sts.,* ☎ *212/496–6280. AE, DC, MC, V.*

$ ✕ **Firehouse.** There's a reason this find calls itself a firehouse: The sauce
they use on the jerk-chicken pizza has enough kick to get you to Jamaica without an airplane (you can get tamer varieties of pizza, too).
You'll also find good buffalo wings, chili, and burgers. Be sure to
check out the microbrewery beers. It's open until 4 AM. ✉ *522 Columbus Ave., between 85th and 86th Sts.,* ☎ *212/595–3139. AE, MC, V.*

Asian

$ ✕ **Rain.** Conjuring up memories of the writings of Somerset Maugham,
who wrote a short story called "Rain," this pleasant restaurant has a

friendly bar, rattan chairs with pillows in chintz, and wooden floors covered with Oriental runners. Share first-rate Thai- and Vietnamese-inspired food: steamed ravioli called bahn cuon, with lump crab, bean sprouts, and chili sauce; crispy whole fish in three-flavor sauce; and tantalizing charred-beef salad. ⊠ *100 W. 82nd St.,* ☎ *212/501–0776. Reservations essential. AE, DC, MC, V. No lunch.*

Chinese

$ ✕ **China Fun.** This cheerful dining spot has clean white walls decorated with captivating swirls of bright colors. As you enter, you pass by the steaming kitchen with its hanging cooked ducks. The extensive menu features a variety of regional cuisines and encompasses a savory array of barbecued food, 18 kinds of noodle soup, dumplings with all sorts of fillings, and a number of Chinese standards. The taro-shrimp cakes and pineapple-curry fried rice are both highly recommended. Save room for the terrific sesame-peanut-butter pancake for dessert. The East Side branch is at 1239 2nd Avenue, at 65th Street (☎ 212/752–0810). ⊠ *246 Columbus Ave., between 71st and 72nd Sts.,* ☎ *212/580–1516. AE, DC, MC, V.*

Contemporary

$$$ ✕ **Two Two Two.** On the ground level of a brownstone, this oak-paneled dining room with its skylight, polished-wood floor, and massive chandelier is classy for any neighborhood—and the garden is a pleasure. Representative offerings include spicy salmon tartare with red caviar, lobster risotto with black truffles, filet mignon with wild mushrooms in a red wine sauce, and baked apple in phyllo with raspberry coulis. ⊠ *222 W. 79th St.,* ☎ *212/799–0400. Reservations essential. AE, DC, MC, V. No lunch.*

Continental

$$$ ✕ **Terrace.** About as off the beaten path as you can get (unless you happen to go to Columbia University), this old-world charmer on the 16th floor possesses a studied elegance. Diners enjoy two large dining rooms, a wraparound balcony, staggering views, and occasional harp music; the Continental cuisine isn't bad, either. It's ideal for special occasions (like popping the question). ⊠ *400 W. 119th St., between Amsterdam and Morningside Aves.,* ☎ *212/666–9490. Jacket required. AE, MC, V. Closed Sun. No lunch Sat. and Mon.*

French

$–$$ ✕ **Le Select.** The dining room of this bustling bistro overseen by Eric Demarchelier has a large bar and dining room in front with sconces, globe lights, ceiling fans, exposed brick walls, bare wood floors, and changing photography exhibitions. Hardy bistro dishes such as steak frîtes share the menu with Thai-inspired dumplings, spring rolls, and sensuous satays (skewered and grilled meats or chicken). For a singular dessert, sample the floating island. ⊠ *507 Columbus Ave., between 84th and 85th Sts.,* ☎ *212/875–1993. AE, MC, V.*

$–$$ ✕ **Savann.** Executive chef Danforth Houle (formally of Bouley) per-
★ forms culinary magic at what is possibly the best small restaurant on the west side. The dining area has exposed brick, brass ceiling fans, and track lighting. Among the superb entrées are cornmeal-crusted oysters on creamy celery-root puree and pan-roasted medallions of salmon with spaghetti squash in a roasted tomato vinaigrette. Apple tarte Tatin with cinnamon ice cream makes a wonderful finale. (Savann Est is found at 181 East 78th Street (☎ 212/396–9300). ⊠ *414 Amsterdam Ave., at 80th St.,* ☎ *212/580–0202. AE, MC, V. No lunch.*

Italian

$–$$ ✕ **Carmine's.** Dark woodwork and old-fashioned black-and-white
★ tiles make this hot spot look like an old-timer. It isn't. Still, savvy West
Siders are only too glad to line up for its home-style cooking, served
family style. Kick off a meal with fried calamari or stuffed artichoke;
then move on to the pastas or lobster *fra diabolo* (in a spicy tomato
sauce). ⊠ *2450 Broadway, between 90th and 91st Sts.,* ☎ *212/362–
2200;* ⊠ *200 W. 44th St., between Broadway and 8th Ave.,* ☎ *212/221–
3800. Reservations only for 6 or more. AE. No lunch.*

Japanese

$$ ✕ **Fujiyama Mama.** White-slipcovered side chairs line up like statues
in the vitrine of this creative restaurant with a high-tech design. In the
startling spirit of the place, dishes have names like "Poseidon Adven-
ture" and "Bermuda Triangle." Tell the waiter it's your birthday and
your tempura deep-fried ice cream comes with flickering sparklers
while the DJ lays on a "Happy Birthday to You" from his collection
of weird recordings of the classic tune. ⊠ *467 Columbus Ave., between
82nd and 83rd Sts.,* ☎ *212/769–1144. Reservations essential. AE. No
lunch.*

Malaysian

$–$$ ✕ **Penang Columbus.** Although it lacks the dramatic decor of its SoHo
counterpart, this often crowded eatery with exposed brick walls and
lacquered columns serves more assertively spiced (and more authentic) Malaysian food than the one downtown. A good place to start is
with the house drink, "Coconut Scream," made with light and dark
rum, coconut milk, lotus jelly, and coconut shavings. Follow this with
roti canai, a flaky flat bread to dip in chicken curry. For the main entrée, sample the whole steamed striped bass or one of the many noodle dishes. *Ice kacang,* made with ice cream, shaved ice, red beans, corn,
palm seeds, herbs, lotus jelly, red-rose syrup, and milk, is a refreshing
dessert. ⊠ *240 Columbus Ave., at 71st St.,* ☎ *212/769–3988. AE,
MC, V.*

Mediterranean

$–$$ ✕ **Isabella's.** French doors lead to a pleasant sidewalk café, while in-
side, the charming dining area has Mediterranean-yellow walls, a balcony, French café chairs, and potted palms. Proprietor Steven Hanson
also owns Coconut Grill, Blue Water Grill, Park Avalon, and the Honest Baker, all of which are sources of the house's pasta, bread, and
desserts, which are practically guilt-free; try, for instance, the reduced-
fat chocolate decadence, a flourless chocolate cake with raspberry
sauce, fresh berries, and yogurt. The grilled meat, seafood, and pasta
dishes are all tasty; try, for instance, the three-peppercorn Black Angus
steak with garlic mashed potatoes or penne with eggplant and mushrooms. ⊠ *359 Columbus Ave., at 77th St.,* ☎ *212/724–2100. AE, DC,
MC, V.*

Mexican

$ ✕ **Gabriela's.** This modest cantina with ceramic parrots hanging from
★ the ceiling and a desert wall mural will reward lovers of authentic Mexican cuisine. The menu has wonderful tacos, stuffed with beef tongue
and *chicharron* (deep-fried pork skins) in a memorable bath of tomatillo
and serrano sauce. The house specialty is a whole rotisserie chicken,
Yucatán style, with rice, beans, and plantains. ⊠ *685 Amsterdam
Ave., at 93rd St.,* ☎ *212/961–0574. AE, DC, MC, V.*

Seafood

$$ ✕ **Mad Fish.** This seafood spot has a skylit shingled roof and amusing
murals depicting cocktail parties with fish as the guests. At the long

mahogany bar, patrons can sample boiled periwinkles, steamed lobster, seasonal oysters, and more. The kitchen produces stylish food, such as barbecued bluefish and fish-and-chips—cured fresh cod, gently coated with tempura and quickly deep-fried. Be sure to sample the warm flourless chocolate cake. ⊠ *2182 Broadway, between 77th and 78th Sts.,* ☎ *212/787–0202. AE, DC, MC, V. No lunch.*

$–$$ ✕ **Stingray.** This trendy restaurant has mottled gold walls, a copper-colored tin ceiling, and comfortably upholstered redwood chairs. The most commanding area is the lounge with its cane chairs, colorful tile mosaics, and small cocktail tables. The eclectic food runs the gamut from oysters on the half shell with caper mignonette and green horseradish sour cream to grilled lobsters with roasted corn and tomato salsa. ⊠ *428 Amsterdam Ave., between 80th and 81st Sts.,* ☎ *212/501–7515. AE, DC, MC, V.*

$ ✕ **Joe's Fish Shack.** After you're seated, the menu arrives attached to a clip board and a free small paper cup of cornbread and fried calamari is set before you. The rustic dining room has sawdust on the floor, tables covered with lacquered newspapers, an old rowboat suspended from the ceiling, and fish-related memorabilia. Dig into creamy oyster stew, delicious fried belly clams, and shrimp steamed in beer and Old Bay Spice. ⊠ *520 Columbus Ave., between 85th and 86th Sts.,* ☎ *212/873–0341. AE, DC, MC, V. No lunch.*

Soul

$ ✕ **Emily's.** At this neat and pleasant eatery, the bare Formica tables, paper napkins, and minimalist decor obviously aren't the draw. This bargain-priced Harlem discovery serves some of the best chopped barbecue sandwiches, deep-fried chicken livers (dunk them into the zesty house sauce), corn-bread stuffing (spiked with hot peppers and spices), and homemade potato salad this side of the Mason-Dixon Line. It's also a good bet for breakfast and brunch. ⊠ *1325 5th Ave., at 111th St.,* ☎ *212/996–1212. AE, DC, MC, V.*

Southern

$$ ✕ **Shark Bar.** Since 1990 this popular restaurant has attracted a multicultural clientele and African-American celebrities. The long series of three dining areas includes a friendly bar, portraits of southern farm workers, and an intimate room with red velvet drapes and velvet striped banquettes. The chicken wings, not to be missed, come in three styles: jerked, Harlem-style (floured and deep-fried),and barbecued. Also check out the soul roll, a playful variation on an egg roll made with chicken, collard greens, and black-eyed peas. ⊠ *307 Amsterdam Ave., between 74th and 75th Sts.,* ☎ *212/874–8500. AE, DC, MC, V. No lunch Fri.–Tues.*

$–$$ ✕ **Savannah Club.** Lightened-up soul food is dished out to an attractive crowd at this airy restaurant with ceiling fans, French doors, and a bar flanked by columns rimmed with colored neon. Homemade corn bread and biscuits are giveaways, served with onion jam and sweet-potato butter. But leave room for the house specialty: a bowl of tender chicken and puffy dumplings. For dessert, the dark chocolate pie is a must. ⊠ *2420 Broadway, at 89th St.,* ☎ *212/496–1066. AE, DC, MC, V. No lunch.*

Worth a Special Trip

Contemporary

$$$$ ✕ **River Café.** This is one of New York's most romantic restaurants.
★ Sipping a perfect cocktail or a glass of wine from the extensive list and watching the sun set over lower Manhattan, just across the East River in Brooklyn, is one of the city's great treats. So is the food by Rick

Laakkonen. Favorite dishes include fruitwood-smoked salmon and grilled jumbo quail on white hominy puree. Desserts are dramatic, such as the "Brooklyn Bridge," sculpted out of a chocolate-mousse cake. Although prices are high—there's a three-course dinner or a more elaborate six-course tasting—the service is among the best in the business. Sunday brunch is a joy, lunch less hectic. ✉ *1 Water St., at the East River, Brooklyn,* ☎ *718/522–5200. Reservations essential. Jacket required. AE, DC, MC, V.*

COFFEE BARS AND CAFÉS

Cafés have been a New York institution since beat days. Yet only recently have coffee bars on the Seattle model taken off. Still, they're multiplying at an exponential rate. Plain and decaffeinated drip coffee and espresso are standard. (Note: "Regular coffee" in New York comes with milk or cream; you must add your own sugar if you want your brew sweetened.) You will also find appellations that were never uttered in Italy: *ristretto,* a highly refined espresso; *macchiato,* espresso with just a bit of foam; caffe latte, espresso with steamed milk; cappuccino, half espresso and half steamed milk, with foam; caffe mocha, espresso with steamed chocolate milk; *mochaccino,* cappuccino flavored with chocolate. Most come in a decaf variant or with skim, low-fat, and soy milk, half-and-half, and cream as well as plain whole milk. Many coffee bars offer snacks; others are restaurants in coffee-bar drag. While prices can top more than $2 for an espresso, all offer a bit of civilized sipping.

Starbuck's, Timothy's, and New World Coffee are among the upscale coffee-bar chains around the city. The listings below serve desserts and snacks and cater to tea drinkers as well.

Greenwich Village
✗ **Bruno Bakery** (✉ 506 La Guardia Pl., between Houston and Bleecker Sts., ☎ 212/982–5854). Espresso and pastries are prima at this festive café near New York University; it has 20 marble-topped tables, a stand-up espresso bar, and an oven to warm up the great sandwiches.
✗ **Caffè Dell'Artista** (✉ 46 Greenwich Ave., ☎ 212/645–4431). This West Village Italian café has dark, romantic back rooms, delirium-inducing desserts, and mismatched wooden writing desks doubling as tables, complete with past patron's poems discarded in the drawers.
✗ **Caffè Dante** (✉ 79–81 MacDougal St., between Houston and Bleecker Sts., ☎ 212/982–5275). A longtime Village hangout, this convivial spot has superlative espresso and knockout tiramisu.
✗ **Caffè Reggio** (✉ 119 MacDougal St., between 3rd and Bleecker Sts., ☎ 212/475–9557). In the neighborhood's oldest coffeehouse, where a huge antique machine steams forth espresso, the tiny tables are close together, perfect for eavesdropping on the interesting crowd.
✗ **Caffè Vivaldi** (✉ 32 Jones St., at Bleecker St., ☎ 212/691–7538). Soak up West Village atmosphere in this peaceful café serving coffee, tea, cannoli, and lovely toasted sandwiches.

East Village, Little Italy, SoHo
✗ **Caffè Roma** (✉ 385 Broome St., at Mulberry St., ☎ 212/226–8413). At Manhattan's most authentic Italian coffeehouse, with worn walls and marble tables, the cappuccino is strong, bracing, and foamy.
✗ **Dean and Deluca** (✉ 121 Prince St., ☎ 212/254–8776). The owner of a gourmet market operates this spacious, skylit café, where you can join the well-heeled SoHo shoppers and gallery hoppers and have coffee, a Brie baguette, or a wicked sweet.

✕ **Internet Cafe** (✉ 82 E. 3rd St., between 1st and 2nd Aves., ☎ 212/614–0747). Relax in cyberspace with a PC or Mac, munch sandwiches with names like NetScape, and enjoy computer magazines over a cup of java.

✕ **Le Gamin** (✉ 50 MacDougal St., between Houston and Prince Sts., ☎ 212/254–4678). Enjoy this hip little haven for surprisingly good crepes, café au lait, and conversation.

✕ **Marquet Patisserie** (✉ 15 E. 12th St., between 5th Ave. and University Pl., ☎ 212/229–9313). At this friendly café, you can savor a French pastry and a steaming bowl of café au lait; the menu also includes inventive salads, thick sandwiches, healthy soups, and *croque monsieur*.

✕ **Veniero's Pasticceria** (✉ 342 E. 11th St., near 1st Ave., ☎ 212/674–7264). Now a century old, this bustling bakery-café sells every kind of Italian *dulce,* plus irresistible cheesecakes and pies.

Chelsea

✕ **Big Cup** (✉ 228 8th Ave., between 21st and 22nd Sts., ☎ 212/206–0059). *The* place to meet in Chelsea—grab a chair or sofa, hang out for hours, sip café au lait, and start writing that novel.

✕ **Milan Café and Coffee Bar** (✉ 120 W. 23rd St., ☎ 212/807–1801). A serious chef makes knockout sandwiches, salads, and desserts in this striking eatery with knotty-pine tables and a ceiling of flags.

✕ **Newsbar** (✉ 2 W. 19th St., ☎ 212/255–3996). This ultracasual resting place with four other Manhattan locations has good coffee and tea, a generous offering of magazines, and even Cable News Network.

East Side

✕ **Café Bianco** (✉ 1486 2nd Ave., between 77th and 78th Sts., ☎ 212/988–2655). White tables fill this popular meeting place with excellent coffee, sinful desserts, and small meals; in warm weather, try the back garden.

✕ **Cinema Cafe Coffee Bar.** (✉ 1453 York Ave., at 77th St., ☎ 212/737–9200). Relax on Victorian red sofas or in a cigar lounge with antique lamps as you sip freshly squeezed fruit juices and cappuccino; each menu cover honors a different movie classic.

✕ **Columbus Bakery** (✉ 957 1st Ave., between 52nd and 53rd Sts., ☎ 212/421–0334; ✉ 474 Columbus Ave., between 82nd and 83rd Sts., ☎ 212/724–6880). In an airy space with chandeliers that look like loaves of bread, you can enjoy the same delicious bread, muffins, and pastries that are served at Lutèce.

✕ **Corrado Café** (✉ 1013 3rd Ave., between 60th and 61st Sts., ☎ 212/753–5100). A branch of a successful West Side restaurant, this convenient spot near cinemas and Bloomingdale's has pastries, cookies, and cakes that outshine the coffee.

✕ **Fleur de Jour** (✉ 348 E. 62nd St., ☎ 212/355–2020). Lace curtains, patterned wallpaper, wonderful wicker baskets full of cookies, and an owner who seems to be everybody's best friend make this New York's most welcoming café; there are just five small tables.

✕ **Sant Ambroeus** (✉ 1000 Madison Ave., between 77th and 78th Sts., ☎ 212/570–2211). You'll swear you're in Milan at this very Italian café with red leather banquettes and Maurano chandeliers, where you can enjoy magnificent coffee and desserts, including gelato (Italian ice cream).

✕ **Trois Jean** (✉ 154 E. 79th St., between Lexington and 3rd Aves., ☎ 212/988–4858). Straight out of Paris, this lower-level patisserie in an expensive bistro provides a romantic respite from the standard coffeehouse, with sensational and classy desserts.

West Side

✕ **Café La Fortuna** (✉ 69 W. 71st St., ☏ 212/724–5846). Weary Columbus Avenue strollers have long flocked to this comforting refuge offering Italian pastries, serious coffee, and opera music.

✕ **Café Lalo** (✉ 201 W. 83rd St., ☏ 212/496–6031). Linger over cappuccino, cake, and crossword puzzles at this flashy, Lautrec-themed spot just off Broadway.

✕ **Coffee Pot** (✉ 350 9th Ave., at 49th St., ☏ 212/265–3566). Overstuffed sofas and chairs, mirrors, brass chandeliers, good deals on coffee of the day, and pleasant service make this joint one of the theater district's most pleasant options.

✕ **Cupcake Café** (✉ 522 9th Ave., at 39th St., ☏ 212/465–1530). Although it's in a desolate neighborhood, this funky place is worth the trek for the old-fashioned cupcakes, doughnuts, coffee cake, and hearty soup, accompanied by strong coffee.

✕ **Drip** (✉ 489 Amsterdam Ave., between 83rd and 84th Sts., ☏ 212/875–1032.) Housed in an old auto-parts store, this café has a kitschy atmosphere replete with vintage couches from the '70s, where you can indulge in remarkable Toll House cookies and other delights.

✕ **French Roast Café** (✉ 2340 Broadway, at 85th St., ☏ 212/799–1533). In a re-creation of a Parisian Left Bank café, you can relax over light bistro fare, decent sweets, and coffee; it's open around the clock.

7 Lodging

New York visitors have a fine choice of places to stay—from elegant grand old hotels and bustling modern giants to friendly boutique hotels and money-saving bed-and-breakfasts. Several of the city's best restaurants are now found in hotels. Though Manhattan lodging tends to be expensive, it often offers unique experiences. Where else can you lie in bed while gazing out at the Empire State and Chrysler buildings, or dine in the room where Dorothy Parker and the Algonquin Round Table once held court?

By Amy
McConnell

IF ANY SINGLE ELEMENT OF YOUR TRIP to New York City will cost you dearly, it will be your hotel room. Unlike many European cities, New York offers few low-priced lodgings. Real estate is at a premium here, and labor costs are high, so hoteliers start out with a lot of expenses to cover. And there are enough well-heeled visitors to support competition at the premium end of the spectrum. Considering the healthy occupancy rate, market forces are not likely to drive current prices down. Fleabags and flophouses aside, there's precious little here for less than $100 a night. The city doesn't charge the highest hotel tax in the country, but you should not fail to figure the 13¼% combined taxes plus $2 per room, per night (city occupancy charge) into your calculations. We have scoured the city for good-value hotels and budget properties, but even our $ category includes hotels that run as high as $135 for one night's stay in a double.

Our price categories are based on the "rack rate," or the standard room cost that hotels print in their brochures and quote over the phone. You almost never need to pay this much. If you book directly with the hotel, ask about corporate rates, seasonal special offers, or weekend deals. The last typically include such extras as complimentary meals, drinks, or tickets to events. Ask your travel agent for brochures, and look for advertisements in travel magazines or the Sunday travel sections of major newspapers such as the *New York Times,* the *Washington Post,* or the *Los Angeles Times.* Of course, booking any all-inclusive package, weekend or longer, will reduce the hotel rate.

If you should be unfortunate enough to arrive in New York City without a hotel reservation, you can also try the most direct method of lowering the room rate: asking. In periods of low occupancy, hotels—especially at the expensive end of the market—will often reduce the price on rooms that would otherwise remain empty.

In general, Manhattan hotels don't measure up to those in other U.S. cities in terms of room size, parking, or outside landscaping. But, since this is a sophisticated city, New York hotels usually compensate with fastidious service, sprucely maintained properties, and restaurants that hold their own in a city of knowledgeable diners.

Common sense should tell you not to anticipate the same kind of personal service from even a top-flight convention hotel, such as the New York Hilton, as you would from a smaller, sedate property like the Doral Tuscany, even though both have rooms in the same price range. Know your own taste and choose accordingly.

Note: Even the most exclusive hotels have security gaps. Be discreet with valuables everywhere, and stay alert in public areas.

CATEGORY	COST*
$$$$	over $260
$$$	$190–$260
$$	$135–$190
$	under $135

All prices are for a standard double room, excluding 13¼% city and state taxes.

Reservations

New York is constantly full of vacationers, conventioneers, and business travelers, all requiring hotel space. Try to book your room as far in advance as possible, using a major credit card to guarantee the reservation; you might even want to work through a travel agent. Because this is a tight market, overbooking can be a problem, and "lost" reservations are not unheard of. When signing in, take a pleasant but firm attitude; if there is a mix-up, chances are the outcome will be an upgrade or a free night.

Hotels with famous restaurants appreciate it when guests who want to use those facilities book tables when they make their room reservations. All chefs mentioned were in charge at press time. Call to confirm the name under the toque. It can make *all* the difference.

Services

Unless otherwise noted in the individual descriptions, all the hotels listed have the following features and services: private baths, central heating, air-conditioning, private telephones, no-smoking rooms or floors, on-premises dining, room service (though not necessarily 24-hour or short-notice), TV (including cable and pay-per-view films), and a routine concierge staff. Almost all hotels now have dataports and phones with voice mail. Hotels in the higher price categories generally offer baby-sitting (arranged through the concierge) and valet service. Most large hotels have video or high-speed checkout capability.

Pools are a rarity, but most properties have fitness centers; we note only those that are on the premises, but other hotels usually have arrangements for guests at nearby facilities, for which a fee is sometimes charged.

Those bringing a car to Manhattan should note the lack of hotel parking. Many properties in all price ranges *do* have parking facilities, but they are often at independent garages that charge as much as $20 or more per day. A few hotels offer free parking; they are noted in the following reviews.

Midtown East

$$$$ 🖫 **The Drake.** This Swissôtel property caters to business travelers. Just off Park Avenue in the heart of corporate Manhattan, it provides conveniences such as fax machines in every room and two hours' use of the extensive business center. A complete renovation has brought spanking-new carpets and wooden furnishings to the modern, art deco rooms, all of which have oversized desks and overstuffed chairs and couches. Visitors and locals alike thoroughly enjoy Swiss specialties and hard-to-find Swiss wines at the convivial Drake Bar. ⊠ *440 Park Ave., 10022,* ☎ *212/421–0900 or 800/372–5369,* 🖷 *212/371–4190. 508 rooms. Restaurant, bar, in-room safes, refrigerators, health club, business services, meeting rooms. AE, D, DC, MC, V.*

$$$$ 🖫 **Four Seasons.** Architect I. M. Pei—responsible for the Louvre Pyra-
★ mid, among other modernist icons—designed this limestone-clad stepped spire amid the prime shops of 57th Street. Everything here comes in epic proportions—from the prices (it's New York's most expensive hotel); to the guest rooms, which average 600 square ft; to the aptly named, sky-high Grand Foyer, with its French limestone pillars, marble, onyx, and acre upon acre of blond wood. The soundproof guest rooms offer the ultimate in luxury, with enormous English sycamore walk-in closets, 10-ft-high ceilings, and spacious bathrooms with tubs that fill in 60 seconds. ⊠ *57 E. 57th St., 10022,* ☎ *212/758–5700 or 800/332–3442,* 🖷 *212/758–5711. 370 rooms. Restaurant, bar, in-room safes, minibars, spa, business services, meeting rooms. AE, DC, MC, V.*

$$$$ 🖫 **New York Palace.** A multimillion-dollar renovation completed in spring 1997 transformed this hotel into one of New York's finest. Long known for its landmark 1882 Villard House, which houses many of the hotel's public rooms, the Palace now offers one of the city's most

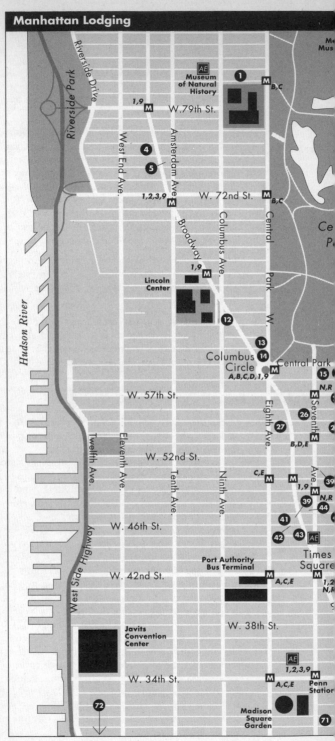

Manhattan Lodging

KEY

AE American Express Office

E. 79th St.

E. 72nd St.

Fifth Ave.

Madison Ave.

Park Ave.

Lexington Ave.

Third Ave.

Second Ave.

First Ave.

York Ave.

FDR Dr.

Queensboro Br.

E. 59th St.

E. 57th St.

Sutton Pl.

E. 52nd St.

East River

E. 46th St.

Grand
Central
Terminal

E. 42nd St.

E. 38th St.

Rockefeller
Center

Public
Library

Empire
State
Building

E. 34th St.

Avenue of the Americas

(Sixth Ave.)

rald
uare

0   800 yards

0   800 meters

elaborate hotel health clubs and a new lobby restaurant; in addition, the celebrated Le Cirque restaurant now occupies the Villard House. The newly redecorated guest rooms are large by Manhattan standards; those on the west side afford views of St. Patrick's Cathedral and Rockefeller Center. All are equipped with fax machines. ☒ *455 Madison Ave., 10022,* ☏ *212/888–7000 or 800/697–2522,* FAX *212/303–6000. 900 rooms. 2 restaurants, 2 bars, breakfast room, in-room safes, minibars, spa, business services, meeting rooms. AE, D, DC, MC, V.*

$$$$ ⌷ **Omni Berkshire Place.** Omni Berkshire's flagship hotel brought a new level of sophistication to the Omni name when it reopened in 1995. Though the cavernous reception area is less than inviting, there's a dramatic, two-story atrium lounge with a fireplace and an elaborately stained dark-wood floor; here you can sip tea while watching Siamese fighterfish swimming in little bowls at your table. The spacious guest rooms (all 375 square ft) have a contemporary, Asian-influenced simplicity and high-tech comforts such as fax machines and bedside comfort controls. ☒ *21 E. 52nd St., 10022,* ☏ *212/753–5800 or 800/843–6664,* FAX *212/754–5020. 396 rooms. Restaurant, bar, minibars, health club, business services, meeting rooms. AE, D, DC, MC, V.*

$$$$ ⌷ **The Peninsula.** Step into the marble Art Nouveau lobby off 55th Street and you'll be transported back to the 1940s, when bell captains wore sailor suits and afternoon tea was an institution. Guest rooms are decorated with rose-colored velour, mahogany furnishings, and framed art nouveau prints; many have sweeping views down 5th Avenue. Bathrobes and slippers are provided in all rooms, along with a welcome box of handmade truffles. The sumptuous marble bathrooms have bidets, contoured soaking tubs (many of them Jacuzzis), and collectible Molton Brown English bath products. The rooftop health club has been called the Rolls-Royce of hotel fitness centers; it's truly a knockout. ☒ *700 5th Ave., 10019,* ☏ *212/247–2200 or 800/262–9467,* FAX *212/903–3943. 243 rooms. 2 restaurants, bar, in-room safes, minibars, indoor pool, beauty salon, spa, meeting rooms. AE, D, DC, MC, V.*

$$$$ ⌷ **St. Regis.** When Sheraton restored this 5th Avenue Beaux Arts land-
★   mark, planners set a high standard for themselves, with prices to match. Public spaces are ultrachic—from the celebrated restaurant, Lespinasse (☞ Chapter 6); to the Astor Court tea lounge, with its trompe-l'oeil cloud ceiling; to the King Cole Bar, an institution in itself, with its famous Maxfield Parrish mural. Guest rooms, all serviced by butlers, are straight out of a period film, with high ceilings, crystal chandeliers, silk wall coverings, Louis XV–style furnishings, and expensive amenities such as Tiffany silver services. Marble bathrooms, with tubs, stall showers, and double sinks, are outstanding. ☒ *2 E. 55th St., 10022,* ☏ *212/753–4500 or 800/759–7550,* FAX *212/787–3447. 213 rooms. Restaurant, bar, in-room safes, minibars, beauty salon, massage, sauna, health club, business services, meeting rooms. AE, D, DC, MC, V.*

$$$$ ⌷ **U.N. Plaza–Park Hyatt.** It's easy to miss the entrance to this favorite among the business and diplomatic set—it's on a quiet side street near (naturally) the United Nations. Rooms, which begin on the 28th floor, have breathtaking views and framed tapestries donated by various missions. The delightful 27th-floor pool (also with dazzling views) and the rooftop tennis courts attract top athletes. Service throughout the hotel is first-rate, and the business center is open 24 hours a day. ☒ *1 United Nations Plaza, 10017,* ☏ *212/758–1234 or 800/223–1234,* FAX *212/702–5051. 427 rooms. Restaurant, in-room safes, minibars, pool, health club, business services, meeting rooms. AE, D, DC, MC, V.*

$$$–$$$$ ⌷ **Waldorf-Astoria.** This landmark Art Deco masterpiece serves as a hub of city life; the lobby, with its original murals and mosaics and elaborate plaster ornamentation, is a meeting place for the rich and powerful. Guest rooms, each individually decorated but all traditional

and elegant, start at the low end of the $$$ category. Astoria-level rooms have the added advantages of great views, fax machines, and access to the Astoria lounge, where a lovely afternoon tea is served free. The Tower section, well known to heads of state and discerning business travelers, is the most exclusive and grand section of the hotel. ⊠ *301 Park Ave., 10022,* ☎ *212/355–3000 or 800/925–3673,* FAX *212/872–7272. 1,380 rooms. 4 restaurants, minibars, health club, business services, meeting rooms. AE, D, DC, MC, V.*

$$$ ⊞ **The Fitzpatrick.** This cozy hotel just south of Bloomingdale's, the
★ first American venture for an established Irish company, is a winner in terms of value and charm. More than half of the units are true suites that are priced well below the market average, even on weekdays. All have emerald green carpets and traditional furnishings and modern, well-equipped bathrooms. The mostly Irish staff is exceptionally friendly and cheerful, which might explain why Gregory Peck, Liam Neeson, various Kennedys, Sinead O'Connor, and the Chieftains have all been guests. ⊠ *687 Lexington Ave., 10022,* ☎ *212/355–0100 or 800/367–7701,* FAX *212/355–1371. 92 rooms. Restaurant, bar, meeting room. AE, D, DC, MC, V.*

$$$ ⊞ **Loews New York Hotel.** This moderately priced hotel is lively and fun, attracting visitors from around the globe. Rooms are comfortable and well designed. During low-occupancy periods, you can book rooms here for the upper end at less expensive prices; even suites are below $250. ⊠ *Lexington Ave. at 51st St., 10022,* ☎ *212/752–7000 or 800/836–6471,* FAX *212/752–3817. 722 rooms. Restaurant, in-room safes, refrigerators, barbershop, beauty salon, health club, business services, meeting rooms. AE, D, DC, MC, V.*

$$$ ⊞ **The Tudor.** Run by the London-based Sarova Hotel Group, this charming, medium-size property is close to the United Nations and Grand Central Terminal. Interior spaces are classic and unassuming, with hardwood reproduction furniture upholstered in brocades and velvets, marble floors, and handmade carpets in the public areas. The 20-story landmark building dates from the '20s and is part of Tudor City, with its private park and fanciful Englishness. ⊠ *304 E. 42nd St., 10017,* ☎ *212/986–8800 or 800/879–8836,* FAX *212/986–1758. 300 rooms. Restaurant, in-room safes, minibars, health club, business services, meeting rooms. AE, D, DC, MC, V.*

$$ ⊞ **The Beverly.** This suite-dominated hotel's plush wood-paneled lobby, with a crystal chandelier, an original terrazzo floor, and Art Deco furniture, inspires confidence in what's upstairs. The spacious accommodations here are popular with visitors to the nearby United Nations, Euro-tourists, and business travelers. Corner suites (Nos. 1801, 1805, and about six more) cost slightly more but are especially grand; some have terraces and carved wooden beds. There is a complimentary Continental breakfast. ⊠ *125 E. 50th St., 10022,* ☎ *212/753–2700 or 800/223–0945,* FAX *212/759–7300. 163 rooms. Restaurant, in-room safes, kitchenettes, beauty salon. AE, DC, MC, V.*

$$ ⊞ **San Carlos.** Comfortable and plain, this small residential-style property has friendly service, a safe and convenient location, and clean modern rooms with plenty of space. Every room has a kitchenette, a walk-in closet, and two phones. Continental breakfast is complimentary. ⊠ *150 E. 50th St., 10022,* ☎ *212/755–1800 or 800/722–2012,* FAX *212/688–9778. 146 rooms. Breakfast room. AE, DC, MC, V.*

$ ⊞ **Pickwick Arms Hotel.** This convenient East Side establishment charges $99 a night for standard doubles and has older singles with shared baths for as little as $50. The marble-clad lobby is often bustling, since this place is routinely booked solid by bargain hunters. Privations you endure to save a buck start and end with the Lilliputian size of some rooms, all of which have cheap-looking furnishings. However, the place is well run and safe, and some rooms look over the Manhattan skyline. ⊠ *230 E. 51st St., 10022,* ☎ *212/355–0300 or 800/742–5945,* FAX *212/755–5029. 370 rooms. Café. AE, DC, MC, V.*

$ 🖵 **Vanderbilt YMCA.** Of the various Manhattan Ys offering accommodations, this one has the best location and facilities, including a full-scale fitness center. Rooms are little more than dormitory-style cells, each with a bed (bunks in doubles), a dresser drawer, and a TV; singles have desks. There are no private baths, but communal showers and toilets are clean. The Turtle Bay neighborhood is safe, convenient, and interesting (the United Nations is a few blocks away). ⊠ *224 E. 47th St., 10017,* ☎ *212/756–9600,* FAX *212/752–0210. 370 rooms. Restaurant, 2 indoor pools, sauna, health club, coin laundry, meeting rooms. MC, V.*

Midtown West

$$$$ 🖵 **Le Parker Meridien.** This dramatic, modern French hotel boasts one of the city's more striking lobbies: Here are two-story arched mirrors with palms and Doric columns, an Islamic-style stained-glass roof, three colors of marble, full-size trees, and a sheer cliff of blond wood at the registration desk. Other standout features are the rooftop swimming pool, comprehensive Club La Raquette health club, and the congenial '30s-style Bar Montparnasse, with nightly entertainment. Upstairs, the well-kept rooms have an elegant neoclassical motif in soothing tans and browns; most rooms face the park. ⊠ *118 W. 57th St., 10019,* ☎ *212/245–5000 or 800/543–4300,* FAX *212/708–7477. 698 rooms. Restaurant, in-room safes, minibars, indoor pool, spa, business services, meeting rooms. AE, D, DC, MC, V.*

$$$$ 🖵 **The Michelangelo.** Italophiles will feel right at home at this deluxe hotel, with its very long, wide lobby lounge full of multihued marble and Veronese-esque oil paintings. Upstairs, rooms are bigger than you'd expect and come in a range of styles, from art deco to French country. All have king-size beds, multiline phones, and marble bathrooms equipped with bidets, TVs, phones, and 55-gallon tubs. The staff is helpful; the concierge is a cut above those found in other New York City hotels. ⊠ *152 W. 51st St., 10019,* ☎ *212/765–1900 or 800/237–0990,* FAX *212/581–7618. 178 rooms. Restaurant, bar, minibars, exercise room, meeting rooms. AE, DC, MC, V.*

$$$$ 🖵 **Rihga Royal.** The Rihga Royal Hotel group has long been recog-
★ nized for its luxury properties in Japan, and its New York property has remained a low-profile favorite among celebrities and business travelers since its opening in 1990. Each of its luxurious, contemporary-style suites has a spacious living room with bay windows and a bedroom enclosed by French doors; the large marble bathrooms have glass-enclosed showers and separate tubs. Every suite has a fax machine, but big spenders prefer the Pinnacle Suites, which have CD players, cellular phones, and "miniature business center" machines that print and copy. ⊠ *151 W. 54th St., 10019,* ☎ *212/307–5000 or 800/937–5454,* FAX *212/765–6530. 500 suites. Restaurant, in-room safes, minibars, in-room VCRs, exercise rooms, business services, meeting rooms. AE, D, DC, MC, V.*

$$$ 🖵 **The Algonquin.** This beloved landmark hotel, where the Round Table group of writers and wits once met for lunch, still shelters celebrities, particularly literary types visiting nearby publishing houses or the *New Yorker* magazine offices. The heartbeat of the hotel is the lobby, with its grandfather clock, overstuffed chairs, and house cat, Matilda. Rooms have homey, Victorian-style fixtures and furnishings; specialty suites are dedicated to Dorothy Parker, James Thurber, and *Vanity Fair.*

Continental breakfast is complimentary. ✉ *59 W. 44th St., 10036,* ☎ *212/840–6800 or 800/548–0345,* 𝔽𝔸𝕏 *212/944–1618. 165 rooms. 2 restaurants, bar, in-room safes, cabaret, library, business services, meeting rooms, free parking (weekends only). AE, D, DC, MC, V.*

$$$ ▦ **The Mansfield.** Built in 1904 as lodging for well-heeled bachelors, this small hotel is Victorian and clublike. Turn-of-the-century details abound here: from the column-supported coffered ceiling, warm ivory walls, and yellow limestone floor in the lobby to the guest rooms' black marble bathrooms, ebony-stained floors and doors, dark wood venetian blinds, and sleigh beds. There are movies in the audiovisual lounge and nightly piano and harp recitals in the intimate concert salon, where complimentary breakfast and after-theater dessert are served. ✉ *12 W. 44th St., 10036,* ☎ *212/944–6050 or 800/255–5167,* 𝔽𝔸𝕏 *212/764–4477. 123 rooms. In-room VCRs, cinema, concert hall, library, free parking. AE, MC, V.*

$$$ ▦ **Marriott Marquis.** This giant in the heart of the theater district is one of the places New Yorkers love to hate. It's obvious, brash, and bright, with a virtual minicity of restaurants, shops, meeting rooms, ballrooms, and even a large theater within its vast confines. As at other Marriotts, every room looks alike, but they are clean, pleasant, and functional, with desks, swivel chairs, and soothing framed prints. Some rooms have dramatic urban views. ✉ *1535 Broadway, at 45th St., 10036,* ☎ *212/398–1900 or 800/843–4898,* 𝔽𝔸𝕏 *212/704–8966. 1,911 rooms. 3 restaurants, 3 bars, café, coffee shop, in-room safes, beauty salon, health club, business services, meeting rooms. AE, D, DC, MC, V.*

$$$ ▦ **The Paramount.** The work of the team responsible for the Royal-
★   ton (☞ *below*) and Morgans (☞ *below*), the fashionable Paramount caters to the forever young and arty. In the Philippe Starck lobby, a sheer platinum wall and a glamorous sweep of staircase lead to a mezzanine gallery of squashy seating, tiny nightclub-style table lamps, and a restaurant—the perfect place to spy on the glitterati below. Rooms are minute, but they have framed headboards, several of them bearing the print of Vermeer's *The Lacemaker,* and conical steel sinks in the bathrooms—all bearing the Starck stamp. ✉ *235 W. 46th St., 10036,* ☎ *212/764–5500 or 800/225–7474,* 𝔽𝔸𝕏 *212/575–4892. 610 rooms. 2 restaurants, bar, café, in-room VCRs, exercise room, nursery, business services. AE, D, DC, MC, V.*

$$$ ▦ **Renaissance.** The former Ramada Renaissance was redone to suit the business community, though vacationers often take advantage of its low off-season rates and its proximity to Broadway. Elevators lead from street level to the third-floor art deco reception area. On the second floor are two bars and the new Foley's Fish House, a restaurant with panoramic views of Times Square. Rooms are warm and inviting, with dark cherry wood and a tan-and-black color scheme. The marble bathrooms have deep soaking tubs. ✉ *2 Times Sq., 10036,* ☎ *212/765–7676 or 800/628–5222,* 𝔽𝔸𝕏 *212/765–1962. 305 rooms. Restaurant, bar, in-room safes, minibars, in-room VCRs, exercise room, business services, meeting rooms. AE, D, DC, MC, V.*

$$$ ▦ **The Royalton.** Ian Schrager and the late Steve Rubell's second Manhattan hotel (Morgans came first) is a second home to the world's media, music, and fashion-biz folk. The centerpiece of each Philippe Starck–designed guest room is a low-lying, custom-made bed with built-in pin lights; there are also geometrically challenged but comfy blue velvet chairs, and window banquettes. The staff here does a good job catering to people who feel it's their lot in life to be waited on. The restaurant, 44, is predictably booked solid by New York–style gurus. ✉ *44 W. 44th St., 10036,* ☎ *212/869–4400 or 800/635–9013,* 𝔽𝔸𝕏 *212/575–*

0012. 168 rooms. Restaurant, bar, minibars, exercise room, meeting rooms. AE, DC, MC, V.

$$$ ☆ 🏨 **The Shoreham.** This is a miniature, low-attitude version of the Royalton—and it's comfortable to boot. Almost everything is metal or metal colored, from perforated steel bed headboards (lit from behind) to the steel sink in the shiny, tiny bathrooms to the silver-gray carpets. Other pleasant touches include black oval night tables with digital gadgetry and a single red rose, and in-room VCRs and CD players. And, darling, those cedar-lined closets are to *die for.* ✉ *33 W. 55th St., 10019,* ☎ *212/247–6700,* 📠 *212/765–9741. 84 rooms. Breakfast room, in-room VCRs. AE, DC, MC, V.*

$$$ ☆ 🏨 **The Warwick.** Catercorner from the New York Hilton and well placed for theater and points west, this handsome, cozy classic belongs to a Paris-based chain. The decor is the familiar, comforting hotel version of Regency style, with thick carpets and floral drapes. Amenities include two-line phones, marble bathrooms, and mahogany armoires in surprisingly ample rooms. ✉ *65 W. 54th St., 10019,* ☎ *212/247–2700,* 📠 *212/489–3926. 427 rooms. Restaurant, minibars, exercise room, meeting rooms. AE, DC, MC, V.*

$$–$$$ 🏨 **New York Hilton.** You could easily spend a week in New York without setting foot outside this vast hotel, whose myriad business facilities, eating establishments, and shops are designed for convenience. Hilton spends vast sums to keep the hotel trim, and it shows: There's a distinctive landscaped driveway and a sprawling, brassy lobby—more businesslike than beautiful but always buzzing. Considering the size of this property, guest rooms are surprisingly well maintained, if not always spacious or fashionable. ✉ *1335 6th Ave., 10019,* ☎ *212/586–7000 or 800/445–8667,* 📠 *212/261–5902. 2,041 rooms. 2 restaurants, café, sports bar, in-room safes, minibars, barbershop, beauty salon, health club, business services, meeting rooms. AE, D, DC, MC, V.*

$$ 🏨 **Ameritania.** This hotel's proximity to popular nightspots such as the Ritz ensures a youthful clientele. Rooms were renovated in 1997; they're simple and modern, with bright emerald green, rose, and blue color schemes; the black marble bathrooms are small but functional. A new theme restaurant, Characters, offers entertainment based on characters from the movies. ✉ *1701 Broadway, 10019,* ☎ *212/247–5000 or 800/922–0330,* 📠 *212/247–3316. 209 rooms. Restaurant, bar, exercise room. AE, D, DC, MC, V.*

$ ☆ 🏨 **Broadway Bed & Breakfast.** In the heart of the theater district, this reasonably priced B&B is friendly and comfortable. Continental breakfast is served in the Victorian-style lobby, whose brick walls, stocked bookshelves, and framed photos of old New York encourage lingering. The building, which dates from 1918, was completely renovated in 1995, and everything from the freshly painted and carpeted rooms to the gleaming dark-wood stair banisters is meticulously maintained. ✉ *264 W. 46th St., 10036,* ☎ *212/997–9200 or 800/826–6300,* 📠 *212/768–2807. 40 rooms. Breakfast room. AE, D, DC, MC, V.*

$ 🏨 **Herald Square Hotel.** Sculpted cherubs on its facade and vintage magazine covers adorning the hallways inside lend character to this historic hotel, which is housed in the former *Life* magazine building. Rooms are basic and clean, with deep-green carpets and floral-print bedspreads; all have TVs, phones with voice mail, and in-room safes. There's no concierge and no room service, but what does it matter when rooms cost as little as $89? ✉ *19 W. 31st St., 10001,* ☎ *212/279–4017 or 800/727–1888,* 📠 *212/643–9208. 127 rooms. In-room safes. AE, D, MC, V.*

$ 🏨 **Hotel Edison.** This offbeat old hotel is a popular budget stop for tour groups from here and abroad. The loan-shark murder scene in *The Godfather* was shot in what is now Sophia's restaurant, and the pink-plaster coffee shop is a hot place to eavesdrop on show-business gossip. Guest rooms are clean and fresh; bathrooms are miniscule. There's no room service, but this part of the theater district has so many restaurants and delis that it doesn't matter much. ✉ *228 W. 47th St., 10036,* ☎ *212/840–5000 or 800/637–7070,* FAX *212/596–6850. 1,000 rooms. Restaurant, bar, coffee shop, beauty salon, airport shuttle. AE, D, DC, MC, V.*

$ ⊞ **Park Savoy.** Rooms here cost as little as $57 (rates go up to $126), and you're in close proximity to Central Park, Carnegie Hall, and the caviar at Petrossian. All of this more than makes up for the lack of room service, direct-dial phone, and cable TV channels. Room decor is eclectic (William Morris–pattern drapes, wine-color carpet, and rock-hard beds). The staff (okay, the guy at the desk) knows all the guests, and there's a lot of repeat business. ✉ *158 W. 58th St., 10019,* ☎ *212/245–5755,* FAX *212/765–0668. 96 rooms. AE, MC, V.*

$ ⊞ **Portland Square Hotel.** You can't beat this theater district old-timer for value, with its clean, simple rooms, exercise facility (albeit tiny), coin laundry, and business services. James Cagney lived in the building, and—as the story goes—a few of his Radio City Rockette acquaintances lived upstairs. Rooms have green carpets and floral-print bedspreads; those on the east wing have oversize bathrooms. ✉ *132 W. 47th St., 10036,* ☎ *212/382–0600 or 800/388–8988,* FAX *212/382–0684. 142 rooms. In-room safes, exercise room, coin laundry. AE, MC, V.*

$ ⊞ **Quality Hotel and Suites.** This relatively small prewar hotel is near many theaters, Rockefeller Center, and some of the city's best-known Brazilian restaurants. The lobby is mighty peculiar with its narrow corridor that snakes off for a mile or so around the corner, its school of photo-realist cityscape murals, and some rather handsome Art Deco Bakelite lights. The rooms are very plain, but most are well maintained and clean. This is a popular stop for South Americans, although you'll see a few U.S. business travelers, too. Single women might find the area eerie at night. ✉ *59 W. 46th St., 10036,* ☎ *212/719–2300 or 800/848–0020. 90 rooms. Café, business services. AE, D, DC, MC, V.*

$ ⊞ **Wellington Hotel.** This large, old-fashioned property's main advantages are reasonable prices and a location near Carnegie Hall (both are draws for many budget-conscious Europeans). Rooms are small but clean; baths are serviceable. ✉ *871 7th Ave., at 55th St., 10019,* ☎ *212/247–3900 or 800/652–1212,* FAX *212/581–1719. 700 rooms. Restaurant, coffee shop, beauty salon. AE, DC, MC, V.*

Central Park South/59th Street

$$$$ ⊞ **Essex House.** The owners, Japan's Nikko Hotels, have done won-
★ ders for this stately Central Park South property. The public areas are Art Deco masterpieces fit for Fred and Ginger. The talented Christian Delouvrier oversees the cuisine, both in the informal Café Botanica (which faces Central Park and resembles a lush prewar English greenhouse) and in the acclaimed Les Célébrités, where art painted by luminaries covers the walls. Guest rooms resemble those in a splendid English country home, elegant and inviting. The staff is discreet, efficient, and friendly. ✉ *160 Central Park S, between 6th and 7th Aves., 10019,* ☎ *212/247–0300,* FAX *212/315–1839. 597 rooms. 2 restaurants, bar, in-room safes, minibars, in-room VCRs, spa, business services, meeting rooms. AE, D, DC, MC, V.*

$$$$ ⊞ **The Plaza.** With its unsurpassed location opposite Central Park and F.A.O. Schwarz, the Plaza is probably the most high-profile of all New York hotels. Donald Trump bought it (in 1988), the fictional Eloise ran riot in it, and film upon film has featured it. Its legendary reputa-

tion is well deserved: Even the smallest guest rooms have crystal chandeliers and 14-ft-high ceilings. A stroll by the fin-de-siècle Palm Court or a view of the park and 5th Avenue from a table in the Edwardian Room will give you a sense of what makes the city tick. ⊠ *5th Ave. at 59th St., 10019,* ☎ *212/759–3000 or 800/759–3000,* ☏ *212/546–5324. 805 rooms. 3 restaurants, 2 bars, café, minibars, exercise room, business services, meeting rooms. AE, D, DC, MC, V.*

$$$$ ▦ **Ritz-Carlton.** Everything about this hotel is first-class, from the pres-
★ tigious Central Park South address to the very polished service to the fine art that covers virtually every wall. Guest rooms are graced with rich brocades, polished woods, and marble bathrooms; some have breathtaking Central Park views. The restaurant, Fantino, serves award-winning cuisine on china designed by Gianni Versace. ⊠ *112 Central Park S, 10019,* ☎ *212/757–1900 or 800/241–3333,* ☏ *212/757–9620. 214 rooms. Restaurant, bar, health club, business services, meeting rooms. AE, D, DC, MC, V.*

Upper East Side

$$$$ ▦ **The Carlyle.** European tradition and Manhattan swank shake hands
★ at New York's least hysterical grand hotel. Everything about this Madison Avenue landmark suggests refinement, from the Mark Hampton–designed rooms, with their fine antique furniture and artfully framed Audubons and botanicals, to the first-rate service, which combines old-school elegance with genuine friendliness. Many guests head straight to the beloved Bemelmans Bar, named after Ludwig Bemelmans, illustrator of the beloved children's book character Madeline and the "twelve little girls in two straight lines"; he created the murals here. Others come just to hear Barbara Cook or Bobby Short perform at the clubby Café Carlyle. ⊠ *35 E. 76th St., 10021,* ☎ *212/744–1600 or 800/227–5737,* ☏ *212/717–4682. 190 rooms. Restaurant, bar, café, kitchenettes, minibars, spa, meeting rooms. AE, DC, MC, V.*

$$$$ ▦ **The Lowell.** You may be tempted to check in long term at this elegant, pied-à-terre–style landmark on a tree-lined street between Madison and Park avenues. Guest rooms, more than half of which are suites, have all the comforts of home, from kitchenettes (or minibars) to stocked bookshelves to umbrellas; 33 of the suites have working fireplaces, and 10 have private terraces. In addition to a gym suite with its own private fitness center, there's a brand-new Hollywood suite with an entertainment center and framed photos of Hollywood stars. The Pembroke Room serves a fine high tea, and the Post House is renowned for its steaks. ⊠ *28 E. 63rd St., 10021,* ☎ *212/838–1400 or 800/221–4444,* ☏ *212/319–4230. 65 rooms. Restaurant, breakfast room, kitchenettes, minibars, in-room VCRs, health club. AE, D, DC, MC, V.*

$$$$ ▦ **The Mark.** You'll find this friendly baby grand hotel a block north
★ of the Carlyle and steps from Central Park. The feeling of calm that pervades the Biedermeier-furnished marble lobby follows you into the deep-green and burgundy bar, where even lone women travelers feel comfortable. The serenity continues at Mark's Restaurant, where afternoon tea is an institution. Bedrooms are elegant and serene, with cream-colored walls, museum-quality prints, plump armchairs, a potted palm or two, and Belgian bed linens. ⊠ *25 E. 77th St., 10021,* ☎ *212/744–4300 or 800/843–6275,* ☏ *212/744–2749. 180 rooms. Restaurant, minibars, in-room VCRs, health club, meeting rooms. AE, D, DC, MC, V.*

$$$$ ▦ **The Pierre.** Before Canada's Four Seasons hotel group opened its eponymous flagship on 57th Street, the Pierre was its pride and joy, and it remains a high-profile presence. Quite the opposite of the understated Four Seasons, the Pierre owes a lot to the Palace of Versailles,

with its chandeliers and handmade carpets, murals depicting putti, and Corinthian columns in the Rotunda lounge (great for tea). Guest rooms are grand and traditional, with much chintz and dark wood; the gleaming Art Deco bathrooms are spacious for New York. You'll appreciate the polished yet unpretentious staff. ⊠ *5th Ave. at 61st St., 10021,* ☎ *212/838–8000 or 800/332–3442,* ‍‍‍‍‍FAX *212/758–1615. 202 rooms. Restaurant, bar, in-room safes, beauty salon, health club, meeting rooms. AE, D, DC, MC, V.*

$$$$ ⊞ **Plaza Athénée.** The French half of Forte Hotels' New York offerings used to be snooty to noncelebrities, but much of that has changed. What hasn't changed is the quiet elegance of the guest rooms and marble baths. Even small rooms are well thought out, if not opulent, in soothing hues of beige and coral, with French Directoire–style mahogany furniture and hand-painted silk drapery and bedspreads. The clubby lounge has faux-leopard-skin chairs and an Old World ambience. ⊠ *37 E. 64th St.,* ☎ *212/734–9100 or 800/447–8800,* ‍‍‍‍‍FAX *212/772–0958. 153 rooms. Restaurant, bar, in-room safes, exercise room, meeting rooms. AE, D, DC, MC, V.*

$$$$ ⊞ **The Westbury.** The English half of Forte Hotels' New York empire combines understated British formality with genuine friendliness. Many come just to have drinks in the clubby Polo Restaurant and Bar, which has leather banquettes and a fine view of Madison Avenue. Rooms and suites have the feel of an English manor, with floral chintz, Oriental rugs, and mahogany furnishings. Bathrooms are less than spacious, but most have windows that keep them from feeling stuffy. The small but immaculately maintained exercise room overlooks Madison Avenue. ⊠ *69th St. at Madison Ave., 10021,* ☎ *212/535–2000 or 800/321–1569,* ‍‍‍‍‍FAX *212/535–5058. 228 rooms. Restaurant, exercise room, meeting rooms. AE, D, DC, MC, V.*

$$–$$$ ⊞ **Hotel Wales.** In the tony neighborhood of Carnegie Hill, this modestly priced hotel is a pleasant surprise. It occupies a landmark building, and every effort has been made to retain the turn-of-the-century mood—from the fin-de-siècle–style lobby to the "Pied Piper" parlor, where vintage children's illustrations cover the walls. Bathrooms are miniscule, and guest rooms are slightly worse for the wear, but fireplaces and fine oak woodwork make up for these faults. A generous European-style breakfast and nightly dessert buffet are served in the parlor. ⊠ *1295 Madison Ave., 10128,* ☎ *212/876–6000 or 800/528–5252,* ‍‍‍‍‍FAX *212/860–7000. 86 rooms. Breakfast room, in-room VCRs. AE, MC, V.*

$$ ⊞ **The Franklin.** It's like sleeping in an art installation. This former seedy, low-rent hostel was transformed into its current incarnation as a ravishing, funky, uptown version of the Paramount. The lobby feels like a private club, with black granite, brushed steel, and cherry-wood decor. Rooms can be very, very small (some measuring 100 square ft), but they have pleasant grape-colored carpeting, custom-built steel furniture, gauzy white canopies over the beds, and cedar closets. ⊠ *164 E. 87th St., 10128,* ☎ *212/369–1000 or 800/428–5252,* ‍‍‍‍‍FAX *212/369–8000. 47 rooms. Breakfast room, in-room VCRs, library, free parking. AE, MC, V.*

Upper West Side

$$$$ ⊞ **Trump International Hotel and Towers.** Sure, it's the most expensive hotel in New York City—but if you've got the money, why not splurge on a one- or two-bedroom mini-apartment? Blast tunes on the Sony sound system, flip through coffee-table books, or just sit and gaze at the park through floor-to-ceiling windows in the living room (minitelescopes are provided). Or lounge in the tub with bath salts and loofahs;

afterward, send for an in-house chef to prepare a meal in your suite. For business travelers there are complimentary cellular phones and personalized stationery and business cards. The restaurant Jean Georges—named for celebrity chef Jean-Georges Vongerichten—has a seasonal, French-inspired menu and an incredible view of Columbus Circle. ⊠ *1 Central Park W, 10023,* ☏ *212/299–1000,* ℻ *212/299–1150. 168 suites. Restaurants, bar, in-room modem lines, in-room safes, kitchens, minibars, in-room VCRs, indoor pool, spa, business services, parking (fee). AE, D, DC, MC, V.*

$$ ⊞ **Mayflower.** After you step under this hotel's green awning into the
★ long, low, wood-paneled lobby, with its gilt-framed oils of tall ships and flowers, you can take an apple from the basket on the registration desk and feel truly welcomed to New York. Such is the charm of this friendly hotel on Central Park. Rooms are large, with thick carpeting, fruit-and-flower-print drapes, dark wood Colonial-style furniture, and walk-in closets; most include walk-in pantries with a fridge and sink. Spend an extra $20 for a spectacular park view. ⊠ *15 Central Park W, 10023,* ☏ *212/265–0060 or 800/223–4164,* ℻ *212/265–2026. 365 rooms. Restaurant, bar, refrigerators, exercise room, meeting rooms. AE, DC, MC, V.*

$$ ⊞ **Radisson Empire Hotel.** The Empire's English country–style lobby is warm and inviting, with its crimson carpet and hanging tapestry. Rooms and suites are small but nicely furnished; all have textured teal carpets, dark-wood furnishings, and high-tech electronics. Guests can work out at a nearby health club for a small fee. This hotel is one of the city's better buys, and you can't beat its location across from Lincoln Center. ⊠ *Broadway at 63rd St., 10023,* ☏ *212/265–7400 or 800/333–3333,* ℻ *212/244–3382. 375 rooms. Restaurant, bar, minibars, in-room VCRs, meeting rooms. AE, D, DC, MC, V.*

$ ⊞ **The Excelsior.** The Excelsior is like one of those faded atmospheric hotels you often find on Parisian backstreets, but it's in a prime New York location: directly across from the American Museum of Natural History. Bedrooms are painted icy blue—a color that's made colder still by the harsh light of electricity-saving bulbs. Still, you can't beat the great staff, great neighborhood, and great rates. ⊠ *45 W. 81st St., 10024,* ☏ *212/362–9200 or 800/368–4575,* ℻ *212/721–2994. 160 rooms. Coffee shop. AE, MC, V.*

$ ⊞ **Hotel Beacon.** Three blocks from both Central Park and Lincoln Cen-
★ ter, this lodging offers many more amenities than you'd expect in this price category. The large rooms and the suites, which have kitchenettes with coffeemakers, full-size refrigerators, and stoves, cost only $40 more than standard rooms. The closets are huge, the dark-wood furniture is elegant, and the bathrooms come complete with Hollywood dressing room–style mirrors. There is no restaurant or bar, but with so much in the neighborhood, this isn't a problem. ⊠ *2130 Broadway, at 75th St., 10023,* ☏ *212/787–1100 or 800/572–4969,* ℻ *212/724–0839. 198 rooms. Refrigerators, meeting room. AE, D, DC, MC, V.*

$ ⊞ **The Milburn.** Convenient to Lincoln Center, Central Park, and Zabar's, this bohemian little hotel has a lobby that looks like a small Bavarian castle, with salmon-pink walls, black-and-white marble floor, heraldic doodads, and abundant gilt. The homey, spacious rooms are a chaotic but cozy assemblage of, say, burgundy carpet and blue drapes, a glass-top brass table, and framed posters on pink floral walls. All have kitchenettes equipped with, among other things, a microwave and coffeemaker. ⊠ *242 W. 76th St., 10023,* ☏ *212/362–1006 or 800/833–9622,* ℻ *212/721–5476. 102 rooms. Kitchenettes. AE, DC, MC, V.*

Murray Hill and Gramercy Park

$$$–$$$$ **Doral Court** and **Doral Tuscany.** These two sisters are not only neigh-
bors in the off-the-tourist-map, peaceful Murray Hill, but they allow
guests to sign up for food and drinks at one another's facilities. Which
to choose? Both have the feel of a small European hotel, with oak-pan-
eled lobbies and English country–style rooms. The Tuscany is the
pricier of the two ($20 more), and its rooms have entrance halls, Ital-
ian marble baths, dressing rooms with a sink, walk-in closets, and three
phones. At the Court, you forego the marble and dress in a mere al-
cove. *Doral Court: ⊠ 130 E. 39th St., 10016, ☎ 212/685–1100 or
800/223–6725, FAX 212/779–0148. 248 rooms, 50 suites. Restaurant,
refrigerators. AE, DC, MC, V. Doral Tuscany: ⊠ 120 E. 39th St., 10016,
☎ 212/686–1600 or 800/223–6725, FAX 212/779–0148. 122 rooms,
24 suites. 2 restaurants, 2 bars, minibars, meeting rooms. AE, DC, MC,
V.*

$$$ **Doral Park Avenue.** This stately little hotel on Park Avenue is stylish
★   in an amusing way. The look is neoclassical meets Miami—from the
lobby rotunda, with its giant painting of an ancient Greek city offset
by palm trees and art deco details, to the renovated guest rooms, some
of which combine neoclassical headboards with faux-leopard-skin
windowseat coverings. Newer rooms have a French country–style
decor. The swank Odyssey Lounge has black carpeting and bright red
walls topped with a neoclassical frieze as well as big windows facing
Park Avenue. *⊠ 70 Park Ave., at 38th St., 10016, ☎ 212/687–7050
or 800/223–6725, FAX 212/973–2497. 188 rooms. Restaurant, breakfast room, health club, meeting rooms. AE, D, DC, MC, V.*

$$$ **Morgans.** The first hotel in nightclub mavens Ian Schrager and the
★   late Steve Rubell's triumphant triumvirate is the perfect place to stay
if you want privacy or care deeply about style. There's no sign out-
side, which is a turn-on for many guests, some of them famous. The
stunning rooms have a minimalist, high-tech look, with low-lying,
futon-like beds and 27-inch Sony TVs on wheels; the exquisite, tiny
bathrooms have crystal shower doors, steel surgical sinks, and poured-
granite floors. *⊠ 237 Madison Ave., 10016, ☎ 212/686–0300 or
800/334–3408, FAX 212/779–8352. 113 rooms. Restaurant, bar, mini-
bars. AE, D, DC, MC, V.*

$$–$$$ **Manhattan East Suite Hotels.** These nine full-service hotels are res-
idential with low rates for long stays. They vary in character and price,
though most reach the upper end of the $$$ category in busy seasons.
Best bets are **Beekman Tower** (⊠ 3 Mitchell Pl.), near the United Na-
tions; **Dumont Plaza** (⊠ 150 E. 34th St.); **Surrey Hotel** (⊠ 20 E. 76th
St.), which is close to Madison Avenue and borders on truly elegant;
Southgate Tower (⊠ 371 7th Ave.), which is attractive and secure, is
near Madison Square Garden, and has the lowest rates; and **Eastgate
Tower** (⊠ 222 E. 39th St.). Except for the contemporary Eastgate and
the Art Deco Beekman Tower, all have traditional guest-room decor.
Most accommodations have completely equipped pantries; larger units
have dining areas with full-size tables. Most properties have restaurants, on-site fitness centers, and coin laundry. *⊠ Sales office, 500 W.
37th St., 10018, ☎ 212/465–3600 or 800/637–8483, FAX 212/465–
3663. AE, DC, MC, V.*

$$ **Gramercy Park Hotel.** This Queen Anne–style hotel is a little worse
for the wear; rooms have dreary, worn furnishings and old-fashioned
baths. Still, it's almost the only hotel in this elegant neighborhood, which
boasts the city's least-populated park. The park remains thus because
it's locked, but hotel guests can use it. Further advantages to staying
here include a bar with a pianist, hot hors d'oeuvres (at happy hour
only), and wicked martinis. *⊠ 2 Lexington Ave., 10010, ☎ 212/475–*

4320 or 800/221–4083, ℻ 212/505–0535. *509 rooms. Restaurant, bar, beauty salon, meeting rooms. AE, D, DC, MC, V.*

$$ ⊡ **Jolly Madison Towers.** The Italian Jolly Hotels chain continually works on this little Murray Hill bargain, with improvements such as glass shower stalls in the tiny bathrooms; fresh carpets and bedspreads in the unobjectionable, if unspectacular, bedrooms; and a good restaurant serving northern Italian cuisine. A separate concession on the premises offers shiatsu massage and Japanese sauna. ✉ *22 E. 38th St., 10016,* ☎ *212/802–0600 or 800/225–4340,* ℻ *212/447–0747. 222 rooms. Restaurant, bar, massage, sauna. AE, DC, MC, V.*

$ ⊡ **Carlton Arms.** It isn't arty, it's art—every wall, ceiling, and other surface is engulfed by murals, commissioned over the years by the hip, free-spirited managers. Each room has a theme: The Versailles Room (5A) by Fabian Compton is an outré symphony of trompe l'oeil trellises and classical urns; the Cow Spot Room (3C) by Heinz Burkhardt has a Holstein motif of cow-spotted rugs, bedspreads, and walls. All rooms have double-glazed windows but are phoneless, TV-less, almost free of furniture, and sometimes bathless. But that's hardly the point. ✉ *160 E. 25th St., 10010,* ☎ *212/684–8337 or 212/679–0680 for reservations. 54 rooms. Fans. MC, V.*

$ ⊡ **The Gershwin.** Young, foreign travelers flock to this hip budget hotel,
★ housed in a converted 13-story Greek Revival. Enter, and be visually assaulted by a giant primary-colored cartoony sculpture, one of many works by house artist Brad Howe. Rooms are all painted in custard yellow and kelly green and are somewhat crumbly in places, with no air-conditioning. Dormitories have four or eight beds and a remarkable $22 rate. You won't be spending much time in your room, however, because of all the activities here: band appearances, film series, summer rooftop barbecues in summer, and the like. ✉ *7 E. 27th St., 10016,* ☎ *212/545–8000,* ℻ *212/684–5546. 160 rooms. Restaurant, bar. MC, V.*

Chelsea, Greenwich Village, SoHo, Chinatown

$$$ ⊡ **SoHo Grand.** SoHo's first hotel has an appropriately high-style aes-
★ thetic. Starting from the first floor, the grand, self-suspended staircase of translucent bottle glass and iron recalls the vast, columned interiors and fanciful cast-iron embellishments of the neighborhood's 19th-century buildings. Upstairs in the Grand Salon, 16-ft-high windows and overscaled furniture complement the immense stone pillars that rise from below. Guest rooms have custom-designed furnishings, including drafting table–style desks, nightstands that mimic sculptors' stands, and minibars made of old campaign chests. In the tavern-style Canal House, superb gourmet renditions of American favorites (macaroni and cheese, crab cakes) are served at surprisingly palatable prices. ✉ *310 W. Broadway, 10013,* ☎ *212/965–3000 or 800/965–3000,* ℻ *212/965–3244. 367 rooms. Restaurant, bar, exercise room, meeting rooms. AE, D, DC, MC, V.*

$$ ⊡ **Holiday Inn Downtown.** In the heart of Chinatown and just a few steps from Little Italy and SoHo, this is one of the few hotels between midtown and the financial district. Though the Asian-decorated lobby and the excellent dim sum at Pacifica Restaurant attract a healthy sampling of Asian business travelers, you'll also find many foreigners and young budget travelers. Rooms and suites have high ceilings, pastel walls and carpets, black-framed furniture, and framed watercolors with an Asian motif. ✉ *138 Lafayette St., 10013,* ☎ *212/966–8898 or 800/465–4329,* ℻ *212/966–3933. 223 rooms. Restaurant, bar. AE, D, DC, MC, V.*

$ ⊞ **Larchmont Hotel.** You might miss the entrance to this Beaux Arts ★ brownstone, whose geranium boxes and lanterns blend right in with the old New York feel of West 11th Street. If you don't mind shared bathrooms and no room service or concierge, the residential-style accommodations are all anyone could ask for at this price, which includes Continental breakfast. Rooms have a tasteful safari theme, with rattan furniture, ceiling fans, and framed animal or botanical prints; your own private sink and stocked bookshelf will make you feel right at home. ⊠ *27 W. 11th St., 10011,* ☎ *212/989–9333,* FAX *212/989–9496. 77 rooms. Breakfast room, kitchen. AE, D, DC, MC, V.*

$ ⊞ **Washington Square Hotel.** This cozy Greenwich Village hotel has ★ a true European feel and style, from the wrought iron and gleaming brass in the small, elegant lobby to the personal attention given by the staff. Rooms are simple but pleasant and well maintained; request one with a window. Continental breakfast is included in the room rate. There's also a good, reasonably priced restaurant, C3. The manager has strong ties to the local jazz community and enjoys providing tips about what's happening at the nearby Blue Note. ⊠ *103 Waverly Pl., 10011,* ☎ *212/777–9515 or 800/222–0418,* FAX *212/979–8373. 150 rooms. Restaurant, bar, exercise room. AE, MC, V.*

Lower Manhattan

$$$$ ⊞ **Millenium Hilton.** This sleek black monolith is the class act of downtown, outdoing the elegance of both the Marriott and the Vista. The modern, beige-and-wood rooms have a streamlined look, with contoured built-in desks and night tables; almost all have expansive views of landmark buildings and both the Hudson and the East rivers. The health club has an attractive pool with windows that look out on St. Paul's Church. The lobby lounge is a popular spot for martinis. ⊠ *55 Church St., 10007,* ☎ *212/693–2001,* FAX *212/571–2317. 561 rooms. 2 restaurants, bar, minibars, indoor pool, health club, business services, meeting rooms. AE, D, DC, MC, V.*

$$$ ⊞ **New York Marriott World Trade Center.** Formerly the New York Vista, this hotel was thoroughly renovated after the World Trade Center bombing in 1994; as a result, rooms and public areas look spanking new. The fabulous skylit lobby has a contemporary green-granite and marble entrance, a grand curved staircase, and a fountain. Rooms are sleekly modern and spacious by Manhattan standards. The 22nd-floor health club has phenomenal views of Lower Manhattan. ⊠ *3 World Trade Center, 10048,* ☎ *212/938–9100 or 800/550–2344,* FAX *212/321– 2107. 820 rooms. Restaurant, in-room safes, minibars, indoor pool, health club, business services, meeting rooms. AE, D, DC, MC, V.*

$$ ⊞ **Best Western Seaport Inn.** This thoroughly pleasant, restored 19th- ★ century building is one block from the waterfront—close to South Street Seaport. With its cozy, library-like lobby, it has the feel of a Colonial sea captain's house, though the reasonably priced rooms are clearly those of a chain hotel—with dark wood, white walls, and floral nylon bedcovers. For less than $20 extra you can have a room with a whirlpool tub and an outdoor terrace with a view of the Brooklyn Bridge. ⊠ *33 Peck Slip, 10038,* ☎ *212/766–6600 or 800/468–3569,* FAX *212/766–6615. 72 rooms. In-room safes, refrigerators, in-room VCRs. AE, D, DC, MC, V.*

Airport

$$ ⊞ **La Guardia Marriott Airport Hotel.** A quarter-mile from the airport and—barring traffic—about 20 minutes from Manhattan, this hotel is out of the direct line of most flights. ⊠ *102–05 Ditmars Blvd., East Elmhurst 11369,* ☎ *718/565–8900 or 800/882–1043,* FAX *718/899–*

0764. 436 rooms. Restaurant, indoor pool, health club. AE, D, DC, MC, V.

$$ ☎ **Newark Airport Marriott.** The Marriott is right on airport premises and provides free 24-hour shuttle service to all terminals; it's only 30 minutes, in light traffic, from Manhattan. ✉ *Newark International Airport, Newark, NJ 07114,* ☎ *201/623–0006 or 800/228–9290,* FAX *201/623–7618. 590 rooms. 2 restaurants, indoor-outdoor pool, health club. AE, D, DC, MC, V.*

Bed-and-Breakfasts

Hundreds of bed-and-breakfast rooms are available in Manhattan and the other boroughs, principally Brooklyn. B&Bs often cost well below $100 a night, though there is also the type with its own kitchen, washer-dryer, whirlpool, and sauna in somebody's priceless brownstone for double or triple that (the price of a room at the Waldorf). But accommodations, amenities, service, and privacy may fall short of what you get in hotels. Sometimes you really do get breakfast, and sometimes you don't. And you usually can't pay by credit card.

A few reservation agencies book B&B accommodations in and near Manhattan. There is no fee for the service, but they advise you to make reservations as far in advance as possible. Except for Abode Bed and Breakfasts Ltd., all of the following agencies book both furnished apartments and guest rooms.

Abode Bed and Breakfasts Ltd. (✉ Box 20022, 10021, ☎ 212/472–2000 or 800/835–8880). **Bed and Breakfast Network of New York** (✉ 134 W. 32nd St., Suite 602, 10001, ☎ 212/645–8134 or 800/900–8134). **City Lights Bed and Breakfast** (✉ Box 20355, Cherokee Station, 10021, ☎ 212/737–7049, FAX 212/535–2755). **Manhattan Home Stays** (✉ Box 20684, Cherokee Station, 10021, ☎ 212/737–3868, FAX 212/265–3561). **New World Bed and Breakfast** (✉ 150 5th Ave., Suite 711, 10011, ☎ 212/675–5600 or 800/443–3800 in the U.S., FAX 212/675–6366). **Urban Ventures** (✉ Box 426, 10024; ✉ 38 W. 32nd St., 10001; ☎ 212/594–5650 for both locations, FAX 212/947–9320).

8 Nightlife

The city that never sleeps has enough diversions to keep even the most gung-ho night owls occupied for weeks. In the same evening you can head for a classic West Village jazz haunt, a sleek TriBeCa bar, a sophisticated uptown cabaret, a grungy East Village club, or a raucous comedy club. Whether you're in the mood for loud rock, Broadway ballads, Brazilian beat, blues, or bluegrass, you're sure to find it in Manhattan.

KAY, SO YOU'VE TAKEN THE STATEN ISLAND ferry,
you've lunched at the Plaza, visited the Met. But
don't tuck yourself in just yet. Get yourself truly
attuned to the Big Apple's schedule, which runs more by New York
nocturnal than by eastern standard time. Even if you're not a night owl
by habit, it's worth staying up late at least once, because by night, Manhattan takes on a whole new identity.

Revised by
Anastasia Mills

CLUBS AND ENTERTAINMENT

New York nightlife really started to swing in 1914, when a pair of ballroom dancers, Florence and Maurice Walton, took over management
of the Parisian Room, in what is today's theater district. At Chez Maurice, as their new club was called, the city's café society learned a sen-
sual dance at Tango Teas. Then came the Harlem Renaissance of the
1920s and '30s, and the New York jazz scene shifted north of 110th
Street. In the 1950s, nightspots mushroomed in Greenwich Village and
the East 50s. Along 52nd Street in those years, recalls columnist Pete
Hamill, "you could walk down a single block and hear Art Tatum, Billie Holiday, and Charlie Parker. And you could go to the Latin Quarter and see girls running around with bananas on their heads."

Well, fruit as headgear is out, but night-owling in the look of the moment never will be. The nightclub scene is now downtown—in the drab-
by-day East Village dives, classic jazz joints in the West Village, and
trendy TriBeCa see-and-be-seen boîtes. Preppy hangouts are also still
alive and well on the Upper East and Upper West sides.

There are enough dedicated club-hoppers in Manhattan to support
nightspots for almost every idiosyncratic taste. But keep in mind that
when you go is just as important as where you go in clubland. These
days, night prowlers are more loyal to floating parties, DJs, even party
promoters, than they are to addresses. A spot is only hot when it's hopping, and you may find the same club or bar that raged last night completely empty tonight.

Style can be a tricky issue. An appropriate costume for a night on the
town could include a rubber mini, a Balenciaga gown, or chains and
leather. Fortunately, Velvet Rope Syndrome—that is, gimlet-eyed bounc-
ers arbitrarily picking and choosing the "right" clientele at the door—
has largely gone the way of the big-money '80s. The atmosphere now
is looser and more accepting. So even if you do wind up wearing the
wrong shoes, you probably won't be left standing out in the cold in
them. Two quick fashion tips to help you blend: wear black and leave
your sneakers at home.

For the tattooed and pierced, *Paper* magazine's "P.M. 'Til Dawn" and
bar sections have as good a listing as exists of the roving clubs and the
best of the fashionable crowd's hangouts. *Time Out New York* offers
a comprehensive weekly listing of amusements by category. The more
staid Friday *New York Times*'s "Weekend" section carries a "Sounds
Around Town" column that can clue you in to what's in the air, as can
the *Village Voice,* a weekly newspaper that probably has more nightclub ads than any other rag in the world. The *Village Voice* is now free
and disappears from its red kiosks on street corners all over the city
often by the afternoon it arrives there (Wednesday). Some newsstands
and bookstores also stock it, but you'll have to search pretty hard—
it's worth the effort. Or stop by Tower Records (⊠ Broadway and E.
4th St., ☎ 212/505–1500; ⊠ Broadway and W. 66th St., ☎ 212/799–

2500), where flyers about coming events and club passes are stacked in the entry. You may also get good tips from a suitably au courant hotel concierge. Just remember that events change almost weekly. We've tried to give you a rounded sample of reliable hangouts—but clubs have the life span of the tsetse fly, so phone ahead to make sure your target nightspot hasn't closed or turned into a polka hall. Most charge a cover, which can range from $2 to $25 or more depending on the club and the night. Take cash, because many places don't accept plastic.

Putting on the Ritz

You are wearing Oscar de la Renta and Armani, your transport is a stretch limo, and you've just come from dinner at Lutèce. Just remember to hide this guidebook so people won't guess that you're not regulars.

The Carlyle (⊠ 35 E. 76th St., ☎ 212/744–1600). The hotel's discreetly sophisticated Café Carlyle is where Bobby Short plays when he's in town; otherwise, you might find Barbara Cook or Eartha Kitt purring by a piano. Bemelmans Bar, with murals by the author of the Madeline books, regularly stars pianists Barbara Carroll and Peter Mintun.
Oak Room (⊠ Algonquin Hotel, 59 W. 44th St., ☎ 212/840–6800). You'll hear that the Algonquin has faded, but this room still offers yesteryear's charms. Just head straight for the long, narrow club-cum–watering hole; you might find the hopelessly romantic singer Andrea Marcovicci, or pianist Steve Ross playing Berlin or Porter.
Rainbow Room and **Rainbow & Stars** (⊠ 30 Rockefeller Plaza, ☎ 212/632–5000). You can find two kinds of heaven high up on Rockefeller Center's 65th floor. The Rainbow Room serves dinner (☞ Chapter 6) and dancing to the strains of a live orchestra and occupies a floor right out of an Astaire-Rogers musical. At the intimate Rainbow & Stars, classy singers such as Maureen McGovern and Rosemary Clooney entertain, backlit by twinkling city lights.
Supper Club (⊠ 240 W. 47th St., ☎ 212/921–1940). Note the last four digits of the telephone number. This huge, prix-fixe dinner-and-dancing club specializes in cheek-to-cheek big band sounds on Friday and Saturday nights, complete with a full orchestra. You wouldn't recognize it the rest of the week when touring alternative and rock-and-roll acts like Mazzy Star and the Black Crowes take the stage.
Tatou (⊠ 151 E. 50th St., ☎ 212/753–1144). This pleasing addition to the supper-club scene, with red velvet decor, offers dinner, dancing, jazz, and cabaret under one stylish roof.

Clubbing

The city's busiest clubs are as much places to bump and grind as to see and be seen. Revelers come to socialize, to find romance, to scream business deals over the music, to show off their glad rags, or to be photographed rubbing shoulders with stars. Some are cavernous spaces filled with throbbing music and writhing bodies. Others are clubs in a different sense, like parties thrown by a mutual friend for people who don't know one another; comers are drawn by a common interest, a likeness of spirit, that can be created almost anyplace. The venues mentioned below are dance clubs, but parties—with or without dancing—with DJs and themes ranging from '60s bossa nova nights to soul-and-drag galas have been known to crop up at places like **Circa** (☞ Watering Holes, *below*) and **Irving Plaza** and **Coney Island High** (☞ Rock Your World, *below*). So read some rags and make some calls.

Denim and Diamonds (✉ 511 Lexington Ave., ☎ 212/371–1600). Break out your boots, y'all, and get out on the dance floor for country line dancing every night of the week. If you need help strutting your stuff, come between 7 and 8 PM for lessons. There are two pool tables and a DJ spinning C&W on the main floor; upstairs in the Roadhouse, there's live music Friday and Saturday. Southwestern food is served here, too.
Le Bar Bat (✉ 311 W. 57th St., ☎ 212/307–7228). This bamboo-encrusted, multitiered monster of a club fits right in with the Planet Hollywoods on 57th Street's Theme Restaurant Row, but a flashy good time can be had here among the Euro and prepster poseurs.
Live Psychic (✉ 209 E. 84th St., ☎ 212/744–5003). The clientele, in their late twenties and thirties, dance to all-time favorites from every music genre in this small club with two floors and three bars.
Nell's (✉ 246 W. 14th St., ☎ 212/675–1567). Back in vogue, Nell Campbell (of *Rocky Horror* fame) reintroduced sophistication to nightlife with her club. The tone in the upstairs live-music jazz salon is Victorian; downstairs, you can dance to a DJ. The boîte opens at 10 PM and closes at 4 AM nightly.
Palladium (✉ 126 E. 14th St., ☎ 212/473–7171). A native New Yorker hasn't crossed its threshold in years, but it's still a hoot with the suburban bridge-and-tunnel set. Expect lit stairs—as in a '30s Hollywood extravaganza—and pounding popular dance music.
Robots (✉ 25 Ave. B, ☎ 212/995–0968). So it's 3 AM on a Saturday morning and you're all tanked up with no place to go. Stop in here, where the absence of alcohol from 4 to 9 AM permits patrons to party all night long. Work off that buzz to hip-hop on the dance floor, or nod off in the upstairs lounge.
Roseland (✉ 239 W. 52nd St., ☎ 212/247–0200). This famous old ballroom dance floor is still open for ballroom dancing Thursday (music provided by a DJ) and Sunday (music by a live orchestra and a DJ).
Roxy (✉ 515 W. 18th St., ☎ 212/645–5156). Roller disco on Tuesday and Wednesday, bridge-and-tunnel dance club Friday and Saturday, this huge hall is gay-centric on Tuesday and draws a mixed rave crowd on others.
Webster Hall (✉ 125 E. 11th St., ☎ 212/353–1600). This fave among NYU students and similar species boasts four floors and five eras of music. Go for the live bands on Thursday, the dance DJs on Friday and Saturday—or the trapeze artists any night.

Jazz Notes

Jazz players always come home to Manhattan. Somehow, the city evokes their sound. Greenwich Village is still the mecca, with more than 12 jazz nightclubs, although plenty of others are strewn around town.

Birdland (✉ 315 W. 44th St., ☎ 212/581–3080). From 5 PM to midnight you'll find up-and-coming groups here—plus dinner.
Blue Note (✉ 131 W. 3rd St., ☎ 212/475–8592). This club is considered by many to be the jazz capital of the world. Just an average week could bring Spyro Gyra, the Modern Jazz Quartet, and Jon Hendricks. Expect a steep music charge, except on Monday, when record labels promote their artists' new releases for an average ticket price of $7.50.
Cajun (✉ 129 8th Ave., ☎ 212/691–6174). This landlocked Chelsea restaurant with a riverboat feel dishes New Orleans–style jazz alongside Cajun-Creole grub. Live music from the likes of former Louis Arm-

strong clarinetist Joe Muranyi will make you feel like you've ducked in off of Bourbon Street. Dixieland is on tap every night save Wednesday, when modern swing takes over.

Knitting Factory (⊠ 74 Leonard St., ☎ 212/219–3055). This eclectic gem of a cross-genre music café in TriBeCa features avant-garde jazz in a homey, funky setting.

Red Blazer Too (⊠ 349 W. 46th St., ☎ 212/262–3112). Roaring '20s, Dixieland, and swing are on tap. It's hot post-theater, when you can sup as well.

Smalls (⊠ 183 W. 10th St., ☎ 212/929–7565). Where can you find jazz 'til dawn and beyond? After the Village Vanguard closes, poke your head around the corner, and you'll find this pocket-size club, where the music keeps coming until 8 AM.

Sweet Basil (⊠ 88 7th Ave. S, ☎ 212/242–1785). A little ritzy, though reliable, this nightspot runs from swing to fusion. Sunday brunch (2– 6 PM) with trumpeter Doc Cheatham is truly a religious experience.

Village Vanguard (⊠ 178 7th Ave. S, ☎ 212/255–4037). This former Thelonius Monk haunt, the prototype of the old-world jazz club, lives on in a smoky cellar, in which jam the likes of Wynton Marsalis and James Carter, among others.

Zinno (⊠ 126 W. 13th St., ☎ 212/924–5182). The food (northern Italian) is actually as good as the jazz (usually duos and trios) at this mellow village club, which boasts a stellar wine list.

Rock Your World

The roots of rock may lie in America's heartland, but New York has added its own spin. Crowds at the Big Apple's rocketerias are young, enthusiastic, and hungry; the noise is often deafening, but you can catch many a rising star in this lively scene. In summer you can also find live music when **Central Park SummerStage** (⊠ Rumsey Playfield, Central Park at E. 72nd St., ☎ 212/360–2777) presents everything from alternative to rap to world music.

Bitter End (⊠ 147 Bleecker St., ☎ 212/673–7030). This old Village standby still serves up its share of new talent; Lisa Loeb, Joan Armatrading, and Warren Zevon once played here. Check before arriving; blues, country, rock, and jazz all make appearances here.

Brownie's (⊠ 169 Ave. A, ☎ 212/420–8392). It's catch-as-catch-can at the East Village dive, but the hard thrashing sounds occasionally pull people in off the street to join the greasy-haired throngs.

CBGB & OMFUG (⊠ 315 Bowery, ☎ 212/982–4052). American punk rock (Ramones, Blondie) was born here, in this long, black tunnel of a club featuring bands with inventive names: Shirley Temple of Doom, Trick Babies, and Xanax 25. **CB's Gallery,** next door at 313 Bowery, attracts a quieter crowd with mostly acoustic music.

Coney Island High (⊠ 15 St. Mark's Pl., ☎ 212/674–7959). Murals of Coney Island amusement-park sideshow acts don't add much cheer to the black and red walls of this hardcore rock haven, which is not nearly as venerable as its state of decrepitude suggests.

Continental (⊠ 25 3rd Ave., ☎ 212/529–6924). This knockdown version of CBGB appeals to thrifty college kids on their last nickel.

The Cooler (⊠ 416 W. 14th St., ☎ 212/229–0785). You've got your trendy bar, live music dive, and DJ dance party all in one at this former meat cooler in the shady yet happening meat-packing district. Come here for a mix of rap, reggae, techno, and jazz.

Don Hill's (⊠ 511 Greenwich St., ☎ 212/334–1390). At this TriBeCa favorite, you'll find bands both popular and not yet signed. Squeeze Box parties on Friday nights are genius.

Irving Plaza (⊠ 17 Irving Pl., ☎ 212/777–6800 or 212/777–1224 for concert hot line). Looking for Marilyn Manson, the Jesus Lizard, or Better Than Ezra? You'll find them in this perfect-size place for general-admission live music. There's a small balcony with a bar and a tiny lounge area.

Mercury Lounge (⊠ 217 E. Houston, ☎ 212/260–4700). With one of the best sound systems in the city, this East Village club holds a quiet cachet with bands and industry insiders.

New Music Café (⊠ 380 Canal St., ☎ 212/941–1019). Their mission is to promote new music, but they've learned how to schedule the bands from totally green (early in the evening) to new but news (around 10 PM). Look out for Milo-Z and the Authority.

Rock 'n' Roll Café (⊠ 149 Bleecker St., ☎ 212/677–7630). Nostalgic for the Doors, Led Zep, Hendrix, or Clapton? Choose a night and the appropriate sleeveless concert T and rock out.

Wetlands (⊠ 161 Hudson St., ☎ 212/966–4225). If you can ignore the environmental murals and the hokey broken-down-VW-bus–cum–gift-shop, this hard-to-find club rules, mostly because it draws great, often danceable, often psychedelic bands. Dave Matthews and Hootie and the Blowfish both "developed" here.

World of Music

A former mayor once called New York a "gorgeous mosaic" for the rich ethnic mix of its inhabitants, and the music in some of its clubs reflects that. Brazilian, Celtic, and of course Latin—salsa, samba, merengue—integrate with the ever-present urban energy of the streets.

Belmont Lounge (⊠ 117 E. 15th St., ☎ 212/533–0009) Come here Tuesday for classic salsa, mambo, and charanga spun by DJ Frankie Inglese. Perry Farrell and Trent Reznor have been spotted at this unpretentious, new-in-'96 watering hole and music venue.

Copacabana (⊠ 617 W. 57th St., ☎ 212/582–2672). Music and passion were always in fashion at this legendary nightclub, but now it's in the form of Latin music by such performers as the three Titos: Ruiz, Riojas, and Nieves. Women often pay less, so give a call.

Knitting Factory (⊠ 74 Leonard St., ☎ 212/219–3055). This cross-genre music café (☞ Jazz Notes, *above*) regularly features performers from far and wide.

Paddy Reilly's Music Bar (⊠ 519 2nd Ave., ☎ 212/686–1210). Irish rock-and-roots hybrid Black 47 (named for the year of the great famine) has a standing Saturday night gig at this cramped but congenial club. Or stop in on Thursday for a traditional Irish jam session.

SOB's (⊠ 204 Varick St., ☎ 212/243–4940). Since 1982, this has been the—and we mean *the*—place for reggae, Trinidadian carnival, zydeco, African, and especially Latin tunes and salsa rhythms. The initials stand for Sounds of Brazil, just in case you wondered. The decor is à la Tropicana; the favored drink, a Brazilian *caipirinha*.

Down-Home Sounds

If you're in the mood for something acoustic, folksy, bone-warming, or bluesy, there are multiple options all over the Village. Many a lonesome cowboy carrying nothing but a tune has hitched his horse in front of the following saloons.

Bottom Line (⊠ 15 W. 4th St., ☎ 212/228–7880). Clubs come and go, but this granddaddy prevails. Its reputation is for showcasing talents on their way up, as it did for both Stevie Wonder and Bruce Springsteen. Recent visitors include Buster Poindexter and Jane Siberry. When a name pulls in a crowd, patrons are packed like a sardine at mostly long, thin tables. This intimate club also hosts singer-songwriter nights when artists share their creative experiences.

Chicago Blues (✉ 73 8th Ave., ☎ 212/924–9755). Big Time Sarah, Jimmy Dawkins, the Holmes Brothers, and others have cozied into this nothing-fancy, just-plain-folksy West Village blues club.

Louisiana Community Bar & Grill (✉ 622 Broadway, ☎ 212/460–9633). It's not exactly the Big Easy, but there's swing on Monday, western swing Wednesday, and dancing Friday and Saturday at this restaurant, where you're sure to have a down-home good time.

Manny's Car Wash (✉ 1558 3rd Ave., ☎ 212/369–2583). Powerhouse blues jams on Manhattan's soul-free Upper East Side? Sounds shocking, but such is the scene at Manny's. Jams are only on Sunday, but live bands dish up the blues seven nights.

Rodeo Bar (✉ 375 3rd Ave., ☎ 212/683–6500). There's never a cover at this full-scale Texas roadhouse, complete with barn-wood siding and a BBQ/Southern Texan menu and featuring "music with American roots"—country, rock, rockabilly, and blues.

Sidewalk Bar–Restaurant (✉ 94 Ave. A, ☎ 212/473–7373). Depending on who's playing, this salon will be packed with bikers, slackers, finger-snapping neo-beatniks, or other fans of the mix of poetry and acoustic blues, rock, and folk, which goes under the label of anti-folk.

Tramps (✉ 45 W. 21st St., ☎ 212/727–7788). For more than two decades Tramps has delivered bands like the Dixie Dregs and NRBQ; now it's got Sponge and George Clinton. Come for Chicago blues or most any other kind of music around.

Comic Relief

Neurotic New York comedy is known the world over, and a few minutes watching these hilarious Woody Allen types will make your own problems seem laughable. Comedy isn't pretty, nor is it especially cheap. Expect to pay around $15 per person on a weekend, sometimes on top of a drink minimum, and reservations are usually necessary. One warning: Only those skilled in the art of repartee should sit in the front. The rest are advised to hide in a corner, or be relentlessly heckled. The *Village Voice* covers the comedy scene well, and it's worth checking its listings because lots of music clubs book comedians for periods between sets. The clubs below are devoted exclusively to comedy.

Boston Comedy Club (✉ 82 W. 3rd St., ☎ 212/477–1000). It's so named because the owner's from Beantown, but comedians come here from all over the country to test their stuff. Monday is open-mike night (amateur night).

Caroline's Comedy Club (✉ 1626 Broadway, ☎ 212/757–4100). This high-gloss club features established names as well as comedians on the edge of stardom. Joy Behar, Sandra Bernhard, and Gilbert Gottfried have appeared.

Catch a Rising Star (✉ 253 W. 28th St., ☎ 212/462–2824). You may indeed catch a rising comedy star at this local link of a chain, but you might also catch established headliners such as Janeane Garafalo, Denis Leary, or *Saturday Night Live* cast members. The restaurant serves contemporary American cuisine Tuesday through Saturday at good prices.

Chicago City Limits (✉ 1105 1st Ave., ☎ 212/888–5233). This troupe's been doing improvisational comedy for a long time, and it seldom fails to whip its audiences into a laughing frenzy. Chicago City Limits performs in a renovated movie theater and is very strong on audience participation.

Comedy Cellar (⊠ 117 MacDougal St., ☎ 212/254–3480). This spot has been running for 17 years now beneath the Olive Tree Café, with a bill that's a good barometer of who's hot.

Comic Strip Live (⊠ 1568 2nd Ave., ☎ 212/861–9386). The atmosphere here is strictly corner bar ("More comfortable than a nice pair of corduroys," says daytime manager J. R.). The stage is brilliantly lit but minuscule; the bill is unpredictable but worth checking out.

Dangerfield's (⊠ 1118 1st Ave., ☎ 212/593–1650). Since 1969, this has been an important showcase for prime comic talent. It's owned by comedian Rodney Dangerfield.

Freestyle Repertory Theater (various theaters; ☎ 212/642–8202 to find out locations). On "Spontaneous Broadway" nights, when an audience member shouts out a song title, the troupe will improvise a show tune—and then a whole musical—around it; on other evenings, teams compete to outperform one another in head-to-head "theater sports" matches.

Gotham Comedy Club (⊠ 34 W. 22nd St., ☎ 212/387–9000). Housed in a landmark historic building in the Flatiron district, this classy venue—complete with a turn-of-the-century chandelier and custom copper bars—attracts an upscale crowd that enjoys such popular headliners as Chris Rock and David Brenner. Once a month, there's a Latino comedy show.

New York Comedy Club (⊠ 241 E. 24th St., ☎ 212/696–5233). This intimate club, chock-full of comedy memorabilia and talent such as Brett Butler, Colin Quinn, and Damon Wayans, has been referred to as "the Wal-Mart of comedy," as covers are low or nonexistent.

Original Improvisation (⊠ 433 W. 34th St., ☎ 212/279–3446). The Improv is to comedy what the Blue Note is to jazz. Lots of now-famous comedians got their first laughs here, among them Richard Pryor.

Stand-Up NY (⊠ 236 W. 78th St., ☎ 212/595–0850). The Upper West Side option for comedy devotees, this club books bright faces off recent TV gigs. Robin Williams has stopped in.

Show and Tell

Cabaret takes many forms in New York City, from a lone crooner at the piano to a full-fledged song-and-dance revue. Various nightspots have stages; here are some of the most consistently entertaining.

Arcimboldo (⊠ 220 E. 46th St., ☎ 212/972–4646). This peachy Italian restaurant dishes out more than spaghetti on Sunday, when it offers its "Opera with Taste" entertainment series, serving up singers from Lincoln Center along with a prix-fixe dinner for a mere $40.

Danny's Skylight Room (⊠ 346 W. 46th St., ☎ 212/265–8133). Housed in Danny's Grand Sea Palace, a fixture on Restaurant Row, this venue offers a little bit of everything: jazz, crooners, and ivory-tinklers.

Don't Tell Mama (⊠ 343 W. 46th St., ☎ 212/757–0788). At this convivial theater district spot, composer-lyricist hopefuls and established talents show their stuff until 4 AM. Extroverts will be tempted by the open-mike policy of the piano bar in front. In the two cabaret rooms you might find singers, comedians, or female impersonators.

Downstairs at the West Bank Café (⊠ 407 W. 42nd St., ☎ 212/695–6909). Below an attractive bistro-type restaurant across from Theater Row, moonlighting musical-comedy triple threats (actor-singer-dancers) show off; on occasion, new plays are read.

The Duplex (⊠ 61 Christopher St., ☎ 212/255–5438). Catch a singing luminary on the rise, a drop-in fresh from Broadway at the open mike, or a comedienne polishing up her act at this longtime Village favorite on Sheridan Square. Plays and rock bands round out the scope of entertainment offerings. Opened in 1951, it's New York's oldest continuing cabaret.

Eighty Eight's (✉ 228 W. 10th St., ☎ 212/924–0088). Come here to hear (among other things) songs by the best of Broadway's tunesmiths, and inventively assembled programs.

Fez (✉ 380 Lafayette St., ☎ 212/533–2680). Tucked away in the trendy Time Café, this Moroccan-themed Casbah offers everything from drag shows to readings and jazz amid a polished young crowd.

55 Grove Street (✉ Near Bleecker and 7th Ave. S, ☎ 212/366–5438). On top of Rose's bar, this landmark cabaret offers a piano bar, singers, and sketch comedy. You may see a Judy Garland impersonator sparring with an Ann Miller impersonator, or a mother-and-daughter team who decided all anyone needs to succeed in show business is nerve—but you'll find good entertainment as well.

Judy's Restaurant and Cabaret (✉ 49 W. 44th St., ☎ 212/764–8930). This cabaret and piano bar next to the Hotel Iroquois is known for singing pianists in the Michael Feinstein mold.

Michael's Pub (✉ Parker Meridien Hotel, 118 W. 57th St., ☎ 212/758–2272). Woody Allen often moonlights on the clarinet here on Monday nights when he performs with his New Orleans Jazz Band. Tuesday through Saturday, the Eddie Davis Dixieland Jazz Band has a standing gig. The crowd is very monied, very uptown.

Nuyorican Poets Café (✉ 236 E. 3rd St., ☎ 212/505–8183). "Nuyorican" means a New Yorker of Puerto Rican descent, but poets of all backgrounds spout their often amazing stuff at this loud, packed Alphabet City haunt. Open-mike "slam" nights give you a chance to read your works—and hear audience opinions. You may also find Latin jazz, comedy, and play readings here.

BARS

Although the health-club craze may have hit New York hard, there's little danger that Manhattanites will abandon their bars. Drinking establishments thrive and multiply, particularly in TriBeCa, where it appears bar design has become a minor art. The city's liquor laws allow bars to stay open until 4 AM, so it's easy to add on a watering stop at the end of an evening's merriment.

Vintage Classics

Algonquin Hotel Lounge (✉ 59 W. 44th St., ☎ 212/840–6800). This is a venerable spot, not only because it was the site of the fabled literary Round Table but also because it has an elegant tone. (☞ Oak Room *in* Putting on the Ritz, *above*.)

Café des Artistes (✉ 1 W. 67th St., ☎ 212/877–3500). This restaurant, as well known for its glorious Art Nouveau murals as for its food (☞ Chapter 6), has a small, warm bar where interesting strangers tell their life stories and the house drink is pear champagne.

Elaine's (✉ 1703 2nd Ave., ☎ 212/534–8103). The food's nothing special, and you will be relegated to an inferior table, but go to gawk; try it late when the stars rise in Elaine's firmament. Woody Allen's favorite table is by the cappuccino machine.

Fantino (✉ Ritz-Carlton, 112 Central Park S, ☎ 212/757–1900). This restaurant bar is dressy and traditional—a very double-martini sort of place.

Four Seasons (✉ 99 E. 52nd St., ☎ 212/754–9494). Miró tapestries in the lobby greet you as you enter this power bar in the Grill Room (☞ Chapter 6). Watch for Kissingers and Trumps.

King Cole Bar (✉ St. Regis Hotel, 2 E. 55th St., ☎ 212/753–4500). The famed Maxwell Parrish mural is a welcome sight at this gorgeous midtown rendezvous spot.

Oak Bar (✉ Plaza Hotel, 5th Ave. and 59th St., ☎ 212/759–3000). Bedecked with plush leather chairs and oak walls, this old favorite continues to age well. Its great location draws sophisticates, shoppers, businesspeople, tourists in the know, and stars.

Pen Top Bar and Lounge (✉ Peninsula Hotel, 700 5th Ave., ☎ 212/247–2200). Take a break from 5th Avenue shopping at this glass-lined penthouse hotel bar on the 22nd. Drinks are pricey ($9.75 for a Tanqueray and tonic), but the views are impressive. Especially nice is the open-air rooftop seating area.

River Café (✉ 1 Water St., Brooklyn, ☎ 718/522–5200). An eminently romantic spot hidden at the foot of the Brooklyn Bridge, this restaurant offers smashing views of Wall Street and the East River.

Top of the Tower (✉ Beekman Tower, 3 Mitchell Pl., near 1st Ave. at 49th St., ☎ 212/355–7300). There are higher hotel-top lounges, but this one on the 26th floor still feels halfway to heaven. The atmosphere is elegant and subdued.

"21" Club (✉ 21 W. 52nd St., ☎ 212/582–7200). Famous for its old-time club atmosphere even before it was filmed in *All About Eve,* this isn't exactly a swinging joint, but its conservative environs evoke a sense of connections, power, and prestige.

Watering Holes

Exploring neighborhood by neighborhood, you'll find a glut of mahogany-encrusted historic old-town taverns in the West Village; chichi wine bars in SoHo and TriBeCa; yuppie and collegiate minifrats on the Upper West and East sides; and terribly trendy kitsch bars in the East Village and Alphabet City. Happy hunting.

SoHo and TriBeCa

Bridge Café (✉ 279 Water St., ☎ 212/227–3344). This busy little restaurant flanks the Brooklyn Bridge, a hop, skip, and a jump from South Street Seaport. The bar is small, but its inventory is huge: you can choose from a list of 80 domestic-only wines and 43 single-malt Scotches.

Broome Street Bar (✉ 363 W. Broadway, at Broome St., ☎ 212/925–2086). A classic hangout, this SoHo standard attracts local artsy types on weekdays, the same from other boroughs on weekends.

Ear Inn (✉ 326 Spring St., ☎ 212/226–9060). There's nothing fancy in this 1817 Federal house. It's the artsy crowd that makes the place, along with Saturday afternoon poetry readings—"lunch for the ear."

El Teddy's (✉ 219 W. Broadway, ☎ 212/941–7070). You can't miss the gigantic Lady Liberty crown out front, and the Judy Jetson Goes to Art Camp decor at this former mob haunt. The margaritas (on the rocks, *por favor*) at this enduring TriBeCa bar are phenomenal.

Fanelli's (✉ 94 Prince St., ☎ 212/226–9412). This is a casual SoHo neighborhood bar where many come on Sunday with the fat *New York Times* under their arms. The food's good, too.

I Tre Merli (✉ 463 W. Broadway, ☎ 212/254–8699). Happy drinkers spill out of the massive doors of this wide, inviting restaurant-bar.

Lucky Strike (✉ 59 Grand St., ☎ 212/941–0479). Formerly a see-and-be-seen scene, this SoHo bistro has calmed into a mere scene.

Max Fish (✉ 178 Ludlow St., ☎ 212/529–3959). This crowded, grungy kitsch palace on an artsy East Village strip boasts a twisted image of a grimacing Julio Iglesias over the bar and a pool table in back. Downtown mainstays like the Ramones have been spotted here.

Merc Bar (✉ 151 Mercer St., ☎ 212/966–2727). A chic European crowd and New Yorkers in the know come to this dark, rather nondescript bar for the wonderful martinis. Its street number is barely visible—look for the French doors.

Naked Lunch (✉ 17 Thompson St., ☎ 212/343–0828). Dazzlingly successful, this Burroughs-inspired, earth-tone SoHo haunt is said to be often graced by Robert De Niro, among others.

Pravda (✉ 281 Lafayette St., ☎ 212/226–4696). Martinis are the rule at this Russian-theme trendy bar and lounge, where there are more than 70 brands of vodka and nearly as many types of martinis on offer.

Screening Room (✉ 54 Varick St., ☎ 212/334–2100). As people often have dinner and/or drinks on a night out at the movies, it makes sense to hold that audience captive as is often done in Britain. The movie theater here is small but inviting, and this spot has made a splash with the TriBeCa crowd since its 1996 opening. Think well-worn velvet and you'll get the picture.

SoHo Kitchen and Bar (✉ 103 Greene St., ☎ 212/925–1866). Pass on the food but sidle up to the long bar, where you can get flights of wine (e.g., a tasting of three South American reds), a million wines by the glass, and myriad beers and scotches.

Sporting Club (✉ 99 Hudson St., ☎ 212/219–0900). The six 10-ft screens and 11 TV monitors here stay tuned to the evening's major sports event. Aficionados come in after punching out on Wall Street.

Spy (✉ 101 Greene St., ☎ 212/343–9000). Part of the lounge trend going on in Manhattan at press time, Spy celebrated its first birthday in 1996 with a celebrity-filled bash. Settle into a plush couch and enjoy the baroque parlor setting and pretty people.

Walker's (✉ 16 N. Moore St., ☎ 212/941–0142). First-precinct NYPD detectives, TriBeCa artists, Wall Street types, and the odd celeb somehow all manage to call this cozy restaurant-bar home.

Wax (✉ 113 Mercer St., ☎ 212/226–6082). Candles create a soft glow on tables in this doorman-guarded lounge with bare wooden floors and rather uncomfortable settees.

Chelsea and the Village

For perhaps the most bizarre bar crawl Manhattan has to offer, consider a mug-hoisting stroll along the West Village's esoteric and enchanting Washington Street, which is one street east of the West Side Highway. Begin while it's light out at the dingy corner of West 13th Street with a visit to **Hogs & Heifers** (✉ 859 Washington St., ☎ 212/929–0655). This seems to be Gotham's homage to the movie *Deliverance,* but it still manages to attract starpower like Drew Barrymore, Julia Roberts, and Harrison Ford. Next, walk south through the meatpacking district to **Braque** (✉ 775 Washington St., ☎ 212/255–0709). Have a seat at the outdoor café frequented by the likes of RuPaul or in a leather club chair in the adjoining indoor restaurant. Across the street, pop into **Tortilla Flats** (✉ 767 Washington St., ☎ 212/243–1053) and check out the backroom "Vegas Lounge," a tribute to the stars of Vegas, from Lewis and Martin to Siegfried and Roy. Proceed next to the French bistro–inspired **Black Sheep** (✉ 344 W. 11th St., ☎ 212/242–1010). Then stumble on to the always hopping **Automatic Slim's** (✉ 733 Washington St., ☎ 212/645–8660), a gritty bar that gets patrons dancing on bars to loud music and eating surprisingly sophisticated food. From here you can finish off an A-1 evening by calling a cab.

Chelsea Commons (✉ 242 10th Ave., ☎ 212/929–9424). An old-fashioned pub in front and a small tree-shaded courtyard in back, this West Chelsea bar draws a disparate but friendly crowd of bookworms, sports fans, and slackers.

Chumley's (✉ 86 Bedford St., ☎ 212/675–4449). There's no sign to help you find this place—they took it down during Chumley's speakeasy days—but when you reach the corner of Barrow Street, you're very close. A fireplace warms this relaxed spot, where the burgers are hearty and the clientele collegiate.

Cornelia Street Café (✉ 29 Cornelia St., ☎ 212/989–9319). A streetside table on this quaint West Village lane is a romantic spot to share a bottle of Merlot—or two. Inside you can groove to live jazz on Wednesday and Saturday.

Dix et Sept (✉ 181 W. 10th St., ☎ 212/645–8023). They say they're "*comme à* Paris—without the attitude," but what they mean is they've subbed a New York attitude, which suits this lively spot just fine.

Flight 151 (✉ 151 8th Ave., ☎ 212/229–1868). This popular, unpretentious neighborhood hangout serves lunch, dinner, and a bargain all-you-can-eat brunch on weekends. The polished wood bar, candlelit booths, and friendly staff create a welcoming atmosphere. Don't miss Tuesday's Flip Night or Thursday's Trivia Night, when you can get your drink on the house if you play along.

Flowers (✉ 21 W. 17th St., ☎ 212/691–8888). In this ultratrendy model hangout, you, too, can escape your fans by taking to the roof, which overlooks the hip photo district.

McSorley's Old Ale House (✉ 15 E. 7th St., ☎ 212/473–9148). One of New York's oldest saloons (opened in 1854), this is a must-see for first-timers to Gotham.

Peculier Pub (✉ 145 Bleecker St., ☎ 212/353–1327). Here, in the heart of the Village, you'll find nearly 400 brands of beer, from Anchor Steam to Zywiec.

Slaughtered Lamb (✉ 182 W. 4th St., ☎ 212/727–3350). A none-too-subtle haunted mansion is the theme here (the paintings have roving eyes, skeletons are strewn here and there).

White Horse Tavern (✉ 567 Hudson St., ☎ 212/989–3956). Here's where Dylan Thomas drained his last cup. From April through October, there's outdoor café drinking.

East Village through East 20s

Bowery Bar (✉ 358 Bowery, ☎ 212/475–2220). Long lines peer through venetian blinds at the fabulous crowd within. If the bouncer says there's a private party going on, more likely than not, it's his way of turning you away nicely.

Beauty Bar (✉ 231 E. 14th St., ☎ 212/539–1389). If you've ever wanted to try out the beauty parlor in *Steel Magnolias,* this is your chance.

Café Tabac (✉ 232 E. 9th St., ☎ 212/674–7072). Practice your glare before entering the ground-floor lounge of this pretentious salon, the site of many Madonna visits as well as fights between Christian Slater, Ethan Hawke, and whichever models they are dating at the moment. Good luck trying to get in a game at the pool table.

Circa (✉ 103 2nd Ave., ☎ 212/777–4120). Blond and tony, with c-shape velvet banquettes and high ceilings, Circa supplies a surprising slice of the Upper East Side on ever-gentrifying 2nd Avenue.

Cloister Café (✉ 238 E. 9th St., ☎ 212/777–9128). With one of Manhattan's largest and leafiest outdoor gardens, the Cloister is a perfect perch for stargazing and elbow-bending.

Coffee Shop (✉ 29 Union Sq. W, ☎ 212/243–7969). The moonlighting models bringing your food and drinks may not be the fastest waitpeople in the city, but a flashy, gorgeous crowd makes for an unbelievable, if attitudinal, spectacle.

Coyote Ugly (✉ 153 1st Ave., ☎ 212/477–4431). The name is appropriate for this dive, where the raucous regulars can be heard across the 'hood singing along with the Skynyrd wailing from the jukebox.

Flamingo East (✉ 219 2nd Ave., ☎ 212/533–2860). Kidney-shape sofas, style-mad patrons, and moody lighting make this haute downtown restaurant and bar a cool good time. Upstairs starts late and is only sporadically open to the public, but the balcony overlooking 2nd Avenue is a treat, and the food is delicious.

Jules (✉ 65 St. Mark's Pl., ☎ 212/477–5560). A *très* français, *très* romantique wine bar with a perfect people-watching patio out front.

Lucky Cheng's (✉ 24 1st Ave., ☎ 212/473–0516). Have a bite beside the goldfish pond downstairs, or mingle amid the gilt and leopard and be served by lovely waiters and bartenders in drag at this Pacific Rim restaurant–cum–cross-dressing cabaret .

Nation (✉ 50 Ave. A, ☎ 212/473–6239). Despite the enormous signs proclaiming NO DANCING and POT SMOKING IS NOT ALLOWED, this smoke-saturated bar still manages to feel friendly. Grab a two-top (table with two seats) by the window and watch the parade of passers-by on Avenue A.

Old Town Bar and Restaurant (✉ 45 E. 18th St., ☎ 212/529–6732). Proudly unpretentious, this watering hole is heavy on the mahogany and redolent of "old New York." True to its name, the Old Town has been around since 1892.

Pete's Tavern (✉ 129 E. 18th St., ☎ 212/473–7676). This saloon is famous as the place where O. Henry is alleged to have written "The Gift of the Magi" (at the second booth to the right as you come in). These days, it's still crowded with noisy, friendly souls.

Republic (✉ 37 Union Sq. W, ☎ 212/627–7172). This trendy noodle shop right on Union Square has an elegant and active bar up front. The concept took on so well that at press time, two more Republics were scheduled to open in Manhattan.

Telephone Bar (149 2nd Ave., ☎ 212/529–5000). Imported English telephone booths and a polite, handsome crowd mark this pub.

Temple Bar (✉ 332 Lafayette St., ☎ 212/925–4242). Romantic and upscale, this unmarked haunt is famous for its martinis and is a treat at any price.

Midtown and the Theater District

Barrymore's (✉ 267 W. 45th St., ☎ 212/391–8400). At this pleasantly downscale theater-district spot, you'll see the requisite show posters on the wall. Listen in on the conversations at the bar and you'll hear a few tawdry, true stories of what goes on behind Broadway stage doors.

Café Un Deux Trois (✉ 123 W. 44th St., ☎ 212/354–4148). This old hotel lobby, charmingly converted, is chicly peopled. The bar itself is small, but it's a hot spot before and after the theater.

Century Café (✉ 132 W. 43rd St., ☎ 212/398–1988). An immense vintage neon sign lights up the bar at this trendy, friendly theater-district bistro, where you *won't* find the requisite show posters.

Halcyon Bar (✉ Rihga Royal Hotel, 151 W. 54th St., ☎ 212/307–5000). A big, airy restaurant and bar, Halcyon has large and well-spaced tables and is great for a private chat.

Joe Allen (✉ 326 W. 46th St., ☎ 212/581–6464). At this old reliable on Restaurant Row, celebrated in the musical version of *All About Eve*, everybody's en route to or from a show. Its "flop wall" offers a change of pace: The posters that adorn it are from Broadway musicals that quickly bombed.

Landmark Tavern (✉ 626 11th Ave., ☎ 212/757–8595). This aged red-brick pub (opened in 1868) is blessed by the glow of warming fireplaces on each of its three floors.

The Royalton (✉ 44 W. 44th St., ☎ 212/768–5000 or 212/869–4400). If you can't find an open seating area in the lobby of this modernistic, Phillipe Starck–designed hotel, search for the tiny, very cool Vodka Bar. Hint: It's to the back and right of the dipped table and chairs on the right as you walk in off the street. Second hint: The hotel is not ·marked—look for the double silver curved railings. (Can you tell that hip celebrities stay here?)

Sardi's (⊠ 234 W. 44th St., ☎ 212/221–8440). "The theater is certainly not what it was," croons a cat in *Cats*—and he could be referring to this venerable spot as well. Still, if you care for the theater, don't leave New York without visiting this establishment.

The Whiskey (⊠ Paramount Hotel, 235 W. 46th St., ☎ 212/764–5500). Small, dark, and crowded, the Whiskey nevertheless remains a favorite Times Square area bar among hipsters. It's hard to find; look for the potted plants outside.

East Side

American Trash (⊠ 1471 1st Ave., ☎ 212/988–9008). The name refers to the decor, not necessarily to the clientele—old pipes, bike wheels, and golf clubs line the walls and ceilings.

Dakota Bar & Grill (⊠ 1576 3rd Ave., ☎ 212/427–8889). A mix of yuppies fresh out of college and neighborhood lifers congregate around the 52-ft, 4-inch bar, one of the longest in Manhattan.

Divine Bar (⊠ 244 E. 51st St., ☎ 212/319–9463). You'll feel like you've died and gone to SoHo, what with the zebra-striped bar chairs, cigar area, and cozy velvet couches upstairs. There's also a great gourmand's selection of tapas and wines and beers.

Harglo's (⊠ 974 2nd Ave., ☎ 212/759–9820). The spicy Cajun food and bright neon sign attract white collars who just can't seem to go straight home after a long day at the office.

Jim McMullen's (⊠ 1341 3rd Ave., ☎ 212/861–4700). A young, quintessentially Upper East Side watering hole, McMullen's has a large, busy bar decked with bouquets of fresh flowers. Here you'll find lots of Gold Cards, tennis talk, and alumni-fund gatherings.

P. J. Clarke's (⊠ 915 3rd Ave., ☎ 212/759–1650). New York's most famous Irish bar, this establishment comes complete with the requisite mirrors and polished wood. Lots of after-workers like unwinding here, in a place that recalls the days of Tammany Hall.

Polo Lounge and Restaurant (⊠ Westbury Hotel, 840 Madison Ave., ☎ 212/439–4835). This place is, in a word, classy; it's frequented by European royalty and Knickerbocker New York.

Twins (⊠ 1712 2nd Ave., ☎ 212/987–1111). Owned by twin sisters Debbie and Lisa Ganz and actor Tom Berenger, this restaurant employs 37 additional pairs of twins and often sees as many as 15 sets of twins as customers a night. Enjoy the double-chocolate fondue—as well as some singular food delights—and cigars.

Water Club (⊠ 500 E. 30th St., ☎ 212/683–3333). Right on the East River, with a pleasing outside deck (you're not on a boat, but you'll somehow feel you are), this is a special-occasion kind of place—especially for those who've already been to all the special landlocked spots in town.

Upper West Side

On the Yupper West Side, as it's sometimes referred to, Amsterdam Avenue between 79th and 86th streets is a promenade for young revelers, many still wearing their college sweatshirts. Weave up and down the avenue, and be sure to stop in at the classy, racially mixed **Shark Bar** (⊠ 307 Amsterdam Ave., ☎ 212/874–8500). Then try **Hi-Life** (⊠ 477 Amsterdam Ave., ☎ 212/787–7199), big with the nabe's bon vivants.

Black Bass (✉ 370 Columbus Ave., ☎ 212/362–3559). Every night is a big, nasty fraternity party that leaves you smelling like a beer-sodden cigarette the next day—hence its popularity.

Chaz & Wilson's (✉ 201 W. 79th St., ☎ 212/769–0100). There must be a reason for the line out the door of this otherwise unremarkable but enduringly popular bar. Perhaps it's the live music (R&B and disco) Wednesday and Friday or the possibility of forging a formidable connection.

China Club (✉ 2130 Broadway, ☎ 212/877–1166). If you don't spot someone famous here within 30 minutes, you just aren't trying hard enough. On Monday night it's the place to be on the Upper West Side.

Iridium (✉ 48 W. 63rd St., ☎ 212/582–2121). The owners spent untold sums to make this lavish restaurant and jazz club near Lincoln Center stand out, which it does. If nothing else, take a look inside for an eyeful of Gaudíesque construction.

Museum Café (✉ 366 Columbus Ave., ☎ 212/799–0150). Trendy, overdesigned joints on Columbus Avenue come and go, but this oasis across from the American Museum of Natural History endures thanks to nice street-side windows and high, airy ceilings.

O'Neal's Lincoln Center (✉ 49 W. 64th St., ☎ 212/787–4663). Mike O'Neal, the owner of the beloved but now defunct Ginger Man, has moved the bar from that establishment down the street and created a series of rooms (one with a fireplace) serving good pub food.

The Saloon (✉ 1920 Broadway, ☎ 212/874–1500). The menu goes on and on; the bar is large and informal; and the waitresses and waiters cruise around on roller skates. It may be gimmicky, but the spirit of fun is infectious, and the people-watching is second to none.

Theme Dreams

In some ways, concept restaurants are as un–New York as it gets. Things that come on strong with a gimmick but can't back up the bluster tend to get eaten alive in the Big Apple, while the true hot spots are all action, no talk (just buzz). While these after-dark theme parks may be tacky and touristy, they do draw some famous faces—if, perhaps, not as many as they'd like you to think—and a visit to one (or several) can become a classically campy evening's adventure.

Fashion Café (✉ 51 Rockefeller Plaza, ☎ 212/765–3131). Backed by supermodels Elle MacPherson, Claudia Schiffer, Naomi Campbell, and Christy Turlington, this joint tries hard (but does not succeed) to be glamorous with its catwalk and displays of clothes in which models have strutted their stuff.

Hard Rock Cafe (✉ 221 W. 57th St., ☎ 212/459–9320). This spot was formerly embraced by the kids of stars—now, in fact, its clientele seems to be eternally prepubescent kids accompanied by muttering parents who find it big, crowded, and far too noisy for talk.

Harley-Davidson Cafe (✉ 1370 6th Ave., ☎ 212/245–6000). Motorcycles are not allowed to park outside, which should give you an idea of the authenticity of this upholstered showroom-size restaurant. Still, rock stars and other biker fans do drop in on occasion.

Jekyll & Hyde Club (✉ 1409 6th Ave., ☎ 212/541–9505). "A restaurant and social club for eccentric explorers and mad scientists," this multiple-story eating and ogling extravaganza features 250 varieties of beer and actors dressed as horror meisters.

Motown Café (✉ 104 W. 57th St., ☎ 212/581–8030). The food is actually quite tasty in this dining homage to the music that puts a smile on everyone's face.

Planet Hollywood (✉ 140 W. 57th St., ☎ 212/333–7827). It's touristy, it doesn't take reservations, and waiting lines are long. Still, the place has cachet, an undeniable star quality, and such movie memorabilia as C-3PO and Dorothy's red shoes.

Gay and Lesbian Bars

For advice on the bar scene, health issues, and other assorted quandaries, call the **Gay and Lesbian Switchboard** (☎ 212/777–1800) or stop by the **Lesbian and Gay Community Services Center** (⊠ 208 W. 13th St., ☎ 212/620–7310). Check out *HomoExtra, Next* magazine, *Metro Source, Sappho's Isle, Time Out New York,* the *Village Voice,* or *Paper* for what's what.

Dance Clubs and Parties

Clit Club (⊠ Mother, 432 W. 14th St., ☎ 212/366–5680). Leather-vested and well-pierced Harley dykes as well as lipstick lesbians dance Friday night away. Call first, because this club roves.

Her/She Bar (⊠ 229 W. 28th St., ☎ 212/631–1093). Dance with drag kings every Friday in the self-proclaimed "nation's largest dance club for women."

Jackie 60 (⊠ Mother, 432 W. 14th St., 212/366–5680). This gay-friendly house dance party on Tuesday is so hip, there's a hot line (☎ 212/929–6060) for the theme of the week so you don't feel left out.

1984 (⊠ Pyramid, 101 Ave. A, no phone). On Friday, relive the '80s here in all its new-wave syntho-trash glory.

The Roxy (⊠ 515 W. 18th St., ☎ 212/645–5156). Tuesday night is boys' night, but girls "won't be turned away" from this huge roller disco-cum-club.

Men's Bars

The Break (⊠ 232 8th Ave., ☎ 212/627–0072). The scene is usually quite young and swells according to the number and generosity of the night's drink specials.

Cleo's 9th Avenue Saloon (⊠ 656 9th Ave., ☎ 212/307–1503). Near the theater district, this small, narrow neighborhood bar draws a convivial, laid-back older crowd.

Crowbar (⊠ 339 E. 10th St., ☎ 212/228–4448). Gay grungers and NYU students mingle happily at this East Village hot spot, which is especially sizzling on Friday.

Eagle's Nest (⊠ 142 11th Ave., ☎ 212/691–8451). This leather-and-Levi's bar is serious about three things: drinking, glaring, and shooting pool.

The Monster (⊠ 80 Grove St., ☎ 212/924–3558). Upstairs, the tone-deaf gather and sing around the piano; downstairs, the rhythm-impaired gyrate in a campy pitch-black disco. This place has been at it for more than a decade, though, and continues to draw a busy mix of ages, races, and genders.

Nuts & Bolts (⊠ 101 7th Ave. S, ☎ 212/620–4000). Upscale gents converge on this classy lounge, which features live performances and a video lounge.

Rawhide (⊠ 212 8th Ave., ☎ 212/242–9332). The older Wild West crowd of this Chelsea nook is mostly local and usually leathered up.

The Spike (⊠ 120 11th Ave., ☎ 212/243–9688). Here, at the ultimate parade of black leather, chains, and Levi's, the bark is always bigger than the bite.

Splash Bar (⊠ 50 W. 17th St., ☎ 212/691–0073). The staggering popularity of this hangout is due as much to its size as to anything else. Most nights go-go dancers writhe in translucent shower-cubicles.

Stonewall (⊠ 53 Christopher St., ☎ 212/463–0950). With its odd mix of tourists chasing down gay history and down-to-earth locals, the scene is everything but trendy.

The Townhouse (✉ 236 E. 58th St., ☎ 212/754–4649). On good nights it's like stepping into a Brooks Brothers catalog—cashmere sweaters, Rolex watches, distinguished-looking gentlemen—and it's surprisingly festive.

Ty's (✉ 114 Christopher St., ☎ 212/741–9641). Though its clientele is close-knit and fiercely loyal, this small, jeans-and-flannel neighborhood saloon never turns away friendly strangers.

The Works (✉ 428 Columbus Ave., ☎ 212/799–7365). Whether it's Thursday's $1 margarita party or just a regular Upper West Side afternoon, the crowd is usually J. Crew–style or disco hangover at this bar, which has been around for nearly two decades.

Women's Bars

Crazy Nanny's (✉ 21 7th Ave. S, ☎ 212/366–6312). The crowd is wide-ranging—from urban chic to shaved head—and tends toward the young and the wild. Wednesday and Friday find the crowd grooving to a house DJ while Thursday is C&W line-dancing night.

Henrietta Hudson (✉ 438 Hudson St., ☎ 212/924–3347). A little more upscale than Crazy Nanny's, this place has two huge rooms and a pool table.

Julie's (✉ 204 E. 58th St., ☎ 212/688–1294). Popular with the sophisticated-lady, upper-crust crowd, this brownstone basement has a piano bar—and dancing on Sunday and Wednesday nights.

Shescapes (✉ Various locations, ☎ 212/686–5665). This roving dance party is probably the most popular of Manhattan's lesbian soirées.

9 Outdoor Activities and Sports

New Yorkers are stopped by nothing in their passion for sports: You can see them jogging in the park when it's sleeting, or heading for a tennis bubble on the most blustery of Sunday winter afternoons. From boccie to croquet, no matter how esoteric the sport, there's a place to pursue it in New York.

YOU'LL FIND OASES OF GREENERY you'd never imagine here (13% of the city, in fact, is parkland). And if you strike up a conversation while waiting to rent a boat or a bike at the Loeb Boathouse, or while stretching before a jog around the Reservoir in Central Park, you'll discover a friendly, relaxed side of New Yorkers that you might not otherwise get the chance to see.

By Karen Cure

Updated by
Margaret
Mittelbach

Just one word before you set out: Weekends are very busy. If you need to rent equipment or secure specific space—for instance, a tennis court—go very early or be prepared to wait.

BEACHES

Fine weather brings sun-worshiping New Yorkers out in force. Early in the season, the nearest park or even a rooftop is just fine for catching rays, but later on everyone heads for New York City beaches. Before you go, call to check on swimming conditions.

City Beaches

The tame waves of **Coney Island** (☎ 718/946–1353) are the closest many New Yorkers get to a surf all year. The last stop in Brooklyn on the B, D, F, and N lines, the beach here, which has the boardwalk and the famous amusement-park skyline of the Cyclone and the Wonder Wheel as its backdrop, is busy every day that the sun shines. If you want to see surfers riding the waves in wet suits, venture out on the A train to the beaches in the **Rockaways** (☎ 718/318–4000) section of Queens—at 9th Street, 23rd Street, or 80–118th streets.

Long Island

New Yorkers' favorite strand may be **Jones Beach** (☎ 516/785–1600), one of the great man-made beaches of the world, built during the era of famous parks commissioner Robert Moses. In summer the Long Island Railroad (☎ 718/217–5477) runs regular trains from Penn Station to Freeport, where you can catch a bus to the beach. On the western end of Fire Island, there's a good beach at **Robert Moses State Park** (☎ 516/669–0449), which can be reached in summer via the Long Island Railroad (☎ 718/217–5477).

PARTICIPANT SPORTS

For information about athletic facilities in Manhattan as well as a calendar of sporting events, pick up a complimentary copy of *Metrosports* magazine at sporting goods stores and health clubs.

Bicycling

Although space comes at a premium in Manhattan apartments, many locals keep a bicycle around for a few of the glorious rides that this city has to offer. A sleek pack of dedicated racers zooms around Central Park at dawn and at dusk daily, and on weekends, parks swarm with recreational cyclists. **Central Park** has a 6-mi circular drive that is closed to traffic from 10 AM to 3 PM and 7 to 10 PM on weekdays, and from 7 PM Friday to 6 AM Monday. On holidays it's closed from 7 PM the night before until 6 AM the day after. In **Riverside Park,** the promenade between 72nd and 110th streets, with its Hudson River view, gets an easygoing crowd of slow-pedaling cyclists—many of them with training wheels. The **Hudson River bike path** runs along the waterfront from 41st Street down to the **Hudson River Park promenade.** From there cyclists will enjoy exploring the **Wall Street** area, which is deserted on weekends. The winding roads in Brooklyn's beautiful **Prospect Park** are closed to cars on the weekends in summer from 10 AM to 3 PM and 7 to 10 PM on weekdays.

Bike Rentals

Expect to leave a deposit or a credit card when renting a bike. **AAA Bikes in Central Park** (✉ Loeb Boathouse, midpark, near E. 74th St., ☎ 212/861–4137) provides cycles for the whole family. **Larry and Jeff's Bicycles Plus** (✉ 1690 2nd Ave., ☎ 212/722–2201) features 10-speeds, mountain bikes, and "hybrids" designed for city riding. **Metro Bicycles** (✉ 1311 Lexington Ave., at 88th St., ☎ 212/427–4450) offers five-speed hybrids, a good choice for urban cycling. **Pedal Pusher** (✉ 1306 2nd Ave., between 68th and 69th Sts., ☎ 212/288–5592) has everything from clunky three-speeds to racing bikes to hybrids.

Group Trips

For organized rides with other cyclists, call or write before you come to New York. **Transportation Alternatives** (✉ 92 St. Mark's Pl., New York, NY 10009, ☎ 212/475–4600) can provide an ongoing update of group rides throughout the metropolitan area. **Hosteling International–American Youth Hostels** (✉ 891 Amsterdam Ave., at 103rd St., ☎ 212/932–2300) runs the Five-Borough Bicycling Club, which organizes day and weekend trips on a regular basis. The **New York Cycle Club** (✉ Box 199, Cooper Station, 10276, ☎ 212/886–4545 or 212/242–3900) sponsors weekend rides around Manhattan and Central Park for every level of fitness. **Time's Up** (☎ 212/802–8222) leads free recreational rides twice a month for cyclists as well as skaters. The **Staten Island Bicycling Association** (☎ 718/815–9290) sponsors trips in New York's most countrified borough, as well as other pretty spots.

Billiards

It used to be that pool halls were dusty, grimy, sticky places—and there are still a few of those around. But they've been joined by a group of oh-so-chic spots with deluxe decor, high prices, and even classical music or jazz in the background. Most halls are open late.

Amsterdam Billiard Club (✉ 344 Amsterdam Ave., between 76th and 77th Sts., ☎ 212/496–8180) is particularly fashionable and part-owned by comedian David Brenner. **Amsterdam Billiard Club East** (✉ 210 E. 86th St., between 2nd and 3rd Aves., ☎ 212/570–4545) has 38 tables, a café, and an international beer bar. **Billiard Club** (✉ 220 W. 19th St., between 7th and 8th Aves., ☎ 212/206–7665), in Chelsea, has a classy look and loud rock music. **Chelsea Billiards** (✉ 54 W. 21st St., between 5th and 6th Aves., ☎ 212/989–0096) has 53 tables on two floors. **East Side Billiard Club** (✉ 163 E. 86th St., between 3rd and Lexington Aves., ☎ 212/831–7665) serves up pizza and beer. **Julian's Famous Poolroom** (✉ 138 E. 14th St., ☎ 212/598–9884) has 29 pool tables, two Ping-Pong tables, and a jukebox. **West Side Billiard Club** (✉ 601 W. 50th St., at 11th Ave., ☎ 212/246–1060) has 12 pool tables and eight Ping-Pong tables.

Bird-Watching

Manhattan's green parks and woodlands provide habitats for thousands of birds, everything from fork-tailed flycatchers to common nighthawks. Since the city is on the Atlantic flyway, a major migratory route, you can see birds that nest as far north as the High Arctic.

May is the best season, since the songbirds are in their freshest colors—and so many are singing at once that you can hardly distinguish their songs. To find out what's been seen where, call the Rare Bird Alert (☎ 212/979–3070). For information on best bird-watching spots in various parks, call the **Urban Park Rangers,** a uniformed division of the Parks Department: Citywide (☎ 800/201–7275); Manhattan (☎ 212/427–4040); the Bronx (☎ 718/548–7070 or 718/885–3466); Brooklyn (☎ 718/438–0100); Queens (☎ 718/353–2460 or 718/520–5316); and Staten Island (☎ 718/667–6042).

Birders will like the 1,146-acre **Van Cortlandt Park** (☎ 718/430–1890) in the Bronx, with its varied habitats, including freshwater marshes and upland woods. In Brooklyn, **Green-Wood Cemetery** (☎ 718/768–7300 for permission to enter grounds) features Victorian-era headstones, as well as a nice woodland that attracts hawks and songbirds. The Ramble in Manhattan's **Central Park** is full of warblers in springtime and may attract as many birders as it does birds. In Queens, try **Jamaica Bay Wildlife Refuge,** where birds are drawn to the 9,155 acres of salt marshes, fresh and brackish ponds, and open water; stop by the visitor center (✉ Crossbay Blvd., Broad Channel, Queens, ☎ 718/318–4340) to get a permit. In Staten Island, head for the fairly undeveloped 317-acre **Wolfe's Pond Park** (☎ 718/984–8266), where the pond and the nearby shore can be dense with geese and ducks during the annual migrations.

Guided Walks

The **New York City Audubon Society** (✉ 71 W. 23rd St., ☎ 212/691–7483) has occasional bird-watching outings; call Monday–Thursday 10–4 PM for information. Also check with the Urban Park Rangers at the numbers listed above.

Boating

The boating available on New York City's ponds and lakes conjures up 19th-century images of a parasol-twirling lady rowed by her swain.

In **Central Park,** the boats are rowboats (plus one Venetian gondola for nighttime glides in the moonlight) and the rowing terrain is the 18-acre Central Park Lake. Rent your boat at **Loeb Boathouse** (☎ 212/517–2233), near 74th Street, from spring through fall.

Boccie

This pinless Italian version of bowling thrives in New York, with 100 city courts. The easiest courts to reach from midtown are at 96th Street and 1st Avenue; at East River Drive and 42nd Street; and at the Thompson Street Playground (at Houston Street) in Greenwich Village. There's also a boccie court at **Il Vagabondo** (✉ 351 E. 62nd St., ☎ 212/832–9221), a vintage Italian restaurant east of Bloomingdale's.

Bowling

The **Leisure Time Bowling & Recreation Center** (✉ 625 8th Ave., at 42nd St., ☎ 212/268–6909) offers 30 lanes on the second floor of the Port Authority Bus Terminal. **Bowlmor** (✉ 110 University Pl., ☎ 212/255–8188) is a funky 44-lane operation frequented by a colorful Village crowd; many stay until closing time: 4 AM on weekends.

Boxing

The recent trendiness of the sport is reflected in its availability to the casual participant. **Chelsea Piers Sports Center** (✉ 23rd St. and the Hudson River, ☎ 212/336–6000) has a boxing ring and equipment circuit. Day passes are $26. **Crunch Fitness** (✉ 404 Lafayette St., ☎ 212/614–0120; ✉ 54 E. 13th St., ☎ 212/475–2018) has a boxing ring at its Lafayette Street location and kickboxing classes at its gym on East 13th St. Brooklyn's venerable **Gleason's** (✉ 75 Front St., ☎ 718/797–2872), home of 106 world champs, including Jake LaMotta and Muhammad Ali, also instructs visitors.

Chess and Checkers

In **Central Park,** the Chess & Checkers House is picturesquely situated atop a massive stone outcrop. Twenty-four outdoor tables are available during all daylight hours. Bring your own or pick up playing pieces at the **Dairy** (midpark at 64th St., ☎ 212/794–6565) Tuesday–Sunday 11–5; there is no charge, but a $20 deposit is required.

Downtown in Greenwich Village, the **Village Chess Shop** (✉ 230 Thompson St., between Bleecker and W. 3rd Sts., ☎ 212/475–9580) has 20 boards that it rents by the hour, along with timers for those who play speed chess. Uptown, the **Manhattan Chess Club** (✉ 353 W. 46th St., between 8th and 9th Aves., ☎ 212/333–5888) sponsors tournaments and exhibitions.

Dance and Aerobics

Naturally enough, New York gives birth to many a new fitness trend, and an aerobics class here may turn out to be executed on in-line skates or to the accompaniment of live gospel singing. **Crunch Fitness** (✉ 404 Lafayette St., ☎ 212/614–0120; ✉ 54 E. 13th St., ☎ 212/475–2018; ✉ 162 W. 83rd St., ☎ 212/875–1902) offers everything from straight-up aerobics to African dance and body sculpting. **Equinox** (✉ 344 Amsterdam Ave., at 76th St., ☎ 212/721–4200; ✉ 205 E. 85th St., between 2nd and 3rd Aves., ☎ 212/439–8500; ✉ 2465 Broadway, at 92nd St., ☎ 212/799–1818; ✉ 897 Broadway, between 19th and 20th Sts., ☎ 212/780–9300) has power yoga, martial arts, and meditation, along with general fitness classes. The **Vanderbilt YMCA** (✉ 224 E. 47th St., ☎ 212/756–9600) schedules more than 100 different drop-in aerobics and exercise classes every week. None requires membership for classes.

Golf

Bethpage State Park (☎ 516/249–0700), in the Long Island town of Bethpage, about one hour and 20 minutes from Manhattan, is home to five golf courses, including its 7,065-yard par-71 Black, generally ranked among the nation's top 25 public courses. Reservations for tee times are accepted 24 hours a day on the course's automated reservation hot line (☎ 516/249–0707). Reservations can be made up to four days in advance. However, getting a tee time is often a matter of luck, since all five courses are busy seven days a week.

Of the 13 city courses, the 6,215-yard Split Rock in **Pelham Bay Park,** the Bronx, is considered the most challenging (☎ 718/885–1258). Slightly easier is its sister course, the 6,405-yard Pelham, which has fewer trees to contend with. **Van Cortlandt Park** in the Bronx has the nation's first municipal golf course, established in 1895—the hilly 6,052-yard Van Cortlandt (☎ 718/543–4595). Queens has a 5,431-yard course at **Forest Park** in Woodhaven (✉ Park La. S and Forest Pkwy., ☎ 718/296–0999). Staten Island has the links-style 6,050-yard **Silver Lake** golf course (✉ 915 Victory Blvd., 1 block south of Forest Ave., ☎ 718/447–5686).

Driving Range

In midtown you can take lessons or practice your swing in netted cages, with bull's-eye backdrops, at the **Richard Metz Golf Studio** (✉ 425 Madison Ave., at 49th St., 3rd floor, ☎ 212/759–6940). Jutting right out into the river, the **Golf Club at Chelsea Piers** (✉ 23rd St. and the Hudson River, ☎ 212/336–6400) has a 200-yard artificial-turf fairway, a computerized tee-up system, and heated hitting stalls—so you can keep right on swinging even in winter.

Miniature Golf

At **Hackers, Hitters & Hoops** (✉ 123 W. 18th St., ☎ 212/929–7482), you can outsmart the obstacles on all 18 holes.

Horseback Riding

A trot on the bridle path around Central Park's Reservoir provides a pleasant look at New York. The carefully run **Claremont Riding Academy** (✉ 175 W. 89th St., ☎ 212/724–5100) is the city's oldest riding academy and the only riding stable left in Manhattan. Experienced English riders can rent horses, at $33 per hour, for an unescorted walk, trot, or canter in nearby Central Park; call ahead to reserve.

Hotel Health Clubs

Although space is tight in Manhattan hotels, most of them offer some kind of fitness facility, even if it's just an arrangement enabling guests to use a nearby health club.

Doral Fitness Center (✉ 90 Park Ave., ☎ 212/370–9692) is available to guests of the **Doral Park Avenue, Doral Court,** and **Doral Tuscany.** This serious health club offers a number of workout programs. The **Four Seasons** (✉ 57 E. 57th St., ☎ 212/758–5700) has a spacious and high-tech facility, including an aerobics room with video, free weights, StairMaster, and Cybex machines. **Holiday Inn Crowne Plaza** (✉ 1605 Broadway, at 49th St., ☎ 212/977–8880) has a fitness center operated by the New York Sports Club, with a lap pool, weights and cardiovascular equipment, and an aerobics studio. The **Peninsula** (✉ 700 5th Ave., ☎ 212/247–2200) reserves floors 21–23 for its health club and spa, with a pool on the 22nd floor, plus exercise machines, a poolside dining terrace, and a full range of bodywork. **Sheraton Manhattan** (✉ 790 7th Ave., at 51st St., ☎ 212/581–3300) has a health club including a large pool, aerobics and aquatic exercise equipment, swimming lessons, and a sundeck. The **Millenium Broadway** (✉ 145 W. 44th St., ☎ 212/768–4400) and the **Millenium Hilton** (✉ 55 Church St., ☎ 212/693–2001) each offer a fitness center with Lifecycles, treadmills, StairMaster, free-weights, and a steam room.

Ice-Skating

Each of the city's rinks has its own character, but all have scheduled skating sessions. Lockers, skate rentals, music, and snack bars complete the picture. Major rinks include the outdoor one in **Rockefeller Center** (✉ 50th St. at 5th Ave., lower plaza, ☎ 212/332–7654), which is fairly small yet utterly romantic, especially when the enormous Christmas tree towers above it. The beautifully situated **Wollman Memorial Rink** (✉ 6th Ave. at 59th St., ☎ 212/396–1010) offers skating in the open air beneath the lights of the city. Be prepared for crowds on weekends. **Sky Rink** (✉ 23rd St. and the Hudson River, ☎ 212/336–6100) has two year-round rinks in the Chelsea Piers complex.

In-Line Skating

New York is wild over in-line skating. **Peck & Goodie** (✉ 917 8th Ave., at 54th St., ☎ 212/246–6123) sells and rents skates. **Blades** has several Manhattan stores, including East (✉ 160 E. 86th St., ☎ 212/996–1644), 2nd Avenue (✉ 1414 2nd Ave., ☎ 212/249–3178), West (✉ 120 W. 72nd St., ☎ 212/787–3911), and TriBeCa (✉ 128 Chambers St., ☎ 212/964–1944); they give lessons and sell and rent skates along with all the appropriate protection.

Those who think skates should be used for disco dancing can be found, whirling and twirling and wearing headphones, weekends in Central Park between the Mall and Bethesda Fountain. Two outdoor roller rinks at the **Chelsea Piers** complex (✉ 23rd St. and the Hudson River, ☎ 212/336–6200) have free-skates, classes, Rollaerobics, and hip-hop dance parties. The **Roxy** (✉ 515 W. 18th St., ☎ 212/645–5156), a downtown dance club, goes roller-disco on Tuesday and Wednesday nights.

Jogging and Racewalking

Jogging

In New York, dog-walkers jog, librarians jog, rock stars jog, and parents jog (sometimes pushing their toddlers ahead of them in speedy strollers). Publicity notwithstanding, crime is not a problem as long as you jog when and where everybody else does. On Manhattan streets, figure 20 north–south blocks per mile.

In Manhattan, **Central Park** is the busiest spot, specifically along the 1½-mi track circling the **Reservoir**. A runners' lane has been designated along the park roads, which are closed to traffic weekdays from 10 to 3 and 7 to 10, and from 7 PM Friday to 6 AM Monday. A good 1¾-mi route starts at Tavern on the Green along the West Drive, heads south around the bottom of the park to the East Drive, and circles back west on the 72nd Street park road to your starting point. **Riverside Park,** along the Hudson River bank in Manhattan, is glorious at sunset. You can cover 4½ mi by running from 72nd to 116th streets and back.

Other favorite Manhattan circuits are around **Gramercy Park** (⅓ mi), **Washington Square Park** (½ mi), the **Battery Park City Esplanade** (about 2 mi), and the **Hudson River Esplanade** (about 1½ mi). In Brooklyn, try the **Brooklyn Heights Esplanade,** facing the Manhattan skyline, or the loop in **Prospect Park** (about 3½ mi).

A year-round schedule of races and group runs is organized by the **New York Road Runners Club** (✉ 9 E. 89th St., ☎ 212/860–4455), including group runs at 6:30 PM on weekdays and at 10 AM Saturday, starting at the club headquarters. One of the most popular events is the 5-km Runner's World Nike Midnight Run, held on New Year's Eve with many of the runners wearing inventive costumes.

Racewalking

Elbows pumping vigorously at their sides, racewalkers can move as fast as some joggers, the great difference being that their heels are planted firmly with every stride. A number of competitive racewalking events are held regularly; for information, contact the **Park Race Walker's Club** (✉ 320 E. 83rd St., Box 18, New York, NY 10028, ☎ 212/628–1317).

Swimming

The **Carmine Street Recreation Center** (✉ 7th Ave. S and Clarkson St., ☎ 212/242–5228) has a 23-yard indoor pool and a 105-yard outdoor pool. For the $25 membership fee, you can use the pools daily while you're in town, but you have to bring your own padlock and towel. **Asphalt Green** (✉ York Ave. between 90th and 92nd Sts., ☎ 212/369–8890) is a fairly new facility with a pool and some fitness equipment; the drop-in fee for the day is $15 for adults, $7 for children. **Chelsea Piers Sports Center** (✉ 23rd St. and the Hudson River, ☎ 212/336–6000) has a six-lane, 25-yard lap pool, with an adjacent whirlpool. Day passes are $26. The **U.N. Plaza–Park Hyatt** (✉ 1 United Nations Plaza, ☎ 212/702–5016) has a lovely rooftop swimming pool that can be used by nonguests for a $25-a-day fee. The **YWCA** (✉ 610 Lexington Ave., at 53rd St., ☎ 212/755–4500) has a sparkling 75-ft lap pool available at $10 to members of all YWCAs and $15 to nonmembers.

Tennis

The New York City Parks Department maintains scores of tennis courts. Some of the most scenic are the 26 clay courts and four hard courts in **Central Park** (midpark, near 94th St., ☎ 212/280–0206), set in a thicket of trees with the skyline beyond. Same-day admissions are available for $5 an hour per person.

You can also play where Steffi Graf and Monica Seles do: at the **USTA National Tennis Center** (☎ 718/760–6200) in Flushing Meadows–Corona Park, Queens, site of the U.S. Open Tournament. The center has 47 outdoor courts (and nine indoor courts, all Deco Turf II). Reservations are accepted up to two days in advance, and prices range from $14 to $40, depending on when you play.

Several local clubs will book courts to nonmembers:

Crosstown Tennis (✉ 14 W. 31st St., ☎ 212/947–5780) has four indoor hard courts that are air-conditioned in summer. **Midtown Tennis Club** (✉ 341 8th Ave., at 27th St., ☎ 212/989–8572) provides lessons and sponsors a tennis camp. It's best to make reservations for one of their eight courts a couple of days in advance. **HRC Tennis** (✉ Piers 13 and 14, East River at Wall St., ☎ 212/422–9300) has eight Har-Tru courts under two bubbles, which are air-conditioned in summer. HRC Tennis also owns **Village Tennis Courts** (✉ 110 University Pl., between 12th and 13th Sts., ☎ 212/989–2300), with two hard rubber courts that are air-conditioned in summer. **Manhattan Plaza Racquet Club** (✉ 450 W. 43rd St., ☎ 212/594–0554) offers five hard surface courts on which WTA and U.S. Open players have been known to practice—not to mention a soap opera star or two, since many actors live in special housing near the club. **Roosevelt Island Racquet Club** (✉ 281 Main St., Roosevelt Island, ☎ 212/935–0250) has 12 air-conditioned green clay courts, group and private lessons, clinics, tennis parties, and game arranging.

SPECTATOR SPORTS

Many sporting events—ranging from boxing to figure skating—take place at **Madison Square Garden** (✉ 7th Ave. between 31st and 33rd Sts.); tickets can be ordered by phone through the box office (☎ 212/465–6000) or TicketMaster (☎ 212/307–7171). Both of New York's professional football teams and one of its basketball teams perform across the Hudson River at the **Meadowlands** (✉ Rte. 3, East Rutherford, NJ, ☎ 201/935–3900 for box office and information). When events are sold out, you can sometimes pick up a ticket on the day of the game outside the venue from a fellow sports fan whose guests couldn't make it at the last minute. Ticket agencies, listed in the Manhattan Yellow Pages phone directory and the sports pages of the *Daily News* can be helpful—for a price.

Baseball

The **New York Mets** play at Shea Stadium (☎ 718/507–8499) at the penultimate stop on Subway 7 in Flushing, Queens. Although owner George Steinbrenner keeps threatening to move the team out of town, the world-champion **New York Yankees** still have their home at Yankee Stadium (☎ 718/293–6000), accessible by Subway 4, D, or C to the 161st Street station in the Bronx. The baseball season runs from April through October.

Basketball

Currently, the **New York Knickerbockers** (the "Knicks") arouse intense hometown passions, which means tickets for home games at Madison Square Garden (✉ 7th Ave. between 31st and 33rd Sts.) are *extremely* hard to come by. For up-to-date game roundups, phone the New York Knickerbockers Fan Line (☎ 212/465–5867). The **New Jersey Nets,** New York's second NBA team, play at the Meadowlands in the Continental Airlines Arena (✉ Rte. 3, East Rutherford, NJ). For tickets—which are remarkably easy to obtain—call the Meadowlands box office (☎ 201/935–3900) or TicketMaster (☎ 201/507–8900). The basketball season is late October through April.

Boxing and Wrestling

Major and minor **boxing** bouts are staged in Madison Square Garden (✉ 7th Ave. between 31st and 33rd Sts., ☎ 212/465–6000). **Wrestling,** a more frequent presence at Madison Square Garden (✉ 7th Ave. between 31st and 33rd Sts., ☎ 212/465–6000) since the days of "Gorgeous" George and "Haystack" Calhoun in the late '50s, is stagy and outrageous, drawing a rowdy but enthusiastic crowd.

Football

The enormously popular—if underachieving—**New York Giants** play at Giants Stadium in the Meadowlands sports complex (✉ Rte. 3, East Rutherford, NJ; ☎ 201/935–8111). Most seats for Giants games are sold on a season-ticket basis—and there's a waiting list for those. However, single tickets are occasionally available at the stadium box office. The hapless **New York Jets** play at Giants Stadium (✉ Rte. 3, East Rutherford, NJ; ☎ 516/560–8100). Although they're nowhere near as scarce as Giants tickets, most Jets tickets are snapped up by hopeful fans before the season opener. The football season runs from September through December.

Hockey

The **New York Rangers** play at Madison Square Garden (✉ 7th Ave. between 31st and 33rd Sts., ☎ 212/465–6741; 212/308–6977 for Rangers hot line). The **New York Islanders** skate at Nassau Veterans Memorial Coliseum in Uniondale, Long Island (☎ 516/888–9000 for tickets). The area's third hockey team, the **New Jersey Devils,** fights for the puck at the Continental Airlines Arena at the Meadowlands (✉ Rte. 3, East Rutherford, NJ, ☎ 201/935–3900). Tickets for the Islanders and Devils are usually available at game time; Rangers tickets are more difficult to find. The hockey season runs from October through April.

Horse Racing

Modern **Aqueduct Racetrack** (⊠ 110th St. and Rockaway Blvd., Ozone Park, Queens, ☎ 718/641–4700), with its spate of lawns and gardens, holds Thoroughbred races late October–early May from Wednesday to Sunday. In May the action moves from Aqueduct Racetrack to **Belmont Park** (⊠ Hempstead Turnpike, Elmont, Long Island, ☎ 718/641–4700), home of the third jewel in horse racing's triple crown, the Belmont Stakes. The horses run here May–July, from Wednesday to Sunday. Then after a few weeks upstate at Saratoga, they return to Belmont from late August through October.

The **Meadowlands** (⊠ Rte. 3, East Rutherford, NJ, ☎ 201/935–8500), generally a trotting venue, also has a flat-racing season from Labor Day through December.

Yonkers Raceway (⊠ Central Ave., Yonkers, NY, ☎ 718/562–9500) features harness racing every evening except Wednesday and Sunday year-round. The **Meadowlands** (⊠ Rte. 3, East Rutherford, NJ, ☎ 201/935–8500) has both trotters and pacers from late December until mid-August.

Running

The **New York City Marathon** has taken place annually on a Sunday in early November since 1970, and New Yorkers love to cheer on the pack of nearly 35,000 (some 95% of them finish). Racewalkers, "jogglers," oldsters, youngsters, and competitors with disabilities help to make this what former Olympic Organizing Committee president Peter V. Ueberroth called "the best sporting event in the country." Spectators line rooftops and sidewalks, promenades, and terraces all along the route—but don't go near the finish line in Central Park around 2 PM unless you relish mob scenes. Contact the **New York Road Runners Club** (☎ 212/860–4455).

Tennis

The annual **U.S. Open Tournament,** held from late August through early September at the USTA National Tennis Center (⊠ Flushing Meadow/Corona Park, Queens, ☎ 718/760–6200), is one of the high points of the tennis buff's year, and tickets to watch the late rounds are some of the hottest in town. Early-round matches are entertaining, too, and with a stadium-court ticket you can also view matches in outlying courts, where the bleachers are so close you can almost count the sweat beads on the players' foreheads, and in the grandstand, where bleacher seating is first-come, first-served. Wherever you sit, the eclectic mix of casual visitors, tennis groupies, and celebrities makes for terrific people-watching. Moreover, a $234 million expansion, including a new state-of-the-art tennis stadium completed in 1997, means the U.S. Open can accommodate even more fans. Tickets go on sale in May through Tele-charge (☎ 800/524–8440).

The tennis year winds up with the **WTA Tournament,** a major women's pro event held at Madison Square Garden (⊠ 7th Ave., between 31st and 33rd Sts., ☎ 212/465–6000) in mid-November. Tickets go on sale in September.

10 Shopping

More than ever before, New York is the place to shop—from small boutiques to gleaming international flagship stores to discount chains. Welcome the era of the superstore and the specialty boutique, each complementing the other in an ever-changing market. Such singular variety makes the retail landscape of New York an eyeful.

Revised by
Jennifer J. Paull

THERE'S SOMETHING FOR EVERYONE in every price range in New York. Fancy a pair of official spoons salvaged from the Kremlin vaults? Just call the **Sovietski Collection** (☎ 800/442–0002). A selection of skulls? **Danse Macabre** downtown can outfit you nicely. Or if you favor high-end designers (especially Italian), the recent store openings along Madison Avenue will keep your credit cards busy.

One of Manhattan's biggest shopping lures is the bargain—a temptation fueled in recent years by the Manhattan openings of discount divas such as Loehmann's. Hawkers of not-so-real Gucci watches are stationed at street intersections (even on Madison Avenue), and Canal Street is lined with faux Prada backpacks. There are thrift shops where well-known socialites send their castoffs and movie stars snap up antique lace; while resale prices are definitely higher than in smaller cities, the sheer selection can make up for it. Designers' showroom sales allow you to buy cheap at the source; auctions promise good prices as well.

Sales

Sales take place late June and July (for summer merchandise) and late December and January (for winter wares); these sales are announced in the papers. Be sure to check out *New York* magazine's "Sales and Bargains" column; it often lists sales in manufacturers' showrooms that are otherwise never promoted publicly. The *Village Voice* is also a good source for tip-off sale ads. If your visit is planned for April or October, when many manufacturers' sales take place, you might phone your favorite designer and ask whether one is in the offing. Find out before you go if you can try on the clothes and whether the seller requires cash or accepts credit cards and checks (local or out-of-state).

Shopping Neighborhoods

New York shops are, for the most part, collected in neighborhoods rather than in malls, so take advantage of good weather to prowl the stores—not only are the odds good that you'll find an irresistible something, but you'll get a strong sense of an area's personality as well. The following sections single out shopping highlights in each neighborhood. Addresses for shops, if not included here, can be found in store listings below.

South Street Seaport

The Seaport's shops are located along the cobbled, pedestrians-only extension to Fulton Street; in the Fulton Market building, the original home of the city's fish market; and on the three levels of Pier 17. Stores in this area tend toward the conservative upscale; for dependable women's clothing try **Ann Taylor** and **Liz Claiborne** (⊠ 133 Beekman St., ☎ 212/346–9190) which includes the Elisabeth line for sizes 14 to 22. The big catalog house **J. Crew** opened its first Manhattan retail outlet in one of the Seaport's old waterfront hotels. Pier 17 has few surprises, but there are some few-of-a-kind shops, including the **Mark Reuben Gallery** (☎ 212/964–6300) for hand printed sepia-toned photographs of both modern and old-time subjects (heavy on the Yankees); **Mariposa** (☎ 212/233–3221) for rare butterflies mounted under Lucite; and **Swatch** (⊠ 89 South St., ☎ 212/571–6400) for mischievous timepieces.

World Financial Center

Although the nearby World Trade Center bills its concourse as the city's busiest shopping center, the World Financial Center in Battery Park City is a shopping destination to reckon with, thanks to stores such as **Barneys New York** for clothing, **Godiva Chocolatier** for chocolates, **Platypus** for unique gifts, **Ann Taylor,** and **Caswell-Massey. Rizzoli** has books and magazines stocked on handsome wooden shelves, and **Quest Toys** (☎ 212/945–9330) has a wonderful selection of wooden and educational playthings.

Lower East Side/East Village

Once home to millions of Jewish immigrants from Russia and Eastern Europe, the Lower East Side is New Yorkers' bargain beat. The center of it all is narrow, unprepossessing Orchard Street, which is crammed with tiny, no-nonsense clothing and shoe stores ranging from kitschy to elegant. Don't expect to schmooze with salespeople, especially on Sunday, the busiest day of the week (on Saturday shops in the Orchard Street area are closed). Start at Houston Street, walk down one side as far as Canal Street, and then walk back up. Essential stops include **Fine & Klein** for handbags and **Forman's** for women's clothing. Grand Street (off Orchard Street, south of Delancey Street) is chockablock with linens, towels, and other items for the home; the Bowery (between Grand Street and Delancey Street), with lamps and lighting fixtures. The East Village offers diverse, off-beat specialty stops, including **Little Rickie** for collectible kitsch. Elizabeth Street in particular is beginning to feel the approving scrutiny of housewares-hunters.

SoHo

The mallification of SoHo has become increasingly evident. Chain stores such as **Victoria's Secret** and **Eddie Bauer** now have Broadway addresses, and **J. Crew** has an outpost on Prince Street. However, there's still a strong percentage of unique shops, especially for housewares and fashion. Recent additions such as **Miu Miu** for double-take worthy clothes hone the creative edge. Some well-known stops include **Wolfman-Gold & Good Company** for decorative items; **Dean & DeLuca,** a gourmet food emporium; **Zona** and **Moss,** full of well-designed home furnishings and gifts; **Williams-Sonoma Grande Cuisine** for kitchenware and gourmet specialties; and the remarkable **Enchanted Forest** toy store. On Lafayette Street below Houston, a hip new strip includes shops outside the mainstream, mainly dealing in home furnishings. Many stores in SoHo are open seven days a week.

Lower 5th Avenue/Chelsea

Fifth Avenue south of 23rd Street, along with the streets fanning east and west, is home to a lively downtown crowd. Many of the locals sport clothes from the neighborhood—a mix of the hip like **Emporio Armani, Paul Smith,** and **Matsuda** (for Japanese designer clothing) as well as discount clothiers such as **Moe Ginsburg.** The sudden surge of gallery openings in the low 20s between 10th and 11th avenues handily provides more events to merit the latest fashions—and more opportunities to go home with a de Kooning. In the same latitudes on 6th Avenue are a cluster of superstores, including **Barnes & Noble, T. J. Maxx, Filene's Basement, Burlington Coat Factory,** and **Old Navy,** as well as the colossal **Bed, Bath & Beyond. Barneys, Loehmann's, Williams-Sonoma,** and **Pottery Barn** are within walking distance on 7th Avenue.

Herald Square

Reasonable prices prevail at this intersection of 34th Street and Avenue of the Americas (6th Avenue). Giant **Macy's** has traditionally been the linchpin. Opposite is Manhattan's first **Toys "R" Us.** Next door on 6th Avenue, the seven-story Manhattan Mall is anchored by **Stern's** department store, which makes for wonderful browsing, as do **Lechter's,** for home furnishings, and **HMV,** for its large music selection. The concentration of shops in a small area makes it a good bet in nasty weather.

5th Avenue

The boulevard that was once home to some of the biggest names in New York retailing may have lost some ground to neighboring Madison Avenue, but 5th Avenue from Central Park South to Rockefeller Center still has the goods. Strong proof lies in the luster of the multistory **Versace** store, opened in late August 1996—not to mention the renovation of the **Bergdorf Goodman Men** store (at 58th St.) and **Salvatore Ferragamo**'s expansion. The perennial favorites will eat up a lot of shoe leather: **F.A.O. Schwarz** and **Bergdorf Goodman** (at 58th St.); **Tiffany** and **Bulgari** jewelers (at 57th St.); **Ferragamo** and other various luxury stores in **Trump Tower** (at 56th St.); **Steuben** crystal (at 56th St.); **Henri Bendel,** across the street; **Takashimaya** (at 54th St.); **Cartier** jewelers (at 52nd St.); and so on down to the flag-bedecked **Saks Fifth Avenue** (at 50th St.). **Rockefeller Center** itself provides plenty of smaller specialty shops. To the south (at 47th St.) is the shiny 575 atrium mall, named for its 5th Avenue address, and the venerable **Lord & Taylor** department store (at 39th St.).

57th Street

The short section of 57th Street between 5th and Madison Avenues seems to have gotten a sudden injection of steroids—and a nose job into the bargain. The coveted block is no longer limited to top-echelon fashion houses, as more affordable (and sizable) stores have muscled their way in. The cartoon-crammed **Warner Bros. Studio Store** finished a massive expansion in fall 1996; not to be outdone, **NikeTown** has opened the largest of its high-tech U.S. sportswear emporiums. Exclusive stores such as **Chanel, Burberrys, Escada,** and **Hermès** have closed ranks on the north side of the street; when an **Original Levi's Store** opened next to Chanel a couple of years ago, the grande dame of couture houses edged a few doors closer to Madison Avenue, opening a lofty town house in 1996. **Louis Vuitton** is following suit with an impressive space just next door. Above many of these jostling stores perch top art galleries such as **André Emmerich** and **Pace.** To the west of 5th Avenue are more human-scale shops, such as the **Compleat Strategist** game store (between 8th and 9th Aves.), **Coliseum Books,** a very classy branch of **Rizzoli**'s bookstores, and **Paron Fabrics** (⊠ 56 W. 57th St., ☎ 212/247–6451).

Columbus Avenue

Between 66th and 86th streets, this former tenement district is now home to a rich shopping strip. Stores are mostly modern in design, upscale but not top-of-the-line. Clothing runs the gamut from traditional for men and women (**Frank Stella Ltd.**) to high funk (**Betsey Johnson**) and high style (**Charivari**).

Upper East Side

Madison Avenue, roughly between 57th and 79th streets, can satisfy almost any couture craving. The magnetic center has shifted a bit in the past year, ratcheting down a few blocks toward the pull of **Giorgio Armani** (at 65th St.), whose spacious new digs opened in fall 1996. Other Italian design houses are making themselves felt; **Moschino, Valentino, Prada** and the less familiar but tantalizing **Etro** also opened flagship stores here in 1996. And evidently, one Madison storefront wasn't enough for the irrepressible Gianni Versace, who added a **Versus** boutique next to his men's and women's store in fall 1997 (the specialized men's boutique closed in spring 1997). The majority of these new stores engulf much larger spaces than traditional, one-level Madison boutiques. With such opulent new neighbors, a ripple effect is under way; relative old-timers such as **Coach** have freshened up their long-run establishments. Madison isn't just a fashion funnel, however; there

298

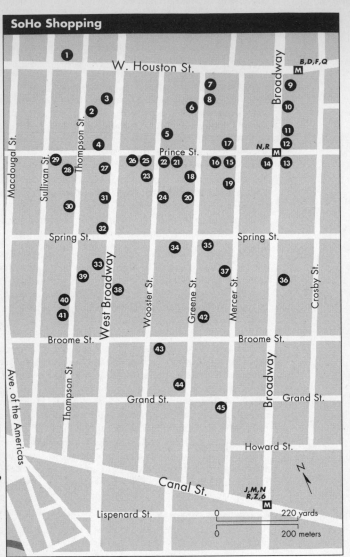

SoHo Shopping

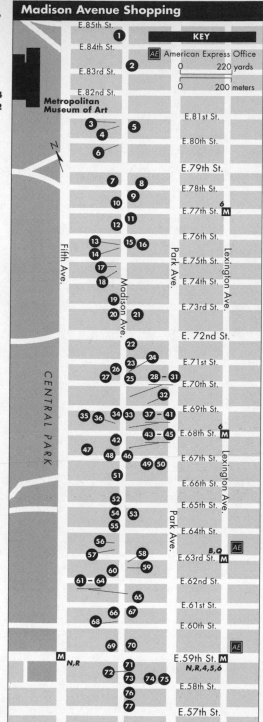

57th Street/5th Avenue Shopping

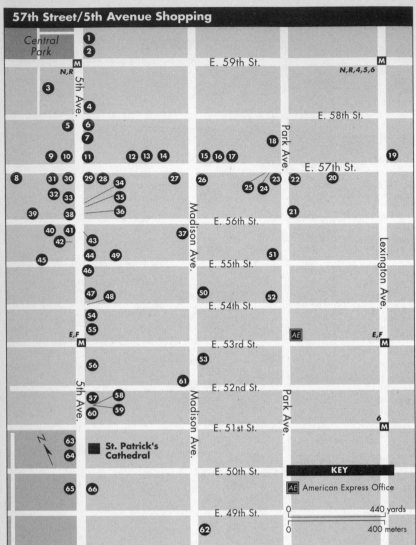

Central Park

E. 59th St.

N,R 5th Ave.

E. 58th St.

Park Ave.

E. 57th St.

Madison Ave.

E. 56th St.

E. 55th St.

Lexington Ave.

E. 54th St.

E. 53rd St.

E,F

St. Patrick's Cathedral

E. 52nd St.

E. 51st St.

N

E. 50th St.

KEY

AE American Express Office

E. 49th St.

0 .... 440 yards

0 .... 400 meters

A La Vieille Russie, **2**
Alfred Dunhill of London, **23**
André Emmerich Gallery, **15**
Asprey, **36**
Aveda, **53**
Bergdorf Goodman, **5, 6**
Blum Helman, **31**
Bulgari, **30**
Burberrys, **12**
Cartier, **57**
Chanel, **14**
Charivari 57, **32**
Cole-Haan, **63**
Christian Dior, **46**
Church's English Shoes, **62**
David Webb, **22**

Dempsey & Carroll, **20**
The Disney Store, **45**
F.A.O. Schwarz, **4**
Façonnable, **48**
Felissimo, **40**
Fortunoff, **55**
Galleri Orrefors Kosta Boda, **24**
Geoffrey Beene, **1**
Gianni Versace, **58**
Gucci, **54**
H. Stern, **60**
Hammacher Schlemmer, **19**
Harry Winston, **41**
Hélène Arpels, **18**
Henri Bendel, **42**
Hermès, **13**
Holland & Holland, **25**

Israel Sack, **33**
J.N. Bartfield, **8**
Librairie de France/Libraria Hispanica, **64**
Louis Féraud, **38**
Louis Vuitton, **17**
Manolo Blahnik, **44**
Mark Cross, **59**
Mary Boone Gallery, **7**
Morrell & Company, **50**
Neuchatel Chocolates, **3**
Niketown, **28**
Norma Kamali O.M.O., **39**
Pace Gallery, **27**
Prada, **16**
Richart Design et Chocolat, **49**

Rizzoli, **9**
Saks Fifth Avenue, **66**
Salvatore Ferragamo, **35, 56**
Sony Style, **37**
Steuben, **43**
Sulka, **51**
Syms, **52**
T. Anthony, **21**
Takashimaya New York, **47**
Teuscher Chocolates, **65**
Tiffany & Co., **29**
Tourneau, **26, 61**
Trump Tower, **34**
Van Cleef & Arpels, **10**
Warner Bros. Studio Store, **11**

are several outstanding antiques and art dealers as well. And just one avenue away, on Lexington, you'll find a healthy number of intriguing stores—where the prices aren't always sky-high. The industrial-edged **Diesel Superstore,** for instance, has its first sizable U.S. location at Lexington and 60th Street.

Blitz Tours

Get your subway tokens ready, and save enough cash for cab fare to lug all your packages home from these shopping itineraries. They're arranged by special interest; addresses, if not included here, can be found in the store listings below.

Antiques
Spend two hours at the **Manhattan Art & Antiques Center** on 2nd Avenue (at 55th St.); then swing over to 57th Street for an even posher array of European, American, and Asian treasures. Stroll westward across 57th Street, stopping at **Lillian Nassau** of Tiffany lamp and Art Nouveau furniture fame and **Israel Sack,** nearby on 5th Avenue, with superb American antique furniture. Then head up Madison to **Didier Aaron** (on 67th St.), **Stair & Company** (near 74th St.), **DeLorenzo** and **Leo Kaplan** (near 75th St.), **David A. Schorsch** (on 76th St.), **Florian Papp** (at 76th St.), **Leigh Keno** (near 76th St.), and **Barry Friedman** (at 83rd St.).

Bargains
Start early at **Century 21** or **Syms** in lower Manhattan. Take a cab to Hester and Orchard streets and shop along Orchard to Houston Street. (Prowl along Grand Street if you're more interested in goods for your home than in clothing.) Leave at 2:30 and take a cab to **S&W** in Chelsea; shop the new Chelsea discounters—**Old Navy, Bed, Bath & Beyond,** and others, for everything from clothes to housewares; then tackle the new **Loehmann's.** But remember: On Saturday, most shops on the Lower East Side are closed.

Kitchen Supplies
Browse in **Zabar's** (⊠ 2245 Broadway, at W. 80th St.) for a couple of hours beginning at 8 AM; then go across town to **Kitchen Arts & Letters** bookstore (⊠ 1435 Lexington Ave., between 93rd and 94th Sts.) and proceed down to **Bridge Kitchenware** (⊠ 214 E. 52nd St.). Order an enchanting fruit basket from **Manhattan Fruitier** (⊠ 105 E. 29th St.), and if you're in the professional-kitchen category, visit **Lamalle Kitchenwares** (⊠ 36 W. 25th St., 6th floor, ☏ 212/242–0750). Keep heading downtown to hit **Balducci's** in the Village; **Williams-Sonoma Grande Cuisine** (⊠ 580 Broadway, between Houston and Prince Sts.), **Dean & DeLuca** (⊠ 560 Broadway, at Prince St.), and **Broadway Panhandler** (⊠ 477 Broome St., between Greene and Wooster Sts.) in SoHo; and **Kam-Man** (⊠ 200 Canal St.) in Chinatown. Or head uptown to **Macy's Cellar** (⊠ Herald Sq., Broadway at 34th St.)

Home Furnishings
For a French accent, start at the luscious, two-story **La Maison Moderne** (⊠ 144 W. 19th St.) for distinctive home furnishings and one-of-a-kind gifts, also complimentary espresso and cappuccino; on weekends, mimosas. Head to Greenwich Village to **William–Wayne & Co.** (⊠ 40 University Pl.) for elegant decorative gifts for the home and garden. Then take a cab to SoHo, making sure not to miss an irresistible trio on Greene Street: **Wolfman-Gold & Good** (⊠ 116 Greene St.), **Moss** (⊠ 146 Greene St.), and **Zona** (⊠ 97 Greene St.). For cross-cultural finds, walk east and poke around the truly small boutiques on Elizabeth Street. Cab it back uptown to **Crate & Barrel** (⊠ 650 Madison Ave., at 59th St.) for great, lower-priced selections and finally head over

to **Bloomingdale's** (⊠ 3rd Ave. at 59th St.), open late on Thursday, and to **Macy's** (⊠ Herald Sq., Broadway at 34th St.), open late Monday, Thursday, and Friday.

Department Stores

Most of these stores keep regular hours on weekdays and are open late (until 8 or 9) at least one night a week. Many have personal shoppers who can walk you through the store at no charge.

ABC Carpet & Home (⊠ 888 Broadway, at 19th St., ☎ 212/473–3000). This store is definitely not a chain; its theatrical quality would be next to impossible to duplicate. And with its recently expanded home decoration selection, this immense emporium just gets bigger and better. From vintage tea sets to trimmings to meditation cushions, good taste prevails.

Barneys New York (⊠ 660 Madison Ave., at 61st St., ☎ 212/826–8900; ⊠ World Financial Center, ☎ 212/945–1600). Like a true gentleman, Barneys does not betray its financial woes (the company filed for bankruptcy in 1996). The Chelsea space may have closed, but the Madison Avenue branch has a chi-chi new restaurant, Fred's. The extensive menswear selection is introducing a handful of edgier designers such as Alexander McQueen. (Made-to-measure is always available.) The women's department is a showcase of cachet names like Armani, Jil Sander, and Vivienne Westwood.

Bergdorf Goodman (⊠ 754 5th Ave., between 57th and 58th Sts., ☎ 212/753–7300). Good taste reigns in an elegant and understated setting; you can visit the salon in the former Goodman family penthouse apartment. The home department has rooms full of wonderful linens, tableware, and gifts. The expanded men's store, across the street, is the perfect companion.

Bloomingdale's (⊠ 1000 3rd Ave., at 59th St., ☎ 212/355–5900). Only a handful of department stores occupy an entire city block; Macy's is one, and this New York institution is another. The main floor is a stupefying maze of cosmetic counters, mirrors, and black walls; elsewhere the racks are overfull and the salespeople overworked. Still, selections are dazzling at all but the lowest price points, and the markdowns on designer goods can be rewarding.

Henri Bendel (⊠ 712 5th Ave., between 55th and 56th Sts., ☎ 212/247–1100). Bendel's continues to charm with its stylish displays and its Lalique windows, even as it temporarily discombobulates the uninitiated with its swirling floor plan. Shoe lovers should be forewarned that there is no true footwear department.

Lord & Taylor (⊠ 424 5th Ave., between 38th and 39th Sts., ☎ 212/391–3344). This store can be relied upon for the wearable, the fashionable, and the classic in clothes and accessories for women. It's refined, well stocked, and never overwhelming.

Macy's (⊠ Herald Sq., Broadway at 34th St., ☎ 212/695–4400). Macy's main store claims to be the largest retail store in America. It recently embarked on a three-year renovation program that is sprucing up departments one by one; a new restaurant will also be added. Fashionwise, there's a concentration on the mainstream rather than the luxe, and its main floor is reassuringly traditional. For cooking gear and housewares, the freshened-up Cellar nearly outdoes Zabar's.

Saks Fifth Avenue (⊠ 611 5th Ave., between 49th and 50th Sts., ☎ 212/753–4000). This wonderful store still embodies the spirit of service and style with which it opened in 1926. Saks believes in good manners, the ceremonies of life . . . and dressing for the part.

Stern's (⊠ 33rd St. and 6th Ave., ☎ 212/244–6060). What was the old Gimbel's, a block south of Macy's, lives again as home to an atrium mall, whose nine floors are anchored by Stern's, which is working hard to become as well established here as in the outer boroughs.
Takashimaya New York (⊠ 693 5th Ave., between 54th and 55th Sts., ☎ 212/350–0100). This pristine branch of Japan's largest department store carries stylish clothes and fine household items, all of which reflect a combination of Eastern and Western designs. The gardening-section–cum–front-window-display is one of 5th Avenue's most refreshing sights.

Specialty Shops

Many specialty stores have several branches in the city; in those cases, we have listed the locations in the busier shopping neighborhoods.

Antiques

Antiquing is fine sport in Manhattan. Goods run the gamut from rarefied museum-quality to wacky and eminently affordable. Premier shopping areas are on Madison Avenue north of 57th Street, 57th Street east of 5th Avenue, and 60th Street between 2nd and 3rd avenues, where more than 20 shops, dealing in everything from 18th-century French furniture to Art Deco lighting fixtures, cluster on one block. Around 11th and 12th streets, between University Place and Broadway, a tantalizing array of settees, tables, bedsteads, and rocking chairs can be seen in the windows of about two dozen dealers, many of whom have TO THE TRADE signs on their doors; a card from your hometown architect or decorator, however, may get you inside. Most dealers are open on Saturday.

Many small dealers cluster in three antiques "malls."

Chelsea Antiques Building (⊠ 110 W. 25th St., ☎ 212/929–0909). With a full 12 floors of antiques and collectibles, the options run the gamut from antique books to vintage Georg Jensen silver to lunch boxes.
Manhattan Art & Antiques Center (⊠ 1050 2nd Ave., between 55th and 56th Sts., ☎ 212/355–4400). Some 100 dealers stocking everything from paisley and Judaica to satsuma, scientifica, and samovars jumble the three floors here. The level of quality is not, as a rule, up to that of Madison Avenue, but then neither are the prices.
Metropolitan Arts and Antiques Pavilion (⊠ 110 W. 19th St., between 6th Ave. and 7th Aves., ☎ 212/463–0200). Good for costume jewelry, off-beat bric-a-brac, and '50s kitsch, this antiques mall holds regularly scheduled auctions and specialty shows featuring rare books, photography, tribal art, Victoriana, and other lots.

AMERICAN AND ENGLISH

Beshar's (⊠ 1513 1st Ave., at 79th St., ☎ 212/288–1998). There's a sprinkling of Asian pieces among the English and American antiques here—as well as a good Asian rug selection.
City Barn Antiques (⊠ 269 Lafayette St., between Prince and Spring Sts., ☎ 212/941–5757). Come for your fill of Heywood-Wakefield originals and streamlined pieces from the '30s to the '50s.
David A. Schorsch (⊠ 30 E. 76th St., No. 11A, ☎ 212/439–6100). This specialist in Early American furniture and folk art sees clients by appointment only.
Florian Papp (⊠ 962 Madison Ave., between 75th and 76th Sts., ☎ 212/288–6770). This store has an unassailed reputation among knowledgeable collectors.

Hyde Park Antiques (✉ 836 Broadway, between 12th and 13th Sts., ☎ 212/477–0033). This store features English decorative arts from the 18th and 19th centuries.

Israel Sack (✉ 730 5th Ave., between 56th and 57th Sts., ☎ 212/399–6562). This is widely considered one of the very best places in the country for 18th-century American furniture.

Kentshire Galleries (✉ 37 E. 12th St., ☎ 212/673–6644). Elegant furniture in room settings is displayed on eight floors, with an emphasis on formal English pieces from the early 18th and 19th centuries, particularly the Georgian and Regency periods.

Leigh Keno American Antiques (✉ 980 Madison Ave., between 76th and 77th Sts., 2nd floor, ☎ 212/734–2381). Before he was 30, Leigh Keno set a new auction record in the American antiques field by paying $2.75 million for a hairy-paw-foot Philadelphia wing chair. He has a good eye and an interesting inventory.

Stair & Company (✉ 942 Madison Ave., between 74th and 75th Sts., ☎ 212/517–4400). Period rooms stylishly show off fine 18th- and 19th-century English mahogany and other pieces.

Steve Miller American Folk Art (✉ 17 E. 96th St., ☎ 212/348–5219). This gallery is run by one of the country's premier folk-art dealers, the author of *The Art of the Weathervane*.

Thomas K. Woodard (✉ 506 E. 74th St., ☎ 212/794–9404). Americana and antique quilts are among the specialties of this prestigious dealer.

ECLECTIC

Newel Art Galleries (✉ 425 E. 53rd St., ☎ 212/758–1970). Located near the East Side's interior-design district, this gallery, the city's biggest antiques store, has a huge collection that roams from the Renaissance to the 20th century.

EUROPEAN

Barry Friedman (✉ 32 E. 67th St., ☎ 212/794–8950). Wiener Werkstätte, Bauhaus, De Stijl, Russian Constructivist, and other European avant-gardists star.

DeLorenzo (✉ 958 Madison Ave., between 75th and 76th Sts., ☎ 212/249–7575). Come here for the sinuous curves, strongly articulated shapes, and highly polished surfaces of French Art Deco furniture and accessories.

Didier Aaron (✉ 32 E. 67th St., ☎ 212/988–5248). This highly esteemed gallery specializes in superb 18th- and 19th-century French furniture and paintings.

L'Antiquaire & The Connoisseur, Inc. (✉ 36 E. 73rd St., ☎ 212/517–9176). Proprietress Helen Fioratti has written a guide to French antiques, but she is equally knowledgeable about the Italian and Spanish furniture and decorative objects from the 15th through the 18th centuries, as well as the medieval arts, that compose her stock.

Leo Kaplan Ltd. (✉ 967 Madison Ave., between 75th and 76th Sts., ☎ 212/249–6766). The impeccable items here include Art Nouveau glass and pottery, porcelain from 18th-century England, stunning antique and modern paperweights, and Russian artwork.

Malmaison Antiques (✉ 253 E. 74th St., ☎ 212/288–7569). This gallery has the country's largest selection of Empire furniture and decorative arts.

Pierre Deux Antiques (✉ 369 Bleecker St., at Charles St., ☎ 212/243–7740). The company that brought French provincial to a provincial America still offers an excellent selection.

FUN STUFF

Back Pages Antiques (✉ 125 Greene St., between W. Houston and Prince Sts., ☎ 212/460–5998). To acquire a restored antique jukebox or slot machine, just drop in.

Darrow's Fun Antiques (✉ 1101 1st Ave., between 60th and 61st Sts., ☎ 212/838–0730). The first of the city's nostalgia shops, the store is full of whimsy: antique toys, animation art, and other collectibles.

John T. Johnston's Jukebox Classics (✉ 6742 5th Ave., near 68th St., Brooklyn, ☎ 718/833–8455). You'll find oodles of vintage jukeboxes, pinball machines, gum-ball machines, slot machines, and other goodies, all expertly restored.

Art Galleries

America's art capital, New York has numerous wealthy collectors, so many galleries are minimuseums that welcome browsing. Be sure to delve into Chelsea's art scene, which is rapidly taking on shape and substance—and call ahead for hours, since some galleries run on "SoHo time" (Tuesday through Saturday) and some on "Chelsea time" (Wednesday through Sunday).

André Emmerich Gallery (✉ 41 E. 57th St., ☎ 212/752–0124). Located in the Art Deco Fuller Building, this gallery displays major works by major modern artists.

Art in General (✉ 79 Walker St., ☎ 212/219–0473). Come here for works in a variety of mediums by emerging contemporary artists.

Blum Helman (✉ 20 W. 57th St., ☎ 212/245–2888). Contemporary art by Brian Hunt, Robert Moskowitz, Joe Andoe, and Ellsworth Kelly, among others, is displayed here.

A Clean, Well-Lighted Place (✉ 363 Bleecker St., at Charles St., ☎ 212/255–3656). Drop in here for prints by well-known artists, including Sean Scully, Susan Rothenberg, Robert Motherwell, and David Hockney.

David Zwirner (✉ 43 Greene St., between Broome and Grand Sts., ☎ 212/966–9074). Strong proof that SoHo's art scene still has some lifeblood, this gallery has very high-caliber contemporary shows.

First Peoples Gallery (✉ 114 Spring St., ☎ 212/343–0166). Paintings, sculpture, and magnificent pottery by many of the country's top Native American artists are showcased here.

Gagosian (✉ 980 Madison Ave., 6th floor, between 76th and 77th Sts., ☎ 212/744–2313; ✉ 136 Wooster St., between W. Houston and Prince Sts., ☎ 212/228–2828). Works on display are by such established artists as Richard Serra, Willem de Kooning, and Jasper Johns.

Hirschl & Adler (✉ 21 E. 70th St., ☎ 212/535–8810). A respected dealer of American painting and sculpture, this gallery also offers American decorative arts. Among the celebrated artists whose works are featured: Thomas Cole, Childe Hassam, Ralston Crawford, John Storrs, and William Merritt Chase.

Isselbacher (✉ 41 E. 78th St., ☎ 212/472–1766). This gallery offers prints by late-19th- and 20th-century masters such as Henri Toulouse-Lautrec, Henri Matisse, Marc Chagall, Joan Miró, Pablo Picasso, and Edvard Munch. Call ahead for an appointment.

James Danziger Gallery (✉ 130 Prince St., ☎ 212/226–0056). Stop here to see the work of high-profile photographers; a past glitzy show profiled supermodel Kate Moss.

Leo Castelli (✉ 420 W. Broadway, between Prince and Spring Sts., ☎ 212/431–5160; ✉ 578 Broadway, near Prince St., ☎ 212/431–6279). He's the man who discovered pop. Look for art by Jasper Johns, Roy Lichtenstein, Ed Ruscha, and Ed Rosenquist.

Margo Feiden Galleries (✉ 699 Madison Ave., between 62nd and 63rd Sts., ☎ 212/677–5330). The specialty here is drawings by theatrical caricaturist Al Hirschfeld, who has been delighting readers of the *New York Times* for more than 60 years.

Mary Boone Gallery (⊠ 745 5th Ave., between 57th and 58th Sts., ☎ 212/752–2929). A hot gallery from the '80s, it's now uptown and still intriguing, with such artists as Eric Fischl and Richard Tuttle.

Matthew Marks Gallery (⊠ 522 W. 22nd St., ☎ 212/243–1650; ⊠ 513–515 W. 24th St., ☎ 212/243–0200; ⊠ 1018 Madison Ave., between 78th and 79th Sts., ☎ 212/861–9455). In each of his three spaces, Marks shows prominent modern artists such as Ellsworth Kelly. On 24th Street, a two-story former garage is newly divided among three noteworthy dealers collectively nicknamed MGM: Matthew Marks, Barbara Gladstone, and Metro Pictures.

Multiple Impressions (⊠ 128 Spring St., ☎ 212/925–1313). Twentieth-century American, European, Asian, and South American paintings and prints are offered here at reasonable prices.

O. K. Harris (⊠ 383 W. Broadway, between Spring and Broome Sts., ☎ 212/431–3600). The oldest gallery in SoHo, opened in 1969, O. K. Harris showcases paintings, sculpture, and photography by contemporary artists.

Pace Gallery (⊠ 32 E. 57th St., ☎ 212/421–3292). This gallery features such well-known modern and contemporary artists as Picasso, Alexander Calder, and Julian Schnabel.

Pat Hearn Gallery (⊠ 530 W. 22nd St., ☎ 212/727–7366). Emerging and established artists are showcased here.

Paula Cooper Gallery (⊠ 534 W. 21st St., ☎ 212/255–1105). A SoHo groundbreaker, Cooper has moved to a grand new space complete with skylights, wood-beamed ceilings, a bookstore—and vast amounts of wall space able to accommodate museum-scale shows.

Spanierman Gallery (⊠ 45 E. 58th St., ☎ 212/832–0208). More than a half-century old and now in handsome quarters, this gallery deals in 19th- and early 20th-century American painting and sculpture.

Books

With so many of the country's publishing houses, magazines, and writers based here, there is an abundance of bookshops, small and large. Of course, all the big national chains are here, with branches all over town—**Barnes & Noble, B. Dalton, Borders,** and **Waldenbooks.**

Biography Bookshop (⊠ 400 Bleecker St., at W. 11th St., ☎ 212/807–8655). Published diaries, letters, biographies, and autobiographies fill this neighborly store.

Coliseum Books (⊠ 1771 Broadway, at 57th St., ☎ 212/757–8381). This supermarket of a bookstore has a huge, quirky selection of remainders, best-sellers, and scholarly works.

Corner Bookstore (⊠ 1313 Madison Ave., at 93rd St., ☎ 212/831–3554). This friendly small shop has been a favorite with local book lovers for years.

Drama Book Shop (⊠ 723 7th Ave., between 48th and 49th Sts., ☎ 212/944–0595). The comprehensive stock here includes scripts, scores, and libretti.

Gotham Book Mart (⊠ 41 W. 47th St., ☎ 212/719–4448). The late Frances Steloff opened this store years ago with just $200 in her pocket, half of it on loan. But she helped launch James Joyce's *Ulysses,* D. H. Lawrence, and Henry Miller and is now legendary among bibliophiles—as is her bookstore.

Librairie de France/Libraria Hispanica (⊠ 610 5th Ave., in Rockefeller Center, ☎ 212/581–8810). These huge collections of foreign-language books, videos, and periodicals, some in quite exotic tongues, are among the country's largest. Books in French and Spanish predominate.

Madison Avenue Bookshop (⊠ 833 Madison Ave., between 69th and 70th Sts., ☎ 212/535–6130). Serious contemporary fiction and biographies are sold here in pleasant surroundings.

Rizzoli (⊠ 31 W. 57th St., ☎ 212/759–2424; ⊠ 454 W. Broadway, near Prince St., ☎ 212/674–1616; ⊠ World Financial Center, ☎ 212/385–1400). Uptown, an elegant marble entrance, oak paneling, chandeliers, and classical music accompany books and magazines on art, architecture, dance, design, photography, and travel; the downtown stores come with fewer frills, though the SoHo location has a quirky gift shop.

Shakespeare & Co. (⊠ 939 Lexington Ave., between 68th and 69th Sts., ☎ 212/570–0201; ⊠ 716 Broadway, at Washington Pl., ☎ 212/529–1330). The stock here represents what's happening in publishing today in just about every field. Late hours are a plus.

GAY AND LESBIAN

A Different Light (⊠ 151 W. 19th St., ☎ 212/989–4850). This is a popular source for fiction, nonfiction, periodicals, calendars, posters, and information about gay life in New York.

Oscar Wilde Memorial Bookshop (⊠ 15 Christopher St., ☎ 212/255–8097). Opened in 1967, this was the first gay and lesbian bookstore in the city. It's just steps away from the site of the Stonewall riots.

MUSIC

Carl Fischer (62 Cooper Sq., ☎ 212/777–0900; ⊠ 44 W. 62nd St., at Columbus Ave., ☎ 212/265–8662). The landmark East Village store is famous for its excellent selection of sheet music for all instruments, including music for choir and band. Julliard students and West Side musicians flock to the Lincoln Center branch.

Joseph Patelson Music House (⊠ 160 W. 56th St., ☎ 212/582–5840). A huge collection of scores has long made this the heart of the music lover's New York.

MYSTERY AND SUSPENSE

Murder Ink (⊠ 2486 Broadway, between 92nd and 93rd Sts., ☎ 212/362–8905). Mystery lovers have relied on this Upper West Side institution for years; ask the knowledgeable staff for recommendations.

Mysterious Bookshop (⊠ 129 W. 56th St., ☎ 212/765–0900). Come here to uncover one of the largest selection of mystery, suspense and detective fiction in the city—new, used, and out-of-print volumes, as well as first editions.

Partners & Crime (⊠ 44 Greenwich Ave., between 10th and 11th Sts., ☎ 212/243–0440). This inviting shop has a helpful staff and whodunits galore—new, out-of-print, and first editions; revered mystery writers give readings here. Check out the imported British paperbacks, the rental library, and the "radio mystery hour" on Saturday evenings.

RARE AND USED BOOKS

Academy Book Store (⊠ 10 W. 18th St., ☎ 212/242–4848). Out-of-print, used, antiquarian, scholarly, and art books overflow here. Academy also deals with autographs and carries a selection of classical and jazz records and CDs.

Archivia (✉ 944 Madison Ave., between 74th and 75th Sts., ☎ 212/439–9194). The shop stocks new, used, and out-of-print books on all sorts of design and decorative arts.

Argosy Bookstore (✉ 116 E. 59th St., ☎ 212/753–4455). This sedate landmark, established in 1921, keeps a scholarly stock of books and autographs.

Bauman Rare Books (✉ Waldorf-Astoria, lobby level, 301 Park Ave., at 50th St., ☎ 212/759–8300). This successful Philadelphia firm now offers New Yorkers the most impossible-to-get titles, first editions, and fine leather sets.

J. N. Bartfield (✉ 30 W. 57th St., 3rd floor, ☎ 212/245–8890). A legend in the field offers old and antiquarian books distinguished by binding, author, edition, or content.

Pageant Book and Print Shop (✉ 114 W. Houston St., ☎ 212/674–5296). This old, reliable shop carries a broad selection of used books, prints, and maps.

Skyline Books & Records, Inc. (✉ 13 W. 18th St., ☎ 212/675–4773). Come here for out-of-print and unusual books in all fields. The store handles literary first editions, as well as jazz and rock records.

Strand (✉ 828 Broadway, at 12th St., ☎ 212/473–1452; ✉ 95 Fulton St., ☎ 212/732–6070). The Broadway branch proudly claims to have 8 mi of books; craning your neck among the tall-as-trees stacks will likely net you something. The Fulton Street branch is close to South Street Seaport.

Cameras and Electronics

Harvey Electronics (✉ 2 W. 45th St., ☎ 212/575–5000; ✉ 888 Broadway, at 19th St. inside ABC Carpet & Home, ☎ 212/982–7191). A well-informed staff offers top-of-the-line audio equipment.

SONY Style (✉ 550 Madison Ave., between 55th and 56th Sts., ☎ 212/833–8800). Audio and video equipment comes in a glossy package here; plunge into the blue-velvet-swathed downstairs area for a demonstration.

Willoughby's (✉ 136 W. 32nd St., ☎ 212/564–1600). Calling itself the world's largest camera store, Willoughby's rates high among amateurs and pros for selection and service.

CDs, Tapes, and Records

The city's best record stores provide browsers with a window to New York's hipper subcultures.

Bleecker Bob's Golden Oldies (✉ 118 W. 3rd St., ☎ 212/475–9677). The staff sells punk, new wave, progressive rock, and reggae, plus good old rock on vinyl, until the wee hours.

Downstairs Records (✉ 35 W. 43rd St., ☎ 212/354–4684). At this gold mine of old 45s, you can track down original and reissued vinyl from the past four decades.

Footlight Records (✉ 113 E. 12th St., ☎ 212/533–1572). Stop here to browse through New York's largest selection of old and new musicals and movie soundtracks, as well as a good choice of jazz and popular recordings.

Gryphon Record Shop (✉ 251 W. 72nd St., 2nd floor, ☎ 212/874–1588). One of the city's best rare-record stores, it stocks some 90,000 out-of-print and rare LPs.

HMV (✉ 57 W. 34th St., ☎ 212/629–0900; ✉ 2081 Broadway, at 72nd St., ☎ 212/721–5900; ✉ 1280 Lexington Ave., at 86th St., ☎ 212/348–0800; ✉ 5th Ave. at 46th St., ☎ 212/681–6700). These state-of-the-art record superstores stock hundreds of thousands of discs, tapes, and videos.

House of Oldies (✉ 35 Carmine St., ☎ 212/243–0500). The specialty here is records made between 1950 and the late 1980s—45s and 78s, as well as LPs; there are more than a million titles.

Jazz Record Center (✉ 236 W. 26th St., 8th floor, ☎ 212/675–4480). Here is the city's only jazz-record specialist; it also stocks collectibles.

J&R Music World (✉ 23 Park Row, ☎ 212/732–8600). This store offers a huge selection with good prices on major releases. Jazz recordings are sold at 25 Park Row, classical at No. 33. You can even buy music by telephone.

Midnight Records (✉ 263 W. 23rd St., ☎ 212/675–2768). This rock specialist stocks obscure artists from the '50s onward.

Tower Records and Videos (✉ 692 Broadway, at 4th St., ☎ 212/505–1500; ✉ 1961 Broadway, at 66th St., ☎ 212/799–2500; ✉ 725 5th Ave., basement level of Trump Tower, ☎ 212/838–8110). The selection of CDs and tapes can get overwhelming here. The scene is pure New York: At the Village location, you'll see many customers in head-to-toe black. The Lincoln Center branch is now larger than ever, with its own café.

Virgin Megastore Times Square (✉ 1540 Broadway, between 45th and 46th Sts., ☎ 212/921–1020). Touted as the largest music-entertainment complex in the world (big enough to hold 938 taxis), this glitzy emporium will impress you or give you a headache, depending on your mood. A 50-ft DJ tower cuts through three levels of consumer frenzy. There's a café, a travel shop, an interactive game wall, and even a special section on New York–theme movies.

Children's Clothing

Bambini (✉ 1367 3rd Ave., at 78th St., ☎ 212/717–6742). Mostly European imports, the clothes here are sophisticated in the old child-like way—not a miniadult look but instead beautiful fabrics and cuts.

Exclusive Oilily Store (✉ 870 Madison Ave., between 70th and 71st Sts., ☎ 212/628–0100). Brightly colored play and school clothes designed in Holland supposedly make children unwilling to wear anything else (if you believe the ad copy).

Greenstones et Cie (✉ 442 Columbus Ave., between 81st and 82nd Sts., ☎ 212/580–4322). **Greenstones Too!** (✉ 1184 Madison Ave., between 86th and 87th Sts., ☎ 212/427–1665). Catering to junior yuppies, these stores offer some handsome clothes, particularly sweaters.

Ibiza Kidz (✉ 42 University Pl., between 9th and 10th Sts., ☎ 212/505–9907) and **Ibiza** (✉ 46 University Pl., between 9th and 10th Sts., ☎ 212/533–4614). Come here for clothing handmade from lovely materials, plus shoes and toys.

Little Eric (✉ 1331 3rd Ave., at 76th St., ☎ 212/288–8987; ✉ 1118 Madison Ave., at 83rd St., ☎ 212/717–1513). Moms who love Eric can introduce their daughters to this happy footwear shop styled in an adult mode.

Space Kiddets (✉ 46 E. 21st St., ☎ 212/420–9878). Casual trendsetting clothes for kids are carried here.

Tartine et Chocolat (✉ 746 Madison Ave., between 64th and 65th Sts., ☎ 212/744–0975). These little French imports might cost as much as dinner at one of the neighboring French cafés, but they are unique and very well made.

Wicker Garden's Children (✉ 1327 Madison Ave., near 93rd St., ☎ 212/410–7001). Top-of-the-line pretties for boys, girls, and babies can be found here.

Wynken, Blynken & Nod's (✉ 306 E. 55th St., ☎ 212/308–9299). The clothes here are especially kid-friendly; for example, "My Little Friend" sweaters have a secret pocket with a small doll inside.

Crystal

Baccarat (✉ 625 Madison Ave., between 58th and 59th Sts., ☎ 212/826–4100) "Life is worth Baccarat," say the ads—in other words, the quality of crystal shown here is priceless.

Galleri Orrefors Kosta Boda (✉ 58 E. 57th St., ☎ 212/752–1095). Stop here for striking Swedish crystal, including work from the imaginative and often brightly colored Kosta Boda line.

Hoya Crystal Gallery (✉ 689 Madison Ave., at 61st St., ☎ 212/223–6335). The stunningly designed vases beg for an exotic bloom or two.

Rogaska (✉ 685 Madison Ave., between 61st and 62nd Sts., ☎ 212/980–6200). The understated classic wares made in Slovenia carried here are sold at relatively modest prices.

Steuben (✉ 717 5th Ave., at 56th St., ☎ 212/752–1441). The stunning and adventurous designs on display often go beyond the basic vase.

Food

CHOCOLATE AND CANDY

Black Hound (✉ 149 1st Ave., at 9th St., ☎ 212/979–9505). The hottest new place to buy truffles and unusual sweets for the sweet is found in the East Village.

La Maison du Chocolat (✉ 25 E. 73rd St., ☎ 212/744–7117). This is the New York branch of the famous Parisian chocolatier, whose bonbons have been described in *Vogue* as "the most refined and subtle in the world."

Li-Lac Chocolates (✉ 120 Christopher St., ☎ 212/242–7374). This charming nook feeds the Village's sweet tooth with homemade selections in the French tradition.

Neuchatel Chocolates (✉ Plaza Hotel, 2 W. 59th St., ☎ 212/751–7742). Velvety chocolates come in five dozen varieties here—all made in New York to approximate the Swiss chocolates.

Perugina (✉ 520 Madison Ave., between 53rd and 54th Sts., ☎ 212/688–2490). This Italian confectionery is most famous for its Baci, hazelnut chocolates wrapped in a multilingual love note—a tradition begun during a secret love affair of an heir to the company.

Richart Design et Chocolat (✉ 7 E. 55th St., ☎ 212/371–9369). The dark, cacao-rich, and very well designed tablets are irresistible at this chic chocolate boutique.

Teuscher Chocolates (✉ 620 5th Ave., in Rockefeller Center, ☎ 212/246–4416; ✉ 25 E. 61st St., ☎ 212/751–8482). Fabulous chocolates made in Switzerland are flown in weekly for sale in these jewel-box shops, newly decorated each season.

GOURMET MARKETS

Balducci's (✉ 424 6th Ave., at 9th St., ☎ 212/673–2600). In this former mom-and-pop food shop, now one of the city's finest food stores, mounds of baby carrots keep company with frilly lettuce, feathery dill, and superlative cheeses, chocolates, baked goods, pastas, vinegars, oils, and Italian specialties.

Dean & DeLuca (✉ 560 Broadway, at Prince St., ☎ 212/431–1691). This huge SoHo trendsetter, splendidly bright white, has an encyclopedic selection, from the heady array at the cheese counter to the exotic produce (baby albino eggplant?!) and the display cases of prepared foods.

Greenmarket Farmers' Market (✉ Union Sq., 17th St. between Broadway and Park Ave. S). Farms truck organic produce, fresh bread, and other homemade goods to this outdoor bastion of fresh food, open Monday, Wednesday, Friday, and Saturday year-round.

Kam-Man (✉ 200 Canal St., ☎ 212/571–0330). The city's premier Chinese market, Kam-Man is filled with exotic foods, the staccato sound of Chinese, and mysterious smells.

Vinegar Factory (✉ 431 E. 91st St., ☎ 212/987–0885). This mouth-watering place carries bread from yeast master Eli Zabar. There's a great selection of vinegars and oils (naturally), plus fresh produce, cheeses, and prepared foods. And in case you lack the proper instruments for slicing and dicing, a housewares section was added in spring 1997.

Zabar's (✉ 2245 Broadway, at 80th St., ☎ 212/787–2000). This is undoubtedly one of New York's favorite food markets. Dried herbs and spices, chocolates, and assorted bottled foods coexist with a fragrant jumble of fresh breads and the cheese, meat, and smoked-fish counters—and every year, there's a "caviar war" with Macy's. Upstairs is a large selection of kitchenware.

WINE

Acker Merrall & Condit (✉ 160 W. 72nd St., ☎ 212/787–1700). Known for its selection of red burgundies, this store has knowledge-able, helpful personnel.

Best Cellars (✉ 1291 Lexington Ave., between 86th and 87th Sts., ☎ 212/426–4200). In a novel move, the stock here is organized by the wine's characteristics (sweet, fruity) rather than region—and not only that, the prices are amazingly low.

Garnet Wines & Liquors (✉ 929 Lexington Ave., between 68th and 69th Sts., ☎ 212/772–3211). Its fine selection includes champagne at prices that one wine writer called "almost charitable."

Morrell & Company (✉ 535 Madison Ave., near 54th St., ☎ 212/688–9370). Peter Morrell is a well-regarded and very colorful figure in the wine business; his store reflects his expertise.

Sherry-Lehmann (✉ 679 Madison Ave., between 61st and 62nd Sts., ☎ 212/838–7500). It's a New York institution.

Union Square Wine & Spirits (✉ 33 Union Sq. W, near 16th St., ☎ 212/675–8100). The store stocks a great selection and has a regular schedule of wine seminars and special tasting events.

Fragrance Shops

Aveda Aromatherapy Esthetique (✉ 509 Madison Ave., between 52nd and 53rd Sts., ☎ 212/832–2416; ✉ 456 W. Broadway, between Prince and Houston Sts., ☎ 212/473–0280). **Aveda Environmental Lifestyle Store** (✉ 140 5th Ave., at 19th St., ☎ 212/645–4797). Concoct your own perfumes from the impressive selection of essential oils.

Caswell-Massey (✉ 518 Lexington Ave., at 48th St., ☎ 212/755–2254). The original displays its fragrant toiletries in polished old cases; branches are in the World Financial Center and at South Street Seaport.

Floris (✉ 703 Madison Ave., between 62nd and 63rd Sts., ☎ 212/935–9100). Floral English toiletries beloved of such beauties as Cher and Catherine Deneuve fill this re-creation of the cozy London original.

Kiehl's (✉ 109 3rd Ave., ☎ 212/677–3171). A favored haunt of top models and hairstylists, it's been a purveyor of quality skin and hair products since 1851.

L'Occitane (✉ 1046 Madison Ave., at 80th St., ☎ 212/639–9185). Ex-tramild soaps, shampoos, and creams here pack an olfactory punch with Provençal scents (think sage, thyme, and the ever-present lavender).

Fun and Games

These are stores by adults, for adults, but with such humor and whimsy that kids will like them, too.

B. Shackman & Company, Inc. (⊠ 85 5th Ave., at 16th St., ☎ 212/989–5162.). Opened in 1898, this gem of a store is filled with hard-to-find Victoriana and other fun items, including paper dolls, flip books, toys, and games.

Compleat Strategist (⊠ 11 E. 33rd St., ☎ 212/685–3880; ⊠ 342 W. 57th St., ☎ 212/582–1272). All kinds of strategy games are supplied for the serious enthusiast.

Darts Shoppe Ltd. (⊠ 30 E. 20th St., ☎ 212/533–8684). Exquisitely crafted English darts and boards are sold here.

Flosso Hornmann (⊠ 45 W. 34th St., Room 607, ☎ 212/279–6079). This modest magic shop offers museum-class memorabilia, including a hand-painted crate used by Harry Houdini.

Little Rickie (⊠ 49½ 1st Ave., at 3rd St., ☎ 212/505–6467). This fun spot is packed with wacky novelties and vintage treasures.

Tannen Magic Co. (⊠ 24 W. 25th St., ☎ 212/929–4500). At this magicians' supply house, you'll find sword chests, dove-a-matics, magic wands, and crystal balls, not to mention the all-important top hats with rabbits.

Uncle Futz (⊠ 408 Amsterdam Ave., at 79th St., ☎ 212/799–6723; ⊠ 1054 Lexington Ave., at 75th St., ☎ 212/535–4686). These delicious toy shops are crammed with supercool puzzles, board games, and souped-up yo-yos.

Gadgets

Hammacher Schlemmer (⊠ 147 E. 57th St., ☎ 212/421–9000). The store that offered America its first pop-up toaster still ferrets out the outrageous, the unusual, and the best-of-kind in-home electronics.

Sharper Image (⊠ Pier 17, South Street Seaport, ☎ 212/693–0477; ⊠ 4 W. 57th St., ☎ 212/265–2550; ⊠ 900 Madison Ave., between 72nd and 73rd Sts., ☎ 212/794–4974). This retail outlet of the catalog company stocks gifts for the pampered executive who has everything.

Home Decor and Gifts

Avventura (⊠ 463 Amsterdam Ave., at 82nd St., ☎ 212/769–2510). Glory in Italian design in all its streamlined beauty here. Tabletop items and handblown glass accessories are all stunning.

Be Seated (⊠ 66 Greenwich Ave., near 11th St., ☎ 212/924–8444). Manhattan's source for new and vintage African and Asian baskets also stocks cotton fabrics from India and Indonesia.

Bed, Bath & Beyond (⊠ 620 6th Ave., between 19th and 20th Sts., ☎ 212/255–3550). This huge Chelsea emporium has some 80,000 different household items at reasonable prices.

Crate & Barrel (⊠ 650 Madison Ave., at 59th St., ☎ 212/308–0011). At this fabulous emporium, you'll find one of the best selections of practically everything imaginable for the home and kitchen, including glassware, kitchen and bath items, and stylish furniture.

Eclectic Home (⊠ 224 8th Ave., between 21st and 22nd Sts., ☎ 212/255–2373). The first contemporary home design store in Chelsea has an especially grand range of decorative (and sometimes downright silly) lighting.

Felissimo (⊠ 10 W. 56th St., ☎ 212/247–5656). Spread over four stories of a Beaux Arts town house are unusual items, many handcrafted, that reconcile classic European and modern Asian sensibilities.

Gates of Marrakesh (⊠ 8 Prince St., ☎ 212/925–4104). Sharpen your acquisitive streak in this small Moroccan shop, where light filters through henna-painted sheepskin lamps.

La Maison Moderne (⊠ 144 W. 19th St., ☏ 212/691–9603). This inviting two-level store is a sumptuous stop filled with elegant gifts for the home and bath.

Let There Be Neon (⊠ 38 White St., between Broadway and Church St., ☏ 212/226–4883). Browse among the terrific collection of new and antique neon signs, clocks, and tabletop accessories.

MacKenzie-Childs Ltd. (⊠ 824 Madison Ave., between 68th and 69th Sts., ☏ 212/570–6050). If the fantastical windows haven't convinced you that this is a store unlike any other, the palatial birdcage containing elegant chickens will. Handmade majolica ware, table settings, and trimmings are done with a Victorian exuberance for detail.

Miya Shoji Interiors (⊠ 109 W. 17th St., ☏ 212/243–6774). This shop offers a superb selection of beautifully crafted Japanese folding screens.

Moss (⊠ 146 Greene St., ☏ 212/226–2190). Your view of toilet brushes and lemon squeezers will be changed forever, after you see what designers like Philippe Starck can do with them. This sleek boutique is decidedly contemporary, putting a fantastic spin on even the most utilitarian objects.

The Pillowry (⊠ 132 E. 61st St., ☏ 212/308–1630). The selection of decorative, one-of-a-kind pillows is vast. It opens weekdays at 11:30, Saturday by appointment.

Pottery Barn (⊠ 600 Broadway, at Houston St., ☏ 212/219–2420; ⊠ 117 E. 59th St., ☏ 212/753–5424; ⊠ 1965 Broadway, at 67th St., ☏ 212/579–8477; ⊠ 250 W. 57th St., ☏ 212/315–1855; ⊠ 231 10th Ave., between 23rd and 24th Sts., ☏ 212/206–8118; and other locations). Come here for contemporary-style items. The Broadway at 67th Street and SoHo locations do double time as concept stores with large home-design studios. Overstocks are discounted at the 10th Avenue location.

Scully & Scully (⊠ 504 Park Ave., between 59th and 60th Sts., ☏ 212/755–2590). The style here is high WASP, whether it's the leather footstools in animal shapes or the small pieces of reproduction antique furniture.

Troy (⊠ 138 Greene St., between W. Houston and Prince Sts., ☏ 212/941–4777). In this spare space, the clean lines of wicker, leather, and wood furniture and home accessories may well wreak havoc with your credit card.

William-Wayne & Co. (⊠ 40 University Pl., at 9th St., ☏ 212/533–4711; ⊠ 846 Lexington Ave., ☏ 212/737–8934; ⊠ 850 Lexington Ave., ☏ 212/288–9243). The highly tasteful, irresistible selection of gifts for home and garden here includes many collectibles with a monkey theme.

Wolfman-Gold & Good Company (⊠ 117 Mercer St., between Prince and Spring Sts., ☏ 212/431–1888). Half antique and half contemporary in spirit, this chic SoHo shop focusing on tableware is a major New York trendsetter.

Zona (⊠ 97 Greene St., between Prince and Spring Sts., ☏ 212/925–6750). SoHo's airy, high-ceilinged bastion offers Solieri bells, earth-toned textiles, expensive furniture, and terra-cottas, all artfully displayed.

LINENS

Madison Avenue has an inviting handful of high-end linen shops; move downtown for less expensive—and less conventional—lines. Grand Street on the Lower East Side has a spate of dry-goods merchants.

Ad Hoc Softwares (⊠ 410 W. Broadway, at Spring St., ☏ 212/925–2652). You'll feel very SoHo as you browse here—natural fibers and nubbly textures abound. The merchandise continues to expand into the home accessory arena.

Century 21 (⊠ 22 Cortlandt St., between Broadway and Church St., ☏ 212/227–9092; ⊠ 472 86th St., Bay Ridge, Brooklyn, ☏ 718/748–3266). If you can handle the crowds, this is an indefatigable source.

D. Porthault (⊠ 18 E. 69th St., ☏ 212/688–1660). Porthault's showcase beds are virtual cocoons of pale, crisp linens and pillows.

Frette (⊠ 799 Madison Ave., between 67th and 68th Sts., ☏ 212/988–5221). Thread counts mount well above 250 here.

Pratesi (⊠ 829 Madison Ave., at 69th St., ☏ 212/288–2315). To complement its pristine bedding, Pratesi introduced layettes, fragrances, and a home gift line in 1996.

Jewelry, Watches, and Silver

Most of the world's premier jewelers have retail outlets in New York, and the nation's wholesale jewelry center is on 47th Street.

A La Vieille Russie (⊠ 781 5th Ave., between 59th and 60th Sts., ☏ 212/752–1727). Stop here to behold bibelots by Fabergé and others, enameled or encrusted with jewels.

Asprey (⊠ 725 5th Ave., at 56th St., ☏ 212/688–1811). The only branch of the distinguished London jeweler, which holds three royal warrants, this store is just the place to go when seeking crystal, silver, leather goods, or, perhaps, a brooch fit for a queen.

Beads of Paradise (⊠ 16 E. 17th St., ☏ 212/620–0642). Enjoy a startlingly rich selection of African bead necklaces, earrings, and rare artifacts. Also, you can create your own designs.

Bulgari (⊠ 730 5th Ave., at 57th St., ☏ 212/315–9000; ⊠ 2 E. 61st St., in the Hotel Pierre, ☏ 212/486–0326). The expertly crafted jewelry here has an understated, tailored look.

Cartier (⊠ 653 5th Ave., at 52nd St., ☏ 212/446–3400). Legend has it that Pierre Cartier obtained this stately mansion by trading it with Mrs. Morton Plant for two rows of natural pearls. Having passed the 150-year mark, Cartier's work continues on its classically designed way— the dazzling gems do the talking.

David Webb (⊠ 445 Park Ave., at 57th St., ☏ 212/421–3030). Featured here are gem-studded pieces, often enameled and in animal forms.

Fortunoff (⊠ 681 5th Ave., between 53rd and 54th Sts., ☏ 212/758–6660). Good prices on gold and silver jewelry, flatware, and hollowware draw crowds to this large store.

Harry Winston (⊠ 718 5th Ave., at 56th St., ☏ 212/245–2000). The moneyed clientele here appreciates this store's oversize stones and impeccable quality.

H. Stern (⊠ 645 5th Ave., between 50th and 51st Sts., ☏ 212/688–0300). Gemstones in contemporary settings are the specialty of this Brazilian firm.

James Robinson (⊠ 480 Park Ave., at 58th St., ☏ 212/752–6166). This family-owned business sells handmade flatware, antique silver, fine estate jewelry, and 18th- and 19th-century china.

Jean's Silversmiths (⊠ 16 W. 45th St., ☏ 212/575–0723). Where to replace the butter knife that's missing from your great-aunt's set? Try this dusty, crowded shop.

Robert Lee Morris (⊠ 400 W. Broadway, near Spring St., ☏ 212/431–9405). Striking originals in silver, gold, and gold plate can be discovered at this SoHo jewelry and accessory mecca.

Tiffany & Co. (⊠ 727 5th Ave., at 57th St., ☏ 212/755–8000). The display windows can be elegant, funny, or just plain breathtaking. Along with the $80,000 platinum-and-diamond bracelets, a lot is affordable on a whim—and everything comes wrapped in that unmistakable Tiffany blue.

Tourneau (✉ 500 Madison Ave., at 52nd St., ☎ 212/758–6098). Browse through this recently expanded store for any number of excellent watches. Another space, including a timepiece museum, was scheduled at press time to open on 57th Street and Madison Avenue in late spring of 1997.

Van Cleef & Arpels (✉ 744 5th Ave., at 57th St., ☎ 212/644–9500). The jewelry here is sheer perfection.

Luggage and Leather Goods

Altman Luggage (✉ 135 Orchard St., between Delancey and Rivington Sts., ☎ 212/254–7275). Come here for reasonable prices.

Bottega Veneta (✉ 635 Madison Ave., between 59th and 60th Sts., ☎ 212/371–5511). The superb Italian goods here are for people who know real quality.

Coach (✉ 710 Madison Ave., at 63rd St., ☎ 212/319–1772; ✉ 595 Madison Ave., at 57th St., ☎ 212/754–0041; ✉ 725 5th Ave., in Trump Tower, ☎ 212/355–2427; and other locations). Coach's classic glove-tanned leather goes into handbags, briefcases, and dozens of other accessories.

Crouch & Fitzgerald (✉ 400 Madison Ave., at 48th St., ☎ 212/755–5888). Since 1839, this store has offered a terrific selection in hard- and soft-sided luggage, as well as handbags.

Fine & Klein (✉ 119 Orchard St., ☎ 212/674–6720). Fabulous handbags are discounted here.

Lederer Leather Goods (✉ 613 Madison Ave., at 58th St., ☎ 212/355–5515). The excellent selection here includes exotic skins.

Louis Vuitton (✉ 49 E. 57th St., ☎ 212/371–6111). Vuitton's famously monogrammed pieces range from purses to extravagant steamer trunks. A new (and larger) store, on 57th Street between 5th and Madison Avenues, was under construction at press time.

T. Anthony (✉ 445 Park Ave., at 56th St., ☎ 212/750–9797). This store's hard- and soft-sided luggage of coated fabric with leather trim has brass fasteners that look like precision machines.

Men's Clothing

Alfred Dunhill of London (✉ 450 Park Ave., at 57th St., ☎ 212/753–9292). Corporate brass comes here for finely tailored clothing, both ready-made and custom-ordered, and smoking accessories; the walk-in humidor stores top-quality tobacco and cigars.

Brooks Brothers (✉ 346 Madison Ave., at 44th St., ☎ 212/682–8800). Here's an American menswear institution, with conservative styles in both suits and sportswear.

Façonnable (✉ 689 5th Ave., at 54th St., ☎ 212/319–0111). Designed in France, the well-made traditional clothing and sportswear have an international appeal.

Holland & Holland (✉ 50 E. 57th St., ☎ 212/752–7755). This is no Ralph-Lauren-does-country-squire; Holland & Holland provides the Prince of Wales (and some very wealthy colonials) with country clothing and accessories such as leather falcon hoods. There's a special safari tailoring section and a gun room on the fifth floor.

J. Press (✉ 7 E. 44th St., ☎ 212/687–7642). This store emphasizes the oxford-cloth shirt, natural-shoulder suit, madras-patch Bermuda shorts, and amusing club tie.

Paul Smith (✉ 108 5th Ave., at 16th St., ☎ 212/627–9770). Dark mahogany Victorian cases display downtown styles.

Paul Stuart Inc. (✉ Madison Ave. at 45th St., ☎ 212/682–0320). The fabric selection is interesting, the tailoring superb, and the look traditional but not stodgy.

Sulka (✉ 430 Park Ave., at 55th St., ☎ 212/980–5200). Most of the elegant clothes here are Italian—and the silk robes are so swank they've shown up on Broadway in a Noël Coward play.

Worth & Worth (✉ 331 Madison Ave., at 43rd St., ☎ 212/867–6058). This classy shop stocks stylish handmade hats.

DISCOUNTS

Eisenberg and Eisenberg (✉ 85 5th Ave., at 16th St., 6th floor, ☎ 212/627–1290). Bargain hunters have relied on this store for decades.

Moe Ginsburg (✉ 162 5th Ave., at 21st St., ☎ 212/242–3482). Come here for a large selection of discounted American and European suits and outerwear. An even-deeper-discount floor opened in 1997, where prices are dirt cheap.

Syms (✉ 400 Park Ave., at 54th St., ☎ 212/317–8200; ✉ 42 Trinity Pl., ☎ 212/797–1199). Designer labels are sold at cut-rate prices; its Park Avenue location is heavy on classic suits.

MEN'S SHOES

Billy Martin's (✉ 810 Madison Ave., at 68th St., ☎ 212/861–3100). Quality hand-tooled and custom-made boots are carried here.

Church's English Shoes (✉ 428 Madison Ave., at 49th St., ☎ 212/755–4313). This store has been selling beautifully made English shoes since 1873.

Cole-Haan (✉ 620 5th Ave., at Rockefeller Center, ☎ 212/765–9747; ✉ 667 Madison Ave., at 61st St., ☎ 212/421–8440). The look in both dress and casual shoes is smart and stylish, yet not at all trendy.

John Fluevog Shoes (✉ 104 Prince St., ☎ 212/431–4484). The inventor of the Angelic sole (protects against water, acid . . . and Satan), Fluevog designs chunky shoes and boots that are much more than mere Doc Marten copies.

Salvatore Ferragamo (✉ 725 5th Ave., at Trump Tower, ☎ 212/759–7990). This Ferragamo branch has traditional, classy men's shoes, plus a limited line of equally swell clothes and accessories.

Stuart Weitzman (✉ 625 Madison Ave., between 58th and 59th Sts., ☎ 212/750–2555). The specialty here is hard-to-find sizes and widths. This store carries the designer's entire line.

To Boot (✉ 256 Columbus Ave., between 71st and 72nd Sts., ☎ 212/724–8249). Here you'll find stylish shoes and boots for a fashionable business look.

Men's and Women's Clothing

A/X: Armani Exchange (✉ 568 Broadway, near Prince St., ☎ 212/431–6000). Here's Giorgio Armani's answer to the Gap.

Calvin Klein (✉ 654 Madison Ave., at 60th St., ☎ 212/292–9000). This huge, stark store showcases Calvin Klein's latest design collection.

Diesel Superstore (✉ 770 Lexington Ave., at 60th St., ☎ 212/308–0055). The display windows styled like washing machines will tip you off as to Diesel's industrial edge; men's and women's clothes sizes tend to be generous (but they don't all shrink).

Dolce & Gabbana (✉ 825 Madison Ave., between 68th and 69th Sts., no phone at press time). It's easy to feel like an Italian movie star in this two-level store (opened in fall 1997), which features attractive men's and women's collections.

Emporio Armani (✉ 601 Madison Ave., between 57th and 58th Sts., ☎ 212/317–0800; ✉ 110 5th Ave., at 16th St., ☎ 212/727–3240). The uptown boutique was part of Armani's double-barreled reinforcement of Madison Avenue. The clothes are (relatively) more casual, often in the ever-cool shades of soot.

Etro (✉ 720 Madison Ave., between 63rd and 64th Sts., ☎ 212/317–9096). This store opened in 1996 with a memorable window display of 18th- and 19th-century men's and women's costumes. You'll see echoes of this period luxury in the clothing for men and women carried here; vest dandies will be particularly happy.

Gianni Versace (✉ 647 5th Ave., between 51st and 52nd Sts., ☎ 212/317–0224). Housed in a restored turn-of-the-century landmark building, this five-story Versace boutique hums with colored neon light. While the exuberant designs and colors of Versace's clothes might not be to everyone's taste, they're never boring. If this isn't enough, there are also two more boutiques, one for the women's and men's lines (✉ 817 Madison Ave., between 68th and 69th Sts., ☎ 212/744–6868) and one carrying the (relatively) lower-end Versus line (scheduled to open in fall 1997).

Giorgio Armani (✉ 760 Madison Ave., between 65th and 66th Sts., ☎ 212/988–9191). Armani managed to beat out Calvin Klein on the exterior-minimalism front; inside, the space has a museumlike quality, reinforced by the stunning cuts of the clothes.

Gucci (✉ 685 5th Ave., at 54th St., ☎ 212/826–2600). Designer Tom Ford's revamp campaign shows no signs of slowing down—the venerable name has an increasingly svelte edge.

Hermès (✉ 11 E. 57th St., ☎ 212/751–3181). Patterned silk scarves, neckties, and the sacred "Kelly" handbags are hallmarks.

Issey Miyake (✉ 992 Madison Ave., at 77th St., ☎ 212/439–7822). Tightly pleated fabrics have become the Miyake signature—some in ultra-high-tech textiles.

J. Crew (✉ 99 Prince St., ☎ 212/966–2739; ✉ 203 Front St., ☎ 212/385–3500; ✉ 91 5th Ave., ☎ 212/255–4848. At these pristine showcases for East Coast chic, the 14 labels for men and women range from flannels to the Collection, an exclusive, Calvin Klein–ish women's line.

Matsuda (✉ 156 5th Ave., between 20th and 21st Sts., ☎ 212/645–5151). Kudos go out for wonderful cuts and fine muted hues.

Polo/Ralph Lauren (✉ 867 Madison Ave., at 72nd St., ☎ 212/606–2100). Lauren's flagship store is one of New York's most distinctive shopping experiences, in a grand, carefully renovated turn-of-the-century town house. Across the street at 888 Madison Avenue is another Ralph Lauren boutique, this one carrying casual clothes and sportsgear.

Prada (✉ 841 Madison Ave., at 70th St., ☎ 212/327–4200). The interior pulses with pale "verdolino" green walls and lighting. The '60s-inspired clothes have proved to be another major Italian fashion coup—even the shoes and leather goods have become international status symbols. A smaller boutique is located at 45 East 57th Street.

Spazio Romeo Gigli (✉ 21 E. 69th St., ☎ 212/744–9121). More gorgeous Italian design reigns here, this time with decadently rich fabrics and a hint of Renaissance about the cut.

Valentino (✉ 747 Madison Ave., between 68th and 69th Sts., ☎ 212/772–6969). The mix here is at once audacious and beautifully cut, with the best of France and Italy on its racks.

Yohji Yamamoto (✉ 103 Grand St., ☎ 212/966–9066). Severe, sleekly designed fashions come from fashion's Zen master.

Odds and Ends

Danse Macabre (✉ 265½ Lafayette St., between Prince and Spring Sts., ☎ 212/219–3907). You could have an interest in radiology. Or you could be morbid enough to want an interesting skull or two. This ossiferous collection also includes Mexican Day of the Dead folk art, African death masks, and the like.

Kate Spade (⊠ 59 Thompson St., ☎ 212/965–0301). Kate Spade's only boutique doesn't exactly stock leather goods—instead, the eminently desirable (and oft-copied) handbags come in various fabrics.

Keiko New York (⊠ 62 Greene St., ☎ 212/226–6051). End bathingsuit trauma once and for all by getting your swimsuit customized here—or pick out one of the brightly colored numbers already made.

Spoken Word (⊠ 285 W. Broadway, between Canal and Lispenard Sts., ☎ 212/431–6121). The size of this tiny shop belies the breadth of its holdings: an amazing collection of famous voices on CD and cassette. Snap up a poet (Kerouac, Eliot, Frost) reading his own work, a stirring speech (FDR, Martin Luther King Jr.), or a 1940s radio comedy show.

Uncle Sam Umbrella Shop (⊠ 161 W. 57th St., ☎ 212/582–1976). This is the only store devoted to umbrellas in the whole country. Umbrellas of all sorts are not only sold here, they're also repaired. In the back are cases of antique walking sticks.

Paper, Greeting Cards, Stationery

Dempsey & Carroll (⊠ 110 E. 57th St., ☎ 212/486–7526). Supplying New York's high society for a century, this firm is always correct but seldom straitlaced.

Kate's Paperie (⊠ 561 Broadway, at Prince St., ☎ 212/941–9816; ⊠ 8 W. 13th St., ☎ 212/633–0570). These wonderful spots feature fabulous wrapping papers, some handmade; bound blank books; and more.

Untitled (⊠ 159 Prince St., ☎ 212/982–2088). The stock here includes thousands of tasteful greeting cards and art postcards.

Performing-Arts Memorabilia

Motion Picture Arts Gallery (⊠ 133 E. 58th St., 10th floor, ☎ 212/223–1009). Vintage posters enchant collectors here.

Movie Star News (⊠ 134 W. 18th St., ☎ 212/620–8160). The film memorabilia emphasizes Hollywood glamour.

One Shubert Alley (⊠ Shubert Alley, between 44th and 45th Sts. west of Broadway, ☎ 212/944–4133). Souvenirs from past and present Broadway hits reign at this theater district shop.

Richard Stoddard Performing Arts Books (⊠ 18 E. 16th St., Room 305, ☎ 212/645–9576). This veteran dealer, who offers out-of-print books, also has the largest stock of old Broadway *Playbill*s in the world.

Triton Gallery (⊠ 323 W. 45th St., between 8th and 9th Aves., ☎ 212/765–2472). Theatrical posters large and small can be found here for hits and flops.

Souvenirs of New York City

Ordinary Big Apple souvenirs can be found in and around major tourist attractions. More unusual items can be found at:

City Books (⊠ 61 Chambers St., ☎ 212/669–8245). Discover all kinds of books and pamphlets that have to do with New York City's government and its various departments (building, sanitation, etc.), as well as pocket maps, Big Apple lapel pins, and sweatshirts featuring subway-token motifs. It's closed on weekends.

New York City Transit Museum Gift Shop (⊠ Boerum Pl. and Schermerhorn St., Brooklyn Heights, ☎ 718/243–5068). This museum shop was built mostly by transit employees. All the merchandise is somehow linked to the MTA, from "straphanger" ties to old subway tokens.

The Pop Shop (⊠ 292 Lafayette St., near E. Houston St., ☎ 212/219–2784). World-famous artist Keith Haring had a particular link to New

York; images from his unmistakable pop art pieces cover all sorts of paraphernalia.

Sporting Goods

Chain stores such as **Eastern Mountain Sports** (✉ 611 Broadway, near Houston St., ☎ 212/505–9860; ✉ 20 W. 61st St., ☎ 212/397–4860), **Speedo Authentic Fitness** (✉ 1 World Trade Center, ☎ 212/775–0977; ✉ 150 Columbus Ave., ☎ 212/501–8140; ✉ 90 Park Ave., ☎ 212/682–3830; ✉ 330 E. 61st St., ☎ 212/888–1130) and the **Sports Authority** (✉ 401 7th Ave., ☎ 212/563–7195; ✉ 845 3rd Ave., ☎ 212/355–9725; ✉ 57 W. 57th St., ☎ 212/355–6430) are reliable, but here are a couple of unique spots to try.

NikeTown (✉ 6 E. 57th St., ☎ 212/891–6453). A fusion of high-tech and school gym, Nike's "motivational retail environment" is its largest sportsgear emporium to date. What with the inspirational quotes in the flooring, the computer-driven NGAGE foot sizers, and the heart-pumping movie shown every 20 minutes on an enormous screen in the entry atrium, it's hard to leave without something in the latest high-tech wick-away fabric or footwear design.

Tent & Trails (✉ 21 Park Pl., ☎ 212/227–1760). There are no slick visuals here, just the rough-and-ready beckoning of crampons, climbing ropes, wilderness survival kits, and good advice.

Toys

Many toy companies are headquartered here, and the windows of the Toy Center at 23rd Street and 5th Avenue display the latest thing, especially during February's Toy Week, when all the out-of-town buyers come to place orders for the next Christmas season (☞ Fun and Games, *above*).

Disney Store (✉ 711 5th Ave., ☎ 212/702–0702; ✉ 210 W. 42nd St., at 7th Ave., ☎ 212/221–0430; ✉ 39 W. 34th St., ☎ 212/279–9890; ✉ 147 Columbus Ave., at W. 66th St., ☎ 212/362–2386). All branches carry merchandise relating to Disney films and characters. The enormous main 5th Avenue store is designed to be a "house" for the characters, with living-room areas and the like; it has the largest single collection of Disney animation art in the country.

E.A.T. Gifts (✉ 1062 Madison Ave., between 80th and 81st Sts., ☎ 212/861–2544). Piñatas hang from the ceiling, and the shelves are full of toys, gizmos, and knickknacks. Tintin fans will have a field day.

Enchanted Forest (✉ 85 Mercer St., between Spring and Broome Sts., ☎ 212/925–6677). Stuffed animals peer out from almost every corner of this fantastic shop. There's all manner of curiosity-provoking gizmos, plus old-fashioned tin toys and a small but choice selection of children's books.

F.A.O. Schwarz (✉ 767 5th Ave., at 58th St., ☎ 212/644–9400). This sprawling, two-level store begins its all-out sensory bombardment as soon as you walk in the door to the tune of "Welcome to Our World of Toys." Beyond a wonderful mechanical clock with many dials and dingbats are tons of stuffed animals, dolls (including an inordinate number of Barbies), things to build with (including blocks by the pound), computer games, and much, much more.

Geppetto's Toy Box (✉ 161 7th Ave. S, between Perry and Charles Sts., ☎ 212/620–7511). Most toys here are handmade, ranging from extravagant costumed dolls to tried-and-true rubber duckies.

Kidding Around (✉ 60 W. 15th St., ☎ 212/645–6337; ✉ 68 Bleecker St., ☎ 212/598–0228). This unpretentiously smart shop is full of old-fashioned wooden toys, fun gadgets, craft and science kits, and a small selection of infant clothes.

Warner Bros. Studio Store (⊠ 1 E. 57th St., ☎ 212/754–0300). A block-buster expansion has given Bugs Bunny a very high 5th Avenue pro-file. Besides seemingly endless amounts of entertainment-related merchandise, there's a 3-D movie theater.

West Side Kids (⊠ 498 Amsterdam Ave., at 84th St., ☎ 212/496–7282). The shrewd selection here mixes educational toys with a grab bag of fun little playthings.

Women's Clothing

CLASSICS

Ann Taylor (⊠ 2015–2017 Broadway, near 69th St., ☎ 212/873–7344; ⊠ 2380 Broadway, at 87th St., ☎ 212/721–3130; ⊠ 4 Fulton St., ☎ 212/480–4100; ⊠ 805 3rd Ave., at 50th St., ☎ 212/308–5333; ⊠ 645 Madison Ave., at 60th St., ☎ 212/832–2010; and other locations). This chain has nearly cornered the market for moderately priced, of-fice-appropriate clothing and shoes.

Burberrys (⊠ 9 E. 57th St., ☎ 212/371–5010). The look is classic and conservative, especially in the Burberrys signature plaid—and nobody does a better trench coat.

Laura Ashley (⊠ 398 Columbus Ave., at 79th St., ☎ 212/496–5110). Old-fashioned English frocks abound here.

DESIGNER SHOWCASES

Chanel (⊠ 15 E. 57th St., ☎ 212/355–5050). The flagship Chanel store, opened in 1996, has often been compared to a classic Chanel suit—slim, elegant, and timeless. The building includes fashion and jewelry boutiques, as well as a five-story, Provence-saturated Frédéric Fekkai salon.

Christian Dior (⊠ 703 5th Ave., at 55th St., ☎ 212/223–4646). An el-egant, two-level, gray-hued outpost of one of France's most venerable fashion houses, this shop offers both daytime and evening clothes, plus all the accessories (and scents) to enhance them.

Comme des Garçons (⊠ 116 Wooster St., between Prince and Spring Sts., ☎ 212/219–0660). This SoHo shop showcases Japanese designer Rei Kawakubo.

Emanuel Ungaro (⊠ 792 Madison Ave., at 67th St., ☎ 212/249–4090). The style here is body-conscious, but it's never flashy.

Geoffrey Beene (⊠ 783 5th Ave., between 59th and 60th Sts., ☎ 212/935–0470). A splendid-looking boutique houses exquisite day and evening wear by America's master designer.

Gianfranco Ferre (⊠ 845 Madison Ave., at 70th St., ☎ 212/717–5430). This Italian designer throws a strong dash of old-style Hollywood ex-travagance into his women's prêt-à-porter line.

Louis Féraud (⊠ 3 W. 56th St., ☎ 212/956–7010). The couturier's deft hand is seen in the superb cut and colorations at his only freestanding North American boutique.

Max Mara (⊠ 813 Madison Ave., between 68th and 69th Sts., ☎ 212/879–6100). Think subtle colors and enticing fabrics—photo ex-hibits lend to the genteel atmosphere.

Morgane Le Fay (⊠ 746 Madison Ave., between 64th and 65th Sts., ☎ 212/879–9700; ⊠ 152 Spring St., ☎ 212/925–0144). The clothes here borrow from centuries past (swaddlings of silk, high waists); you almost have to be either tall and willowy or French to carry it off.

Moschino (⊠ 803 Madison Ave., between 67th and 68th Sts., ☎ 212/639–9600). "It's Better to Dress As You Wish Than As You Should!" proclaims one of the walls of the multistory Moschino flag-ship. People with a penchant for comedic couture won't have any trouble finding their wardrobe soul mate in this whirligig store.

Nicole Miller (✉ 780 Madison Ave., between 66th and 67th Sts., ☎ 212/288–9779; ✉ 134 Prince St., ☎ 212/343–1362). Known for her silk prints spoofing almost any topic imaginable (French wine, Dalmatians, dentistry), Nicole Miller also sells some simple dresses.

Norma Kamali O.M.O. (✉ 11 W. 56th St., ☎ 212/957–9797). The look here ranges from sweatshirts to evening gowns.

Sonia Rykiel (✉ 849 Madison Ave., between 70th and 71st Sts., ☎ 212/396–3060). Paris's "queen of knitwear" created an exclusive line of poor-boy sweaters for the 1996 opening of her first U.S. boutique.

Todd Oldham (✉ 123 Wooster St., near Prince St., ☎ 212/219–3531). The cutting-edge designer's SoHo shop is the perfect antidote to too much beige.

TSE Cashmere (✉ 827 Madison Ave., at 69th St., ☎ 212/472–7790). Soft delicacy doesn't stop at the fabric; the sweaters are hopelessly refined.

Vera Wang (✉ 991 Madison Ave., at 77th St., ☎ 212/628–3400). Sumptuous, made-to-order bridal and evening wear is shown here by appointment only. Periodic prêt-à-porter sales offer designer dresses for a (relative) song.

Yves Saint Laurent Rive Gauche (✉ 855 Madison Ave., between 70th and 71st Sts., ☎ 212/988–3821). The looks range from chic to classic for day and evening. The men's boutique is right next door, at 859 Madison.

DISCOUNT

Aaron's (✉ 627 5th Ave., at 17th St., Park Slope, Brooklyn, ☎ 718/768–5400). If your taste runs to expensive labels, you'll appreciate the significant savings. You'll have your own salesperson assigned to you.

Century 21 (✉ 22 Cortlandt St., between Broadway and Church St., ☎ 212/227–9092; ✉ 472 86th St., Bay Ridge, Brooklyn, ☎ 718/748–3266). Spiffy quarters make bargain-hunting a pleasure, and there are fabulous buys on very high fashion.

Forman's (✉ 82 Orchard St., ☎ 212/228–2500; ✉ 145 E. 42nd St., between Lexington and 3rd Aves., ☎ 212/681–9800; ✉ 59 John St., ☎ 212/791–4100). This is an unexpectedly attractive longtime mainstay of the Lower East Side.

Loehmann's (✉ 101 7th Ave., at 16th St., ☎ 212/352–0856). Bargain hunters throughout Manhattan rejoiced when the legendary Loehmann's finally opened a branch downtown. The highest fashion is concentrated in the "Back Room," and there are both communal and private dressing rooms. You'll have an especially good shot at a winter coat.

S&W (✉ 165 W. 26th St., ☎ 212/924–6656). Prices here are good to great on coats, suits, shoes, handbags, and other accessories.

HIP STYLES

Agnès B. (✉ 116 Prince St., ☎ 212/925–4649; ✉ 13 E. 16th St., ☎ 212/741–2585; ✉ 1063 Madison Ave., near 81st St., ☎ 212/570–9333). This Euro-style boutique has maintained its SoHo popularity for several years. In December 1996, the company added a line of makeup.

Alicia Mugetti (✉ 999 Madison Ave., between 77th and 78th Sts., ☎ 212/794–6186; ✉ 186 Prince St., 212/226–5064). These designs are unmistakable—layers of lush fabrics and lots of silk, often hand painted.

Anna Sui (✉ 113 Greene St., between Prince and Spring Sts., ☎ 212/941–8406). The violet-and-black salon, hung with Beardsley prints and neon alterna-rock posters, is the perfect setting for Sui's flapper- and gangster-influenced designs.

Betsey Johnson (✉ 130 Thompson St., between W. Houston and Prince Sts., ☎ 212/420–0169; ✉ 251 E. 60th St., ☎ 212/319–7699; ✉ 248 Columbus Ave., between 71st and 72nd Sts., ☎ 212/362–3364; ✉ 1060 Madison Ave., between 80th and 81st Sts., ☎ 212/734–1257). The look here is still hip and quirky.

Canal Jean (✉ 504 Broadway, between Spring and Broome Sts., ☎ 212/226–1130). Casual funk draws hip shoppers.

Charivari (✉ 257 Columbus Ave., at 72nd St., ☎ 212/787–7272; Charivari 57, ✉ 18 W. 57th St., ☎ 212/333–4040). Founder Selma Weiser has made a name for herself internationally for her eagle eye on the up-and-coming and avant-garde.

Harriet Love (✉ 126 Prince St., ☎ 212/966–2280). This is the doyenne of the city's faux-vintage/retro clothing scene.

Label (✉ 265 Lafayette St., between Prince and Spring Sts., ☎ 212/966–7736). Familiar logos take on very different meanings after a scalding wit treatment by designer Laura Whitcomb.

Miu Miu (✉ 100 Prince St., ☎ 212/334–5156). Responding to the huge appetite for the designs of Miuccia Prada, the company opened its first North American Miu Miu boutique here. You can get the same straight-edged look for a little less money.

Patricia Field (✉ 10 E. 8th St., ☎ 212/254–1699). This store collects the essence of the downtown look—lots of marabou, techno-fabrics, and humor.

Trash and Vaudeville (✉ 4 St. Mark's Pl., ☎ 212/982–3590). Black, white, and electric colors are the focus here—and you never know when you might see Lou Reed buying jeans.

United Colors of Benetton (✉ 542 5th Ave., between 48th and 49th Sts., ☎ 212/398–1205; ✉ 666 48th St., at 5th Ave., ☎ 212/317–2501; ✉ 805 Lexington Ave., at 62nd St., ☎ 212/752–5283; and other locations). After years of having small boutiques scattered throughout the city, Benetton opened a three-level flagship store in the old Scribner building on 5th Avenue in 1996. Besides the colorful, casual clothes, you'll find an extensive sporting goods section.

LINGERIE

Joovay (✉ 436 W. Broadway, near Prince St., ☎ 212/431–6386). Stop here for exquisite little things in silk and lace, both naughty and nice.

La Petite Coquette (✉ 52 University Pl., between 9th and 10th Sts., ☎ 212/473–2478). You'll find fine lingerie here for yourself or someone special.

Le Corset (✉ 80 Thompson St., at Spring St., ☎ 212/334–4936). This lovely boutique naturally stocks its namesake.

VINTAGE

The 1909 Company (✉ 63 Thompson St., between Spring and Broome Sts., ☎ 212/343–1658). Some excellent vintage clothing picks are for sale here—a special display case holds the Gucci and Pucci, while the racks have classy '60s suits, all in great condition.

Screaming Mimi's (✉ 382 Lafayette St., between 4th and Great Jones Sts., ☎ 212/677–6464). Vintage '60s and '70s clothes and retro-wear include everything from lingerie to prom dresses.

Women's Shoes

DESIGNER SHOES

Hélène Arpels (✉ 470 Park Ave., between 57th and 58th Sts., ☎ 212/755–1623). This is the grande dame of fine footwear for the well heeled.

Manolo Blahnik (✉ 15 W. 55th St., ☎ 212/582–3007). It's possibly the hautest—and costliest—footwear in town, by England's top shoe designer.

Peter Fox (✉ 105 Thompson St., between Prince and Spring Sts., ☏ 212/431–7426; ✉ 806 Madison Ave., between 67th and 68th Sts., ☏ 212/744–8340). Looks here are outside the fashion mainstream—really fun.

Robert Clergerie (✉ 681 Madison Ave., between 61st and 62nd Sts., ☏ 212/207–8600). Try on exquisite, high-style French footwear; the Joseph Fenestrier line of men's shoes is available here as well.

Salvatore Ferragamo (✉ 661 5th Ave., between 52nd and 53rd Sts., ☏ 212/759–3822). Join the ranks of Sophia Loren and the late Audrey Hepburn as a Ferragamo customer. Lately, the line has featured several reinventions of the designer's most distinctive styles, such as his scalloped heel.

Tanino Crisci (✉ 795 Madison Ave., between 67th and 68th Sts., ☏ 212/535–1014). Well-made shoes in classic styles and subtle variations of basic colors are the highlight here. All are made in Italy.

MODERATELY PRICED SHOES

Eighth Street between 5th and 6th avenues is crammed with small shoe-storefronts, hawking funky styles from steel-toed boots to outrageous platforms.

Joan & David (✉ 816 Madison Ave., at 68th St., ☏ 212/772–3970; ✉ 104 5th Ave., at 16th St., ☏ 212/627–1780) can always be relied on for classy flats.

Maraolo (✉ 782 Lexington Ave., between 60th and 61st Sts., ☏ 212/832–8182; ✉ 551 Madison Ave., ☏ 212/308–8793; ✉ 835 Madison Ave., ☏ 212/628–5080) is filled with clothing designers' footwear (Armani, Donna Karan).

Patrick Cox (✉ 702 Madison Ave., between 62nd and 63rd Sts., ☏ 212/759–3910) stocks shoes with a retro, slightly ironic feel.

Sacco (✉ 324 Columbus Ave., between 75th and 76th Sts., ☏ 212/799–5229; ✉ 94 7th Ave., between 15th and 16th Sts., ☏ 212/675–5180; ✉ 111 Thompson St., between Prince and Spring Sts., ☏ 212/925–8010; and other locations) has some incredible sales.

DISCOUNT AND LOWER-PRICE SHOES

Discount shoe stores dot Reade Street between Church and West Broadway, including **Anbar** (✉ 60 Reade St., ☏ 212/227–0253). Several Orchard Street stores also discount uptown shoe styles.

Secondhand Shops

Thrift Shops
The thrift shops listed below are run for charity; the closet-cleanings of affluent New Yorkers often result in high-quality donations. Hours are limited, so call ahead.

Council Thrift Shop (✉ 246 E. 84th St., ☏ 212/439–8373).

Everybody's Thrift Shop (✉ 261 Park Ave. S, between 20th and 21st Sts., ☏ 212/674–4298).

Housing Works Thrift Shop (✉ 143 W. 17th St., ☏ 212/366–0820; ✉ 202 E. 77th St., ☏ 212/772–8461; ✉ 307 Columbus Ave., ☏ 212/579–7566). These shops benefit housing services for people with AIDS.

Irvington Institute for Medical Research Thrift Shop (✉ 1534 2nd Ave., at 80th St., ☏ 212/879–4555).

Memorial Sloan-Kettering Cancer Center Thrift Shop (✉ 1440 3rd Ave., between 81st and 82nd Sts., ☏ 212/535–1250).

Flea Markets

The season runs from March or April through November or December at most of these markets in school playgrounds and parking lots.

Annex Antiques Fair and Flea Market (⊠ 6th Ave. at 26th St., ☎ 212/243–5343). Weekends year-round.

The Garage (⊠ 112 W. 25th St., between 6th and 7th Aves., ☎ 212/647–0707). The newest flea market in town, this one is indoors in a 23,000-square-ft, two-story former parking garage. Weekends year-round.

Green Flea (IS 44 Market: ⊠ Columbus Ave. at 77th St., ☎ 212/721–0900 evenings; PS 183 Market: ⊠ E. 67th St. and York Ave.). Green Flea runs the PS 183 market on Saturday, and the IS 44 market on Sunday.

11 Portrait of New York City

The New York Babel

Books and Videos

THE NEW YORK BABEL

IF PARIS SUGGESTS INTELLIGENCE, if London suggests Experience, then the word for New York is Activity. York itself is an almost intolerably famous name, but adding New to it was one of the lucky prophetic insights of nomenclature, for newness, from day to day, was to be the moral essence of the place. There is no place where newness is so continuously pursued.

What is not naturally active in New York soon has to turn to and become so. There is not an inactive man, woman, or child in the place. It might be thought that a contemplative, passive New Yorker, one who is inhabited by his feelings and his imaginings, who lives in an inner world, or was born torpid, must be immune to the active spirit. This is not so in New York, where states like passivity, contemplation, vegetativeness, and often sleep itself are active by prescription. Pragmatism sees to that. The prime example is the bum or derelict. There he lies asleep or drunk on the doorstep or props himself against a wall in the Bowery, an exposed, accepted, but above all an established figure of a 51st state. In a city where all activity is specialized, he has his specialty: he must act in protest against activity, which leads him from time to time on a chase for alcohol, a smoke, or a coin as persistent as a salesman's, but in solitude. Virginia Woolf used to ask where Society was; the notion was metaphysical to her. But Skid Row exists as a recognized place. You go there when the thing comes over you. You graduate in dereliction. You put in a 20-hour day of internal fantasy-making in your studied rejection of the New York norm. The Spanish mendicant has his rights and takes his charity with condescension; the bum grabs with resentment. He is busy. You have upset his dream. The supremely passive man in theory, he will stop in the middle of the street as he crosses the Bowery, holding up his dirty hand at the traffic, and scream in the manner of madness at the oncoming driver. Screaming like that—and New York is dotted with screamers on a scale I have seen in no other city in the world, though Naples has its share—reveals the incessant pressure of the active spirit.

For ourselves who are trying to settle first what we see before our eyes, this active, practical spirit has curious manifestations. New York City is large, but Manhattan is small in extent, so small that a large part of its population has to be pumped out of it every night by bridges and tunnels. Despite the groans about the congestion of its traffic, it is easy to dash from one end to the other of the island and to drive fast all around it. And most people do dash. The only real difficulty is in the downtown tangle of named streets in old New York; the grid has settled the rest. The grid is an unlovely system. It is not originally American: Stuttgart and Berlin hit upon this method of automatically extending cities in the 17th century. By the 18th century Europe had discovered that cities must be designed before they are extended: mere pragmatism and planning will not do. It absolutely will not do if left to engineers, soldiers, or what are called developers. The makers of the New York grid confused the idea that parallel lines can be projected into infinity without meeting, with the idea of design. The boredom this has inflicted upon the horizontal life of Manhattan has turned out to be endurable to the primarily active man who is impatient of the whole idea of having neighbors. The striping, unheeding avenues of the grid have given one superb benefit. They cut through long distances, they provide long vistas that excite the eye, and these are fine where the buildings are high, if they are featureless where the buildings are low. No other city I can think of has anything like the undulating miles that fly down Park Avenue from 96th Street to Grand Central, blocked now though it is by the brutal mass of the Metropolitan Life Building—a British affront to the city and spoken of as a revenge for Suez—or the longer streak of Madison. These two avenues impress most as a whole, other avenues in part, by their assurance as they cleave their way through the cliffs.

OF COURSE, BEING A stranger, you have been living it up, for if you want a night city, this is preeminently the one. There is a large fluorescent population of pale faces—who is that old man sitting alone in the Automat at this late hour? Where are all those taxis streaking to endlessly through the night? You have been listening to the jazz in Birdland perhaps, listening to the long drumming that says "Encroach, encroach, encroach, encroach, overcome, come!" or to that woman with the skirling voice which is shoving, pushing, and struggling cheerfully to get all her energy out of her body and into her mouth as she sings what is really the theme song of the city: "And it's good. It's all good, good, good." She was wired in to some dynamo.

Those words never fade from the mind. In sleep you still hear them. You are a receiving station for every message Babel sends out day and night. The sirens of the police cars, the ambulances and fire engines, mark the hours, carrying the mind out to fantasies of disaster. I say "fantasies," for surely all these speeding crews are studiously keeping alive the ideal of some ultimate dementia while the rest of us sleep. New York demands more than anything else that one should never fail to maintain one's sense of its drama; even its social manners, at their most ceremonious, have this quality. Where the crowds of other cities are consolidating all day long, filling up the safes and cellars of the mind, the New York crowd is set on the pure function of self-dispersal. A couple of cops idling through the night in a police car will issue their noise as if it were part of the uniform and to keep up their belief in their own reality and in the sacred notion of the Great Slaying or the Great Burglarization. Then there is light traffic on the highways, with its high, whipping, cat-gut whine. On 104th Street on the West Side I used to have the sensation of being flayed alive all night by knives whipping down Riverside Drive; it was not disagreeable. City life is for masochists. On many other avenues the trucks bulldozed the brain. There were bursts of noctambulist shouting off Madison and 60th at 3 or 4, followed by the crowning row of the city, the clamor of the garbage disposers, successors to Dickens's gentlemanly swine, that fling the New York garbage cans

across the pavement and grind the stuff to bits on the spot. Often I have sat at my window to watch these night brutes chew up the refuse. The men have to rush to keep up with its appetite. As a single producer of shindy this municipal creature is a triumph.

The only way of pinning some sort of identity onto the people is to think of them as once being strangers like yourself and trace them to their districts. The man who used to bring my breakfast, saying, every morning, "Lousy day," was a 115th Street Puerto Rican, of five years' standing. You learn to distinguish. You know where the Ukrainians, the Sephardic Jews, early and late Italians, degrees of Irish, live. You build up a map of the black and Puerto Rican pockets. You note the Germans are at 86th Street and yet the Irish are there, too; that, at the bottom, on East End Avenue, the neighborhood has become suddenly fashionable. The Greenwich Village Italians are pretty fixed; the several Harlems have established their character, for they have stuck to their district for 60 years, which must be a record for New York. You know the Greeks are on 9th Avenue. The Lower East Side, now largely transformed, is Jewish and Puerto Rican. But large groups break away; poor give place to poorer. Sometimes poor give place to rich. In Sutton Place they cleared the poor away from that pleasant little cliff on the East River. But one must not understand these quarters as being the old parishes or the ancient swallowed-up villages of European cities, though they were sometimes the sites of farms. Topographically they are snippings of certain avenues and cross streets. For the avenues stripe the city and the groups live on a block or two along or across the stripe. One would have to analyze New York street by street, from year to year, to know the nuances of racial contact.

Statistics deceive, but it is clear that the oldest American stock of Dutch, British, and German, though dominant in wealth and traditional influence, is a small minority in New York. The question no one can answer is how far the contents of the melting pot have really melted and whether a new race has yet been created. For a long time the minorities resist, huddle into corners. Some foreign groups of New Yorkers melt slowly or not at all. O. Henry in his time called Lower Manhattan "Bagdad-on-the-Subway," thinking then of the unchanging Syrians and Armenians around Rector Street, but they have almost vanished. The Ukrainians still have their shops and churches near Avenue A. The Russian Orthodox priest walks down the street. The Poles shout from their windows or sit on the cagelike fire escapes east of Greenwich Village. Slowly these people, no doubt, merge; but the tendency for social classes to be determined by race is marked. Many groups of Orthodox Jews remain untouched. Over in Williamsburg you see a sect wearing beards, the men in black hats and long black coats, their hair often long, with curls at the ears, walking with a long loping shuffle as if they traveled with knees bent. They look like a priesthood, and the boys, curled in the same way, might be their acolytes. You will meet them with their black cases of treasure between their feet standing on the pavement outside the diamond markets of 47th Street.

The foreign are tenacious of their religions—there must be more Greek Orthodox and Russian Orthodox churches than in any other city outside of Europe—and of their racial pride. The old Romanian who cleans your suit has never seen Romania, but he speaks with his old accent; as one looks at his settled, impersonal, American face, one sees the ghost person of another nation within its outlines, a face lost, often sad and puzzled. The Italian cop stands operatically in the full sun at the corner of Union Square; the nimble Greek with his four pairs of hands in the grocer's has the avidity of Athens under that slick, standard air of city prosperity. It occasionally happens that you go to restaurants in New York kept by the brother-in-law or uncle, say, of the man who has the founding place in London, Naples, or Paris; you fall into family gossip, especially with Italians, who are possibly more recent but who are still entangled in the power politics of the European family system. I once talked to an Irish waiter who rushed away into the bar, crying, "D'ye see that bloody En-

glishman? He knows me father." I didn't, but I did know that his father was a notorious leader of one of those "columns" of the IRA in the Irish Civil War.

In this quality of being lost and found there is the mixture of the guilt, the sadness, the fading mind of exile with the excited wonder at life is an essential New York note. New York tolerance allows the latitude to civilization. People are left alone and are less brutally standardized than in other cities. "Clearly"—these foreigners tell you with resignation—"this is not Europe. But"—they suddenly brighten, tense up, and get that look of celebration in their eyes—"it is New York." That is to say, the miracle. Although New Yorkers of all kinds curse the city for its expense and its pressures, and though all foreigners think it is the other foreigners who make it impossible, they are mad about the place. There is no place like it in the world. And although a Londoner or a Parisian will think the same about their cities, here the feeling has a special quality: that of a triumphant personal discovery of some new thing that is getting bigger, richer, higher, more various as every minute of the day goes by. They have come to a ball. And this is felt not only by the New Yorker with the foreign strain but also by the men and women who come in from the other states, drawn by its wealth but even more by the chances, the freedom, and the privacy that a metropolis offers to human beings. Its very loneliness and ruthlessness are exciting. It is a preemptive if not a literal capital. Scott Fitzgerald speaks of his wife, Zelda, coming up because she wanted "luxury and largeness beyond anything her world provided," and that precisely describes the general feeling of many a newcomer.

— V. S. Pritchett

One of the great masters of English prose, V. S. Pritchett (1900–1997) expounded delightfully on his impressions of the city in *New York Proclaimed*. The choice passages above were taken from the book.

BOOKS AND VIDEOS

Suggested Books

Some of the best full-length accounts are *Christopher Morley's New York,* a mid-1920s reminiscence; *Walker in the City,* by Alfred Kazin; and *Apple of My Eye,* a 1978 recollection of writing a New York guidebook, by Helene Hanff. Dan Wakefield recalls his early literary days in *New York in the 50s. Back Where I Came From* brings together essays on the city that A. J. Liebling wrote for the *New Yorker. Up in the Old Hotel* is a collection of stories by another *New Yorker* writer, Joseph Mitchell, who etches memorable portraits of several colorful city characters. Other recent literary memoirs include *New York Days,* by Willie Morris, and *Manhattan When I Was Young,* by Mary Cantwell. And don't forget E. B. White's excellent 1949 essay "Here Is New York."

For a witty early history of New York, turn to the classic *Knickerbocker's History of New York,* by Washington Irving. The heavily illustrated *Columbia Historical Portrait of New York,* by John Kouwenhoven, provides a good introduction to the city. Another profusely illustrated history of the metropolis is Eric Homberger's *The Historical Atlas of New York City,* full of maps, photographs, drawings, and charts. *You Must Remember This,* by Jeff Kisseloff, is an oral history of ordinary New Yorkers early in this century.

Fiorello H. La Guardia and the Making of Modern New York, by Thomas Kessner, is a biography of the charismatic depression-era mayor. Robert Caro's *The Power Broker* relates the fascinating story of parks commissioner Robert Moses. In *Prince of the City,* Robert Daley covers New York police corruption. Highly critical accounts of recent politics can be found in *The Streets Were Paved with Gold,* by Ken Auletta; *The Rise and Fall of New York City,* by Roger Star; *Imperial City,* by Geoffrey Moorhouse; and *City for Sale,* by Jack Newfield and Wayne Barrett. *A License to Steal,* by Benjamin J. Stein, concerns Wall Street's Michael Milken, as does *Den of Thieves,* by James B. Stewart.

Theater lovers will want to look at *Act One,* the autobiography of playwright Moss Hart; *The Season,* by William Goldman; David Mamet's *The Cabin;* and Neil Simon's *Rewrites. From Manet to Manhattan,* by Peter Watson, explores the city's art world. *Literary New York,* by Susan Edmiston and Linda D. Cirino, traces the haunts of famous writers, neighborhood by neighborhood. Shaun O'Connell's *Remarkable, Unspeakable New York, A Literary History* discusses writers who wrote about the city. *The Heart of the World,* by Nik Cohn, is a vivid block-by-block account of the high- and low-life of Broadway.

AIA Guide to New York City, by Elliot Willensky and Norval White, is still the definitive guide to the city's myriad architectural styles; Paul Goldberger's *The City Observed* describes Manhattan building by building.

Many writers have set their fiction here. Jack Finney's *Time and Again* is a delightful time-travel story illustrated with 19th-century photos; *Winter's Tale,* by Mark Helprin, uses surreal fantasy to create a portrait of New York's past. Novels set in 19th-century New York include Henry James's *Washington Square,* Edith Wharton's *The Age of Innocence* (also available as an audio book), Stephen Crane's *Maggie, A Girl of the Streets,* and two more recent works, *The Alienist,* by Cabel Carr, and *The Waterworks,* by E. L. Doctorow (both available as audio books). O. Henry's short stories depict the early years of this century, while Damon Runyon's are set in the raffish underworld of the 1930s and 1940s. F. Scott Fitzgerald (*The Beautiful and the Damned*), John Dos Passos (*Manhattan Transfer*), John O'Hara (*Butterfield 8*), and Mary McCarthy (*The Group*) all wrote about this city. J.D. Salinger's *Catcher in the Rye* partly takes place here, as does Thomas Pynchon's *V.* Truman Capote's 1958 novella *Breakfast at Tiffany's* is a favorite of many New Yorkers.

John Cheever, Bernard Malamud, Grace Paley, and Isaac Bashevis Singer have written many wonderful short stories celebrating New York and its singular inhabitants. More current New York novels include *Bonfire of the Vanities*, by Tom Wolfe (also available as an audio book); *The Mambo Kings Play Songs of Love*, by Oscar Hijuelos; *The New York Trilogy*, by Paul Auster; and *People Like Us*, by Dominick Dunne.

The black experience in Harlem and New York City has been chronicled in Ralph Ellison's *Invisible Man*, James Baldwin's *Go Tell It on a Mountain*, and Claude Brown's *Manchild in the Promised Land*. For a portrait of 1920s Harlem, try *When Harlem Was in Vogue*, by David Levering Lewis. The history of New York's Jewish population can be traced in such books as *World of Our Fathers*, by Irving Howe; *Call It Sleep*, by Henry Roth; *The Promise*, by Chaim Potok; and *Our Crowd*, by Stephen Birmingham.

Greenwich Village and How It Got That Way is an affectionate investigation by Terry Miller. Francine Prose's novel *Household Saints* uses Little Italy as its setting. *The New Chinatown*, by Peter Kwong, is a recent study of the community across Canal Street. Kate Simon's memoir *Bronx Primitive*, Laura Cunningham's autobiographical *Sleeping Arrangements*, and E.L. Doctorow's novel *World's Fair* are all set in the Bronx. Brooklyn's history is lovingly unfolded in *Brooklyn: People and Places, Past and Present*, by Grace Glueck and Paul Gardner. Part of William Styron's novel *Sophie's Choice* takes place in 1940s Brooklyn. *Patchwork of Dreams*, edited by Morty Sklar and Joseph Barbato, is a collection of fiction, poetry, essays, and photography by residents and former residents of Queens.

Mysteries set in New York City range from Dashiell Hammett's urbane 1933 novel *The Thin Man* to Rex Stout's series of Nero Wolfe mysteries. More recent picks include *While My Pretty One Sleeps*, by Mary Higgins Clark; *Greenwich Killing Time*, by Kinky Friedman; *Dead Air*, by Mike Lupica; and *Unorthodox Practices*, by Marissa Piesman.

Suggested Videos

Perhaps the quintessential New York City movie is *Breakfast at Tiffany's* (1961), directed by Blake Edwards and based on Truman Capote's novella. Anyone who sees the film cannot forget the opening scene,

in which Audrey Hepburn as party-girl Holly Golightly, dressed in a long black Givenchy evening gown, window-shops at Tiffany's jewelry store at dawn. *On the Town* (1949) stars Gene Kelly and Frank Sinatra as sailors on a 24-hour leave; directed by Kelly and Stanley Donen, this was one of the first Hollywood musicals to be shot on location.

Filmmaker Woody Allen has photographed many of his movies in Manhattan, and many of his characters are shown walking the city streets. *Annie Hall* (1977), *Manhattan* (1979), *Broadway Danny Rose* (1985), *Hannah and Her Sisters* (1987), *Another Woman* (1988), *Crimes and Misdemeanors* (1989), *Alice* (1990), *Manhattan Murder Mystery* (1993), *Bullets over Broadway* (1994), *Mighty Aphrodite* (1995), and *Everyone Says I Love You* (1996) are a few.

Director Martin Scorsese, who attended New York University's film school, has made some of his best films in New York. *Mean Streets* (1973) and *Taxi Driver* (1976), both starring Robert De Niro and Harvey Keitel, show a darker side of the city.

Sidney Lumet films often deal with misfits and police corruption. Look for *Serpico* (1973) and *Dog Day Afternoon* (1975, both starring Al Pacino; *Prince of the City* (1981); *Q&A* (1990); and *Night Falls on Manhattan* (1997).

Some of director Paul Mazursky's most entertaining films have New York settings: *Next Stop, Greenwich Village* (1976), *An Unmarried Woman* (1978), *Moscow on the Hudson* (1984), and *Enemies, A Love Story* (1989), based on the novel by Isaac Bashevis Singer.

Neil Simon films with city locations are *Barefoot in the Park* (1967), *The Odd Couple* (1968), *The Sunshine Boys* (1975), *The Goodbye Girl* (1977), and *Brighton Beach Memoirs* (1986).

Joan Micklin Silver portrays the Lower East Side in *Hester Street* (1975) and *Crossing Delancey* (1988). For a look at the African-American experience in Manhattan and Brooklyn, try the films of Spike Lee: *She's Gotta Have It* (1988), *Do the Right Thing* (1990), *Jungle Fever* (1991), and *Crooklyn* (1994). *I Like It Like That* (1994), directed by Darnell Martin, deals with a Latino woman in the Bronx.

Other NYC-set movies include *Sweet Smell of Success* (1957), *Love with a Proper Stranger* (1963), *A Thousand Clowns* (1965), *Up the Down Staircase* (1967), *Wait Until Dark* (1967), *Midnight Cowboy* (1969), *Kramer vs. Kramer* (1979), *Fame* (1980), *Tootsie* (1982), *Moonstruck* (1987), *New York Stories* (1989), *True Believer* (1989), *Sea of Love* (1989), *Metropolitan* (1990), *Night and the City* (1992), *Household Saints* (1993), *A Bronx Tale* (1993), *Little Odessa* (1994), *City Hall* (1996), *Smoke* (1996), *Walking and Talking* (1996), *Ransom* (1996), *Basquiat* (1996), *The First Wives Club* (1996), *Sleepers* (1996), *The Mirror Has Two Faces* (1996), *One Fine Day* (1996), *Donnie Brasco* (1997), and *The Devil's Own* (1997).

INDEX

NOTES

NOTES

NOTES

NOTES

NOTES

NOTES

NOTES

NOTES

NOTES

Fodor's Travel Publications

Available at bookstores everywhere, or call 1–800–533–6478, 24 hours a day.

Gold Guides

U.S.

Alaska

Arizona

Boston

California

Cape Cod, Martha's Vineyard, Nantucket

The Carolinas & Georgia

Chicago

Colorado

Florida

Hawai'i

Las Vegas, Reno, Tahoe

Los Angeles

Maine, Vermont, New Hampshire

Maui & Lāna'i

Miami & the Keys

New England

New Orleans

New York City

Pacific North Coast

Philadelphia & the Pennsylvania Dutch Country

The Rockies

San Diego

San Francisco

Santa Fe, Taos, Albuquerque

Seattle & Vancouver

The South

U.S. & British Virgin Islands

USA

Virginia & Maryland

Walt Disney World, Universal Studios and Orlando

Washington, D.C.

Foreign

Australia

Austria

The Bahamas

Belize & Guatemala

Bermuda

Canada

Cancún, Cozumel, Yucatán Peninsula

Caribbean

China

Costa Rica

Cuba

The Czech Republic & Slovakia

Eastern & Central Europe

Europe

Florence, Tuscany & Umbria

France

Germany

Great Britain

Greece

Hong Kong

India

Ireland

Israel

Italy

Japan

London

Madrid & Barcelona

Mexico

Montréal & Québec City

Moscow, St. Petersburg, Kiev

The Netherlands, Belgium & Luxembourg

New Zealand

Norway

Nova Scotia, New Brunswick, Prince Edward Island

Paris

Portugal

Provence & the Riviera

Scandinavia

Scotland

Singapore

South Africa

South America

Southeast Asia

Spain

Sweden

Switzerland

Thailand

Toronto

Turkey

Vienna & the Danube

Special-Interest Guides

Adventures to Imagine

Alaska Ports of Call

Ballpark Vacations

Caribbean Ports of Call

The Official Guide to America's National Parks

Disney Like a Pro

Europe Ports of Call

Family Adventures

Fodor's Gay Guide to the USA

Fodor's How to Pack

Great American Learning Vacations

Great American Sports & Adventure Vacations

Great American Vacations

Great American Vacations for Travelers with Disabilities

Halliday's New Orleans Food Explorer

Healthy Escapes

Kodak Guide to Shooting Great Travel Pictures

National Parks and Seashores of the East

National Parks of the West

Nights to Imagine

Rock & Roll Traveler Great Britain and Ireland

Rock & Roll Traveler USA

Sunday in San Francisco

Walt Disney World for Adults

Weekends in New York

Wendy Perrin's Secrets Every Smart Traveler Should Know

Fodor's Special Series

Fodor's Best Bed & Breakfasts

America
California
The Mid-Atlantic
New England
The Pacific Northwest
The South
The Southwest
The Upper Great Lakes

Compass American Guides

Alaska
Arizona
Boston
Chicago
Colorado
Hawaii
Idaho
Hollywood
Las Vegas
Maine
Manhattan
Minnesota
Montana
New Mexico
New Orleans
Oregon
Pacific Northwest
San Francisco
Santa Fe
South Carolina
South Dakota
Southwest
Texas
Utah
Virginia
Washington
Wine Country
Wisconsin
Wyoming

Citypacks

Amsterdam
Atlanta
Berlin
Chicago
Florence
Hong Kong
London
Los Angeles
Montréal
New York City

Paris
Prague
Rome
San Francisco
Tokyo
Venice
Washington, D.C.

Exploring Guides

Australia
Boston & New England
Britain
California
Canada
Caribbean
China
Costa Rica
Egypt
Florence & Tuscany
Florida
France
Germany
Greek Islands
Hawaii
Ireland
Israel
Italy
Japan
London
Mexico
Moscow & St. Petersburg
New York City
Paris
Prague
Provence
Rome
San Francisco
Scotland
Singapore & Malaysia
South Africa
Spain
Thailand
Turkey
Venice

Flashmaps

Boston
New York
San Francisco
Washington, D.C.

Fodor's Gay Guides

Los Angeles & Southern California
New York City
Pacific Northwest
San Francisco and the Bay Area
South Florida
USA

Pocket Guides

Acapulco
Aruba
Atlanta
Barbados
Budapest
Jamaica
London
New York City
Paris
Prague
Puerto Rico
Rome
San Francisco
Washington, D.C.

Languages for Travelers (Cassette & Phrasebook)

French
German
Italian
Spanish

Mobil Travel Guides

America's Best Hotels & Restaurants
California and the West
Major Cities
Great Lakes
Mid-Atlantic
Northeast
Northwest and Great Plains
Southeast
Southwest and South Central

Rivages Guides

Bed and Breakfasts of Character and Charm in France
Hotels and Country Inns of Character and Charm in France
Hotels and Country Inns of Character and Charm in Italy
Hotels and Country Inns of Character and Charm in Paris

Hotels and Country Inns of Character and Charm in Portugal
Hotels and Country Inns of Character and Charm in Spain

Short Escapes

Britain
France
New England
Near New York City

Fodor's Sports

Golf Digest's Places to Play
Skiing USA
USA Today The Complete Four Sport Stadium Guide

Your
Window
To The
World
While You're
On The
Road

Keep in touch when you're traveling. Before you take off, tune in to CNN Airport Network. Now available in major airports across America, CNN Airport Network provides nonstop news, sports, business, weather and lifestyle programming. Both domestic and international. All piloted by the top-flight global resources of CNN. All up-to-the-minute reporting. And just for travelers, CNN Airport Network features intriguing segments such as "Travel Facts." With an information source like Fodor's this series of fascinating travel trivia will definitely make time fly while you're waiting to board. SO KEEP YOUR WINDOW TO THE WORLD WIDE OPEN. ESPECIALLY WHEN YOU'RE ON THE ROAD. TUNE IN TO CNN AIRPORT NETWORK TODAY.

WHEREVER YOU TRAVEL, *H*ELP IS NEVER FAR AWAY.

From planning your trip to providing travel assistance
along the way, American Express® Travel Service Offices
are always there to help.

New York City

American Express Travel Service
New York Hilton Hotel
1335 Sixth Avenue
212/664-7798

American Express Travel Service
American Express Tower
200 Vesey Street
212/640-5130

American Express Travel Service
150 East 42nd Street
212/687-3700

American Express Travel Service
200 Fifth Avenue
212/691-9797

American Express Travel Service
New York Marriott Marquis Hotel
1535 Broadway
212/575-6580

American Express Travel Service
374 Park Avenue
212/421-8240

American Express Travel Service
JFK International Airport
Main Lobby
718/656-5673

Travel

http://www.americanexpress.com/travel

**American Express Travel Service Offices are located throughout
New York City. For the office nearest you, call 1-800-AXP-3429.**